A Companion to the City

Edited by

Gary Bridge and Sophie Watson

Blackwell Companions to Geography

Blackwell Companions to Geography is a blue-chip, comprehensive series covering each major subdiscipline of human geography in detail. Edited and contributed by the disciplines' leading authorities each book provides the most up to date and authoritative syntheses available in its field. The overviews provided in each Companion will be an indispensable introduction to the field for students of all levels, while the cutting-edge, critical direction will engage students, teachers and practitioners alike.

Published

A Companion to the City
Edited by Gary Bridge and Sophie Watson

A Companion to Economic Geography
Edited by Eric Sheppard and Trevor J. Barnes

A Companion to Political Geography
Edited by John Agnew, Katharyne Mitchell, and Gerard Toal (Gearoid Ó Tuathail)

A Companion to Cultural Geography
Edited by James S. Duncan, Nuala C. Johnson and Richard H. Schein

A Companion to Tourism
Edited by Alan A. Lew, C. Michael Hall and Allan M. Williams

Forthcoming

A Companion to Feminist Geography
Edited by Lise Nelson and Joni Seager

This Companion contains commissioned pieces from a deliberately broad range of established academics and new researchers. There are considerable attempts to include both western and non-western perspectives as well as more traditional established approaches and contemporary theorizations of the city. In combination with *The Blackwell City Reader* (2002) the full range of approaches to the city and key contributors to the field are covered.

"The Companion merits a prominent place on the bookshelves of every academic and planner who is concerned with the contemporary city."

Area

"I know of no other book that better captures the assertions of the new urban studies. This is an intriguing marker of the new urban studies; I highly recommend it."

Urban Studies

BLACKWELL PUBLISHING
350 Main Street, Malden, MA 02148-5020, USA
9600 Garsington Road, Oxford OX4 2DQ, UK
550 Swanston Street, Carlton, Victoria 3053, Australia

First published 2000
First published in paperback 2003

4 2007

Library of Congress Cataloging-in-Publication Data

A companion to the city / edited by Gary Bridge and Sophie Watson.
p. cm.
Includes bibliographical references and index.
ISBN 0-631-21052-0 (hardback); ISBN 0-631-23578-7 (paperback)
1. Cities and towns. 2. Cities and towns—Cross-cultural studies. I. Bridge, Gary.
II. Watson, Sophie.

HT111. C65 2000
307.76—dc21

00-024885

ISBN-13: 978-0-631-21052-8 (hardback); ISBN-13: 978-0-631-23578-1 (paperback)

A catalogue record for this title is available from the British Library.

Advisory Editors: Peter Marcuse, Columbia University; Geraldine Pratt, University of British Columbia

Set in 10 on 12pt Sabon
by Kolam Information Services Pvt Ltd, Pondicherry, India
Printed and bound in India
by Replika Press Pvt Ltd, Kundli

The publisher's policy is to use permanent paper from mills that operate a sustainable forestry policy, and which has been manufactured from pulp processed using acid-free and elementary chlorine-free practices. Furthermore, the publisher ensures that the text paper and cover board used have met acceptable environmental accreditation standards.

For further information on
Blackwell Publishing, visit our website:
www.blackwellpublishing.com

Contents

Contributors

Riad Akbur   has completed 3 years of a PhD at Queen Mary and Westfield College, University of London

Asu Aksoy   Goldsmith's College, University of London

Ash Amin   University of Durham

Alessandro Aurigi   University College, London

Harriot Beazley   Visiting Scholar at the University of Cambridge

Giedrius Blagnys   Ecofin Vilnius Research Centre, Vilnius, Lithuania

Liz Bondi   University of Edinburgh

M. Christine Boyer   Princeton University

Gary Bridge   University of Bristol

Nick Buck   University of Essex

Lesley Caldwell   University of Greenwich

Bob Catterall   University of Newcastle

Hazel Christie   Edinburgh College of Art and Heriot-Watt University

William Clark   University of California, Los Angeles

Allan Cochrane   The Open University

Phil Cohen   University of East London

Philip Cooke   University of Wales, Cardiff

James Donald   Curtin University of Technology, Western Australia

Michael Edwards   University College, London

Susan Fainstein   Rutgers University

Katherine Gibson   Australian National University, Canberra

Ian Gordon   University of Reading

Stephen Graham   University of Newcastle

Patrick Guinness   Australian National University

Annette Hamilton   Macquarie University in Sydney

Chris Hamnett   King's College, London

Alan Harding   Salford University

Michael Harloe   Salford University

Patsy Healey   University of Newcastle

Chua Beng Huat Singapore National University
John Paul Jones III University of Kentucky
Maria Kaika Associate Researcher at the University of Oxford, Junior Research Fellow at Linacre College, Oxford, and Lecturer at St. Peter's College, Oxford
Raite Karnite Latvian Academy of Sciences, Riga, Latvia
Michael Keith Goldsmith's College, University of London
Anthony D. King Binghamton University, State University of New York
Lily Kong National University of Singapore
Alan Mabin Witwatersrand University, Johannesburg
Peter Marcuse Columbia University, New York City
Andy Merrifield Clark University
Steve Pile The Open University
Kevin Robins Goldsmith's College, University of London
Alisdair Rogers Keble and St. Catherine's Colleges, Oxford University
Benjamin Rossiter studied sociology and cultural studies at La Trobe and Monash Universities, Melbourne, and recently finished his PhD
Charles Rutheiser Johns Hopkins University
Saskia Sassen University of Chicago and Centennial Visiting Professor at London School of Economics and Political Science
Richard Sennett London School of Economics and Political Science
John Rennie Short Syracuse University
Edward W. Soja University of California, Los Angeles
Erik Swyngedouw Reader in Geography at Oxford University and Fellow of St. Peter's College, Oxford
Erik Terk Estonian Institute for Future Studies, Tallinn, Estonia
Nigel Thrift University of Bristol
Alison Todes University of Natal, Durban
Fran Tonkiss Goldsmith's College, University of London
Patrick Troy Australian National University
John Urry University of Lancaster
Anthony Vidler University of California, Los Angeles
Sophie Watson The Open University
Chung-Tong Wu University of New South Wales

Illustrations

Introduction

At the start of the new millennium cities are firmly back on the agenda. More people live in cities and more people are affected by urban processes than ever before. Cities are the sites of complex global/local interconnections producing a multiplicity of social, cultural, political, and economic spaces and forms. It is no longer possible, if it ever was, to look at the city from one perspective – be it cultural or economic. Instead cities need to be understood from a variety of perspectives in the recognition that the cultural/social constructs, and is constructed by, the political/economic and vice versa. It is only when we adopt such a complex and textured reading of cities that we will begin to be able to address the pressing social, economic, and environmental questions faced by cities across the world – be it the postindustrial city of North America or the rapidly growing megacity in China.

This Companion sets out precisely to think about cities in these more complex ways and to bring together scholars from a range of different fields to create a multidisciplinary approach to cities. No longer is the city the privileged terrain of urban studies or geographical analysis. Instead academics and thinkers from disciplines as diverse as film studies and economics or philosophy and geography have turned their attention to the city and generated exciting new ways of thinking. This Companion has deliberately included voices from this diverse terrain in order to promote a dialog that for many years of urban analysis was dormant. Poststructuralist and feminist writers thus rub shoulders with Marxists and neoclassical economists in order, hopefully, to provoke lively debate and new intellectual spaces.

The Companion does not aim to map the field historically or to provide a chronology of major writing on cities – there are other excellent readers that do precisely that (see Le Gates and Stout 1996; Short 1996). Neither does it aim to provide a geographical catalog of the conditions of contemporary cities, since that is done very well by Habitat and other regional collections. This Companion instead deals with contemporary analysis *of* cities as well as some of the key issues *in* cities. There has been a tendency within urban studies historically to develop an analysis and argument based on Western cities and Western assumptions of cultural, social, and economic life, with little attention paid to the profound differences of social, cultural, and economic processes and the local specificity of cities across the world. This universalizing approach has come under growing criticism and scrutiny from postcolonial writers, feminists, poststructuralists and others who have pointed out how western, male, and white assumptions have produced a global homogenous discourse which has masked and ignored difference. It has also perpetuated dominant power/knowledge relations and written whole groups of people, cities, and countries out of the picture.

This Companion aims to redress this imbalance. It does not purport to be comprehensive in its coverage or analysis of cities across the globe. It does however aim to consider the key themes of the book in a variety of contexts, places, and spaces. Its aim therefore is to give a taste at least of the complexity and texture of cities, city spaces, and city interventions at the beginning of the millennium.

All the chapters in this Companion were commissioned by the editors and are thus original pieces of work. They range from discursive and reflective pieces to discussions of original empirical research. The Companion is organized around five themes which we consider to be a useful way of mapping the field: imagining cities, the economy and the city, division and difference, public cultures and everyday space, urban policy and interventions. Each of the sections is introduced by a think piece by the editors which is not intended as an introduction to the chapters in the section, but rather is an attempt to lay out the dimensions of discussion and suggest new ways of approaching the city. Each section includes chapters from non-western[1] cities in order to highlight the variety and diversity of cities and analyses of cities globally rather than to provide a comprehensive coverage of cities across the world.

Cities are feats of the imagination and they affect the ability to imagine. The first section, "Imagining Cities," looks at the different ways cities have been imagined in planning and design as well as media representations and the effects on the built form and the social, cultural, and esthetic realms. These are not just cognitive and creative but unconscious and uncanny. They are not just confined to planning and cultural discourse but influence ways of thinking the economic, identity, and difference, constructions of the public and the private, and the sphere of politics. Each section of the Companion is intended to cohere sufficiently to examine the main currents of discussion within each theme but also to provide openings, connections, and productive juxtapositions with the other sections of the book. So "The Economy and the City" is not just understood in terms of academic disputes about material processes (between neoclassical, Marxist, and post-Marxist analyses) but also as acts of the imagination and political will – as much the terrain of cultural studies as conventional political economy. "Cities of Division and Difference" explores the distinctions of age, class, gender, "race" and ethnicity, sex, citizenship in relation to urban space, and the disruptions of western and nonwestern understandings of productive recognition and prejudiced separation. The extent to which these interrelations result in a depleted public realm in cities is a concern that runs through the chapters in the section "Public Cultures and Everyday Space." Rumors of the death of public space might be a little exaggerated as the contributors seek the possibilities of a rejuvenated public realm in the mundane, the unnoticed, and the everyday practices of city life. These insights give us new ways of thinking about urban politics and the interrelations between formal, institutional policy-making, and informal political activity in the uncelebrated spaces of the city.

In all these arguments on the city and imagination, economy, division, the public, and politics we are seeking to unsettle assumptions and cross boundaries, not in the pursuit of endless displacement, but rather to identify new connections that lie at the confluence of the imagination as economy, globalization as cultural difference and as productive, and the political in acts that are normally ignored. These disruptions and juxtapositions are at the heart of the urban experience and offer a beginning for a reconstituted understanding of the city in the third millennium.

NOTE

1. There have been a number of ways of regionalizing discussion of cities such as the division between cities of the north and cities of the south. Here we choose western and non-western to connote not just geographical location but sets of intellectual histories and assumptions in traditional literatures on cities.

REFERENCES

Le Gates, R. and Stout, F. (eds.) 1996: *The City Reader.* London: Routledge.
Short, J. 1996: *The Urban Order: An Introduction to Cities, Culture and Power.* Oxford: Blackwell.

Part I Imagining Cities

Chapter 1

City Imaginaries

Gary Bridge and Sophie Watson

Cities are not simply material or lived spaces – they are also spaces of the imagination and spaces of representation. How cities are envisioned has effects. Urban designers and planners have ideas about how cities should look, function, and be lived, and these are translated into plans and built environments. Cities are represented in literary, art, and film texts, and these too have their effects. The public imaginary about cities is itself in part constituted by media representations as much as by lived practices. Ideas about cities are not simply formed at a conscious level; they are also a product of unconscious desires and imaginaries. This Companion starts with these city imaginaries to illustrate the power of ideas, the imagination, representations, and visions in influencing the way cities are formed and lived.

Here we pursue two themes which organize thinking on the relationship between the city and the imagination: *how the city affects the imagination* and *how the city is imagined*. Although there are obvious links between these two they are a useful way to think about imagining cities.

The effect of the city on the imagination contains a tension between the conditions of the city *stimulating* or *constraining* the imagination. On the one hand cities are creative, places that encourage the imagination, sites of stimulation. People with different ideas come together in cities and their webs of interconnection and sharing of knowledge and ideas are productive creatively. These ideas have material effects – in the form of economic innovation (for example in manufacturing) and profits from selling ideas in the innovation and informational economy (see, for example, in this volume Amin, chapter 11, Catterall, chapter 17). The idea of the city as a crucible for ideas and innovation has a long history – back to the very origins of urbanism in fact. Soja (chapter 3) argues that the stimulating effects of urban agglomeration (what he calls synekism) resulted in innovations in cultivation that produced the agrarian revolution. Here the interactive conditions of the city encourage bright ideas to overcome settled ways of thinking.

Settled ways of thinking can be powerful acts of the imagination in themselves. Cities might act to constrain the imagination or to consolidate it in collective imagination as tradition and authority. Cities, like nations, can be the locus for imagined communities. This collective imagination might be held in place through the exercise of discipline and authority. One of Short's three urban discourses (chapter 2) looks at the city as a source of authority, repression, and compunction. These influences act as chains on the imagination. On the other hand such an authoritarian city can be a source of identity and security. The tensions between authority and identity are evident in Patrick Guinness's account (chapter 9) in which the figure of the sultan acts as a powerful locus for the imagination on the "subjects" of Yogyakarta. In many non-Western cities (and increasingly in many Western ones) the religious or spiritual imagination is a key locus of identity and impacts on the built form of the city. This cosmic city (as Short puts it) can come into conflict with the dominant urban imaginary in the West which is that of capital accumulation. This also challenges conventional Western views of modernity and the city (via Weber 1966; Simmel 1995, and others) on the secularization of society and forms of individual alienation or anomie. If Western urbanism was facilitated by the individualism that came with a disenchantment with the world, the interaction of capitalism with other collective imaginations and representations (such as those based on religious faith) give a more unpredictable mix of confrontation or cooptation of capital and culture, and vice versa.

It is clear that forms of collective imagination can be both positive and negative (Boyer 1994). Prejudiced imaginaries of "the other" are a source of racism, and the untrammeled domination of certain collective imaginaries work to exclude others – as the burgeoning literature on postcoloniality points out (see Akbur, chapter 7; King, chapter 22). Similarly notions of community assume a homogeneity of population and can entail an idea of purification where those designated as outside become the site of prejudice and segregation. Postcolonial and feminist writing reveal the degree to which Western imaginaries of the city and the other were overwhelmingly *visual* in nature (the colonial gaze, the watching *flâneur*). Anthony Vidler (chapter 4) shows the extent to which this was true for the conceived space of the city in Western architecture and planning: Le Corbusier's imagination was fed by airplane flights above Paris.

The speed of growth and the kaleidoscope of capital and culture in non-Western cities challenges the visual imaginary through the synesthesia of the city and the importance of other senses. What makes cities extraordinary is that they contain sites where the senses are bombarded and these can be read as a source of pleasure: the Spice Market in Istanbul, or the street markets of Hanoi; or displeasure, as in the rush-hour spaces of underground stations.

The city in its complexity and abundance of sensory data can also be seen as a space which contributes to our sense of fragmented subjectivity or overload. In Simmel's exploration of the relation between the subject's inner life and the city he suggests that in the modern metropolis the individual becomes saturated with stimuli: "There is no psychic phenomenon which is so unconditionally reserved to the city as the blasé attitude" ([1903] 1995: 329). Yet with the influence of postmodernist thought the notion of fractured selves, lives, and complexity has shifted from being constituted as a negative trope to a more positive one. Thus Simmel's notion of the city as a site of overstimulation and excess of feeling has been substituted by an imagination of the city as vibrant and exciting and a space where the play of the senses and bodily pleasures can be celebrated and explored.

Contemporary discourses of the city as constituting sites of pleasure are perhaps one of the many reasons that Benjamin's writings have received so much recent attention by urbanists. For him the city and its crowds are intoxicating, fascinating, productive, and creative, while the commodity culture of the nineteenth century is conceived as a dreamworld. The modern metropolis for Benjamin was the principal site of the phantasmagoria of modernity and the new manifestation of myth, which is illustrated particularly in his writings on the covered shopping arcades of Paris which were constructed from glass and intricate ironwork which shone and sparkled. The dreamworld and unconscious of the bourgeoisie, with its dreams of progress, abundance, desire for pleasure and consumption are materialized in the architecture, commodities, and fashion of the city. But the city for Benjamin is also an ambiguous place – at once alluring and threatening (Buck-Morss 1995: 66):

> As a social formation, Paris is a counter image to that which Vesuvius is as a geographic one: A threatening, dangerous mass, an ever-active June of the Revolution. But just as the slopes of Vesuvius, thanks to the layers of lava covering them, have become a paradisiacal orchard, so here, out of the lava of the Revolution, there bloom art, fashion and festive existence as nowhere else.

His writings are not explorations of memory as such and the metropolis is not simply a space remembered by Benjamin; rather memory is intricately interwoven with particular sites (Gilloch 1997: 11, 66). Memory shapes the city at the same time as being shaped by it.

City and the Realization of Self

So far we have considered the city's effect on the collective imagination. But urban imagination can also be read in terms of *realization* or *nonrealization* of the individual – *the self*. It was in the ordinary spaces of the city that James Joyce's characters achieved self-realization – those epiphanies or moments of insight and revelation, so extraordinary, came in the everyday spaces of the city. Equally those urban writers and scholars of the cosmopolitan school look to the encounter with others as a form of psychic development and enlightenment (Sennett 1970; Young 1990; Jacobs 1962). On the other hand the city and urban experience may also act to separate the self from imagination and creativity. Alienation is estrangement. For Marx this was a material process, an outcome of the social relations of production in capitalism. In this sense much experience for many urban dwellers in western and non-Western cities is a distance from the imagination and a denial of imagination. Yet even in the spaces of alienation, shackled to the production line, acts of the imagination like daydreams form sites of resistance (see Figure 1.1).

This distance from the imagination was enforced through bricks and mortar for Engels (Engels 1971). In his study of Manchester of 1844 the separation of workers in different quality housing and separate districts led to the separation of their imaginations and suppressed the possibility of them coming together to form a revolutionary consciousness. These city trenches (to borrow Katznelson's 1981 term) are trenches in the imagination. In contemporary cities such trenches take new forms in the fortress architecture of the gated communities, or exclusionary suburbs, all of which act to block imaginative identifications with the other.

Alienation is one modernist trope; other imaginative influences on understanding the city look to the fragmentation of self and suggest that there is no real self to be estranged from. We could also argue that the notion of the self is a Western problem, or at least a Western conceit when set against life on the Bombay pavements or in the squatter settlements of Manila. Nevertheless, the distance of self from deeper impulses, desires, and fears continues to be a theme in understanding the urban condition. Here we encounter the relation of the imagination to the subconscious. Deep desires and fears can emerge in the city – hence its representation as a crucible of civilization, as promethean, but also as the site of sin (as in Sodom and Gomorrah), or as unruly spaces that have to be managed. The fabric of the city might provide glimpses of deeper psychic drives but it might also operate to keep them in check. The city might be the dreamwork that keeps those urges at a distance (see Pile, chapter 8), or it might help reinforce our distance from the unconscious. The city is a dream, a trance full of ghosts and traces and possibilities that never (literally) materialize.

We can also think of the city as a space of anxiety and fear, or drawing, as Vidler (1992) does, on Freud, as the site of the uncanny. Richard Sennett sees the modern city as reflecting the divide between subjective experience and worldly experience, or between the self and the city. Thus cities reflect a great fear of exposure, and are constructed instead to protect our inner (even spiritual) selves from the threat of social contact and from differences. There is some resonance here with the idea of the fortress city (Davis 1992) of more recent construction which plays on fear of "the other" and of violence to entice people into private gated communities. Suburbs are imbued with a similar imagery counterposed to the dangerous, congested, and criminal inner city as imagined spaces of community, safety and family.

Early feminist writers looked to the city as a source of self-realization away from the constraints of the gendered space of the home and patriarchal relationships. Rather than following conventional views of the city as spaces of immorality, threat, and danger for women, feminists have also articulated the city as a space of freedom and possibility away from the shackle of domestic life, constraint and suffocation (Wilson 1991). Thus in the Australian context Barbara Brooks (1989: 33–5) writes:

> Coming from the country to the city was an escape into a freer more varied and tolerant way of life... the private and the public landscape interact, release each other. Moving to a different place gives you the chance to shift habits and routines, move into a different persona. An urban or semi-urban environment gives more variety, more chance to move around between different groups and get lost in between.

Other feminist writers and idealists have imagined new urban designs and city forms as a potentially liberating force whereby women can be freed from domestic drudgery (Hayden 1981). The fantasy here is that more collective built forms will enable and even determine a more collective and shared way of life. Many utopian novels written by women embody similar ideas.

Figure 1.1 Aboriginal inscription, Sydney (© Steve Pile)

Clearly for people living outside of conventional norms, such as gays or single women, or for those seeking to break the bonds of earlier ties, the city can represent a space of liberation. A different fantasy comes into play for many intercountry migrants or rural–urban migrants leaving an impoverished rural life where agricultural opportunities have been stripped away, who may see the city as a potential source of livelihood and a better life. The fact that many such migrants end up living in the poor areas of the American, British, or European city or ramshackle dwellings on the sidewalks of Johannesburg, does not dilute the force of the imagined advantages of the city to those who follow.

Cities, then, operate as sites of fantasy. So also subjectivities are constructed in the spaces (both formal and interstitial, imagined and real) of the city and certain kinds of feelings or a sense of self are made possible, and we remember these as emerging in a particular site. In Woolf's (1938: 119) *The Years* Rose is standing by the Thames:

> As she stood there, looking down at the water, some buried feeling began to arrange the stream into a pattern. The pattern was painful. She remembered how she had stood there on that night of a certain engagement, crying.... Then she had turned... and she had seen the churches, the masts and roofs of the city. There's *that*, she had said to herself. Indeed it was a

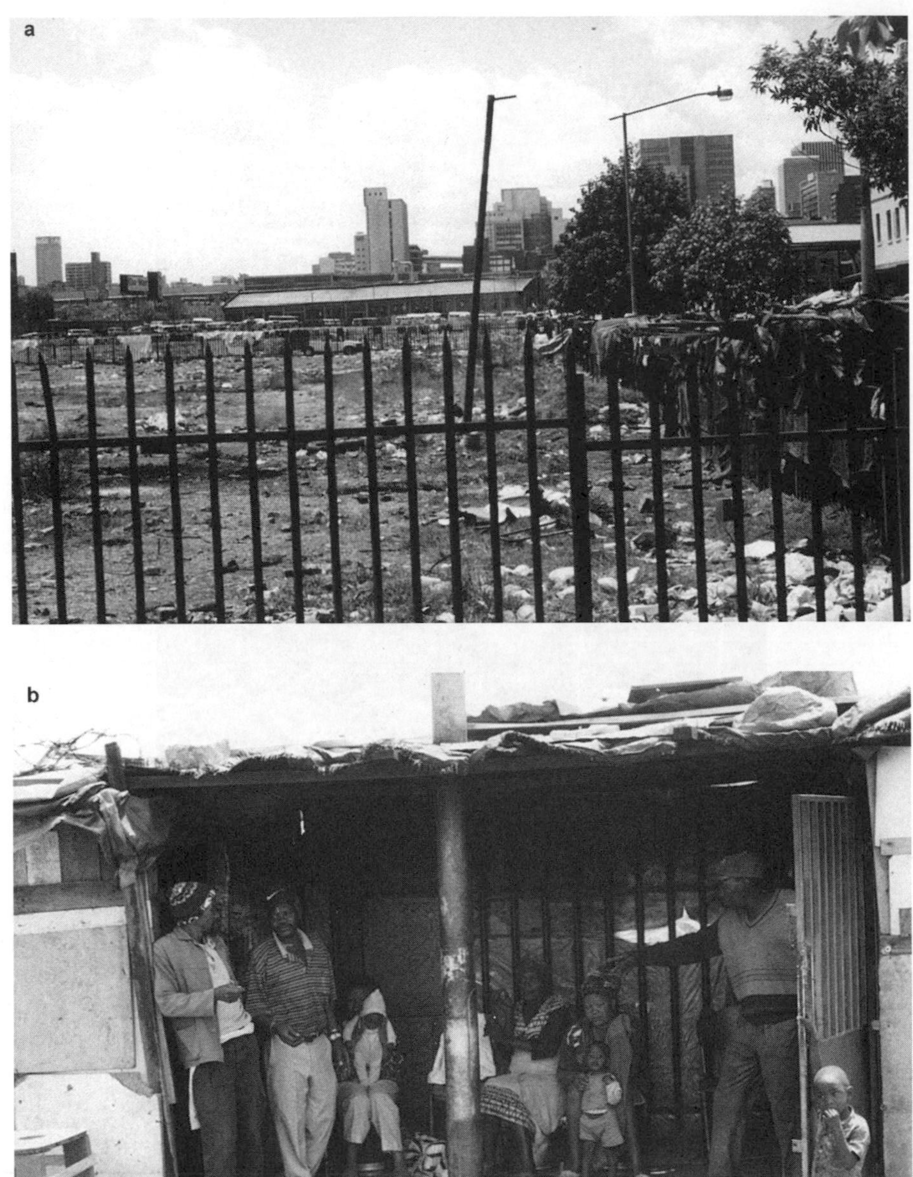

Figure 1.2a,b Sidewalk dwellers, Johannesburg (© Sophie Watson)

splendid view... she looked, and then again she turned. There were the Houses of Parliament. A queer expression, half frown, half smile, formed on her face and she threw herself slightly backwards, as if she were leading an army.

The buildings and spaces of the city are formed in, and themselves form, memory, while memory becomes spatialized.

Drawing on memory, learning from the past in one's relationship with the city is part of this self-development and self-actualization. Memory plays a part in the way that cities are imagined. At the level of the everyday a smell in the street or the sound of a piano from a room we are passing can evoke another place and time. The complex textures of the city are a rich source of memory for urban dwellers which may represent an absence for new migrants disembedding them, at least initially, from a sense of place and belonging. Antony Vidler (1992: 176) suggests that urban memory in the traditional city was easy to define as the image of the city which made it possible for the individual citizen to identify with its past and present as a cultural, social, and political entity: "it was neither the 'reality' of the city nor a purely 'imaginary' utopia but rather the complex mental map or significance by which the city might be recognised as 'home,' as something not foreign, and as constituting a (more or less) moral and protected environment for actual daily life." In this scenario monuments come to act as crucial signifiers constructing particular meanings – whether it is the triumphal arch or the splendor of government buildings. Once again this aspect of cities is captured by Viriginia Woolf (1938: 165):

The omnibuses swirled and circled in a perpetual current round the steps of St Paul's. The statue of Queen Anne seemed to preside over the chaos and to supply it with a centre, like the hub of a wheel. It seemed as if the white lady ruled the traffic with her sceptre, directed the activities of the little men in bowler hats and round coats; of the women carrying attache cases; of the vans, the lorries and the motor omnibuses.

This view of the significance of monuments giving cultural location is questioned by Thrift (chapter 34) when he argues for the inconspicuousness of monuments and encourages us to look to other everyday spaces in the city to find the extraordinary.

As cities have become more complex, more global, and more diasporic it is harder to construct cultural markers which make for a simple image of the city with which to identify. At whose imagination, we may ask, is the statue, the poster, the building facade, or the pavement mosaic directed, and for what purpose? And what and whose past are we drawing on in the construction of city monuments? As Vidler points out (1992: 179), for modernists it was as much a story about erasing the past, forgetting the old city and what it stood for, its chaos and corruption, as it was a story about referencing earlier urban forms. Le Corbusier's Ville Radieuse, for example, maintained the body as the central organizing principle and central reference point echoing the classical tradition. In a similar way current urban regeneration initiatives are also drawing on cultural imaginaries of earlier times, be it invoking earlier traditions of local employment and industries – as is classically seen in the reconstruction of dockland areas – or cultural life.

Representing Cities

All these tensions – between imaginative innovation or constraint, between actualization or remoteness, between the individual or the collective imagination – emerge not just in the effects of the city on imagination but in the way that the city is imagined, the way it is *represented* in film and literature, in urban scholarship, and in urban planning and politics. City narratives can come in many forms. Cities take their shape through representation and the discursive practices which construct them, and the boundary between real and imagined cities is difficult to draw. Jonathan Raban (1974: 10) puts it thus:

> Cities, unlike villages and small towns, are plastic by nature. We mould them in our images: they, in their turn, shape us by the resistance they offer when we try and impose a personal form on them.... The city as we might imagine it, the soft city of illusion, myth, aspiration, nightmare, is as real, maybe more real, than the hard city one can locate in maps and statistics, in monographs on urban sociology and demography and architecture.

Different theoretical approaches tell different stories which purport to some kind of truth about cities but which are themselves only one way of understanding the complexities that constitute a city. There is no one narrative of a city, but many narratives construct cities in different ways highlighting some aspects and not others.

There has been a long tradition of the urban sociological imagination with writers as diverse as Simmel ([1903] 1995), Benjamin (1985), Wirth (1938), and Lefebvre (1991) representing the city in a diversity of ways. In the early days of urban analysis the dominant imagining of cities was the Chicago School and the ecological approach. In this formulation, Burgess (1925), Park (1925), and others conceived the city as a plantlike organism which was ordered according to certain principles which divided the land into specific populations and uses thus achieving some form of balanced growth. In this model the analogy was of the city as a living organism operating according to given laws. Contained within this approach was an evolutionary model of economic growth and change where Chicago was taken as the epitome of the modern industrial city which was the culmination of a long evolutionary process dating back to much earlier historical periods. The new spatial divisions in cities were imagined as the product of the complex divisions of labor in modern industrial society.

The Chicago narrative was superseded by two dominant theoretical imaginaries to understanding cities; one of these derived from Weber's work, the other from Marx. Ray Pahl (1975), among others, drawing on Weber, emphasized the importance of institutions and the decisions of urban managers in determining the shape and distribution of resources and services in the city. This was a relatively benign imaginary, wherein resided the possibility for change and reform. David Harvey (1973) and Manuel Castells (1977) are two of the Marxist urban analysts who have played a significant role in developing a political economy approach to the city. In his work Harvey developed Marx's theory of capital accumulation to draw out the implications for urban structures. In the early texts he set out to explore the importance of land in three circuits of capital: the primary circuit of production of commodities, the secondary circuit where capital is fixed in the built environment, and the tertiary circuit of scientific knowledge and expenditures related to the reproduction of labor power. Other Marxist writers developed different but related approaches to understanding the city, but within each the prevailing imaginary was of a city that worked in the interests of capital accumulation and exploitation. In this period, from the early 1970s to mid-1980s many writers sought to construct true representations of the city, rather than recognizing that any representation of the city could only ever be partial.

More recently the cultural turn has meant the emergence of new city stories and imaginaries which foreground cities as spaces of cosmopolitanism, multiculturalism, as well as spaces of the psyche, memory and the imaginary. Much of this writing has turned back to the earlier analysts of the city in modernity to develop new paradigms and new insights. Other texts draw on postmodern writers such as Foucault, Lyotard, and Baudrillard to shift the focus from the material and economic spheres to the imaginary, the cultural, and the hyper-real. These paradigms self-consciously disrupt the boundaries between real and imagined cities and discursive and non-discursive terrains. Notions of difference, fragmentation, complexity, virtuality, hyper-reality, simulacra, and cyberspace surveillance are thus now embedded in these contemporary stories. Cities have always been the repository of all sorts of myths and fantasies, some of which tend to the utopian-cities as sites of desire, others to the dystopian–cities as sites of fear. Pro- and anti-urban representations and mythologies have been as much a feature of literary and film texts as they have a been a feature of the texts of social reformers, philanthropists, and politicians. For pro-urbanists and city lovers, cities are imagined as spaces of opportunity, of the co-mingling of strangers, as spaces of excitement, difference, cosmopolitanism, and interconnection; and as spaces of culture, engagement, enchantment, fluidity, and vibrancy. These pro-urban imaginaries themselves have translated into policies to encourage and enhance city living (see chapter 42 in this volume).

Another positive representation is the city as polis. A political imaginary of the city dates from the early days of cities from the Mayan and Aztec cities of Central and South America to the cities of the Greek and Roman empires. The archetypal city of Athens stood, and continues to stand, for notions of democracy, civic culture, human fulfillment, and urbanity. For Marx the city represented a potential space of freedom for the masses away from the conservatism and idiocy of rural life. Taking seriously the politics of difference in the contemporary city Iris Marion Young (1990), among many other political theorists (Sennett 1990), proposes a political imaginary of the city as a space of "the being together of strangers." Different political imaginations find their way into urban design and form. Harlow new town, for example, was built after the Second World War near London with a socialist vision of democracy and inclusion and with innovative ideas as to how the city could enable a more egalitarian way of life. Similarly Brasilia was conceived as a symbol of modernity, where squatting was to be abolished, and order was paramount (Hall 1988: 219).

Anti-urban imaginaries have been forcefully in play in literary, art, and political texts for as long as there have been cities. Here the associations are with the city as a site of anomie, alienation, corruption, ill health, immorality, chaos, pollution, congestion, and a threat to social order. In these imaginaries, the urban masses need to be contained and controlled, for if they are left to their own devices the city will become a site of crime and potential revolution. Fear and anxiety lie close to the surface of these representations, whether it be fear of cities as spaces of disease or as spaces of disorder. The role of the social reformer or politician in this scenario is to impose order in the midst of chaos, harmony in the face of disharmony, and cleanliness out of squalor. This attitude is characterized in the reforming zeal of the mid- to late nineteenth century of philanthropists in the mould of William Booth and Octavia Hill in England.

Urban designs and city plans (such as those of Le Corbusier, Lloyd Wright, and Ebenezer Howard) have often embodied, implicitly or explicitly, some version of anti-urbanism which evokes the city as a place to be tamed and ordered and made predictable. It is interesting to question what is at stake in the different discourses and interpretations of the city and whose interests they serve. Or to put this another way, what power/knowledge relations are in play in these representations? Plans and designs are never neutral tools of spatial ordering. We can illustrate this point by considering the strategy deployed by the Republican Mayor of New York in the 1990s, Rudolf Giuliani, to clean up the city. Dominant representations of the city as dangerous, dirty, and derelict legitimated fairly draconian measures to clear the streets of unwanted people. Rather than tackle the problem of the homeless through housing policy, homeless people were simply forced off the streets of Manhattan – to other parts of the city – so that Manhattan residents could walk the streets without encountering beggars. In this case this representation acted in the interests of businesses and established residents of the city both financially – in the case of businesses or property owners – and in terms of quality of life. As a result homeless people were further marginalized. A dominant imaginary of Black people as threatening and violent similarly legitimated an apartheid system in South Africa where Black people were cast to marginal settlements on the edge or outside of the city. If we take seriously the power of the imagination, then questions also need to be asked regarding in which sites and institutions different imaginings are produced and with what effects.

Representations of the city have tended to be dominated by the Western imaginary – Peter Hall's mammoth text on cities (1998) is a case in point, where the only non-European or non-American city to warrant a chapter is Tokyo. Western rationalist planning imaginaries have also failed to cope with the conditions and particularities of many non-Western cities. This Companion has deliberately set out to include explorations and discussion of different kinds of cities not in an attempt to be comprehensive or even comparative, but in order both to shift the dominance of western cities in contemporary urban collections and also to illustrate the diversity and specificity of cities across the globe. This is all the more necessary as processes of globalization have disrupted cities as imagined homogenous spaces. So too new racial imaginaries have begun to destabilize predominantly White representations of city life and experience.

In conclusion, imaginings of cities are powerful and have their effects. In some instances they may represent an attempt to overcome our sense of alienation from the city; in others they are an outcome of that, and no doubt these responses exist in some kind of tension. So too our imagination can be either an escape from the problems of cities, or an act of resistance, or both. Any representations and imaginaries are bound to be in a state of flux and will also be subject to contestation by those who feel excluded or on the margins of the dominant imaginary. Increasingly cultural geographies of locality are revealing the multiple stories of how space is lived and imagined by different sections of the population from youth to small migrant communities, by women, and by gays. There are many cities and many stories to be told.

Not only are cities constituted in imagination and different forms of representation, they are also themselves sites of imagination and creativity. The very maelstrom of the city to which Benjamin and others have drawn attention can itself be a creative influence, while in other circumstances it may be constraining. Imagination and the city are mutually constitutive and interwoven in countless ways and, as we have seen, the membrane between specific sites of the city and memory and the imaginary is a porous one. We see in Part 5 how imagination is translated into policy and how through the mechanisms of governance it has its effects.

REFERENCES

Benjamin, W. 1985: *One Way Street and Other Writings*. London: Verso.
Boyer, C. 1983: *Dreaming the Rational City*. Cambridge, MA: MIT Press.
Boyer, C. 1994: *The City of Collective Memory: Its Historical Imagery and Architectural Entertainments*. Cambridge, MA: MIT Press.
Brooks, B. 1989: Maps. In D. Modjeska (ed.), *Inner Cities: Australian Women's Memory of Place*, Sydney: Penguin, 29–42.
Buck-Morss, S. 1995: *The Dialectics of Seeing Walter Benjamin and the Arcades Project*. Cambridge, MA: MIT Press.
Burgess, E. W. [1925] 1969: The growth of the city: an introduction to a research project. In R. Park et al. (eds.), *The City*, Chicago: University of Chicago Press, 3rd edn, 47–62.
Castells, M. 1977: *The Urban Question: A Marxist Approach*. London: Edward Arnold.
Davis, M. 1992: *City of Quartz: Excavating the Future in Los Angeles*. London: Verso.
Engels, F. [1845] 1971: *The Condition of the Working Class in England*. Oxford: Basil Blackwell.
Gilloch, G. 1997: *Myth and Metropolis: Walter Benjamin and the City*. Cambridge: Polity.
Hall, P. 1988: *Cities of Tomorrow*. Oxford: Blackwell.
Hall, P. 1998: *Cities in Civilisation*. London: Weidenfeld and Nicholson.
Harvey, D. 1973: *Social Justice and the City*. London: Edward Arnold.
Hayden, D. 1981: What would a non-sexist city be like? Speculations on housing, urban design, and human work. *Signs*, 5(3) supplement, S170–S187.
Jacobs, J. 1962: *The Death and Life of Great American Cities*. London: Jonathan Cape.
Katznelson, I. 1981: *City Trenches*. New York: Pantheon Books.
Lefebvre, H. 1991: *The Production of Space*. Oxford: Blackwell.
Pahl, R. 1975: *Whose City?* Harmondsworth: Penguin.
Park, R. et al. (eds.) [1925] 1969: *The City*. Chicago: University of Chicago Press, 3rd edn.
Raban, J. 1974: *Soft City*. London: Hamish Hamilton.
Sennett, R. 1970: *The Uses of Disorder*. Harmondsworth: Penguin.
Sennett, R. 1990: *The Conscience of the Eye*. London: Faber and Faber.
Simmel, G. [1903] 1995: The metropolis and mental life. In P. Kasnitz (ed.), *Metropolis: Center and Symbol of our Times*, Basingstoke: Macmillan, 30–45.
Vidler, A. 1992: *The Architectural Uncanny*. Cambridge, MA: MIT Press.
Weber, M. 1966: *The City*, tr. and ed. by D. Martindale and G. Neuwirth. New York: Free Press.
Wilson, E. 1991: *The Sphinx and the City*. London: Virago.
Wirth, L. 1938: Urbanism as a way of life. *American Journal of Sociology*, 44(1), 1–24.
Woolf, V. 1938: *The Years*. London: Penguin, 1998.
Young, I. 1990: *Justice and the Politics of Difference*. Princeton: Princeton University Press.

Chapter 2

Three Urban Discourses

John Rennie Short

In this chapter I want to consider three fundamental discourses of the city: the authoritarian city, the cosmic city, and the collective city. These are ideas of the city as well as urban social relations, intellectual discourses as well as political forces. They are chosen from the many possible, because I feel they have a special resonance at this millennial juncture.

The Authoritarian City

Cities are sites of social aggregation that involve compulsion, order, and discipline as well as freedom, anarchy, and self-realization. In recent years, the latter rather than the former have been stressed. While it is important to see the city as a site of individual and collective emancipation, a tradition that incorporates Marx and Engels as well as Nozick and Milton Friedmann, it is just as important to remember that the city is an imposition and adherence to a series of master narratives. From Rameses II to Frank Gehry, through Baron Haussmann and Le Corbusier the city has been inherently authoritarian, sometimes totalitarian and occasionally fascistic.

All ideas are relational. However, this notion of the urban as discipline is not contrasted to a pastoral freedom. I am not counterpoising a brutal urban with an idealized rural. If comparisons need to be made I draw upon Bruce Chatwin's notion of the nomadic alternative. In a series of essays and particularly in his book *The Songlines* he argued that nomadism was the "natural" human condition (Chatwin 1987). The urban revolution was not a leap forward but a tethering of the human need to move. While Chatwin's biologizing of social relations needs to be treated with extreme care, or we will fall into the reactionary, antimodern lauding of the idealized nomad apparent in the work of Wilfred Thesinger and Laurens van der Post, he raises an important point about cities as places of compunction.

The debate on urban origins has long fascinated me. The traditional view was that the urban revolution was predicated upon the agricultural revolution. Agricultural surplus created cities. An alternative was outlined by Jane Jacobs (1969) who proposed a reversal of the process; urban trade created agriculture. We can think of an urban–agricultural revolution in which trade played a key role. However, the work of Marshall Sahlins (1972) has convincingly shown that hunting-gathering societies that prefigured this revolution spent less time working than agricultural societies; he calls them the original affluent society. In other words, pre-urban, pre-agricultural societies had more free time, more freedom. The urban–agricultural revolution marks a loss of freedom, a greater work discipline and more time devoted to the drudgery of work and the compulsion of social order. Cities are a Nietzschian will to power. An example.

In the desert South West of the United States, there are remains of an important urban culture. They were called the Anasazi and their independent urban civilization was centered on Chaco Canyon, New Mexico. The traditional rendition goes like this: between the tenth and twelfth centuries the Anasazi culture, based on efficient agriculture, flowered into cities with vast cliff dwellings, and major feats of engineering, architecture, and art. Brilliant pottery, sophisticated irrigation systems, and keen solar and astronomical observations round out a picture of an urban civilization that follows the old precept that cities equal civilization.

There is another interpretation of the Anasazi. The work of anthropologist Christy Turner presents a darker side of Anasazi culture (Preston 1998). It appears that the Anasazi culture was prefigured by the Toltec empire which lasted from the ninth to the twelfth century in central Mexico. This was an empire centered on human sacrifice and cannibalism. Thugs from the Toltec empire moved north into what is now New Mexico and found a pliant population of docile farmers whom they terrorized into a theocratic society. Social control was maintained through acts of cannibalistic terror. The Anasazi culture, so long admired, was a Charles Manson-type social order where the bad and powerful controlled the weak. The great feats of art and astronomy, road building, and city formation were less sparks of human ingenuity and more the mark of organized social terrorism.

An extreme example. But the past is less a fixed reality than a mirror of contemporary concerns. While others would want to remind us of the ingenuity in Çatal Hüyük, I want to remind us of the terror of Chaco Canyon.

The authoritarian project is not always successful. The city is a place of resistance and contestation. And while these have emerged as important topics in recent years, it is well to remember that something is being resisted, something is being contested. There is a structure to all this agency.

Neither am I suggesting that the authoritarian project is always bad. We may agree with the classical liberal theorists like Locke and Hobbes that we need some form of social contract in order to save us from the excesses of the more powerful. The city is the embodiment of the social contract.

Cities have an authority embedded in them. Street layouts, traffic lights, police, the location of things; there is an imposed structuring to our lives, our behaviors, the paths that we trace through time and across space. Whatever the question, Lenin suggested, the answer is always power. The city both reflects and embodies power. Urban society involves an order in time and space, a discipline of space and time. The urban built form is a system of boundaries and transgressions, centers and peripheries, surveillances and gestures, gazes and performances. At a fundamental level there is something inherently fascistic about architecture and urban planning.

The authoritarian city is a useful corrective to the idea of urbanism as a sort of unbound Prometheus breaking through the bonds of tradition and established order, a theme best exemplified by Peter Hall (1998). This has been the dominant rendering of the city for the past two hundred years including the socialist emancipatory project, the gaze of the *flâneur*, modernist sensibilities and a post-modern irony. In recent years it has morphed into a market-driven, so-called neoliberal narrative that has called for loosening planning controls and deregulation. The implied call of freedom has now been attached to the unfettered operation of the market. I want to stress very strongly that this discourse needs to be challenged. Because the city is inherently authoritarian, the calls for less planning and deregulation should be challenged for what they are: struggles over who is doing the planning and what are the redistributional consequences of regulation. Deregulation is always reregulation that reflects economic and political power. And the real question is not whether urban planning is done or not, but who is doing the planning. If planning controls over land use disappear more power is transferred to private interests. When we have a view of the city as the operation of power; then debates become released from the phoney dichotomy of control versus freedom to the more politicized debate concerning the question Who is in control?

Power is a practice, a ritual, a process, wielded by some people over others. It is unevenly distributed and unequally imposed. Work on the authoritarian city such as that of Michel Foucault has revived interest in the practices of power, the operation of discipline, the spaces of exclusion, and the sites of control. An edited book by Nicholas Fyfe (1998), for example, draws together interesting contributions on surveillance and policing, and ties in the *connection between* control and identity in public spaces. These are the more obvious uses of power. Power is exercised in a number of ways from direct coercion through adherence to community standards. At one extreme are the personnel and techniques of the coercive state and corporatist apparatus, at the other the social norms that define what is proper. The nature of the authoritarian city varies from the direct operation of centralized power including imprisonment, punishment, and bodily torture to the individual incorporation of values and standards into a taken-for-granted view of the world. A thumbnail history of the authoritarian city would show a reliance on both but in democratic capitalist societies a greater use of the latter.

The authoritarian city comes in a number of thicknesses. Authority is thickest when everyday practices are overlain with the practice of power and thinnest when power is part of people's desires. Consider the contrasting utopia/dystopias imagined by Aldous Huxley and George Orwell in their respective novels *Brave New World* and *1984*. These are arguably the most emblematic political novels of the twentieth century. Huxley describes a place where order is maintained by sexual promiscuity and easy availability of drugs. Orwell's world is puritanical, harsh, and bitter. Orwell's depicts a thick authoritarian city, Huxley presents a thin authoritarian city.

While the obvious and direct uses of power are worthy of investigation, especially as new more subtle forms of surveillance are introduced and employed, it is also important to realize that the more powerful chains are ones that we impose on our own imagination. When we internalize power relations we become our own repressive police state. There are connections between *Brave New World* and *1984*.

Excavating previous intellectual debates can be useful, not so much for providing answers but for posing questions. After the First World War when the first flush of the revolutionary impulse had fizzled throughout much of Western Europe, a number of radical thinkers sought to understand how the social order was maintaining itself. The Marxist belief in the the inexorable dynamic of revolution was being shattered by the tenacity of the capitalist system to survive. It was in this context that Gramsci developed his notion of hegemony, the Frankfurt School was developing a critical theory, and in particular Herbert Marcuse (1964), in *One Dimensional Man*, sought to understand the process of introjection in which the values of a capitalist society become embedded into an individual psyche.

A succession of French theorists, rarely seduced by the notion of participatory democracy, have outlined similar ideas. Althusser wrote of an ideological state apparatus, including schools and universities that maintained loyalty to the capitalist order. And Pierre Bourdieu (1998), echoing a theme of Noam Chomsky, argued that social consent is manufactured, representative democracy is an illusion, and that the struggle for domination is less in the marketplace and more in the media place where bourgeoisie culture perpetuates itself.

The very notion of struggle has been displaced. While local struggles over working and living conditions will always occur, we have lost, at least for the moment, the sense of big struggles over the shape of the social order. The real success of capitalism has been to persuade us of its rightness and to embrace us in its working. We are all capitalists now. Through the creation of an all-embracing market mentality, the seductive power of the commodity and the wrapping of fulfillment and desire with purchase and consumption, capitalism has shown itself so infinitely adaptable that even resistance and contestation is commodified and sold. There is now a strong and binding connection between commodities and identity, satisfaction and consumption. A linkage between political economy and psychoanalysis, first outlined by Eric Fromm and Charles Reich, would seem to be an important way for us to unravel some of the strands that bind us to this tenacious social order.

We should be wary, however, of accepting a hermetically sealed connection between order and consent. If consent is manufactured how does radical change come about? How does any change come about? One view is that we are recycling notions: from focus groups come advertising campaigns and media strategies that package our beliefs and fears into commodities, a closed cycle of desire and satisfaction, endlessly repeating itself from dream to commodity back to desire and commodity. But change does occur and it takes place when people interact; when discourse is "real"; and that occurs when people come together, or are brought together to talk, discuss, share, complain; and when individual fears and dreams are shared and shaped by comparison and contrast, empathy and argument. And this takes place most palpably in cities. Taking to the streets is not only an age-old political strategy, it has become a necessary corrective to the imposed media images. Resistance takes place when lived urban space conflicts with the dictates of the marketplace and the commodified images of the media place.

The Cosmic City

The city is a religious artifact. For modernists this sentence may seem strange, even incomprehensible. Religion has been too long counterpoised to the continuing enlightenment project of rationality. The city has been so long associated with the modern and the contemporary in the Western imagination that it is read as the site of the irreligious and the secular. But cities have always reflected and embodied cosmologies. The earliest cities mirrored the world. Indeed they were the world. The size, shape, orientation, location, siting, and naming of cities were tied to a deeper vision of the connection between the sacred and the profane. The Athens of Pericles, often depicted as the birthplace of Western rationality, was named after the goddess Athene. She was glorified and worshiped by the citizens and the success of the city was seen as a mark of her benevolence. The Parthenon was dedicated to her and once a year citizens marched in a long procession to the Parthenon atop the Acropolis and presented a sacred garment to the 40-foot-high statue of the goddess made from gold and ivory. The ancient Chinese cities such as Changan and Beijing were laid out on precise rectangular lines orientated to the four points of the compass that embodied the shape of the world and the symbol of order in Chinese cosmology. The Aztec city of Tenochtitlan was also laid out in four equal parts, four being a magical number in Aztec cosmology indicating the completeness of the world. The boundaries of the four quarters of the city met at a central point occupied by the Great Temple and imperial palaces. City layout and building design were a homology with the wider cosmos. In the Hindu city of Angkor Wat each step on the temples marked a stage in the solar cycle, each terrace represented a tier of the world. The earliest cities were marketplaces and living places but above all they were ceremonial sites of religious recollection and cosmic narrative. The site and shape echoed religious cosmology. Even the grid, a seemingly secular form of urban design, contains a fantasy of turning chaos into order, transforming topography into geometry. The very act of founding a city and planning a city was connected to how the wider world worked; human involvement in and responsibility for the world were embodied in city location, city form, and city shape. The city was the cosmos, the cosmos was embodied in the city. This macrocosm–microcosm also extended from city to body. The walled, quartered medieval city was a microcosm of a larger world but also a metaphor for a bounded, divided self.

The urban cosmologies justified (they still do) the social hierarchy. The cities gave substance to the line from the gods to the people through the ruling classes. Through the built form of the city and urban rituals the social hierarchy was sanctified and legitimized. Festivals, ceremonies, and rituals tied the people, the rulers, and the gods together in spectacular urban connections.

The long history of urbanism would reveal a steady secularization of the city, a growing disenchantment. In the West, the advent of the merchant city, the humanist city, and the capitalist city all undermined the city as *the* site of cosmic narrative. Religious observance did not disappear, it often increased in outbreaks of religious fervor, but the city itself lost its religious significance. There were individual churches and religious communities but the city was reduced to a meaningless background for human behavior. The city became illegible as a religious document;

it was no longer a religious artifact, a text for understanding the world; less and less was it a site for taking part in rituals of cosmic significance that tied together people and place, the sacred and the profane. The word "profane," by the way, means "outside the temple." Over time more of the city was outside the temple. The city became part of the God-shaped hole of the modern world.

The market city, based on individual adherence to the power of the market (I am what I consume), provides little in the way of cosmic significance. Consumption- and wealth-display provide only one layer of meaning and little by the way of spiritual depth and resistance to the contingencies of human life and suffering. The market gives us social positioning, not human understanding; social ranking, not communal meaning. At its existentialist bleakest the city becomes a setting for the meaningless passage of the individual through a blind universe, bereft of meaning. One of the more dramatic images is provided in James Kelman's (1994) novel *How Late It Was, How Late*: a man wakes up in jail, blind. He stumbles his way through a Kafkaesque nightmare. There is something heroic about the will to "batter on" but it is tragically heroic, an act of blind individual will in the face of an indifferent, cold world. A meaningless life beyond the will to survive.

This existential crisis is not a global phenomenon. In many non-Western cities, religion has survived; and even in the West many are looking at religions, less as false consciousness – the opiate of the people – and more as acts of collective identity and resistance to globalization. More accurately it is an accommodation with globalization as extended communities around the world shape their sense of themselves through religion. The postcolonial city is becoming the more religious city. Many cities are becoming enlivened by new faith communities, new sites of religious observance; even club culture can be seen as a Dionysian celebration as acolytes orgiastically dance the night away. In the city there are many and varied attempts to fill the God-shaped hole at the center of our materialistic culture. Thomas Moore (1997), for example, writes of the need for, and practice of, more soulful cities. The postmodern city has become the site for a rich variety of religious cosmologies.

The Collective City

Cities are sites of collective provision, collective consumption, and the workings of civil society. They are shared spaces, a place of parallel and sometimes intertwined lives, joint projects, externalities, and neighborhood effects. The organization of this collective project has varied over time and across space. I will examine briefly two issues: collective goods and services, and the notion of civil society.

The city is a site for the provision and consumption of collective goods and services. Two basic divisions can be identified in the organization of collective goods and services: private or public provision, and private or public consumption. The resultant fourfold division provides a basic anatomy of the city. Take the case of transport, which can be either provided by the market or by the state. In most cases the large, capital investment projects, such as highway construction or mass transit systems, tend to be handled by the state. The market shies away from such big, long-term risky projects. The work of David Harvey (1982) has pointed to the connections and tensions of this public/private split in the production and configuration of the capitalist space economy. The consumption can vary from the more private, such as the automobile, to the more public, the subway or bus. Around the world the shift has been from public to private consumption and it is tied to trends of individualism and the decline of civic engagement.

These divisions are more than just alternative ways of providing or consuming goods and services – they have become the epicenters of fundamental debates about the social contract. In recent years there has been an assault on the notion of the public provision of the collective. Collective provision and consumption has been associated with the discredited Left. Socialist cities were meant to take away the power of the market to influence social and spatial outcomes. The defeat of communism, the decline of the Eastern bloc and the apparent failure of the socialist agenda to garner mass support has meant a withering away of the collective ideal. To be sure this has not prevented the state from assuming huge influence and spending power. In the US, for example, critics of big government and government spending see no apparent paradox in their demands for less government, but call for more government spending on "defense" and on giving the the power of capital punishment to the state. Governments cannot be entrusted with providing basic human services but seemingly they can be given carte blanche to spend billions of dollars on armaments or to take human life.

Collective goods are described less by fiscal realities and more by social and political power. Subsidies to corporate interests, corporate welfare, are less discussed than income support to low-income households. Subsidies to home owners are seen as less destructive to the social order than subsidies to the unemployed. One is legitimized, the other is delegitimized. The big debate about political control of the market is made most vivid in our discussions on collective goods and services. There has been a decline of the Keynsian city and a withering away of the socialist city. At this millennial juncture we are in the process of a fundamental shift in the collective organization of the city. Civil society has emerged from the set of rules and practices established in the shared space of the city. The first cities were gated communities and notions of a public good or civic order were slow to develop, always it seems, able to be undermined by family and group loyalties.

There is now a great deal of interest in civil society, social capital, and all those interstitial areas between the realm of formal politics and the marketplace. Civil society operates between the state and the market. The decline of the Keynsian state has undermined reliance on the state, while the operation of the market creates inequalities in social and spatial outcomes. For a number of commentators civil society has now become a terrain of social opportunity providing one of the few possibilities of maintaining an emancipatory project. A number of commentators have stressed the positive forms of civil society. Robert Putnam's (1993) notion of social capital, for example, refers to the ability of civil society to transcend family and group ties; and John Friedmann (1998) has written on the possibly emancipatory connections between civil society and urban planning.

While civil society is important we should be careful of seeing it as a panacea. Janet Abu-Lughod (1998) reminds us that civil society contains the Michigan Militia and Ku Klux Klan as well as chess clubs and benign neighbor groups. Moreover, underlying many of the debates concerning civil society and the state is a Greek notion of the polis, a small, almost homogeneous, community. The contemporary city, however, has always been a problem for the workings of democracy. Growing heterogeneity, suburbanization, and the fragmentation of city governments have undermined the urban community. The Greek polis was small and unitary. The contemporary city, in contrast, has a metropolitan fragmentation that separates out center from edges, cities from suburbs, blacks from whites, rich from poor.

A number of years ago, Kenneth Galbraith (1958) wrote of the growing disparity between private affluence and public squalor. In many cities around the world the disparity seems to be growing. As the city becomes balkanized, architecturally into gated communities, and politically into exclusive suburbs and abandoned inner cities, simply calling for civic engagement, a major chord in social commentary on the city, is to miss this wider structural context. To be actively involved in your all-white suburban neighborhood may be public involvement, but it is not civic engagement.

The city has always been full of paradoxes: affluence with squalor, civic obligations with individual needs, and public duties with private actions. The precise mix has varied over the years. The cities of classical Greece, almost two-and-a-half millennia ago, combined public affluence and private squalor, private actions were circumscribed with civic obligations, and the marketplace did not dominate over the temple or the agora. Contemporary cities are marked by the power of the market over the polis and the temple, private affluence (of a minority) with public squalor and the lauding of individual rights over civic obligations. It will be interesting to note the changing balance of this urban equation over the new millennium, with the city center stage of the evolving, contested social order.

REFERENCES

Abu-Lughod, J. 1998: Civil/uncivil society: confusing form with content. In M. Douglas and J. Friedmann (eds), *Cities For Citizens*, Chichester: John Wiley Press, 227–38.
Bourdieu, P. 1998: *On Television*. New York: New Press.
Chatwin, B. 1987: *The Songlines*. New York: Viking.
Friedmann, J. 1998: The new political economy of planning: the rise of civil society. In M. Douglas and J. Friedmann (eds), *Cities For Citizens*, Chichester: John Wiley Press, 19–35.
Fyfe, N. (ed.), (1998): *Images of The Street*. London and New York: Routledge.
Galbraith, J. K. 1958: *The Affluent Society*. London: Hamish Hamilton.
Hall, P. 1998: *Cities in Civilization*. London: Weidenfeld and Nicholson.
Harvey, D. 1982: *The Limits to Capital*. Oxford: Blackwell.
Jacobs, J. 1969: *The Economy of Cities*. New York: Random.
Kelman, J. 1994: *How Late It Was, How Late*. London: Secker and Warburg.
Marcuse, H. 1964: *One Dimensional Man: Studies in the Ideology of Advanced Industrial Society*. Boston: Beacon Press.
Moore, T. 1997: *The Re-Enchantment of Everyday Life*. New York: HarperCollins.
Preston, D. 1998: Cannibals of the Canyon. *The New Yorker*. November 30, 76–89.
Putnam, R. 1993: *Making Democracy Work: Civic Traditions in Modern Italy*. Princeton: Princeton University Press.
Sahlins, M. 1972: *Stone Age Economics*. Chicago: Aldine-Atherton.

Chapter 3

Putting Cities First: Remapping the Origins of Urbanism[1]

Edward W. Soja

The development of society is conceivable only in urban life, through the realization of urban society.

Henri Lefebvre, translated from *Le droit à la ville. Éspace et politique,* 1968

What I am saying is that every city has a direct economic ancestry, a literal economic parentage, in a still older city or cities. New cities do not arise by spontaneous generation. The spark of city economic life is passed on from older cities to younger. It lives on today in cities whose ancestors have long since gone to dust... These links of life may extend – perilously tenuous at times but unbroken – backward through the cities of Crete, Phoenicia, Egypt, the Indus, Babylonia, Sumeria, Mesopotamia, back to Çatal Hüyük itself and beyond, to the unknown ancestors of Çatal Hüyük.

Jane Jacobs, *The Economy* of Cities, 1969

To investigate the city is therefore a way of examining the enigmas of the world and our existence.

Lea Virgine, in Mazzoleni, *La città e l'immaginario,* 1985[2]

My intent in this brief essay is not simply to re-explore the ancient origins of cities, but also to encourage a critical rethinking of the ways scholars have written about cities and the role of urbanization in the historical development of human society. The sequence of quotes presented above sets the scene for this double enquiry, beginning with Lefebvre's assertive premise that the development of society is conceivable only in urban life, in and through the creation and realization of a specifically urban society. Jane Jacobs expands on this to connect contemporary urbanism and the "spark of city economic life" to a virtually unbroken chain of urban societies stretching back over 10,000 years to her choice for the first known city, Çatal Hüyük in south-central Anatolia. The concluding premise is even bolder and more challenging. It expands the scope of urban studies well beyond its traditional domain to suggest that investigating the city leads to new ways of understanding the "enigmas of the world and our existence," the ultimate aim of all practical and theoretical knowledge.

The Precession of Urbanism: Putting Cities First

The conventional picture of the origins of cities begins around 15,000 years ago in Southwest Asia. After the retreat of Pleistocene glaciation, egalitarian hunting and gathering bands began to intensify their exploitation of wild plants and animals and to settle in more permanent camps. Between 9,000 and 10,000 years ago in such places as Jericho and Çatal Hüyük, plant and animal domestication had advanced to the point of intentional cultivation and herding, leading to a more stratified and larger-scale social order. Farming villages multiplied and spread through a T-shaped region from the Taurus to the Zagros Mountains (Turkey to Iran) and south through the Levant to the Lower Nile Valley, initiating the first great breakthrough in the development of human societies, the Agricultural or Neolithic Revolution.

In these now agrarian societies, organized around kinship ties and small "village states," innovations and adaptations to the environment increased. Villages became larger and larger, but there were no true cities until agricultural development shifted, around 6,000 years ago, from the highland arc of Mesopotamia to the fertile alluvial valleys of the Tigris and Euphrates in the area known as Sumeria. Symbolized and stimulated by the local invention of writing and larger-scale irrigation technology, the city, the state, and class-structured urban society "crystallized" together in the first city-states, giving birth to what we call today "civilization," from the Latin *civitas*, or city. From this base in Sumeria and the lowland "Fertile Crescent," the so-called Urban Revolution spread in many different directions, including into Europe where Western scholars argue that the city-state and civilization reached its most advanced early forms in classical Athens and Rome. In this process and its historical extensions and reinventions, the monarchial and patriarchal state and empire, and much later the nation-state, increasingly subsumed the importance of the city as a developmental force in human society.

Many archeologists and prehistorians describe the crystallization of the first cities and city-states as a "synoecism." In *The Emergence of Civilization* (1990: 155), a text that creatively reflects and expands upon the canonical sequence described above, Charles Keith Maisels defines synoecism (pronounced sin-ee-sism) as "interdependence arising from dense proximity" and uses it to explain the urban origins of state government and administration based on writing, the hallmark of civilization. In *Postmetropolis* (2000) I adapt this term to refer more generally to *the stimulus of urban agglomeration* and call it *synekism*, to recapture the hard k-sound of the original Greek *synoikismos*. In ancient Greek, *synoikismos* literally meant the condition arising from dwelling together in one house, or *oikos*, the root term for such words as economics, ecology, ecumene, and ekistics, coined by the Greek architect and planning theorist Doxiades to describe the comprehensive study of all human settlements from the household to the global scales. More expansively, *synoikismos* was used to describe the union of several smaller urban settlements under a dominant or "capital" city, thus implying some form of urban-based governmentality and a regional network of settlements (region derives from the Latin *regere*, to rule). Combining these meanings, synekism connotes the economic and ecological interdependencies and the positive as well as negative synergies that arise from the purposeful clustering and collective cohabitation of people in space, in a "home" habitat.

Aside from its obvious affinities to notions of "agglomeration economies," this expanded idea of synekism relates to several other concepts of significance in contemporary urban studies. As a force shaping political governance, economic development, social order, and cultural identity, synekism has a definite *regionality* in the sense of occurring within a multilayered hierarchy of nodal regions, an *urban system* of settlements. There is also a kinship here to the original Greek term *metropolis*, literally "mother city," the dominant *polis* of a colonized constellation of cities, towns, villages, and less densely settled hinterlands that defines a regional or territorial *homeland*, a larger scale *oikos*. Even the first cities can thus be seen as inherently metropolitan, as dominant nodal centers of a network of settlements defining a *city-region*. The concept of synekism also focuses attention on what can be called the *spatial specificity of urbanism* and its role in the dynamic processes of innovation, development, and change associated with what can be broadly defined, following Lefebvre, as the *social production of cityspace*.

There has been a long debate among urban scholars concerning the spatial specificity of urbanism, hinging on the question of whether the city and cityspace can be the specific object of theoretical inquiry or whether it is merely the outcome and reflection of more general social processes. When seen only as fixed spatial forms arising from externally generated forces (social, ecological, historical), cityspace becomes little more than a receptive container, a place in which and to which things happen, with no intrinsic theoretical significance. Cityspace and its specific geography are thus something to be explained, not a source of explanation in and of itself. But seen as a dynamic and problem-filled process of "making geographies" that are capable of generating innovation, growth, and both societal and individual development from within their regional domain, the synekistic social production of cityspace and the evolving spatial specificities of urban life take on a more powerful theoretical and explanatory significance. Building on these more robust conceptualizations of urban spatiality, we can return with a different perspective to the debates on the origins of cities.

A first step in rethinking the geohistory of cityspace is to release the force of synekism from its confinement to the moment of city-state formation, and to see it as a fundamental and continuous factor in the entire history of human society, from the deepest past to the immediate present. When this is done, the traditionally defined sequence from hunting and gathering to domestication and the formation of farming villages to the full-blown Agricultural Revolution and only then to the Urban Revolution becomes open to alternative interpretations. There is now sufficient evidence to suggest the possibility, at least in Southwest Asia, of *putting cities first*, that is, pushing back the origin of cities to a time before the Agricultural Revolution, and recognizing synekism, the stimulus of urban agglomeration, as one of the indispensable foundations not only for the development of agriculture but also for the appearance of agricultural villages, rural life, pastoralism, large-scale irrigation systems, writing, class formation, and the state. In opening up this revisioning, I am not suggesting that the conventional sequence must be discarded, but rather that another course of originating events may also have been involved, unrecognized by scholars who have overly narrowed the definition of the city and synekism, as well as the importance of a critical spatial perspective, in understanding the historical development of human societies. To illustrate and develop this argument here, let us look at the remarkable site of Çatal Hüyük.

Learning from Çatal Hüyük

Çatal Hüyük (alternatively Çatalhöyük, the mound or *tell* of Çatal, pronounced cha-TAHL-hu-yook) since its major excavation in the 1960s has become the focal point for a much larger interpretive literature not just on the origins of cities but on more general aspects of the human condition. Although its peak development was probably predated by the biblically trumpeted Jericho, it is today widely recognized as the world's first significant urban center and for the key role it played in the early development of agriculture and many other major technological, social, and artistic innovations. Leading its first round of excavation was James Mellaart, a British archeologist who first brought this remarkable site to worldwide attention in an article in *Scientific American* in 1964, entitled "A Neolithic City in Turkey."

As Mellaart states, beginning at least 9,000 years ago the central Anatolian Plateau became the most culturally advanced region of the Neolithic world, with a developing network of settlements spread over thousands of square miles and a local urban society which he described as having "a definitely metropolitan air." Trade was already well developed, based mainly in obsidian, the hard volcanic glass used primarily for tools, but also involving wild varieties of cereal grains, legumes, and animals. Recent DNA evidence has confirmed that there was a remarkably concentrated rush of plant and animal domestication between 10,000 and 9,500 years ago, centered in eastern Anatolia but extending throughout the T-shaped region mentioned earlier. Found in and around this area are the first "founder crops" of domesticated barley, wheat (einkorn, emmer, and bread varieties), chickpeas, vetches of various sorts, peas, lentils, broad bean, grapes, olives, and flax, as well as the first domesticated sheep, goats, cattle, and pigs. Less than a hundred sites have been excavated in this Neolithic core region, but Çatal Hüyük is among the oldest and is by far the largest, with a population that some now estimate to have been as many as 10,000 permanent residents.

This is a significant point, for Jericho and Çatal Hüyük certainly did not originate as agricultural villages and *no specialized agricultural villages have yet been discovered anywhere in the world that predate them*. In other words, the city and urban life appear to have come first, built by sophisticated and relatively egalitarian bands of hunters, gatherers, and traders. Full-scale agriculture and agrarian society came later, more as a consequence than a cause. Not only does this "precession" of the urban challenge the established model of human sedentism (moving from kraals to more permanent camps to hamlets and villages growing ever larger to become towns and then cities), it goes against the grain of those interpretations of history that emphasize social relations of production. What is suggested here is not that an agricultural surplus was necessary for the creation of cities, but that cities *were necessary for the production of an agricultural surplus*. Also contrary to many contemporary expectations is another implication, that major innovations and substantial societal development can come from relatively egalitarian, weakly stratified, and nonpatriarchal communalist cultures.

Many contemporary archeologists contend with these possibilities by simply rejecting the definition of Jericho and Çatal Hüyük as cities, even with the recent estimates of the latter's population size. This may work for some to sidestep the challenge, but there is much more evidence to be noted that sustains the view that an extraordinary synekism was operating in these first cities. The pueblo-like settlement of Çatal Hüyük, unlike Jericho, was never surrounded by massive stone fortifications. Cityspace consisted of a dense agglomeration of attached houses without any streets or paths between them, at least at ground level. Access and movement within the settlement occurred on the laddered roofs, with defense against human and natural intrusions provided simply by the continuous perimeter of timber-reinforced and doorless house walls. There was at least one public square, which may have served as a marketplace, and many small open courts probably used mostly as refuse pits. There was also an abundance of shrines, about one to every four houses, but no indication of a dominant religious center or temple. The shrines and many homes were elaborately decorated with wall paintings, plaster reliefs, small cult statues, animal heads, and bull horns.

Female deities and cult statuettes become more prominent over time in Çatal Hüyük, and wall paintings depicting hunting scenes decline significantly in number in favor of realistic and abstract representations of fertility symbols, agricultural production, and urban life. These changes suggest not only the transition from hunting and gathering to agriculture but also the consolidation of a new gender-based, and possibly matricentric, division of labor associated with the early stages of urbanization. Permanent and stable urban settlement made women's work and especially their religious and secular power more central to the production and reproduction of urban spatiality and sociality, leading Mellaart to conclude that the religious culture of Çatal Hüyük was mainly created by women. The relative openness of the town plan, the absence of monumental fortifications such as those at Jericho, the fact that no signs of violent death were found among the abundant skeletal remains excavated, and other indications that urban society in Çatal Hüyük was remarkably peaceful and productive for nearly a millennium, probably continued to enhance, and also to be enhanced by, the social power of women, at least until the rise of the first more formally institutionalized Mesopotamian city-states around 4,000 BC.[3]

Within this built environment was an extraordinary collection of highly skilled artists, craftworkers, manufacturers, and merchants, among them the first known weavers of cloth and tapestry, the first crude pottery-makers and carvers of elaborated wooden bowls, the first metalworkers along with the beginnings of a substantial weapons industry, and the carvers of some of the best religious statuary of the Neolithic, including the now famous "Mother Goddess." Perhaps even more iconically revealing, here we also find the first handcrafted mirrors, hemispheres of polished obsidian backed with plaster, and what all major art history textbooks, as well as the *Guiness Book of Records*, recognize as the first painting of a humanized landscape. The latter is of particular significance in the geohistory of cityspace. This very special – and very spatial – fresco was found on a wall in one of the oldest shrines, and brilliantly expresses the emerging popular awareness of the spatial specificity of urbanism. It depicts in the foreground a creatively cartographic representation of cityspace, stunningly detailed yet abstractly perceived, with about

Figure 3.1 Reconstruction and original of cityscape painting at Çatal Hüyük (Source: (*top*) James Mellaart, *Çatal Hüyük* 1967: Plate 60; (*bottom*) de la Croix, Tansey, and Kirkpatrick, *Art through the Ages*, 9th edn, New York: Harcourt Brace Jovanovich 1991: 46, figure 2–8, landscape with volcanic eruption (?), detail of a copy of a wall painting from Level VII, Çatal Hüyük, ca. 6150 BC)

75 separate building footprints set against a backdrop dominated by a gently erupting vermilion-colored volcano: the world's first known example of a self-consciously panoramic urban art form. What is even more remarkable is that the Çatal Hüyük panoramic cityscape remained the only true painting of the humanized landscape to be found anywhere in the world for the next 7,000-plus years.

In *The Economy of Cities* (1969), Jane Jacobs drew on Mellaart's work to launch her own richly imaginative revisioning of the Urban Revolution and the evolution of cities. She describes New Obsidian, her ancestral site for Çatal Hüyük, as a "pre-agricultural city of hunters" established more than 11,000 years ago and centered around the crucial obsidian trade. New Obsidian was not simply a home base for hunting and gathering but also a performatively urban agglomeration that was capable of generating economic growth from its own internal resources, from the construction of a cityspace that both stimulated and reflected economic innovation, new forms of productive work, and an expanding division of labor, the hallmarks of her definition of the urbanization process and very close to what I have called synekism. Of particular interest is her detailed tracing of the endogenous process that led to the domestication of wild cereal grains and the subsequent development of intentional cultivation and full-scale agriculture, as well as the budding off of the first farming and herding villages as satellites of the City.[4] For Jacobs, the product of this synekistic social and spatial process is the specifically *urban* origin of the Agricultural Revolution and along with it the development of subordinate networks of agricultural, pastoral, trading, and service settlements, and the beginnings of what we define today as rural life.

Jacobs's imaginative scenario, increasingly supportable in the light of recent archeological findings, contains within it not only the seeds of such contemporary ideas about economic expansion as import-substitution strategies and export-base models, but also, by putting cities first, she constructed a comprehensive, powerful, and pervasively spatial theory of agglomeration economies that would significantly influence a more contemporary generation of geopolitical economists and economic geographers. It was not agriculture that was the salient invention of the Neolithic for Jacobs, but rather the stimulus of urban agglomeration, "the fact of sustained, interdependent, creative city economies that made possible many new kinds of work, agriculture among them" (1969: 34). This self-generating capacity of city-regions, the "spark" of city economic life, emerges directly from the social production of cityspace, from the purposeful clustering and collective cohabitation of people in distinctively urban-regional agglomerations. In *The Regional World* (1997), Michael Storper updates our understanding of synekism, the stimulus of urban agglomeration, in a theory of "conventions" and "untraded interdependencies." He centers this work around the notion of economic *reflexivity*, defined as the ability to shape the course of economic evolution through reflexive human action and what he calls "competitive learning." This ability to reflect creatively on the human condition (I am reminded here of the first mirrors of Çatal Hüyük), is most acute in the "context of proximity" that is the city-region. Although Storper concentrates his attention on contemporary urban-regional worlds of production and globalization, what he has to say echoes back 10,000 years to the origins of the city and urbanism as a way of life, to use that famous phrase of the Chicago School. Combining the past and the present enables us to understand better the title and head quotes of this chapter, "Putting Cities First." The mention of globalization also makes me recall the first sentence in Lewis Mumford's *The City in History* (1961), still the standard work on the subject despite Jane Jacobs's valiant attempt to revise its underlying premises.[5] Mumford writes, "This book opens with a city that was, symbolically, a world: it closes with a world that has become, in many practical aspects, a city." It is this quote that begins the first chapter of my *Postmetropolis*, which by no coincidence has the same title as the chapter you are reading.

An interesting epilog to the story of Çatal Hüyük is unfolding today in the Çatalhöyük Research Project, conceived and directed by Ian Hodder, a former student of Mellaart and one of the English-speaking world's leading critical and creatively postmodern theoretical archeologists. For more than 20 years, Hodder has been constructing what he calls a "postprocessual" and "contextual" archeology based on new theoretical perspectives derived from critical theory, structuralism, neo-Marxism, hermeneutics, and, more recently, poststructuralism, the new ethnography, feminism, postcolonial critiques, and critical postmodernism.[6] Through these contextual readings, the objects studied by archeologists are seen as both materially and conceptually constructed, simultaneously real-and-imagined, to refer back to the phrase I have used to describe the critical study of lived spaces in *Thirdspace* (1996). The Çatalhöyük Research Project is Hodder's first major attempt to put his theories to work at what he calls the "trowel's edge." The entire project is now online, taking advantage of multimedia technology to keep its work open to the world and to multiple forms of interpretation, reflecting one of the principles of postprocessual archeology.[7]

Thus far relatively little that is new and surprising has been found at Çatal Hüyük and nothing significant has been added specifically to the debate on putting cities first.[8] What is most notable, however, is not the preliminary findings but rather that this site is being excavated and interpreted by archeologists and other scholars who are unusually well informed in critical theory; acutely aware of the relevance of the past to contemporary issues of democracy, citizenship, gender, race, and class; assertively spatial in their outlook and methods; and equipped with a salient "postmodern attitude," which Hodder describes as an openness to difference, alterity, multivocality, and experimentation aimed at "the empowerment of marginal political and cultural constituencies"(Hodder et al. 1995: 241–2). Very rarely has the distant past become so vitally relevant to contemporary debates not only in specifically urban studies but also with respect to our more general understanding of the "enigmas of the world and our existence." This adds significantly to the ways we can learn from putting Çatal Hüyük first.

NOTES

1. Extracted from Introduction to Part 1 and chapter 1 in *Postmetropolis: Critical Studies of Cities and Regions,* Oxford, UK, and Cambridge, US: Blackwell, 2000.
2. Quoted in Chambers 1990: Some Metropolitan Tales. Chapter 3 in *Border Dialogues: Journeys in Postmodernity.* London and New York: Routledge. 51.
3. Çatal Hüyük and its Mother Goddess statues have become an important symbolic focus for academic feminist critiques of established patriarchal religions and androcentric power, as well as for the recent expansion of popular interest in Goddess theories and cults. See, for example, Gimbutas 1974 and 1989.
4. Jacobs sees this process of domestication as arising from selective trading and planting of wild cereal grains in the local household economy, leading to full-scale intentional cultivation. She also speculates that the first village settlements were not primarily agricultural but based on animal herding, which demanded much more space than farming and could not so easily be maintained in the vicinity of the city.
5. Mumford and Jacobs were probably the best known and most competitively combative urban critics and public intellectuals writing about the city in the 1960s. *The City in History,* first published by Harcourt, Brace in 1961, appeared before Mellaart's major

publications on Çatal Hüyük and before the most explosive period of urban crises and uprisings, both of which had a significant influence on Jacobs and her writings.

6. Through his position as Professor of Archeology at Cambridge University, Hodder has had many contacts with Anthony Giddens, until recently Professor of Sociology at Cambridge and now Director of the London School of Economics. Giddens's work features prominently in Hodder's retheorizations of archeology. For some of his more recent publications, see Hodder 1991; Hodder 1995; and Hodder and Preucel 1996.
7. The web pages for the project can be found at http://catal.arch.cam.ac.uk/catal. Of particular note are "Discussions with the Goddess Community" and the papers presented at a Liverpool conference in 1996 on "Postprocessual Methodology at Çatal," which include Hodder's keynote address engaging with current ideas about globalization and critical postmodernism entitled "Glocalising Çatal."
8. The first major publication of the project's early findings is Ian Hodder (ed.) 1996: *On the Surface: Çatalhöyük 1993–1995*. Cambridge: McDonald Institute for Archeological Research, and British Institute of Archeology at Ankara.

REFERENCES

Chambers, Ian 1990: *Border Dialogues: Journeys in Postmodernity*. London and New York: Routledge.

Gimbutas, Marija 1989: *The Language of the Goddesses: Unearthing the Hidden Symbols of Western Civilization*. San Francisco: Harper and Row.

—— 1974: *The Goddesses and Gods of Old Europe, 6500–3500 BC*. Berkeley: University of California Press.

Hodder, Ian 1991: *Reading the Past: Current Approaches to Interpretation in Archeology*. Cambridge: Cambridge University Press.

Hodder, Ian and Preucel, Robert 1996: *Contemporary Archeology in Theory*. Oxford and Cambridge, US: Blackwell.

Hodder, Ian et al. (eds.) 1995: *Intepreting Archeology: Finding Meaning in the Past*. London and New York: Routledge.

Jacobs, Jane 1969: *The Economy of Cities*. New York: Random House.

Lefebvre, Henri 1968: *Le droit à la ville / Éspace et politique*. Paris: Éditions Anthropos.

Maisels, Charles Keith 1990: *The Emergence of Civilization: From Hunting and Gathering to Agriculture, Cities, and the State in the Near East*. London and New York: Routledge.

Mellaart, James 1967: *Çatal Hüyük: A Neolithic Town in Anatolia*. London: Thames and Hudson.

—— 1964: A Neolithic City in Turkey. *Scientific American*, 210–14, 94–194.

Mumford, Lewis 1961: *The City in History*. New York: Harcourt, Brace.

Soja, Edward 1996: *Thirdspace: Journeys to Los Angeles and Other Real-and-Imagined Places*. Oxford and Cambridge, US: Blackwell.

—— 2000: *Postmetropolis: Critical Studies of Cities and Regions*. Oxford, UK, and Cambridge, US: Blackwell.

Storper, Michael 1997: *The Regional World: Territorial Development in a Global Economy*. New York and London: The Guildford Press.

Chapter 4

Photourbanism: Planning the City from Above and from Below

Anthony Vidler

Photography shows cities in aerial shots, brings crockets and figures down from the Gothic cathedrals. All spatial configurations are incorporated into the central archive in unusual combinations which distance them from human proximity.

Siegfried Kracauer, "Photography."[1]

Aerial photography, in its context as an extension of the traditional "view from above" as it had been established in Paris from the first balloon flights of the 1780s to the photographic surveys from balloon by the photographer Nadar, served from the outset as at once a machine of the "real" and agent of the surreal, an increasingly privileged instrument of the double desire of planners – utopian and projective.[2] As Kracauer noted, this viewpoint, entirely distanced from the ground, tended necessarily to increase the natural "distance" inherent in the photographic medium, and thus to increase its assumed objectivity and of course its inherent manipulability devoid of the difficult and intractable individual or social subject.

And yet, the camera, with its real effect, is also a primary instrument of resistance to this view from above, and, building on the tradition of street photos, after the rediscovery of Atget in the 1920s increasingly served to counter the aerial views of planners with the "on the ground" views of radicals and nostalgics who called for the art of city planning to recognize the historical and social context. In this sense the debates and uses of photography in urban planning replayed in a new key the debates over demolition and reconstruction that had begun long before Baron Haussmann. Here I want to focus on two moments in the modernist history of this discussion (which still goes on): that of the confirmation of the aerial view in its planning role by Le Corbusier in the 1920s and 1930s, and that of the not entirely successful opposition to this vision in the 1950s and 1960s.

It is well known that Le Corbusier had a penchant for airplanes: the illustrations and text of *Vers une architecture* (G. Crès et Cie, Paris, 1923), his sketches of Latin America from the air, his photographic album *Aircraft* (The Studio, London, 1935), are only a fraction of the instances when his "complexe de Saint-Exupéry" was unequivocally demonstrated.[3] His enthusiasm for flight was, as he recalled in 1935, provoked by hearing the roar of Le Comte de Lambert's airplane passing over his student garret in the Quai Saint Michel in 1909: "I heard a noise which for the first time filled the entire sky of Paris. Until then men had been aware of one voice only from above – bellowing or thundering – the voice of the storm." Later, when working for Perret he remembered that "Auguste Perret... burst into the atelier... 'Blériot has crossed the Channel! Wars are finished: no more wars are possible! There are no longer any frontiers!' "[4] From then on the aerial view, if not actual aerial vision, became a part of Le Corbusier's representational and conceptual technology. Airplanes, indeed, rapidly came to surpass cars in his lexicon of enthusiasms. If in *Vers une architecture*, the Delage grand sport was a modern equivalent to the Parthenon, the airplane stood as the model for the conception of the new house – "I place myself, from the point of view of architecture, in the state of mind of the inventor of airplanes,"[5] hence the presentation of the Maisons Voisin (not as the Maison Citrohan house *like* a car, but house *made* by an airplane manufacturer and according to the same principles). By 1932, indeed, the car had even been supplanted with respect to the Parthenon, as a photo from *La ville radieuse* (Vincent, Fréal et Cie, Paris, 1933) of two seaplanes seen through the columns attests.

We can trace a distinct evolution in Le Corbusier's thought, as he found in the airplane a model for architecture and a machine of planning. Thus in *Vers une architecture* the airplane was illustrated on the ground, in details and in flight throughout the second part of chapter 4, under the title "Eyes which do not see..." The first part of the book, "Liners," had been dedicated to the question of "organization," organization on the scale of a small city according to the implacable rules of the machine – "the liner is the first stage of a world organized according to the new spirit."[6] The last part, "Autos," had been dedicated to the emergence of standards and types, the quasi-Darwinian rules of evolution that governed the perfecting of Greek architecture from Paestum to the Parthenon, and equally auto design from the Humbert to the Delage. The second part, "Airplanes," by contrast, was about solving problems:

> The lesson of the airplane is not so much in the forms created, and, above all, one must learn not to see in an airplane a bird or a dragonfly, but a machine for flying; the lesson of the airplane is in the logic which presides over the enunciation of the problem and which has led to the success of its realization. When a problem is posed, in our epoch, it inevitably finds its solution. The problem of the house is not posed.[7]

The rest of the chapter deals centrally with the problem of the house – how to pose it and how to solve it, and deals not at all with the airplanes that profusely illustrate its principled argument. As Beatriz Colomina has pointed out, Le Corbusier's aim here was "the insertion of architecture into the contemporary conditions of production," conditions which included the publicity necessary to consumption.[8] Not a word, in a chapter entitled "Eyes which do not see" on the view from the plane itself – Le Corbusier had likely not yet been up in one; nor on the special world that is revealed from above, despite the fact that the frontispiece to Part II, taken by Le Corbusier from a publicity brochure for the Farman Goliath, dramatically illustrates this theme.[9] With respect to architecture, the airplane was important for what it represented as design submitted to the powerful functional determinants of flight.

But if this was true for Le Corbusier's understanding of architecture, it was certainly not the case for his developing theory of urbanism. Here the airplane was no longer so important as an analog of production methods – as in the Maisons Voisin described in *L'Esprit Nouveau* as models of serial production, the house as static airplane, the airplane as a flying house – as it was as a technique and visual instrument of planning. It was what the airplane revealed as a visual instrument, equivalent to the camera, the telescope, and the microscope that made it important. And most important to the design and planning of cities. If, as Colomina has argued, the photograph was more than a simple "record" of architecture for Le Corbusier, wherein the building itself might be envisaged as a kind of camera obscura through which to view the surrounding landscape, the aerial photograph, standing in for the planner's eye view, was the key for city form. This is evident from the illustrations to the *L'Esprit Nouveau* articles that made up the volume *Urbanisme* (G. Crès et Cie, Paris, 1925). Here, the idea of airplanes as simply the analogs of house design in their functionality and precision has been supplanted by the idea of the airplane as a central vehicle of knowledge, analysis, conception, and design.

In the various representations of the Ville Contemporaine, the diorama, so powerful a vehicle for the representation of the nineteenth-century metropolis, is challenged by the aerial view as the preferred representational device for the big city plan, a plan which is among the first to embed an airport at its center, significantly enough in the form of Saint Peter's, Rome. The photographic evidence for the new scale of the city is equally aerial: "At the same scale and at the same angle, view of the *Cité* of New York and of the *Cité* of the 'Ville Contemporaine.' The contrast is striking."[10] Le Corbusier had selected an aerial photo made of the Eiffel Tower from a balloon flight in 1909 for the cover of *L'Art Décoratif d'aujourd'hui*, a photograph that had already served Robert Delaunay for his painting of 1922, *La Tour Eiffel*, and in *Urbanisme* such views from the Eiffel Tower are used to simulate views from the office windows – "From these office windows will come to us the feeling of lookouts [*vigies*] dominating a world in order."[11] Other aerial photos are used, again to draw scale comparisons: a view of Venice and the Piazza San Marco to point to the "common measure of uniform quarters" contrasting with "the squares of splendor"; the aerial view of traditional settlements – Timgad, Kairouan; Chicago tenements contrasted with the "lotissments 'redents'"; and of Paris, the Place Vendôme. Two photos in particular, taken from the collection of the Compagnie Française aérienne, show, respectively, the quarter of the Archives, and the quarter of the Champs Élysées. They are compared with respect to the urban conditions they reveal. The captions read: "Is this a view of the seventh circle of Hell of Dante? No, alas, it is the terrifying shelter (*gîte*) of hundreds of thousands of inhabitants. The City of Paris does not possess these denouncing photographic documents. This view of the whole (*vue d'ensemble*) is like a sledge-hammer blow." Le Corbusier is sarcastic at the expense of the historicized romanticism of the tourist: "As for our promenades, we follow the labyrinth of streets, our eyes are ravished by the picturesque of these rugged landscapes, evocations of the past rise up," and pits such sentimental emotions against the rampant "tuberculosis, demoralization, poverty, shame" that "triumphs satanically" while the "Commission du Vieux Paris" nostalgically does nothing but collect and list examples of old wrought iron work.[12]

The aerial photograph (an accusatory document not yet owned by the City of Paris) is now an instrument of battle, a legal submission in a trial over the proper nature of urban space. For Le Corbusier an aerial photograph alone reveals the whole truth, shows what is invisible from ground level, demonstrates the case against overcrowding decisively. The final "blow" of the Corbusian sledgehammer is to juxtapose the aerial view of the proposed area of redevelopment, the Marais, against the plan for renewal at the same scale.[13] The tailpiece of *Urbanisme*, a seventeenth-century engraving showing Louis XIV planning the Invalides, shows the figure of Fama hovering over Paris; Le Corbusier has simply substituted the airplane's eye for that of the absolute monarch.

The martial analogy is apt enough, for of course it was as an instrument of reconnaissance that the airplane photo came into its own in 1914–18. Gradually, as the war developed, aerial bombardment and aerial surveillance became indissolubly linked. As Le Corbusier reflected, in 1935: "The bird can be dove or hawk. It became a hawk. What an unexpected gift to be able to set off at night under cover of darkness, and away to sow death with bombs upon sleeping towns . . . to be able to come from above with a machine-gun at the beak's tip spitting death fanwise on men crouched in holes."[14] At the start of hostilities, a camera found in the wreckage of a captured German Zeppelin inspired the French to set up a photographic corps under the Armée de l'air, with the help of a former professor of photographic science at the University of Paris, Louis-Philippe Clerc. Together with a new aerial intelligence section of the Service Géographique de l'Armée under General Bourgeois, these two services thenceforward became the primary source of aerial images, classified and popular, well into the 1920s. Towards the end of the war, the development of military information began to support new archeological studies. In Syria, archeologists from France and Britain, themselves trained in aerial reconnaissance, started to use "aerial discovery photography" in their surveys.

This combination of the military and the urban, not new in the politics of replanning Paris since Haussmann, was consolidated by Le Corbusier in *La ville radieuse* (The Radiant City), published in 1933 and written after his own flight to Moscow. As he wrote in *Aircraft*, Le Corbusier had discovered the potential of the airplane, practically and conceptually on this trip: "I thought I would shorten the journey by taking an airplane. I discovered the airports at Le Bourget, Cologne, and Berlin. I perceived that persons by dint of faith and determination had little by little, higgledy-piggledy, equipped hangars, instruments, buildings, and staff. And that airports were stations like railway stations. One set off at a given time, and lo! One arrived with chronometric exactitude."[15]

The book *La ville radieuse* celebrates the new aerial experience with gusto. A photo of Coste having just crossed the Atlantic, October 1930, opens the book,[16] as does the example by the engineer Mopin of the project for a reinforced concrete cantilevered airplane hangar.[17] In keeping with the war ideology of the plan, The Radiant City itself was not simply conceived from the air; it was also conceived with a view to its survivability under aerial attack, sensed to be an increasing danger in the 1930s. Citing the evidence of French and German military strategists – Lt. Col. Paul Vauthier, *Le danger aérienne et l'avenir du pays* (Paris, 1930) and Dip. Ing. Hans Schoszberger, *Bautechnischer Luftschutz* (Berlin, 1934) – Le Corbusier argues for the Ville Radieuse as defensible space, defensible that is from air attack. Against the "sinister apotheosis" heralded by aerial warfare, Le Corbusier argued that the type of city "Ville Radieuse," would, with its thin ribbons of buildings offering little surface for bombardment, its concrete flat roofs offering shelterlike protection, its air conditioning and elevation on pilotis protecting against poison gas, and its open parkland in which bombs might drop harmlessly, be the only kind of city "capable of emerging victorious from an air war."[18]

For the new forms of regional city, built along freeways or sinuously following the contours of coasts and mountain ranges, the aerial photograph afforded even more dramatic support. Here Le Corbusier's experience in South America was decisive. He was lyrical in recounting his second major flight experience undertaken in 1929 in a wooden airplane piloted by Mermoz and Saint-Exupéry for the inaugural voyage of passenger service between Buenos Aires and Paraguay. From above Le Corbusier noted all the landscape features of Latin America, the colonial settlements, the forests, the rivers, and pampas.[19] The spectacle was, he wrote, "cosmic." The sight gave rise to an interesting analogy: "The Earth is like a poached egg, it is a spherical liquid mass surrounded by a wrinkled envelope," and, "like the poached egg, the Earth is saturated with water on its surface, it is in a constant process of evaporation and condensation."[20] The dawn over Uruguay, the dispersal of the mist and dew by the sun, seen always with respect from the infinite horizon line, is "vertiginous." But beyond this spectacle, there lay another – that of an earth decaying beneath the waters and jungles that covered it. Here, by contrast, "the poached egg inclined us towards melancholy, to despair; I think even to a neurasthenia of 'the poached egg'. The earth is marked with all the marbling of a body in putrefaction."[21]

Looking back in 1964 Le Corbusier remembered that Saint-Exupéry had warned him: "Be prepared M. Le Corbusier; the airplane has now endowed man with an eye that can look down from 12,000, from 30,000 feet above the ground." Le Corbusier retorted, accurately enough as we have seen, "For years I have been using an eye that is 30,000 feet above the ground!" The architect was now endowed with a new eye: the eye of a bird transplanted into the head of a man; a new way of looking: the aerial view. What the rational intelligence had acquired in the way of knowledge by analysis, by comparison, by deduction, suddenly becomes a matter of total and first-hand experience for the eye. And to see is a mode of perception unutterably more forceful than simply conceiving with the brain.[22]

The calm and purifying effect of travel at an altitude of 1,000 meters, supports, in Le Corbusier, what he terms "human visions," as opposed to those "infernal visions" from a train or car, a state of sight that approximates to that detachment necessary for calm reflection: "I exist in life," Le Corbusier concluded, "only on the condition of *seeing*."[23]

The philosophy of the poached egg joined to the "law of the meander", observed by Le Corbusier in his sketches of the Parana delta, was of course to inform his plans for Rio, and later for North Africa. The view from the air has enabled the colonial occupation of the landscape to be realized as a kind of infinite apotheosis of technical space. As Manfredo Tafuri described Plan Obus for Algiers, the spatial environment is taken over, in a "stream of fluxes": "By spreading like a magma into reality, technology – or its image – subsumes it." Viewed from the heights of the "new Acropolis" created by the airplane, "the battle of technology against nature" is grasped "with a sense of vertigo."[24]

As Le Corbusier uses it such an eye was, in Latin America, but above all in Algeria, not simply a surveying eye, but also a surveillance eye. The ethnologist Marcel Griaule, who had led the expedition to study the Dogon in 1936, underlined this in his eulogy of aerial photography to the Paris geographical society: "De toute évidence les documents qu'elle établit constituent des instruments de travail de premier ordre pour *l'Administration coloniale*: gouverner un peuple, c'est d'abord le connaître. . . . les études de l'ethnologie aidera, par le fait même, les gouvernements coloniaux dans l'exercice d'une tâche difficile et aux multiples aspects."[25] A means of understanding the indigenous population, of course, but also as colonial oversight. By means of aerial photography Griaule was able to survey the territory of the Niger, the land of the Dogons, with the help of the Air Ministry and the military air arm of Gao, in a third of the time that a land survey would have cost. From *Ville radieuse* to *Les quatre routes*, from 1935 to 1945, Le Corbusier increasingly expands this colonial/territorial/aerial vision to encompass the planning of Europe and the World, creating in the process a species of what Hans Speier, the political sociologist, and New York colleague in exile of Siegfried Kracauer, termed "Magic Geography" in an important article in the 1941 volume of *Social Research*.[26] A comparison of Le Corbusier's map of the aerial routes of Europe in *Les quatre routes* with Speier's illustration of the German use of maps in war propaganda is sufficient to make the point.

With the close of hostilities, and with the enormous advances in technology stimulated by military reconnaissance in 1941–5, the aerial view became institutionalized as a central tool of planning, and, in France, largely through the efforts of Paul Chombart de Lauwe, a geographer and ethnologist at CNRS, attached to the Musée de l'Homme, who had himself crossed the Sahara in a tourist plane to aid the *mission ethnographique* of Griaule in 1936 and who was dubbed "le pilote ethnographe" (the enthnograph pilot) as he fought in the Free French Army from 1942–5.[27] Writing in 1948 in his edited volume *La découverte aérienne du monde* (Horizons de France, Paris, 1948) Chombart claimed "La vision aérienne du monde" (the aerial vision of the world) as *the* vision of modernity.[28] In the same volume Michel Parent, conservateur du Musée des plans en relief, wrote on "L'utilisation de la photographie aérienne par l'urbaniste" (the use of aerial photography by the urbanist) both as a tool to criticize Haussmannization, and as a way to celebrate the three-dimensional modernity of Le Corbusier's projects for La Porte Maillot, and the visionary perspectives of Le Corbusier whose spatial slogans and representations, he notes, are derived from aerial photography.[29] "The aerial view of the center of Paris," wrote Parent, "demonstrates to what extent Haussmann was led to disembowel the old quarters, to sometimes denature sites that the centuries had patiently harmonized."[30] This did not prevent him from eulogizing the projects of Le Corbusier, who had succeeded, he claimed, in realizing the perfect intersection of the "aerial vision and three-dimensional urbanism," against what he called "mole urbanism," the view from too close to the ground:

> Le Corbusier, great visionary of architecture and of future urbanism, has for the last twenty years oriented us to such researches. All his slogans, on the architecture of three dimensions, the synthesis of the major arts, are expressed in drawings derived from aerial photography. From the terraces of the great administrative blocks to come, aerial vision is called upon to

become the everyday vision of the city, and whatever one says, this vision is by no means despondent.[31]

Two years later, Chombart followed with a technical manual on *Photographies aériennes* that would, he claimed, lead to a new understanding of "the study of man on the earth," of human geography, ethnology, and archeology, but also of urban sociology and planning.[32] Accompanied by a detailed case study of the village of Urt in the Southwest of France, analyzing the relations between Basque and Gascon inhabitants through their spatial traces, Chombart systematically studies the method of local and regional aerial surveys, and the interpretation of photographs at all scales. But he is most concerned with the different technologies and geometries of vision appropriate to each specialization – special filters, colored screens, fast films, infrared views, and, above all different angles of view. A careful exposition of angles, of flight patterns, and of the distortions produced on irregular terrain, is followed by a geometrical analysis of correction techniques, stereoscopic views and their examination, in order to serve the needs of different disciplines.

Turning from the territory as a whole, to the city of Paris, Chombart, in a work that greatly influenced the Situationists after 1958, found that one of the best forms of documentation not only of the physical milieu, but also of social processes, was the aerial survey: "In the study of social space, an important part of its explication is linked to aerial views and graphic documentation. The aerial survey and research by comparative maps allows, not only the representation of the social space, but also the study of certain processes."[33]

The aerial view of a city, indeed, is, in Chombart's terms, the only means of developing a synthetic vision of its social space – "l'espace social" – which is the theme of the first part of his Paris study, a work influenced strongly by Maurice Halbwachs. Le Corbusier's *Plan Voisin* for Paris, conceived from this point of view, is for Chombart, "however exaggerated it has been from certain points of view," admirable, and the first to open up a "true debate" over planning, especially as it takes account of the value of the "essential symbolic monuments" of the city and their accessibility by the whole population. Chombart continued his interest in Le Corbusier in research into the housing solutions and their social results in the built *Unités d'habitation* after 1949.

The Chombart de Lauwe of whom I have been speaking, pilot, ethnographer and sociological expert in the aerial view, is also, interestingly enough the source of much of the evidence cited by the Situationists between 1958 and 1968 as they sought to develop a radical critique of urbanism and of Le Corbusier in particular. The first issue of the *International Situationist*, of June 1958, republishes Gilles Ivain's "Formulaire pour un urbanisme nouveau," illustrated by a large-scale aerial photograph of Southeast Paris (pp. 6–17) and a "map" showing typical geographical features (p. 20). Immediately following this article, was another, entitled "Venice a vaincu Ralph Rumney" (p. 28), who was reported as having set out to make a psychogeographic map of Venice, but finally reduced (by boredom) to a "purely static position" and lost in the Venetian "jungle," again illustrated by a map taken directly from Chombart showing all the movements of a young girl student living in the sixteenth arrondissement (PAP, I, 106), where the spatial limits are represented by her house, her piano lessons, and her courses at Sciences politiques. The Situationists, of course, argued strongly for the breaking of these spatial and psychological boundaries and the creation of a new "psychogeographic map" of the city, broken up into psychically unified quarters linked by arrows representing vectors of more rapid or random movement. Guy Debord recommended taxis. Here again Debord's map seems inspired by one of Chombart's, delineating the social organization of a sector of Paris.

Here, as Peter Wollen has argued (in a conversation with me), the Situationists are espousing, and with very similar methods, an equal if opposite vision of urbanism as totalizing, and from above, as that of their enemy Le Corbusier. It was not until 1961 that Raoul Vaneigem, in "Commentaires contre l'urbanisme," *International situationist*, 6 (1961), 33–7, finally developed the Situationist critique of Chombart in detail. Between 1961 and 1968, the *IS (International Situationist)* increasingly avoided propositions of a physical kind (Constant was expelled already in 1960 for daring to fix the Situationist vision in the concrete terms of an architectural project), and espouses an urbanism which is like no urbanism ever before conceived – a "unitary urbanism" of the streets and of the psychological and political desires and needs of the populace. Photos now celebrate the "unpaved street" – "Under the street the beach" – and the graffiti revolution of 1968.

Here there emerges the other side, so to speak, of the photographic revolution – that which inherently criticized the view from above: for photography, as the surrealists had demonstrated, was an equally powerful instrument of critique, employing all the modernist techniques of "making strange" and relying specifically on the "real effect" of the camera, whose increasing portability (the Leica) allowed the fleeting moments of the everyday to be captured as verité. As Pierre Mac-Orlan noted in his preface to the republishing of Atget's work in 1930, such photographs reveal the intimacy of a city – not its "official personality": "It is not through official architecture that cities impose their personalities, but by that indefinable appearance of popular streets which are so many little songs of a very delicate kind of patriotism." The little popular chanson, the small street, the familiar streetcry, has since the thirties been opposed to official culture with all the nostalgia of music halls, photo-magazines, both on the Left and the Right. Adrian Rivkin in his *Street Noises* has characterized this sensibility with respect to Maurice Chevalier; René Clair in film, and Robert Doisneau in photography fixed the genre.

One would think then, that so powerful a movement as this, fueled by Poujardism on the Right and the Popular Front mentalité on the Left, and doubly fueled by post-Second World War nostalgia for a settled France and a peaceful empire, would have brought the view from above decisively down to earth. And in one sense of course this happened, especially for the generation of the fifties and sixties. Many leaders of the uprising in 1968, readers of the *IS*, and influenced by Henri Lefebvre's call for the citizen's "right to the city" and his emphasis on the delicate and important structures of everyday life, were drawn from the student body of the Ecole des Beaux Arts. Influenced by the Situationists, these were increasingly open to revise principles of architecture that had so seriously damaged the centers of cities and created wastelands in the *banlieue*. Architects and theorists such as Antoine Grumbach, Roland Castro, Christian de Porzamparc, and others, began to revise their notions of urban intervention, developing a theory of the "impure" as against the "purity" of conventional modernism, and arguing that the city should build on itself as a continuation of the process of transformation over centuries, as opposed to the idealistic rupture installed by modern development.

Opposed to the wholesale demolition of quarters, however, this generation was unsuccessful in saving the nineteenth-century market of Les Halles, torn down to make way for a commercial development. And no amount of debate around this act of "vandalism" hindered the government in instigating the Centre Pompidou which, designed by the British architect Richard Rogers in partnership with the Italian Renzo Piano, was to influence the nature of French Modernism to the present. Completed in 1977 this high-tech fantasy, with its inner tubes, so to speak, revealed on the outside as a multicolored framework, and accessible to the public by way of banks of transparent escalators that form a "facade" from which to view the city, has set the tone for a generation of architects, and guided the style and method of President Mitterand's *grands projets*.

In this sense, from the vantage point of the end of the twentieth century, the aerial vision of Le Corbusier, and his posthumous "effect", has never ceased to inform French Modernism. Indeed, the entire program of Mitterand's *grands projets* implemented by Bernard Tschumi, which encompassed the development of the Parc de La Villette on the site of the former nineteenth-century abattoirs of Paris – the glass pyramid serving as the new entrance to the Louvre by I. M. Pei, the cubic "arch" at La Défense, the new "popular" Opera on the Place de la Bastille and the library – seems to have been conditioned by the sense that, from the air, the prismatic forms of the new projects will become comprehensible as a set of modern insertions. By a combination of high-tech construction and services, geometric purism, and a dedication to transparency given material emphasis in the case of the Louvre pyramid by the effort to manufacture a nonreflective glass and, in the case of the library, the attempt to make the towers transparent against all the programmatic needs of sheltering the books from daylight, these projects were, as selected personally by Mitterand himself, symbolic of centuries of French rationalism. Heirs to the grand building programs of Louis XIV, to the revolutionary cult of geometrical forms in the architecture of Claude-Nicolas Ledoux and the festivals of Jacques-Louis David, to the glass and iron architecture of architects like Henri Labrouste and Victor Baltard, to the large-scale planning projects of Haussmann, and finally, to Le Corbusier's brilliant absorption of these traditions into an abstract modernism, the *grands projets* summarize more than three centuries of state-centralized sponsorship of modernity and its architectural representation.

Perhaps we might have to recast the apparent opposition between the view from above and that from below in a more complementary way, say, for example in terms such as those presented by Lamorisse's classic movie *Le Ballon Rouge*. On the one hand, the stills from the film echo those of the Doisneau school; the grimy but familiar quarters, the romanticism of the "zone" pervasive *sine Apollinaire*, the everyday routine punctuated by moments of truancy all found their place in a vision of "situation" and small events; the *mineur* as opposed to the *majeur*. On the other hand, if we look at Pascal and notice where he is looking, it is always up, to the sky, and to the magic floating spheres that inhabit it. And when Pascal finally escapes from his tormentors – mother, school officials, local bullies – it is to the sky that he eventually ascends, holding onto the balloons that will enable him to look down with comfort at the world he has escaped. Back then to where Nadar started. We might well imagine that in later life Pascal settled down to a professional career as an architect or planner, maybe taking his revenge on the quarters of his repression, by razing them and replacing their small alleyways with big spaces. Certainly, the generation following 1968 seems to have no qualms over reviving the omnipresent view from above, the Corbusian gaze, as the successful visual polemics of the photo collages of Dominique Perrault's Bibliothèque de France bear witness.

NOTES

1. Siegfried Kracauer, *The Mass Ornament: Weimar Essays*, tr., ed., and with an introduction by Thomas Y. Levin (Harvard University Press, Cambridge, MA, 1995), p. 62.
2. The history of aerial photography has often been written – the elegant volume by Beaumont Newhall, *Airborne Camera: The World from the Air and Outer Space* (Hastings House, New York 1969) is perhaps the most concise. It begins with the first balloon photograph taken by Nadar in 1856 and ends with the photos taken from the *Gemini IV* spacecraft in 1968.
3. See the important summary by Bruno Pedretti, "Il volo dell'etica," *Casabella*, 531–2 (January–February, 1987), pp. 74–80.
4. Le Corbusier, *Aircraft* (The Studio, London, 1935), pp. 6–7. The original, unpublished, French text, "En frontispice aux images de l'épopée aérienne," is printed in *Casabella*, 531–2, pp. 111–13.
5. *Vers une architecture*, p. 85.
6. Ibid., p. 80.
7. Ibid., p. 86.
8. Beatriz Colomina, *Privacy and Publicity: Modern Architecture as Mass Media* (MIT Press, Cambridge, Mass., 1994), p. 159.
9. *Vers une architecture*, p. 81. See Stanislaus von Moos, (ed.), *L'Esprit Nouveau: Le Corbusier und die Industrie 1920–1925* (Ernst and Sohn, Zurich, 1987), pp. 248–9.
10. Le Corbusier, *Urbanisme*, p. 164.
11. Ibid., p. 177.
12. Ibid., p. 268.
13. Ibid., p. 274.
14. *Aircraft*, pp. 8–9.
15. Ibid., p. 10.
16. Le Corbusier, *La ville radieuse*, p. 15.
17. Ibid., p. 20.
18. Ibid., pp. 60–1.
19. Le Corbusier, *Précisions: Sur un état présent de l'architecture et de l'urbanisme* (Vincent, Fréal of Cie, Paris, 1930), pp. 4–7.
20. Ibid., p. 5.
21. Ibid., pp. 6–7.
22. Ibid., p. 83.
23. Ibid., p. 8.
24. Manfredo Tafuri, "*Machine e mémoire*": The City in the Work of Le Corbusier," in *Le Corbusier*, ed. H. Allen Brooks (Princeton University Press, Princeton: 1987), p. 210 (203–18). This remains the most incisive and suggestive analysis of Le Corbusier's urbanism and its relation to 19th and 20th century thought.
25. "It is fully apparent that the documents it establishes constitute working tools of the first importance for the official administration: to govern a people is first to know

it . . . studies in ethnology will help, by the same token, colonial governments in the exercise of a difficult task with different aspects." (Marcel Griaule, "L'emploi de la photographie aérienne dans la recherche scientifique," *L'Anthropologie* 1937), pp. 474–5. The *Géographie universelle* of the geographer P. Vidal de La Blache filled with aerial photos as a result of the development of this "cartographie aérienne" between 1935–9.

26. Hans Speier, "Magic Geography", *Social Research*, 8 (1941), 310–30.
27. Emmanuel de Martonne, *Géographie aérienne* (Paris, 1948), p. 15.
28. Paul-Henri Chombart de Lauwe, ed., *La découverte aérienne du monde* (Horizons de France, Paris, 1948), pp. 19–56.
29. Michel Parent, "L'utilisation de la photographie aérienne par l'urbaniste," in *La découverte aérienne du monde*, pp. 316–26.
30. Ibid., p. 316.
31. Ibid., p. 325.
32. Paul-Henri Chombart de Lauwe, *Photographies aériennes. Méthode – Procédés – Interprétation. L'étude de l'homme sur la terre* (Armand Colin, Paris, 1951).
33. Chombart de Lauwe, *Paris et l'agglomération parisienne*, 2 vols. (Puf: Paris, 1952), vol. 2, p. 5. In his bibliography Chombart cites Le Corbusier's article, "L'habitation moderne," in *Population*, Paris, 1948, as well as *La ville radieuse*, 1935 and the *Destin de Paris* (Sorlot, Paris, 1941).

Chapter 5

The Immaterial City: Representation, Imagination, and Media Technologies

James Donald

I

J.-K. Huysmans's *À Rebours* (*Against Nature*) is a fictional study of a certain type of dandy in the latter part of the nineteenth century, exemplified in the character of its hero, Des Esseintes.[1] Published in 1884, the novel recounts in exquisite detail his love of artifice, his fetishistic obsession with material objects, his often perverse pleasures, and his retreat from the hurly-burly of Paris into a private, interior reality.

As Des Esseintes teeters towards nervous collapse, he turns from his usual literary taste for obscure Latin authors to – surprisingly, perhaps – the works of Charles Dickens. The English writer fails to soothe his nerves as he had hoped. Gradually, however, "an idea insinuated itself in his mind – the idea of turning dream into reality, of travelling to England in the flesh as well as in the spirit, of checking the accuracy of his visions" (p. 132). Impulsively, he packs a trunk, takes a train into central Paris and, in weather foul enough for England, hails a cab.

> ...his mind conjured up a picture of London as an immense, sprawling, rain-drenched metropolis, stinking of soot and hot iron, and wrapped in a perpetual mantle of smoke and fog. He could see in imagination a line of dockyards stretching away into the distance, full of cranes, capstans, and bales of merchandise...Up above, trains raced by at full speed; and down in the underground sewers, others rumbled along, occasionally emitting ghastly screams or vomiting floods of smoke through the gaping mouths of air-shafts. And meanwhile, along every street, big or small, in an eternal twilight relieved only by the glaring infamies of modern advertising, there flowed an endless stream of traffic between two columns of earnest, silent Londoners, marching along with eyes fixed ahead and elbows glued to their sides (pp. 133–4).

Having bought a guide book to London, Des Esseintes seeks refuge from the rain and cold in the Bodega, a cellar in one of the Paris arcades so beloved of Walter Benjamin. It is full of English customers drinking port and sherry.

> His senses dulled by the monotonous chatter of these English people talking to one another, he drifted into a daydream, calling to mind some of Dickens' characters, who were so partial to the rich red port he saw in glasses all about him, and peopling the cellar in fancy with a new

set of customers ... He settled down comfortably in this London of the imagination, happy to be indoors, and believing for a moment that the dismal hootings of the tugs by the bridge behind the Tuileries were coming from boats on the Thames (p. 138).

From the cellar Des Esseintes moves on to a tavern where, despite months of near fasting, he indulges in what he imagines to be an English meal: oxtail soup, smoked haddock, roast beef and potatoes accompanied by pints of pale ale, Stilton cheese, and rhubarb tart (with porter) rounded off by coffee laced with gin. When the time comes to catch his train, he cannot bring himself to move.

When you come to think of it, I've seen and felt all that I wanted to see and feel. I've been steeped in English life ever since I left home, and it would be madness to risk spoiling such unforgettable experiences by a clumsy change of locality (p. 143).

He gathers together his luggage, his packages, his rugs and his umbrellas, and takes the cab and the train back home.

II

Des Esseintes is able to experience London, a city he has never visited, because he is already familiar with its representation in literature and in paintings. London exists for him as a collection of signs – "smells, weather, citizens, food, and even cutlery" (p. 143) – that connote an idea of the place. The intensity of his imagining may be extreme. Even so, and this is the first reason for starting with Huysmans, this tantalizing passage from *À Rebours* is a reminder that representations have real consequences. The way we experience cities is profoundly shaped by the immaterial city of word, image, and myth.[2] It is through them that we learn not only to see cities, but also how to live in them.

The question is therefore less representations of the city, than mediated pedagogies of urban life. Rather than assuming that there is a real city and then a representation of it, my starting point is that we experience cities as what Henri Lefebvre calls "representational space," and that this space comes into being through the interaction of inextricably entwined realities. The theorist and art practitioner Victor Burgin explains this approach in his book *In/Different Spaces*:

The city in our actual experience is at the same time an actually existing physical environment, and a city in a novel, a film, a photograph, a city seen on television, a city in a comic strip, a city in a pie chart, and so on.[3]

The important point is not just this simultaneity, but above all the productive transactions between urban realities. The traffic between fabric, representation and imagination fuzzies up epistemological and ontological distinctions and, in doing so, produces the city between, the imagined city where we actually live.

III

The second reason for starting with *À Rebours* is because it enables us to see that the immaterial city has its own histories just as much as any actual city.

The Dickensian London conjured up by Des Esseintes seems to refer to the opening of *Bleak House*, with its imagery of fog over the city, gas lamps dimly lighting an implacable November afternoon, and ill-tempered pedestrians negotiating muddy streets behind their umbrellas. Tracing the particular reference is less important, however, than the general observation that novels, at least from the eighteenth century on, helped to produce "the city" as an experiential category for a reading public. The structure and form of the genre disseminated certain ways of seeing of the urban landscape, certain perspectives on the life of its citizens, and so (I would argue) instituted certain structures of imagination. The earliest of these was probably the opposition between rural utopia and urban nightmare. Gradually, this was supplemented and to some extent displaced by the *Bildungsroman* narrative of heroic self-creation in the great city. The logic of Dickens's novels is a search for subterranean networks of community beneath the obscure and irrational surface of the class-divided city. To some extent they also share with the tradition of French novelists from Balzac to Zola an attempt to grasp the social complexity of the city by recording the variety of its demotic idioms and slang.

Behind the particular Dickensian London conjured up by Des Esseintes, then, there stands a sprawling, composite novel-city. As the nineteenth century progressed, this city of texts came to be characterized by frenetic activity and a growing degree of social opacity. Nevertheless, it continued to be peopled by a type of personality that is recognizably and pedagogically urban. From one perspective, the novel's structural openness to the city's multiple points of view and to the Babel of linguistic diversity gives the genre a semblance of democratic inclusiveness, an urban tolerance of difference. Viewed from another angle, the formal organization of this plenitude often appears to embody a powerful will to domination, a desire to subjugate urban heterogeneity to the design of an omnipotent, panoptic narrator. This mix of tolerance and paranoia produced a repertoire of responses to the city, from popular melodramas about master criminals and secret conspiracies to the *flâneur's* contemplative, estheticizing gaze.[4]

Dickens's mid-nineteenth-century London already contained many of these tensions and ambiguities. For all the detail of its description and the acuity of its observation, this city is already modern to the extent that it exists as a mental landscape as well as a geographical space or a complex but ultimately decipherable web of social networks. This is what is brought out by Huysmans in his account of Des Esseintes's relationship to the city. It is a view of an urban imagination that prefigures the representation of the city in the modernism of the early twentieth century.

Forty years on from *À Rebours*, in 1922, T. S. Eliot's *The Wasteland* shows how completely the city has been absorbed into the mental landscape of the observer. In the poem, London's fog and river and anonymous crowds are still there as they had been in *Bleak House* 70 years earlier. But now the city has become unreal.

> Unreal City,
> Under the brown fog of a winter dawn,
> A crowd flowed over London Bridge, so many,
> I had not thought death had undone so many.
> Sighs, short and infrequent, were exhaled,
> And each man fixed his eyes before his feet.

"The city is a state of mind," wrote the Chicago sociologist Robert Park in 1915. "The forces of the action have become internal," as Raymond Williams observes of James Joyce's novel *Ulysses*, like *The Wasteland* published in 1922, "in a way there is no longer a city, there is only a man walking through it."[5]

What is evident in the increasing emphasis on interiority between *Bleak House* and *The Wasteland* or *Ulysses* is a sense that, by the twentieth century, the narratives and images of the nineteenth-century novel were no longer adequate to the new realities of the city. They had been outstripped by the new rhythms and routines instituted by new modes of transport (the train and the automobile), the appearance of artificial lighting, new forms of communication, the rebuilding of many great city centers, and many of the phenomena analyzed by Walter Benjamin – advertising, expositions, department stores, and so forth. It was no longer possible to make sense of this new reality of speed and artifice using the old representational conventions. That is not to say those old forms and genres – and so the old ways of imagining – disappeared overnight. Rather, they were put into question by modes of literary and visual representation that gave expression to the sense that the city had become illegible. The city could not be represented in a single image. It could not be reduced to an encompassing narrative. In a sense, it had become unimaginable. From that crisis of representation were born cubism in painting, stream of consciousness in literature, and movements like constructivism and surrealism. The question they posed was whether "the city" was itself sustainable as a coherent concept or as a category of experience.

IV

Des Esseintes imagines London from Paris. In the 1880s, this existential dislocation was, it seems, still eccentric enough to be worthy of note. By the early decades of the twentieth century it had become almost a norm. Nor was this urban state of mind explored only by artists and writers. It was a way of being both encouraged and managed by new and largely urban technologies of communication: the newspaper, cinema, and, later, broadcasting.

In his 1903 essay "The metropolis and mental life," with Berlin in mind, the sociologist Georg Simmel attempted to explain the crisis of inner life produced by the modern city. This he attributed to a complex and demanding objective world that made unprecedented demands on subjective resources: the "overwhelming fullness of crystallised and impersonalised spirit."[6] The problem was intensified for the many provincial newcomers to the metropolis. With every crossing of the street, argues Simmel, the great city "sets up a deep contrast with small town and rural life with reference to the sensory foundations of psychic life." Elsewhere, outside the metropolis, "the rhythm of life and sensory mental imagery flows more slowly, more habitually, and more evenly." Unlike the detached *flâneur*, these new migrants were especially susceptible to "the intensification of nervous stimulation which results from the swift and uninterrupted change of outer and inner stimuli."[7]

The typical response to this intensity of urban experience was both defensive and creative: on the one hand, a blasé and expedient relationship to others, on the other, a sometimes extravagant degree of superficial individualization. In the rapidly growing Berlin of Simmel's day, however, there was another means for managing the illegibility and anxiety of the city. This was the mass circulation newspaper.

In the early twentieth century – and especially in Berlin, apparently[8] – these newspapers were a pedagogic medium that compensated for the impersonality and overstimulation described by Simmel. It provided dislocated city-dwellers with two things. One was a practical guide to surviving, exploiting, and also enjoying the city. The papers advertised jobs, and they listed sporting events and entertainment. The other was a collage of fragmentary stories to be consumed distractedly at home, in the workplace, or on the move in tram or train between them. Mass newspapers packaged a view of the world that not only mirrored, but actually made sense of, their readers' hurried and often uneasy experience of the metropolitan landscape.

Again it was not just through practices of representation that the newspaper shaped people's experiences of the city. They were affected more profoundly by symbolic structures and media technologies. In "The metropolis and mental life," Simmel was not concerned with modern media like the newspaper. Note, however, the terms in which he describes the experience of the metropolis. The modern city-dweller, he suggests, is overwhelmed by "the rapid crowding of changing images, the sharp discontinuity in the grasp of a single glance, and the unexpectedness of onrushing impressions." Might he not equally well be describing the new experience of the movie theater? For Walter Benjamin, like Robert Park a pupil of Simmel's, this experience of remorseless visual stimuli is what created the need for the film theater. Moviegoers and city-dwellers both equally embody the perceptual experience of the man of the crowd as defined by the poet Charles Baudelaire in nineteenth-century Paris: "a kaleidoscope equipped with consciousness." Film renders this experience, argues Benjamin. In the new medium, "perception in the form of shocks was established as a formal principle." In cinema "multiple fragments . . . are assembled under a new law."[9]

This "new law" for assembling multiple fragments in film to create a reality that transcends time and space was the cinematic principle of montage. This takes us back to the normalization of Des Esseintes's curious adventure. For, as the Harvard psychologist Hugo Münsterberg noted in his pioneering study of film spectatorship in 1916, cinematic editing allowed the viewer to have the experience of being "simultaneously here and there." Benjamin's famous description in "The work of art in the age of mechanical reproduction" of the liberating potential of the cinema might thus be read almost as a gloss on Des Esseintes's fantasy trip to London. However, Benjamin sees in the cinema not just the lure of distraction or daydreaming, but an explosive epistemological power. Montage arms cinema with an analytic light that can reveal the labyrinthine constraints of the ordinary, of commonsense knowledge, and so expand the spectator's field of possibilities:

> Our taverns and our metropolitan streets, our offices and furnished rooms, our railroad stations and our factories appeared to have us locked up hopelessly. Then came the film and burst this prison-world asunder by the dynamite of the tenth of a second, so that now, in the midst of its far-flung ruins and debris, we calmly and adventurously go travelling.[10]

V

Simmel and Benjamin, like Eliot and Joyce, were interested in the city as the locus of modernity. The mass newspaper and the cinema emerged as distinctively modern media. Does that mean that the representations, technologies, and pedagogies I have been describing have now become irrelevant, of interest only to cultural historians? Hasn't everything been changed utterly by the shift from an age of mechanical reproduction (the newspaper, the photograph, the movie) to an age of electronic communication (television, the fax, the Internet)? The question might suggest a different lesson to be learned from the instructive figure of Des Esseintes. From this point of view, he could be read not just as a portent of the transubstantiation of the city into a state of mind, but as prefiguring a solipsistic virtual reality that displaces the physicality of the city and of bodies moving through cities. Personally, I don't believe it. Why not?

Towards the end of *In/Different Spaces*, Victor Burgin talks about the city, cinema, and television. To be specific, he chides Fredric Jameson for structuring his discussion of space allegorically around the cinema, not television. He does so on the grounds of a comparison between the temporalities of the two media, and their relationship to the time of the city.

> The urban dweller who turns away from the image on her or his television screen, to look out of the window, may see the same program playing on other screens, behind other windows, or, more likely, will be aware of a simultaneity of different programs. Returning from this casual act of voyeurism they may "zap" through channels, or "flip" through magazines. Just as Benjamin refers to architecture as appreciated "in a state of distraction", so television and photography are received in much the same way. The cinematic experience is temporally linear. For all that narrative codes may shuffle the pack of events, the spatial modulations that occur in the diegesis are nevertheless successively ordered and experienced as a passage through space and time. The global space-time of television, however, is fractured and kaleidoscopic.[11]

The affinities Burgin notes between television and contemporary urban life could be attributed to changes in the city as well as to changes in the media. The media sociologist Roger Silverstone, for example, believes that too much fuss is made about the twentieth-century city, at the expense of any serious attempt to understand the unspectacular but massive growth of suburbs. As he points out, "for millions, and mostly by choice, the city was too much to bear. It was a place to leave."[12] Like Burgin, however, he is especially interested in the ontological implications of domestically based media like radio, television above all, but increasingly the Internet and other forms of electronic communication. For Silverstone, "suburbia offers a coincidence of the architectural and the televisual." This televisual reality of the suburb then grounds his view that political ideals like Habermas's public sphere are also too city-bound: both backward looking and too literally spatial. The reality of political community in suburbia is less the refeudalization predicted by Habermas than "a new kind of neo-participatory politics based on self-interest and grounded in defensive anxiety."[13] A similar point is made by the media theorist and cultural critic Margaret Morse. A posturban ontology of television, mall and freeway has rendered any notion of publicness hopeless: "older notions of the public realm and of paramount reality have been largely undermined, and a return to a pre-televisual world of politics, the street, or the marketplace is unlikely."[14]

Historically and sociologically, of course, Burgin, Silverstone, and Morse are right. More people watch television than go to the cinema (even if they watch a lot of films on television.) Fewer people live in city centers than in suburbs – or whatever term fits the sprawling agglomerations spreading across urban regions.

For all that, I still want to defend the cinema as a uniquely powerful prism through which to think the city. For one thing, I think that Burgin is wrong about the temporality of cinema. Of course, the experience of watching a film is temporally linear. But the cinema isn't the experience of a single film, any more than a cinema is the only place films are viewed. Cinema (the introjected cinema that we inhabit and that inhabits us) is the layered and worked over archive of all those narratives, all those images, all those occasions of viewing. Secondly, and more importantly, just as Burgin argues that we should think with television because its temporality is like the "global space-time" on the other side of the urban window (whereas cinema supposedly isn't), Silverstone and Morse too imply that the argument should start from the spatio-temporal homologies between television and urban reality. This is where I disagree. Whereas they seem to assume that the media–city relationship is an ontological one, I go back to Benjamin's account of cinema and insist that we are dealing with an epistemological question. That question, for me, is neither any similarity between geography and medium, nor even urban representations in various genres and media. Rather, it is how to construct a perspective, or a technology, through which to think the city critically.

So, for example, I can agree with Silverstone and Morse that publicness is not now, if it ever was, a matter of face-to-face conversation between citizens in coffee-shop or piazza. For me, though, "the public" doesn't (or shouldn't) refer either to a physical space or to a lost reality or to a dead community. To put it another way, "the public" – like "the city" – refers to the question of community, not the fact of community. It is an immaterial yet effective social force. The public domain is always, inherently, a phantom sphere.[15] In a discussion of public art, Rosalyn Deutsche, with an echo of Simmel and a feminist twist, underlines that it is an epistemological concept: "In the phantom public sphere, man is deprived of the objectified, distanced, knowable world on whose existence he depends and is presented instead with unknowability, the proximity of otherness, and, consequently, uncertainty in the self."[16]

That helps to explain why I think that the homology between television's "global space-time" and urban reality may be the problem, not the solution. Television confirms time-space, it doesn't question it. It renders "the objectified, distanced, knowable world" on which, says Deutsche, man depends. Television doesn't help me to understand the imaginative space, the analytical space, between our private worlds and the public world of the city; the space of proximity, unknowability, and uncertainty.[17]

On my side of the argument, the cultural and media geographer Kevin Robins too holds out against the "death of cinema," against the denial of its imaginative and creative possibilities, and defends "the need to continually transform – to de-integrate – structures of vision and visibility."[18] He quotes Italo Calvino's recollection that the cinema "satisfied a need for disorientation, for the projection of my attention into a different space, a need which I believe corresponds to a primary function of our assuming our place in the world."

Also in the cinema party is the Australian literary and cultural theorist John Frow. He cites the enthusiasm for television by the fictional academic Murray in Don DeLillo's novel *White Noise*. Murray's students do not share his postcritical celebration of the medium. They see television as "worse than junk mail. Television is the death throes of human consciousness, according to them. They're ashamed of their television past. They want to talk about movies." "Murray is a postmodernist," comments Frow. "His students, wishing to return to the high modernism of cinema, are postpostmodernists."[19]

From the preposterous position of postpostmodernism, my argument is that the very fact that cinema (or the novel, for that matter) is in some sense out of date may be one of the things that makes it good to think with, and especially good for thinking the city. Gilles Deleuze argues the epistemological case for subverting temporal homologies:

> To think means to be embedded in the present-time stratum that serves as a limit: what can I see and what can I say today? But this involves thinking of the past as it is condensed in the inside, in the relation to oneself (there is a Greek in me, or a Christian, and so on). We will then think the past against the present and resist the latter, not in favour of a return but "in favour, I hope, of a time to come" (Nietzsche), that is, by making the past active and present to the outside so that something new will finally come about, so that thinking, always, may reach thought.[20]

The philosopher John Rajchman links this style of thinking on behalf of future times and future people to the questions about the city, representation and the media I have sketched here:

> The principle of such other, invisible, future peoples is not some recognition withheld by a state or its majority. Rather, we can invent the other peoples that we already are or may become as singular beings only if our being and being-together are indeterminate – not identifiable, given, recognizable in space and time – in other words, if our future remains unknown and our past indeterminate such that our very narratives can go out of joint, exposing other histories in our histories, releasing the strange powers of an artifice in our very "nature". Fiction and cinema have both explored the powers, the times, the spaces of this principle of the future city.[21]

Des Esseintes's daydream about London suggests how representations inform our capacity, and our need, to imagine "the city" – cities elsewhere, but also the pedagogic city we inhabit physically and as a state of mind. Fiction and cinema (rather than representation as such) suggest another capacity and a different need. The "principle of the future city" is conceivable even if it resists any attempt to represent it. That is why we are still haunted and provoked by abstract utopian ideals like the City of God, the republican polis, the Ville Radieuse, or the public sphere. The immaterial city is a disconcerting yet hopeful reminder of imagination beyond images.

NOTES

1. J.-K. Huysmans, *Against Nature*, tr. Robert Baldick (Penguin, Harmondsworth, 1959).
2. "The immaterial city" is Ihab Hassan's phrase. See "Cities of mind, urban words," in Michael C. Jaye and Ann Chalmers Watts (eds.), *Literature and the Urban Experience* (Rutgers University Press, New Brunswick, 1981), p. 94.
3. Victor Burgin, *In/Different Spaces* (University of California Press, Berkeley, 1996), p. 48.
4. Christopher Prendergast, *Paris and the Nineteenth Century* (Cambridge University Press, Cambridge, 1992), p. 221. See also Raymond Williams, *The Country and the City* (Chatto and Windus, London, 1973); D. A. Miller, *The Novel and the Police*, (University of California Press, Berkeley, 1988); and Klaus R. Scherpe, "The city as narrator: the modern text in Alfred Döblin's Berlin Alexanderplatz," in Andreas Huyssen and David Bathrick (eds.), *Modernity and the Text: Revisions of German Modernism* (Columbia University Press, New York, 1989).
5. Williams, *The Country and the City*, p. 243.
6. Georg Simmel, "The metropolis and mental life," in David Frisby and Mike Featherstone (eds.), *Simmel on Culture* (Sage, London, 1997), p. 184.
7. Simmel, "The metropolis," p. 175.
8. See Peter Fritzsche, *Reading Berlin 1900* (Harvard University Press, Cambridge, Mass., 1996).
9. Simmel, "The metropolis," p. 175; Walter Benjamin, "The work of art in the age of mechanical reproduction," in *Illuminations* (Fontana, London, 1973), p. 227; Benjamin, *Charles Baudelaire: A Lyric Poet in the Era of High Capitalism* (NLB, London, 1973), p. 132.
10. Benjamin, "Work of art," p. 229.
11. Burgin, *In/Different Spaces*, p. 34.
12. Roger Silverstone (ed.), *Visions of Suburbia* (Routledge, London, 1997), p. 4.
13. Silverstone, *Visions*, pp. 11–12.
14. Margaret Morse, "An ontology of everyday distraction," in Patricia Mellencamp (ed.), *Logics of Television* (BFI, London, 1990), p. 213.
15. See Bruce Robbins (ed.), *The Phantom Public Sphere* (University of Minneapolis Press, Minnesota, 1993), especially Thomas Keenan, "Windows: of vulnerability."
16. Rosalyn Deutsche, "Agoraphobia," in *Evictions: Art and Spatial Politics* (MIT, Cambridge, Mass., 1996), pp. 325–6.
17. See Kevin Robins, *Into the Image: Culture and Politics in the Field of Vision* (Routledge, London, 1996), p. 143.
18. Robins, *Into the Image*, p. 145.
19. John Frow, *Time and Commodity Culture* (Clarendon, Oxford, 1997), p. 26.
20. Gilles Deleuze, *Foucault*, (University of Minnesota Press, Minneapolis, 1988), p. 119; quoted in Nigel Thrift, *Spatial Formations* (Sage, London, 1996), p. 295.
21. John Rajchman, *Constructions* (MIT Press, Cambridge, Mass., 1998), p. 113.

Chapter 6

Imagining Naples: The Senses of the City

Lesley Caldwell

In this article I discuss two movies by the Italian director Mario Martone which illustrate the centrality of place in constituting an understanding of the self. In emphasizing the characters' links with the city of Naples, Martone provides a cinematic exploration of the workings of the past in the present as containing both an individual and a social reality. He uses the images and sensations of the city as an externalization of the protagonists' introspective fantasies, and, in so doing, presents the public arena as the repository of both individual and collective history. When Susan Sontag describes Walter Benjamin as "not trying to recover his past, but to understand it: to condense it into its spatial forms, its premonitory structures" (1979: 13), she identifies one of the many echoes that resonate between Martone's and Benjamin's own account of Naples, written in 1924.

A different strand in recent work on location and identity has involved some questioning of previously assumed links between place and the understanding of self. This work registers the transformation of perceptions of local and national, individual and collective ideas about self and other, occasioned by the dislocations, migrations, movements, and diasporas of the twentieth century. It emphasizes the modern condition as a universalizing experience which has had the effect of partially detaching the individual from any continuous sense that identity has connections with a particular place (Carter, Donald, Squires 1993; Morley and Robins 1993). Martone's two movies not only set the narratives in a particular city, they use images of Naples to represent personal, individual memory and to begin to think about the memories of past generations of Italians and a different Italy. In this way, they highlight some of the changes in Italian society since the Second World War.

A Neapolitan Director

Martone's first feature-length movie *Morte di un matematico napoletano* (hereafter *Death of a Neapolitan Mathematician*, 1990) is a movie with a distinctly local ambience organized around the symbolic importance of city space. His next film, *L' amore molesto* (1995), also assigns a primacy to the city. Both movies, through their narratives and through their representation of Naples, explore the links between place and identity. The city is strongly signaled as desired, the intimate possession of a creative artist who has attempted to represent his own city, one with a strong, lasting grasp on the European imagination, in a distinctively different way. The massing of details, fragments, and impressions, as it were, from the inside, extends considerably the complex of associations brought to mind by the idea of "Naples". In this respect these movies form part of a more general cinematic, cultural, and political opening which happened in Naples during the 1990s.

The European art cinema has often been regarded as a tool for the elaboration of the personal issues of its directors as they are articulated through the creativity of movie making. (Bordwell 1985; Neale 1981). This tradition has emphasized the director as the authorizing presence and the condition of coherence for a form of moviemaking whose ambiguities often stress a self-conscious narration and an overt concern with psychological states.

The concentration on visual style, character, and the interiorization of dramatic conflict in Martone's two movies asserts the links between personal, psychological identity and its local and regional roots. Memory and time appear as possessing both personal and collective attributes and meanings. The crowded allusions to which they give rise, materially and geographically, but also mentally, form the focus for a set of interlocking concerns – the lives of the characters and their relation with the past of the city in the diegesis, the transformations in Naples, and in Italy, from the fifties to the nineties, and the director's younger self and interest in his city.

Each movie identifies one central character as its focus, a man in the first, a woman in the second. Through their encounters with themselves and their past in the streets of Naples, the city is established as the other major protagonist, a setting through which the emotions and conflicts of living are encountered, enacted, recognized/misrecognized, and thought about by the characters themselves, but also by the spectator. The shifting between past and present registered through physical locations becomes a visual rendering of states of mind, and of a process of self-realization. The characters, Renato the mathematician, and Delia the daughter, are played by two actors with long associations with Naples and with the theater. This offers Martone, a theater director himself, another area for exploration: the overlap of actor and role (Martone 1995: 14).

Versions of Naples

Some of Martone's themes in these first two feature-length movies mirror the preoccupations Sontag proposes as central to Walter Benjamin: "Benjamin had adopted a completely digested analytical way of looking at the past. It evokes events for the reactions to the events, places for the emotions one has deposited in the places, other people for the encounter with oneself, feelings and behaviour for intimations of future passions and failures contained in them" (1979: 9–13). Benjamin's own account of Naples written with his lover Asja Lacis, emphasizes "the interpenetration of buildings and action" (p. 169). Furthermore, "What distinguishes Naples from other large cities is that each private attitude or act is permeated by streams of communal life; similarly dispersed, porous and commingled, is private life. To exist, for the northern European the most private state of affairs, is here a collective matter. So the house is far less the refuge into which people retreat, than the inexhaustible reservoir from which they flood out." (1979: 167).

This idea of Naples as a city which shapes private lives through the dominance of public spaces is an image which brings together architecture, geography, and people. Since the center of Naples contains one of the highest territorial densities in Europe, this further adds to a set of dramatically shifting parameters between lives conceived in conventional private terms and their existence in a public domain. Until the postwar period and the extension outwards of the speculation of the sixties, a geographical separation of poverty from wealth, a separation of classes in a separation of zones or areas, was strictly limited. In Naples it was one of higher and lower, with the rich above the poor, and the poor often, literally, below ground.

The vertical organization of Naples and the architectural choices that have followed its physical forms certainly contribute to the particular social relations identified by Benjamin, but Martone has mainly chosen not to represent this, just as other familiar images of the city – the volcano, the bay, the ruins of antiquity – are also absent from his movies.The touristic picture of Naples, part of a legacy predating the photograph and the film, stresses this combination of geographical, natural, and architectural features, and such associations have been the basis of many other cinematic representations, often shaping them as a kind of residuum of the folkloric (Bruno 1997: 47–9). Various commentators, including the director himself, have insisted that these movies represent an attempt to engage with an alternative tradition, and, by rendering Naples from the inside, to introduce another reality (Fofi 1997; Martone 1997).

In the first film, *Death of a Neapolitan Mathematician*, Naples appears uncharacteristically empty, in *L'amore molesto* it is full and noisy. In both, the encounter of character and city embodies the space of individual experience and precipitates the decisions following upon it. An intimacy and a distance between the two protagonists of each movie – the character and the city – are constructed by the camera's way of locating them relationally in the pro-filmic space. But this is also the construction of a mental space, a space of thought, rumination, association, and sensation first for the characters, then for the spectators. Artistic choices in the construction of the personal narratives emphasize them as narratives of the city. Naples emerges both as dream-like terrain and as a constellation of different and distinctive cultural arenas and groups, a visual reinforcement of the claim that "the mental and the social find themselves in practice in *conceived* and *lived* space" (Lefebvre 1996: 197).

In offering a sense of the very different lives of Neapolitans of different classes and genders in an earlier period and in the nineties, these movies stress the perception of what Lefebvre and Regulier (1986; reproduced in Kofman and Lebas 1996) have described as a city's "rhythms," as fundamental. In their delineation of some general characteristics of Mediterranean cities, "persistent historical links . . . fated to decline, to explode into suburbs and peripheries," they propose that such cities have more discernible rhythms than others, rhythms that are both "historical and daily", "closer to the lived" (p. 228).

Naples is an obviously Mediterranean city, a city of immense beauty and reputation, which has been pictured as containing and encouraging a fullness and extravagance, elsewhere already considered impossible or lost. The idea that lives of passion and melodramas of raw emotions exist in the midst of wretchedness, squalor, and misery, condenses an array of beliefs, fantasies, prejudices, and expectations about "the Neapolitans." Naples, as a place where Europe' s Other is to be met within its own territory, is one of its most longstanding myths. It is often regarded as changing and loosening up the outsider who encounters the combination of city and people together (Goethe 1987, and many others). Martone's representation of a local Naples ultimately also serves to confirm this view.

The simultaneity of a visible past written into a present is one theme that Martone's movies develop, and one which links him directly with Roberto Rossellini who conveys a similar sense of Naples in *Viaggio in Italia* (1953). Starring his then wife Ingrid Bergman and George Sanders, this study of a marriage and how it was affected by a northern couple's exposure to Naples and its environs, made the city and its environs the other character whose influence becomes decisive. Bazin said of this movie, "It is a Naples filtered through the consciousness of the heroine.... Nevertheless, the Naples of the movie is not false...It is rather a mental landscape at once as objective as a straight photograph and as subjective as pure personal consciousness (quoted in Brunette 1987: 160). In *Viaggio*, Catherine's (Bergman's) journey becomes that of the spectator (Kolker 1983: 132) and in each of Martone's movies something similar is involved. *Death of a Neapolitan Mathematician* is a loose interpretation of the last week of the life of Renato Caccioppoli (1904–59), a well-known mathematician, the son of a Neapolitan surgeon and a woman known as the daughter of the Russian anarchist Bakhunin. Renato was a well-known intellectual and political figure, with a colorful history, first of antifascism, and later, of relations with the Italian Communist party (PCI). Played by the Tuscan stage actor Carlo Cecchi, who has a long association with Naples, Renato is shown at work and at meetings in the university, in restaurants, at the opera, with friends, comrades, ex-wife, brother and, crucially, alone. Warmth, concern and conviviality in the life of a leftist bourgeois intellectual in the fifties are set beside the solitude of the man and his progressive withdrawal from the world around him. The passing of the days of his last week lived within the streets and spaces of the old center of Naples provides the film's structure, and a certain labyrinthine aspect of the city conveyed through the streets and the angles of the buildings, becomes the condition of its representability.

L'Amore molesto is based on a book by Elena Ferrante. It recounts the events following the return to Naples of Delia/Anna Buonaiuto, a designer of comics living in Bologna. Delia returns the day after her birthday on hearing the news of her mother Amalia's mysterious death in the sea. The daughter seeks out the facts of her mother's last few days, meets up with her father, her uncle, a petty criminal type – her mother's possible long-term lover – and his son, her childhood companion. She imagines, remembers, invents, and encounters her loved, known mother, along with other possible mothers and other possible selves. It is the return to Naples which proves decisive for this engagement with the past and its shaping of her present and future. The film's notionally investigative structure is a personal journey in which a noisy, modern Naples is the setting for a fraught internal encounter. The encounter with the mother in the mind is occasioned by the encounter with the city, a city often associated with the maternal and the feminine (Gribaudi 1996; Ramondino 1991).

In the spaces of its buildings and streets, its language and its sounds, its inhabitants and their customs, its relationship to an illustrious set of traditions, and its place in a national culture (although, in the case of the latter, it is largely to be inferred from the well-nigh complete absence of any explicit reference to it) a city which is simultaneously local and particular, national and general is pictorialized. In the first movie the status of Naples as an intensely cosmopolitan city ties it to a particular Italian and European past. In the second, local intensities, bodies, words, sounds, and images are immersed in the more general anonymity of shops, transport, cars, and crowded streets. The appropriation of the body of one by the eye of another, and of course the eye of the camera, is common to both, but, in the first, the concentration of looks is more from camera and spectator to (male) actor and city; in the second, the looks at, and between, the characters, especially at Delia, the heroine, record an invasive intimacy, a visual aggression and an awareness of bodies through a regime of looking that renders the physicality and sensuality of Naples through an explicitly hierarchical relation between the sexes.

As a central component of both movies, time figures in three different ways. There is the severely proscribed time in which the events of each narrative emerges – a week in the first film, two days in the second; the pace of the movies – slow thoughtful, distanced, and introspective in the case of the first, frenetic, noisy, overbearing, and externalized in the second. Finally there is the presence of an earlier historical era within the temporality of each movie. Through this juxtaposition of a filmic present, and a remembered past, the different renderings of time make available different ways of living and thinking. "Pastness" forms an intractable aspect of Mediterranean cities and their associations, and this is utilized by Martone as the terrain for a kind of public and personal memoir where the past both facilitates and constrains the life of the present.

Death of a Neapolitan Mathematician

In *Death* the movie reveals a Naples of the fifties, still existent today, a living recollection, in stone and buildings, of a different Naples and a different Italy from that of the movie's construction. Renato's visual confinement within a small area of the city center suggests the mathematician's despairing evaluation of his life and himself, but Martone's use of an intensely personal Naples makes the overall mood one of nostalgia rather than despair. Piantini (1993) sees the civility and behavior of family and friends and the shots of Naples which express such conviviality and warmth as creating a regret for the passing of the fifties. The movie is shot in a golden light, described by Roberti (1992) as a permanent sunset, and its color spectrum provides a setting of gentleness, luminosity, warmth, and beauty, that is markedly at odds both with the suicide of the hero and with the associations of enclosure and entrapment sometimes conveyed by the camera angles. It lends support to the sense in which thinking about the life of the man is the occasion for an essay about the city and its past, and the director and his. For the character Naples is ultimately confining, loving but irrelevant.The man of thought, mathematics, politics, music, culture is permanently clad in an old raincoat that echoes the feel of the street and the color of the buildings. "Fantastic reports by travellers have touched up the city. In reality it is grey: a grey red or ochre, a grey-white. Anyone who is blind to forms sees little here" (1992: 169). Martone explained the film's color as the suggestion of Bigazzi, the cinematographer, who, in sorting out locations, had been struck by the yellowness of Naples. "I was immediately convinced because this yellow seemed to gather together another instance of the double aspect of the city, the comforting yellow of the sun's rays, and the pallid dusty yellow of illness" (1992: 132). The emptiness and silence may act as signifiers of the inner despair of the man, but, paradoxically, they register the richness and beauty of the city itself.

The local sites in this movie are mostly confined to a particular area of Naples, that of Via Partenope, Via Chiaia and the Spanish quarter. Palazzo Cellamare, where the protagonist, Renato Cacciopoli, lived, is shot from inside, outside, by night, by day; a constant visual reference. It may have once been the home of Goethe, but, far more significantly, Martone himself lived his adolescence there, and it is still his family home. His Naples, like that of his mathematician, is part of the intense intellectual artistic, musical, and commercial culture that has long distinguished the city; but it is not one that has seen much cinematic attention. "How is a field of memory formed? It needs frontiers, milestones, seasons... Otherwise, days flood in, each erasing the previous one, faces are interchangeable, pieces of information follow, and cancel one another. It's only in a defined space that there is room for an event, only in a continuum that beginnings come into view and ruptures occur" (Pontalis 1993: 79).

Martone's use of the city/person connection in this movie depends upon an inversion of the traditional theatricality and spectacle of Naples, mentioned by Benjamin, but the movie echoes him in another: "buildings and action interpenetrate in the courtyards, arcades and stairways. In everything they preserve the scope to become a theater of new, unforeseen constellations" (1992: 169). As Renato withdraws, the city becomes the theater for the staging of the troubled mind of a ruined political and intellectual hero and it is no suprise that Renato is reading Beckett with friends the night before his death.

L'Amore Molesto

The second movie makes the modern anonymous city the external impetus for the uncovering of a particular personal history which is part of a social one. The story of Delia, her mother, and family figures is also an account of a Naples of women's work, men's violence and jealousy, of poverty, postwar shortages and hardship, and of the differences and similarities between the nineties and earlier decades. While the wish that guides the narrative of *L'amore molesto* appears as the clarification of the circumstances of the mother's death, questions of past and present are here laid, the one upon the other, from sequence to sequence, in an attempt to capture the fluidity and apparent randomness of individual mental processes through the cinematic codes of editing and color.

L'amore molesto contains a fantasy or a memory of a possible past event, but, overall, this seems less significant than the more general accession of Delia to her younger self through the recollection of a former Naples and the encounter with a present one, both ordered on gendered lines. The gestures, assumptions, and behavior of the old men seem ludicrous and inappropriate, but their continuity in relations between the sexes is underlined by the persistent looking of the young men in the streets and on public transport. The fantasies, memories, recollections, flashbacks, the status of the possible personal pasts of the protagonist, Delia, remain open, and in this too, the film's structure offers an analogy with the mind and the kaleidoscopic transformations provoked in fantasy by memories. That they originate in a vital, gutsy Naples does nothing to detract from this oneiric sense.

The relation of past and present in the second movie is a complexly shifting affair; the female character involves a less directly personal dimension for the director, and the movie inscribes a Naples described by him as "sometimes unknown disquieting and foreign" (Martone 1995), a Naples of the margins, not only the geographical margins – Delia's father lives in the periphery – but peopled with the old, whose language, gestures, and behavior Martone has identifed as setting them apart "like an ancient tribe barricaded inside the hostile modern city" (1995).

Noise is one of the most notable elements of contemporary Naples and constant sound is the accompaniment of most of the second film, especially its exterior scenes.The sounds of dialect and the level and timbre of the voices, together with the omnipresence of the car and other modes of transport, carry the sensation of the modern city. The exceptions are the scenes signaled as memory and the past. In *L'amore molesto* the physical and architectural aspects of Naples more often appear in Delia's memories, most of which are staged below ground, a reference to the social conditions of her family, though also available to a symbolic reading given the film's engagement with memory.

A cool color spectrum is employed throughout, and in the tinted sequences that signify memory or recollection or fantasy, Amalia, the mother, is always in blue except in the scenes of her death, imagined by Delia on the rail journey away from Naples. In them, Amalia, wearing the red lingerie the old admirer had returned to the daughter earlier in the film, dances round a fire on the beach, first laughing, then crying, finally walking into the sea as the old man sleeps. Delia imagines these scenes of her mother's enjoyment, and discovers a facet of her own, as, once more dressed in the gray/blue suit, she shares the beer offered to her by the young men.

This is one of the few Italian movies to feature the mother-daughter relation and it makes its embeddedness in Naples central, so that a general interrogation of the maternal and what it means also runs through the film. "There still exists today a series of stereotypes in the Italian imagination; Naples as a female city, a belly city, a city of the heart: in short, a mother city . . . the city willingly accepts the image of mother which is frequently assigned to it" (Niola 1994, quoted and translated by Green 1999). A fantasy of shifting identifications in the condensation of memories, events, and sexual encounters of both mother and daughter is continually alluded to through their clothes. The mother's birthday present was a clinging red dress which Delia wears for most of the film, replacing the gray/blue suit in which she arrived. In fantasy, and in the time of the film, red and blue garments move between mother and daughter, paralleling visually the intricacies of the relationship. For Delia/Anna Buonaiuto, encountering the city and its inhabitants forces a revisiting of her mother, and herself, and her own past. The intensity of the individual situation emerges through the amalgam of social meanings, experiences and knowledge comprised in the images of the city.

In its public spaces, after an absence of three years, and immediately following her mother's death, Delia becomes a sexualized body, almost as a present from her mother. Her decision to wear the dress is queried by her old uncle, "We've just buried your mother!" She replies, "Don't you like it? I was depressed. I wanted to give myself a present." In this dress the female protagonist negotiates the streets of Naples and her own mind, as it gathers around her the accumulated connotations of such a garment. Putting it on parallels the revival of memories of family and self, but it also bequeaths to Delia a sexual persona and a bodily enjoyment. In it, the relation with the dead mother and with her own and her mother's sexuality is revived.

An economy of sex is introduced in the stark contrast of the individualized woman's body and the masses of other bodies, and Bo reads the corporeality of Naples as the frame across which *L'amore molesto*'s taking on both of bodies and of love develops (1997: 15). It is this connectedness that the movie appears to insist upon, even in the midst of the everyday violence of the remembered domestic scenes. Through the involvement in the city as repository of her past life and that of her family, especially her mother, Delia's own life appears to become a life more vital and available for living. The exchanges between mother and daughter and their inscription in the red garments propose a potentially conservative and unchanging account of the place of sexuality in the lives of these women of different generations – Delia, after all, inherits her mother's position as the object of the look – yet what is released by the mother's death and the daughter's return appears as the possibility of a fuller life rather than its opposite. That Naples and the South should be its propeller contributes to those myths about the transformations that city has been associated with facilitating.

Conclusion

In *Civilisation and its Discontents* Freud first imagines (1930: 70) the layering of one famous Rome upon another as paradigmatic of the mind, but then dispenses with the possibility of the city as metaphor and rejects the idea that, outside the mind, the same space can contain different contents. Through the visual evocation of Naples in different decades as they are held in the characters' individual memories, Martone establishes the link between place and person over time and offers an exploration of the relation between body and mind, feeling and thought. Like Freud's Roman ruins, the residues and results of individual and collective mental life are evident in the filmed spaces of the city.

Apart from period, the past these movies explore is radically other in terms of class, cultural norms, and customs, quarters of the city, family relations, sex, and intellect.

Martone speaks of the double aspect of Naples: warmth and generosity, and harshness and toughness; and the two movies, in revolving around the one or the other, offer a double-sided vision of the city (Roberti 1992: 130). The fluctuating aspects of masculinity and femininity, and of what might be called the maternal function, are represented as a quality of the city itself, where, like human sexuality, there is little neat confinement or traditional division between rationality, the mind, and the male (ostensibly the territory of *Death*), and emotionality, the body, and the female (that of *L'amore molesto*).

The different emotional registers constitute an ongoing investigation of life and living, as complexly inscribed in the the simultaneity in the mind, of a person's past and present places. But Martone also claims that the individual trajectories of these characters offer access to "the sense, feel, atmosphere of Naples," something he sees as residing "not in ethnic roots, but in the movement between the people of the city, given through its cinematic representation" (Addonizio 1997: 341).

The lives of the two protagonists may be incommensurable in terms of family and domestic life, but the rhythms of Naples and of the South are consistent across the cinematic imaging. Language, cityscapes, noise, bodies, the presence of death – the first movie ends with a funeral, the second begins with one – reveal, at the same time, a regional city of the South, and an Italian city like any other. In the emotional geography the movies map, external differences shape internal scenarios, locally and nationally.

REFERENCES

Addonizio, A. et al. 1997: *Loro di napoli il nuovo cinema napoletano 1986–1997*. Edizioni della battaglia, percorsi in collaboration with FICC, Bologna.

Bazin, A. 1976: *What is Cinema?* 2. Berkeley: University of California Press.

Bo, F. 1997: Una lucida vertigine. *Cinecritica*, 2(8), 13–25.

Bordwell, 1985: *Narration in the Fiction Film*. London: Methuen.

Brunette, P. 1987: *Roberto Rossellini*. London: Oxford University Press.

Bruno, G. 1997: City views: the voyage of movie images. In D. Clarke (ed.), *The Cinematic City*, London: Routledge.

Carter, E., Donald, J., and Squires, J. (eds.) 1993: *Space and Place Theories of Identity and Location*. London: Lawrence and Wishart.

Fofi, G. 1997: Introduction. In A. Addonizia et al., 3–8.

Forgacs, D. and Lumley, B. 1996: *Italian Cultural Studies, an Introduction*. Oxford: Oxford University Press.

Freud, S. 1930: Civilization and its discontents. In *Standard Edition*, 21. London: The Hogarth Press and the Institute of Psychoanalysis, 59–148.

Green, P. 1999: Neapolitan bodies in Italian cinema. Che c'è di nuovo nel nuovo cinema napoletano? Paper given to movie studies seminar, Birkbeck College, University of London, May.

Goethe 1987: *Italian Journey*. London: Penguin.

Gribaudi, G. 1996: Images of the South. In Forgacs and Lumley, 72–87.

Kofman, E. and Lebas, E. (eds.) 1996: *Henri Lefebvre. Writings on Cities*. Oxford: Blackwell Publishers.

Lefebvre, H. 1986: Rhythmanalysis of Mediterranean cities. In Kofman and Lebas, 228–40.

Lefebvre, H. 1996: Introduction to E. Kofman and E. Lebas, ch. 18.

Lefebvre, H. and Réguliar 1996: Rhythmanalysis of Mediterranean cities. In E. Kofman and E. Lebas, 228–40 (ch. 23).

Lèvi-Strauss, C. 1963: The structural study of myth. In *Structural Anthropology*. London: Penguin, 206–31.

Macchiocchi, M. A. 1973: *Letters from Inside the Italian Communist Party to Louis Althusser*. London: NLB.

Martone, M. 1995: Le due anime del cinema italiano contemporaneo: the two souls of Italian cinema. Handout to Deparment of Italian, University of Warwick.

Martone, M. 1997: interview in Addonizio, 79–103.

Mazzoleni, D. 1993: The city and the imaginary. In E. Carter et al. 285–302.

Montini, F. and Spila, P. 1997: Mario Martone: la liberta è il rigore. Interview in *Cinecritica*, 2(8), 6–12.

Morley, D. and K. Robins 1993: No place like Heimat: images of Home(land) in European Culture. In E. Carter et al., 3–31.

Neale, S. 1981: Art cinema as institution. *Screen*, 21(1), 11–40.

Niola, M. 1994: *Totem e ragù*. Naples: Pironti.

Penz, F. and Thomas, M. (eds.) 1997: *Cinema and Architecture*. London: BFI.

Piantini, L. 1993: Sulla morte di un matematico napoletano. *Cinema Nuovo*, 42(1), 26–7.

Pontalis, J. B. 1993: *Love of Beginnings*. London: Free Association Books.

Ramondino, F. 1991: *Star di casa*. Milan: Garzanti.

Ramondino, F. and Martone, M. 1992: *Morte di un matematico napoletano*. Milan: Ubulibri.

Roberti, B. 1992: Lui, una città, dei compagni di strada, nel tempo. Conversazione con Mario Martone. In Ramondino and Martone, 130–6. Reprinted from *Filmcritica*, 425, April, 1992.

Sennett, R. 1991: *The Conscience and the Eye*. London: Faber and Faber.

Sontag, S. 1979: Introduction. In W. Benjamin, *One Way Street and Other Writings*. London: NLB, 7–28.

Chapter 7

The City as Imperial Centre: Imagining London in Two Caribbean Novels

Riad Akbur

I propose to examine, here, the representation of the urban as it occurs in the highly convention-bound creative discipline of novel writing. The central aim is to highlight the creative activity of imagining cities as potentially a problematic undertaking, occasionally at odds with the surroundings imagined, and inevitably involving the nonrepresentation or imaginative exclusion of aspects of an urban totality.[1]

The materials I have chosen for this task are Samuel Selvon's novel *The Lonely Londoners* and V. S. Naipaul's *The Mimic Men*. Following a brief summary of the two novels, I will attempt to isolate the imaginative context producing the portrait of the city, the city in this case being London. The main part of the chapter discusses some of the problems encountered in the literary mediation of urban settings. I will use my concluding remarks to engage the question of whether we should look to literary works to enhance our critical knowledge of urban environments.

*

Samuel Selvon and V. S. Naipaul are arguably the most distinguished of the generation of Caribbean writers who rose to prominence during the 1950s. Selvon's 1956 work *The Lonely Londoners* has been called 'one of the seminal West Indian novels'. Its loosely structured episodic narrative relating the adventures of a group of Caribbean immigrants living in London broke new ground in being among the first to address the topic in fiction. The novel's linguistic inventiveness, especially its favouring of the syntax and vocabulary of Caribbean diction over the conventional narrative voice of the English novel, marked a watershed in the development of a distinctive Caribbean literary aesthetic and made it a classic work of cultural decolonisation. *The Mimic Men*, V. S. Naipaul's 1967 novel, is the autobiography of Ralph Singh, a former government minister of the fictional Caribbean state of Isabella who, manoeuvred out of political office, turns over the events of his life from a hotel room in the English Home Counties. *The Mimic Men* has been acclaimed by post-colonial literary critics for its documenting of the damaging impact of imperial structures on the psyche of the colonised subject. Detractors criticise its unflattering portrait of Third World societies, attributing it to the novel's entrapment within the system it sets out to analyse.[2]

*

I want to begin by describing the spatial idea monopolising the portrait of the city in the two novels. In *The Mimic Men* and *The Lonely Londoners* there is one term which seems to dominate and restrict the portrayal of London. This is the notion of the 'Motherland' or the 'imperial centre'.

The dominance of the 'Motherland' category in Selvon and Naipaul's texts results in a very specific construction of London. In these works the image of the city is inextricably associated with the 'mother country'. The city in their novels, is immediately identified with the nation, and the nation's imperial identity in particular (or exclusively). It is the place which the original Greek word embodies (metropolis = mother + city/state, i.e. *metro* + *polis*, *OED*). This view of London as an undifferentiated expression of the British nation as a whole (with the nation-state itself defined as merely the location or venue for the reproduction and enjoyment of imperial privilege) is not confined to the novels.

Use of the term 'metropolis' to describe a national territory as opposed to a large urban settlement coincides with distinctions peculiar to the geographical ordering of the imperial realm. In English, this usage dates back to at least the sixteenth century. The French variant 'la métropole' carries the same meaning. The national territory the word refers to is in each case the parent state of a colony.[3]

In addition, independent of the contingencies of language use, Britain does experience, over time, a veritable convergence of metropolitan and national space. Use of the term 'metropolis', undeniably, recurs as propaganda: the establishment of this and other links to the ancient empires of the past belongs to a larger rhetorical system functioning to dignify modern acts of territorial expansion and political and economic hegemony. On the other hand, the term is applied quite legitimately in the sense that from the late nineteenth century onwards little, if anything, remained of a Britain untouched and unenhanced by the profits of overseas conquest. The Marxist literary critic, Raymond Williams, in his study *The Country and the City* isolates this particular definition of the 'metropolis':

> In current descriptions of the world, the major industrial societies are often described as 'metropolitan'. At first glance this can be taken as a simple description of their internal development, in which the metropolitan cities have become dominant. But when we look at it more closely in its real historical development, we find that what is meant is an extension to the whole world of that division of functions which in the nineteenth century was a division of functions within a single state. The 'metropolitan' societies of Western Europe and North America are the 'advanced', 'developed', industrialised states; centres of economic, political and cultural power. In sharp contrast with them, though there are many intermediate stages, are other societies which are seen as 'underdeveloped': still mainly agricultural or 'under-industrialised'. The 'metropolitan' states, through a system of trade, but also through a complex of economic and political controls, draw food and, more critically, raw materials from these areas of supply, this effective hinterland, that is also the greater part of the earth's surface and that contains the great majority of its people. . . . Thus one of the last models of 'city and country' is the system we now know as imperialism.[4]

London, in this and other versions of the 'metropolis', designates moreover an ideal type. Any part of Britain may of course claim an imperial identity in the sense that it enjoys a material advantage or infrastructural dominance over its equivalent in the subordinate region. The distinction, however, is conveyed by some places better, or less ambiguously, than others. Indeed, the 'metropolis' is a more tangible proposition as a composite of the landscape – 'Englands of the Mind' to use Seamus Heaney's phrase[5] – elevated and separate from the inferior world of the periphery, comprising a similar condensation of topographic variety and inter-/intra-regional discontinuities. London, for example, as Britain's capital, expresses this comparative supremacy with relatively few qualifications. Other sites, besides London, also amplify the division.

Numerous examples from *The Mimic Men* and *The Lonely Londoners* register the assimilation of London to the features of the 'Motherland'. The conflation is achieved, for instance, with reference to a utopia/dystopia organisation. Images which exalt the city are evident in *The Lonely Londoners* in this extract concerning the character, Sir Galahad:

> He had a way, whenever he talking with the boys, he using the names of the places like they mean big romance, as if to say 'I was in Oxford Street' have more prestige than if he just say 'I was up the road'. And once he had a date with a frauline, and he make a big point of saying he was meeting she by Charing Cross, because just to say 'Charing Cross' have a lot of romance in it...Jesus Christ, when he say 'Charing Cross', when he realise that is he, Sir Galahad, who going there, near that place that everybody in the world know about (it even have the name in the dictionary) he feel like a new man. It didn't mater about the woman he going to meet, just to say he was going there made him feel big and important, and even if he was just going to coast a lime, to stand up and watch the white people, still, it would have been something. (pp. 83–4)[6]

The depiction of Piccadilly Circus in Selvon's novel registers a similar fetishised image, conferring on the 'big city' both the ideological attributes and the radial configuration of a centre:

> Always, from the first time he went there to see Eros and the lights, that circus have a magnet for him, that circus represent life, that circus is the beginning and ending of the world.... Galahad Esquire, in all this, standing there in the big city, in London. Oh lord. (p. 90)

Proof that *The Mimic Men* venerates London can be gleaned from the portrait the novel produces from the use of such synonyms as 'the great city' (pp. 19, 26, 27), 'the big city' (p. 45), 'the great city, centre of the world' (p. 18), 'the city of magical light' (pp. 229, 243) and 'a city of such a miraculous light' (p. 26).[7]

Stigmatising of the periphery, reinforcing this version of the imperial centre, is evident in both novels. Trinidad is scornfully described as '[t]his small place' based on 'small-time village life' in *The Lonely Londoners* (p. 94). Disordered (pp. 55, 118, 192, 206), obscure (pp. 118, 146), fraudulent (pp. 50, 118, 146), and barbarous (p. 118) are some of the many faults attached to Isabella in Naipaul's novel.

Formulations of the imperial centre dominating these literary accounts of London are also highlighted by the distinctive narrative preoccupations of each novel. *The Lonely Londoners*, for example, in presenting its principal subject of Britain's post-war Caribbean settlers, constructs the city as a landmark of an inside/outside spatial order, that is to say, as a destination enclosed within the British Empire. The novel makes no attempt to connect settlement in Britain to the contemporary occurrence of Caribbean emigration to other parts of the world. There is one reference to a former girlfriend of one of the characters absconding to Venezuela from Jamaica (p. 67), but otherwise *The Lonely Londoners* suppresses any mention of the continuing flight of West Indians to the North American and South American mainland. Similarly, the chart defined by the immigrants' journey does not accommodate other movements of labour to Britain. Insofar as the novel avoids portraying the immigrants as guest workers recruited by the British Government, it does not invoke the supply lines of surplus labour supporting the British economy, which in the decade after the war encompassed the British West Indies, but also overlapped the imperial sphere to include labour intakes from Eire and Southern and Eastern Europe. Typically, as in the view asserted by the main character Moses, the map of Empire dominates the narrative setting, on the one hand, uniting the location of arrival and departure, and on the other prescribing the notion of 'abroad' and the circumstances in which Britain can be classed a foreign country: 'In fact, we is British subjects and he is only a foreigner, we have more right than any people from the damn continent to live and work in this country, and enjoy what this country have, because is we who bleed to make this country prosperous.' (p. 40)[8]

The effect of the dominance of this geographical convention is firstly the editorial exclusion or non-representation of aspects of the urban totality. The permanent equating of London with the 'Motherland' or the imperial state – in other words, the construction of a narrative setting defined or over-determined by the centre-margin metaphor – registers a continuum which is vertical, its particular items ranked in a hierarchy in which London and the imperial capital are absolutely identical to the extent that competing spatial languages which signify London as another kind of place are subordinated.

The failure of vision in these terms adopts the form of absent or missing spatial registers. Some of the geographical styles marginally placed by the 'London–Mother-country' continuum in these works might be listed as follows: the north–south of England divide invoking London in regional terms; the capital city system of political geography in which London signifies the national capital of England in relation to Edinburgh, Cardiff, and Belfast – the capital cities of the other countries in the United Kingdom; the world economy's alignment of sites in which London as a supranational figure of trade exists only in relation to Tokyo, New York, Paris, Zurich and Bonn; the structure of concentric rings differentiating the city in terms of 'Central London', the 'inner city' and 'the outer London Boroughs'; the mosaic made up of the local cultures of North, East, West and South London; the historical geography delineating London from the provincial towns of the industrial revolution, the nineteenth-century garden cities, the mid-twentieth-century greenfield conurbation and the commuter towns of the mid-twentieth-century, and the contemporary hyperpolis (e.g. the autonomous, self-enclosed universe of the shopping city, the industrial estate, the theme park, the multi-complex entertainment village, and so on).[9] There are many other contexts distinguishing the city's other identities. The point to emphasise, however, is not the infinite range of urban discourses available for creative adaptation, but the scale of repression necessarily involved in privileging a single geographical style. The concepts the novels employ to invoke the city – 'London', 'the mother country', 'the old Brit'n', 'the centre', 'the centre of the world' – insofar as they are interchangeable in these works register this diminution, in that linguistically a spatial order distinct from a geography of overseas territorial conquest is unattainable, but also to the extent that they make up a vocabulary whose words fail to delineate a multi-faceted view of place. The lack of a more varied account of London only partially describes the imaginative deficiency. In addition to the failure to accommodate and synthesise an inclusive account of city life, these literary portraits of the imperial centre contain other problems.

A second effect of London's assimilation to the features of the Motherland is the inability of the novels to register territorial borders. A third effect is the imaginative loss of the sense of the 'local', that is to say, the loss of the creative facility to conceive surroundings as unique and original. Landscape, regardless of where the narrative action occurs, all appears the same, that is to say, is alike, repetitive, ubiquitous. Instead of the perception of the local and locality, the narrative consciousness is unable to cohere a distinction between places, or register a sense of having moved when geographic boundaries are crossed.

The Mimic Men with its emphasis on dislocation and placelessness documents this loss of a certain spatial order, or of a symbolic geography suspended in a state of dismemberment:

> I thought that this absurd disorder, of placelessness, was part of youth and my general unease and that it would go as soon as I left Isabella. But certain emotions bridge the years. It was unease of just this sort which came to me when I began this book... the red brick houses became interchangeable with those others in our tropical street, of corrugated iron and fretted white gables, which I had also once hoped never to see again. Certain emotions bridge the years and link unlikely places. Sometimes by this linking the sense of place is destroyed, and we are ourselves alone: the young man, the boy, the child. The physical world, which we yet continue to prove, is then like a private fabrication we have already known (p. 154).

The mode of perception which categorised the colonial society of Isabella as derivative and unreal, an inferior copy of the real world of the metropole, similarly resists inscribing, first the metropole, and then the hotel from which Ralph Singh composes his memoirs, with any distinguishable individuality.

The Lonely Londoners also registers this blurring of geographic difference:

> Ah, in you I see myself, how I was when I was new to London. All them places is like nothing to me now. Is like when you back home and hear fellars talk about Times Square and Fifth Avenue, and Charing Cross and gay Paree. You say to yourself, 'Lord, them places must be sharp'. Then you get a chance and you see them for yourself and is like nothing (p. 85).

Here, creativity is trapped or preoccupied by the process of undermining the definition of landscape, so much so that although particular locales receive intense narrative attention – for instance, the topography of Isabella is vividly detailed – it is nonetheless very difficult to bridge the gap between the meaninglessness of place insisted on by the narrator and the meaningful expression of place in the text, that is between on the one hand the rejection of geography as a trick of ideology (colonial or otherwise), and on the other the status that might be ascribed to an image of London still possible to assemble from a discourse analysis of the landmarks comprising the narrative setting: the attic room, the factory, the cinema, the bomb site, the pub, the registry office, the weather, and so on.

The problem, in this last sense, is deciding whether these signposts contradict or affirm a narrative commentary that is asserting the artificiality of the specifically local. Do these landmarks amount to a description of place – a grim, depressed capital, symbolising Britain's decline as an international power; or a shabby, seedy landscape subverting the illusion of a cultured civilisation which, despite claims to the contrary, is seen to suffer the same problems as the dysfunctional colony on the periphery? Or are these spatial motifs anti-representational/counter-discursive, expressions of the fictionality or the ultimate illusion of the idea of 'London', in the sense that while located within the city limits, the landmark itself is arbitrary, not inevitably synonymous with London, that is to say, a symptom of the city's lack of originality?

This inability to conceive London as a place different from other places is particularly acute in *The Lonely Londoners* with its depiction of a Caribbeanised London, indistinct from Port of Spain, or Kingston or Bridgetown. The novel derives its narrative idiom from cultural sources specific to the West Indies – the novel, for example, is narrated in a Caribbean linguistic register eschewing standard English, the narrative style is based on the calypso ballad, and the conventions of fête or carnival define the structure of the novel's set-piece scenes. As a consequence, the novel fails to attach a symbolic system to place that provides access to the local. The imported forms seemingly domesticate London, serving to mystify or exclude environmental features which exceed their descriptive capability. At the same time, this naturalising manoeuvre reproduces London in Caribbean terms. 'Selvon's characters', as one commentator notes, 'reconstruct the language of the lime and through imposing their language on the great city, they remake it in their own image'.[10] The domestication of the local and the diminishing of its specificity through this impressionistic technique is illustrated in these passages describing Tanty's excursions in Harrow Road:

> Well Tanty used to shop in this grocer every Saturday morning. It does be like a jam-session there when all the spade housewives does go to buy, and Tanty in the lead. They getting on just as if they in the market-place back home: 'Yes child, as I was telling you, she did lose the baby... half-pound saltfish please, the dry codfish... yes as I was telling you... and two pounds rice, please, and half-pound red beans, no, not that one, that one in the bag in the corner...' (p. 78).

> She used to get into big oldtalk with the attendants, paying no mind to people waiting in the queue. 'If I know Montego Bay!', she say. 'Why, I was born there, when I was a little girl I used to bathe in the sea where all those filmstars does go. If we does have a Winter there? Well no, but it does be cold sometimes in the evening. Not like this cold! Lord, I never thought in my old age I would land up in a country like this, where you can't see where you going and it so cold you have to light fire to keep warm! Why I come to London? Is a long story, child, it would take up too much time, and people standing in the queue waiting. But I mind my nephew from when he a little boy, and he there here in London, he have a work in a factory...' (p. 80).

A symbolic landscape dissimilar to the Caribbean is only recoverable in this sense to the extent that the narrative setting dominated by a Caribbean identity also constructs an exterior segment absent from the novel, formed from the symbolic surplus including the missing or excised signifiers of London's geographical difference, i.e. the local. The novel's imaginative organisation, therein, distinguishes with regard to the definition of place a fugitive or insular aesthetic: a way of seeing that is, perhaps, provisionally useful as an aid for self-location and orientation in new surroundings yet with prolonged and uninterrupted use suggesting a defensive and petrified rhetorical convention, that is to say a refuge from, or avoidance of other formal languages which represent the world differently. Both novels' mediation of London from an initiate's perspective – in other words, a portrayal from the viewpoint of a first-time encounter, and hence the domination of its codification by the narrow circumstances of the narrative event in which akin to virgin territory it is as it were discovered and named – should be mentioned here in addition to the techniques of Caribbeanisation as a further conceptual device employed in the erosion of geohistorical depth and detail.

The fourth and ultimate creative failure *The Lonely Londoners* and *The Mimic Men* distinguish in their representation of London is the inability to imaginatively access the world of the metropolis, and, especially, to register an informed understanding of the city's geography of economic, ideological, and political power. The outsider's perspective mediating the image of London in both novels (not to be confused with the penetrative vision of an excluded subject documenting mainstream society from the periphery), is here consistent with the stranger or alien's outlook, in the sense of a gaze denied admission and barred from inspecting the universe of the ruling executive. It is an untrained perspective, unfamiliar with and incapable of detecting the identity and location of institutions of power. London mirrors the lack of his tiny island, London, Ralph Singh decides – it is an absent centre, 'the greater disorder, the final emptiness':

> Here was the city, the world. I waited for the flowering to come to me.... Excitement! Its heart must have lain somewhere. But the god of the city was elusive. The tram was filled with individuals, each man returning to his own cell. The factories and warehouses, whose exterior lights decorated the river, were empty and fraudulent. I would play with famous names as I walked empty streets and stood on bridges. But the magic of names soon faded. Here was the river, here the bridge, there that famous building. But the god was veiled. My incantation of names remained unanswered. In the great city, so solid in its light, which gave colour even to unrendered concrete – to me as colourless as rotting wooden fences and new corrugated-iron roofs – in this solid city life was two-dimensional (pp. 18–19).

This perspective in failing to depart from the impoverished fringes of the host society to engage the metropolis is restricted to merely displacing the centre, as distinct from disproving its authority or effectively challenging its existence. Passing off the demimonde for the totality of the city, the rhetorical manoeuvre bars from its portrayal all but the landmarks of the immigrant's milieu. Metropolitan power is based on no more than a *myth* of superiority that is possible to abolish by *demythologising* the centre. The inability to conceive the social and political interior of London and in particular to apprehend and represent the network of power that resides there seriously compromises the decolonising claims of both novels.

*

The above assessment of literature's ability to imagine the city has engaged imaginative practice in the restricted sense of the task of synthesising the poetic and the critical. Works of fantasy were asked to present facts, to contribute and support the production of critical knowledge. Imaginative acts which did not satisfy the formula were presented as instances of imaginative failure, of a perceptual block, a creative deficit. Expecting fictional texts to discharge such duties might seem unrealistic. Literature is after all no better equipped to contribute new knowledge of the city than more conventional branches of learning. It teaches nothing about cities which cannot also be discovered through the research of non-literary materials. There are limits, in other words, to what urban studies can hope to learn from literary works.

It would also have to be conceded that the representation of place in literary works serves a variety of rhetorical ends unrelated to an accurate or truthful account of urban surroundings. Narrative setting, for example, is, finally, a technical device which together with other textual artefacts such as character, plot and theme is subordinate to the task of conveying a story. Structurally defined, these narrative elements are, moreover, not bound to any particular content. Thus, in Balzac's writing for instance, it is 'the city', according to one commentator that takes the role of the 'main character'.[11] Besides narrative production, the mediation of place in literary works can perform other creative duties too. For example, it has been observed that the description of Rouen in Flaubert's *Madame Bovary* serves no material purpose apart from the ideological function of promoting the impression that the text depicts reality.[12] Instrumentalised in such ways, a spatio-linguistic register appears to have the potential to support literary effects without necessarily advancing a knowledge of urban settings.

Literary works nevertheless are engaged in producing knowledge about cities which invite evaluative responses. Technical criteria such as those referred to above may well determine the features chosen to comprise the portrayal of place. At the same time, processes of editorial selection seem also to define the identity of the setting. A referential value or information item is cohered for critical reception, notwithstanding the formal role it might also be asked to fulfil. It is evident, for example, that recognising the city in literature involves attaching to certain language items a lived and/or a learnt knowledge of urban space. The associating of words with an actual place or at least its topographical type is a convention of language use. As with all language artefacts the meanings invested in these words are decided by their immediate enunciative context as well as the cognitive value language users recall from one or more of their former investments in these words, whether in an occurrence of creative/non-creative writing or in a speech situation.

Context-led investments tend to be regulated and arbitrary. These are passive investments on the whole, influenced to a large extent by the text's own agency. Accounts of place with an identifiable textual function – i.e. those responsive to recuperation and integration in the overall work – are dependent on this type of preordained anticipated participation in the creation of meaning.

Exogenous investments, meanwhile, whereby individual words receive a semantic load, comprised of the meaning language users have known them to express, are much harder to predict and anticipate. This much more active investment, may potentially invite language items to display their full repertoire of referential values.

These two types of codifying practice may, inspite of their differences, produce identical meanings: versions of place privileged by the text's symbolic economy may well coincide with the reader's own notions of place. Literature operates, in such circumstances, to affirm and reinforce the expectations and beliefs of an 'implied', 'intended'/'ideal' reader. This said, textual endorsements should be weighed against their strategic quality. The authority conferred on particular readers may be no more than tactical – a device, for example, which enlists and licenses the knowledge of particular readers in order to entrust creative responsibilities to them elsewhere in the work, thus freeing texts to economise on the information content of narrative details, and exploit the productive tensions of ellipsis and allusion. Place, in this alternative sense, offers a resource for engaging an individual, or community of reading subjects potentially for the purposes of challenging their value systems at a later point in the work.

These two types of encoding activity are also potential occasions of dispute. Instances exist of disjunction between syntagma-derived and paradigm-derived inscriptions of place. In post-colonial literary studies, these instances of conflict furnish very fertile conditions for critical intervention. It is evident, for example, in Chinua Achebe's analysis of *Heart Of Darkness* that Achebe's personal image of the African Congo is vastly different from the setting militated by the formal arrangement of Conrad's novella. Unauthenticated by the text, this other knowledge of Central Africa informs a wide-ranging polemic on the reactionary bias of both the work and its author.[13] In this case it would seem that a personal knowledge of place ceases to fulfil a compositional role in the work, and instead supplies the evidence of the distortions of place the work's rhetorical organisation invites. It appears, in addition, that this sensitivity to the empirical flaws in the portrayal of place is a direct, albeit uninevitable, product of the symbolic regime which prevents or obstructs particular acts of creative investment.

If aesthetic disciplines lack unique insights to contribute to urban studies, these last remarks should indicate the important role the specialist knowledge of urban scholars and geographers can have in heightening critical thinking about, and experience of, cultural objects. Greater attentiveness to the existence of literary artifice is encouraged, simply by the depth and diversity of urban scholarship highlighting the constructed, arbitrary quality of the city's representation in literary works. Of course, an increased materialist emphasis needs to be combined with the practices of formalist critique. Understanding the depiction of urban space is only obscured by ignoring the wider textual ends the mediation of these representations can be found to serve: the current reductive applications of Foucauldian theories of 'representation' are clearly not sufficient, in this respect, for studying the variety of rhetorical work the city is employed to undertake in literary works. On the other hand, a materialist perspective must not be restricted by self-censorship. Social science has to avoid setting artificial limits on the application of its training and subject knowledge. A materialist input needlessly undermines its authority and diminishes its benefits, if disengaged from the reading project. Traditional empirical research about cities needs to be deployed not merely in critical but also compositional labour – even when the latter is invested at the expense of cohering meaning. Raising the standard of debate concerning writing and the city starts with the totality of the reading experience, with all its contradictions, being reported.

NOTES

1. I use the term 'totality' to mean 'all of it', to refer, that is, to an intact entity made incomplete by an event of repression or exclusion. The word is also employed in the Marxist sense of a critical definition of 'reality', that is, to describe the product of an evaluative facility whose aspirations oppose analytic methods which perceive the various ways of knowing urban space as equally valid.
2. A selection of critical responses to the two novels can be found in Susheila Nasta, ed. *Critical Perspectives on Sam Selvon* (Three Continents Press: Washington, 1988), Edward Baugh, ed. *Critics on Caribbean Literature: Readings in Literary Criticism* (George Allen and Unwin: London, Boston and Sydney, 1978), and Bill Ashcroft et al., *The Empire Writes Back: Theory and Practice in Post-Colonial Literatures*, (Routledge: London and New York, 1989, repr. 1993), pp. 88–91.
3. See *OED* and *Le grand Robert de la langue Française.*
4. Raymond Williams, *The Country and the City* (Hogarth Press: London, 1993), p. 279.
5. The phrase is the title of Heaney's 1976 lecture collected in Seamus Heaney, *Preoccupations: Selected Prose, 1968–1978* (Faber and Faber: London, 1984), pp. 150–69.
6. Page references are taken from Samuel Selvon, *The Lonely Londoners* (Longman: Harlow, 12th imp., 1993).
7. Page references are taken from V. S. Naipaul, *The Mimic Men* (Penguin Books: London, New York, Victoria, Toronto, Auckland, 1969).
8. A summary of research into the factors governing Caribbean emigration to Britain can be found in Margaret Byron, *Post-War Caribbean Migration to Britain: The Unfinished Cycle* (Avebury: Aldershot, Brookfield, Hong Kong, Sydney, Singapore, 1994), pp. 6–7. Examples of Britain's overseas recruitment programmes together with data on the ethnic breakdown of British immigration in this period is presented in Colin Holmes, *John Bull's Island: Immigration and British Society, 1871–1971* (Macmillan: Basingstoke and London, 1988), pp. 210–28.
9. The place 'Hyperpolis' in J. M. G. Le Clézio's 1973 novel *Les Géants* is a vast supermarket similar to a British Tesco Superstore. I am extending its original meaning to include other buildings, firstly, because its lexical properties seem already to refer to hyperreal Baudrillardian amusement parks, and secondly (and more importantly) because its association in Le Clézio with technocratic terror, regimented consumerism, and sublime social control offers a useful proper noun to label this insidious architectural aesthetic.
10. See Gordon Rohlehr's essay in Baugh, pp. 159–60.
11. See Italo Calvino, 'The city as protagonist in Balzac', *The Literature Machine: Essays*, tr. Patrick Creagh (Secker and Warburg: London, 1987), pp. 182–9.
12. See Roland Barthes, 'The reality effect' in Tzvetan Todorov, ed. *French Literary Theory Today* (Cambridge University Press: Cambridge, 1982), pp. 11–17, tr. R. Carter from Roland Barthes, 'L'effet de réel', *Communications*, 11, (1968), pp. 84–9.
13. Chinua Achebe, 'An image of Africa: racism in Conrad's *Heart of Darkness*', *Hopes and Impediments: Selected Essays* (Doubleday: New York, 1989), pp. 1–20.

Chapter 8

Sleepwalking in the Modern City: Walter Benjamin and Sigmund Freud in the World of Dreams

Steve Pile

There were a hundred thousand slopes and substances of incompleteness, wildly mingled out of their places, upside down, burrowing in the earth, aspiring in the air, mouldering in the water, and unintelligible as any dream.

Charles Dickens describing a suburb of London in 1848

The reform of consciousness consists *entirely* in making the world aware of its own consciousness, in arousing it from its dream of itself, in *explaining* its own actions to it.

Karl Marx, in a letter to Arnold Ruge, 1843

A dream is an answer to a question we haven't learnt how to ask.

Scully reminding Mulder of an observation he'd made in an earlier episode of the *X Files*, 1997

Never mind Charles, Karl, Dana, and Fox. In his novel *Invisible Cities*, Italo Calvino imagines a meeting between Marco Polo and Kublai Khan. In the course of their conversations, Marco Polo conjures up images of many fabulous and incredible cities. At one point, however, the Great Khan challenges Marco Polo. He has begun to notice that these cities have begun to resemble one another. The Khan's mind now sets out on its own journey. Interrupting Marco Polo, the Khan begins to describe a wondrous city. And he wonders whether it exists. But it appears the Khan had not been paying attention, for it seems that Marco Polo had been telling the Khan about precisely that city. Intrigued, or perhaps in disbelief, the Khan asks Marco Polo the name of the city:

"It has neither name nor place. I shall repeat the reason why I was describing it to you: from the number of imaginable cities we must exclude those whose elements are assembled without a connecting thread, an inner rule, a perspective, a discourse. With cities, it is as with dreams: everything imaginable can be dreamed, but even the most unexpected dream is a rebus that conceals a desire or, its reverse, a fear. Cities, like dreams, are made of desires and fears, even if the thread of their discourse is secret, their rules are absurd, their perspectives deceitful, and everything conceals something else."

"I have neither desires nor fears," the Khan declared, "and my dreams are composed either by my mind or by chance."

"Cities also believe they are the work of the mind or of chance, but neither the one nor the other suffices to hold up their walls. You take delight not in a city's seven or seventy wonders, but in the answer it gives to a question of yours" (Calvino 1972; 37–8).

As with cities, so it is with dreams. Marco Polo's analysis is clear: the randomness of cities – their absurd or deceitful realities – has an inner meaning, an inner rule, a perspective, a discourse, in the same ways as dreams. Underlying the production of cities are the hidden workings of desire and fear. In other words, cities are desire and fear made concrete, but in deceitful, disguised, displaced ways. It is the same with dreams. Kublai Khan cannot accept this interpretation, either of dreams, or of the city. And, surely, dreams and cities have nothing to do with one another. Dreams are illusions, unreal. Cities are very real, the work of the conscious mind, not the random, absurd juxtaposition of astonishing images. But this chapter sides with Marco Polo. And not only Marco Polo. With Walter Benjamin and Sigmund Freud too. Out of these elements, it might be possible to discover the deceitful discourses, to uncover the hidden desires and fears, to dream again of/about the city. Let's start with Walter B.

Dreaming the Modern City

Much has been said about Benjamin's use of dream analysis to interpret modernity and the city – the best commentators are Buck-Morss 1989; Gilloch 1996 and Weigel 1996, and this chapter follows determinedly in their wake. However, rather than simply trail these analyses, I would like to demonstrate how Benjamin's ideas about dreams and his theory of revolution are provocatively combined in one of his best known (and loved) works, *One Way Street* (written between August 1925 and September 1926: Benjamin 1985).

We should start at the beginning. The title of *One Way Street* refers to the "street" that his lover, Asja Lacis, had driven through him. The title is already a metaphor, one which evokes a one-way flow of ideas through Benjamin and through the city. But towards what? The work is filled with shorter and longer pieces of writing: each piece is an anecdote or metaphor, hewn from the natural history of modernity; each observation has its own heading, each heading is drawn from a detailed observation of the modern city. These fragments are bizarre, absurd, juxtaposed in odd, puzzling ways, their meaning not immediately apparent – and, when it is apparent, it becomes curious for being so obvious. The effect is deliberate. By juxtaposing these fragments in this way, Benjamin is attempting to bring seemingly unrelated things into a dialectical relationship. Through this process of dialectical imaging, Benjamin is seeking to use the tension between fragments to break them out of their isolation, their stasis. In this way, objects would be placed back in the flow of history, as if the dust had been shaken off them. The effect is almost city-like. Or, maybe, dreamlike. Marco Polo would be proud.

Let's take a closer look at the opening shots in Benjamin's analysis of the modern city (and it is important to remember that the pieces are named after features found in cities, since many of the pieces are seemingly not about cities). The first one is titled Filling Station. In it, Benjamin effectively introduces the work. It begins by talking about how the present is constructed out of facts, but facts that sterilize literary activity. The task of the critic, then, is to detonate this state of letters. In part, this is to be achieved through the use of opinions, which give writing both influence and the capacity to act. Such writing acts not in universal ways but through its specific, careful, accurate, and effective application – much as one applies oil to a complex machine (hence the title of the fragment). It can be easily surmised, then, that *One Way Street* is the drop-by-drop application of criticism to "the vast apparatus of social existence" (1985: 45). Through this process, the work can become a significant literary work. Another lesson to draw is this: these fragments are not assembled without connecting threads, without a perspective. These fragments are a rebus. Locked in the puzzle are the desires and fears of the modern city. Let us proceed down the street.

The next observation is headed Breakfast Room. Benjamin begins:

> A popular tradition warns against recounting dreams on an empty stomach. In this state, though awake, one remains under the sway of the dream. For washing brings only the surface of the body and the visible motor functions into the light, while in the deeper strata, even during the morning ablution, the grey penumbra of dream persists and, indeed, in the solitude of the first waking hour (1985: 45–6).

You might balk at this claim, but it is possible to glimpse Benjamin's understanding of modernity, cities and revolutionary practice in this tiny fragment of a fragment. Like a railroad station whose lines lead in many directions, so too we can tease out many themes from this apparently simple point of departure: the breakfast room.

In one direction, we can see that there is a tale about dreaming. Benjamin continues:

> The narration of dreams brings calamity, because a person still half in league with the dream world betrays it in his words and must incur its revenge. Expressed in more modern terms: he betrays himself (1985: 46).

In a nutshell, it can be said that Benjamin is describing the alienation experienced by people in modernity. They betray themselves by articulating their dreams and the revenge that is wreaked on them is that they have to exist in the dreamworld of modernity. And from which they cannot awake:

> He has outgrown the protection of dreaming naïveté, and in laying clumsy hands on his dream visions he surrenders himself... The fasting man tells his dream as if he were talking in his sleep (1985: 46).

The "moderns" – after betraying their (innermost) dreams – are doomed to walk in a gray, alienated dreamworld as if in their sleep. The problem is that they have no way of knowing that they are still half in league with the world of dreams. It is, therefore, the (revolutionary) task of the critic to shock the dreamers awake: to act as an alarm

Figure 8.1 *Heavenly Dinner* (© Sygma-Keystone-Paris 1989)

clock, to make the hammer strike the bell. For Benjamin, the desires and fears of the sleepwalker in the modern city have to be materialized, but this is not as easy as it might be. The modern individual is perfectly capable of articulating a whole series of needs and wants, fears, and anxieties. Indeed, the endless production of commodities taps directly into the conscious wishes of modern individuals. Unfortunately, though commodities seemingly embody people's wishes, they remain unconnected to the desires and fears that surround them. It is as if the moderns are talking in their sleep: talking, asking, wishing, but unaware of the meaning of the words. In this sense, commodities become fetishes: they are worshipped, but no one knows why, nor what they stand for.

One might think that the late nineteenth-century city was terrible enough to wake anyone from their slumbers. But Simmel's analysis of the modern city and its effects on human psychology (1903) suggests exactly the opposite to be true. From Simmel, Benjamin learns that the urbanite becomes indifferent to the shocks of city life and blasé about the sheer number of – absurd and surprising, dreadful and exciting – things that cities bring into close proximity. Despite the clarion calls of injustice and inequality, then, the modern individual is indifferent. Worse, citydwellers become subject to the revenge of dreams, for once they learn indifference, their desires and fears become a secret discourse in which everything conceals something else. Though they can speak their wishes, the moderns have no way to make them real. The modern world becomes a never-ending cycle of dreamlike figures, none of which ever fulfills their promise. Fashions come and go, ever more rapidly, in ever more absurd forms. Buildings are put up and torn down, their façades become make-up in a clown's parade of architectural forms. Just admit it: nothing's shocking.

In Benjamin's analysis, "dreaming" has two apparently contradictory meanings. It describes, on one hand, a state of sleeping and, on the other, a state of waking. Both asleep and awake, however, the mind dreams. So, Benjamin searches in the idea of the dream for a resource of (revolutionary) hope. He finds it in the possibility that the dreamer might awake: in a real way, dreams must anticipate a waking. Analytically, then, Benjamin was concerned to discover and interpret dreams, both past and present. He sought these in artifacts – especially old-fashioned objects (that embodied redundant dreams) – and in the sites that housed, or contained, dream-artifacts. It is worth looking in a little more detail at the dreamhouses of modernity, since this is where the dreamwork in the production of modern urban spaces is most apparent.

For Benjamin, the dream is most vivid at the point of waking. In practice, this means that Benjamin was most interested in those parts of the city that were being torn down or being altered, since it was as if people were waking up from the dreams that these spaces embodied. Such places included, famously, the once-fashionable arcades of Paris. But also the temporary structures put up for the great exhibitions of London and Paris. However, Benjamin also found modern dreams in museums (which contained artifacts – dreams – from the past) and railroad stations (where there were dreams of travel). He uncovered dreams of previous generations in the ruins of the city: in their castles and churches. Like an archeologist, he dug deeper and deeper into the historical layers of the city, to find the persistence of its dreams. Benjamin was searching for a memory. He was attempting to travel in time – *and space* – to recover the long history of a society's desires and fears. Through the labyrinths of the city's streets, through the journeys undertaken, Benjamin would piece by piece, piece together the unconscious strivings of social and urban imagination.

Benjamin was optimistic. If he could bring the pieces into tension, through "dialectical imaging," by putting the pieces side by side, Benjamin thought it would be possible to induce a shock that would wake up the moderns. In *One Way Street* this revolutionary task manifests itself in the juxtaposition of ideas within observations, but also in the juxtaposition of observations. Here, we see the world of dreams (significantly he recounts his dreams) and the world of waking (his analysis of the dreamlike connections between things) in direct relation to one another. The Breakfast Room, for example, becomes a space which contains two apparently unconnected ideas: the premodern folk-tale and an interior space in the bourgeois home set aside for the timed and localized activity of breakfasting, now regimented by capitalist labor relations.

Reading this work is almost like walking through a city: along any path, you find places built out of different stories (see Keith, chapter 35 this volume), sometimes side by side, sometimes in the same place (say, as one use blends into another). So, in London today, if you go to the corner of Marlborough Crescent and Bedford Road, you can see two different dreamworlds: one is the bricks and gardens of the first garden suburbs built in the late nineteenth century, the other is the concrete and function dream of the 1960s high rise. Meanwhile, a local house in the same area now houses the local Victorian society, both appropriately (it's in a Victorian building) and ironically (since the Society has changed the use and look of the building). In this understanding, the city is an assemblage of absurdities that have lost their impact, and we can no longer see the dreams that are embodied in their bricks and concrete, their flowers and smells.

Through montage, through shocking juxtapositions, Benjamin was attempting to wake the modern world up, so that it could act on its dreams, rather than simply live in them. In this way, it might be possible to produce utopia, to make the dream real. Or so he hoped. But the dialectic of dreaming and awakening has never quite played itself out (at least, in Benjamin's terms). People seem to have remained relentlessly asleep, indifferent to the shocks of modernity. *But maybe the moderns are not sleepwalking in the city.* Maybe they have been walking open-eyed through the streets, fully aware of the poverty and brutality of modern life (like many of the chapters in this volume). So, it may be that Benjamin's understanding of dreams could usefully gain from another perspective. Benjamin was not adverse to psychoanalysis, though he knew very little about it (as Buck-Morss, Gilloch and Weigel have noted). Perhaps now is a good time to put Benjamin and Freud side by side. Let's see what Sigmund Freud might have to say about walking in the city, as if in a nightmare.

By Another Détour, the Dreamcity

Freud is not renowned for his analyses of urban life (see Smith 1980). In fact, it is more common to complain about Freud's lack of appreciation of his own context (for a review of these criticisms, see Elliott 1998). Freud did use the city as a metaphor to describe mental life (Pile 1996, chapter 8), but it is more useful for this chapter that he described a walk in the city in his essay on the uncanny (1919). More generally, Freud's account of the uncanny has been taken up in many analyses of urban space (see, for example, Vidler 1992; Jacobs 1996 and Pile 2000). However, it is the dreamlike qualities of Freud's urban anecdote that concern us here, because this will allow us to pursue an interpretation of the dreamlike quality of cities and the city-like quality of dreams. In this way, it might be possible to progress Benjamin's project of uncovering the secret discourses of the city, the hidden desires and fears in the city's dreaming. First, let us examine Freud's uncanny story. While walking in Genoa,

> ... one hot summer afternoon, through the deserted streets of a provincial town in Italy which was unknown to me, I found myself in a quarter of whose character I could not long remain in doubt. Nothing but painted women were to be seen at the windows of the small houses, and I hastened to leave the narrow street at the next turning. But after having wandered about for a time without inquiring my way, I suddenly found myself back in the same street, where my presence was now beginning to excite attention. I hurried away once more, only to arrive by another *détour* at the same place yet a third time. Now, however, a feeling overcame me which I can only describe as uncanny, and I was glad enough to find myself back at the piazza I had left a short while before, without any further voyages of discovery (Freud, [1919] 1985: 359).

Of course, we should realize quickly that this "uncanny" experience is clearly the experience of a repressed bourgeois man who is afraid to be associated with "painted women." But Freud at least was prepared to admit a secret desire: to "be with" the women whose character was not in doubt. Now, we can see in this tale how the return of a repressed desire might lead to a feeling of dread. It might be possible, quickly, to observe that the experience of the city – and perhaps of modernity in general – is ambivalent (about the interplay of desire and fear) or paradoxical (about the apparent contradiction between conscious desires and unconscious motivations). Among Victorian bourgeois men, this experience was certainly not unusual (see Walkowitz 1992). However, I would like to apply another form of interpretation to this situation, one derived from Freud's interpretation of dreams ([1900] 1976). In part, this is a legitimate move because it was this that Benjamin drew on in his interpretation of the dreamworld of the modern city, However, in Freudian terms, the move is illegal. So, let's proceed with enthusiasm!

Using Freud's story, it is possible to investigate the relationship between dreaming, waking and the geography of the city (for related discussions, see Pile 1998; 2000). To begin with, we can note that Freud's stance on dreams correlates quite nicely with Marco Polo's and Walter Benjamin's:

> ...in spite of everything, every dream has a meaning, though a hidden one, that dreams are designed to take the place of some other process of thought, and that we have only to undo the substitution correctly in order to arrive at this hidden meaning ([1900] 1976: 169).

For Freud, dreams are the "*(disguised) fulfilment of a (suppressed or repressed) wish*" ([1900] 1976: 244). However, dreamwork responds to this imperative in such a way that the wish does not wake the dreamer. Dreams, therefore, are also "the *GUARDIANS of sleep*" (1976: 330). It is presumed that the basic thought constituting the dream would trouble the dreamer enough to wake her/him up: so, the dream takes on a disguised form because the revelation of the dream's secret wish would, presumably, be disturbing and wake the dreamer up. This is certainly Benjamin's understanding of the modern individual, sleepwalking in the city. Thus, dreams are the guardians of a sleeping modern world.

In Freud's waking nightmare, we can see that he arrives at, then returns to, a place – with women – of a certain character. The scene is important. Freud carefully constructs a story out of a sequence of images, but his experience of uncanniness lies in the way in which time and space shift, dreadfully (in the city). Time becomes circular, while space is strangely connected. Both time and space take on character that is in doubt. Moreover, Freud's repeated returns to the same place indicate the labyrinthine nature both of the narrow streets of the city, and also of his unconscious wishes. The city becomes the "show place"of his desire/fear. More than a stage on which the vicissitudes of mental life play out, the city constructs the experience (in mind and body). It was as if Freud had voyaged into some mythic labyrinth, only narrowly escaping intact. Perhaps this is more of a nightmare than a dream, but Freud found it hard to wake up from the torment.

For Freud dreams work mainly (though not only) through the use of images: "Dreams construct a *situation* out of these images; they represent an event which is actually happening...they 'dramatize' an idea" (1976: 114). Such a view accords neatly with Benjamin's. The city is a collection of images, which can be produced in different forms. The city is put together as a situation – or series of situations – in which desire can be dramatized. However, these desires are dramatized in disguised ways. Thus, commodities represent a desire, but not directly. So it is, too, with physical infrastructure: homes, skyscrapers, overpasses, subways, piazzas, and the like. It is evident that, in the production of the dreamcity, some serious thinking has to take place: the wish has to be felt, then thought, then represented through images that disguise the thought, then the multifarious images have to be carefully assembled into a dream that has a (un)believable story line (however absurd the images and story seem). Freud calls this mental process dreamwork and identifies within it some key components: condensation, displacement, and the means of representation. It is this idea of dreamwork that might help us progress Benjamin's analysis of the work of modern cityspaces.

For Freud, dreamwork transcribes the dreamthought from one mode of expression (the desire/fear) into another mode of expression (the dream) by using images (or elements). Freud suggests that the process of transcription (dreamwork) allows for a complex (and duplicitous) interweaving of wishes, thoughts, and images:

> Not only are the elements of the dream determined by the dream-thoughts many times over, but the individual dream-thoughts are represented in the dream by several elements. Associative paths lead from one element of the dream to several dream-thoughts, and from one dream-thought to several elements of the dream. Thus... a dream is constructed... by the whole mass of dream-thoughts being submitted to a sort of manipulative process in which those elements which have the most numerous and strongest supports acquire the right of entry into the dream-content... (1976: 389).

As for dreams, so it is for the city. As Freud walks through Genoa, he makes an element – the street – suddenly take on a character that he might not have noticed on another day. An associative path has been opened up that suddenly gives the place connotations it might not otherwise have had. A train of thought has been set in motion, at both a conscious and an unconscious level, each leading in opposite directions. Consciously, Freud wants to leave; unconsciously, he wants to return. Despite being fully awake, Freud would appear to be sleepwalking. This suggests that the street is dreamlike: a site of both condensation, displacement, and an image through which meaning comes to be represented – a meaning which is not immediately apparent. We can pick specific instances of this, though it should be remembered that these are just examples. In the street, we can see how one idea "painted women" is substituted for another "sex" and how "the street" itself takes on this meaning, without it ever being said. In this way, the "sexual energy" associated with the street is expressed only when the thought gains access to Freud's conscious thoughts, before that he was indifferent. However, the emotional intensity of city life can quickly make itself felt – and we see this in Freud's increasing discomfort.

Of course, Freud draws on a whole repertoire of images to tell his story and these contain or channel his story in particular ways. Others would tell Freud's story differently. Others, of course, have their own stories to tell. Their experiences would be different (see Keith, this volume). Nevertheless, their experiences would also be partial, whether dream- or nightmare-like. This is an important point. This chapter stresses that people's experiences of the city – and of dreaming – are very differently located and localized. This point was paid insufficient attention by both Benjamin and Freud. Now, of course, it is less easy to make credible arguments about

Figure 8.2 Gustave Caillebotte, *Paris Street: Rainy Day*, oil on canvas, 1876–77 212.2 × 276.2 cm, Charles H. and Mary F. S. Worcester Collection, 1964.336. Photograph © 2000 The Art Institute of Chicago, All Rights Reserved

collective experiences, or collective dreams, of the city or modernity. Instead, we are more likely to see a crosscutting web of power relations, defining class, race, gender, sexuality, able-bodiedness, and so on (as this book amply demonstrates). However, this should not allow us to ignore how "dreaming"is bound up in the "regulatory fictions" [fixions?] that determine how people are seen and how people see themselves, whether they feel at home, where they feel out of place, what mobilizes them, and so on.

Freud's story is significant not because his uncanny experience is *the* experience of cities, but because it suggests that the tension between ordinary indifference and shocking realization is all too rare. A view with which Benjamin would despairingly concur. In Benjamin's terms, this is a revolutionary moment: by putting two and two together, Freud is shocked to discover his own motivations and awakes to the secret discourse of his desires and fears. Indeed, it might be that the city affords the opportunity for such self-realizations, but for most these experiences will be privatized, cast in shadows, as if under an umbrella.

Even awake, the moderns talk – and walk – as if sleeping. The city is like a scene in a dream, not a passive backdrop, but an active constituent of the story itself. Indeed, the street activates the story. Each element a condensation of many meanings, a moment of intense indifference and potential shock, the full meaning of which is never quite realized. Dreams – and cities – remain the guardians of the moderns' sleep: an elaborate play of remembering and forgetting; showing and disguising. In this understanding, both displacement and condensation work (to make dreams; to make cities) by using associative paths to combine and recombine thoughts, and also to decenter both meanings and feelings. In this way, dreamcity-work enables the dreamcity to be woven out of seemingly desireless, fearless, and absurd elements.

Even awake, then, the most intricate structures (of dreams, of cities) are created, all of which are the points of articulation of many associative paths of meaning, all of which displace the intensity that realized them elsewhere. For sure, an understanding of the city must trace the social relations that produce "things" (from buildings to emotions) – as political economists since Marx have pointed out. But now we must be sure that we understand that the "things" that make (up) the city also have secret discourses of desire and fear, desires and fears that have been displaced along disparate paths. For Benjamin, as for Freud (and Marco Polo!) these paths can be reconstructed. And, in this reconstruction, it is possible to understand the paradoxical motivations that made the dreamcity possible; to map out the yearnings that cannot yet be realized – corporealized – in the dreamcity.

On another day Freud could have walked through the street in Genoa and been oblivious to its character. And he might have found his refuge piazza first time. Someone else walking the street would have experienced it very differently. And the "painted women" were almost certainly having much more fun (at Freud's expense) than Freud! So, we can quickly surmise that *there is no one dream that articulates the city, nor one aspect of the city that defines its dreaming*. Instead, like a dream – or a city – the interpretation of cities must rely on the capacity to trace the lines of "work" that emanate from urban spaces, an understanding of their production in multiple social relations and of how the dreamcity condenses and displaces meanings in their very form. But we know a little more than this too – and on this, I will conclude.

Conclusion

At the outset of this chapter, it was suggested that cities are like dreams, for both conceal secret desires and fears, for both are produced according to hidden rules which are only vaguely discernible in the disguised and deceitful forms (of dreams; of cities). There is of course a difference between the world of dreams and the waking world: to begin with, the world of dreams pays no attention to other people – a rare luxury in waking life! Nevertheless, Benjamin's allegory of the persistence of dreams, suggests that modernity – while constantly proclaiming its open-eyed objective gaze on the world – is just as prone to sleepwalking as the worlds of religion and the worlds of myths (see also Thrift, chapter 34 this volume).

From Freud, it can be recognized that the mind, far from operating in completely incompatible and unrelated ways, in sleep and awake, works in parallel ways. Simmel was the first to suggest that mental life in cities is characterized by indifference, reserve, and a blasé attitude, but this only reinforces the idea that mental life in cities is characterized by displacement, condensation, and the use of images to represent *and effectively disguise* desires and fears – as in dreams. Freud's experience in Genoa suggests that elements of the city resemble dream elements – for not only can sites in cities be visited many times and the meanings of the locality change depending on the "orientation" of the visit, but also cities bring together elements from different places and urban spaces are produced through the intersection of crosscutting social relations, which combine to produce meaningful places – whether these are Benjamin's arcades or multiplex cinemas, the Ministry of Defence or home sweet home. This is to say that, like the dream, the city is produced in time and space by fervently traced paths, made and unmade connections, and the composition and position of elements.

But to what purpose is all this musing? For Benjamin, we can see that his desire was to shock modernity into waking up. No such option would appear to exist in Freudian thought. Perhaps this means there is no future for cities. On the other hand, it is possible to draw other lessons from Benjamin, Freud, and co. In this, we can think again of the paradox of dreaming: that it occupies both our sleeping and waking worlds. Through dreaming, it might be possible to imagine different transformative possibilities (see also Robinson 1998). Thus, instead of waking (to realize those secret wishes), or, instead of returning to the dream (to find those hidden messages), the significant move may be to pursue with greater enthusiasm the unconscious logics of the city. These will not be singular, nor universal, nor capable of being circumscribed by a master narrative of urban development. Instead, we would be forced to recognize that cities will have contradictory, incommensurable logics. And perhaps this is why cities are like dreams, both because they are never simply works of the mind or of chance, and also because they embody paradoxical and ambivalent elements.

It still feels like musing, all this talk of dreams. The alarm bells are ringing loud and clear: cities are wrecked by earthquakes, riots, (not so) smart bombs, pervasive disease, abject poverty. The problems confronting cities are so vast that they seem absurd: Western-dominated neoliberal economic strictures force people off the land and into the shanty towns of the poorest countries of the world, so cities of 20 million plus are created where there isn't enough food. But it is important to remember that neoliberal dreamings are not the only ones, nor the inevitable ones. Perhaps the scale of the problem explains why it is so easy to forget what the dreams of the city are all about – what it means to live in cities, their freedoms and opportunities, their new communities and cosmopolitanism. This suggests a revolutionary practice that relies as much on imagining and mobilizing better stories as on shocks to the system. Collapsing neither into the waking world of rationalizations and instrumental logic, nor into the dreamworld of barbaric desires and satisfying fears, the transformation of urban space would instead necessitate an understanding of vicissitudes of the dreamcity.

REFERENCES

Benjamin, W. 1985: *One Way Street and Other Writings*. London: Verso.

Buck-Morss, S. 1989: *The Dialectics of Seeing: Walter Benjamin and the Arcades Project*. Cambridge, MA: MIT Press.

Calvino, I. 1972: *Invisible Cities*. London: Faber and Faber.

Dickens, C. 1848: *Dombey and Son*. Harmondsworth: Penguin.

Elliott, A. 1998: Introduction. In A. Elliott (ed.), *Freud 2000*, Cambridge: Polity, 1–12.

Freud, S. [1900] 1976: *The Interpretation of Dreams*, vol. 4. Harmondsworth: Penguin Freud Library.

Freud, S. [1919] 1985: The "uncanny". In *Art and Literature: Jensen's "Gradiva", Leonardo Da Vinci and other works*, vol. 14. Harmondsworth: Penguin Freud Library, 339–76.

Gilloch, G. 1996: *Myth and Metropolis: Walter Benjamin and the City.* Cambridge: Polity.

Jacobs, J. M. 1996: *Edge of Empire: Postcolonialism and the City.* London: Routledge.

Marx, K. [1843] 1975: Letters from the Franco-German Yearbooks. In K. Marx, *Early Writings*. Harmondsworth: Penguin, 199–209.

Pile, S. 1996: *The Body and The City: Psychoanalysis, Subjectivity and Space*. London. Routledge.

Pile, S. 1998: Freud, dreams and imaginative geographies. In A. Elliott (ed.), *Freud 2000*, Cambridge: Polity, 204–34.

Pile, S. 2000: The un(known)city... or, an urban geography of what lies buried below the surface. In I. Borden, J. Kerr, A. Pivaro and J. Rendell (eds.), *The Unknown City.* Cambridge, MA: MIT Press.

Robinson, J. 1998: (Im)mobilizing space-dreaming (of) change. In H. Judin and I. Vladislavić (eds.), *Blank: Architecture apertheid and after* (Amsterdam: Netherlands Architecture Institute), 163–71.

Simmel, G. [1903] 1995: The metropolis and mental life. In P. Kasinitz (ed.), *Metropolis: Centre and Symbol of our Times*. Basingstoke: Macmillan, 30–45.

Smith, M. P. 1980: *The City and Social Theory.* Oxford: Basil Blackwell.

Vidler, A. 1992: *The Architectural Uncanny: Essays in the Modern Unhomely.* Cambridge, MA.: MIT Press.

Walkowitz, J. R. 1992: *City of Dreadful Delight: Narratives of Sexual Danger in Late-Victorian London*. London: Virago.

Weigel, S. 1996: *Body- and Image-Space: Re-reading Walter Benjamin*. London: Routledge.

Chapter 9

Contested Imaginings of the City: City as Locus of Status, Capitalist Accumulation, and Community: Competing Cultures of Southeast Asian Societies

Patrick Guinness

In 1997–8 many of the cities and towns of Indonesia were rocked by riots and demonstrations. The political dynamics of these riots lay in the maneuverings of armed forces, "pro-democracy," and "Islamic" forces, but they were marked also by the burning and sacking of symbols of capitalism and foreign influence, first the churches and then the shopping plazas, particularly those associated with the Chinese. One of the characteristics of these sackings was that people brought out store merchandise and burnt it together with motor vehicles on the streets. Siegel (1986: 232–54) in describing a similar phenomenon that occurred in Solo, Indonesia, in 1980 suggested that the Chinese were seen as a sign of money and money was seen as being their "natural" language. Yet they were charged with not deserving their wealth, and with holding it inappropriately. For Javanese people *pamrih*, "personal indulgence," as in personal acquisitiveness, sexual indulgence, or political ambition, is disavowed. The burning of Chinese goods was thus a disavowal of such a materialist focus, an admission by the rioting Solo youth that they had been taken in by Chinese-generated consumerism.

This chapter looks at the imaginings of the Southeast Asian city espoused by indigenous citizens and reflected in the urban literature, where "imagining" refers to images and metaphors of the city that provide a locus for diverse ideas and concepts (Low 1996). Sahlins (1976: 20) suggests that a culture can have "a privileged institutional locus . . . whence emanates a classificatory grid imposed upon the total culture." In the West, he argues, this locus is the economy, and until recently focus on the tiger economies of Southeast Asia indicated that many presumed the economy to be the locus there too. O'Connor (1995), in contrast, argues that in Southeast Asia status differentiation expressed principally through city forms and normative behavior is the privileged institutional locus. As in the above examples these two, and possibly other, imaginings are currently being contested.

City as Locus of Capitalist Accumulation

Armstrong and McGee in *Theatres of Accumulation* described Southeast Asian cities as principally the locus of the economy, the principal theater of action for those decision makers concerned with the operation of capital, corporate business and the state (1985: xiii). Cities, they stated, act as

> the crucial elements in accumulation at all levels . . . providing both the institutional framework and the locus operandi for transnationals, local oligopoly capital and the modernizing national state. . . . . On the other hand . . . [they] also play the role of diffusers of the lifestyles, customs, tastes, fashions and consumer habits of modern industrial society. Cities are the arenas in which foreign and local capital market, advertise and sell the philosophy of modernization, efficiency and growth through imitative lifestyles and consumerism and in so doing undermine non-capitalist production systems and cultural values. (1985: 41–2)

Indeed capital accumulation was so central to Armstrong and McGee's understanding of cities that they labeled a pre-1970s urban population expansion in the absence of capital accumulation as "pseudo-urbanization."

Pinches in writing on Manila (1987, 1994) supports this emphasis on capitalist accumulation as the prime cultural force. Modernization is evident in the massive investment of capital in suburban expansion and industrial production, and the proletarianization of the city workforce. The lives of Filipinos, he suggests, are "increasingly circumscribed by the flux and uncertainty of commodity production, commercialisation and a nation-state whose political economy orientates them to a global market in goods, labour and cultural values" (1994: 36). He instances the investment of private capital in the luxury housing estates and thriving business centre of Makati on the fringes of Manila, a "showcase to the world" and the pride of the Philippines (1994: 18).

In Malaysia such real-estate developments have mushroomed throughout the Peninsula. The larger of these boast industrial and commercial centers, shopping plazas, sporting facilities such as golf course or swimming pool, and mosque. These are the urban expressions of capitalism, where personal space is purchased as individualized lots of house, security, and services. In these new constructions of capitalist culture the elite and middle classes rely on exclusivity, by means of protected walled housing, exclusive shopping malls, personal automobile travel, and the like, rigidly based around capitalist values.[1]

The 1997–8 targeting of Chinese shops and churches in Indonesia demonstrated a rejection of these values by a sizable number of city-dwellers. The most ready explanations from looters for their actions was the sudden increase in prices, seen to be lining the pockets of the Chinese merchants. They were seen to be prioritizing the continued accumulation of capital even as the general populace struggled to survive. They were also the importers of those very items of white goods, clothes, food, and the like that had come to characterize the emerging middle class, themselves a product of economic growth. The lootings frequently were galvanized by street marches protesting the excessive wealth of the president, his family, and favored elite. Such self-indulgence was alien to a cultural imagining where status was defined through interpersonal relations and acknowledged in elaborate expressions of respect.

City as Pinnacle of Status Differentiation

In Southeast Asia cities have existed for two millennia.[2] The majority of the early cities were based on an Indian model, with its concept of kingship, the court, the army, the civil and religious bureaucracy and royal overlordship of the land. Administration centered on a primate royal capital city supported by the wealth from land taxes. Great monuments provided centralizing symbols of statehood, among them none better recognized today than Angkor Thom and Angkor Vat, the Khmer capital of the ninth century (Kirk 1990: 18–21). Richard Fox identified such cities as regal-ritual, the essential element of which was its ideological role, emerging from the "prestige and status of the state rule or the cohesive power of state religious ideology" (1977: 41). The royal court provided an image of ordered and ritualized existence as a model for the rest of society, and its ceremonials and elaborate rituals were occasions on which the king dramatized the ideal organization of the world for his followers (1977: 55). This cultural logic has thus been the dominant arrangement in Southeast Asia for centuries, and persists today in contestation with other imaginings of the city, the most powerful being that of the city as locus of capital accumulation.

Leeds (1984) was particularly scathing of an ethnocentric tendency in social analysis to equate the urban only with the features of capitalist systems, pointing out that feudal and capitalist integrations of urban society were radically different. While capitalist integration of urban society is marked by concentrations and mobility of capital and labor, with minimum intervention by the state, the feudal alternative is marked by the public display of elite pomp and wealth, an immobility of labor and fixity of class relationships.

While Leeds drew his examples of feudal society from medieval Europe O'Connor (1995) draws attention to similar distinctions in his analysis of Southeast Asian cities. The city's dominance is not to be explained by higher economic logic but by a cultural logic whereby society represents itself in symbols that presume a center. It is as status distinctions that urbanism imposes itself strictly and deeply on how people live (O'Connor 1995: 37). Many of the towns of Java (Indonesia) were, and some like Yogyakarta still are, centered symbolically in the palace of the Sultan. In Yogyakarta the palace wall encompasses a number of neighborhoods traditionally granted to princes, nobility, or power holders, or occupied by *kraton* (palace) servants. Ringing the palace was a larger city domain symbolically ordered by the presence of the sultan (Sullivan 1992: 22–3). In contrast the sultan's power was seen as much diminished in the outside ring of surrounding villages. Within the palace wall is the great park square with its banyan trees, symbols of the shelter and security afforded by the sultan.[3] In towns without an active *kraton* such a "palace" park still forms the symbolic and ritual center of the town, "a still center in a turbulent world" as Javanese might put it.

The status of the center was constructed around the conferring of privileges, awards, and titles to court loyalists, such as the titles in past and contemporary

Malay states by which the sultan rewards allies and co-opts rivals. C. Geertz's (1980) study of the traditional Balinese state indicated how rulers there conferred status down from the top even while lesser folk ceded power up from the bottom by their presence at the royal rituals. The modern Southeast Asian state, in order to consolidate its control and shore up its status, has manufactured jobs in the civil service that incorporate the newly educated into its ranks (Evers 1987). These emerging middle classes appear to rely heavily on social forms inherited from earlier and especially founding groups, combining colonial-derived Western style with the outlook of the traditional elite. The Thai military and civil service is built around the ascetic values and self-discipline originating in the Thammayut Order. More generally the Thai middle class is dependent on borrowed royal forms and attitudes and a style of Buddhism "whose gift-giving is better suited to court politics than bourgeois practicality" (O'Connor 1995: 42–43).

Koentjaraningrat, the foremost Indonesian anthropologist through the 1960s and 1970s, and himself a member of the Javanese nobility, wrote of urban culture entirely in terms of the *priyayi* (later called *pegawai negeri*), the class of administrative officials and intelligentsia, because, as he said, it is this culture, this "grandeur-addicted life style" (1985: 281), which today dominates the urban sector of Javanese society (1985: 233). This *priyayi* culture experienced its greatest elaboration under Dutch colonial government, when the elite, stripped of direct power, focused on the refinement of status distinctions. Brenner (1991: 60)[4] pointed out that the Javanese merchants of Solo, Central Java, traditionally outsiders to the royal court, "have done their utmost to uphold what they see as the most basic pillars of Javanese cultural life and tradition, particularly in their tireless attention to linguistic and behavioral etiquette and ritual detail" associated with the *priyayi*. It was the status distinctions constructed in the space and lifeways of the city that symbolized the city and beyond the city the society at large. In such a conception of the city promoted by elite urbanites the city person is seen as a person of wealth and status. Others who live in contiguous spaces but have neither wealth nor status are not of the city.

In Indonesia congested off-street neighborhoods called *kampung* are home to about half of all city residents. Some of these *kampung* are squatter settlements; in others a minority of residents or outsiders hold title to large sections of the neighborhood. The term *kampungan* is a derisory one, referring to nonsophisticates, those uncultured in speech, social habits, those separated from the true urbanite by a wide social and cultural chasm. In Yogyakarta, where I did my research (Guinness 1986, 1991) many *kampung* elders had never been inside the local shopping mall. It was not for them. Nor had they been in McDonald's or Kentucky Fried Chicken, where prices were aimed at the urban middle and upper classes rather than the masses. Despite their central location these *kampung* residents, being of low status as defined by this dominant urban imagining, were not of the city. Although they comprised an important part of the capitalist economy, in the dominant imagining focused on status distinctions their standing in the city was more ambiguous. Geertz (1957) suggested that although the social structural forms in which *kampung* people participate are for the most part urban, their cultural patterns are rural. The *slametan,* communal feast that marked rites of passage based on the principle of propinquity, no longer suited an urban society where *kampung* dwellers were

Figure 9.1 A poor kampung by the river's edge in Yogyakarta (© Harriot Beazley)

increasingly drawn into extra *kampung*, citywide, religio-political factions. *Kampung* people are thus, he summed up, not quite urban, "half rural, half urban."

For Pinches and his Filipino informants the distinction is one based on modernity rather than "urban"-ness. In Manila the squatters and slum-dwellers constitute the other of modernity, the underside, the alternative future into which the whole country could slide. They present a "moral and physical threat to social well-being, stability and development in Manila," under the so-called New Society of development and social and political order (1994: 26). To Pinches the spatiality and architecture of intimacy, improvization and flux which marked Manila's squatter settlements were a result primarily of the exclusionary and hostile stand of the Philippine state and propertied classes towards the city's disinherited (1994: 36). The elite of the Filipino New Society attempted to cancel out such settlements by hiding them behind white boards or demolishing them. The recent history of cities in Indonesia is replete with attempts by the city elite to exclude the masses. *Kampung* were demolished and their residents moved out of the city (Jellinek 1991), while pedicab drivers had their means of livelihood confiscated, and later destroyed, and were themselves trucked out of the city. Various Jakarta governments have attempted to close the city. What appears to motivate these attempts to marginalize the poor is the desire of the city's elite to display the city as modern as defined by the West and as the exemplar of the nation's civilization. The city elite moved against those elements that threatened that image.

O'Connor argued that the localisms and ethnicities that comprise Southeast Asian societies are subordinated to a higher status incorporated in the city. In this conceptualization the city, and within the city the sultan, the president or the governor is the pinnacle, or the "axis," or the "lap," of the whole society. Located within the city the elite generates the status distinctions that govern the city and larger society. "Urbane, yet insular, elites can imagine peasantries and nations to suit themselves" (O'Connor 1995: 38). Thus the city not only subordinates but also encompasses the larger society. A much-cited illustration of the capacity of the center to incorporate and represent the whole is the Taman Mini complex in Jakarta. The brainchild of Mrs. Soeharto, the former president's wife, this Mini Park required that every provincial governor have a building representative of his province designed and constructed there. In their diverse architectural forms these were arranged around a lake on which the archipelago of Indonesia was mapped out. In this imaginative way the whole of Indonesia had come to Jakarta. It became popular for families in Jakarta to visit the Park rather than taking the more costly journey home to their province (Pemberton 1994: 159). Kahn (1992) identified a similar phenomenon in Malaysia where Taman Mini Malaysia outside Melaka attracted a largely Malay middle-class consumer of culture.

Recent attempts of the Malay elite to construct an ideal Malay society drew on the notion of a romanticized village society, ruled by harmony and cooperation. As Kahn points out (1992: 164) "the revived interest in a traditional, rurally-based Malay culture is taking place in a social setting characterised by a massive decline in what is considered to be the traditional Malay peasant community." The positive features of Malay culture highlighted by the urban Malay middle class in this imaginary included ethnic homogeneity, absence of conflict, differentiation by age and gender rather than class, communalism, and a morality that expects politeness and fairness. These urban elite reconstructions of Malay village life are being advocated as the ideal for all Malays, and actively promoted in the nation's cities.

In 1975 Imelda Marcos directed the construction in Manila of a cluster housing project called Kapithahayan (neighborliness), a project that was supposed to embody the Filipino traditions of *bayanihan* (mutual help) and *barangay* (precolonial local community) and to become the prototype for community housing throughout the country. Its significance however was as a showcase that demonstrated to domestic and foreign observers the status of the city, the president and first lady, and the nation (Pinches 1994: 31).

The superiority of the city is expressed in its adoption of foreign idiom such as the foreign languages, art, and architecture commonly espoused in contemporary Southeast Asian cities. While their origin may lie in colonial or mercantile contacts the continued currency of these cultural symbols is explicable in terms of the need for the center to express itself in an idiom different from, and superior to, that of localisms (O'Connor 1995). Jakartan and other Indonesian urban elites elaborate a "metropolitan superculture" that favors facility with Dutch, English, and other foreign languages, classical Western art forms and political ideologies, nonindigenous voluntary associations, travel abroad and Western luxury goods (H. Geertz 1963). In Yogyakarta palace guards continue to dress in a variety of uniforms of Dutch and Portuguese origin.

Manila's elite adopted first Malay, then Spanish, and finally English as its favored foreign tongue. The adoption of foreign idioms was particularly evident in the showcase architecture of Manila during the Marcos era. In the early 1970s President Marcos and the First Lady were busy constructing a New Society that found its symbolic core in Manila. This expression of grandeur was associated with the West but designed to impress indigenes by claiming equality or resemblance to foreign symbolic status. Their efforts led to extraordinary transformations in urban architecture. Pinches (1994: 14) suggests that the design and building of the Cultural Centre complex reflected "a strong desire by the Marcos regime to win recognition from the affluent industrial West by emulating its forms of architectural modernism. Yet there is also an important sense in which the Cultural Centre and Folk Arts Theatre in particular, sought to encapsulate, dignify and display a cultural heritage that was uniquely Filipino." This was an architecture of display, where the city represented, as Imelda Marcos proclaimed in 1977, "the crown of civilisation . . . not for ourselves alone nor for city dwellers . . . [but] for an entire people" (Pinches 1994: 29).

Contesting Imaginings: Capitalist Accumulation or Status Distinctiveness?

Within this metropolitan superculture we can identify both the establishment of status through foreign idiom and a consumerist mentality central to capitalist transformations. Contrary to Armstrong and McGee's assertions quoted earlier it is not clear that capitalist accumulation is providing the dominant cultural locus. There is even a hint that commoditization and modernization provide yet other foreign idioms in which the ruling center expresses its superior status. Where society's structure arises performatively "modernization just like other exogenous changes functions as an indigenous urbanization that breaks down the local only to build up the urban" (O'Connor 1995: 35).

Pinches recognizes that these two principles have been in contention in the refashioning of Manila. The first, as an architecture of display, is exemplified by the Cultural Centre Complex, associated with a visionary language of utopian humanism. The complex is a statement of progress, national identity, and state power. The second, as a pursuit of capitalist accumulation, was exemplified by the rational planning that sought to reorder Manila along technical-bureaucratic lines, sponsored by the World Bank. Despite Pinches' earlier emphasis on capital accumulation as the dominant cultural process he admits that neither approach proves able "to harness the dynamic and complexity of Manila's urbanisation," resulting in the "deeply divided and ambiguous way in which members of Philippine elite and civil servants have approached the construction of national identity" (Pinches 1994: 37).

The interplay of these two concepts of the city is evident in the real estate complexes that have sprung up all over Southeast Asia. In constrast to Western portrayals of such complexes as "villages" (retirement villages, Greenwich village, etc.) Malaysians focus on their urbanness by terming them *bandar* (town) or *taman* (town park) and Indonesians focus on their foreignness by terming them *ril estet*. They are both the creation of capital investment and the carriers of urban status values. In 1996 the sales manager of a luxury housing estate outside Yogyakarta volunteered to me that the sultan and top military figures had purchased houses in this estate, illustrating how capitalist interests have integrated the fascination with status into their marketing. The large number of recently constructed banks and hotels in Yogyakarta were conspicuous by the lavishness of their construction. The stately facades and spaciousness of their approaches and entrance halls seemed to appeal more to a logic of status display than of capitalist profit-accumulation.[5]

The contestation between such urban principles is clearly illustrated in the construction of new towns by mining companies. Initially mining companies appeal to exaggerated statements of status through housing design and segregation, privileged access to urban facilities such as schools, leisure centers, and health clinics, and distinctive uniforms and transportation. Such an approach attempts to engage a labor force in a new location under a feudalistic regime where the company is often both the investor and the state representative (Robinson 1986). My own research in an Indonesian mining town in 1998 indicated that as the Indonesian labor force becomes more skilled and state administration more widespread companies do not need to focus as strongly on labor retention and may attempt to surrender control of the town. However, "deconstructing" the status structures of the mining town is not readily acceptable to its citizens who preferred a "closed" town and a fixity of status symbols to a more market-driven arrangement.

All the cities of Southeast Asia have been reconstructed according to elite aspirations. The city they fashion has the symbols of urban opulence found elsewhere in the world, the highway overpasses, the world's tallest tower (Kuala Lumpur), the shopping malls, and international hotels. In its exemplary role within the society and nation the city has been fashioned by its elite to appeal to sentiments of grandeur and pride. National monuments and institutions have been created. From precolonial palaces to contemporary skyscrapers urban elites have sought to construct symbolic capital within the city. Thus the growth of capitalism in Southeast Asian cities has been marked by other priorities, those of the display of status in which the audience is not so much the foreign capitalist or the tourist but the imagined community of the nation (Anderson 1991). In this performance the tourist and the businessman are part of the display. It would be blind to ignore the dominance of capital, both foreign and indigenous, in the construction of the city. Village migrants, city factories, shopping centers, and tourist facilities are evidence enough of that strength. Yet the city as locus of capitalist accumulation feeds on, and contests with, other major, perhaps dominant, cultural forces generating urbanism in Southeast Asia.

City as Locus of Community

The anti-Chinese riots dramatized the conflict between these two conceptualizations of the city. While the Chinese stood for capitalist accumulation, their overthrow represented the triumph of indigenous values and status distinctions. There was a further key urban imagining revealed in these riots. For the *kampung* residents who no doubt formed the bulk of the rioters the Chinese were outsiders to the communities of residents that characterize these cities. They are outsiders because they do not participate in community events (Sullivan 1992; Guinness 1986). For urban low-income residents community is a stronger cultural locus than either the capital accumulation or status distinctions of other imaginings. In Yogyakarta there is a strong norm of community cooperation in *kampung* relations. Such communities are based on female-centric cell groups (Sullivan 1992) or on neighborhoods. *Kampung* residents referred to the mutual help expected in *slametan* rites of passage, or the cooperation in public works such as building stairways or public wells, or the aiding of those in need. In one neighborhood of about one hundred households I researched in 1996 community endeavors were particularly evident. Youth, women, and men conducted separate savings groups, and two sections of the neighborhood had instituted savings and loans associations. Under these a member could borrow up to one million rupiah (roughly $A500) to do such things as renovate houses, purchase pedicabs, or pay school expenses. Residents collectively reorganized a key ritual. Neighborhood youth were building up their joint fund by organizing the payment of electricity and water bills for neighbors for a small commission. The neighborhood community held a lavish concert to celebrate Independence Day, and provided scholarships to meet school costs of poorer children. Residents had also constructed impressive safety fences along the upper pathway. On one occasion while I was there community labor was called to repair the house of a poor widow and clean up the surrounding area, with over one hundred neighbors attending. These neighborhoods exist as a form of community that downplays the status distinctions that invigorate middle-class and elite "streetside" residents. In these communities wealth is for sharing rather than reinvestment. This is evident in the obligation to invite neighbors to rites of passage, to share one's kitchen or gardening utensils, and to oblige neighbors with credit at the local shop or stall.

Kampung residents also saw a clear distinction between their principles and those that appeared to govern the outside city bent on status differentiation. In the 1970s streetsiders were seen by *kampung* people as being of high social status, reflected in their brick houses, privileged position in civil service or private business, and the foreign idiom which permeated their culture. In the 1990s, after two decades of capital accumulation, *kampung* residents counterposed their world to that of real-estate complexes. Both streetsiders and real-estate residents, however, were characterized as living an isolated, individualistic existence, where neighbors rarely spoke and family rites rarely attracted the assistance of the community. In contrast, even within their own neighborhoods *kampung* residents dealt strongly with neighbors who vaunted their wealth or their status, particularly if that restricted their participation in community.

Their idea of the city was of a mass of *kampung* communities, between which there was a minimum of interaction, but which all espoused a similar discourse. Interestingly the sultan was also incorporated within this community perspective. His person and the symbols of his presence such as royal regalia and ceremonies were focal points uniting the various communities of the city. *Kampung* residents perceived the sultan and the royal regalia that symbolized his presence in the city as protecting their communities, as for example when such royal regalia were carried about the city during an epidemic or when water from washing royal carriages was carried back to the community to be used for healing or sacralizing. The sultan in this context was seen as benevolent "father," rather than the apex of an elaborate status hierarchy. At the major royal rituals there was, in a sense, no one between themselves and the sultan, as people milled around the royal *gamelan* (orchestra) displayed in the palace park or received the food carried from the palace to the mosque for distribution. As half a million of Yogyakarta's populace rallied in early 1998 to oppose the president the sultan himself offered to lead the march, so providing to the military authorities his personal guarantee that no looting of property would take place.

In 1996 I identified among *kampung* residents widespread dissatisfaction with the growing wealth and power disparities within society. Among the poor there was widespread cynicism about the wealth of the Soeharto family, the corruption of the local police force, and the nepotism of local officials. Bribery had become a way of life in the city that effectively excluded the poor, but was largely tolerated by the emerging middle class indulging in their own wealth and status accumulation. Those who lived in city neighborhoods dominated by a community cultural focus rejected the wealth polarities seen to result from Indonesian capitalist expansion and the foreign idiom of urban status. The goods they burnt would not have a place in homes without running water, high voltage electricity supply, and street access. Instead they were burnt as symbols of personal indulgence and of corrupted status. The 1997–8 shopburnings and lootings in Jakarta were preceded by streetmarches calling for greater democracy and the indictment of the president and his family for unfair accumulation of wealth.

Conclusion

The recent toppling of the Indonesian president, like earlier expressions of people power in the Philippines, is a demonstration of the bitterness that such status distinctions have generated in contemporary society. Under the influence of capital accumulation high status no longer carries the responsibilities and obligations to those of lower standing. Ties of patronage across social classes have collapsed, leaving the elite vulnerable to the criticism of the poor and *kampung* people regretting the loss of "connections" that could find them a niche in the city economy. The poor have always insisted on the responsibilities of patrons towards their clients in their construction of community, and in their recognition of the elite construction of the city as expressing status distinctions. That mutual respect has been undermined in contemporary urban society, leading to more overt demonstrations of violence in people's contesting of the city

NOTES

1. For real estate and shopping-mall developments in contemporary Indonesian cities see Robison (1996: 80).
2. In the early centuries AD cities existed along the Irawaddy and Sittang deltas in present-day Burma, on the Menam Chao Phraya in present-day Thailand, in the lower valley and delta of the Mekong in Cambodia, and on the Champa coast in present-day Vietnam. In the seventh century the port city states of Jambi, Drivijaya, and Palembang were found in Southeast Sumatra.
3. The dominant civil service party, Golkar, adopted the Waringin as their symbol.
4. Brenner introduced her article with a quote from Arwendo Atmowiloto's novel *Canting*: "Rank, wealth, title, that's what being priyayi is about."
5. Much of the analysis of the present Indonesian economic crisis is focused on poor banking practices.

REFERENCES

Anderson, Benedict 1991: *Imagined Communities: Reflections on the Origin and Spread of Nationalism*. New York: Verso.

Armstrong, Warwick and McGee, T. G. 1985: *Theatres of Accumulation: Studies in Asian and Latin American Urbanization*. London: Methuen.

Bowen, John 1986: On the political construction of tradition: gotong royong in Indonesia. *Journal of Asian Studies*, 45 (3), 545–61.

—— 1989: *Muslims through Discourse*. Princeton: Princeton University Press.

Brenner, Suzanne A. 1991: Competing hierarchies: Javanese merchants and the priyayi elite in Solo, Central Java. *Indonesia*, 52, 55–83.

Dumont, Louis, 1986: *Essays on Individualism: Modern Ideology in Anthropological Perspective*. Chicago: University of Chicago Press.

Evers, Hans-Dieter, 1987: The bureaucratisation of Southeast Asia. *Comparative Studies in Society and History*, 29, 4.

Fox, Richard 1977: *Urban Anthropology: Cities in their Cultural Settings*. Englewood Cliffs, N. J.: Prentice-Hall.

Geertz, Clifford 1957: Ritual and social change: a Javanese example. *American Anthropologist* 59, 32–54.

—— 1963: *Peddlers and Princes: Social Development and Economic Change in Two Indonesian Towns*. Chicago: University of Chicago Press.

—— 1980: *Negara: The Theatre State in Nineteenth-century Bali*. Princeton: Princeton University Press.

Geertz, Hildred 1963: Indonesian cultures and communities. In Ruth McVey (ed.), *Indonesia*, New Haven, Conn.: Southeast Asian Studies, Yale University Press.

Guinness, Patrick 1986: *Harmony and Hierarchy: In a Javanese Kampung*. Singapore: Oxford University Press.

—— 1991: Kampung and streetside: Yogyakarta under the new order. *Prisma 51, 86–98.*

—— 1992: *On the Margin of Capitalism: People and Development in Mukim Plentong, Johor, Malaysia*. Singapore: Oxford University Press.

Jellinek, Lea 1991: *The Wheel of Fortune: The History of a Poor Community in Jakarta*. Sydney: Allen and Unwin.

Kahn, Joel 1992: Class, ethnicity and diversity: some remarks on Malay culture in Malaysia. In Joel Kahn and Francis Loh (eds.), *Fragmented Vision*, North Sydney: Allen and Unwin, 158–78.

Kirk, William 1990: South East Asia in the colonial period: cores and peripheries in development processes. In D. J. Dwyer (ed.) *South East Asian Development*, New York: Longman Scientific and Technical, 15–47.

Koentjaraningrat 1985: *Javanese Culture*. Singapore: ISEAS/OUP.

Leeds, Anthony 1984: Cities and countryside in anthropology. In L. Rodwin and R. Hollister (eds.), *Cities of the Mind*. New York: Plenun Press.

Low, Setha 1996: The anthropology of cities: imagining and theorizing the city. *Annual Review of Anthropology*, 25, 383–409.

Murray, Alison 1991: *No Money, No Honey: A Study of Street Traders and Prostitutes in Jakarta*. Singapore: Oxford University Press.

O'Connor, Richard 1995: Indigenous urbanism: class, city and society in Southeast Asia. *Journal of Southeast Asian Studies*, 26 (1), 30–45.

Peattie, Lisa Redfield and Robbins, Edward 1984: Anthropological approaches to the city. In L. Rodwin and R. Hollister, *Cities of the Mind*. New York: Plenum Press, 83–95.

Pemberton, John 1994: *On the Subject of "Java"*. Ithaca: Cornell University Press.

Pinches, Michael 1987: "All that we have is our muscle and sweat": the rise of wage labour in a Manila squatter community. In M. Pinches and S. Lakha (eds.) *Wage Labour and Social Change: The Proletariat in Asia and the Pacific*, Clayton: Centre of Southeast Asian Studies, Monash University, 103–40.

—— 1994: Modernisation and the quest for modernity: architectural form, squatter settlements and the new society in Manila. In Marc Askew and William Logan (eds.), *Cultural Identity and Urban Change in Southeast Asia: Interpretative Essays*, Geelong, Victoria: Deakin University Press, 13–42.

Robinson, Kathryn 1986: *Stepchildren of Progress*. Albany: State University of New York Press.

Robison, Richard 1996: The middle class and the bourgeoisie in Indonesia. In R. Robison and D. Goodman (eds.), *The New Rich in Asia: Mobile Phones, McDonalds and Middle-class Revolution*, London, New York: Routledge 79–104.

Sahlins, M. 1976: *Culture and Practical Reason*. Chicago: University of Chicago Press.

Soemardjan, Selo 1962: *Social Change in Yogyakarta*. New York: Cornell University Press.

Siegel, James T. 1986: *Solo in the New Order: Language and Hierarchy in an Indonesian City*. Princeton, N.J.: Princeton University Press.

Sullivan, John 1990: Community and local government on Java: facts and fictions. Clayton: Centre of Southeast Asian Studies Working Papers, Monash University.

—— 1992: *Local Government and Commmunity in Java*. Singapore: Oxford University Press.

Part II The Economy and the City

Chapter 10

City Economies

Gary Bridge and Sophie Watson

In urban theory and analysis the economy has occupied a privileged status as the real, the material and, in early Marxist writings, the underlying structure which in the last instance determines all other phenomena. The economy, it could be said, is the hard stuff – the given – against which culture and the social is othered as soft and more malleable and open to change. This bifurcation has now started to shift as poststructuralist and feminist theory has fractured the notion of the economy as a monolithic space, and social/cultural analysis has come into its ascendancy. At the same time culture and economy are recognized as far more mutually constitutive than once was thought. Cultural readings of the economy meet the influential arguments from Marxist political economy. In all these cases the question arises as to whether we are seeing adjustments to capitalism or is capitalism itself taking on a decisively different character? Is Confucian capitalism the same as American capitalism? Will the effects of the market have the same impact on the form and function of cities in those two countries? Are arguments about globalization testament to the triumph of Western capitalism (Wallerstein 1974; 1991) and the "end of history" (Fukuyama 1992) or just the beginning of new cultural economic forms?

Some even question the notion of capitalism itself. Is it no longer something we can hold together in a unitary conceptual discourse or do its discontinuities open up the space for resistance and change? As Gibson-Graham (1996) argue this might not be the end of capitalism but the end of capitalism as we knew it. These debates bring out the contrasts between neoclassical, Marxist, and poststructuralist understandings of city economies that we will consider in the first part of this chapter.

Theoretical divisions map onto various key trends in city economies. In this chapter we group them into three related themes: materiality/embeddedness, location/relational space, and the city. First are the arguments about what we might call the dematerialization of the economy. These contrast with understandings of markets as socially and culturally embedded and indeed corporeal. Then there are important questions over the degree to which economic activity is localized or set in relational networks. The implications of materiality and territory for understandings of urbanization, urban growth and the urban experience in city economies will be considered. These themes consume our attention in the second part of the chapter.

Neoclassical, Marxist and Poststructuralist Understandings of City Economies

Neoclassicists and Marxists take certain (but different) elements of capitalism as given. For neoclassicists these are consumer sovereignty and markets as price-fixing mechanisms. For Marxist authors such as David Harvey it is capital logic that is invariant, such as accumulation for accumulation's sake and rent as an unequal social relation (Harvey 1982; 1985). For poststructuralists such as Trevor Barnes, capitalism exists through discursive constructions and the specificities of context and location (Barnes 1996).

Before the Marxist revolution in urban studies in the 1970s most economic analysis of cities was decidedly neoclassical in tone. The spatial form of cities was an outcome of competing demand for space, and land uses changed from commercial, to industrial to residential at the margins of the ability of different users to "bid" for the land (see Alonso 1964; Muth 1969). Rent was an equilibrium mechanism that sorted out competing bids on land uses. Equally the geographical location of settlements relative to each other was determined by the spatial extents of consumer markets for different goods (e.g. Christaller 1966).

Neoclassical analysis is still a significant part of urban analysis, though there is a theoretical and political divide between the neoclassical and Marxist, and post-Marxist camps with often little dialog between them. There are exceptions to this – for instance Sayer's (1995) call for greater connections between Marxist political economy and liberalism and Merrifield's Marxist analysis that accommodates the market, at least for the time being (see chapter 12 in this volume).

A good example of the neoclassical approach is given by Bill Clark (chapter 13) in which he analyses changing consumer tastes, accessibility and locational trade-offs, and their impact on urban form. He argues that issues of demand and accessibility are just as important in explaining the form of the decentralized city as they were in the 1960s when agglomeration and accessibility to the center was the key. Consumer demand explains the more fragmented form of the contemporary city.

Concurrently Marxist political economy has mounted a sustained critique of neoclassical assumptions. Rather than consumer demand being the key explanatory variable in the form and location of cities, Marxists looked to factors of production of commodities and the social relations that were involved in production processes. The canon of David Harvey's work (Harvey 1973; 1982; 1989; 1996) has had a profound effect on the interpretation of capitalism and the role of cities in capitalist accumulation – what he calls the urban process in capitalism. Harvey and others have argued that cities have distinctive roles in the circulation of capital. They are concentrated centers of exploitation and the class-based extraction of surplus value from workers (the spatial equivalent of the length of the working day). They also act as coordination centers for the control of investment between the various circuits of capital in commodity production, the built form, services, finance, and credit. Indeed much of the built form of the city itself is seen as an outcome of investment in the second circuit of capital to overcome overaccumulation crises in the first

Figure 10.1 Hairdressing salon, South African township (© Sophie Watson)

circuit of commodity production. Rent here is not seen as a market clearing mechanism in the demand for land as it is in the neoclassical models. Rather it is a social relation that is an outcome of the unequal struggle between landowners and land users who are able to exact a surplus given their monopoly control of land. In this spirit Edwards (chapter 50) attacks the neoclassical naturalized view of markets to argue for their historical and material construction, in this case through planning systems. More latterly cities are seen as sites of spectacle (world fairs, the Olympics) and other cultural accumulation strategies which are themselves sources of rapid profits.

In recent years Marxist political economy has been criticized from several directions for being too much of a grand narrative seeking to encompass everything in its explanations and too rigid about social factors, particularly class (Laclau and Mouffe 1985; Resnick and Wolff 1987). Gibson-Graham (1996) argues that the discourse about capitalism in Marxism is so concentrated on the unitary and all-encompassing nature of capitalist processes that it stymies any radical political resistance. Marxist metaphors and analyses are male (domination, penetration, invasion) and Gibson-Graham's feminist critique seeks to reorientate debate to find a discursive space for resistance to the monster of capitalism. Barnes (1996) argues that total knowledge cannot be had – our understandings are at best partial and situated in a cultural context and this leads us to view capitalism as a potentially fragmented and particular process, rather than being unitary and universal.

Postcolonial studies have also questioned Western-oriented understandings of markets and capitalism (see King, chapter 22). Occidental assumptions are evident in variants of "modernization theory" (e.g. Rostow 1971) that are applied from the "developed" to the "developing" world. From the sub discipline of development economics to ideas of dependency and Marxist interpretations of the "development of underdevelopment" – these diverse theoretical approaches all infer the experience of non-Western economies from prior western experience. The idea of overurbanization for instance, in which the level of urbanization of a country was much higher than its GDP compared with a similar stage of "development" in the West in the end revealed more about the nature of Western assumptions than any experience of urbanization in many non-Western countries. In the West the "economy" is assumed to be separate from the domestic. This ignores the fact that in non-Western, and to some extent also in Western cities, one part of the economy is a combination of household/family production, home based but conducted in public. Western assumptions about the marginality of the "informal economy" ignore the fact that an increasing amount of economic activity is informal, undocumented, and even illegal.

The possibility that cultural differences make a decisive difference to this thing called capitalism, or even that Western capitalism itself is an exception, has been considered by economists and sociologists and more recently economic sociologists (e.g. see Weber 1958; 1978; Polanyi 1957; Smelser and Swedberg 1994). The new socioeconomics and earlier institutional approaches argue that categories of economic action are culturally variable and socially constituted. Perhaps we should look to Weber as well as Marx for our understanding of the inner workings of capitalism. In *The Protestant Ethic and the Spirit of Capitalism* Weber argued that there was an "elective affinity" between certain puritan forms of Protestantism that had an emphasis on the individual, on thrift, on wealth as a sign of discipline and the investment behavior required in capitalism. These ideas of human nature were secularized as capitalism took off in a process of rationalization and disenchantment.

That economic system is now global. Embedded within it are certain conceptions of the person, rational action, economic convention. These cultural assumptions meet other ways of seeing the person (and therefore constituting the economic actor) along with other understandings of the significance of the commodity, other ways of coordinating economic activity, and other ideas of the role of the economic in the rest of life. In China Confucian values emphasize the significance of roles (in balanced hierarchies) rather than individuals, and an orientation to an adjustment to the world rather than a mastery of it (Hamilton 1994).

In theoretical terms the key engagement is likely to be the degree to which these economic/cultural differences locate capitalism in its specificity or whether the relations between these processes are sufficiently similar that we can talk of trans-cultural processes. If culture is a critical component in the organization and form of capitalism Marxist urban theory will need rethinking if it is to deal with these new economic forms. This is a key theoretical encounter and is beginning to be worked through. It is represented by the scope of this Companion.

City economies: Materiality/Embeddedness, Location/Relational Space, and the City

The relations between conceptions of the economy and cities are considered here in terms of materiality and embeddness, locational and relational space. To what extent is the economic a material realm? To what extent is it composed of matter, of objects, of touchable things? This question underlies a good deal of contemporary argument about the economy and the economic role of cities.

There is one fundamental sense in which the economy has materiality – the outcome of economic activity in terms of the material wealth and poverty of populations. At the broadest level real income per person in 1991 varied from $US14,860 in "the North" to $US2,730 in "the South" with a world average of $US5,490. The poorest countries (mostly in sub-Saharan Africa had per capita income of $US880). In the last 20 years countries with economies that have grown fastest have had fastest urban growth. In 1990 the world's 25 largest economies also had over 70 percent of the world's 281 millionaire cities and all but one of its 12 urban agglomerations with 10 million or more inhabitants (Habitat 1996). Growth has been especially rapid in what have been termed the Dynamic Asian Economies (Republic of Korea, Taiwan, Hong Kong, Singapore, Thailand, Indonesia, and Malaysia). Of course the economic downturn of the late 1990s has arrested economic growth in many of these countries and this has had a real impact on cities where building development of offices, apartments, and infrastructures has been halted. The Chinese economy is growing fast and East Asia contains ever-larger proportions of the world's urban population and of its largest cities (Habitat 1996). In contrast, between 1980 and 1991 per capita income was negative for three regions: sub-Saharan Africa, the Middle East and North Africa, and Latin America and the Caribbean, much of this a result of higher interest rates on debt repayments to the West. Although the increase in urban populations was more modest, the living and working conditions of those populations deteriorated. The numbers living in poverty increased sharply in many countries during the 1980s and 1990s, up to 40 percent of the urban population of Zambia and Mozambique, for example, and 68 percent of the population in Bangladesh.

Despite the stark reality of these material outcomes of economic processes the key drivers of economic change seem ever more elusive. This feeling of the dematerialization of the economy can be explained in a number of ways. First, changes in production processes have led to the unbundling of the commodity. This happened in manufacturing first of all with separation of manufacturing functions, subcontracting and just-in-time production – the flexible specialization of post-Fordism (see Scott 1988ab; Lovering 1990; Amin 1995). Ford's Hermosillo plant in Mexico that made Mazda cars is a good example (Harris 1998). Just-in-time stock policies ensured that there was no accumulation of parts in any of the thousands of contributing factories in the Kansai region of Japan or en route to Mexico. Export of the parts was monitored and conducted at such a speed so as not to interrupt vehicle assembly in Mexico.

Unbundling has now spread to services. As Harris again illustrates, "The design of Walt Disney cartoons starts in Hollywood, but part of the drawing is done in Manila. Mumbai handles SwissAir's accounting, Barbados that of American Airlines. Manila processes British criminal records; Shenzhen, Japanese land transactions (1998: 11).

The disaggregation of manufacturing and service provision has profound territorial effects. Most contributing regions don't have a grasp on the entire production process and so control of production comes from afar and is more elusive. For some this means a complete deterritorialization, the demise of the nation-state and the concentration of economic decision making on a few global cities. Harris, for example, argues that "the overall result of unbundling has been the spread of manufacturing capacity world-wide – binding the globe into a single manufacturing system directed from cities" (Harris 1998: 11). Others argue that the nation-state determines the impact of external economic forces (Weiss 1998) or point to the significance of government trade and foreign relations departments in doing the diplomatic groundwork to assist national or transnational corporations in their investment strategies abroad – what is called "the new diplomacy" (Stopford, Strange and Henley 1991).

Yet others reassert the importance of territory as the intricacies of supply in post-Fordist production create industrial regions as a new form of urbanism. Scott (1988ab) argues that just-in-time production and the industrial networks of sub-contracted supply it demands have resulted in a new geography of urban nuclei in dispersed regional systems in which firms seek to minimize their transaction costs. Scott (1988b) defines this as a new urban form in which transaction costs between subcontractors and suppliers are minimized across a region. Whether we see this as a new form of urban concentration which is tied together by rapid transport routes or as dispersed urbanization in new edge cities (Garreau 1991) is open to question. Others even see it as the coming of the postmetropolis where the degree of urbanization and decentralization is such that the world in some senses has become a city (Soja 1999).

The second sense of dematerialization comes from the growth of new commodities to be traded. The most important of these is knowledge. In *The Coming of Post-Industrial Society*, Bell (1973) defined postindustrialism in terms of knowledge-intensive production. Over the last 20 years there has been a rapid expansion in the production, consumption, and exchange of knowledge and information. In this informational economy the action of knowledge upon knowledge itself is the main source of productivity (Castells 1996: 17). This is a set of economic processes based on reflexivity (see Amin, chapter 11 in this volume). Especially important in this new mode of development are informational cities that act as hubs of knowledge-intensive activity and the infrastructure required to support it (Castells 1989).

There is a tension between an idea of the economic assets of a city resting on its location, accessibility, and history and its increasing irrelevance in international flows of capital – a dilemma that Amin points out in chapter 11. These dilemmas can be seen in terms of cities that are changing from one form of economic order (state socialism) to another (capitalism), and the changes have different borderlands, to use Sassen's metaphor. In Havana, Cuba, there are dual spaces that consist of government-sponsored activities and those of the parallel economy. The spaces of sociocapitalism are uneasy ones (Rutheiser, chapter 19 of this volume). The capital cities of the Baltic states are being used as cultural and historical locational assets to attract inward investment and "adjust" to the market (Cooke et al., chapter 20). Tong Wu (chapter 18) notes the significance of the international migration of the Chinese. These migrants invest in their destination cities outside China and also repatriate investments to home regions in China. The transnational investment strategies of the wealthiest migrants reveal the importance of networks of family and cultural inflections on capitalist processes.

The informational economy is a network economy, where place is not important but connectedness is. The network metaphor has been significant in a number of ways. Post-Fordist flexible specialization production relies on a network of production units and subcontractors. The informational economy stresses the significance of network effects and cities themselves are networked in an (increasingly global) urban network hierarchy. Economic competitiveness relies on innovation and creative clusters that are networked. These networks are seen to be most rich and productive in the city (see Comedia and Demos 1997). It is networks of advantage or disadvantage that can exist in the teeth of spatial juxtapositions of wealth and poverty in our cities. Networks and connectedness, rather than location, seem to be the economic metaphor of the age (see Castells 1996–8).

Many of the new commodities based around knowledge working add to the images that confront individuals – pop videos, computer games, cable TV, the Internet. This proliferation of images in an economy of signs (Lash and Urry 1994) either increases the reflexive sense of self (Giddens 1991) or adds to their sense of disembeddedness in an experience of hyperreality (Baudrillard 1981). This is a set of esthetic processes where design, finish, and niche marketing to specific taste groups become important. The media economy is increasingly self-referential – advertisements draw on allusions to other advertisements, or TV programs, or videos – in a form of intertextual economy. Knowledge is traded, images are traded, images of images are traded. Economies become spectral.

Cities become sites for the production of images and the cultivation of spectacle. In the competition for inward investment they must market themselves as desirable places for business (Kearns and Philo 1993; see also chapter 20) and tourism (Urry 1990). They also sell their desirability to young professionals through the marketing of consumption landscapes of gentrification (Mills 1988; Zukin 1991; 1982). The city is sold as a bundle of consumption assets. The keen competition between cities for events such as World Fairs or the Olympics is testimony to the significance of spectacle, city name recognition, and a global audience. Harvey argues that signs and spectacle have the added significance of reducing the turnover time between investment and return in the global race for profit.

A third sense in which the economy is dematerialized is the changed character of money. Money is increasingly disconnected from material things. The advent of floating exchange rates, the expansion of credit, and the futures and derivatives market means that money as a form of value is more and more distanced from commodity production, more and more tied to forms of speculation (Harvey 1989). Money is more mythical. Yet with the growth of securities and deregulation of financial markets money (as a form of information) is moving around the globe in greater quantities instantaneously.

The free and rapid movement of capital investment reduces the significance of territory in the "space of flows" as Castells (1996) calls it. At the same time these rapid and proliferating movements have to be coordinated. In recent years urban debates have proliferated around global cities and the processes of globalization. Globalization is variously posited as an inevitable homogenizing force – a kind of juggernaut discourse, but similar to the internationalization of earlier periods (Hirst and Thompson 1996), as generally beneficial (Giddens 1998) – or as having vastly spatially differentiated effects (Castells 1997). The place of certain cities as

Figure 10.2 Chicago (© Steve Pile)

command-and-control centers for the flow of finance capital has been extensively explored in Western cities (see Sassen, chapter 15; and Fainstein and Harloe, chapter 14) and increasingly in a non-Western context (see Tong Wu, chapter 18). The fact that such cities are fully immersed in the daily movements of the global stock market and are sites of producer services is argued to have separated them off from other cities in their nations. As a result new forms of proximity in the space of flows have emerged. New York, London, and Tokyo have more in common (in some respects) with each other than their hinterlands or other regions of their respective countries. They are more like city-states separate in many respects from their hinterlands and with enormous significance for their national economies. In global cities we see the clearest signs of cities becoming independent economic actors.

However easy it is to be seduced by the gleaming towers, bustle, hypermobility, and sophisticated consumption landscapes of New York, Tokyo, London, and Hong Kong or Shanghai, there is another side to globalization. Cities in this global arena rely on local populations (cleaners, maintenance personnel and other low-grade service jobs supporting the professional employees). These workers are also characteristic of processes of globalization in which immigrant and refugee populations are as central to the global narrative as the city slicker. These contrasts and relations form the "analytic borderlands" which disrupt dominant discourses of globalization in which the economy has been constructed as the center while culture is othered as marginal (chapter 15).

The transnational city is the other face of the global city. While stricter immigration controls have meant a decline in immigration to many Western countries over the last 20 years, international migration has increased worldwide. 100 million people were estimated to live outside their country of origin in 1992, 20 million of whom were refugees and asylum-seekers. Many of these people are concentrated in low-wage sectors of the economy, or in the informal economy. Immigrants' experiences are explored throughout this volume in terms of the politics of citizenship (see chapters 24 and 27) and political action in the transnational city.

Global cities might not be that exceptional. Economic changes (in industry, labor, and property markets) that affect cities defined as global are not necessarily distinct from those impacting on other urban areas. Susan Fainstein and Michael Harloe (chapter 14) challenge the simplistic binary notion of a dual labor market consisting of highly paid professionals and underpaid service workers in the city. They point to the missing mass of the suburban middle class who are involved as workers and consumers in the city economy but are often forgotten in the analyses. Recent work in London (Nick Buck and Ian Gordon, chapter 16) points to processes of turbulence (high turnover) in employment and sedimentation where people with skills are bumped down to jobs for which they are overqualified. This process then forces less qualified people to take jobs that are below their skills level. This reveals the instability of the postindustrial labor market.

Labor market divisions within transnational cities reflect wider international divisions of labor (Froebel et al. 1980). This has been understood as the decline in manufacturing jobs in the West and their growth in non-Western nations, especially East Asia and the growth of routinized service occupations in non-Western countries supporting higher order nonroutinized services in the West. There is also the staggering growth in informal activities where jobs in the formal economy are too few, or in the illegal economy. The burgeoning economy of crime and corruption (drugs, money laundering, and so on) was estimated to be worth $US750 billion in 1994 (for a discussion see Castells 1998: chapter 3).

Analyses of changing labor markets worldwide are matched in numbers by discussions of work, or rather the transformation of work (Castells 1996; Sennett 1999). Castells summarizes this as "networkers, jobless and flextimers" (1996: chapter 4). Overall this represents a loosening of the relationship between people and work, either because they cannot get access to employment, or they have a more flexible experience of both time at work and "careers" as a whole. Work becomes a less structuring element of life and identities are forged in realms other than employment and the economic. The declining significance of work for identity (and politics arguably) can be seen as another form of dematerialization.

The transformation of work is again uneven. Sassen also points to the sharper valorization and devalorization of different parts of the city. Devalorized spaces speak of dematerialization in another sense. It is a dematerialization in the sense of absence of material goods or access to them. Thrift (1995) gives the illustration of the African-American and Latino neighborhoods of South Central Los Angeles where banks, automatic cash machines, mortgage finance, and credit facilities are largely absent.

Lack of investment on a larger scale is symptomatic of those former industrial cities which have lost manufacturing employment and which have no compensating service sector to take up the employment loss. Rustbelt cities in the northeastern US, northern England, or Wollongong and Newcastle in Australia, have experienced prolonged economic decline and physical decay.

On a greater scale still, whole regions of the world can be seen as excluded from the flows of hypermobile capital. Thus Smith (1984) talks of the redlining of sub-Saharan Africa. Even where investment or aid is forthcoming it is couched in neoliberal terms. The assumptions of open competition, the hidden hand of the market and minimal interference in market mechanisms have certainly prevailed politically over the last quarter century. This neoliberal hegemony in many countries has broken down labor market regulation, weakened labor representation, and reduced so-called obstacles to competition. Such assumptions have also lain behind the activities of the IMF and the World Bank as they credit rate countries and cities and enforce conditions of competition on non-Western nations in return for loans and debt rescheduling. The net flow of monies from non-Western to Western nations in the form of debt repayments can be seen as a form of neocolonialism reinforcing the subaltern status of these economies.

From this discussion of the dematerialization of the economy it might be easy to gain an impression (supported by writers such as Giddens 1998) that in some senses the world is like finance capital. But that is far from the case. As the previous examples have shown, the terrain of the modern international economy is uneven. Materialization and commodification continue apace. In East Asia rapid industrialization, urbanization, and urban growth dominate certain regions. Infrastructure connections between Hong Kong, Shenzen, Guandgzhou, Zhuhai, Macau, and the small towns in the Pearl River Delta lead to an emerging megacity of 40 to 50 million people. This urban region encompasses preindustrial, industrial, postindustrial, and postmodern landscapes of street trading, manufacturing, light industrial and commercial enterprises, and IT and other consumer services. The prior settlements were connected up by improved rapid transport infrastructure and information technology to produce a wired urban region. Most regions of the world are experiencing unprecedented material transformations.

Equally the materiality of cities in terms of the substances that go into making them, and their effect on the environment – as possible limits to the economy – is of heightened concern. As Harvey (1996) has remarked the environmental movement has assumed that cities are anti-ecological, but given the fact that most of the world's population will be living in them, the density and compactness of cities must also be seen as a solution to environmental problems. Nature is not separate from cities (see especially Cronon 1991; Swyngedouw and Kaika, chapter 47 of this volume). What the conditions of Western and rapidly urbanizing areas shows is the different meanings attached to the environment in different regions of the world. The environmental movement has been concerned with big questions such as the depletion of the rainforest. This is at the expense of environmental concerns such as good water supplies and sanitation that affect most people in cities. Household environmental concerns tend to be the most pressing for much of the world's urban populations but are less prominent than public global concerns. This discourse constructs the economy and environment as public rather than private, and attaches different values to each side of this binary: the public is constructed as more important. It also reveals a Western bias in conceptions of cities and the environment, since the global environmental agenda is focused on developing non-Western nations. However, the poverty of many rapidly growing cities means that the effective recycling of materials is already a reality of daily life and an important means of subsistence. Sustainability means survival and is an everyday matter of life or death. In contrast, overconsumption of materials in most Western cities means that sustainability is about reducing consumption.

Ideas of dematerialization and a placeless, ethereal economy are also countered by arguments for the social and cultural embeddedness of markets. Institutional economics and the new socioeconomics have combined to argue for the importance of social and cultural factors in the operation, and indeed construction, of markets. Thus Amin and Thrift (1995) see differences in market processes according to their degree of institutional thickness. Networks of relationships are seen as significant in terms of contractual histories between subcontractors and their suppliers in post-Fordist production. Face-to-face contacts and networks of trust are particularly significant when it comes to exchanging nonroutinized information and expertise (see, e.g., Leyshon and Thrift's 1997 analysis of social networks in the City of London). Creative networks can be particularly productive in cities (Comedia and Demos 1997). These are influences in the formal economy but networks and embeddedness are also deemed to be important in the informal economy. Social capital theory (Putnam 1993), which argues that it is possible for social relationships to become sources of productive activity (shared skills), has become a debating point in Western cities. In this sense they are following the networks of self-provisioning that are such a feature of squatter settlements in non-Western cities.

The cultural and social lumpiness of economic activity works against the dematerializing tendencies of the "global" economy. The significance of physicality in the "space of flows" of the global informational economy suggests an emerging interest in what might be called the corporeal economy. The body as a site that bears the marks (or scars) of economic activity was vividly depicted by Engels in Manchester. He was able to identify workers' occupations from the deformities of their bodies (Engels [1844] 1993; and for contemporary arguments see Harvey 1998). In many cities the body is the site of economic exchange, from the sex trade to the international trade in human organs at one extreme, and the cultivation of knowledge and expertise at the other. Processes of globalization commodify and give the first global image of the body. Commodities are more and more sold on sexualized images of the body. Advertising presents a worldwide audience with perfect bodies. Increasing amounts of money are spent in keeping the body presentable and youthful (historically for women and now increasingly for men). All these tendencies are collapsed inwards in cities and affect bodily display or concealment, and the movement or restriction of bodies in urban space.

Contemporary processes create tensions between ethereal and embedded economies, between fixed assets and the advantage of mobility, between signs and traces and immobilized bodies. The discourse of the economic has moved out beyond the material to embrace the cultural. The city, with its concentration of ever more diverse cultural/material objects and subjectivities, is at the center of this creative tension. It maps the terrain of future discussion between political economy and cultural studies.

REFERENCES

Alonso, W. 1964: *Location and Land Use*. Cambridge, MA: Harvard University Press.

Amin, A. (ed.), 1995: *Post-Fordism: A Reader*. Oxford: Blackwell.

Amin, A. and Thrift, N. 1995: Institutional issues for the European regions: from markets and plans to socioeconomics and the powers of association. *Economy and Society*, 24, 41–66.

Barnes, T. 1996: *Logics of Dislocation: Models, Metaphors, and Meanings of Economic Space*. New York: Guilford.

Baudrillard, J. 1981: *For a Critique of the Political Economy of the Sign*. St. Louis: Telos.

Bell, D. 1973: *The Coming of Post-Industrial Society*. London: Heinemann.

Castells, M. 1989: *The Informational City: Information, Technology, Economic Restructuring, and the Urban-Regional Process*. Oxford: Blackwell.

Castells, M. 1996: *The Information Age: Economy Society and Culture*, vol. I: *The Rise of the Network Society*. Oxford: Blackwell.

Castells, M. 1997: *The Information Age: Economy, Society and Culture*, vol. II: *The Power of Identity*. Oxford: Blackwell.

Castells, M. 1998: *The Information Age: Economy, Society and Culture* vol. III: *End of Millennium*. Oxford: Blackwell.

Christaller, W. 1966: *Central Places in Southern Germany*. Englewood Cliffs, NJ: Prentice-Hall.

Comedia and Demos 1997: *The Richness of Cities*. London: Comedia and Demos.

Cronon, W. 1991: *Nature's Metropolis: Chicago and the Great West*. New York: Norton.

Engels, F. [1844] 1993: *The Condition of the Working Class in England*, edited with an introduction by D. McLellan. Oxford: Oxford University Press.

Froebel, F., Henricks, J. and Kreye, O. 1980: *The New International Division of Labor*. Cambridge: Cambridge University Press.

Fukuyama, F. 1992: *The End of History and the Last Man*. New York: The Free Press.

Garreau, J. 1991: *Edge City: Life on the New Urban Frontier*. New York: Doubleday.

Gibson-Graham, J.-K. 1996: *The End of Capitalism (as We Knew it): A Feminist Critique of Political Economy*. Oxford: Blackwell.

Giddens, A. 1991: *Modernity and Self-Identity*. Cambridge: Polity.

Giddens, A. 1998: *The Third Way: The Renewal of Social Democracy*. Cambridge: Polity.

Habitat – United Nations Centre for Human Settlements 1996: *An Urbanizing World: Global Report on Human Settlements* 1996. Oxford: Oxford University Press.

Hamilton, G. 1994: Civilizations and the organization of economies. In N. Smelser and R. Swedberg (eds.), *The Handbook of Economic Sociology*, Princeton: Russell Sage Foundation, 183–205.

Harris, N. 1998: Technologistics. *Urban Age*, 6, 9–11.

Harvey, D. 1982: *The Limits to Capital*. Chicago: Chicago University Press.

Harvey, D. 1985: *The Urban Experience*. Oxford: Blackwell.

Harvey, D. 1973: *Social Justice and the City*. London: Edward Arnold.

Harvey, D. 1989: *The Condition of Postmodernity*. Oxford: Blackwell.

Harvey, D. 1996: *Justice, Nature and the Geography of Difference*. Oxford: Blackwell.

Harvey, D. 1998: Globalization and the body. In R. Wolff, A. Schneider, C. Schmidt et al., *Possible Urban Worlds: Urban Strategies at the End of the Twentieth Century*, Zurich: Birkhauser Verlag for INURA, 26–38.

Hirst, P. and Thompson, G. 1996: *Globalization in Question: The International Economy and the Possibilities of Governance*. Cambridge: Polity.

Kearns, G. and Philo, C. (eds.) 1993: *Selling Places: The City as Cultural Capital, Past and Present*. Oxford: Pergamon.

Laclau, E. and Mouffe, C. 1985: *Hegemony and Socialist Strategy: Towards a Radical Democratic Politics*, tr. W. Moore and P. Cammack. London: Verso.

Lash, S. and Urry, J. 1994: *Economies of Signs and Space*. London: Sage.

Leyshon, A. and Thrift, N. 1997: *Money/Space: Geographies of Monetary Transformation*. London: Routledge.

Lovering, J. 1990: Fordism's unknown successor: a comment on Scott's theory of flexible accumulation and the re-emergence of regional economies. *International Journal of Urban and Regional Research*, 14: 158–71.

Mills, C. 1988: "Life on the upslope": the postmodern landscape of gentrification. Environment and Planning D, *Society and Space* 6, 169–189.

Muth, R. 1969: *Cities and Housing: The Spatial Patterns of Residential Land Use*. Chicago: University of Chicago Press.

Polanyi, K. [1944] 1957: *The Great Transformation*. Boston: Beacon.

Putnam, R. 1993: *Making Democracy Work: Civic Traditions in Modern Italy*. Princeton: Princeton University Press.

Resnick, S. and Wolff, R. 1987: *Knowledge and Class: A Marxian Critique of Political Economy*. Chicago: University of Chicago Press.

Rostow, W. 1971: *The Stages of Economic Growth: A Non-Communist Manifesto*. Cambridge: Cambridge University Press, 2nd edn.

Sayer, A. 1995: *Radical Political Economy: A Critique*. Oxford: Blackwell.

Scott, A. J. 1988a: Flexible production systems in regional development: the rise of new industrial spaces in North America and Western Europe, *International Journal of Urban and Regional Research*, 12: 171–86.

Scott, A. J. 1988b: *Metropolis: From the Division of Labour to Urban Form*. Berkeley: University of California Press.

Sennett, R. 1999: *The Corrosion of Character: The Personal Consequences of Work in the New Capitalism*. London: Norton.

Smelser, N. and Swedberg, R. (eds.) 1994: *The Handbook of Economic Sociology*. Princeton: Russel Sage Foundation.

Smith, N. 1984: *Uneven Development: Nature, Capital and the Production of Space*. Oxford: Basil Blackwell.

Soja, E. 1999: *Postmetropolis: Critical Studies of Cities and Regions*. Oxford: Blackwell.

Stopford, J., Strange, S., and Henley, J. 1991: *Rival States, Rival Firms: Competition for World Market Shares*. Cambridge: Cambridge University Press.

Thrift, N. 1995: A hyperactive world. In R. J. Johnston, P. Taylor, and M. Watts (eds.), *Geographies of Global Change: Remapping the World in the Late Twentieth Century*, Oxford: Blackwell, 18–35.

Urry, J. 1990: *The Tourist Gaze: Leisure and Travel in Contemporary Societies*. London: Sage.

Wallerstein, I. 1974: *The Modern World-System: Capitalist Agriculture and the Origins of the European World Economy in the Sixteenth Century*. New York: Academic.

Wallerstein, I. 1991: *Geopolitics and Geoculture*. Cambridge: Cambridge University Press.

Weber, M. [1904–5] 1958: *The Protestant Ethic and the Spirit of Capitalism*, tr. T. Parsons. New York: Charles Scribner's Sons.

Weber, M. [1922] 1978: *Economy and Society*, ed. G. Roth and C. Wittich, tr. E. Fischoff et al. Berkeley: University of California Press.
Weiss, L. 1998: *The Myth of the Powerless State: Governing the Economy in a Global Era*. Cambridge: Polity.
Zukin, S. 1982: *Loft Living: Culture and Capital in Urban Change*. Baltimore: The Johns Hopkins University Press.
Zukin, S. 1991: *Landscapes of Power: From Detroit to Disneyworld*. Berkeley: University of California Press.

Chapter 11

The Economic Base of Contemporary Cities

Ash Amin

We now find that capital is no longer concerned about cities. Capital needs fewer workers and much of it can move all over the world, deserting problematic places and populations at will.

Harvey 1997: 20

Getting things economically right in our cities is the path towards economic change and economic development, even to economic growth. To treat the cities as the secondary feature of this whole dynamic is essentially wrong.

Harvey 1997: 26

Introduction

These two citations from the same article by David Harvey illustrate our ambivalence about the economic role of contemporary cities. It seems that cities do and do not matter in economic life. The second citation implies that the assets of cities are central for economic competitiveness and economic dynamism in general, while the first implies that the release of capital from the constraints of time and space is reducing its commitment to, and need for, the properties of place.

Certainly a historical glance at the changing economic role of Western cities over the last 100 years might lead to the view that cities have become less important. There can be little doubt that these cities were the workshops and forcing houses of industrial capitalism and imperialist expansion. First London, Manchester, Liverpool, and Rotterdam; then Turin, Düsseldorf, Detroit, and Coventry, sustained the large factories, mass workforces, know-how, social and physical infrastructure, and capital that facilitated industrial modernization and expansion from the late nineteenth century. The Western city was the factory and the center of commercial life, in short, the engine of capital accumulation, with its industrial smog and endless hustle and bustle acting as testimony. The city became the source of "immobile" resources and agglomeration economies for competitive advantage, as Bailly, Jensen-Butler, and Leontidou (1996: 165) explain: "In the Fordist era, competitive advantage was based upon the existence of natural advantage, presence of certain labour qualifications and existence of specific types of capital, all of which has some degree of immobility."

Nowadays, however, we are less certain about the distinctive economic role of cities, possibly because of lack of clarity about their comparative advantage in a world of increasing factor mobility and possibly because they are no longer the powerhouse of the industrial economy. For well over two decades large scale manufacturing has been disappearing from the Western metropolis. This has been due to a number of factors, including the rise of the postindustrial service-based economy, the decentralization of production to peripheral regions and the developing world, and the emergence of smaller factories owing to the availability of labor-saving and space-saving new technologies. As a result of this process of deindustrialization – marked by the many derelict industrial zones or converted factories to be seen in cities – we no longer think of factory life as the economic motor of cities, and, in turn, we think less of the city as the motor of the contemporary economy.

Instead, the urban economy appears to have become a mixed bag of activities. Perhaps the most decisive shift has been the growth of services as the core of urban economic activity. Today's urban hustle and bustle seems to be associated with servicing the needs of consumers and residents through such activities as shopping, leisure, and tourism, supporting the productive economy with business services such as banking, insurance, and accountancy, facilitating social reproduction through welfare services such as education, health care, sanitation, and transport and providing activities related to local and national public administration and governance. The urban economy, increasingly, is associated with the production, exchange, and consumption of services of one sort or another.

Beyond this postindustrial role, however, lie at least three other enduring economic activities which are hard to avoid when thinking about any city. One is of course the continuing millennial role of cities as trading places, that is, their historical role as a marketplace and commercial center for the distribution of goods and services around the world and the rest of the local and national territory. Cities are quintessential places of exchange. Another activity is the enduring presence of manufacturing, notwithstanding large-scale deindustrialization. Cities continue to house sweatshops and small firms which operate for long hours to produce traditional consumer goods such as clothing, furniture, and food. Their revamped inner-city sites attract the location of knowledge or innovation-intensive sectors and activities, while the headquarters and research divisions of international corporations are drawn to central business districts which provide access to specialized expertise and services. Finally, and perhaps the major source of economic support for the growing army of poor, underpaid, unemployed, and marginalized people in cities all over the world, is the informal economy. For a very long time, the backstreets and homes of inner and outer areas of cities have throbbed with precarious and often illegal activities from domestic outworking and fly-by-night contracting to petty crime and trade in illicit ventures of one sort or another (Castells 1996).

Perhaps it is such variegation that makes us less sure about what remains the economic base of the city, especially in terms of its competitive advantage. Indeed, for some observers, processes such as urban deindustrialization and international capital mobility, together with escalating urban poverty and social conflict, confirm that cities are a symbol of economic decline and an impediment to economic dynamism. The critics (see Amin and Graham 1997) stress that the high cost of urban premises as well as the problems of urban congestion – from traffic jams to housing shortages and large class sizes in schools – have become an economic burden on firms, employees, and urban dwellers. They also argue that the threat of crime and other urban disorders such as begging and street peddling are a powerful deterrent on investment, as firms escape to protect their assets, employees, and clients. They describe parts of the city which house the unemployed and other economically inactive groups as sinks in which welfare and other expenditure is poured down without any productive returns. The list of urban disorders is endless.

Without denying the importance of these diseconomies and patterns of urban variegation, is it still possible to see the city as a source of economic vitality, as David Harvey implies in the second caption above? In this chapter, I wish to claim the continued economic salience of the city. The city continues to provide vital assets for economic competitiveness, but as we shall see, these are quite different from those which marked the city as factory. Then, urban density played a vital role in providing the labor, capital, infrastructure and markets to satisfy the voracious appetite of mass industrialization, to make location in the city a source of competitive advantage owing to the offer of externalities and economies of agglomeration associated with all of these factor inputs. Now, the advantages of urban proximity appear quite different, and, on the surface, less narrowly economistic.

The first section of the chapter summarizes three views which stress the city as a source of new "fixed" assets in the contemporary knowledge-intensive and globalizing economy. These assets range from clustering as a source of competitive advantage, to cities as sources of fixity, proximity, and strategic resources in the global information economy. The second section offers an alternative account of city economic assets, by stressing the relational and non-traded aspects of local economic networks, notably the benefits of loose ties and reflexivity. The third section loosens the understanding of the "economic" even further, to discuss the merits of considering "social capital," and the "social economy" as an economic asset of contemporary cities.

Fixed Assets

In the urban literature, more positive economic appraisals of cities seem to draw on three lines of argument. The first is that the net advantages of urban agglomeration outweigh the diseconomies in national economic competitiveness. The second is that city environments offer the core resources of the emerging information age. The third is that cities are the forcing houses or basing points of a globalizing economy characterized by the incessant flow of factors between places as well as the commanding influence of institutions articulated at the transnational level. These three perspectives are discussed in turn below.

Clusters of competitive advantage

In an article that attained cult status almost immediately after its publication, business guru Michael Porter (1995) rejects the dominant view in the US of cities as a drain on economic resources. Focusing his attention on run-down inner-city areas, he argues that they continue to display four unique advantages, which, with remedial policy action, could help not only to revitalize the urban economy, but also to sustain national competitive advantage.

The first is strategic location, associated with the proximity of inner-city areas to central business districts, companies, and the entertainment and tourist centers of cities. The second is an ever-buoyant demand: "At a time when most other markets are saturated, inner city markets remain poorly served – especially in retailing, financial services, and personal services (1995: 58). The third is the scope for integration with regional clusters of competitive advantage, through the supply of upstream products and services to the clusters of interrelated industries and firms and through the downstream delivery of products and services to local markets. The fourth is the mobilization of unique local human resources, notably the entrepreneurial skills of ethnic minorities, and the cost advantages of an abundant supply of semiskilled labor.

Porter is firmly of the view that inner-city revitalization, through the mobilization of latent resources such as those listed above, is possible as long as some of their historic disadvantages are tackled head on. The list of disadvantages which Porter claims can be tackled through appropriate public policy actions includes unusable land and property; high building costs; high cost of utilities, welfare services and insurance; fear of crime; traffic congestion; poor employee and management skills; poor access to capital; and antibusiness attitudes.

Porter's positive spin on the inner city has become symptomatic of a gradual shift in opinion that cities provide vital resources for competitive advantage – from proximity to markets and various factor inputs to economies of agglomeration (Cisneros 1993; Kanter 1995). There is a growing conviction on the part of urban policymakers that firms and networks of firms can draw upon these externalities to underwrite their specialist strengths, while an enriched local supply base might help to spawn further entrepreneurship and economic spin-off. This sense of the city as a growth machine is increasingly endorsed by city leaders and planners across the world, ready to be advised that the city managed as a business can become the competitive city (Thrift 1998) if its agglomeration assets can be mobilized.

Centre of the information age

If there is any truth in the claim that Fordism, based on the routines of mass manufacture and mass consumption, is giving way to the information age, based on the economic centrality of information, knowledge, and innovation as markets become increasingly uncertain, discerning, and contested, then cities are set to return to center stage (Castells 1989). Bailly, Jensen-Butler, and Leontidou (1996) identify at least four shifts associated with this transition which seem to privilege cities. First, the service industries, notably the advanced services such as business, professional, and legal services, are seen to prefer urban locations owing to the access they provide to markets and customers as well as specialized factor inputs such as professional expertise. Second, and as a consequence, the new professional and managerial class is seen to prefer to live in "attractive" cities such as Paris and Amsterdam because they best sustain the consumption, lifestyle, and work patterns of this class (e.g. rapid communications, cultural, and recreational variety). Third, the rising importance of creativity and innovation as a factor of competitive advantage is regarded to privilege the urban milieu owing to its ability to sustain both through its sheer density of educational and research institutions, governance activities, media, and cultural industries, and highly qualified or creative people in the labor market.

In the information age, as Michael Parkinson (1994: 19) puts it, businesses are attracted to cities since:

> they depend on good quality higher education institutions to provide the skilled labour and the technological innovation that can feed into local economies. They seek out urban areas with a good quality of life – in residential, cultural and environmental terms – which attract and retain skilled and potentially mobile workers and provide a magnet to visitors. They require good access to communications facilities such as advanced telecommunications, international airports, high speed trains and efficient motorway networks.

The economic base of the city in the information age, thus, seems to be reconstituted in rather novel ways, as the knowledge industries and the professional and business service sectors gradually dominate the urban economy (Mellor 1997). The new competition finds its sources of information and knowledge in the elements of a city's knowledge fabric linking headquarter functions, media, cultural, and arts industries, education and information organizations, and research, science, and technology institutions. In turn, metropolitan life offers rich transactional opportunities and advantages of interpersonal proximity, to facilitate adjustment in volatile and design-conscious markets. Finally, the cultural assets of cities (from their media, entertainment, sport, and leisure industries, their theaters, restaurants, and cinemas, and their pull upon the creative professions) are re-emerging as an important source of urban economic renewal. The renewal is anticipated not only from the ever-increasing demand for cultural consumption, but also from the potential for economic innovation offered by the city's creative people.

Powers of proximity in a world of flows

Perhaps the best known economic role that has been claimed for contemporary cities relates to the salience of their central business districts as centers of command and control within global industrial and corporate networks, financial markets, producer services industries, and other associated service industries (Sassen 1994; Castells 1989; Friedman 1995). In the emerging information age, characterized by the intense international flow of people, commodities, and information, together with organization of business and institutional networks on a global scale, such districts act as forcing houses and centers of coordination and management. In this context, as Saskia Sassen (1991: 4) explains, major cities: "...now function in four new ways: first, as highly concentrated command points in the organization of the world economy; second, as key locations for finance and for specialized service firms...; third, as sites of production, including the production of innovation...; and fourth, as markets for the products and the innovations produced."

Manuel Castells (1996: 384–5) explains why the global "space of flows" in the new "network society" requires a "space of places" in which cities act as "nodes" of strategic importance and "hubs" of information exchange and communication within the global networks, helping also to sustain the cosmopolitan elites who run these networks:

> These cities, or rather, their business districts, are information-based, value production complexes, where corporate headquarters and advanced financial firms can find both the suppliers and the highly skilled specialized labor they require. They constitute indeed networks... whose flexibility needs not to internalize workers and suppliers, but to be able to access them when it fits, and in the time and quantities that are required in each particular instance.... Other factors seem also to contribute to strengthen concentration of high-level activities in a few nodes: once they are constituted, heavy investments in valuable real estate by corporations explains their reluctance to move... also, face-to-face contacts are still necessary in the age of widespread eavesdropping.... And finally, major metropolitan centres still offer the greatest opportunities for the personal enhancement, social status, and individual self-gratification of the much-needed upper-level professionals, from good schools for their children to symbolic membership at the heights of conspicuous consumption, including art and entertainment.

In the informational city, despite predictions otherwise, the face-to-face work environment, the personal relations between corporate leaders, the satisfaction of elite groups, the access to specialized inputs and the struggle to improve access to changing know-how, innovations, and industry standards, are all crucial for maintaining competitive advantage. These seem to be the new advantages of fixity and proximity in the information age. While Sassen (1991) tends to stress the powers of fixity, that is the places which house command-and-control functions, and Castells (1996) tends to stress the qualities of hubs and nodes within global business networks (Allen 1998), both seem to agree that certain cities succeed in exercising both place-based and network power.

To summarize, there appears little evidence to support the claim that cities are becoming less important in an economy marked by increasing geographical dispersal. All three lines of argument above reassert, in one way or another, the powers of agglomeration, proximity, and density, now perhaps less significant for the production of mass manufactures than for the production of knowledge, information, and innovation, as well as specialized inputs.

It is clear, however, that this positive reading cannot be generalized to all cities, but is based upon the experience of the central business districts of a small number of usually global cities. It does not describe the city of poverty, hardship, informal economic activity, and hand-to-mouth survival, nor the sprawling outer areas of the global cities themselves, struggling for an economic identity and lacking the powers of geographic density and proximity. Indeed, and perhaps this is the central paradox, it is also clear that the dynamism of the central business districts themselves derives in part from their proximity to the "other" city. We can see this, for example, from the dependence of the superstressed professionals and business elites upon the labor, commodities, and cultural products on offer from low-income, displaced, and ethnic minority groups. Nevertheless, in terms of the territorial base of the economy, there can be no question that the city remains the economic motor of postindustrial society also.

Relational Assets

Michael Storper (1997) has criticized interpretations such as the three above for generating a machine-like account of the economic assets of cities. He rejects the distinction between cities as fixed assets and the world as a space of flows, as he does any functionalist account that looks to ascribe agency to isolated aspects of cities. Thus for him the city is not a "mere basing point for globalized, placeless economic forces," a "mere subassembly in the global machine" (1997: 222), but a rich source of untraded interdependencies, notably relational or reflexive assets forged out of ties of proximity and interpersonal contact. He explains (1997: 223): "...when global firms locate in big cities, they do so in part to tap into their distinctiveness, for two reasons. They attempt, on the one hand, to gain access to the local conventionally and relationally distinctive society in order to service it and earn profits there. They try, on the other hand, to gain access to the specific forms of reflexivity that reside there." Defining reflexivity as the deliberate and strategic shaping of the environment by knowledgeable individuals and organizations, Storper argues that the proximity and intensity of concentration of actors and institutions that the city represents – its urbanness in other words – produces particular forms of reflexivity and conventions, based on daily ties, face-to-face contact, and informality. These are the attributes which generate spillovers and feedbacks of a virtuous or negative kind for a city. Positive feedbacks might draw upon the power of the "reflexive classes" to forge or make sense of industrial standards and conventions, or communities of urban consumers and citizens generating local demand and investment through their unique local vernaculars, identities, and spectacles. Negative feedbacks of proximate ties, serving to hinder investment or direct it in often covert directions, might draw on conventions of action and behavior and knowledge networks built around "cultures of criminality, underclass patterns, certain forms of persistent poverty and exclusion" (1997: 254).

Storper's argument seems to be that the economic assets of cities are related to the quality of local relational ties and reflexive capabilities, which serve as the real catalyst for action, rather than to features of presence or absence, such as the density of the professional and managerial class, the location of headquarter and research activities, or the quality of local amenities to support the needs of knowledge workers. These are the factors which help to mobilize local specificity and to shape or make sense of opportunity.

Ties

Regarding relational ties, for example, it could be argued, drawing on Mark Granovetter's work (1985), that contexts dominated by weak ties between economic agents might be economically more innovative than those dominated by strong ties (e.g. enforced loyalty in Mafia networks) or easy escape from ties (e.g. rugged individualism in market-driven relationships). While weak ties offer agents (and networks) the benefits of cooperation and a varied selection environment for new learning, strong ties, such as many crime networks, pose the threat of both lock-in and closure of selection and self-reliance poses very high search costs. We might speculate, therefore, that cities dominated by overlapping networks of loose ties – in the workplace, among firms, between institutions, among households and communities – are likely to exhibit a higher disposition towards search, exploration, and experimentation, as agents are able to draw upon existing collective resources to innovate.

This kind of sensibility is beginning to appear in economic analysis of the city. Speculating on the "good city," Will Hutton (1996) has argued that part of the story of urbanization relates to the need of economic agents for relationships of trust and mutual commitment as a basis for coping with the endemic problem in markets about unequal power relationships, uncertainty, and information asymmetry. He asserts that "where market economies actually work very well you have committed owners, you have long-term relationships, you have heavy penalties for people who cheat on bargains" (1996: 93). He explains that the city, through its physical structures and proximate links, facilitates face-to-face contact in order to build trust: "I like to think of the city, and the growth of urbanization, as . . . a place where actually one sees through physical proximity the construction of relationships of commitments. Or in a good city that's certainly what takes place" (1996: 93).

Trust-based links, mediated by face-to-face contact in the context of the city, is what makes markets work. This is a bold claim, and open to all kinds of challenge, not least its rosy assumption that ties in general are of a virtuous nature (what of shady ties?) and its view that the city promotes face-to-face contact (walls can hide – see Marcuse, chapter 23 – which is why physical proximity should not be equated with relational proximity). It is a claim that also comes perilously close to uncritical rediscoveries of the virtues of trust which fail to acknowledge the negative aspects, such as complacency, blindness, and closure, associated with networks of excessive loyalty, and indeed even the rather tenuous link between trust and economic success (Coleman 1990; Fukuyama 1995). In any discussion of the city, omissions of this sort are risky because no straightforward link is to be found between its multiple networks of varying degrees of trust and their economic performance. Criticisms apart, however, Hutton does seem to be right in incorporating the nature of ties in their urban context into the frame of discussion on the economic assets of cities.

Reflexivity

The same kind of guarded defense can be made of urban reflexivity as an economic asset. Reflexivity is a notoriously difficult concept to define accurately, but there seems to be some consensus that it includes the reliance of contemporary society on non-instrumentalist forms of knowledge (i.e. those without a direct, usually utilitarian, goal) to negotiate an increasingly complex and uncertain socioeconomic environment, which itself has become knowledge-intensive and expertise-based in its daily workings (Beck, Giddens, and Lash 1994). In this regard, the acquisition of knowledge and expertise, together with the potential for learning and adaptation, are premium assets for economic competitiveness and innovation. In addition, actors and networks need to pay considerable attention to interpreting, translating, and operationalizing information, scripts, know-how, and knowledge. This is required not only for economic imitation and innovation, but as a basic condition of survival in an increasingly complex, changing and imperfectly knowable economic environment.

What might constitute reflexivity as an urban economic asset? Clearly, the concentration in cities of research establishments, specialist schools, and universities, skilled and creative people, services, media, and communication organizations, headquarter and strategic activities, and so on, makes them the forcing houses of formal and codified knowledge and learning. All three interpretations above of the city's "fixed" assets can be reinterpreted in this light. But, all else does not automatically follow.

First, as the literature on economic learning reminds us (Lundvall 1992; Storper 1997; Cooke and Morgan 1998; Maskell et al. 1998) it is the combination of formal knowledge with tacit knowledge that really matters for economic dynamism and evolution. Thus, for example, the economic dynamism of a firm is a reflection of how applications of scientific knowledge and scripted information combine with the overall cognitive and behavioral culture, influenced by such factors as employee know-how, managerial routines, corporate norms, and so on. It could be speculated – and no more – that potentially the city is a rich source of tacit knowledge, locked into its varied and dense business networks, cultural sites, diverse knowledge environments, media organizations, social and cultural heterogeneity, and varied connections with the outside world. In this regard, the city can be seen as a large reservoir of different forms of know-how for economic agents to dip into, activate, and mobilize.

Reflexivity, however, involves more than the combination of tacit and formal knowledge. It is also a cognitive attribute that shapes perception and action, and the rationalities it invokes play a vital role in determining the kinds of possible outcome. For example, an instrumentalist rationality is likely to favor reactive responses to problems, based on a largely rule-bound logic (minimum reflexivity). In contrast, a procedural rationality, in which agents actively seek to adapt to the environment, draws upon perceptive powers and generally more complex cognitive arrangements for problem solving. While the latter two rationalities tend to assume an invariant environment (therefore largely problem solving), a recursive rationality is more problem seeking and tends to assume that the environment can be anticipated and to a degree manipulated, through such procedures as strategic monitoring, experimental games, group learning, and so on (maximum reflexivity).

How might the urban environment connect with the cognitive foundations of economic behavior? It would not be accurate to claim that cities privilege a superior rationality, such as recursive, problem-seeking, economic behavior among its firms and institutions. There is no evidence to suggest that cities offer economic actors a supply of inputs which favor strategic, innovation-oriented decision making and action. The knowledge-base of the city is the sum of rule-guided, procedural and recursive behavior, with each appropriate for different economic needs and trajectories (e.g. cost-seeking actions requiring instrumentalist behavior, or incremental innovations requiring procedural behavior, versus path-shaping innovations requiring strategic, recursive behavior). But, perhaps it is this very variety of cognitive settings that is significant, offering as it does, a wide range of economic rationalities and outcomes – a broad pool of options. In this regard, it may be better to claim plural rationalities as an economic strength of the city, rather than a particular, reflexive, order.

Social Capital, Social Economy

Variety in the cognitive options located in a city presupposes variety in the types of economic activity within it. Yet, only too often, discussion of the economic assets of cities has been based on dominant sectors and corporations in the formal economy (from business and professional services to transnational corporations and banks). Much of the earlier discussion on "fixed assets," and to a lesser degree the discussion of "relational assets," presupposes the economic cutting edge. Consequently, the urban foundations of small-scale manufacturing or commercial activities serving local markets, the informal economy, or voluntary and third-sector activities, remain largely ignored, or when discussed, undervalued as economic assets. In most cities, they constitute a very substantial proportion of the entrepreneurial, employment, and income base. Indeed, in the context of the retreat of the formal market economy as a source of full employment (owing to technological substitution, intensified international competition, and globalized production), informal activities are becoming the staple source of employment in many cities.

In part, the disregard of anything other than the economic cutting edge in discussions of the economic base of cities, follows from a tacit assumption that small-scale entrepreneurship, the informal economy, or nonprofit activity, are not sources of economic dynamism and innovation, and market efficiency or aggression. This assumption, however, is open to question from at least two perspectives, which are discussed below: first, that participation in informal and voluntary activity helps to generate the "social capital" necessary for economic efficiency; and second, that experiments in the "social economy" help to generate economic creativity.

Social capital

Until recently, welfare economists have stressed the importance of investment in "human capital," covering such aspects as training, education, skill-formation, and know-how, as a key economic resource. Now, pioneering research by US sociologist James Coleman (1990) and US political scientist Robert Putnam (1993) claims a central economic place for social capital, defined as the productive resource mobilized by interpersonal networks of cooperation and coordination for mutual benefit. These might include informal arrangements such as family support networks, friendship and trust-based networks, and participation in spontaneous mutual help and voluntary activities, as they might include more formally constituted forms of social cooperation such as codes within interlocking business communities (Fukuyama 1995) or various civic associations.

The ideas of Robert Putnam in particular have become enormously influential not only in the academic community, but also in the development of policy community (e.g. World Bank, see Rose 1997). They are based on his research in Italy on societal influences on democracy and economic efficiency. He observes that old republican city-states such as Tuscany and Emilia-Romagna are characterized by efficient, nonbureaucratic, and accountable local government, and a very successful and dynamic local economic system. In contrast, old monarchical or hierarchical regions in southern Italy are dominated by inefficient and corrupt elites, and their economies languish in poverty and state dependence.

His argument, put simply, is that the difference between the two types of region can be explained in large measure by the presence or absence of social capital. The northern regions, which he describes as "civic" regions, are replete with social capital, as can be seen through such indicators as high turnout at elections, participation in popular campaigns and public events, newspaper readership, and, above all, active participation in voluntary activity and civic associations (cultural, leisure, political, etc.) and a generally developed third sector. In these regions, grassroots civic democracy and participation is said to ensure state efficiency and accountability, while their culture of social autonomy and civic responsibility, linked to their disposition towards cooperation and mutuality, is said to allow full exploitation of the economics of association and trust (from long-term commitments within and between businesses, to pooling of resources, and cost advantages of cooperation). In contrast, in "uncivic" regions the culture of self-interest and "amoral familism" allows the state to become inefficient and authoritarian, while the economy comes to be dominated by apathy and free-rider tendencies, resource domination or hoarding, ruthless market control, and other power-based manipulations of economic opportunity. In short, there is no social audit or societal involvement.

Putnam's ideas are not that distant from Machiavelli's Renaissance comparisons in *Discourses*, between the virtues of republican city-states and the vices of principalities. They have immediate relevance to the discussion here on the economic assets of contemporary cities. It could be speculated that "civic" cities (strangely, the classical definition of cities) which are rich with associational life and civic engagement show a greater potential for economic dynamism and prosperity. I am not convinced, however, that a straightforward positive link exists between social capital and economic performance. The negative link is easier to envisage: an absence of social capital – resulting in powerful tendencies to exit from the formal economy, social breakdown and anomie, self-preservation and rugged individualism, rising crime and public insecurity – is a clear deterrent on investment, business confidence, socioeconomic participation, and public scrutiny of the commons, as it is a cost and resource burden for whoever has to cope with the casualties of crime and social breakdown.

But, the positive link is harder to envisage, because social capital need not be mobilized as an economic asset, but can remain a largely civic virtue and source of active citizenship. A typical example is a prosperous city dominated by corporations which draw on their global networks of relational ties, a multitude of small firms scattered around the city in low-cost locations and benefiting from cheap migrant labor, and high-tech businesses which prosper through their in-house access to sophisticated R&D and specialized skills recruited internationally. The same city might possess an intensively active civic life, with relatively well-off individuals and communities given to charitable and public activity, as well as involvement in cultural and recreational associations. At the extreme, the social activity is additional to, or an escape from, everyday economic concerns, and while this city's economic elite and employees may benefit from the public and civic amenities on offer, their economic performance is not dependent upon the trust, cooperation, and other economies of association characteristic of the civic city.

Social economy

The concept "social economy," in contrast, seems to offer a more fruitful way of exploring, above all, the emergent properties of a generally underrecognized economic asset of cities. The social economy refers to "not-for-profit" activities which create jobs and community-owned assets through the delivery of social and welfare services by and for local people. Commonly, it is referred to as the "third sector" as distinct from the market and the public sector, to recognize the activities of co-operatives, charities, nonprofit organizations, voluntary groups, community organizations, religious bodies, trusts, and so on.

Traditionally the third sector has tended to be seen as a "mop up," parallel activity to market and state provision. More recently, usage of the term "social economy" has become more frequent, to stress the potential for social and economic regeneration at the local level in response to market and state failure. The basic argument is that within local communities there exists a substantial latent demand for social and welfare services which are currently not provided by the state because they are considered too specific or too small (and therefore too costly) nor by the market because they offer too low a return. In the context of increasing fiscal stress on the welfare state and the retreat of the formal economy as a source of full and stable employment, it is considered that the fulfillment of such demand could be a vital source of new employment and entrepreneurship. Indeed, a number of recent studies have identified examples of community-based third sector initiatives that are able to deliver cost-effective services directly in response to local need, and in doing so, to create jobs and tackle wider problems of social exclusion and economic marginalization (European Commission 1998; Allen, Cars, and Madani-Pour 1998; West 1996).

It is interesting to note that while the American (and British) debate on economic renewal has turned to the powers of social capital for the formal economy, and in public policy, on compulsive welfare-to-work programs, thus preserving the traditional dualist choice between market and state in the economy, the European debate has begun to recognize the powers of welfare as work (Amin, Cameron, and Hudson 1998), that is, to recognize the considerable scope for a third, independent sphere of economic activity, largely in the hands of the third sector, based on providing socially useful services. This second debate has roots in the community politics of the 1970s' grass-roots attempts to revitalize the economic and social fabric of communities through local empowerment.

The European literature on economic alternatives has identified a number of sources of local renewal through the social economy: environmental improvements – employment created through the improvement of built and natural spaces (Altvater 1993; Lipietz 1995); intermediate labor market policies and new forms of training through "apprenticeship," both geared toward skills, capacity, and confidence building for social economy ventures (Esping-Andersen 1996); the provision of social services beyond the state – such as care for children and the elderly; and the creation of microcredit schemes or nonmonetized metrics of exchange such as LETS (Local Employment and Trade System) and "time dollars, in order to decouple access to cash from access to services (Lee 1996; Leyshon and Thrift 1997). Central to all these suggestions is the idea that the purpose of the initiatives is not to mirror the market or state in providing the socially useful services, but to further the principles of empowerment and capacity building, by employing socially excluded groups (from the unemployed to the disabled and ethnic minorities), experimenting with new forms of democratic participation and involvement in decision making, and helping participants to secure a broad range of skills and capacities for future employment or entrepreneurship (Mayer 1998; Lipietz 1996).

What is the link between the social economy and cities? Most obviously, the mobilization of undermet welfare needs requires action not at the national or regional scale, but at the level of neighborhoods, communities, and localities, with specific service needs and specific capacities. This question of spatial scale of appropriate action is of clear relevance to cities. But, there are also more concrete reasons for considering the social economy as a powerful source of urban economic regeneration. Commencing with the rather obvious point that cities are people, buildings, and services, Alain Lipietz (1996: 89–90) goes on to argue:

> Clearly a policy of the third sector answers a lot of the problems involved in regenerating cities. First, it gives employment to many people. [...] when you can reduce...from 10 per cent...to say, 5 or 3 per cent unemployment by the development of a third sector, you change life in a city completely. Second, I said that the city was buildings, and services. Regenerating buildings...could be done by the third sector. Most of the services – urban services – could be provided by the third sector. [...] the third sector should do what the two others don't do. You know, services for people who can't pay – so it is substitutes for moonlighting, or in large proportion, substitutes for what women don't accept doing any more in the patriarchal relation.... People who are unemployed in the city take charge of a city, maintain the city.

In the same vein, Nigel Thrift writes (1998) of the potential of the alternative economy in cities, based on networks of cooperation and association among those deprived of cash and credit. He refers to the rise, in many cities, of exchange networks (LETS schemes) in which participants exchange products or labor calculated in a local currency that never actually changes hands. He also refers to the rise in cities of economic hardship, of microcredit networks, in particular community development banks and community development loan funds, which direct money from socially minded investors to fund housing rehabilitation, nonprofit housing development, and small businesses. Similarly, George Monbiot (1996: 100) refers to the city as a source of "community intelligence," drawing together local residents, activists, architects, and planners, to launch sustainable, people-centered redevelopment projects in the derelict and other spaces of cities momentarily abandoned by the official development industry.

Through these accounts of the third sector in the city, it is the transformative and creative potential of the social economy that must be stressed. The emphasis falls not only on the ability of the social economy to meet social needs, but also on its potential for economic regeneration. This potential is traced to the necessity and legitimacy of the alternative economy in its own right in cities riddled with state and market failure, and also, more importantly, to the scope that social empowerment and social citizenship offer for economic creativity by unleashing the capabilities and capacities of people in networks of common fate. Thus, one of the key economic assets of cities surely must be the scope they offer for building collective capabilities and social voice.

Conclusion

Returning to the urban paradox noted by David Harvey at the start of this chapter, it is clear that the city continues to play a central role in the post-mass production economy of increasing global flows of resources. But, it is also clear that an orthodox, "land, labor, capital" interpretation of the economic assets of cities has little analytical purchase (has it ever been different?). The literature reviewed in this chapter suggests that the contemporary city finds its realized or potential strengths in new advantages of agglomeration and proximity serving clusters of interrelated industries, strategic resources of the information economy, and "node" and "hub" functions in networks of global flow. While this literature still tends to view economic assets as a fixed and static set of resources, another literature, rooted in evolutionary economics and economic sociology, offers a relational interpretation which stresses the learning and risk-minimization advantages of daily cooperation in networks of reciprocity. Finally, a third reading of the city stresses the civic aspects of cities, both as a check on the formal economy and as a source of new forms of economic activity.

Which perspective we choose rather depends on the kind of economics we find convincing. The strength of the "fixed assets" perspective is that it offers a tangible grasp of the new urban assets, while the relational perspective is more vague in comparison, with its emphasis on the properties of ties. On the other hand, the relational perspective decisively illustrates the social foundations of economic action, by revealing the cognitive, interpersonal, habitual and conventional, civic and communal sources of economic behavior, innovation, and evolution. Perhaps, given the extraordinarily diverse and fluid nature of a city's economic circuits, all three perspectives are in some way relevant. What does seem interesting is that a common thread binding all of them is an emphasis on the powers of density, agglomeration, and proximity in explaining the particularities of the city as an economic place. These powers have always marked the city, but in different forms and with different outcomes (Amin and Graham 1999).

ACKNOWLEDGMENT

I am very grateful to Sophie Watson for her comments on the earlier draft.

REFERENCES

Allen, J., Cars, G., and A. Madani-Pour (eds.) 1998: *Social Exclusion in European Cities: Processes, Experiences and Responses*. London: Regional Studies Association/Jessica Kingsley.

Allen, J. 1999: Cities of power and influence: settled formations. In J. Allen, D. Massey, and M. Pryke (eds.), *Unsettling Cities*, London: Routledge, 181–218.

Altvater, E. 1993: *The Future of the Market*. London: Verso.

Amin, A., Cameron, A., and R. Hudson 1999: Welfare as work? The potential of the UK social economy. *Environment and Planning A*, 31, 2033–51.

Amin, A. and S. Graham 1997: The ordinary city. Transactions of the Royal Geographical Society (Institute of British Geographers), 22, 411–29.

Amin, S. and S. Graham 1999: Cities of connection and disconnection. In J. Allen, D. Massey, and M. Pryke (eds.), *Unsettling Cities*, London: Routledge.

Bailly, A., Jensen-Butler, C., and L. Leontidou 1996: Changing cities: restructuring, marginality and policies in Europe. *European Urban and Regional Studies*, 2, 161–76.

Beck, U., Giddens, A., and S. Lash 1994: *Reflexive Modernisation*. Cambridge: Polity.

Cooke, P. and K. Morgan 1998: *The Associational Economy: Firms, Regions and Innovation*. Oxford: Oxford University Press.

Castells, M. 1989: *The Informational City: Information Technology, Economic Restructuring and The Urban-Regional Process*. Oxford: Blackwell.

Castells, M. 1996: *The Rise of The Network Society*. Oxford: Blackwell.

Cisneros, H. 1993: *Interwoven Destinies: Cities and the Nation*. New York: Norton.

Coleman, J. S. 1990: *Foundations of Social Theory*. Cambridge, MA: Harvard University Press.

Esping-Andersen, G. (ed.) 1996: *Welfare States in Transition: National Adaptations in Global Economies*. London: Sage.

European Commission 1998: The era of tailor-made jobs: second report on local development and employment initiatives. European Commission Working Document, SEC (98), Forward Studies Unit, Brussels.

Friedman, J. 1995: Where we stand: a decade of world city research. In P. Knox and P. Taylor (eds.) *World Cities in a World System*. Cambridge: Cambridge University Press.

Fukuyama, F. 1995: *Trust: The Social Virtues and the Creation of Prosperity*. London: Hamish Hamilton.

Granovetter, M. 1985: Economic action and social structure: the problem of embeddedness. *American Journal of Sociology*, 93 (3), 481–510.

Harvey, D. 1997: Contested cities: social process and spatial form. In N. Jewson and S. MacGregor (eds.) *Transforming Cities*, London: Routledge.

Hutton, W. 1996: The third sector and the stakeholder. *City*, 5–6, 90–6.

Kanter, R. M. 1995: *World Class: Thriving Locally in a Global Economy*. New York: Simon and Schuster.

Lee, R. 1996: Moral money: LETS and the social construction of local economic geographies in Southeast England. Environment and Planning A, 28, 1377–94.

Leyshon, A. and N. J. Thrift 1997: *Money/Space: Geographies of Monetary Transformation*. London: Routledge.

Lipietz, A. 1995: *Green Hopes: The Future of Political Ecology*. Cambridge: Polity.

Lipietz, A. 1996: The third sector and stakeholding. *City*, 5–6, 88–90.

Lundvall, B. A. 1992: *National Systems of Innovation*. London: Pinter.

Maskell, P., Eskelinen, H., Hannibalsson, I., Malmberg, A., and E. Vatne 1998: *Competitiveness, Localised Learning and Regional Development*. London: Routledge.

Mayer, M. 1998: New forms of politics and political action in the city. Paper presented at conference on Globalization, State and Violence, University of Sussex, Brighton, April 15–17.

Mellor, R. 1997: Cool times for a changing city. In N. Jewson and S. MacGregor (eds.), *Transforming Cities*, London: Routledge.

Monbiot, G. 1996: Appropriate development now. *City*, 5–6, 98–102.

Parkinson, M. 1994: European cities towards 2000: The new age of entrepreneurialism? Mimeograph, European Institute for Urban Affairs, Liverpool, UK, John Moores University.

Porter, M. E. 1995: The competitive advantage of the inner city. *Harvard Business Review*, May–June, 53–71.

Putnam, R. 1993. *Making Democracy Work: Civic Traditions in Modern Italy*. Princeton: Princeton University Press.

Rose, R. 1997: Measuring social capital in a post-communist society. Mimeograph, Centre for the Study of Public Policy, University of Strathclyde, UK.

Sassen, S. 1991: *The Global City: New York, London, Tokyo*. Princeton: Princeton University Press.

Sassen, S. 1994: *Cities in a World Economy*. London: Pine Forge.

Storper, M. 1997: *The Regional World*. New York: Guilford.

Thrift, N. J. 1999: Cities and economic change. In J. Allen, D. Massey, and M. Pryke (eds.), *Unsettling Cities*. London: Routledge, 271–308.

West, A. 1996: *The New Strategy: Engaging the Community*. London: CDF/DfEE.

Chapter 12

Flexible Marxism and the Metropolis

Andy Merrifield

Proletarian revolutions ... criticize themselves constantly, interrupt themselves continually in their own course, come back to the apparently accomplished in order to begin afresh, deride with unmerciful thoroughness the inadequacies, weaknesses and paltrinesses of their first attempts.

Karl Marx, *The Eighteenth Brumaire*

We have got on to slippery ice where there is no friction and so in a certain sense the conditions are ideal, but also, just because of that, we are unable to walk. We want to walk: so we need *friction*. Back to the rough ground!

Ludwig Wittgenstein, *Philosophical Investigations*

If it had been possible to build the Tower of Babel without ascending it, the work would have been permitted.

Franz Kafka, *Reflections on Sin, Pain, Hope, and the True Way*

In what follows, I want to argue for a recovered and reconstructed Marxian scholarship in urban studies. Rehearsing in detail why Marxism has disappeared from radical political and intellectual agendas during the last decade isn't, however, something I want to get too involved in here. To frame the existential panic experienced by Marxists we might merely recall Neil Smith's wry observation: "The Enlightenment is dead, Marxism is dead, the working class is dead ... and the author does not feel very well either." After almost two decades of neoconservative rule in many Western countries, imprimatur has been given to "free market" neoliberalism, forcing socialist organizations and unions into decidedly defensive postures. In intellectual milieux, too, new cultural practices and styles of thought – like postmodernism – have hastily swept in and assumed growing hegemony within radical ranks, supplanting class and political-economic issues with those of culture and identity. Meanwhile, the nigh apocalyptical implosion of the former Communist countries meant the panic Smith expressed with such immediacy was effectively to reach meltdown proportions. For while the wide-reaching events in the old Eastern bloc were generally celebrated by socialists, they still posed some very awkward questions for those operating from a broadly anticapitalist stance. It was almost the way Nietzsche had warned: maybe these scholars had been looking too long into the abyss and now the abyss was starting to look back at them.

Urban studies itself – that interdisciplinary field which includes city and regional planning, urban sociology and anthropology, cultural studies, and urban geography – hasn't been immune from the intellectual incredulity and weariness with Marx (see Sayer 1995a, and for the opposite argument Harvey 1987). This strikes me as rather ironical and tragic: ironical, because for a while some of the most original urban research came out of the Marxist tradition; tragic, because undoubtedly some of the best Marxism has been conducted by Marxist urban scholars. Spearheaded by the likes of Henri Lefebvre's *Le Droit à la Ville* (1968) and *La Pensée Marxiste et la Ville* (1972), Manuel Castells's *The Urban Question* (1972) and David Harvey's *Social Justice and City* (1973), the critical edge of a surgent Marxist scholarship emerged during the early 1970s with an imaginative grandeur and sweeping power. A lot of this work, as Marshall Berman has reminded us, "brings us closer to the historical long waves that drive and wreck our lives; and forces us to see ourselves and one another and our whole society and all our inner contradictions in depth face to face. If Marxist thought can do that, I think it has plenty to be proud of. But I know a lot of people for whom that isn't enough; they feel Marxism has to provide a transcendent revolutionary *zap*" (Berman 1991: 420).

This yearning for a transcendent revolutionary zap looks a little distant right now, and such a "Big Bang" theory of Marxism presents radical urbanists with awkward problems. An obvious dilemma is that beyond relentless criticism Marxism has very little constructive to say about cities – except for advocating the exorcism of markets. It apparently has no truck with anything that leaves the capitalist city intact. Now this perspective isn't, I think, so much wrong as rather one-sided, narrow in its vision, closed in its horizons with respect to prospective action and political possibilities, *in the immediate term*. The deepening of market relations in our own society and sheer commodification of daily life certainly requires Marxists, on the one hand, to redouble their denunciations of the city and the power of capital. On the other hand, though, a rethink is maybe in order as well. Indeed, the failure to consider the city *more dialectically* has confined Marxist urban studies to a proverbial Weberian iron cage. And the withering away of Marxist urban scholarship, and the *ennui* currently expressed towards it, isn't unrelated to the conceptual inflexibility and the political straightjacket it has created for itself.

"Street Marxism" and the Practice of Dialectics

One route for understanding, practically negotiating, and contesting actual injustices and assorted forms of domination and exclusion might be to develop a more flexible Marxism *from the street upwards*. This "street Marxism" would amount to something of a "messy" Marxism and would try to understand and confront the raw edges and awkward actuality of people's lives in cities today. It would, above all, tease out and interpolate the *practical* thrust of Marx's own thought. Here, Marx went to pains to stress that the pursuit of justice is not something solvable by speculation or normative theory building – which, he claimed, is a "purely scholarly question." Instead, it is, like all other mysteries in the human world, a question of *practice* and of the comprehension of that practice (see Marx 1978). And this practice would be constituted by actual human activity – organizing, activism, protests, demonstrations, and probably violent struggle – responsive to present historical and geographical conditions, the outcome of which is impossible to predict with certainty. "We must recognize," says Althusser, "that there is no practice in general, but only *distinct* practices" (Althusser 1970: 58). That's why Marx smacks as an anti-utopian: it isn't that socialism will unequivocally lead to the negation of all injustices; more that we have to begin to work through prevailing injustices by practically addressing them in the here and now, in their various guises and complexities, right in front of us. A flexible Marxism, therefore, wouldn't contain any systematic program or prefigurative blueprint, but would assume, as Cohen has suggested, that "[a]ll change in modern conditions of social differentiation and international integration is perforce incremental, 2 percent here, 5 percent there, accumulating after, say, fifteen years, into a revolution" (Cohen 1995: 5). The zap would duly come about doggedly and on the due installments plan. In the meantime, there is plenty of contested terrain between actually existing late capitalism and prospective socialism which can be fought over, here and now, and with reworked Marxian categories.

In practice, this flexible urban Marxism would insist upon an honest conviction to the dialectic and to the street. The dialectic, of course, is a critical view of the world and a workable method for studying problems in our cities. Dialectical thought, more specifically, prioritizes change – everything is evolving and changing over time and space – while positing the world as interconnected at every level. Moreover, various relations between parts of urban reality invariably express contradictions, antagonisms, and ambiguities that need to be understood holistically. Used by Marxists, dialectical analysis abstracts from the directly empirical world and develops concepts that emphasize interconnections and imperceptible patterns between various aspects of society that somehow appear isolated and unrelated. It shows that there's actually more going on in daily life situations, that *unobservable presences* are also active (and destructive), and these have to be understood more fully in order to take action for or against them. Dialecticians suggest that our world appears in a form which often belies *other truths about it*.

That the dialectic can help us glimpse another reality is evident from a contemporary example from urban Britain. More recently, Conservative and Labour politicians alike have castigated aggressive beggars, squeegee merchants, and homeless people. These concerns have caused considerable furore within the British Left because they've been voiced by Labour Home Secretary Jack Straw. (Straw, apparently, had studied "The Year of Change: Reengineering the New York City Police Department," a study written in 1995 by Republican Mayor Rudolph Giuliani and ex-Police Chief William Bratton.) Now, both parties in Britain endorse rights for citizens to walk the streets unharassed by people demanding money and to enter parks that have supposedly become exclusive junkie havens, huddles for winos, scenes of cardboard communities. Henri Lefebvre's "right to the city" thesis has thereby taken on a strange revanchist twist. Not surprisingly, controversy has ensued over this "get tough" policy on street people and over the "clean up" campaign for urban public spaces. New York, the pioneer in these initiatives, is apparently tutoring London's drive. Lee Stringer, a former editor of New York's homeless paper *Street News* and author of the acclaimed *Grand Central Winter: Stories from the Street*, has commented on the tone of this assault: "If you can blame a person for being homeless, you can ignore them... To many New Yorkers that's very attractive." It's an option that now appears very attractive to some Londoners as well. But a dialectical interpretation could give a less fetishized, deeper, and more rounded insight into affairs.

Everyday street life – that directly immediate, palpable, and observable world – is the scale where everybody gives meaning and substance to their lives. To feel safe and happy in the street and in the city's public space is thus an ontological priority. Nevertheless, the street *internalizes* other forces and other realities – abstract forces and processes, which, as Marx warned us in *Capital*, are sometimes "imperceptible to the senses" (Marx 1967: 77–8). Accordingly, it takes a special kind of thinking and person to see and feel at once concrete *experience* and abstract *processes* and then try to live them out and understand them as one world, in their totality. (Gramsci suggested that "organic intellectuals" were equipped with this special kind of sensibility.) True, homelessness, street begging and alcoholism are conditioned by a whole array of complex psychological, personal, and domestic factors. (Homeless women, for instance, have often fled their homes to escape male domestic violence.) As these factors manifest themselves concretely in daily life, out on the street, they're often seen as pathological, as nuisances that have to be endured and experienced by "ordinary" passers-by. And yet, on the other hand, if the personal and individual is taken relationally and embedded in a broader socioeconomic and political context, which both incorporates and constrains individual agency, a different truth bursts forth. In British cities, *The Big Issue* homeless magazine tries to voice such an alternative: it conveys, as it says, a discourse which "comes up from the streets." The paper is a fine example of what Gramsci once called "integral journalism": a criticism and journalism which "seeks to arouse" and "seeks to enlarge its public" (Gramsci 1988: 383). This is grist to the mill for any aspiring Marxist urbanist, yet only if it can be embedded in the larger pattern of things. And a Marxist dialectical framework still has a lot to say about the interconnections and contradictions of this larger political-economic pattern.

Consider, briefly, Britain over the 1980s and 1990s. Here job losses, employment "restructuring" and income deficiencies have prompted enormous mortgage repossessions in many cities. Now, even paying jobs in London aren't reasonable enough to provide affordable and decent accommodation (Harloe 1992: 189–204). Moreover, cuts in public housing (London has lost over 74,000 public sector units since 1985) and the brutal marketization of the private rental housing sector under Conservative rule has meant money and capital exponentially flowing into profitable speculation, thus sanctioning extortionate rental appropriation. Working and nonworking people alike have been priced out of whole sectors of London's housing market. And because local authority and voluntary sectors have been starved of adequate funding by both the Tories and New Labour, there has been little net to break the fall of the needy. When matched with excessive office speculation and reconversion – with large numbers now standing vacant – that homelessness appears as the end *observable reality* is hardly startling.

David Harvey's *Limits to Capital* is invaluable for comprehending the paradoxical coexistence of homeless people huddled in doorways of office and commercial properties festooned with that veritable icon of 1990s British urbanism: "TO LET" signs. In *Limits*, Harvey put forward the powerful thesis that land is a form of fictitious capital, a pure financial asset, intimately entwined with the circulation of interest-bearing capital. Consequently, urban space is increasingly structured around what Harvey calls the "secondary circuit of capital." The insight remains a vital point of reference for Marxists trying to understand the process of capitalist urbanization (see Harvey 1978 and 1982, esp. pp. 367–72). Following Henri Lefebvre's earlier (and underdeveloped) insight from *The Urban Revolution*, Harvey suggests that slow growth and excess capacity – or "overaccumulation" in Marx's terminology – in the manufacturing "primary circuit" of industrial capital has been the main impetus behind "switching" toward short-term speculative pecuniary pursuits. The chasing of rental income through investment in the so-called "secondary" or built environment circuit of capital comes into its own here. Now, real estate has offered particularly profitable returns *vis-à-vis* other investment portfolios, thus engendering a spatial solution – or a "spatial fix" – to potential economic recession and crisis.

Close affinities thereby become apparent between interest rates and anticipated land and rental values. Movements in interest rates impose strong temporal rhythms on the geographical structure of capitalist cities. Links between the supply and demand for money capital and the supply and demand for land become tight. Low interest rates and surpluses of money capital generally signal enhanced land values. The perpetual search for greater future ground rents not only regulates land prices but equally promotes activities on land that conform to the highest and best commercial uses. Land treated as a pure financial asset, Harvey concludes, regulates a "rational" landscape of production, exchange, distribution, and consumption. Land prices, then, dictate the actions of property developers and the myriad of parasitic agents involved in the real-estate sector, and the timing of their specific actions gets determined by the overall rate of interest (see Merrifield 1993).

The speculative character of land and real estate is writ large. To the wily investor, capital can be invested into land at a specific moment in time to produce a new material basis for the appropriation of a higher (differential) rent. Yet this process also realizes a space whose own material viability is then extremely vulnerable to fluctuations in interest rates and vagaries in the global economy. And, of course, with an increasingly integrated and deregulated financial system, inevitable shifts in interest rates, at home and abroad, can dramatically affect investment fortunes everywhere. High interest rates mean high costs of borrowing, depressed demand for commercial space, and generally lower rents. In this climate, too, some developers might be "overexposed." Overinvestment in the real-estate sector and the mountains of unrealized fictitious titles to future rents that pile up are disciplined in much the same way as the circulation of *real* capital disciplines *fictitious* capital: through glut, slump, and devaluation. Devaluation and glut may mean that many landowners and freeholders sit on property, milk their assets, and wait till the financial and real-estate climate becomes more buoyant. Kingsway, in central London, a main North–South boulevard adjacent to an expanding Covent Garden, is a prominent example of this phenomenon right now. Boarded-up properties, dereliction, and general shoddiness of much of its built environment betoken upscaling at some future date, and a possible incorporation into the Covent Garden development. In the interim, it's these empty office spaces under which many homeless bodies now cower and huddle or else try to sell *The Big Issue*. National Health Service cuts, deinstitutionalization, and the patent failure of Care in the Community policies to cater adequately for the mentally ill have, meanwhile, forced many patients out on to the streets, under these vacant doorways, where, unable to cope for themselves, such people too become vulnerable to brutalities of living on the street. And for huge chunks of the nation's population, both young and old, with little hope of a decent job, home or bright future, that some eventually turn to alcohol and drugs and end up as *habitués* of the streets is shocking enough but not entirely unexpected to the vigilant urbanist. "Pauperism," Marx says, is the "hospital" of the working classes (Marx 1967: 603) and its wards are now the streets, doorways, and deserted parks of our cities. Imperceptible structural processes mesh with perceptible daily experience. Two truths reveal themselves to the initiated as one truth, as a paradoxical dialectical truth.

A lot of people nowadays find themselves "set free," tossed out of work, downsized and rightsized and outsourced, downgraded into the ranks of a "contingent worker" – didn't Marx call them "floating relative surplus populations"? Maybe some of these people never thought of themselves as Marx's "modern working class," never dreamt they'd one day join the ranks of the partially employed or wholly unemployed or even homeless, especially because some weren't factory hands nor blue-collar workers, but instead wore suits and were employed in offices or labs or schools or dealing rooms. Yet now they too must sell themselves piecemeal, as a commodity, finding work only insofar as their labor is able to pile up capital for somebody else. Today few workers are safe; many are at the mercy of market demands and vicissitudes in competition for labor-power. This is really what Marx meant by the "working class" and why he saw its ranks growing (see Berman 1998).

The product of this "lean" urbanization inevitably unfurls on the city street itself where it's there for everybody to see, hear, and encounter each day, if not always to fully understand. City streets in Britain, as in the United States, bear the grisly scars of a society which has an ideological and material aversion to public policy and which favors instead corporate greed over civic virtue. Out on the streets, domestic and personal circumstances cascade and become embroiled with, and exacerbated by, macro and structural forces: a relentless and vicious dialectic takes hold leaving many people teetering on the edge of the abyss; and some plunge into it. Yet dialecticians have a distinctive role to play in revealing these ties, of pointing out subtle links as well as brutal interconnections; and making them known to the public at large. Dialecticians, in short, have a responsibility to promote a critical understanding of the world. Why else would Gramsci argue in *Prison Notebooks* that Marxist dialectical analysis shouldn't be an abstract "higher" mode of thought, but must enter into *people's common sense itself* (Gramsci 1971: 328–31)? That way, Marxism as a philosophy of dialectical praxis can give people a better critical handle on their world and on the bigger context of their immediate life situation.

So while some people will still feel threatened and intimidated by the convulsions of the street, with a deeper knowledge of the mechanisms *producing* this grim scenario they might at least be able to look street people in the eyes, have more compassion, show greater patience and caring, be more sympathetic and tolerant towards the homeless, beggars, and the poor. Meantime, greater knowledge of the underlying injustices could spark anger and disgust at a society that either normalizes or criminalizes such circumstances, and seeks to play people off against each other and uses all forms of prejudice and intolerance to motivate wealth creation and prosperity. And who knows, maybe this disgust and anger might even be converted into action that struggles for social change.

Marxists and Marxist urbanists can expose received ideas, reactionary ideologies and fetishized understandings of reality, and show links between individuation and process, between concrete events and abstract forces, between the personal and the political. And yet, to do it, they, we, equally need to be receptive to the sights, sounds, horrors, and experiences of the city street itself. The street really isn't a bad barometer for reflecting what's what in city life, politics, and culture. Streets and urban public spaces have long been the terrain for encounters, protests, and sufferings. That social change is invariably sanctioned in the street and in public was always acknowledged by the former Conservative government; they were forever fearful and paranoid of any public gathering or direct action – like strikes, antiroad and car protests, raves, and animal liberation demos – seeking to contest their once fragile and unconvincing grip on British society. The 1994 Criminal Justice Act was imposed precisely to crush this vital and primal encounter in the street. Notwithstanding, Marxist urbanists can abstract and problematize society from the level of the city street and develop more general concepts and practices and actions that seek to explain and transform present concrete realities there. In so doing, Marxists can try to keep intact all that is inspiring, heroic, and beautiful in city cultural life while attempting to stamp out its horrific economic injustices and political oppressions – which are insidiously abstract and global, and glaringly concrete and particular, in nature. This is maybe one way how urban and dialectical Marxism can be put back to work and inspire new hope.

The City Dialectic, the Dialectical City

There's another challenge and possibility that the dialectical worldview presents for Marxists and Marxist urbanists. For, if being dialectical is to highlight ambiguity and contradiction, then the challenge now is for Marxism to find somehow ways to thrive off ambiguity and contradiction. Sure, Marxists should work against ambiguity and contradiction, but also *make ambiguity and contradiction work for Marxism*. There are many ways this can be done. Consider the market itself. In the past, Marxists have been right to show how markets operate to create and perpetuate inequality and injustice. Throughout the seventies, urban Marxism tended to hold absolute incredulity toward the market and commodity culture. Yet the problem is, for the foreseeable future at least, markets are here to stay. Where does that leave dialectical analysis in the interim? Marx himself used dialectical insight to criticize the market. He recognized the dramatic expansion of the productive forces and market relations as at once liberatory and repressive: new communities were certainly opened up and horizons were broadened and fresh ideas emerge. But these eventually become new communities and ideas dominated by the *real* community of money and markets (Marx 1973: 225). All ideas – radical or otherwise – become commodified and can be used to expand capital and create new markets. Marx realized how capitalism generates a market even for radical ideas. Does it follow that radical ideas can use – as well as be used by – the market to propagate and nourish radical politics? Of course it does. It has to.

Marxists have to give up on the idea of the market as "original sin" or as somehow a source of "inauthenticity." After all, we know enough about commodities, markets, and capital not to leave their concerns exclusively to bourgeois apologists and free-marketeers. Marx left us a colossal intellectual legacy in three volumes of *Capital* and the *Grundrisse*, the bulk of which has formally stood the test of time. The bulky "Chapter on Money" in the *Grundrisse*, for example, offers a brilliant conceptualization of what Marx calls the "transcendental power of money" in bourgeois society. His analysis posits money in its material, symbolic, and representative form, and some of Marx's discussion on money as a "symbol of itself" really prefigures Baudrillard by more than a hundred years (Marx 1973: 141–5).

Thus it is well known to Marxists how commodities are produced and exchanged and how money circulates to become capital, how capital inexorably accumulates and circulates in its different forms, and how it propels people into situations where they are forced to act in ways which they might not have otherwise. Left unchecked, money and markets are forces which create and perpetuate inequality and class power. Marxist research here across various disciplinary spectrums has taught us to know that playing with markets necessarily means playing with fire. Nevertheless, Marxists have little choice now but to use their vast critical knowledge to devise ways of burning their hands minimally and of showing how fire can also warm and create light. The recent work of Andrew Sayer has begun to pose these sorts of questions (see esp. Sayer 1995b). Sayer's aim is, I think, fair enough: that of trying to "go beyond Marxism" – especially its unqualified resistance to markets. That said, unlike Sayer, I am not convinced that Hayekian liberalism helps to transcend the prevailing impasse within Left political-economic thinking. The struggle to develop Marxist ideas and politics has to be an intensely dialectical one: at once a struggle *in* and *against* the market and *in* and *against* the state apparatuses, but also knowing when to be *for* and *against* certain market and investment practices.

Meanwhile, there is absolutely no reason why Marxist urbanists cannot push for more limited "reformist" aims like rent control in the city, explore the strengths and weaknesses of community empowerment and self-management, monitor and lobby against financial institutions to prevent property speculation and gentrification activities, support ventures designed to aid the homeless, like buying *The Big Issue*. Radical change comes, if it comes – Althusser, after all, warned that knowledge and emancipation is never *guaranteed* (Althusser 1970: 54–8) – bit by bit, over the long haul. Likewise, actions geared towards such redistributive justice need to be combined with combating injustices that are not uniquely capitalist in orientation (like racism, homophobia, and sexism). Then, maybe it's possible to foster ideas and actions that seek to humanize or "socialize" the market (Elson 1988) while developing more compassionate forms of human intercourse based around tenderness, tolerance, and generosity rather than hate and selfishness. And – who knows – even at some time in the long run push towards a "postmarket" society. (Raymond Williams, remember, suggested that this might be a "long revolution.") Marx knew how markets were disempowering. But Engels knew, maybe better than Marx himself, how they could empower as well; and empower those seeking to disempower markets! (Don't forget, Engels used money and capital from his father's Manchester textile company tirelessly to support Marx's lifelong revolutionary pretensions.)

Within cities we know how market dictates and capital investment trends can produce sanitized, anodyne "theme park" urban spaces while divestment renders other areas whole urban wastelands. Yet within the ruins, peripheries, and interstices are spaces where struggle and resistance on behalf of the dispossessed can lead to passionate creative activity and collective vibrancy: music, art, graffiti, poetry, and various subcultural tendencies. Some of this, of course, becomes commodified, some does not; some might be burned by its own success and turned into a phony Hollywood scam or undergo utter commodification and corporate reappropriation (like rap music). Still, the dispossessed can use markets to liberate themselves and rise to prominence and even move to another part of town, *yet somehow still stay radical and subversive.*

Inevitably, though, the boundaries between freedom, empowerment, and existential exploration, and tyranny, oppression, and injustice, will be blurry in cities, and are made blurrier again when markets start to impinge and intrude. Sometimes wresting the lever of economic power and manipulating markets can be used to assert political power and just recognition. Certain expressions of freedom in the city – lifestyle affairs, affinity group politics, subcultural and underground activities (e.g. eroticism and S&M) – often don't actively threaten market relations but actually use commodity culture for their own political ends. For example, the "café culture" and healthy development of a "pink economy" in London's Soho has permitted considerable empowerment and freedom for some gay men.

Dialecticians can and should thrive off ambiguity and ambivalence. There's plainly much scope for radical political, intellectual, and artistic maneuver here – maybe more than Marxist urbanists during the 1970s accepted – both against and within the market, where great opportunities reside and daunting threats brood. Markets expose individual inadequacies and so often force people apart and prey off greed to cajole them into competing against each other. But elsewhere the market can bring people together, can compel people to act and struggle collectively to correct its failings and inequities. In a sense, Marx himself tried to reveal the enormous creative power of conflict, of *human dissatisfaction*, of human history and geography progressing with its worst foot forward – as Henri Lefebvre always liked to point out. Paradoxically, it's clear how much art and literature and kinship have developed out of conflict and dissatisfaction. Think of places like Tompkins Square Park in the Lower East Side of Manhattan, especially around homelessness and antigentrification struggles (Smith 1996). The pages of Joel Rose's and Catherine Texier's literary journal *Between C and D* or the *East Village Eye* tell us a lot about an endearing and rugged neighborhood that's been at the cutting edge of life and death for a while now (Rose and Texier 1988; Moore and Gosciak 1990). And it's that conflict, that intensity of experience, which makes for compelling stories, and attracts avid readers and concerned citizens. Here, too, conflict fuels struggle, makes people clash and come together and demand their rights. Political confrontations of this nature, Marx knew, get ultimately sanctioned by *force*: "The matter," he quipped long ago, "resolves itself into a question of the respective powers of the combatants" (Marx 1975: 74). It's only, then, through organizing and campaigning and struggle – individual and collective struggle – invariably out on the street, that people will discover who they are, how much they're really worth, and how much they can take back: businesses and bureaucracies will never give anything up without being forced to. Democracy is seldom about being nice to your opponents.

I am all too aware that this raises a dangerous and bothersome question for Leftists: bereft of dissatisfaction and conflict, what do humans become and how much creative capacity is lost? It's dangerous because this reasoning can be hijacked by the Right who will (and do) claim that inequality and suffering (for certain people anyway) is good insofar as it forces them to struggle. It's bothersome as well, because Left urbanists now have to ask themselves whether a society – particularly an urban society – free from all inner contradictions, visible imperfections, threatening disorders, and desperate strivings, isn't so much possible as *desirable*. Maybe it's this incessant wrestling against societal defects and injustices that – inner and outer perils and traumas notwithstanding – enables us to feel more alive and makes us more complete human beings. Maybe it isn't *despite* these traumas and perils but *precisely because* of them that we get a zest for life?

Flexible Marxism can still provide zest for life, can still be a veritable adventure of the mind and body, can still define the breadth and depth of the radical battlefield, dialectically pinpointing the inner connections and contradictions between the economy and politics, between urbanization and urbanism, between thought and action. Crucially, too, it can also show ways *into* these contradictions while *highlighting the contradictions worth keeping and nourishing*. This emphasis on nourishing certain contradictions has to be the key difference between 1990s urban Marxism and its 1970s forebear. Here, too, Marxism now has to discern how patient negotiations and dialogs can be established with cultural theorists, feminists, antiracists, postcolonialists and those expressing affinity-group concerns, while insisting that political economy still matters a great deal in social life. Then, perhaps, it will be possible to devise ways for developing spiritually alive cities with exciting and differentiated public spaces, open to conflict and debate and which face up to their troubles and sufferings squarely and fairly.

REFERENCES

Althusser, L. 1970: *Reading Capital*. London: New Left Books.

Berman, M. 1991: LA Raw: review of Mike Davis's *City of Quartz*. *The Nation*, April 1.

Berman, M. 1998: Unchained melodies: review of the 150th edition of the "Communist Manifesto." *The Nation*, May 11.

Cohen, G. A. 1995: Back to socialist basics. *New Left Review* 207, 3–16.

Elson, D. 1988: Market socialism or socialization of the market? *New Left Review*, 172, 3–44.

Gramsci, A. 1971: *Selections from Prison Notebooks*. London: Lawrence and Wishart.

Gramsci, A. 1988: Integral journalism. In D. Forgacs (ed.), *A Gramsci Reader*, London: Lawrence and Wishart.

Harloe, M. 1992: Housing inequality and social structure in London. *Housing Studies*, 7, 189–204.

Harvey, D. 1978: The urban process under capitalism: A framework for analysis. *International Journal of Urban and Regional Research*, 2, 101–31.
Harvey, D. 1982: *The Limits to Capital*. Oxford: Basil Blackwell.
Harvey, D. 1987: Three myths in search of reality in urban studies. *Environment and Planning D: Society and Space*, 5, 367–76.
Marx, K. 1967: *Capital*, vol. 1. New York: International Publishers.
Marx, K. 1973: *Grundrisse*. Harmondsworth: Penguin.
Marx, K. 1975: *Wages, Price and Profit*. Peking: Foreign Languages Press.
Marx, K. 1978: II and VIII Theses on Feuerbach. Reprinted in R. Tucker (ed.), *Marx-Engels Reader*. New York: Norton Books, 143–5.
Merrifield, A. 1993: The Canary Wharf debacle: From TINA – There is no alternative – to THEMBA – There must be an alternative. *Environment and Planning*, A 25, 1247–65.
Moore, A. and Gosciak, J. (ed.) 1990: *A Day in the Life: Tales from the Lower East*. New York: Evil Eye Books.
Rose, J. and Textier, C. (eds.) 1988: *Between C and D*. New York: Penguin Books.
Sayer, A. 1995a: Liberalism, Marxism and Urban and Regional Studies. *International Journal of Urban and Regional Research*, 19, 79–95.
Sayer, A. 1995b: *Radical Political Economy*. Oxford: Basil Blackwell.
Smith, N. 1996: *The New Urban Frontier*. London: Routledge.

Chapter 13

Monocentric to Policentric: New Urban Forms and Old Paradigms

William A. V. Clark

The spatial economy of large American cities is changing. Most jobs are not downtown and have not been in the center of the city for at least three decades. Jobs and services have followed the spreading residential communities to outlying centers far from traditional downtowns. In the very large metropolitan complexes like Los Angeles and Dallas/Fort Worth, the second and ninth largest metropolitan areas respectively, less than a tenth of all jobs are in the core of the region. Joel Garreau in his evocative essay on edge cities singled out Los Angeles as an exemplar of future growth: "Every single American city that is growing, is growing in the fashion of Los Angeles, with multiple urban cores" (Garreau 1991). Moreover, evidence from Europe suggests that this process is already in place in the Randstad, in the Ruhr, and the Milan region of northern Italy (Dieleman and Faludi 1998).

The change in structure has led to theoretical adaptations of old models of city structure to account for the emerging new patterns, and to alternative postmodern explanations for the structure and organization of the nature of the twenty-first-century metropolis. This essay reviews the thinking about emerging policentric forms, and evaluates the changing nature and form of edge cities. I come down firmly on the side of the socioeconomic explanations for the changes and I interpret them in the context of changing and increased accessibility, and the changes created by an information-based society. I argue that although the journalistic interpretations of Garreau (1991) help us to visualize the changes, the changes themselves are explained not in the abstractions of postmodernism but firmly in the desire to rationalize the journey to work and to escape the negative externalities of the central city.

New Language, Old Forms?

Some writers have suggested that cities now look different, that there is a new urban form that makes it difficult to discern the social ecologies and bid rent patterns of old urban areas (Knox 1991). But how true is this? Would a nineteenth-century urban observer find our late twentieth-century cities so different? Certainly New York and

London would not be unfamiliar, more spread out of course, with much more of the urban space devoted to transportation, but how different? Even Los Angeles, frequently invoked as the forerunner of the policentric city, had its present makings in the nodes and transportation system of the early twentieth century. The far-ranging Pacific Electric Car system served an area as large as the freeways do today.

There is a large literature[1] which has documented that US metropolitan areas are more dispersed and that the job mix is different from earlier industrial mixes, but the question remains, is it a "new urban structure" or simply a continuation of processes set in place with the emergence of the car as the principal means of urban transport? Is our understanding of past patterns and arrangements as applicable today as they were when regional scientists and urban economists and geographers adapted the bid rent curve to understanding distributions of activities in the urban realm? While Cooke (1990) and Dear and Flusty (1998) argue for new models and new paradigms for our emerging urban forms, there is a strong case to be made for revising the models which have served us well in understanding the urban form and changing structure of the city. It is clear that the monocentric model of the city is no longer relevant but equally surely we do not need to reject the notions of accessibility and economic competition. Reexamining the literature which has shown the continued interaction of residences and multiple workplaces, and the usefulness of multiple density gradients, provides a context within which the less structured suggestions of Dear and Flusty (1998) among others, can be evaluated.

The central argument in the Dear and Flusty (1998) presentation is that the old models are no longer useful and that a postmodern city needs a postmodern structure. They suggest that there is a radical break in the processes of the postmodern city and that highly mobile capital and the emergence of flexism (unfortunately not well defined) requires a new way of thinking about urban structure. They use the term "Keno capitalism" to suggest a board game in which the squares are all equal and urbanism occurs in a quasi-random field of opportunities. But is this a useful new paradigm? Is it even a necessary paradigm?[2]

Comparing old and new urban forms

As most geography and planning students know, three decades ago density gradients and land value curves were pivoted on the Central Business District. The CBD was just that, the center of business, and it was the most accessible point in the city. As early as 1903, Richard Hurd drew out the relationships which explained the rise of concentrations of business industry and population. Hurd (1903) emphasized how the role of economic rent in cities could be used to explain the rise of cities and their tendency to create powerful and privileged centers of commerce. The translation of his verbal explanations to economic principles including well-developed bid rent curves followed (Haig 1926; Ratcliff 1949). It was Haig (1926) who emphasized what has remained at the heart of analyses of urban structure, the strong complementarity between rent and transportation costs. Further expanded by Wingo (1961), Alonso (1964), and Muth (1969), the underlying thesis of the empirical work was that the the monocentric city is the outcome of competition for accessibility (Figure 13.1). Tests of the theory by examining population density gradients and land value gradients showed that the monocentric model was a good fit to empirical data in Chicago (Rees 1970). Correlation coefficients greater than .9 suggested that the models were good fits even in 1960 and were even better fits in the more defined cities of the 1940s and 1950s. Tests across cities (Mills 1972) confirmed the fits for densities and land values though they were clearly declining over time.

As cities spread further from the core and as cities like Los Angeles clearly did not fit these patterns, the diagrams were modified to reflect the changing urban structure (Figure 13.1b). Over time the extreme simplification of the monocentric model was either modified by specifying more than one center (Papageorgiou 1990) or reconceptualized by developing the conditions under which policentric structures might emerge (Ogawa and Fugita 1980; Odland 1978). The theoretical work has been tested in a variety of empirical studies with reformulated density gradients and trend surfaces, and most extensively in a series of papers on Los Angeles by Gordon and others and on Dallas/Ft. Worth by a group of geographers and economists (Berry and Kim 1993).

The work on the urban structure of Los Angeles and Dallas/Ft. Worth provided a new picture of the relevance of a policentric approach to the evolving urban structures of the late twentieth century. Gordon, Richardson, and Wong (1986) used a multicentered version of the monocentric density gradient, and the Wright coefficient derived from the Lorenz curve, to measure the extent of the population dispersion. The empirical results showed that the number of centers had increased between 1970 and 1980, and that a modified policentric model fits the population and employment densities more closely than a monocentric model. In addition the fit of the monocentric model has declined over time as the fit of the policentric model has increased (Table 13.1). Not only does the policentric model fit better; the work-trip data for Southern California show that work trips are increasingly intracounty and more critically, these trips are shorter in the outlying counties. This implies that there are large numbers of jobs in the peripheral areas and that people are behaving rationally by seeking jobs in nearby locations when the jobs are available.

The data from a study of house prices in the Dallas/Ft. Worth area tell a similar story of the inadequacy of the monocentric model. Waddell, Berry, and Hoch (1993) show that "the emergence of new nodes of regional significance has created housing price gradients that far overshadow any residential gradient with respect to the CBD." In fact the research emphasized that the relative location of residential land-use was the critical factor in creating residential gradients. It is the new urban nodes which are creating the price surface for the metropolitan region.

In Europe, the studies by Blotevogel (1998) and Vanhaverbeke (1998) have demonstrated the same processes and outcomes as have been occurring in the United States. In these cases it is often a case of the coalescence of previous patterns of

Table 13.1 Comparing monocentric and policentric models in Southern California

Year	Variable	R2 Monocentric	R2 Policentric
1970	Population	.34	.43
1980	Population	.31	.49
1980	Employment	.40	.52

Source: Gordon, Richardson, and Wong 1986

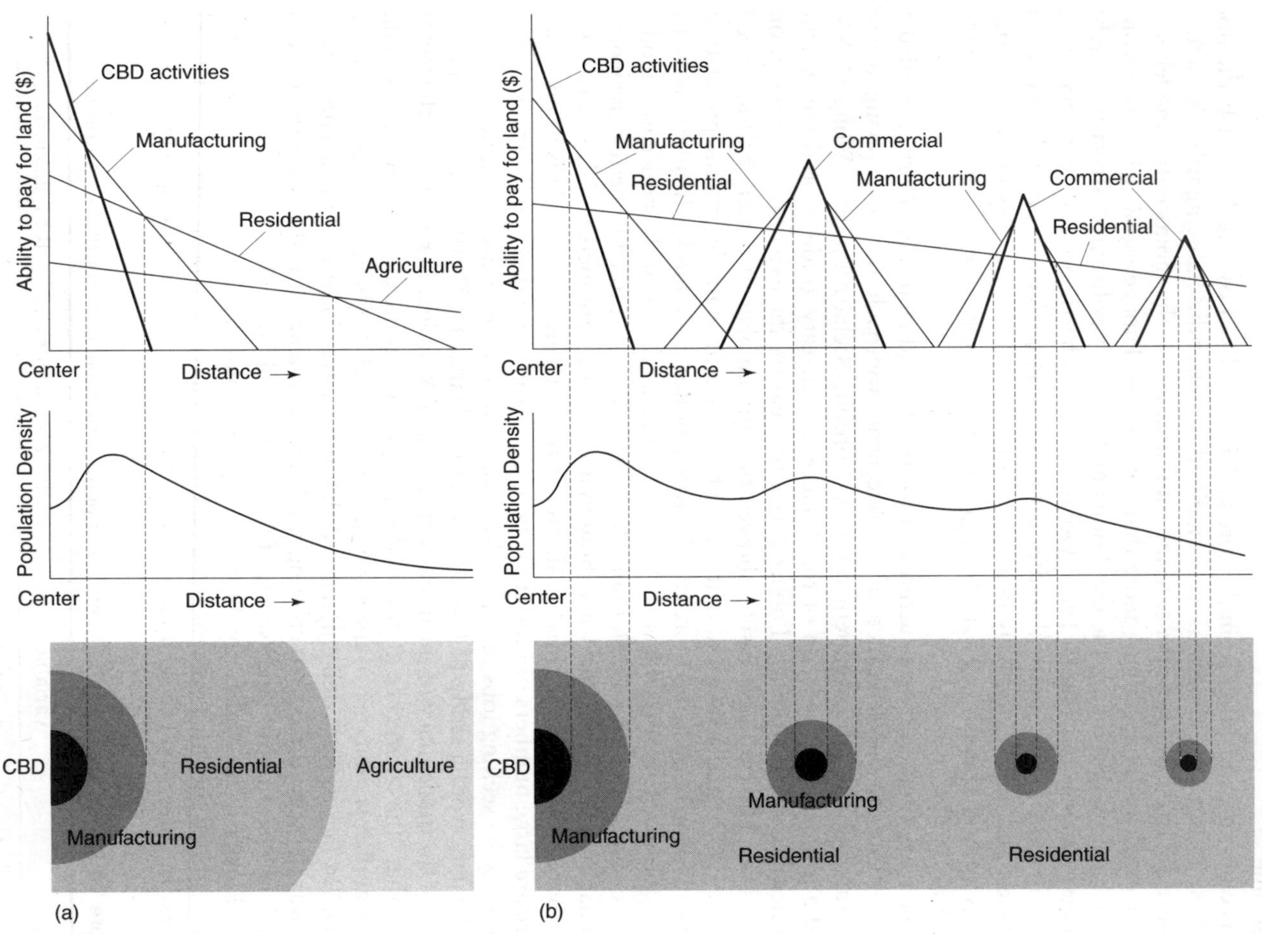

Figure 13.1 Hypothetical monocentric and policentric urban structures (a: adapted from Bourne (1981); b: adapted from Cadwallader (1996))

separated and independent cities. In the Randstad there is increased intercity commuting and localized commuting within the "green heart" at the same time (Clark and Kuijperslinde 1994), indicating little doubt about the generality of multinodal structures in late twentieth-century urbanization.

Edge cities and cities within cities

The increasing spread of the large metropolitan areas necessarily led to a dispersal of new services, especially shopping and associated consumer services, insurance, banking, and medical services. These services, as services in the past, clustered in concentrated locations that were the most accessible to the largest number of potential customers. Because these new services are located in reference to accessibility by the car, it is not surprising that Garreau (1991) identified so many of the new edge cities at the conjunction of interstate highways or at the intersection of important urban throughways. Accessibility is still as powerful a force in creating and sustaining the new nodes as it was in creating the dominance of the Central Business District in the early decades of the twentieth century.

An evocative essay on the nature of edge cities has shown their generality across American urban landscapes (Knox 1991). The analysis of Washington DC emphasizes the way in which new edge cities are so closely connected to the automobile and the continuing development of high-speed urban corridors. Knox goes so far as to suggest that the new patterns are anarchical in nature, lacking order, and so reflect a postmodern conception of urban structure. Leinberger (1990) however, draws us back to the multicentered nature of the new forms by reiterating the message within the Knox discussion, that edge cities are in fact rational responses to evolving urban occupational structures and the way these are being translated into urban form. The essays in Berry and Kim (1993) suggest that the new urban form can still be analyzed with the forces which created the monocentric structures, accessibility, and the trade-off of location and cost, but clearly the monocentric model no longer captures the structure of modern urban areas.

The past into the future

The patterns that we are observing in the Randstad in the Netherlands, in the Ruhr in Germany, in Southern California, Dallas/Ft. Worth, and in the complex of counties around Washington DC are extensions of patterns that were already in place several decades earlier in Los Angeles. Southern California may have been ahead of the curve – it was always a collection of edge cities – but increasing affluence, and our and the world's fascination with, and dependence on, the automobile has strengthened rather than weakened the linkage between work and residence.

The edge cities of Los Angeles in the first decades of the twentieth century – Pasadena (railroads), Long Beach (ports), Huntington Beach in Orange County (oil) – were important commercial and employment centers. While much of the US was still celebrating the high-rise centralization of urban development surrounded by suburban residential districts, Los Angeles was simply avant garde in the way its combination of automobile flexibility, cheap land, and low densities were parlayed into a different and distributed pattern. Many urban commentators have noted that people in Los Angeles voted with their feet and chose not to live in crowded centralized apartments but in small ranch houses with large yards (Monkkonen 1988). Los Angeleans took advantage of the open spaces and the existing interconnections to decenter the metropolis and create a pattern which is now the norm.

It is equally important to recognize that this decentered structure arose with a set of technologies which, while new in Los Angeles (it was the first city to be completely electric), merely were the forerunners of a process which would allow urban residents in any metropolitan area to exercise flexibility in living, and it was only a matter of time before the services would follow. It also arose as a market response to the marketplace. Los Angeles and its edge cities is not a postmodern construction without meaning and explanation; it is the natural evolution of a set of processes put in place seven decades ago. The implication that edge cities are peculiar and require special explanations is mistaken. Typically, smaller "edge cities," incorporated or not, sometimes offer things the centralized metropolis cannot: more accessible school boards, more responsive planning services, and faster police reaction times – even a sense of community (Monkkonen 1988).

These arguments suggest that we view with some caution the alternative suggestions of the postmodern arguments that some chaotic process is creating the new urban structure, and in particular that we view with real caution the notions of inchoate explanations of "Keno capitalism" (Dear and Flusty 1998). That changes in consumer tastes are important elements of the continuing evolution of urban areas is not in dispute; the issue is really whether the old paradigms speak to modern processes. The following empirical analyses suggest that they have, and will continue to do so, although in the end the conclusion will come from the behavior of entrepreneurs and city dwellers.

Population Decentralization and Changing Population Densities

The thesis emphasized by research on Los Angeles and Dallas/Ft. Worth (Berry and Kim 1993; Gordon, Richardson, and Wong 1986: Guiliano and Small 1991) is that there is a continuing and strengthening process of the movement of households further from the city center in search of amenities, and that decentralization is being followed at an accelerating rate by firms who wish to provide services to the dispersed population. In turn firms who wish to access the new suburban labor pools follow the population and the services. In this scenario the new regional shopping centers are the visible centers celebrated in the discussion of edge cities, and the new technopoles of Southern California are the less visible but no less important job centers of the new urban structure (Scott 1990).

Nationally the counties outside of central cities have been growing rapidly in the past three decades, and no more rapidly than in those cities that have been identified as containing clusters of edge cities. Dallas/Ft. Worth, Houston, Washington/Baltimore, Philadelphia, New York/Newark, Chicago, and the greater Southern California region are only the most visible cases of clusters of service and employment nodes outside of the traditional downtown, the new edge cities.

A case study of the population changes in Los Angeles and in the Dallas/Ft. Worth region in the past three decades brings a specificity to the changes which have been described journalistically by Garreau (1991) and demographically by Frey and

Table 13.2 Population Changes in Southern California

	1970	1980	1990	1997	% change 1970–97
Los Angeles City	2,816,061	2,966,850	3,485,398	3,553,638	26
County Ring	4,220,396	4,510,653	5,377,772	5,591,581	32
Contiguous Counties	2,936,980	4,020,015	5,668,365	6,463,667	120

Source: US census of population 1970, 1980, 1990, and US census of population estimates 1997

Table 13.3 Population change in Dallas/Ft. Worth

	1970	1980	1990	1997	% change 1970–97
Dallas	844,401	904,074	1,006,877	1,053,292	25
Ft. Worth	393,476	385,166	447,619	479,716	22
County Ring	805,761	1,129,030	1,568,417	1,817,464	126
Contiguous Counties	221,583	386,460	674,948	930,894	320

Source: US census of population 1970, 1980, 1990, and US census of population estimates 1997

Speare (1988). To reiterate, the changes in Southern California are a continuation of processes put in place seven decades ago. The spread of small towns and "electric car" links to the downtown began a process in which the growth of the interstitial areas created the basis for a continuous urban region (Laslett 1996). Between 1970 and 1997 the five-county Southern California region grew by 5.4 million people, by more than 50 percent (Table 13.2). The numbers are smaller but the magnitudes of change in the vast Dallas/Ft. Worth region are similar (Table 13.3). But it is the relative nature of the growth, the difference between growth in the center and growth in the surrounding communities which is at the heart of the analysis we are pursuing in this discussion.

While the City of Los Angeles grew by about 800,000 persons, it did grow, unlike some other central cities; the area in the county outside Los Angeles grew by 1.4 million. In the four outlying counties the population more than doubled from a little under three million persons to almost 6.5 million persons. The outlying counties grew by 120 percent in contrast to the modest 26 percent growth of the central city. Individual outlying counties outgrew the central city by magnitudes varying from 5 to 10 times. The story is similar in the Dallas/Ft. Worth region (Table 13.3). There the growth of areas outside the cities of Dallas and Ft. Worth was three to ten times the central cores. Again the outlying areas outgrew the central areas by quite large proportions. It is a similar story in all the large metropolitan areas and has been documented by Frey and Speare (1988). To that documentation it is important to add that the growth of the suburban areas has come from depopulation from the center as well as new growth from other regions. For example, the pattern of growth in Prince George's County outside Washington DC has been fueled by out-migration from Washington as well as significant growth from other nearby counties and states. These flows are rearranging the

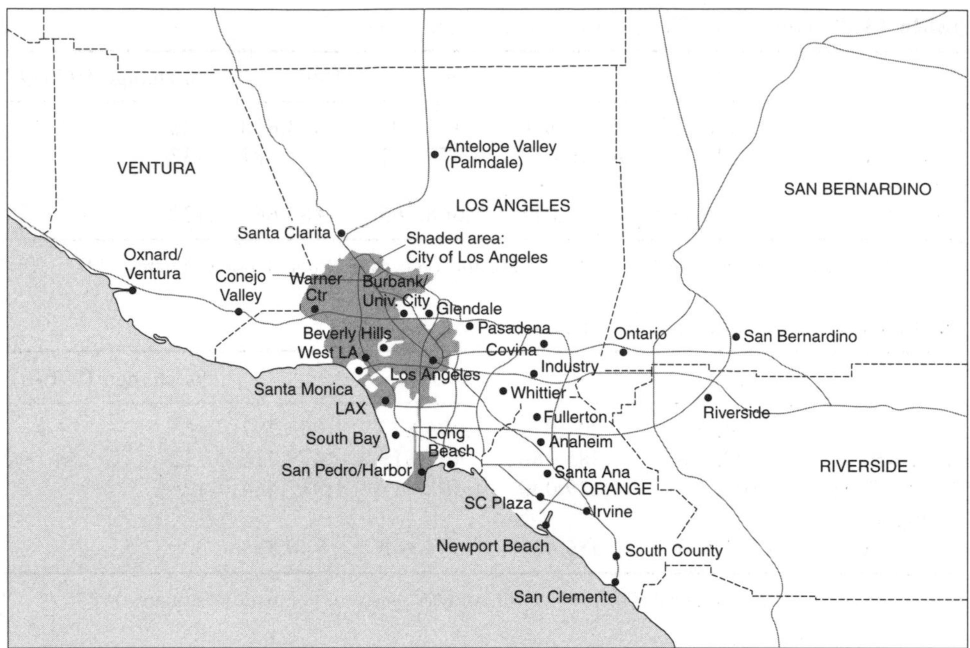

Figure 13.2 The Southern California urban region

distribution of population across the metropolitan areas and changing the densities of both central and outlying communities. While the densities in many inner cities are declining, around the new service and job centers in the suburbs they are increasing.

The changing populations in suburban counties in general is increasing, but the increases in the communities around the new nodes of the policentric city are greater. An examination of the growth around the edge cities in the Los Angeles metropolitan region (Figure 13.2) shows a pattern of substantial population increases. To examine the level of change the study examined the population in a standardized set of neighborhoods around a sample of the edge cities in Los Angeles County. Garreau (1991) identified 19 such edge cities in the Southern California region and the study here is of a sample of those edge cities in Los Angeles and Orange Counties. All the communities close to the edge cities increased their population (Figure 13.3). Densities tripled or nearly tripled in five of the nine case studies. In three other " further out" edge cities, Santa Clarita, Palmdale, and Warner Center, the populations, and consequently the densities increased between five and ten times. Only one relatively close-in edge city (South Bay/Torrance) had an increase of less than 100 percent. These are significant increases given that the county as a whole only increased by 32 percent. There can be no doubt that the clustering of services and jobs in these new nodes is being translated into associated increases in population and population densities and, in turn, an increased emphasis on policentricity.

The evidence of growing residential concentrations around regional service nodes is striking but is it accompanied by an increase in employment?

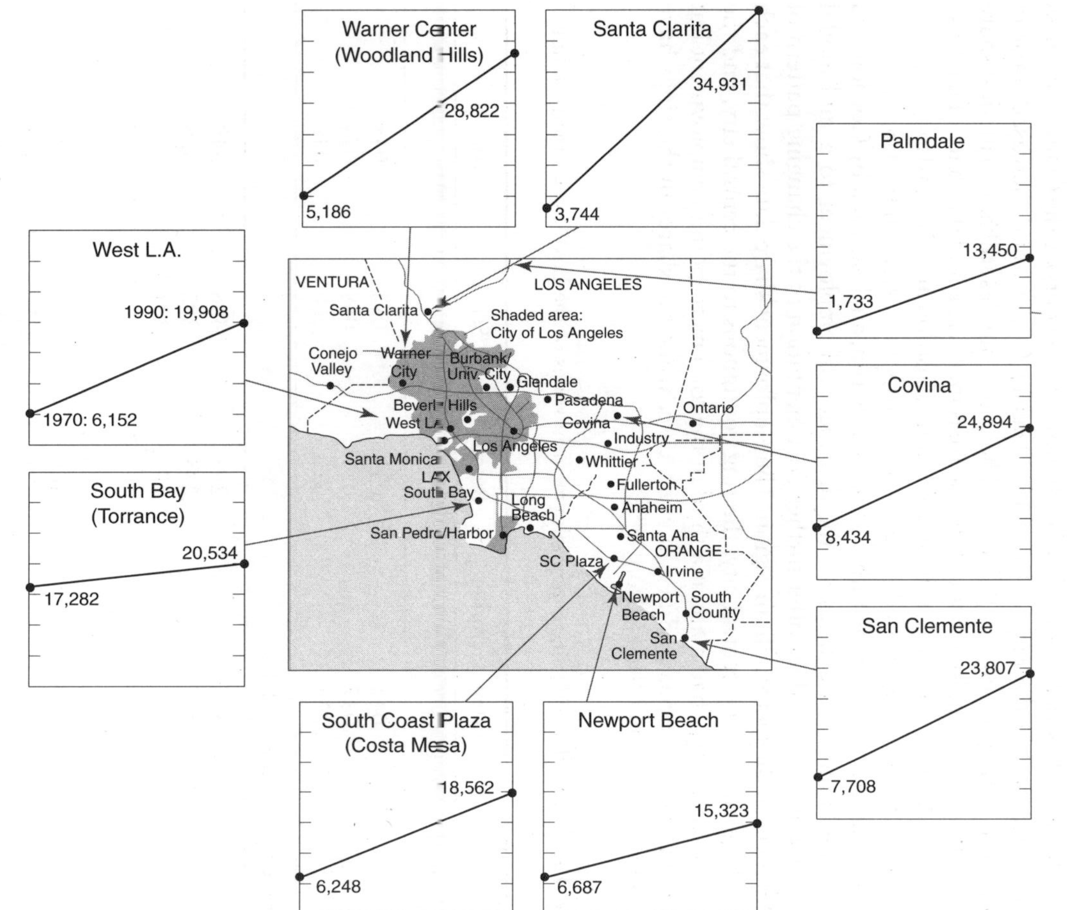

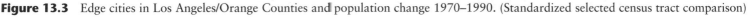

Figure 13.3 Edge cities in Los Angeles/Orange Counties and population change 1970–1990. (Standardized selected census tract comparison)

Job Locations and the Nature of Commuting in Restructuring Metropolitan Areas

The simple tests of monocentric and policentric models suggested that jobs as well as residences were increasingly outside the old cores. A recent refinement of that analysis by Gordon and Richardson (1996) showed that total employment declined in the Central Business District, declined in the central city ring outside the Central Business District, increased in the remainder of Los Angeles County, and increased most in coterminous Orange County (Table 13.4). The outer counties still have a modest share of the total regional employment but that share is increasing and the share of employment in Los Angeles County continues to decline (Gordon and Richardson 1996).

When the analysis is extended to 12 large metropolitan areas in the US the results are quite similar. Although the rather general core ring analysis used by Gordon and Richardson is only a rough test of the dispersion of employment to a multinodal structure, the evidence does offer further documentation of the changing pattern of employment in the metropolitan region. The employment share data show that each of the three zones – the central city, the ring contiguous to the central city, and the suburban outer ring – had a about a third of the total metropolitan employment but the central city share has declined in every case, while the shares in the rings have increased (Gordon and Richardson 1996).

Table 13.4 The changing share in employment in zones of the Los Angeles metropolitan area

	Manufacturing	Retail	Services	All
Central Business District				
1976	.042	.034	.083	.058
1980	.039	.050	.068	.054
1986	.029	.022	.060	.049
Central city (excludes CBD)				
1976	.317	.295	.406	.349
1980	.277	.285	.392	.326
1986	.253	.271	.331	.287
Rest of Los Angeles County				
1976	.470	.468	.357	.426
1980	.479	.428	.370	.425
1986	.492	.450	.390	.437
Orange County				
1976	.171	.203	.153	.167
1980	.205	.237	.170	.195
1986	.226	.256	.219	.227

Source: Gordon and Richardson 1996

The data for US metropolitan areas are not exceptional. Hall (1988) showed that the employment grew most in the furthest rings of communities with each succeeding decade, and Sahling and Anderson (1992) found similar results in Paris. The changes in the increasingly decentralized Mexico City region are an even more dramatic illustration of the pattern of decentralized employment (Rowland and Gordon 1996). The data from Europe confirm these findings. The patterns of the Randstad and the Ruhr are coalescing urban regions in which formerly separated cites are part of a vast network of residences and jobs, and a system in which households juggle locations in response to changing distributions of jobs.

The evidence from commuting patterns is further evidence of the changing structure of late twentieth-century urban regions. Most measures of commuting show that overall distances have either decreased slightly or not increased. For the United States as a whole, commuting travel time was virtually unchanged between 1980 and 1990. The number of workers who traveled less than 20 minutes decreased from a little over to a little under a half of all workers (STF3C, 1990). Given the population growth in counties outside the central city, the number of job opportunities in outlying nodes *must* have increased to maintain an unchanged journey to work. It is worth emphasizing too, that the stability in commuting times occurred in the same interval that there was a very large increase in the number of vehicles in service in the United States.

The data from an analysis of commuting times in the Randstad and Southern California also suggest that commuting reflects changing job distributions. In all Southern Californian counties the proportion of commuters who had short commutes, between 20 and 30 minutes, increased over time. At the same time very long commutes also increased in Southern California, which suggests that there are still insufficient jobs in the outlying counties. The evidence points to a region in transition, to a region in which jobs are dispersing but where there are still a proportion of centrally located jobs out of the county of residence.

Transactions in the New Urban Form

Not only are there a new set of ethnic nodes, but the means of communication are also changing. The development of increasing decentralized living and employment is not independent of the transformations which have been changing the urban form. Castells (1989) uses the notion of the information city to emphasize the changing nature of communication and its impact on urban form. Part of this revolution has been the flexibility imparted by the ease of communication. In particular, the increase in modes and manners of communication has reduced the need for face-to-face contact. The communication city of the twenty-first century will likely further weaken the arguments for a compact urban form with a dominant center. The city will continue to change as communication technology changes the needs for face-to-face contact on a daily basis. The information city – the knowledge city – will privilege accessibility still further and commutes are likely to decrease. Clearly, consumers in America and in Europe have voted with their feet. For knowledge workers the transactions in the new city will likely further increase the decentralized nature of urbanization.

Urban Form in the Twenty-first Century

There is no doubt either from the daily experience of commuters in large American cities, or from the statistical analysis drawn from a variety of sources and presented in the preceding pages, that the work–residence linkages are changing. There is more crosstown, and reverse-direction commuting than three decades ago. The changes in commuting patterns are only the most visible manifestation of the changing structure of metropolitan areas, whether in the United States or Europe. The presentation in the previous sections favors a view of a new urban form in which decentralization will promote greater proximity between work and residence and reduced commuting. There is an alternative view in which decentralization is a force which deprives the low-income central-city residents of access to the best jobs and adequate housing (Cervero 1989). In this view, low densities are associated with economic inefficiency and environmental degradation from excessive automobile use. Thus, the changing urban form requires intervention and planning and a jobs–housing balance, but this is debated by those who point out that commuting is a decreasing proportion of all trips (Guiliano and Small 1991), and those who caution against intervention in the evolving complexity between behavior and urban form (Berry 1993).

The conclusions of this review of urban structure come down clearly on the side of caution in abandoning old models of the urban structure. This review reiterates the value of old paradigms of accessibility and locational trade-offs as central elements in the creation of the urban structure, albeit modified to account for the emergence of multinodal structures and the changing demographics of the late twentieth century. It is also worth reiterating the notion that the structure is emerging as the result of the interplay of capitalist decisions about profit and individual choices about location. The complex interplay of capital and choice is a central element of the emergence of the form of cities in the next century. The processes of accessibility, influenced by new methods of information transmission and modification, have not changed nor have the motivations of households as they transition through the life course. Simply inventing new terms for what can be more clearly enunciated in modified old paradigms will not capture either the way in which the city is changing or its emerging policentricity.

The postmodern interpretations of the city, if they have advanced our understanding of policentric urbanism have done so only at the margins. After all, most of the movement in the city is still intrinsically bound up with the need to move from residence to workplace, or in pursuit of consumer goods and services. Sometimes in the quest to introduce new ways of thinking about the city, of privileging gender and color, it is possible that the basic urban processes are lost. They can be recaptured by using and understanding modifications of accessibility, consumer behavior and market outcomes. The explanation for the new policentric structures is embedded in the past urban structure and present household behavior.

NOTES

1. Examples include reviews by Berry (1973) chapter 2, Frey and Speare (1988), and in Europe by Champion (1989).

2. It is perhaps notable that in the Dear and Flusty (1998) discussion of Los Angeles and the changing urban form of the city there is no reference to Guiliano and Small (1991), Gordon and Richardson (1996), or Muth (1969). It is as if these analyses of the urban form of Los Angeles do not exist. Perhaps even more critical is the notion that case studies are the proper (only?) methods of analysis in economic geography and by implication that the carefully developed analyses of household behavior are somehow not relevant for understanding the dynamics of the modern American metropolis.

REFERENCES

Alonso, W. 1964: *Location and Land Use*. Cambridge, MA: Harvard University Press.

Berry, B. J. L. 1973: *The Human Consequences of Urbanization*. London: Macmillan.

Berry, B. J. L. (ed.) 1993: The multinodal metropolis: special issue. *Geographical Analysis*, 23, 1–82.

Berry, B. J. L. and Kim, H. 1993: Challenges to the monocentric model. *Geographical Analysis*, 25, 1–4.

Blotevogel, H. H. 1998: The Rhine Ruhr metropolitan region: reality and discourse. *European Planning Studies*, 395–410.

Bourne, L. 1981: *The Geography of Housing*. New York: John Wiley.

Cadwallader, M. 1996: *Urban Geography: An Analytical Approach*. New Jersey: Prentice-Hall.

Castells, M. 1989: *The Informational City*. Oxford: Basil Blackwell.

Cervero, R. 1989: *America's Suburban Centers*. London: Unwin-Hyman.

Champion, A. G. (ed.) 1989: *Counterurbanization*. London: Arnold.

Clark, W. A. V. and Dieleman, F. 1996: *Households and Housing. Choices in the Housing Market*. New Brunswick, NJ: Rutgers University, Center for Urban Policy.

Clark, W. A. V. and Kuijpers-Linde, M. 1994: Commuting in restructuring urban regions. *Urban Studies*, 31, 465–83.

Cooke, P. 1990: Modern urban theory in question. *Transactions of the Institute of the British Geographers*, 15, 331–43.

Dear, M. and Flusty, S. 1998: Postmodern urbanism. *Annals of the Association of American Geographers*, 88, 50–72.

Dieleman, F. M. and Faludi, A. 1998: Polynucleated metropolitan regions in Northwest Europe: theme of the special issue. *European Planning Studies*, 365–77.

Frey, W. and Speare, A. 1988: *Regional and Metropolitan Growth and Decline in the United States*. New York: Russell Sage Foundation.

Garreau, J. 1991: *Edge City: Life on the New Frontier*. New York: Doubleday.

Getis, A. 1983: Second order analysis of point patterns: the case of Chicago as a multi center urban region. *Professional Geographer*, 35, 73–80.

Gordon, P. and Richardson, H. 1996: Employment decentralization in US metropolitan areas: is Los Angeles an outlier or the norm? *Environment and Planning A*, 28, 1727–43.

Gordon, P. and Richardson, H. 1997: The communications city. *Urban Land*, 56, September.

Gordon, P., Richardson, H., and Jun, M. 1991: The commuting paradox: Evidence from the top twenty. *Journal of the American Planning Association*, 57, 416–20.

Gordon, P. Richardson, H., and Wong, H. 1986: The distribution of poulation in a polycentric city. *Environment and Planning A*, 18, 161–73.

Griffith, D. 1981: Evaluating the transformation from a monocentric to a policentric city. *Professional Geographer*, 33, 189–196.

Guiliano, G. and Small, K. A. 1991: Subcenters in the Los Angeles region. *Regional Science and Urban Economics*, 21, 163–82.

Haig, R. M. 1926: Toward an understanding of the metropolis. *Quarterly Journal of Economics*, 40, 421–3.
Hall, P. 1988: *London 2001*. London: Unwin Hyman.
Hamilton, B. W. 1982: Wasteful commuting. *Journal of Political Economy*, 90, 1035–53.
Hartshorn, T. and Mueller, P. 1989. Suburban downtowns and the transformation of metropolitan Atlanta's business landscape. *Urban Geography*, 10, 375–95
Hurd, R. 1903: *Principles of City Land Values*. New York: The Record and Guide.
Knox, P. 1991: The restless urban landscape. *Annals of the Association of American Geographers*, 81, 181–209.
Laslett, J. 1996: Historical perspectives: Immigration and the rise of a distinctive urban region, 1900–1970. In R. Waldinger and M. Bozorgmehr, *Ethnic Los Angeles*, New York: Russell Sage.
Leinberger, C. 1990: Urban cores. *Urban Land*, 49, 4–9.
Mills, E. 1972: *Studies in the structure of the urban economy*. Baltimore: The Johns Hopkins University Press.
Monkkonen, E. 1988: *America Becomes Urban*. Berkeley, Calif.: University of California Press.
Muth, R. 1969: *Cities and Housing: The Spatial Patterns of Urban Residential Landuse*. Chicago: University of Chicago Press.
Odland, J. 1978: The conditions for multi-center cities. *Economic Geography*, 54, 234–44.
Ogawa, H. and Fujita, M. 1980: Equilibrium land use patterns in a non monocentric city. *Journal of Regional Science*, 20, 455–75.
Papageorgiou, Y. 1990: *The Isolated City State: An Economic Geography of Urban Spatial Structure*. New York: Routledge.
Ratcliff, R. U. 1949: *Urban Land Economics*. New York: McGraw-Hill.
Rees, P. 1970. The urban envelope: patterns and dynamics of population density. In , B. J. L. Berry and F. Horton, *Geographic Perspectives on Urban Systems*. Englewood Cliffs, NJ: Prentice-Hall, 276–305.
Rowland, A. and Gordon, P. 1996: Mexico City. In A. Gilbert (ed.), *Mega cities in Latin America*, Tokyo: United Nations University Press.
Sahling, L. G. and Anderson, V. 1992: Paris: a bold game plan for the 21st Century. *Urban Land*, 51, 46–51.
Scott, A. J. 1990: The technopoles of Southern California. *Environment and Planning A*, 22, 1575–1605.
Summary Tape File (STF) 1990: Bureau of the Census, US summary STF3C.
Vanhaverbeke, W. 1998: An economic analysis of the Flemish Diamond. *European Planning Studies*, 425–42.
Waddell, P., Berry, B. J. L., and Hoch, I. 1993: House price gradients: The intersection of space and built form. *Geographical Analysis*, 25, 5–19.
Waddell, P. and Shukla, V. 1993: Employment dynamics, spatial restructuring, and the business cycle. *Geographical Analysis*, 25, 35–52.
Wingo, L. 1961: *Transportation and Urban Land*. Washington, DC: Resources for the Future.

Chapter 14

Ups and Downs in the Global City: London and New York at the Millennium

Susan S. Fainstein and Michael Harloe

The early 1980s marked the beginning of a new stage in the development of London and New York. While other economic sectors were dispersing geographically, certain advanced service industries centering around financial activities intensified their presence in the centers of these cities (Friedmann 1986; Friedmann and Wolff 1982; Sassen 1991). This intensification resulted primarily from the enlarged role of financial capital in coordinating the world economy and the extremely active deal-making that accompanied this role. The decade witnessed the birth of new financial markets for the exchange of arcane financial instruments and the raising of huge pools of credit to underwrite speculative activities in property development, mergers, and leveraged buy-outs, as firms themselves became negotiable assets. Physical proximity was needed to facilitate the face-to-face encounters among principals, bankers, brokers, accountants, attorneys, and other consultants necessary for the negotiation of financial packages. New office structures were required to house the activities of the heightened volume of securities trading and ancillary services, resulting in growth in the real-estate development industry. Other industries flourished as well: New York and London continued to be capitals of culture and information production in their respective countries and magnets for world tourism. Although manufacturing, wholesale and retail, and port functions were declining relatively or absolutely, they continued to employ substantial labor forces. The international flavor of the two cities resulted not just from their situation in the global economy but also from their role as receptors of recent immigrants. Their metropolitan areas remained the largest in population in their respective nations, and thus they also comprised the largest markets for consumer products.

Decline and Revival

By the 1970s both cities were widely regarded as being in decline. The simplest indicator of this was the loss of population due to selective out-migration, a process that was a long established trend in London and had recently taken off in New York. More significant were the collapse of large sections of manufacturing industry,

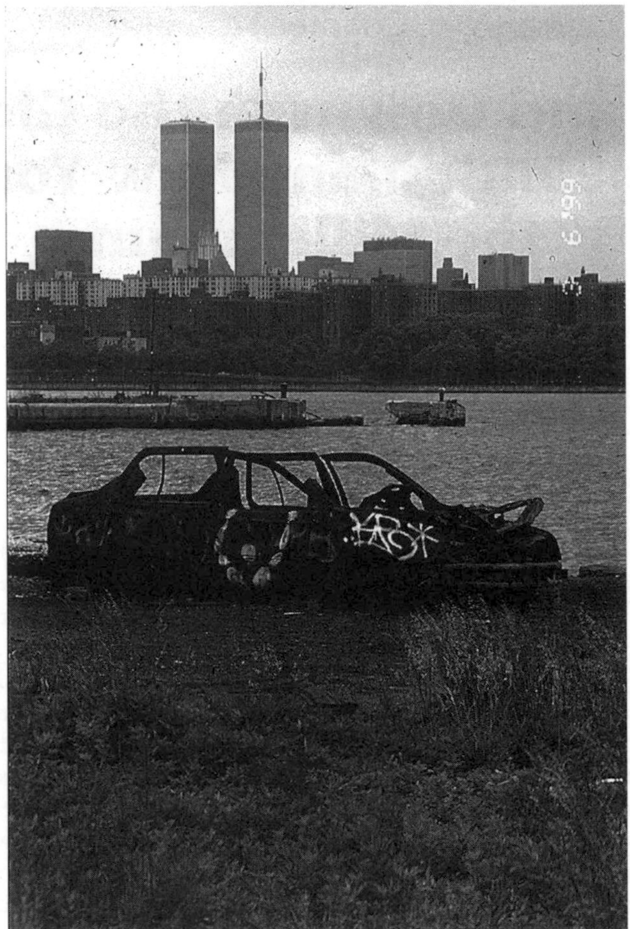

Figure 14.1 New York (© Steve Pile)

disinvestment in the built environment, the growth of the multi-faceted "inner city problem", and the failure of urban policies which attempted to reverse such trends or alleviate their consequences. The timing and detailed nature of the changes were not the same in the two cities. Unlike New York, London had no fiscal crisis, although the subsequent cuts in public services by the Thatcher government, together with its abolition of the Greater London Council, provided a functional equivalent. Likewise, the social and ethnic composition of those most severely affected by decline differed, as did the nature of their political representation. But while such differences affected the intensity and timing of decline, a recognizably similar process was underway.

By the mid-1980s, however, a striking improvement in aggregate economic performance began to take place. Changes in the nature, level, and location of economic activity and jobs, however, suggest that there was no simple revival of the previous urban space economy, as occurs after a downturn in the business cycle, but rather a more radical restructuring and reordering of this economy. The indicators of revival in the 1980s in the two cities had a good deal in common. First, there was the reversal, continuing through the nineties, of previously accelerating population loss. In New York, this gain resulted wholly from replacement of the out-migrating middle class by foreign-born residents. An equally significant change was the shift from employment decline to gain, in New York starting in 1977 and in London beginning in 1983. However, job growth did not fully compensate for previous losses; increases in the metropolitan areas outside the central cities surpassed that in the core; and the new jobs, in services rather than manufacturing and associated activities, were very different from those which they had partially replaced. In the early 1990s this growth was reversed: in the first two years of the decade New York City lost 200,000 jobs, half the total number that had been added during the previous boom (Malanga 1991). Only in 1999 did New York return to the total at the beginning of the decade. In the UK there was a sharp downturn in London and the South East in 1990, ahead of other regions. Between June 1990 and January 1992 over 250,000 jobs were lost in London (Cambridge Econometrics 1992); as in New York it took the rest of the decade to recover the jobs lost.

Changing labor markets

The restructuring of the labor market consisted of a move from what has been termed a "Fordist" (i.e. mass production) industrial organization to a much more "flexible" labor market. The new jobs that have been created in the two cities have many common features: for example, they tend to be occupied by women rather than men, they provide a significant number of well-paid jobs for the highly qualified and many more low-level jobs, but few intermediate-level jobs for skilled manual and supervisory staff. This results in increased inequality in the distribution of earnings. So there has been a change from the more "balanced" distribution of jobs and incomes that existed earlier.

There are, however, some important contrasts between the two cities. To a considerable extent these derive from New York's role as a center for immigrant workers; despite the increase in the immigrant population in the nineties as a result of refugee flows, London's labor force has a substantially larger proportion of native-born workers. In New York the spaces left in the city's labor markets by the out-migration of white workers have been filled by African-Americans and the new ethnic minorities. However, there has not been a balance between in-migration and the demand for replacement labor, leading to high levels of unemployment among the latter two groups. In London the racial and ethnic composition of the labor force has changed less, and the complex pattern of sectoral growth and decline has not led to such extensive and persistent unemployment as has occurred among certain racial and ethnic groups and within particular geographical areas of New York. Despite this, some groups have suffered from a lack of employment opportunities, notably school leavers lacking job qualifications. Another consequence of the immigrant labor phenomenon in New York may have been its declining wage rates in relation to the national average. This has stimulated some growth in lower-paid job categories. London's wage rates have remained high, adding to the cost pressures inducing manufacturing firms to decentralize.

A feature of both labor markets is the growth of much less stable employment conditions. Both cities have historically had quite high levels of labor turnover but the new jobs are often on a short-term or casual basis, employment protection for the worker tends to be far less than in the Fordist era, and in New York there is large-scale informal or unregulated employment. Especially at the bottom of the labor market the balance of advantage has shifted towards the employers, notably in declining sectors of manufacturing and the growing area of consumer services. Job losses in the public sector and the increased resort to contracting out the more routine public service jobs have intensified the situation. The more volatile and less secure employment conditions which affect most severely those at the bottom of the labor market are also experienced by highly paid workers (Ehrenreich 1989; Sennett 1998). Still, the competition which exists for those with relevant skills for the new industries – which has helped them to gain such large salary rises in the past decade – also ensures that the costs of job loss are likely to be less serious for them.

Urban reinvestment

One of the most visible consequences of economic restructuring is the reinvestment which has occurred in the built environment of the two cities. Large-scale projects such as the Docklands development in London and Battery Park City in New York City, and the high volume of investment elsewhere in new offices, retail facilities, entertainment, and leisure complexes and housing, together with the necessary (and largely publicly funded) infrastructure to support them, followed on a period of property disinvestment. This reinvestment was tied to the needs of the growth sectors in the two urban economies and the consumption demands generated by those employed in the better paid jobs. In contrast, little investment has gone into construction of nonluxury housing in the past 25 years.

New patterns of industrial organization and location

London and New York, as discussed above, resemble each other in both the economic and political forces affecting them and in the position they occupy within the international economic system. These in turn have shaped spatial form and social structure. To summarize the argument: London and New York have been affected by the internationalization of capital and the rise of new technologies that have caused the outflow of manufacturing from old urban centers to peripheral areas at home and abroad. They have at the same time profited from the increasing importance of financial and coordinating functions, as well as of tourism and cultural production, saving them from the fate of "rust belt" areas with no compensating economic role. Some theorists have asserted that the recent development of the two regions can be understood as resulting from the reconcentration of industry in a new form of agglomeration. Scott (1988, ch. 4) contends that there has been a change in the overall technology of production away from hierarchical to market forms of control. He argues that "the net effect will be an intricate labyrinth of externalized transactions linking different producers, many of whom will coalesce in geographical space to form clusters and subclusters of agglomerated economic activity" (Scott 1988: 54). The tight agglomeration of the old urban core was produced by the need to lower the costs of internal transactions; the looser connectedness of the new urban region, based on modern transportation and communication technologies, results from the same dynamic. Within both the London and New York regions the last decades of the century witnessed a simultaneous densification of the core and a rapid growth of commercial and industrial agglomerations in "edge cities" on the periphery.

Scott's analysis focuses on the needs of manufacturers rather than the financial, business service, and cultural industries that dominate the cores of the New York and London regions. Sassen, like Scott, argues that changing forms of economic control have produced new spatial patterns and applies this logic to the industries that dominate the London and New York core economies, claiming that global cities are sites for production as well as coordination: "They are sites for 1) the production of specialized services needed by complex organizations for running a spatially dispersed network of factories, offices, and service outlets; and 2) the production of financial innovations and the making of markets, both central to the internationalization and expansion of the financial industry" (Sassen 1991: 5).

Both the New York and London regions during the 1980s proved magnets for economic activity that arrayed itself throughout their territories at differing intensities of concentration. The metaphor has been used of milk in a bottle as representing the earlier mode of economic agglomeration and spilled milk, or perhaps more accurately spilled mercury, as denoting the new model. Fishman (1987) coins the term "technoburb" to capture peripheral zones within metropolitan areas that now contain the complete gamut of productive and reproductive functions and goes so far as to claim that these areas operate independently of the core city around which they have developed. To what extent was revival a consequence of global city status?

To put this question more bluntly, does location at the top of the global hierarchy make a metropolis a winner? To assess this question we need to specify more clearly what is meant by "global city status". We can identify six broad changes in the capitalist economic system which are of relevance. These are as follows:

1. The decline in manufacturing and the partial rise of flexible systems of production.
2. The disaggregation of the geography of production which this development, as well as changes in transport and communications, allows.
3. The rise of producer services (i.e. services such as accounting, management consulting, corporate law, etc. that are sold to businesses) highly concentrated in large cities such as London and New York.
4. The growth of international financial systems even more highly concentrated in the three "first division" global cities – London, New York, and Tokyo.
5. The use of public policy to stimulate private investment, especially through the mechanism of public–private partnerships.
6. The growth of more specialized consumer services to meet the needs of the high status, high income workers in the expanding sectors of the economy, plus the growing demand from international tourism.

Each of these changes has had an impact on New York and London but the extent to which they have only or mainly had an impact in these places varies considerably. Thus the decline in manufacturing (or more accurately the decline in the older manufacturing industries) has been felt across the two national economies and territories; likewise the shift to more flexible production systems. It is true that both cities were especially affected by manufacturing decline because they had high concentrations of some of the types of industry which were hardest hit. However, many other urban areas in both countries were completely devastated by deindustrialization. Again, the effects of the decentralizing geography of production have been especially acute in London and New York, but not uncommon elsewhere. To some extent such decentralization can be seen as a consequence of their far from unique status as very large, high-cost urban areas.

The third factor – the high level of producer services associated with the growth in the planning, controlling, and coordinating needs of geographically dispersed production – exceeds that of cities further down the urban hierarchy in each country. However, although the absolute levels of such services and their share of the urban economy in the two global cities are higher than elsewhere, their rate of growth (from smaller bases) is greater outside the urban cores and in some parts of other regions altogether. Moreover, there are some important differences between the two cities: London's economic primacy and other factors have resulted in its retaining a far higher proportion of major national (although probably not international) corporate headquarters than New York and, more generally, having a higher proportion of the nation's producer services than New York.

The fourth development – the growth of financial services – is the one which marks the two cities most strongly as the preeminent global cities (with Tokyo). Together with producer services, financial services are characterized by the importance of intensive linkages for the exchange of nonroutine information. Consequently, there are great economies of agglomeration in these industries, although the decentralization of routinized back office (i.e. routine processing) functions, aided by developments in transport, computing, and communications, is evident in both cities. Within their regions the old central cities still exert an enormous pull on their surrounding areas, and certain industries – entertainment, financial securities, and legal services – have not decentralized significantly. Nevertheless, even though financial and business services continue to show employment growth and the securities and law subsectors have maintained their position, the cities were outpaced by the rest of their countries in the overall category of finance, insurance, and business services (Schwartz 1989; Rosen and Murray 1997; Gordon 1997). Furthermore, the portions of the region outside the old core (that is, London outside the greenbelt and the New York metropolitan area minus New York City) conform to Fishman's (1987: 185) description of areas that "are often in more direct communication with one another – or with other techno-cities [i.e. metropolitan areas] across the country – than they are with the core." The London and New York regions as a whole therefore conform to a spatial patterning that characterizes expanding regions elsewhere and which some theorists envision as ultimately universal (Hall 1988). Their cores, however, maintain a unique importance that no longer pertains to the central business districts of most other metropolitan regions.

The fifth factor, the significant expansion of the role of the state in economic management, is, like some others noted above, not confined to New York and London, or even to other very large cities (see, inter alia, Squires 1989; Harloe et al. 1990). Nor is the history of especially high levels of public expenditure in these particular cities a purely recent development. What is most significant is the recent switch in the balance of growth-stimulating and welfare-providing state activity, away from the latter and towards the former.

The final trend, the expansion of higher order consumer services, is closely linked to the expansion of producer and financial services. Such services have always been concentrated in the two cities and in recent years they have grown rapidly – stimulated by the high concentration of well-paid employees in the expanding producer and financial services and booming international tourism.

There is, therefore, no simple division between these two global cities and other cities. All of the six aspects of global economic restructuring discussed exist elsewhere, although some, most notably the concentration of financial services, are far less significant in other places. What does, however, make the two cities unique (together perhaps with Tokyo, although see Fujita [1991], Machimura [1998], for some important ways in which Tokyo differs from other "world cities") is the scale of the six factors and their combination in a single urban and regional space economy. It is the extent to which both cities have been affected by all six sets of changes – and hence by the interactions between them as well – that really marks them off from other large cities and links their evolving urban and social structures most closely to changes in global economic organization and its consequences.

One of the most important of these interactions flows from the competition for, and the high price of, urban land. While such competition has always existed in these large cities, the growth of producer and financial services and of the high-income segments of the population which they employ, together with the more specialized consumer services which they require, has intensified the process. High land prices have forced other economic activities, less able to meet the high costs of urban location, to decentralize to the periphery of the two regions and beyond at a rapid rate. They have also caused large sections of the population to be priced out of the housing market or to accept higher housing costs, occupy less housing or endure longer commutes to work than in cities where the transition to the new economic regime has been less rapid and on a smaller scale. The loss of skilled manual and supervisory jobs – evident throughout both national economies – has been amplified by the peculiar conditions which apply in the two cities, leading to the development of the polarized distributions of incomes and life chances to which we have already referred. Evidently then, placement at the top of the world urban hierarchy does not necessarily result in a generally better quality of life for the populations of these cities.

The Social Consequences of Economic Change

Some commentators have sought to encapsulate the social structural changes that have occurred in the image of the "dual city" – the suggestion that London and New York each contained, in the same urban and regional space, two increasingly separate economies, inhabiting increasingly segregated neighborhoods and social systems. Features such as the juxtaposition of homogeneously low and high income areas, the occupation of the sidewalks of well-to-do districts by the homeless, and the simultaneous broadening of employment opportunities for some and their foreclosure for others have encouraged the use of this two-city metaphor. The contrast has perhaps been heightened by a rather selective perception of the inhabitants of these two worlds and a narrow geographic focus. From such a viewpoint the observer has seen, on the one hand, the expansive economy, environment and lifestyle of the "new service class" inhabiting a "reconquered," gentrified inner city, and, on the other hand, the misery of those at the margins of the labor market and outside it, living in close spatial proximity to this first group, but a world away in social and economic terms.

The continued existence of what Pahl has termed the "middle mass" of the population, predominately located in the suburbs and towards the periphery of the two city regions, has hardly rated a mention in such scenarios (see, e.g., Sassen 1991). Instead, the concern has been that a process of social and economic polarization is occurring, a shift away from what Pahl (1988) has described as a pyramidal social structure toward an hourglass pattern. In a pyramidal structure, in principle at least, economic and social mobility from the base to the apex is possible. However, in the polarizing cities of London and New York (and elsewhere) such mobility may be increasingly inconceivable for those trapped in marginal jobs or dependent on state benefits – cut off from the new opportunities opening up in the growth sectors of the urban economies.

Detailed studies of the distributional consequences of economic change lead us to a more complex conclusion than is implied by the dual city thesis. Above all, the changes have benefited the financial and producer services industries, associated higher level consumer services and the people who occupy the high-level positions in these parts of the economy. In addition, throughout the 1980s real-estate investors amassed large fortunes, although the slump in real-estate markets that ended the decade in both cities resulted in sudden financial crises and even bankruptcies in this sector. The late 1990s revival of the property markets resurrected the fortunes of development interests in both cities, although not at the level of the more speculative 1980s. For the middle mass, which constitutes a far larger section of the metropolitan population, the outcome is more ambiguous. It has shared a good deal of the prosperity generated by growth. Middle-income households, however, have difficulty in gaining access to desirable housing, and urban public services such as education and transport have deteriorated. Public safety, even in London but especially in New York, became a critical concern during the 1980s, although a sharp drop in New York's crime rate during the nineties has alleviated this problem.

By far the heaviest consequences of economic change have been experienced by those who are outside, on the margins of or at the bottom of the labor market. Of course, growth has resulted in an expansion of low-skilled and low-paid jobs, but in industries with a missing "middle," chances for upward occupational mobility are limited. One consequence of low-income employment, evident in both cities, is the rise in the average number of household members who are in full- or part-time work.

There has been a significant rise in the proportion of the population of both cities which is in poverty, to around a quarter in London and 30 percent in New York in 1997 (Garfinkel and Meyers 1999). The impact of poverty, however, differs within the cities as a consequence of the more extensive availability in London of state-provided services, especially medical care, which is of crucial importance to the working poor. The provision of public housing and rent subsidies on a large scale has been particularly important in London and is quite low by comparison in New York. Recently, however, there has been something of a shift, as in the late 1980s New York City embarked on a program of affordable housing provision, relying on nonprofit community development corporations and tax benefits for private developers to stimulate construction of units at below-market rents. Nevertheless, the city continued to show a net loss in housing units from 1980 to 1995 (Salins 1999: 56). London, in contrast, saw its stock of subsidized housing decrease as a consequence of the Thatcher government's "right to buy" program, allowing the purchase of council (i.e. public) housing by its occupants. New York's suburban ring, like London's, continues to offer little housing opportunity to low-income people. Moreover, changes in UK policies contributed by the late 1980s and through much of the nineties to a marked convergence between the two cities, or rather to a rate of growth in income inequality in London bringing it nearer to New York's pattern of income distribution. There are other, "softer" indicators showing similar types of deprivation in the two cities, notably large-scale begging and homelessness, formerly confined to people with severe social and personal problems, but now experienced by many more, such as the young and unskilled and families with children.

The economies and social structures of both cities are shaped and divided by class, race and gender. The consequential pattern or system of social stratification is highly complex and this complexity seems to increase as one moves down the system. Fairly clearly, the upper levels of the executive and professional strata have grown (Hamnett 1994). Despite gains by women and minorities, upper-level positions are predominantly filled by white males. Racial and gender discrimination – though eroding at the edges – still presents severe barriers to entry by other sectors of the population, even when they have the necessary skills and training.

At lower levels of the employment hierarchy, women and ethnic minorities have taken over many positions. However, the diversity of situations experienced by these subgroups of the population makes any simple and universally applicable description of their circumstances invalid (Mingione 1991). In both cities a combination of skills, predispositions, social networks, and group resources operates to differentially filter distinctive ethnic groups into a variety of employment niches. Outside the labor market different patterns of advantage and disadvantage also exist. For example, Asian homeowners in London derive some benefit from an appreciating housing asset in comparison with those Afro-Caribbeans concentrated in inner city public housing estates (note though the very different circumstances of Afro-Caribbeans in New York who have a high propensity to become home owners in comparison with other ethnic minorities). Public policies also contribute to varying and shifting patterns of disadvantage – for example, cuts in welfare benefits in both cities at differing times adversely affected, in New York, poor households with dependent children and, in London, young adults.

These and other factors should make us pause before accepting any simple notion of the "dual" city or any equally simple association of certain population groups with the lower end of the system of social stratification. Despite this qualification, however, we can identify a close link between economic change and intensified poverty and deprivation, alongside soaring incomes for limited sections of the population and a more ambiguous combination of costs and benefits for many more.

The Future

The recession of the early nineties called into question the permanence of 1980s revival. Subsequent turnaround indicated that the downturn was cyclical rather than structural. Even so, in the case of New York, "the 1990s expansion has been much weaker and less diverse than the expansion the City experienced in the 1980s" (Parrott 1998). In this context a key consideration must be the long-term prospects for further growth in the financial and producer services sectors, together with those other parts of the two urban economies which are essentially dependent on such growth. A second issue is whether financial and producer service growth will continue to center in London and New York.

The first point to note is the significance of changes in the regional space economy of which London and New York form a part. Much of the remaining manufacturing employment is now located in the outer areas of the two regions, beyond their respective city limits. Changes in the organization of production and the other factors which have encouraged decentralization have already resulted in a new form of regional structure, with a development of relatively self-contained agglomerations outside the two core cities. Although these core cities retain a unique importance no longer found in many other metropolitan regions, they nevertheless must rely on a narrower economic base than in the past. New York, which lacks London's governmental dominance, particularly suffers from a high level of specialization. Thus, Wall Street, which represented only 5 percent of city employment, accounted for 56 percent of the increase in aggregate real earnings in New York City between 1992 and 1997 (Office of the State Deputy Comptroller for the City of New York, 1998).

Continued economic restructuring may bring fewer benefits to the core areas of the London and New York regions than in the past. An important issue here concerns the future location of the existing financial and producer services industries and of possible future growth in them. On the one hand, the information-intensive activities have tended to concentrate in central London and New York City. On the other hand, the growth of these industries in the outer parts of the two regions is now far higher than in the cities themselves and there is a convergence in the proportional share of all economic activity taken by these industries in the inner and outer parts of both regions. So the new industries which provided the basis for the revival of London and New York in the 1980s are, like earlier established industries, now decentralizing (Markusen and Gwiasda 1994). Developments in transport, communications, and information technology aid this process and the cost pressures in the urban cores are also significant in bringing about decentralization. Until now, much of this out-migration has involved "back office" functions, leaving those activities which still require the advantages of agglomeration in the CBDs behind. It remains to be seen, however, whether, with further advances in information technology, some of the latter will also eventually decentralize.

If in the next decade the decentralization of the "new core" industries now located in London and New York does accelerate, both cities may enter another period of relative decline. Any further out-migration of population is likely to be selective, given the massive inflation which has occurred in regional house prices, the lack of public or other subsidized accommodation in the metropolitan fringe and beyond and, especially in New York, the discriminatory barriers which still exist to prevent the outmigration of nonwhite ethnic minorities.

The Effect of Globalization

Their positions as global cities have, as we noted earlier, differentiated London and New York from other cities only in certain limited respects. Nevertheless, this status has important consequences for these two cities. The clusters of industries with global ties have characteristics that produce important externalities: they create a stratum of very high earners, whose spending patterns then affect retail and housing markets; they attract a highly specialized labor force with a disproportionate number of very competitive and/or very creative individuals who spin off new businesses and give these cities their idiosyncratic character; they have strong speculative elements which reinforce cyclical tendencies in the economy; they need highly specialized and expensive kinds of working spaces and their demands for space skew property markets.

Global city theorists regard the impact of these externalities as so enormous as to create a qualitatively unique city form. Our position, however, is more moderate. First, changes in family structure common to every city have been profoundly influential at all levels of the social hierarchy. In both cities the poorest households are those that suffer either from labor force exclusion or meager earnings, most frequently as a consequence of having a single, usually female, wage earner. At the same time households with multiple earners do better even when individual wages are low, and when they have two high-wage earners, they move into the top of the income distribution. The situation of these households cannot be attributed to global city status, nor does it differ from that of similar households in other cities. Second, we find that other factors independent of both globalization and of the global sectors are at least as influential in affecting the economic base and social outcomes within our four cities. Thus, the same economic restructuring that has affected all cities in the developed world has been at the root of many of the changes in socioeconomic configurations in these cities. And while global competition, the potential to create globalized production systems, and global linkages have been among the stimuli to economic restructuring within the cities, that process is not simply attributable to globalization. For the middle mass, most of whom have seen some improvement in their status, primary determinants of their situation lie within the national economic and policy system, including the impact of public-sector and, more broadly, social-service employment.

Both cities are alike in containing a very wealthy segment of their nation's population and supporting the economic and cultural institutions that sustain this group. Their economic bases are similar but by no means identical, and the similarities are only partly a consequence of globalization. New York and London, while similar in economic composition differ in social composition, with New York having a far larger immigrant population and London retaining a larger middle- and upper-class population. Both cities have seen increasing income inequality, but polarization is not the most accurate description of this phenomenon in that, as a term, it fails to capture the improving position of a large proportion of the middle mass. In sum, New York and London share many characteristics with each other, but they also resemble other cities that are not homes to the most important financial institutions and multinational headquarters.[1]

NOTE

1. This chapter draws on the findings of a major research project on London and New York, a full account of which will be found in Susan Fainstein, Ian Gordon, and Michael Harloe (eds.) (1992) *Divided Cities: London and New York in the Contemporary World* (Oxford: Blackwell). This research was supported by the UK Economic and Social Research Council and the US Social Science Research Council.

REFERENCES

Barnekov, T., Boyle, R., and Rich, D. 1989: *Privatism and Urban Policy in Britain and the United States*. Oxford: Oxford University Press.

Cambridge Econometrics, 1992: Press release for *January 1992 Regional Economic Forecast*, January 22.

Ehrenreich, B. 1989: *Fear of Falling*. New York: Pantheon.

Fainstein, S. S. 1990: Economics, politics, and development policy: the convergence of New York and London. *International Journal of Urban and Regional Research*, 14 (4), 553–75.

Fishman, R. 1987: *Bourgeois Utopias*. New York: Basic Books.

Friedmann, J. 1986: The world city hypothesis. *Development and Change*, 17, 69–83.

Friedmann, J. and Wolff, G. 1982: World city formation: an agenda for research and action. *International Journal of Urban and Regional Research*, 6 (3), 309–44.

Fujita, K. 1991: A world city and flexible specialisation: restructuring of the Tokyo metropolis. *International Journal of Urban and Regional Research*, 15 (2), 269–84.

Garfinkel, I. and Meyers, M. K. 1999: *New York City Social Indicators 1997: A Tale of Many Cities*. New York: Columbia University School of Social Work, Social Indicators Survey Center.

Gordon, I. 1997: The role of internationalization in economic change in London over the past 25 years. Paper presented at the meeting of the Global Cities Group, New York, March.

Hall, P. 1988: *Cities of Tomorrow*. Oxford: Basil Blackwell.

Hamnett, C. 1994: Social polarisation in global cities: theory and evidence. *Urban Studies*, 31 (3) (April), 401–24.

Harloe, M., Pickvance, C., and Urry, J. (eds.) 1990: *Place, policy and politics: Do Localities Matter?* London: Unwin Hyman.

Lovering, J. 1991: Theorizing postfordism: why contingency matters (a further response to Scott). *International Journal of Urban and Regional Research*, 15 (2), 298–301.

Machimura, T. 1998: Symbolic use of globalization in urban politics in Tokyo. *International Journal of Urban and Regional Research*, 22 (2), 183–94.

Malanga, S. 1991: N. Y. job losses dim hopes for rebound in '92. *Crain's New York Business*, 7 (50), December 9.

Marcuse, P. 1981: The targeted crisis: on the ideology of the urban fiscal crisis and its uses. *International Journal of Urban and Regional Research*, 5 (2), 330–55.

Markusen, A. and Gwiasda, V. 1994: Multipolarity and the layering of functions in the world cities: New York City's struggle to stay on top. *International Journal of Urban and Regional Research*, 18 (2), 167–93.

Mingione, E. 1991: *Fragmented Societies*. Oxford: Basil Blackwell.

Office of the State Deputy Comptroller for the City of New York 1998: *New York City's Economic and Fiscal Dependence on Wall Street*, Report 5–99, August 13.

Pahl, R. E. 1988: Some remarks on informal work, social polarization and the social structure. *International Journal of Urban and Regional Research*, 12 (2), 247–67.

Parrott, J. A. 1998. Cover letter accompanying Office of the State Deputy Comptroller for the City of New York, *New York City's Economic and Fiscal Dependence on Wall Street*, Report 5–99, August 13.
Rosen, R. D. and Murray, R. 1997: Opening doors: access to the global market for financial sectors. In M. E. Crahan and A. Vourvoulias-Bush (eds.), *The City and the World: New York's Global Future*, New York: Council on Foreign Relations, 39–50.
Salins, P. D. 1999: Reviving New York City's housing market. In M. H. Schill (ed.), *Housing and Community Development in New York City: Facing the Future*, Albany, NY: State University of New York Press, 53–72.
Sassen, S. 1991: *The Global City*. Princeton: Princeton University Press.
Savitch, H. 1988: *Post-Industrial Cities*. Princeton: Princeton University Press.
Schwartz, A. 1989: *The Decentralization of Advanced Service Industries in the New York Metropolitan Area*. Ph.D. thesis, Rutgers University, New Brunswick, NJ.
Scott, A. 1988: *Metropolis*. Berkeley: University of California Press.
Sennett, R. 1998: *The Corrosion of Character: The Personal Consequences of Work in the New Capitalism*. New York: Norton.
Squires, G. (ed.) 1989: *Unequal Partnerships*. New Brunswick, NJ: Rutgers University Press.
Uchitelle, L. 1990: New York City is hurt but still has reserves. *New York Times*, November 12.

Chapter 15

Analytic Borderlands: Economy and Culture in the Global City

*Saskia Sassen**

What happens to place in a global economy? And how is globalization inscribed – in the spaces of the economy and of culture, in built form, and generally in space? I want to use these questions to argue that the dominant narrative about economic globalization is a narrative of eviction because its key concepts – globalization, information economy, and telematics – all suggest that place no longer matters. And they suggest that the type of place represented by major cities may have become obsolete from the perspective of the economy, particularly for the leading industries, as these have the best access to, and are the most advanced users of, telematics. It is an account that privileges the capability for global transmission over the concentrations of built infrastructure that makes transmission possible, that privileges information outputs over the work of producing those outputs, from specialists to secretaries, and the new transnational corporate culture over the multiplicity of cultural environments, including reterritorialized immigrant cultures, within which many of the "other" jobs of the global information economy take place.

The overall effect is to lose the place-boundedness of significant components of the global information economy. This loss entails the eviction of a whole array of activities and types of workers from the account about the process of globalization which, I argue, are as much a part of it as is international finance. And evicting these activities and workers excludes the variety of cultural contexts within which they exist, a cultural diversity that is as much a presence in processes of globalization as is the new international corporate culture. The terrain within which the dominant account represents economic globalization captures only a fraction of the actual economic operations involved. It reconstitutes large portions of the city's economy in "cultural" terms – the spaces of the amalgamated other, the "other" as culture. My purpose (Sassen 2000a; 1998) is to reframe the terrain of the economy, incorporating as an integral part the discontinuity between what is represented as economic and what is represented as cultural in the broad sense of the term – the "center" as

* Revised version of the 1992 Distinguished Visitor Lecture, Department of Art History, State University of New York, Binghamton, originally published in King, A. D. (ed.) *Representing the City* (London: Macmillan 1995).

economy and the "other" as culture. In so doing I reconstitute "the" economy as a multiplicity of economies with distinct organizational patterns. It also invites a rereading of the notion of a unitary economic system, a notion central to mainstream economic thought and encapsuled in the notion of "the" economy.

Recovering Place

How do we reintroduce place in economic analysis? And secondly, how do we construct a new narrative about economic globalization, one which includes rather than evicts all the spatial, economic, and cultural elements that are part of the global economy as it is constituted in cities? For me as a political economist, addressing these issues has meant working in several systems of representation and constructing spaces of intersection. There are analytic moments when two systems of representation intersect. Such analytic moments are easily experienced as spaces of silence, of absence. One challenge is to see what happens in those spaces, what operations (analytic, of power, of meaning) take place there.

One version of these spaces of intersection is what I have called analytic borderlands. Why borderlands? Because they are spaces that are constituted in terms of discontinuities; in them discontinuities are given a terrain rather than reduced to a dividing line. Much of my work on economic globalization and cities has focused on these discontinuities and has sought to reconstitute them analytically as borderlands rather than dividing lines. This produces a terrain within which these discontinuities can be reconstituted in terms of economic operations whose properties are not merely a function of the spaces on each side (i.e. a reduction to the condition of dividing line) but also, and most centrally, of the discontinuity itself, the argument being that discontinuities are an integral part, a component, of the economic system.

Methodologically, the construction of these analytic borderlands pivots on what I call circuits for the distribution and installation of economic operations. These circuits allow me to follow economic activities into areas that escape the increasingly narrow borders of mainstream representations of "the" economy and to negotiate the crossing of discontinuous spaces. Further, these circuits give us one possible representation of the materialization of global economic activity in a place.

These are the instruments through which I want to reread the city's economy in a way that recovers organizational, spatial, and cultural dimensions that are now lost in the dominant representation of that economy. I do this in three sections. The first is a brief discussion as to why cities are useful arenas within which to explore the limitations of this mainstream narrative. Secondly, I explain why crucial aspects of the most advanced sectors of the economy are place-bound, a fact disregarded in the mainstream account of the information economy, and especially its global dimension. Why does this matter? Because recovering place in the analyses of the economy, particularly place as constituted in major cities, allows us to see the multiplicity of economies and work cultures in which the global information economy is embedded. It also allows us to recover the concrete, localized processes through which globalization exists and to argue that much of the multiculturalism in large cities is as much a part of globalization as is international finance. The third section examines how space is inscribed in the urban economy, and particularly how the spaces of corporate culture, which are a representation of the space of power in today's cities, are actually contested spaces. The overall purpose is to bring these various elements together in an effort to move from an economic narrative of eviction to one of inclusion.

Why Focus on Cities in This Inquiry?

These questions can be usefully explored in large cities such as New York and Los Angeles, Paris and Amsterdam, or many other major Western European cities, for at least two reasons. First, cities are the sites for concrete operations of the economy. For now we can distinguish two forms of this. One is about economic globalization and place. Cities are strategic places which concentrate command functions, global markets, and, I add, production sites for the new, advanced information industries. The other form through which this concreteness can be captured is by an examination of the day-to-day work in the leading economic complex, finance and specialized services. Such an examination makes it clear that a large share of the jobs involved in finance, for example, are lowly paid clerical and manual jobs, many held by women and migrants. These types of workers and jobs do not fit the dominant representation of what the premier economic complex of our era is about.

Secondly, the city concentrates diversity. Its spaces are inscribed with the dominant corporate culture but also with multiple other cultures and identities. The slippage is evident: the dominant culture can encompass only part of the city. And while corporate power inscribes noncorporate cultures and identities with "otherness," thereby devaluing them, these are present everywhere. This presence is especially strong in our major Western cities which also have the largest concentrations of corporate power. We see here an interesting correspondence between great concentrations of corporate power and large concentrations of "others." It invites us to see that globalization is not only constituted in terms of capital and the new international corporate culture (international finance, telecommunications, information flows) but also in terms of people and noncorporate cultures. There is a whole infrastructure of low-wage, nonprofessional jobs and activities that constitute a crucial part of the so-called corporate economy.

I now want to move to a rather straightforward account of the distinct ways in which place, and particularly the type of place represented by large cities, matters in today's global economy.

Place in the Global Economy

We can begin this inquiry by asking whether an economic system characterized by pronounced concentration of ownership and control can have a space economy that lacks points of intense agglomeration. Elsewhere (2000a) I have argued at great length that the territorial dispersal of economic activity made possible by global telecommunications creates a need for expanded central control functions – if this dispersal is to occur under conditions of continued economic concentration. Globalization has engendered a new logic for agglomeration, a new spatial dynamic between dispersal and centralization. The neutralization of distance through telematics has as its correlate a new type of central place.

One way of capturing this is through the image of cities as *command centers* in a global economic system. The notion of command centers is actually one that lacks much content. In the specialized literature it is usually thought of in terms of the power and global reach of large corporations. I have sought to give it content, to capture the "production" of global command functions, the work of global control and management. Focusing on production rather than simply on the awesome power of large corporations and banks brings into view the wide array of economic activities, many outside the corporation, necessary to produce and reproduce that power. An exclusive focus on the power of corporations and banks would leave out a number of issues concerning the social, economic, and spatial impacts of these activities on the cities where they are located.

The domestic and international dispersal of loci of growth and the internationalization of finance bring to the fore questions concerning the incorporation of such growth into the profit-generating processes that contribute to economic concentration. That is to say, while in principle the territorial decentralization of economic activity could have been accompanied by a corresponding decentralization in ownership and hence in the appropriation of profits, there has been little movement in that direction. Though large firms have increased their subcontracting to smaller firms and many national firms in the newly industrializing countries have grown rapidly, this form of growth is ultimately part of a chain in which a limited number of corporations continue to control the end product and to reap the profits associated with selling on the world market. Even industrial homeworkers in remote rural areas are now part of that chain.

This is not only evident with firms, it is also evident with places. Thus, the internationalization and expansion of finance has brought growth to a large number of smaller financial markets, a growth which has fed the expansion of the global industry. But top-level control and management of the industry have become concentrated in a few leading financial centers, especially New York, London, Tokyo, Frankfurt, Paris, and other such cities. These account for a disproportionate share of all financial transactions and one that has grown rapidly since the early 1980s.

The fundamental dynamic posited here is that the more globalized the economy becomes the higher the agglomeration of central functions in global cities. The extremely high densities evident in the downtown districts of these cities are the spatial expression of this logic. The widely accepted notion that agglomeration has become obsolete when global telecommunication advances should allow for maximum dispersal, is only partly correct. It is, I argue, precisely the opposite in some of the leading sectors: because of the territorial dispersal facilitated by telecommunication advances, agglomeration of centralizing activities has expanded immensely. This is not a mere continuation of old patterns of agglomeration but, one could posit, a new logic for agglomeration.

Information technologies are yet another factor contributing to the new logic for agglomeration. These technologies make possible the geographic dispersal *and* simultaneous integration of many activities. But the distinct conditions under which such facilities are available have promoted centralization of the most skilled users in the most advanced telecommunications centers. Even though a few newer urban centers have built complex telecommunications facilities, entry costs are increasingly high, and there is a tendency for telecommunications to be developed in conjunction with major users, which are typically firms with large national and global markets (Castells 1989; Graham 2000). Indeed there is a close relationship between the growth of international markets for finance and trade, the tendency for major firms to concentrate in major cities, and the development of telecommunications infrastructures in such cities. Firms with global markets or global production processes require advanced telecommunications facilities. And the acceleration of the financial markets and their internationalization make access to advanced telecommunications facilities essential. The main demand for telecommunication services comes from information-intensive industries which, in turn, tend to locate in major cities which have such facilities.

Besides being command points, I see two additional ways in which major cities are strategic places in the global economy. One is as production sites for finance and specialized services, and the other as transnational marketplaces for these products.

Production sites

Centralized control and management over a geographically dispersed array of plants, offices, and service outlets does not come about inevitably as part of a "world system." It requires the development of a vast range of highly specialized services and of top-level management and control functions. These constitute the components for "global control capability" (Sassen 2000a).

By focusing on the production of this capability, I am seeking to displace the focus of attention from the familiar issue of the power of large corporations over governments and economies; or the issue of supracorporate concentration of power through interlocking directorates or organizations such as the IMF. I want to focus on an aspect that has received less attention, what could be referred to as the *practice* of global control: the work of producing and reproducing the organization and management of a global production system and a global marketplace for finance, both under conditions of economic concentration. This allows me to focus on the infrastructure of jobs involved in this production. Furthermore, while it is typical to think of finance and specialized services as a matter of expertise rather than production, the elaboration of, for example, a financial instrument requires inputs from law, accounting, advertising. There is a production complex in the advanced service economy that benefits from agglomeration. In addition, the actual production process includes a variety of workers and firms that are not usually thought of as being part of the information economy.

The growth of advanced services for firms along with their particular characteristics of production helps to explain the centralization of management and servicing functions that fueled the economic boom of the 1980s in cities such as New York, London, Tokyo, Amsterdam, Toronto, and so on. The face-to-face explanation needs to be refined in several ways. Advanced services are mostly services for firms; unlike other types of services, they are not dependent on vicinity to the consumers served. Rather, economies occur in such specialized firms when they locate close to others that produce key inputs or whose proximity makes possible joint production of certain service offerings. Moreover, concentration arises out of the needs and expectations of the people likely to be employed in these new high-skill jobs. They are attracted to the amenities and lifestyles that large urban centers can offer. The accounting firm can service its clients at a distance, but the production of its service benefits from proximity to specialists of various kinds, lawyers, financial experts, programers. In this sense then, one can speak of *production sites*.

Transnational marketplaces

Globalization does not *only* consist of instantaneous transmission around the globe; much of it takes place in markets and a key part of even the most digitalized market is likely to be located in a particular place. Cities are the location for many of the transactions in global markets for finance and specialized services. These are markets where firms, governments, and individuals from all around the world can engage in transactions that often bypass the "host" country.

Multisite forms of organization in manufacturing, services, and banking have created an expanded demand for a wide range of specialized service activities to manage and control global networks of factories, service outlets, and branch offices. While to some extent these activities can be carried out in-house, a large share is not. High levels of specialization, the possibility of externalizing the production of some of these services, and the growing demand by large and small firms and by governments, are all conditions that have both resulted from, and made possible, the development of a market for freestanding service firms that produce components for "global control capability." This in turn means that not only large but also small firms can buy components of that capability, such as management consulting or international legal advice. And so can firms and governments from anywhere in the world. In brief, while the large corporation is undoubtedly a key agent inducing the development of this capability and is its prime beneficiary, it is not the sole user.

In brief, this focus on the *work* behind command functions, on *production* in the finance and services complex, and on market*places* has the effect of incorporating the material facilities underlying globalization and the whole infrastructure of jobs typically not marked as belonging to the corporate sector of the economy: besides the already mentioned work of secretaries and cleaners, there are the truckers who deliver the software, the variety of technicians, and repair workers, all the jobs having to do with the maintenance, painting, renovation of the buildings where it all is housed.

This can lead to the recognition that there are multiple economies involved in constituting the global information economy. It allows for a valorization of types of activities, workers, and firms that have never been installed in the "center" of the economy or have been evicted from that center in the restructuring of the 1980s and have therefore been devalorized in a system that overvalorizes the "center." Globalization can, then, be seen as a process that involves several economies and work cultures. Yet it is in terms of the corporate economy and the new transnational corporate culture that economic globalization is represented. How can we expand the terrain for this representation to incorporate these conditions? And how can we make a new reading of the locations where corporate power is now installed, a reading that captures the noncorporate presences in those same sites?

Globalization and Inscription

Once we have recovered the centrality of place and of the multiple work cultures within which economic operations are embedded, we are still left confronting a highly restricted terrain for the inscription of economic globalization. Sennett (1992: 36) observes that "the space of authority in Western culture has evolved as a space of precision." And Giddens notes the centrality of "expertise" in today's society, with the corresponding transfer of authority and trust to expert systems (Giddens 1991: 88–91). Corporate culture is one representation of precision and expertise. Its space has become one of the main spaces of authority in today's cities. The dense concentrations of tall buildings in major downtowns or in the new "edge" cities are the site for corporate culture – though as I will argue later they are also the site for other forms of inhabitation, but these have been made invisible. The vertical grid of the corporate tower is imbued with the same neutrality and rationality attributed to the horizontal grid of American cities. Much has been said about the Protestant ethic as the culture through which the economic operations of capitalism are constituted in the daily life of people. Sennett (1992: 46–62) opens up a whole new dimension both on the Protestant ethic and on the American city by suggesting that what is experienced as a form of rational urban organization, the grid, is actually a far more charged event. It is the representation in urban design of a Protestant language of self and space becoming a modern form of power (Sennett 1992: 55).

We can recognize that the neutralization of place brought about by the modern grid contains an aspiration to a modern space of precision. This same aspiration is evident in the self-inscription of corporate business culture as neutral, as ordered by technology, economic efficiency, rationality. This is put in contrast to what is thought of as the culture of small businesses, or, even more so, ethnic enterprises. Each of these is a partial representation, in one case of the city, in the other of the economy.

The dominant narrative presents the economy as ordered by technical and efficiency principles, and in that sense as neutral. The emergence and consolidation of corporate power appears, then, as an inevitable form that economic growth takes under these ordering principles. The impressive engineering and architectural output evident in the tall corporate towers that dominate our downtowns are a physical embodiment of these principles. And the corporate culture that inhabits these towers and inscribes them is the organizational and behavioral correlate to these ordering principles. Authority is thereby "divorced from community" (Sennett 1991: 37). "The visual forms of legibility in urban designs or space no longer suggest much about subjective life..." (1992: 37).

We can easily recognize that both the neutralization of place through the grid in its aspiration to a modern space of precision, *and* the self-inscription of corporate culture as neutral, as ordered by technology and efficiency, are partial representations of the city and of the economy. This inscription needs to be produced and reproduced, and it can never be complete because of all the other presences in the city which are inscribed in urban space. The *representation* of the city contained in the dominant economic narrative can exclude large portions of the lived city and reconstitute them as some amalgamated "other." The lived city contains multiple spatialities and identities, many indeed articulated and very much a part of the economy, but represented as superfluous, anachronistic, or marginal. Through immigration, for instance, a proliferation of, in their origin, highly localized cultures have now become presences in many large cities, cities whose elites think of themselves as cosmopolitan, that is, transcending any locality. An immense array of cultures from around the world, each rooted in a particular country or village, are now reterritorialized in a few single places, places such as New York, Los Angeles,

Paris, London, and most recently Tokyo. Re-territorialized "cultures" are not the same as cosmopolitanism (Sassen 1998: chapter one). Subjective life is installed in a multiplicity of subjectivities, and this undermines the representation of the advanced modern economy as a space of neutrality, the neutrality that comes from technology and efficiency, the ordering principles of a modern economy.

The space of the amalgamated other is constituted as a devalued, downgraded space in the dominant economic narrative: social and physical decay, a burden. In today's New York or Los Angeles, this is the space of the immigrant community, of the black ghetto, and increasingly of the old manufacturing district. In its most extreme version it is the space of the "underclass, full of welfare mothers and drug addicts."

Corporate culture collapses differences, some minute, some sharp, among the different sociocultural contexts into one amorphous otherness, an otherness that has no place in the economy, that holds the low-wage jobs that are, supposedly, only marginally attached to the economy. It therewith reproduces the devaluing of those jobs and of those who hold the jobs. By leaving out these articulations, by restricting the referent to the centrally placed sectors of the economy, the dominant economic narrative can present the economy as containing a higher-order unity. The corporate economy evicts these other economies and its workers from economic representation, and the corporate culture represents them as the other. What is not installed in a corporate center is devalued or will tend to be devalued. And what occupies the corporate building in noncorporate ways is made invisible. The fact that most of the people working in the corporate city during the day are low-paid secretaries, mostly women, many immigrant or, in US cities, African-American women, is not included in the representation of the corporate economy or corporate culture. And the fact that at night a whole other workforce installs itself in these spaces, including the offices of the chief executives, and inscribes the space with a whole different culture (manual labor, often music, lunchbreaks at midnight) is an invisible event.

In this sense, corporate architecture assumes a whole new meaning beyond the question of the economy of offices and real-estate development. The built forms of the corporate economy are representative of its "neutrality" – of being driven by technology and efficiency. Corporate architectural spatiality is one specific form assumed by the circulation of power in the economy, and specifically in the corporate economy. Wigley (1992: 327) notes that the house is not innocent of the violence inside it. And we now have an excellent literature showing how the design of different types of buildings – homes, factories, "public" lobbies – is shaped not only by cultural values and social norms, but also by matters of power in its many instantiations.

The supposedly "rational" organization of office space illustrates certain aspects of Foucault's microtechnologies of power (Rakatansky 1992). But the changes in the details of inhabitation – institutional practices, the types and contents of buildings – indicate there is no univocal relation between these and built form. I agree with Rakatansky's observation that the play of ideologies in architectural form is complex. And I would add that this conception is essential if we are to allow for politics and agency in the built environment. Yes, in some sense, buildings are frozen in time. But they can be reinscribed. The only way we can think of these towers now is as corporate, *if* located downtown (and as failed public housing project if they are in poor ghettos). Can we reinscribe these corporate towers in ways that recover the fact that they are also the workplace of a large noncorporate workforce?

Another dimension along which to explore some of these issues is the question of the body. The body is citified, urbanized as a distinctively metropolitan body (Grosz 1992: 241). The particular geographical, architectural, municipal arrangements constituting a city are particular ingredients in the social constitution of the body; Grosz adds that they are by no means the most important ones. She argues that the structure and particularity of the family and neighborhoods are more influential, though the structure of the city is also contained therein. "The city orients perception insofar as it helps to produce specific conceptions of spatiality" (1992: 250). The city contributes to the organization of family life, of worklife insofar as it contains a distribution in space of the specific locations for each activity; similarly, architectural spatiality can be seen as one particular component in this broader process of the organization of space. I would add to this that the structure, spatiality, and concrete localization of the economy are also influential. In these many ways the city is an active force that "leaves its traces on the subject's corporeality."

But it is citified in diverse ways: it is inscribed by the many sociocultural environments present in the city and it, in turn, inscribes these. There are two forms in which this weaves itself into the space of the economy. One is that these diverse ways in which the body is inscribed by the diverse sociocultural contexts that exist in the city works as a mechanism for segmenting and, in the end, for devaluing, and it does so in very concrete ways. For example, research by the anthropologist Philippe Bourgeois (1996) shows us the case of an 18-year-old Puerto Rican from East Harlem who gets a job as a clerical attendant in an office in downtown Manhattan. He tells us that walking over to the copying machine, past all the secretaries, is humiliating. The way he walks, the way he is dressed, the way he moves present him to the office staff secretaries and managers as someone from the ghetto. Someone who "doesn't know the proper ways."

The other way in which this diversity weaves itself into the space of the economy is that it reenters the space of the dominant economic sector as merchandise and as marketing. Of interest here is Stuart Hall's observation that contemporary global culture is different from earlier imperial cultures: it is absorptive, a continuously changing terrain that incorporates the new cultural elements whenever it can. In the earlier period, Hall (1991) argues, the culture of the empire, epitomized by Englishness, was exclusionary, seeking always to reproduce its difference. At the same time today's global culture cannot absorb everything, it is always a terrain for contestation, and its edges are certainly always in flux. The process of absorption can never be complete.

One question is whether the argument developed earlier regarding the neutralization of space brought about by the grid, and the system of values it entails or seeks to produce in space, also occurs with cultural globalization. As with the grid, "global" culture never fully succeeds in this neutralization; yet absorption does alter the "other" that is absorbed. An interesting issue here that emerges out of my work on the urban economy is whether at some point all the "others" (at its most extreme, the informal economy) carry enough weight to transform the center. In the case of culture one can see that the absorption of multiple cultural elements, along with the cultural politics so evident in large cities, have transformed global culture. Yet it is still centered in the West, its technologies, its images, as Hall argues. Thus absorbed the other cultures are neutralized. And yet . . . they are also present. We can perhaps see this most clearly in urban space, where multiple other work cultures, cultural environments, and culturally inscribed bodies increasingly inhabit a built environment that has its origins visibly in the corporate culture lying behind the grid. Here again, I ask, at what point does the "curve effect," as social scientists would put it, take hold and bring the center down.

In conclusion, we cannot restrict our account of the global information economy to global *transmissions* and information *outputs*. Likewise, we cannot restrict our representations of economic globalization to the new transnational corporate culture and the corporate towers it inhabits. Globalization is a contradictory space; it is characterized by contestation, internal differentiation, continuous border crossings. The global city is emblematic of this condition. In seeking to show that (a) these types of cities are strategic to economic globalization because they are command points, global marketplaces, and production sites for the information economy, and (b) that many of the devalued sectors of the urban economy actually fulfill crucial functions for the center, I try to recover the importance of cities precisely in a globalized economic system and thereby to make a countervailing argument. It is all the intermediary sectors of the economy (such as routine office work, headquarters that are not geared to the world markets; the variety of services demanded by the largely suburbanized middle class) and of the urban population (i.e. the middle class) that can leave and have left cities. The two sectors that have remained, the center and the "other" find in the city the strategic terrain for their operations.

SELECT BIBLIOGRAPHY

Abu-Lughod, J. 1995: Comparing Chicago, New York and Los Angeles: testing some world cities hypotheses. In P. Knox and P. Taylor (eds.), *World Cities in a World-System*. Cambridge, UK: Cambridge University Press, 171–91.

Allison, E. 1996: Historic Preservation in a development-dominated city: the passage of New York City's landmark preservation legislation. *Journal of Urban History*, 22, 350–76.

Allen, John, Massey, Doreen, and Pryke, Michael (eds.) 1999: *Unsettling Cities*. London: Routledge.

Amin, Ash (ed.) 1997: *Post-Fordism*. Oxford: Blackwell.

Appadurai, Arjun 1996: *Modernity at Large*. Minneapolis: University of Minnesota Press.

Ascher, F. 1995: *Metapolis ou L'Avenir des Villes*. Paris: Editions Odile Jacob.

Berner, E. and Rudiger K. 1995: Globalization and local resistance: the creation of localities in Manila and Bangkok. *International Journal of Urban and Regional Research*, 19, 208–22.

Body-Gendrot, S. 2000: *The Social Control of Cities? A comparative perspective*. Oxford: Blackwell.

Bonilla, Frank, Melendez, Edwin, Morales, Rebecca, and de los Angeles Torres, Maria (eds.) 1998: *Borderless Borders*. Philadelphia: Temple University Press.

Bourgeois, P. 1996: *In Search of Respect: Selling Crack in El Barrio*. Structural Analysis in the Social Sciences Series. New York: Cambridge University Press.

Copjec, Joan, and Sorkin, Michael (eds.) 1999: *Giving Ground*. London: Verso.

Corbridge, Stuart, Martin, Ron, and Thrift, Nigel (eds.) 1994: *Money Power and Space*. Oxford: Blackwell.

Castells, M. 1989: *The Informational City*. Oxford: Blackwell.

Cybriwsky, R. 1991: *Tokyo: The Changing Profile of an Urban Giant*. World Cities Series, eds. R. J. Johnson and P. L. Knox. London: Belhaven.

Davison, C. (ed.) 1996: *Anywise*. Cambridge, MA: MIT Press and Anyone Corporation (New York).

Dunn, S. (ed.) 1994: *Managing Divided Cities*. Keele, UK: Keele University Press.

Feldbauer, P., Piltz, E., Runzler, D., and Stacher, I. (eds.) 1993: *Megastädte: Zur Rolle von Metropolen in der Weltgesellschaft*. Vienna: Böhlau Verlag.

Friedmann, J. 1995: Where we stand: A decade of world city research. In Knox and Taylor (eds.), 21–47.

Frost, M. and Spence, N. 1992: Global city characteristics and Central London's employment. *Urban Studies*, 30 (3), 547–58.

Fuchs, G., Moltmann, B., and Prigge, W. (eds.) 1995: *Mythos Metropole*. Frankfurt: Suhrkamp.

Futur Anterieur 1995: Special issue, *La Ville-Monde Aujourd'hui: Entre Virtualité et Ancrage*, ed. by T. Pillon and A. Querrien, vols. 30–2. Paris: L'Harmattan.

Giddens, A. 1991: *The Consequences of Modernity*. Oxford, UK: Polity.

Graham, S. 2000. "On Global Cities, Telecommunications and Planetary Urban Networks." In Sassen (ed.) *Cities and their Cross-Border Networks* Tokyo: United Nations University Press.

Gravesteijn, S. G. E., van Griensven, S., and de Smidt, M. C. (eds.) 1998: Timing global cities. *Nederlandse Geografische Studies*, 241.

Grosz, E. 1992: Bodies-Cities. In B. Colomina (ed.), *Sexuality and Space*, Princeton Papers on Architecture. Princeton, NJ: Princeton Architectural Press, 241–53.

Hall, Rodney Bruce 1999: *National Collective Identity*. New York: Columbia University Press.

Hall, S. 1991: The local and the global: globalization and ethnicity. In A. King (ed.), *Current Debates in Art History 3. Culture, Globalization and the World-System: Contemporary Conditions for the Representation of Identity*, Department of Art and Art History, State University of New York at Binghamton.

Harvey, D. 1985: *The Urbanization of Capital*. Oxford: Blackwell.

Heisler, B. 1991: A comparative perspective on the underclass: Questions of urban poverty, race, and citizenship. *Theory and Society*, 20, 455–83.

Hiss, Tony 1991: *The Experience of Place*. New York: Alfred A. Knopf.

Hitz, Keil, Lehrer, Ronneberger, Schmid, and Wolff (eds.) 1995: *Capitales Fatales*. Zürich: Rotpunkt Verlag.

Holston, J. (ed.) 1996: Cities and citizenship. Special issue, *Public Culture*, 8 (2).

Indiana Journal of Global Legal Studies 1996: Special Issue: Feminism and globalization: the impact of the global economy on women and feminist theory, 4 (1) (fall).

Journal of Urban Technology 1995: Special issue, *Information Technologies and Inner-City Communities*, 3 (19), fall.

Judd, Dennis and Fainstein, S. 1999. *The Tourist City*. New Haven, CT: Yale University Press.

Karatani, Kojin 1995: *Architecture as Metaphor*. Boston: MIT Press.

Katznelson, I. 1992: *Marxism and the City*. Oxford: Clarendon.

King, A. D. (ed.) 1995: *Representing the City: Ethnicity, Capital and Culture in the 21st Century*. London: Macmillan.

Klopp, Brett 1998: Integration and political representation in a multicultural city: the case of Frankfurt am Main. *German Politics and Society*, 49, 16 (4) (winter), 42–68.

Klosterman, R. 1996: Double Dutch: polarization trends in Amsterdam and Rotterdam after 1980. *Regional Studies*, 30, 5: 467–76.

Knox, P. and Taylor, P. (eds.) 1995: *World Cities in a World-System*. Cambridge, UK: Cambridge University Press.

Landrieu, Josee, May, Nicole, Par, Dirige, Spector, Therese, and Veltz, Pierre (eds.) 1998: *La Ville Eclatee*. La Tour d'Aigues: Editions de l'Aube.

Le Debat: 1994 Special issue, Le Nouveau Paris. summer 1994.

LeGates, R. and Stout, F. (eds.) 1996: *The City Reader.* London and New York: Routledge.

McDowell, Linda 1997: *Capital Culture*. Oxford: Blackwell.

Meyer, D. 2000. "Hong Kong: the role of business intermediaries. In Sassen (ed.) *Cities and their Cross-Border Networks*. Tokyo: United Nations University Press.

Mittelman, J. (ed.) 1996: Globalization: Critical Reflections. International Political Economy Yearbook, vol. 9, Boulder, CO: Lynne Rienner Publishers.

Palumbo-Liu, David 1999: *Asian/American*. Stanford: Stanford University Press.

Peraldi, M. and Perrin, E. (eds.) 1996: *Reseaux Productifs et Territoires Urbains*. Toulouse: Presses Universitaires du Mirail.

Petz, U. von and Schmals, K. (eds.) 1992: *Metropole, Weltstadt, Global City: Neue Formen der Urbanisierung*. Dortmund: Dortmunder Beitrage zur Raumplanung, vol. 60, Universität Dortmund.

Pryke, M. 1991: An international city going global: spatial change in the City of London. *Environment and Planning D: Society and Space*, 9, 197–222.

Rakatansky, M. 1992: Spatial narratives. In J. Whiteman, J. Kipnis, and R. Burdett (eds.), *Strategies in Architectural Thinking*, Chicago: Chicago Institute for Architecture and Urbanism, and Cambridge, MA: MIT Press, 198–221.

Roberts, B. 1995: *The Making of Citizens: Cities of Peasants Revisited*. New York: Arnold.

Rotzer, F. 1995: *Die Telepolis: Urbanität im digitalen Zeitalter.* Mannheim: Bollmann.

Roulleau-Berger, Laurence 1999: *Le Travail En Friche*. La Tour d'Aigues: Editions de l'Aube.

Sachar, A. 1990: The global economy and world cities. In A. Sachar and S. Oberg (eds.) *The World Economy and the Spatial Organization of Power,* Aldershot: Avebury, 149–60.

Salzinger, L. 1995: A maid by any other name: the transformation of "dirty work" by Central American immigrants. In M. Burawoy et al., *Ethnography Unbound: Power and Resistance in the Modern Metropolis*, Berkeley: University of California Press, 139–60.

Sandercock, L. and Forsyth, A. 1992. A gender agenda: new directions for planning theory. *APA Journal*, 58, 49–59.

Santos, M. 1993: *A Urbanizacao Brasileira*. São Paulo: Hucitec.

Sassen, S. 2000a: *The Global City: New York, London, Tokyo*. Princeton NJ: Princeton University Press. (New Updated Edition).

Sassen, S. 2000b (ed.) *Cities and their Cross-Border Networks*. Tokyo: United Nations University Press.

Sassen, S. 1998: *Globalization and its Discontents*. New York: New Press.

Sennett, R. 1992: *The Conscience of the Eye: The Design and Social Life of Cities*. New York: Norton.

Smith, D., Solinger, D., and Topik, S. (eds.) 1999: *States and Sovereignty in the Global Economy,* London: Routledge.

Social Justice 1993: Special issue, *Global Crisis, Local Struggles*, 20 (3–4), (fall–winter).

Souza, M. de 1994: *A Identidade da Metropole. A Verticalizacao em São Paulo*. São Paulo: Hucitec.

Stren, R. 1996: The studies of cities: popular perceptions, academic disciplines, and emerging agendas. In M. Cohen, B. Ruble, J. Tulchin, and A. Garland (eds.) 1996: *Preparing for the Urban Future: Global Pressures and Local Forces*, Washington DC: Woodrow Wilson Center Press (distributed by The Johns Hopkins University Press), 392–420.

Taylor, P. 1995: World cities and territorial states: the rise and fall of their mutuality. In Knox and Taylor (eds.), 48–62.

Taylor P. 2000: "World Cities: A First Multivariate Analysis of their Service Complexes." In Sassen (ed.) *Cities and their Cross-Border Networks*.

Todd, G. 1995: "Going Global' in the semi-periphery: world cities as political projects. The case of Toronto. In Knox and Taylor (eds.), 192–214.

Torres, Rodolfo D., Inda, Jonathan Xavier, and Miron, Louis F. 1999: *Race, Identity, and Citizenship*. Oxford: Blackwell.

Toulouse, C. 1993: Politics, planning, and class: the sociology of inner city development in London and New York 1977–1992. Unpublished Ph.D. dissertation, Columbia University.

Veltz, Pierre 1996: *Mondialisation Villes Et Territoires*. Paris: Presses Universitaires De France.

Vergara, C. 1995: *The New American Ghetto*. A Traveling Exhibition Produced by the New York State Museum. Albany: New York State Museum.

Wissenschaft Forum 1995: Special issue, *Global City: Zitadellen der Internationalisierung*. 12 (2).

Wigley, M. 1992: Untitled: the housing of gender. In B. Colomina (ed.), *Sexuality and Space*, Princeton Papers on Architecture. Princeton, NJ: Princeton Architectural Press, 327–90.

Wright, Talmadge 1997: *Out of Place*. Albany: State University of New York Press.

Yeung, Y. (ed.) 1996: *Global Change and the Commonwealth*. Hong Kong: Institute of Asia-Pacific Studies, The Chinese University of Hong Kong.

Chapter 16

Turbulence and Sedimentation in the Labor Markets of Late Twentieth-Century Metropoles[1]

Nick Buck and Ian Gordon

Introduction

The economy and labor market of metropoles such as London, Paris, or New York, at the close of the nineteenth century had a number of characteristics with renewed resonance a hundred years later. In London's case these included a dependence on workshops and service establishments catering for elite consumer markets, and industries linked to an unstable global economy, accompanied by a substantial casual labor market which (now) seems to have been a major contributor to concentrated deprivation and an apparent absence of "social cohesion" in the inner East End. At the time, however, an influential body of opinion attributed the problems to other processes within the city, which over a period of years demoralized initially employable and responsible (rural) migrants to the city, and concentrated a social "residuum" in its inner areas (Stedman Jones 1971). In New York, with a similarly structured economy and comparable social concerns, an additional factor was the rapid influx of (particularly Jewish and southern Italian) migrants into ethnically segmented labor markets (Buck and Fainstein 1992). And in Paris too, though craftworkers exercised more power than elsewhere, this was largely irrelevant to the masses of provincial immigrants for whom the reality was one of competitive individualism in a labor market characterized by small firms and great seasonal instability in employment (Harvey 1985).

For much of this century things have been very different in such cities. In London, for example, much larger, nationally orientated employers emerged, as market orientation and mass production came to the fore in manufacturing (Hall 1962), service functions were increasingly bureaucratized, and the tide of internationalization was reversed (Hirst and Thompson 1996). Thus, particularly in the middle decades, from the 1920s to the 1960s, London appeared simply as the dominant industrial centre, at the heart of its most prosperous region, enjoying relatively low levels of both unemployment and social disorder. In New York an additional stabilizing factor over this time was the halt to large-scale immigration. Since then the tide has turned again, with a particularly early and rapid onset of deindustrialization in London, the continuing dispersal of routinizable jobs as employers (both public and private) pursue spatial and/or organizational divisions of labor, and (especially in New York) a renewed influx of labor from low-wage economies. Unlike other cities exposed to such radical shifts in their economic position, for the metropoles this has meant not simple loss, but a switch back to other sources of competitive advantage. In particular, increased emphases on international linkages, flexibility, marketed expertise, novelty, money, and cultural products all play to their comparative strengths. But the benefits of success in these terms have been very unequally distributed and, in the London case, a sharp deterioration in unemployment levels (relative to the rest of the country as well as the experience of earlier decades) appears as the central factor in growing social exclusion, and is a credible threat to social cohesion in the city (Buck 1997).

Within the context of their national urban systems, these leading centers can seem quite unique, even idiosyncratic, both in their economic history and in the current tension between economic success and social failure. Clearly their experience has been very different from that of cities in the old industrial regions, but these are themselves becoming less and less typical of the cities of advanced (post)industrial societies. Whether or not the experience of the metropoles now has relevance to a much wider set of cities is a matter basically of the weight placed on analyses emphasizing their peculiar role within an emergent global economy (Sassen 1991), as against those focusing simply on agglomeration as an intensifier of pervasive trends toward deregulated and more flexible economic relations in an increasingly competitive world. Though the empirical focus of this paper is on one of the "global cities," namely London, the features which emerge as crucial to labor market developments are essentially those of agglomeration, and of much more general relevance.

In terms of labor market effects, the (exceptionalist) "global city" interpretation focuses largely on an hypothesized polarization of demand growth in these cities (since the early 1980s), on advanced international services *and* low-level local service functions – squeezing out those functions which previously offered both accessible *and* worthwhile jobs.[2] Difficulties with fitting this model to the London case include a lack of actual growth in low-wage services (at least prior to the late 1990s), limited absolute growth in globally oriented services, and a pattern of structural change with considerable continuity over the past 40 years. In fact, a structural shift away from routinizable jobs also figures within the "simple agglomeration" account, as an expected feature of *all* high order centers (not just those with an international orientation). But this account also emphasizes ways in which agglomeration affects labor market processes, particularly in relation to the risks of unemployment. Even in the London case, we shall argue that these labor market processes are more important contributors to social divisions than headlined "global city" developments.

The pure agglomeration effect on labor market processes is to reduce the risks of labor market flexibility, since new jobs and workers are easier to find when required in the external labor market, encouraging higher turnover rates, both directly and also through "natural selection" of firms and workers needing or wanting such flexibility (Gordon 1988; Scott 1988). This can be one of the major competitive advantages of the metropoles, but there may be important side effects, both in terms of underinvestment in skills by free-riding firms, and of unforeseen risks falling on individuals with little organizational support. Two other side effects of some importance are the attraction – both through domestic and international migration – of especially heterogeneous populations, and residential segregation of more and less advantaged groups at a broader scale than in less extensive labor market areas.

In this paper, our focus is on the contribution of labor market processes to a growing concentration of unemployment within the metropoles, as the key factor in increased social inequality within them. In the London case this is indicated by the fact that 10 of the 14 inner boroughs now figure among the 20 districts with the highest unemployment rates in Britain – whereas none did at the start of the 1980s, and other parts of the region have some of the lowest rates. Traditionally, such problems are seen as ones of the inability of a spatially and occupationally constrained labor force to adjust in the face of major structural shocks. With different political perspectives and/or reality judgments, this implies either a need to counteract the processes of change or to absorb them more effectively through promotion of labor market flexibility. By contrast, the hydrological metaphors in our title imply a rather more fluid perspective on metropolitan labor markets, with various forms of flexibility and adjustment actually contributing to an increasing concentration of unemployment and underemployment. Both the concepts of turbulence and sedimentation involve parallels with two alternative sets of ideas invoked to account for problems of unemployment, exclusion and incohesion in late nineteenth-century London, in terms of casualization and demoralization/residualization (Stedman Jones 1971). In this paper, however, where they relate to the downside of a flexible, insecure urban labor market and to a progressive downgrading of status and competitiveness among those affected by job loss, the two concepts are seen as complementary explanations of concentrated urban unemployment.

Turbulence, Turnover, and Urban Labour Markets

We turn first to the issues of turbulence and instability in the labor markets of large metropoles. These have had a particular salience over the past couple of decades because of a number of developments expected to increase general levels of employment instability throughout the advanced economies. First, governments (notably in the UK) have sought to promote greater labor market and wage flexibility. Together with higher levels of unemployment, these increase the pressure on those in the weakest position in the labor market to take poor-quality jobs offering worse conditions of security. Secondly, management practices within large organizations have favored a sharper division (across all grades) between core employees, with substantial job security, and a less secure periphery, including workers on various forms of more flexible contract (though actual numbers on these contracts are still limited in the UK). Recent tendencies to "downsize," and "delayer" bureaucratic organizations have also added to job insecurity among managerial, professional, and technical workers. Nevertheless, detailed empirical research shows that the growth in instability has in fact been greatest for the less skilled workers (Gregg and Wadsworth 1995). Finally, the overall incidence of job instability has also been raised by structural shifts in employment, away from larger organizations and from the public sector, toward small firms and private services sectors, as well as by a growth of self-employment, part-time work, and employment of women in childbearing age groups.

These processes are occurring both inside and outside the metropoles, though some, linked to deindustrialization, will be proceeding faster there. In these cities, however, a number of other factors continue to encourage higher rates of job turnover than are found elsewhere. First among these is the direct effect of agglomeration – appropriately thought of in terms of numbers of business units/employers, as well as numbers of workers – in encouraging higher rates of job turnover. This reflects the fact that with a larger range of employment opportunities available to workers, and a larger external pool of workers (with relevant skills) available to firms, search costs are lower for both, and new jobs/workers can be secured more readily when they are wanted. In consequence firms may be less concerned to retain workers – adjusting employment levels more rapidly to fluctuations in demand, and doing less to avoid natural wastage – while workers will be more willing to leave in search of better jobs, and invest less in a particular employment relationship. A second-order effect is to make survival easier for firms experiencing substantial fluctuations in their product market (including those in new or fashion-related activities), and harder for those needing a more stable environment. Similarly, among the more mobile groups in the population, the metropolitan cores can be expected to attract and retain residents with a stronger preference for flexibility over security.

For most of its history, London's employment structure has been characterized by small firms, and service sector industries, many linked to elite consumer markets or innovative activities, all involving unstable demand at the plant level. The port, which had been a particular source of instability, reflecting global trade fluctuations, is no longer relevant. However, global links through finance seem to have taken over this role, being substantially responsible for the bubble economy of the late 1980s and early 1990s. The speculative character of this boom/bust actually reflected a (misplaced) confidence on the part of many businesses in continuing growth, rather than the uncertainty which encourages the design of shorter-term employment relations. And it is not obvious that dependence on global markets should particularly encourage flexible employment strategies – especially when many of the players are rather large. On the supply side, various factors promote unstable relations. In particular, London's role as an entry point in many professional and managerial careers (see Fielding 1989) encourages a concentration of younger more mobile people in the residential population, as does its role as a consumption center, as a refuge for those fleeing overseas political events or domestic family breakdown, and as a haven for nonconformist lifestyles.

In looking at actual levels of instability in the London labor market, as compared with other parts of the country, we focus on differences in rates of job turnover,[3] as a direct indicator of labor market turbulence, rather than on the incidence of types of "nonstandard" jobs (including part-time jobs of all sorts) which is sometimes misleadingly taken as a general index of labor market flexibility. Three measures of mobility are considered (differing as to whether or not moves into and/or out of employment are considered as well as moves between jobs) in order to allow for different cyclical influences on each type of move. Overall though, the dominant pattern is for higher rates of turnover during years of strong economic performance (when opportunities are greatest and the risks facing voluntary job quitters are least). Depending on the type of move involved, over an average year between 10 and 16 percent of men and between 11 and 21 percent of women in the working age range made one of these transitions, with rather more exits and entrants than direct job changes. As we should expect, the incidence of mobility varies between occupations, industries, and age/sex/marital status groupings as well as spatially. In relation to the workers involved, these variations are likely to reflect differences in career and life-cycle positions, expectations and responsibilities, previous work histories, and the extent to which people possess transferable skills, as well as differing attitudes toward risk and security. From the employers' side, as well as shifting patterns of labor demand, they will reflect different personnel strategies for different segments of the labor force, involving higher or lower planned turnover rates according to a balancing of future uncertainties about needs against costs of hiring, training, and socializing new staff.

Because of this range of influences, in comparing areas, it is necessary to look not only at recorded turnover rates, but also at standardized rates, controlling for identified sources of variation other than area. For the South East region as a whole, which is the probably relevant labor market unit for the London metropole, such comparisons show that rates of mobility are substantially higher than elsewhere in Britain, and this is not simply the result of compositional differences in the population. Controlling for these effects, entry/exit rates are about 20 percent, and interjob moves about 30 percent, above the national average. Within this area inner London stands out, largely as a reflection of the predominance of rented accommodation in its housing stock, as compared with owner-occupation in the suburbs, as well as some lifestyle preferences likely to be associated with different attitudes to security/change. The other British conurbations have turnover rates much closer to the national average, but falling below this in the case of those with particularly high unemployment rates (Merseyside, South Yorkshire, and Central Clydeside). The general pattern within Britain appears to be one of higher turnover rates in both larger/denser labor market areas *and* those with a stronger pressure of demand – a combination yielding the highest expected rates in the London region and the lowest in nonmetropolitan areas outside the South East.

From the worker's point of view this turbulence of the London labor market has both positive and negative consequences. For some workers it provides a context for greater choice between jobs, leading to more rapid career advancement, while for others it may lead to weak human capital formation, insecurity, and ultimately a restricted range of satisfactory job choices. These consequences will be distributed more or less directly by occupational level and type of industry, so it becomes important to know how London's turbulence affects different groups. In fact, the tendency to higher rates of turnover applies to almost all occupations and industry groups in London – being most marked in those types of job which are generally most stable, including professional and managerial jobs, reflecting London's role as an entry point and site for rapid advancement in white collar careers.[4] In relation to age, however, the normal steep decline of mobility rates with age is strongly exaggerated in London, with the tendency to greater instability being concentrated among young workers, and more or less disappearing by the age of 40. By that time it is likely that most of those involved will have successfully made the transition to an established job, rather later than their peers in the provinces, though possibly at a higher level.

Much of this evidence is consistent with a positive view of the role of job turnover in career progression and the accumulation of human capital. While some career progression takes place within the internal labor markets of large organizations, many other occupational career paths, particularly in professional and related occupations, depend on accumulating experience with a variety of employers. It is also likely that there has been some shift towards the latter form of career progression, for which metropolitan labor markets play very important roles.

However, there are real risks associated with a high-turnover labor market, which can have very serious consequences for some of those involved. Involuntary job losses, or the failure of some speculative moves, mean a greater risk of spells of unemployment, which though typically short are liable to leave people in a lower quality job than would otherwise have been expected. This is a particular risk for those in the type of job where short-term experience gives the worker little human capital which can be taken on to future jobs. Thus, although the differential in mobility rates between London and other parts of the UK is most marked for skilled workers, it is those in the lower reaches of the labor market who run the greatest risks of entering downward career paths as a result of the unstable character of employment relations in the metropolitan labor market. As White and Forth (1998) have shown, there is a strong tendency for the unemployed to cycle through more unstable or downgraded parts of the labor market. Indeed even the evidence of stabilization among older workers has ambiguous implications, since it can reflect not only many people finding more stable jobs, with some sort of career prospect, but also longer spells of unemployment among those who fail to achieve this by middle age. And, significantly, it is in these middle age ranges that London exhibits the highest unemployment rates, relative to the national average. For some people at least, youthful turbulence seems to be followed by a form of sedimentation in the sense of downward mobility, leading to possible marginalization. The risks of this occurring are likely to vary with the overall labor market situation, as we show in the next section where we consider the general role of sedimentation in concentrating unemployment within metropolitan communities.

Sedimentation, Bumping Down, and Structural Unemployment

The relatively turbulent character of metropolitan labor markets implies rather higher levels of unemployment, especially among the middle-aged. But the sort of long-term shift toward less stable service jobs discussed in the last section is unlikely to explain the marked increase in the concentration of unemployment which London (at least) has experienced since the early 1980s. Nor in this case can it be blamed on a deteriorating economic performance, since even in the manual sectors employment trends have been no worse than in previous decades. In fact, the general evidence is that the city's "labour market" is too open, particularly in commuting terms, for there to be any close link between employment and unemployment trends at the city level. In this situation, explanations of higher levels of unemployment within inner London in particular, as compared with the regional hinterland, naturally focus on its concentration of residents from groups with limited competitive power in the labor market. This factor could only account for a marked *increase* in the spatial concentration of unemployment, however, if *either* the residential segregation of disadvantaged groups had substantially increased over this period, *or* the competitive position of some of these groups had been substantially worsened. In the London case, there is actually no convincing evidence of an intensification of social segregation – so we shall focus on the ways in which labor market processes might have been responsible for further marginalization of those in initially weak positions.

Our basic argument is that prolonged experience of economic conditions where demand is insufficient to provide full employment leads to a *sedimentation* of the labor supply, with a continual risk of individuals falling into positions below their capacities and limited chances of recovering their position. In extreme cases this leads to people descending beyond long-term unemployment into effective disengagement from the labor market, in some form of concealed unemployment. But the underlying processes are ones which are believed to operate right across the labor market and do not depend on pathological behavior (such as an unwillingness to engage in job search) by those at its margins. The consequences are spatially uneven because of residential segregation of those in the least advantaged positions.

A central process is that of "bumping down,"[5] whereby, with an inflexible wage structure, individuals respond to demand-deficient unemployment by lowering their sights, taking a job one tier down, in a position where they outcompete others displaced to the tier below, and so on. In our analyses of London labor market flows this is indicated by the fact that people are substantially more likely to enter unemployment from higher nonmanual or supervisory jobs than they are to return there, with experience of unemployment causing a net shift downward particularly into personal service and less skilled manual jobs. A consequence is that the unemployed always include disproportionate numbers from the lowest tiers (the "unskilled"), even when falls in demand are equally spread across all types of job. This can give a misleading impression about the causes of unemployment, but would be of limited consequence if cyclical upturns and a relaxation of hiring standards could be counted on to restore everyone (including the unemployed) to their previous position within the labor market. But, particularly if recession has been prolonged there may be several brakes on this process. Those who, under pressure of redundancy, secured permanent jobs at a lower position in the occupational hierarchy may not feel the same pressure to start searching again for a better paid job, particularly if they are middle-aged or older workers. In any case, they (like the unemployed) may now be judged less employable, whether on the basis of their current occupation or a lower valuation of "experience" in the open labor market, and are particularly liable to be overtaken by younger workers on an upward trajectory. Those who have had spells of unemployment are also rather likely to have been forced to take less permanent jobs (White and Forth 1998), thus acquiring an unstable work history which further reduces their chances of regaining stable jobs commensurate with their previous standing and talents, leaving them in a state of subemployment (Norris 1978). Periods of continuing demand-deficiency are thus likely to induce a progressive growth of structural unemployment, reversible only through extended periods of full employment, rather than simply by an upturn in labor demand.

These processes are not peculiar to cities, and are believed to underlie the upward drift in European unemployment rates since the 1980s, accompanied by shifts in the unemployment–vacancy and unemployment–inflation relationships, each implying a reduced efficiency of labor market performance, raising the level of nondemand-deficient unemployment.[6] But they have some particular implications for the metropoles, because these are likely to include extensive areas with concentrations of those individuals most likely to be "bumped" out of regular, secure and reasonably rewarded employment, and because some area-specific processes may exacerbate sedimentation in these areas. One such process involves a deterioration in the (crucial) networks of informal information about jobs when there are fewer local people in such regular employment. Some others operating over more extended timescales involve the impact of (male) unemployment rates on family structures, with knock-on effects both on educational achievement (Gordon 1996) and on the incidence of health problems – both leading to significantly higher risks of unemployment. And all of these have a particular salience for the larger metropolitan areas where the scale of residential segregation increases the likelihood that the personal networks of those at risk of unemployment will be localized within relatively homogeneous areas. How important these area effects may be in quantitative terms is by no means clear, but qualitatively they reinforce the simple expectation, based on individual level processes and housing market geography, that there will be growing differentials in unemployment rates between inner and outer areas during periods of deficient demand.

The London case

In the London case some direct confirmation for this proposition can be found in the relationship between year-by-year changes in unemployment rates in the urban core of Greater London, and in its regional hinterland, the Rest of the South East (ROSE). Twenty-five years ago the officially recorded rates for these two areas were equal,[7] but subsequently a considerable gap opened up, peaking in the mid-1990s when the Greater London rate was 3.5 percent higher than that in ROSE. More detailed examination of the year-to-year changes in this differential shows no substantial association with other developments in the labor markets concerned. There is, however, a clear tendency for it to widen whenever unemployment in the hinterland is above the traditional "full-employment" benchmark of 3 percent,[8] as it was for most of the 1980s and 1990s, with some narrowing in the three short periods of peak employment.[9] Comparisons with developments in other neighboring regions make it clear that this is not simply a matter of changing terms of competition between Londoners and those living in its commuter hinterland, but involves a progressive accumulation of structural unemployment within the urban core, raising the aggregate rate of unemployment across wider areas, including the South East as a whole.

In fact, most of this increasing concentration has occurred within a small number of inner East London boroughs, notably Hackney, Haringey, Newham and Tower Hamlets, where open unemployment rates increased by 6–7 percent between the 1981 and 1991 Censuses, compared with about 2 percent in the typical London borough and 1 percent in the outer metropolitan ring. Increases in the numbers "permanently sick" or on government schemes suggest a further growth of

2–3 percent or so in concealed unemployment in the first group of areas, against apparent reductions of 1–2 percent elsewhere in the region. By 1991 there were a dozen wards in the region with unemployment rates over 25 percent (about 5 times the modal value), all lying in an arc in the inner east, between North Hackney and Brixton. Regression analyses at district level suggest that part of this pattern of change is attributable to more unfavorable trends in labor demand for semi/unskilled groups in this part of London, and partly to differential growth in disadvantaged sections of population, notably some of the newer immigrant groups. But together these account for only about a third of the increased concentration of unemployment, most of which seems simply to reflect sharp increases in those places with a history of unemployment, whether associated with population mix, earlier local job losses or a combination of these factors. One important mediating variable in this appears to be the incidence of limiting health conditions, which seems both to reflect past unemployment rates and to significantly boost current ones.

Two distinct sets of evidence on the changing spatial pattern of unemployment in the London region thus suggest that the processes of sedimentation which we have argued to play a substantial role in the upward drift of unemployment nationally are especially evident in London and bear much of the responsibility for the emergence of very high levels of unemployment within inner east London. Some of these processes clearly bear a relation to that "demoralization" which was supposedly the bane of late Victorian London, though the essential cause of more recent sedimentation has been persistently low levels of demand for labor (in the national and regional economies), and experience of unemployment itself, rather than corrupting effects of urban life. The improvement in London's relative position in unemployment terms over the past three years of stronger demand shows what can be achieved, though these conditions would have to persist for much longer than seems likely (on the brink of another recession) for the bulk of those representing the accumulated sediment to be brought back into circulation.

Conclusions

Concentrated urban unemployment has been one of the key factors in increased inequality in advanced capitalist economies since the 1980s. In the British case, and probably in other northern European cities, it is a much more important factor in the growth of poverty than the potential increases in low-wage service employment that Sassen (1991) drew attention to in the context of New York (Buck 1997). Concentrated urban unemployment has reflected unfavourable macroeconomic developments and policies, but also involves specific labor market processes with an important urban dimension to them. In this paper we have emphasized two characteristic combinations of these processes particularly associated with metropolitan areas. On the one hand, *turbulence*, where high rates of turnover, encouraged by large and flexible metropolitan labor markets, present hazards as well as opportunities for young workers pursuing individualistic strategies, particularly if they fail to make a transition to more durable employment relations in midcareer. On the other, *sedimentation*, where processes of individual adjustment (rather than inertia) in the context of deficient demand lead to a creeping underemployment and marginalization of workers, has its most chronic effects in metropolitan inner areas where disadvantage is reproduced through a combination of local social processes. These two sets of processes interact in a number of ways, both at the individual and aggregate level, jointly contributing to processes of social exclusion. Turbulence at least is directly related to a labor market's flexibility, which is not only ideologically applauded but is a real contributor to metropolitan competitiveness and economic success for the majority. But, if unchecked, the social consequences of sedimentation, and of turbulence's downside, in terms of crime, family fragmentation, and school failure, all pose some degree of threat to the maintenance of this competitiveness and success.

NOTES

1. This is a substantially shortened version of an original conference paper (Buck and Gordon 1998), incorporating a detailed examination of evidence on recent labor market behaviour and performance in the London region which underpins and illustrates the analysis in sections 2 and 3 of this paper. Copies of the full paper are available on request from the authors.
2. Though not emphasized by Sassen, there is also a supply-side aspect of the exceptionalist position in that "global cities" may be particularly attractive to international immigration from lower wage economies.
3. These derive from the UK Labour Force Survey, pooling data from the years 1986-96 to encompass a range of macroeconomic circumstances, and relate to the proportions of workers who have entered, left, and changed their employment during the past 12 months.
4. This is actually the old South East standard region.
5. This is not an effect of having a younger labor force.
6. This stems from the work of Reder (1955)who first focused on the tendency for job applicants to be ranked in terms of characteristics affecting their likely productivity rather than the wage they are prepared to work for, characterized by Thurow (1983) as "job" rather than "price" competition.
7. Because the denominator includes employment counted on a workplace rather than residence basis, rates for the core area are consistently understated, and those in ROSE slightly overstated, so London unemployment was actually a bit higher than in ROSE even at the outset.
8. ROSE unemployment rates are taken as the indicator of demand-deficiency or adequacy in the regional market since they are free of the upward drift between cycles which we associate with the accumulation of structural (non-demand-deficient) unemployment: very similar results are obtained, however, if unemployment rates in the neighbouring semi-rural regions, East Anglia and the South West, are taken as the benchmark.
9. The tipping point is actually a rate of 3.5 percent in ROSE; in the 10 years with rates below that the London differential fell in 5, and showed no change in 3; in the 14 with rates above that level, the London differential increased in 12 and showed no change in 1.

REFERENCES

Buck, N. H. 1997: Social divisions and labor market change in London: national, urban and global factors. *Institute for Social and Economic Research Working Paper series*, 97–25, Colchester: University of Essex.

Buck, N. H. and Fainstein, N. 1992: A comparative history, 1880–1973. In S. Fainstein, I. Gordon, and M. Harloe (eds.), *Divided Cities: New York and London in the Contemporary World*, Oxford: Blackwell, 29–67.

Buck, N. H. and Gordon, I. R. 1998: Turbulence and sedimentation in the labor markets of late 20th century London. Paper presented to the conference on Cities at the Millennium, RIBA, London.

Fielding, A. J. 1989: Inter-regional migration and social change: a study of south east England based upon the Longitudinal Study. *Transactions of the Institute of British Geographers*, 14, 24–36 .

Gordon, I. R. 1988: Unstable people, unstable jobs and unstable places. Paper presented to the IBG/Regional Science Association conference on Geography of Labour Markets, London.

Gordon, I. R. 1989: Urban unemployment. In D. T. Herbert and D. M. Smith (eds.), *Social Problems and the City: New Perspectives*. Oxford: Oxford University Press, 232–46.

Gordon, I. R. 1996: Family structure, educational achievement and the inner city. *Urban Studies*, 33, 407–23.

Gregg, P. and Wadsworth, J. 1995: A short history of labor turnover, job tenure, and job security 1975–93. *Oxford Review of Economic Policy*, 11, 73–90.

Hall, P. G. 1962: *The Industries of London since 1861*. London: Hutchinson.

Harvey, D. 1985: *Consciousness and the Urban Experience*. Baltimore: The Johns Hopkins University Press.

Hirst, P. and Thompson, G. 1996: *Globalization in Question: The International Economy and the Possibilities of Governance*. Cambridge: Polity.

Layard, R., Nickell, R., and Jackman, R. 1991: *Unemployment: Macroeconomic Performance and the Labour Market*. Oxford: Oxford University Press.

Norris, G. M. 1978: Unemployment, subemployment and personal characteristics: (b) job separation and work histories: the alternative approach. *Sociological Review*, 25, 327–47.

Reder, M. W. 1955: The theory of occupational wage differentials. *American Economic Review*, 45, 833–52.

Sassen, S. 1991: *The Global City: New York, London, Tokyo*. Princeton: Princeton University Press.

Scott, A. J. 1988: *Metropolis: From the Division of Labor to Urban Form*. Berkeley, CA: University of California Press.

Stedman Jones, G. 1971: *Outcast London*. Oxford: Oxford University Press.

Thurow, L. C. 1983: *Dangerous Currents: The State of Economics*. Oxford: Oxford University Press.

White, M. and Forth, J. 1998: *Pathways Through Unemployment: The Effects of a Flexible Labour Market*. York: York Publishing Services.

Chapter 17

Informational Cities: Beyond Dualism and Toward Reconstruction[1]

Bob Catterall

...the Informational City is also the Dual City...It opposes the cosmopolitanism of the elites, living on a daily connection to the whole world (functionally, socially, culturally), to the tribalism of local communities, retrenched in their spaces that they try to control as their last stand against the macro-forces that shape their lives out of their reach...[2]

Cyberspace is not a *single* integrated and ubiquitous entity revolving around the Internet. It is a place fractured into *multiple spheres of influence,* each with autonomous priorities of its own. Sometimes these spheres will cooperate, sometimes they will compete, but always they will guard their vital cores.[3]

Information is a slippery concept. In ordinary usage it takes, as does knowledge, an exclusively singular form – information not informations. At one level of analysis, the singular form seems essential. If there is no common basis to all the practices that can be classified as informational, how can we grasp either the phenomenon or the phenomena at all? But at another level of analysis, as we move towards the actual textures of cyberspace and of urban and regional life and its possibilities, we need a strong sense of the plurality of information and accordingly we need to be able to refer to informations as well as information (and knowledges as well as knowledge).[4] This emphasis on the plurality of information and knowledge, as well as their tensions and conflicts (spheres of influence...autonomous priorities... guarded vital cores – see David Brown above), is essential if we are to understand the dualistic imperatives at work in the Informational City as well as the tendencies and possibilities for reconstituted or regenerated cities and regions. We also need to consider the forces that shape the elaboration or, alternatively, the restriction of informations into knowledges as well as determining informational opacity or, alternatively, transparency.[5]

Such considerations have implications for the nature of urban studies itself (or, perhaps, themselves). The analysis of the Informational City is also predominantly dualistic in nature, polarized between social science (including political economy) and cultural (including postmodern) approaches.[6] This analytic duality has a basis in the deep existential division between the socioeconomic and cultural spheres of our lives. But such analyses also reinforces that division. Much mainstream urban analysis is, despite its empirical procedure, also to a significant degree an expression of "the cosmopolitanism of the elites" and does little justice to the struggles of "local communities, retrenched in their spaces that they try to control... against the macro-forces that shape their lives..." (Castells, above). I have in mind both the political program and the empirical basis of such work.

As to political programs, consider the assertion by Scott Campbell and Susan Fainstein that the central question of planning theory is: "*What role can planning play in developing the city and region within the constraints of a capitalist political economy and a democratic political system?*"[7] The acceptance of these constraints, I shall show, results in a certain myopia towards what is happening and pushes more liberatory possibilities off the agenda. As to the empirical basis of such work, there is a failure to represent the actual texture of marginalized voices, and their informations, and to link them to the kinds of analysis of the economy and culture that would supplement and challenge mainstream accounts of what is happening and allow for a more liberatory agenda. The political and "scientific" programs of the mainstream approaches reinforce each other.

This chapter sketches out an alternative agenda, one that requires as agents a broad notion of urbanists, one that includes community activists and journalists as well as architects, planners, and academics. The sketch is presented in six stages. First, there is a brief discussion of urban dualisms. Second, there is an examination of the notion of a "cultural economy," particularly in the work of Peter Hall, which despite its intentions serves "the cosmopolitanism of the elites." Such an economy, a capitalist political economy, though awash with "information," is informationally opaque – it guards its secrets. Third, there is an outline, drawing on some of the speculative and political work of Alain Lipietz, of a more informationally transparent and more socially and ecologically responsible economy. The fourth and fifth stages involve the consideration of two specific sites and processes: the nature of "communication exchanges" such as railway stations and their possible regeneration beyond the imperatives of the Dual City, and, drawing further on the work of Manuel Castells, the significance of the idea of a citizens' movement. In both cases, I have drawn additionally on my own journalistic work. Finally, there are some interim conclusions.

Urban Dualisms

To claim with Castells that the Informational City is also the Dual City is not to deny that there are intermediate strata or a range of social strata, segments or fragments.[8] Nor is it to deny that there is room for social action.[9] If the notions of polarization or dualism are, on occasion, associated with crude either/or implications, their avoidance or rejection can lead instead to a form of bland and disengaged analysis that does no justice to our intellectual and social dilemmas. For the more positivistically inclined, there may be an unsettling metaphysical quality to the range of dualisms – that also include the space of flows and the space of places – and their manner of deployment in Castells' work. But this quality represents an attempt to express actual tendencies, the dynamics, of these processes.

In his account of the Dual City Castells includes occupational polarization, the one-sided location of immigrant labor within that duality, the polarization of age differentials, a surge of social tensions and the emergence of defensive space, and, finally, "the fundamental urban dualism of our time... [which] opposes the cosmopolitanism of the elites... to the tribalism of local communities..." Castells has also expressed a hope for the integration of the duality in urban sociology between "structuralist" and "subjectivist" approaches.[10]

Informational Opacity and the "Cultural Economy"

Rich, affluent, cultivated nations and cities can sell their virtue, beauty, philosophy, their art and their theater to the rest of the world. From a manufacturing economy we pass to an information economy, and from an information economy to a cultural economy. During the 1980s and 1990s, cities across Europe – Montpellier, Nîmes, Grenoble, Rennes, Hamburg, Cologne, Glasgow, Birmingham, Barcelona, and Bologna – have become more and more preoccupied by the notion that cultural industries (a term no longer thought anomalous or offensive) may provide the basis for economic regeneration, filling the gap left by vanished factories and warehouses, and creating a new urban image that would make them more attractive to mobile capital and mobile professional workers.[11]

It might be argued that it is cultural policy that provides the missing link between social-scientific and cultural analyses.[12] Cultural policy is now an increasingly respected concern both in academic research and in governmental (local and national) and business circles. This has, however, been a contradictory development. Its proponents have demonstrated that "culture" can be, on the one hand, a very significant generator of income and image but, on the other, this emphasis has led to policies that in effect restrict the concept and practice of the arts so that they fit into a narrow and ideological conception of economic development. The allied World City perspective takes the social and cultural needs of international finance and business as identifying the necessary path of social progress. But if world cities also contain major divisions of interest, particularly between social elites who are, in a sense, world-city insiders and other citizens who are outsiders with respect to world-city activities, how can such a deeply divided city be reunited? Dedicated *flâneurs* fanning out into the surrounding suburbs? Or perhaps planners?

Planners, as Peter Hall and others see it, could have a major role to play in regenerating the city in a less divisive way. Hall highlights four emerging questions:[13] new sources of economic growth, subsequently conceptualized as the "cultural economy"; sustainable development; private–public partnerships; and polarization and the urban underclass. Planning, Hall argues, could and should have a role in dealing with these questions; but "it will need to learn to adjust to a subtly different socioeconomic system; it may well need to become yet more entrepreneurial..." (p. 186).

Hall's exposition of his agenda is a little thin and piecemeal. Can the "newer, softer informational sectors – culture, the arts, entertainment, education" (p. 183) by themselves lead, as he seems to suggest, to the necessary social and economic growth? Or are new directions in cultural policy required? Is sustainability essentially little more than balanced ITH (industry, transport, and housing)? Does private–public partnership include the third (voluntary, community) sector and, if so, on what terms? Is dispersal the way to *solve* the problems of polarization and the underclass or is it merely a way of shifting it and them around?

The emphasis on entrepreneurialism could be crucial, but it depends on the form that it takes. If it is merely a matter of "adjusting" to a socioeconomic system already set in place by the restructuring of the 1980s and after, then the divisions will deepen. But is there an alternative entrepreneurialism? What is missing in this text of Hall's, and in his subsequent and more extended account in *Cities in Civilization* (1998), is a sense of the sheer contradictoriness of current changes. In the passage quoted above there is, apart from its uncritical celebration of the "virtue" of rich nations and cities, the oxymoronic yoking in "cultural economy" of analytic opposites which can be united only through a far-reaching process of social reconstruction. The possibility that what might be required is the shift to a radically, rather than marginally, different socioeconomic system is not entertained.

There is a contradiction between highlighting the income-generating effect of "culture" in a context of selective "redevelopment" and placing the cultural dimension at the heart of a reconstitutive urban and social policy. An important attempt to find a way out of this contradiction into an approach to cultural policy that can meet deep-seated but marginalized social and economic needs has been made by Franco Bianchini.[14] He states:

> The 1980s saw a flourishing of studies on the economic importance of the cultural sector in different cities, and of the direct and indirect economic impacts of cultural activities and policies on employment and wealth creation. This tradition of studies was undoubtedly important to raise the profile of cultural policies and to advocate for increased public and private sector of investment in culture. In the 1990s, however, new methodologies and indicators will be needed to measure the impact of cultural policies and activities in terms of quality of life, social cohesion and community development.[15]

And, it should be added (taking us beyond Bianchini's analysis), new methodologies, *practices*, and indicators will be needed to sustain cultural initiatives as they impact on the economic domain. The "cultural economy," to revert to Peter Hall's term, is not a relationship of equals. The cultural economy would be one in which culture is commodified. It is not, then, just a question of trying to *balance* economic against social and cultural factors; it is a matter of trying to *integrate* them.[16] What is involved is the refusal to accept the dominant arrangement of social reality in which the category of "the economic" is opaque, impenetrable to noninitiates, and dominant, whereas the category of the social and cultural, which includes the human capacity of people as well as their dreams, occupies a separate dimension which influences but is not allowed to shape, the outcomes delivered by the economic sphere.

Informational Transparancy and the Reconstructed Socioeconomy

Sometimes, a utopian vision is needed to shake the institutions from shortsightedness and stasis and to enable people to think the unthinkable...[17]

Re-recording the work [Schoenberg's Piano Concerto] . . . thirty-six years after my first attempt felt like an act of re-generation, as though I were contributing some continuity and progress to a world which, relapsing into nationalism, fascism and madness, appears to have lost interest in both.[18]

For salamanders, regeneration after injury, such as the loss of a limb, involves regrowth of structure and restoration of function with the constant possibility of twinning or other odd topographical productions at the site of the former injury. The regrown limb can be monstrous, duplicated, potent. We have all been injured, profoundly. We require regeneration not rebirth, and the possibilities for our reconstitution include the utopian dream of the hope for a monstrous world without gender.[19]

A valuable attempt to make the local economic order, particularly the possibilities for citizens locked within it, transparent rather than opaque, and an arena for hopeful action rather than frustrated acquiescence, is made by Alain Lipietz in his *Towards a New Economic Order.*[20] Lipietz sees the need to rethink "economics" in terms of the environment and ecology. Lipietz reminds us of the etymologies of the words "economy" and "ecology." "Economy" is the study of the laws (norms) of the household sphere (*oikos*); "ecology" is the study of the meaning or rationality (*logos*) of the household sphere. Political ecology, which he advocates, emphasizes that that sphere is the whole of the city (*polis*). Whereas the horizon of economics barely extends beyond the human activities of production and distribution, that of political ecology extends to "human beings and nature as a single whole." Political ecology emphasizes that "human beings are nature, that nature is being irresistibly altered and humanized, sometimes for the better, but for the worse if one ceases to be aware of it" (p. 40). What is at stake is not nature pure and simple. "The environment defended by political ecology is mostly artificial: hedgerows, cultivated fruits, attractive residential areas, built-up areas to be protected from noise and fumes. In other words, political ecology is mainly urban ecology" (p. 49).

What Lipietz puts forward is an alternative to Neo-Fordism – in essence, a three-way rather than a two-way (state–market) compromise, in which the third partner, "the community," or the third sector, is given a central role. It may seem that this is just the same notion of "partnership" that has been taken up of late as conventional wisdom (if not as conventional practice). But what is involved is a new approach to how we define both the boundaries and interactions between the three sectors and the basis and nature of their dialog and interactions.

A crucial development in this direction would be the creation of a new sector of activity, a socially useful third sector or "welfare community." Workers in this sector, or rather the "intermediate agencies for socially useful schemes" that would pay them, would continue to receive from the state money equivalent to unemployment benefits. Their work would take up some areas of need that are met by unsatisfactory provision or not met at all at present. These are: (1) those now provided at a high cost by certain sectors of the welfare state: for example, basic medical care or care for convalescents; (2) those now provided by women, for nothing and without their having a say in the matter; (3) those which are provided infrequently or not at all because they are too expensive (improvement of the environment, particularly in deprived areas, and cultural provision).

Lipietz's outline of the nature of this sector – of possibilities, problems, areas of negotiation – arise not only out of his academic work but also from political work in Seine-Saint Denis, "a run-down and crisis-ridden area just outside Paris" (p. 192). He is, then, more than aware of the problems of introducing and developing this third sector. But he is also aware that, once underway, it "would eliminate many of the problems of the Fordist welfare state. Active taxpayers would know what they are paying for: socially useful services. Workers in the third sector would have a useful job which would give them a more positive sense of identity, more social and self-esteem than moonlighting or part-time jobs in fast-food or shoe-polishing" (p. 325). Such a sector would play a major part in the move towards ecological responsibility on the basis of a new social ethic (one that would undermine "the dependency culture"):

> We can only move towards an ecological compromise in a society which perceives itself as a community and which refuses to abandon the marginalized. Fordism had at its disposal a powerful tool of solidarity – the welfare state, social security, various welfare benefits and allowances. These have been attacked, rightly, as bureaucratic. The alternative compromise must take on "individual" aspirations to be responsible for one's affairs, to see things through to their conclusion (p. 92).

The development of the third sector would begin with the opacity of the local economy and polity and seek to make their processes more transparent and open to genuine democratic control.

Lipietz's proposals for the third sector are at the heart of an account of an alternative social order that cannot be dismissed as merely localistic. Other policy-oriented concerns are with related changes in the organization of work, a model of consumption, and a significant role for increased free time, and on the development of a nonaggressive international economic order.

What a noncommodifying cultural economy would involve is – to use Castells' emphasis (above) – a *utopian* notion of regeneration. Such regeneration can be conceptualized along a continuum: at one pole, that "monstrous" reconstitution,[21] to which Haraway refers, and, at the other, that combination of continuity and progress to which Alfred Brendel refers. Reconstitutive regeneration, whether "monstrous" or not, is to be sharply distinguished from the established top-down model of state–capital collaboration, sometimes referred to as partnership or, indeed, as urban regeneration. That would be continuity for some but hardly progress. Whether the alternative is some bottom-up recipe, remains to be seen.

But, if reconstruction and regeneration are required, where, when, and how is this process to be set in motion? In seeking to answer this question, I draw on, in addition to the work of others, insights and "narrative knowledges" or informations derived from investigative visits in the early 1990s to King's Cross, London, and to Barcelona and Paris. Despite the immense significance for urban regeneration of the work of the King's Cross Railwaylands Community Group and of the Citizen Movement from which urban policy developed in Barcelona, they have not been understood. This is, as they say, no accident.

Sites and Processes: (1) Communication Exchanges

The new architectural monuments of our epoch are likely to be built as "communication exchanges" (airports, train stations, intermodal transfer areas, telecommunication infrastructures, harbours, and computerized trading centres.[22]

For many years, and even now, generations of black folks who migrated north to escape life in the south, returned down here in search of spiritual nourishment, healing, that was fundamentally connected to reaffirming one's connection to nature, to a contemplative life, where one could take time, sit on the porch, walk, fish and catch lightning bugs.[23]

One starting point would be at one of the "communication exchanges" in our cities. In the case of railway stations, these are often long-delayed "redevelopment" sites. One step in the reconstitution of such areas would have to begin with a revaluation of what is there. Is it correct to perceive sites like the King's Cross Railwaylands in London, as the developers do, as derelict and degraded property which unquestionably needs "renewal"? Or do such locations in fact play an essential part in the inner-city economy by providing cheap premises for activities ranging from theater scenery storage to cheap hostels, on which the inner-city economy and society depend?[24] Such areas may already have their own social order. The King's Cross Railwaylands Community Group and its associates have researched, documented and conceptualized what they call the "organizational landscape" as a social order.[25]

These continuities need to be maintained, but how can such sites be part of a profound and progressive regeneration? Should they be seen as opaque informational nodes or as relatively transparent "communication exchanges"? Luca Bertolini, in a paper on the redevelopment of railway stations and their surroundings,[26] sets out an account that can be said to begin to answer these questions and to "link the contemporary cultural studies invocations of spatiality with political economies of the production of space . . ."[27]

Bertolini first introduces us to Guido Martinotti's characterization of world cities.[28] Martinotti has explored the significance of the fact that, in addition to the residents, there are three other sets of people that now go to make up the population of a city: the commuters, the "city users" (tourists), and the "metropolitan businessmen" (managers of the global city economy). Bertolini then points out that all these subsets of the city's population "literally meet in the compressed space of railway stations. In and around them metropolitan incongruity gets to a maximum, while redevelopment tends to exacerbate the tensions."

Four walks at King's Cross would illuminate the contrast between established realities and the regenerative potential present there, and the informations and knowledges available. First, for rival informations, one needs a walk around the site informed by the plan for the usual development for cosmopolites (courtesy of the distinguished architect/master planner Norman Foster and the developers), and the Railwaylands Community Group's rival view of what that would have meant (see illustration).

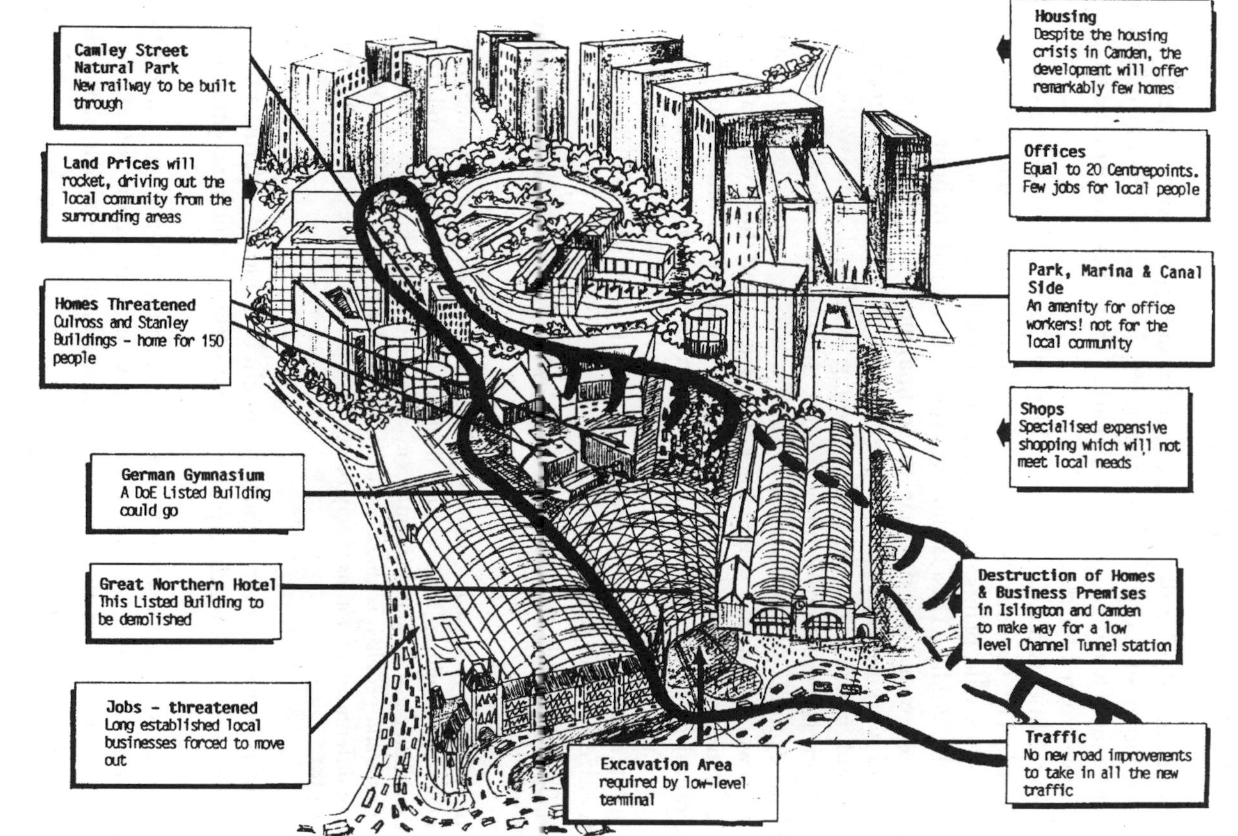
Camley Street
Natural Park
New railway to be built through
Land Prices will rocket, driving out the local community from the surrounding areas
Homes Threatened
Culross and Stanley Buildings - home for 150 people
German Gymnasium
A DoE Listed Building could go
Great Northern Hotel
This Listed Building to be demolished
Jobs - threatened
Long established local businesses forced to move out
Excavation Area
required by low-level terminal
Housing
Despite the housing crisis in Camden, the development will offer remarkably few homes
Offices
Equal to 20 Centrepoints. Few jobs for local people
Park, Marina & Canal Side
An amenity for office workers! not for the local community
Shops
Specialised expensive shopping which will not meet local needs
Destruction of Homes & Business Premises
in Islington and Camden to make way for a low level Channel Tunnel station
Traffic
No new road improvements to take in all the new traffic

Figure 17.1 The cosmopolite development model? An interpretation by the King's Cross Railwaylands Community Group of the London Regeneration Consortium's and British Rail proposal for King's Cross.
Source: Michael Parkers, "Planning Prospects, Planning Education," in *Regenerating Cities*, 3 and 4, p. 23.

Second, a commuter's walk, with its somewhat limited knowledge of the area. As Phil Jeffries, former chair of the Railwaylands Community Group, put it: "They see the gas holders, the concrete batching plants, the buddleia growing out of walls that desperately need re-pointing, the run-down and decayed buildings. As they head for the tube, they see the litter, the people hanging around the station and experience the traffic and noise."[29]

Phil Jeffries offers a third walk, alternative information, to visitors: "I take them just round the corner of the public thoroughfares, just behind the old industrial buildings. I show them where the communities are. I show them some of the facilities the residents have created for themselves."

One of these facilities is the Camley Street Natural Park. This two-acre site was a derelict coalyard. The Camden Wildlife Group found it had been claimed by a remarkable array of wild plants. The Greater London Council bought it in 1981, and, helped by the Wildlife Trust, volunteers put in thousands of hours. This is the fourth category of walk, one that has to be imagined, the frequent purposeful explorations and working visits that have resulted in the creation of a nature park with a large pond, marsh, meadow, areas of young woodland and a well-equipped nature center. This is a breakthrough towards the third sector as envisaged by Alain Lipietz and an example of profound and transformative knowledge/information. "For those who were involved," comments Phil Jeffries, "and those who value it, the commitment is not simply to Camley Street but to the emotional and physical energy, the moral recreation, that went into it." In such locations it is possible to feel that "spiritual nourishment, healing," to which bell hooks refers, that involves "reaffirming one's connection to nature, to a contemplative life," a place where we can walk as citizens rather than *flâneurs*.

In discussing what is at issue at King's Cross between two rival approaches to development, Bertolini comments:

> The high-profit activities proposed . . . may also, at least sometimes, be an authentic contribution to the area's revitalization. However, the liveliness and long-term social and economic viability of the urban place the station identifies also rest on the plurality of its dimensions, on the variety of uses and people it is able to contain. The problem could be defined as one of a "coexistence of differences" if not, as it may be argued with a bit of idealism, of "integrating diversity" (p. 134).

What he considers is the process by which this might be achieved, offering a brief but important account of an approach to planning that seeks to build on contradictions, ambiguities, and conflicts.[30]

Nevertheless, as Michael Edwards has argued, "community-generated alternative plans are no panacea"; but "they can be a benign virus, putting the passion and the social critique, even some of the strategic thinking, back into urban planning."[31] What else is required?

Sites and Processes: (2) Citizen Movements

. . . if innovative social projects, represented and implemented by renewed local governments, are able to master the formidable forces unleashed by the revolution in information technologies, then a new sociospatial structure could emerge made up of a network of local communes, controlling and shaping a network of productive flows. Maybe then our historic time and our social space would converge towards the reintegration of knowledge and meaning into a new Informational City.[32]

Manuel Castells sees such a social project in the Madrid and Barcelona citizen movement of the 1970s and 1980s. It was "the most innovative, powerful and productive movement in terms of its effects, certainly in Europe, and probably in the world."[33] He suggests that three essential lessons can be drawn from the movement (particularly in Barcelona). This strategy relates the knowledge and role of professionals to the wider informational processes of the media and politics through:

[1] ...a symbiotic interaction between people who needed professional experience, to really succeed in their movement and to know exactly what to target, and professionals who needed political support to implement their projects that were not simply an accommodation to the real estate interests or the logic of bureaucracy (p. 142).

[2] ...a very close alliance with the media. The media played a substantial role in making movements that maybe were only a minority in a particular neighbourhood, strike a chord in the society at large... (p. 142).

[3] ...a very complex relationship to politics... the idea is to broaden the participation beyond the usual partnership with business into a broader participation of society, but not eliminating at all the business input (pp. 142, 143).

Castells suggests that the usual approach to participation, codetermination, tends to constant negotiations and sometimes to blockage. His alternative is to build contradictory participation from different sectors around a collective urban project that includes humanistic values as well as economic ones. These humanistic values are essentially concerned with ethics (see below), particularly about what is just. It is the task of opinion leaders and local government to sustain and/or develop a collective urban project on this basis.

Table 1 is a provisional attempt based largely on interviews with a number of the urbanists/architects involved, to set out some major elements of a city-wide approach to urban regeneration. While its instances are from Barcelona and Paris, it was also designed to illustrate what was missing in London.[34] Whereas Paris and Barcelona could be said to have achieved high scores on all points – though with a largely elitist and bureaucratic bias in the case of Paris and a populist one in the case of Barcelona – London had low scores on all points. Paris and Barcelona, though, nevertheless stopped short – far short in the case of Paris – of the regenerative strategy proposed here. But the table begins to point towards a further dimension of the notion of a liberatory informational culture, one of pragmatic elaboration and focus.

A major need for the realization of this dimension of culture is for agencies that will contribute to the nurture, development, and linkages between pockets of innovation such as King's Cross, and to public awareness of them. This is not just a matter of political leadership (aspect 4) but also of intellectual speculation and

Table 17.1 Aspects of comprehensive approaches to urban change

Aspect	Barcelona	Paris
1. Comprehensive vision of the city in relation to its past and future	Olympic focus; return to the waterfront; "strategy of greenery"; "retracing its steps" (retaining qualities from past) as a Mediterranean and European city	1989 focus; and on national monuments (Grands Travaux); recovery of waterfront and green strategy (La Boucle de la Seine)
2. Role of popular experience, interest and action	Parks as confidence builders in anti- and post-Franco movement; subsequent loss of popular impetus	Monuments (Grands Travaux) etc. as sources of interest; suburbs, riots and Suburbs 89; but no popular impetus
3. Role of architects, planners, art, design, intellectual speculation, and research	Initially, a new popular role for planner/architects; art and a theory of urban design plus research	Architects as a new international elite
4. Political leadership, will and sophistication	Pujol and Maragal; an anti-Franco and pro-Catalan project	Chirac and Mitterand; Suburbs 89
5. Approach to public/private collaboration and partnership	Populist	Elitist and bureaucratic
6. Interaction of all aspects; moral/cultural dimension	"The city council got a certain moral power" (Bosquets)	"Ethical commitment" from above (Biasini); culture and urbanism

Source: Bob Catterall, personal research note 1991, revised 1995

action-research (3), and an explicit ethical or moral/cultural commitment (6) that connects and energizes all aspects.

The work that the table to some extent summarizes and interprets gave considerable emphasis to the role of architect-planners in urban redevelopment, but a more general category, as already indicated, is one of urbanists, broadly conceived (so as to include community activists, journalists, and artists as well as architects, planners, and academics). The challenge of such movements is that they take us beyond the predominantly commodified city and towards use-values. Castells has described the process in similar terms in relation to the Citizens Movement in Madrid under Franco:

> ...another dimension had been introduced into the debate: the city as a use-value. If the historic city was to be preserved, if people's effort to urbanise vacant land was to be rewarded, if suburban expansion should be discontinued until all the children could be educated, if feasts were more important than traffic, and if citizens' participation had to become a crucial element in the planning process, then it followed that economic profit and bureaucratic power could not be the ultimate goals. Now there were new priorities...[35]

Some Interim Conclusions

Perhaps, in this next age of capitalism, an original thinker will arise somewhere in the world with a new theory that reconciles the market's imperative with unfilled human needs, without having to destroy the marketplace to do so. This would be an intellectual achievement for the ages – reordering economic rhythms that have governed for five or six centuries and offering capitalist enterprise a way out of its own destructive pathologies.[36]

I return to Castells' account of the Informational City as a Dual City and the duality and lack of integration in urban sociology. In the fractured, and often guarded, realms of Informational Cities, what is the alternative to tensions between social science and cultural analysis and related oscillations at the level of theory? Steven Seidman, presenting *The Postmodern Turn*, urges "a shift from sociological theory as a foundational practice to narrative knowledges which unite moral advocacy and social analysis".[37] But do we have to choose between "subjective" informational narratives and sociological theory and "scientific" procedure?

I have sketched in – with particular reference to King's Cross in London and, to Barcelona[38] – an approach to informational narratives which unites moral advocacy and social analysis. Though it gives sustained attention to bottom-up processes,[39] emphasis has also been given to the role in the overall process of a wide range of "urbanists" (including architects, planners, academics, artists, journalists, community activists). In the two cases considered – King's Cross and Barcelona – a key tool of enquiry has been the interview, conducted in these instances without proper social science rigor, without, for example, an objective approach to sampling or to a standardized procedure, but with sustained attention to the narratives deployed, their situation, and their informational and conceptual implications.

Such a project is seen as focused on urban regeneration/reconstitution involving, to use Castells' words, "the reintegration of knowledge and meaning into a new Informational City."[40] It has been suggested that applied political economy/ecology or the Marxian tradition cannot be simply put aside and that there is a crucial place for cultural analysis. But the focus is a practical one. There is a way out of the polarizations that surge through and around us in the Dualist City.

The dualistic and fragmented Informational City can be reconstructed. It is likely that there will be crucial opportunities early in the twenty-first century.[41] But there are no one-sided and exclusionary deliverances, whether from above or below. There are no short cuts. The process of reconstruction will not so much require original thinkers as urbanists in active dialog with social movements in which they seek to relate social analysis to narrative informations and knowledges.

NOTES

1. This chapter draws on, refines, and extends a paper, "There must be some way out of here – polarized cities and polarized urban studies?" contributed to the 1995 BSA (British Sociological Association) Conference on Contested Cities.

2. Manuel Castells, "European cities, the informational society and the global economy," *New Left Review*, 204 (1994), pp. 29–30.
3. David Brown, *Cybertrends: Chaos, Power and Accountability in the Information Age*, Penguin, 1997, p. 190 (his emphasis).
4. Frank Webster criticizes Castells' use of the notion of information in *The Information Age* and discusses the rival claims of "theoretical knowledge" and "action knowledge" (Giddens) in "Manuel Castells' analysis of the information age," *City* 7, pp. 105–21, and "Is this the information age: towards a critique of Manuel Castells," *City 8*, pp. 70–84.
5. I make use here of Basil Bernstein's powerful distinction between elaborated and restricted speech codes (see his *Class, Codes and Control*, 1–3, Routledge and Kegan Paul, 1971–3). I am grateful to him for many hours of discussion of this and related topics.
6. Susan Fainstein has provided a particularly useful analysis of political economy and post-structuralist approaches in her chapter, "Justice, politics and the creation of urban space," in *The Urbanization of Injustice*, ed. Andy Merrifield and Erik Swyngedouw, Lawrence and Wishart, 1995.
7. Introduction to *Readings in Planning Theory*, ed. Scott Campbell and Susain Fainstein, Blackwell Publishers, 1996, p. 1 and again on p. 11 (their emphasis).
8. Critics of the notion of the polarized or dual city include Manuel Castells and John Mollenkopf, *Dual City: Restructuring New York*, Russell Sage Foundation, 1991; Susan Fainstein, Ian Gordon, and Michael Harloe (eds.), *Divided Cities: New York and London in the Contemporary World*, Blackwell Publishers, 1992 (see the first and last chapters); Chris Hamnet, "Socio-economic change in London: professionalization not polarization," 1994, a paper contributed to the ESRC London seminars; and Peter Marcuse, "Not chaos, but walls: postmodernism and the partitioned city," in Sophie Watson and Katherine Gibson, *Postmodern Cities and Spaces*, Blackwell Publishers, 1995.
9. Castells and Mollenkopf, for example, argue: "Occupational polarization and income inequality become translated into widespread urban dualism... only when public policy mirrors the naked logic of the market." (*Dual City*, 1991, p. 413).
10. Castells, 1994, p. 19.
11. Peter Hall, *Cities in Civilization: Culture, Innovation and Urban Order*, Weidenfeld and Nicholson, 1998, p. 8.
12. I draw here, and later, on parts of my review-article "Urban studies: urban crisis" in *Regenerating Cities*, 6.
13. Peter Hall's concluding chapter to James Simmie (ed.), *Planning London*, University College Press, 1994. I draw here on my review article, "Science cities... cyber cities... citizen cities," in *Regenerating Cities*, 7.
14. Bianchini covered some of this ground in his contributions to issues 1–2 and 3–4 of *Regenerating Cities*. See also Carol Kenna, "Partnership and Community Arts/A perspective from Greenwich," in *Regenerating Cities*, 1(2).
15. Franco Bianchini's concluding chapter to Bianchini and M. Parkinson (eds.), *Cultural Policy and Urban Regeneration: The West European Experience*, Manchester University Press, 1993.
16. This line of criticism also applies to Anthony Giddens on the Third Way (see his *The Third Way: The Renewal of Social Democracy*, Polity, 1998, pp. 99–100.) who also seeks "a balance beween the economic and non-economic..."
17. Manuel Castells, *The Informational City: Information, Technology, Economic Restructuring, and the Urban Regional Process*, 1989, Blackwell Publishers, p. 353.
18. Alfred Brendel, "On playing Schoenberg's Piano Concerto," *New York Review of Books*, February 16, 1995. This passage is repeated in Brendel's liner note to his 1995 CD, Philips 446 683–2.

19. Donna Haraway, "A manifesto for cyborgs: science, technology, and socialist feminism in the 1980s," in Linda Nicholson (ed.), *Feminism/Postmodernism*, Routledge, 1990, p. 223.
20. Alain Lipietz, *Towards a New Economic Order: Postfordism, Ecology and Democracy*, Polity, 1992. See also David Gibbs, *The Green Local Economy: Integrating Economic and Environmental Development at the Local Level*, Centre for Local Economic Strategies, 1992, and the chapter "The economy, stupid! Industrial policy discourse and the body economic," in J. K. Gibson-Graham, *The End of Capitalism (as we know it): A Feminist Critique of Political Economy*, Blackwell, 1996, pp. 92–119
21. A good source for the sociological imagination can be found in Manga videos. See my "Science cities ... cyber cities ... citizen cities," n. 13 above, and "L. A. Blues, Japanimation, architecture and urban analysis," in *City* 1–2.
22. Castells, *The Rise of the Network Society*, Blackwell Publishers, 1996, p. 422.
23. bell hooks, *Sisters of the Yam: Black Women and Self-Recovery*, Southend Press, 1993, p. 180.
24. UCL, Bartlett School, "King's Cross Second Report," 1990 (quoted in Susan Fainstein, *The City Builders: Property, Politics, and Planning in London and New York*, Blackwell Publishers, 1994, p. 128; see her chapter on King's Cross (and Times Square) for background, pp. 124–129 but not for an understanding of the radical implications of the work of the King's Cross Railwaylands Community Group).
25. See Michael Safier, "Leading from the ground up: organizational landscape and community-led urban regeneration," in *Regenerating Cities*, 3, 4.
26. Luca Bertolini, "Knots in the net: on the redevelopment of railway stations and their surroundings," *City* 1–2, pp. 129–37.
27. Michael Keith, "Street sensibility? Negotiating the Political by Articulating the Spatial," Merrifield and Swyngedouw (eds.) op cit., p. 139.
28. See Guido Martinotti, "Urbs Hospitalis. Social morphology and governance in the new metropolis," paper presented to the American Sociological Association, August 5–9, 1994.
29. Extracts from an interview published in Bob Catterall, "All aboard for another docklands?" *New Statesman*, January 10, 1992.
30. Related discussions are by Paolo Fareri, "Consensus building: a research programme in urban policy," and Alessandro Balducci, "Planning *with* the community: the Vicenza Project," both in *Regenerating Cities*, 7; also Alessandro Balducci, "Environmental restoration in central Lombardy: the difficult search for effective planning instruments," *City* 3–4, pp. 49–57.
31. Michael Edwards, "The potentialities of community-generated alternatives to developers' schemes," Economic and Social Research Council London Seminars, n.d.
32. Castells, *The Informational City*, p. 353.
33. "Citizen movements, information and analysis: an interview with Manuel Castells," *City*, 7, p. 141.
34. This was prepared in 1991 on the basis of brief journalistic research forays in Barcelona and Paris undertaken for Mark Fisher and Richard Rogers, *The New London*, Penguin, 1992. Both were at the time proponents of the grands Travaux in Paris and predisposed towards the merits of the Norman Foster masterplan at King's Cross (for the latter point, see the editorial in *City*, 1992, 8, pp. 2–3). The significance of the Barcelona citizen movement has yet to reach them. Nevertheless, they have shown considerable interest in developments in Barcelona, and Pasqual Maragall, the former (urbanistic) mayor of Barcelona, contributes a foreword to the useful final report of the Urban Task Force chaired by Lord Rogers, *Towards an Urban Renaissance*, Department of the Environment, Transport and the Region (distributed by E. and F. N. Spon), 1999.

35. Manuel Castells, *The City and the Grassroots: A Cross-Cultural Theory of Urban Social Movements*, Arnold, 1983, p. 262. One of the results of the collapse of Marxist triumphalism in the social sciences has been a swing away from any of its insights, no matter how valuable. Those unfamiliar with the distinction between use-values and exchange-values in relation to commodities will find a useful starting point in the glossary to Ken Morrison, *Marx, Durkheim, Weber: Formations of Modern Social Thought*, Sage, 1995. See also Lewis Hyde, *The Gift: Imagination and the Erotic Life of Property*, Vintage, 1999.
36. William Greider, *One World, Ready or Not: The Manic Logic of Global Capitalism*, Penguin, 1997, p. 468.
37. Steven Seidman (ed.), *The Postmodern Turn: New Perspectives on Social Theory*, Cambridge University Press, 1994, pp. 9–10. See also my reference to the need to draw "on "history from below" and on approaches that derive from documentary filmmaking, the 'roman vrai' and Latin American testimonial literature" in a review "City life – infotainment, identity and action," in *City*, 7, particularly p. 189 (where I stake a claim for the importance of Paul Berman's book, *A Tale of Two Utopias: The Political Journey of the Generation of 1968*, Norton, 1996).
38. I have limited myself to European developments, in which I have had direct access to the participants and sites. For global and multicultural perspectives see, for example, Roger Burbach, "The (un)defining of postmodern Marxism: on smashing modernization and narrating new social and economic actors," in *Rethinking Marxism*, 10, 1 (1998), pp. 52–65.
39. One of the greatest weaknesses of Anthony Giddens' sociological project is its lack of attention to one crucial form of action knowledge, the deep and often relatively invisible struggles associated with a bottom-up and transformative social movement. Thus, it is hardly surprising that Giddens sees bottom-up development as a "new strategy" (Anthony Giddens and Christopher Pierson, *Conversations with Anthony Giddens: Making Sense of Modernity* Polity, 1998, p. 157). However, he does suggest that it is "surely important and in line with real possibilities generated by the global system."
40. Manuel Castells, *The Informational City*, p. 353. For a valuable preliminary reading of Castells' more recent work, *The Information Age* (1996, 1997, 1998), and with Jordi Borja, *Local and Global: The Management of Cities in the Information Age*, 1997, see Sophie Watson, "New orders, disorders and creative chaos: the information age and the network society," *Policy and Politics*, 26, 2, pp. 227–32, and her close reading of vol. II of *The Power of Identity*, in Watson, "From social movements to the politics of identity," in *City*, 7, pp. 133–9. There is a further need to reread *The City and the Grassroots* (1983) and *The Informational City* (1989). I have offered some preliminary indications above as to what that might involve. Castells himself offers a reading in my interview with him, "Citizen movements, information and analysis," in *City*, 7, pp. 140–55.
41. Peter Hall sets out, in his *Cities in Civilization*, and elsewhere, the possible significance of a fifth major wave (the so-called Kondriatieff wave) of technological, economic and social innovation forecast to begin around 2007–11. Whatever one's doubts about the existence of, and/or predictability, of such waves, future opportunities for "a way out of the destructive pathologies" (Greider) of capitalism can only be taken if urban analysis addresses such tendencies and possibilities. It is one of the many strengths of Hall's work that he addresses such a possibility. However, his consistently negative evaluation of the potential of grass-roots movements and, as argued above, the underdeveloped nature of his concept of "cultural economy" results in a failure to address that possibility effectively.

Chapter 18

Diaspora Capital and Asia Pacific Urban Development

Chung Tong Wu

Studies of the impacts of globalization on urban development have tended to focus on the changes in the economy of the cities and the social consequences of these changes (Sassen 1991). Few studies have examined the urban development impacts of global capital associated with specific ethnic groups. Part of the globalization process is the rush of global capital to invest in urban development, influencing a diverse range of major developments in cities such as Pudong, Shanghai, or inner-city apartments in Sydney and shopping malls in Vancouver. Even lesser cities and towns do not escape the attention of global capital seeking new investment opportunities.

One group of investors, the ethnic Chinese based in Southeast Asia, Taiwan, and Hong Kong, has made significant impacts on the major cities in the Asia Pacific region. Their investment forays in cities such as Los Angeles, Vancouver, and Sydney have attracted considerable press coverage, some scholarly research and occasional controversy (Goldberg 1996; Mitchell 1996) not just because the investments are sometimes extremely large but also due to their new development ideas as well as occasional perceived conflicts with established styles of development. Diaspora Chinese entrepreneurs, similar to other entrepreneurs, are seeking new investment opportunities and safe havens for their investments. Part of that strategy involves investing in global cities. Their decisions are shaped partly by the network of Chinese overseas or perception of opportunities shaped by previous experience through tourism and tertiary education in the relevant global city – personal or through their offspring (Goldberg 1985). For example, during 1996/97 international students studying in tertiary institutions in Canada numbered 65,235 and in Australia, 33,409. Interest in diasporas is not new. Kotkin (1993) argues that in the late twentieth century, networks based on ethnic origins and religion are shaping the new global economy. Skeldon, assessing Asian migration, suggests that diaspora is a concept that can capture the additional nuances of the new migration (Skeldon 1998). Studies of Chinese networks have ranged from studies of industrial development (Zysman and Doherty 1995), of specific industries (Borrus 1997), to those that focus on the real-estate market (Goldberg 1996). Lever-Tracy and others (1996) have examined the economic links of Chinese overseas with Mainland China.

Figure 18.1 Hong Kong skyline (© Sophie Watson)

Works such as the edited volumes by Skeldon (1994) and Sinn (1998) give a much broader overview of identity, settlement, and the activities of the Chinese overseas around the world or in major destination countries such as Australia (Inglis et al. 1992) and Canada (Adelman et al. 1994; Skeldon 1994).

In its first section, this chapter provides an overview of how diaspora Chinese capital has manifested itself in urban development in select locations, examines the ways diaspora Chinese capital changes local practices in real-estate development and explores the ways in which local interests respond to the new investments. The next section gives an overview of the rise of diaspora Chinese capital in Asia Pacific. The third section explores the impacts that diaspora capital has on urban development. The concluding section draws out the key ideas that emerge from this study of diaspora Chinese capital and urban development.

Rise of Diaspora Chinese Capital

In spite of the Asian Financial Crisis which started in Thailand in July 1997 and eventually spread to a number of Asian nations in 1998, there is no dispute that Asia, pronounced not that long ago by the World Bank as the "Asia Miracle" (World Bank 1993), achieved rapid and important economic changes against which the 1997/98 crisis is a counterpoint. Without the sustained and rapid economic growth over the last two decades, there would have been little to constitute a "crisis." This discussion by necessity deals with the situation before what has come to be known as the "Asian Financial Crisis," but it would be a mistake to assume the gains made by the sustained growth of the last three decades have all been swept away, or that the diaspora Chinese capital, which has been immensely enhanced over the same period, has completely dissipated. The significant capital that has been invested in different parts of Asia and outside of Asia will make sure the diaspora Chinese entrepreneurs will weather the storm much better than would have been the case if all or most of the capital had remained within Asia. Indeed, the crisis that started in mid-1997 illustrates well both the benefits and problems associated with globalization.

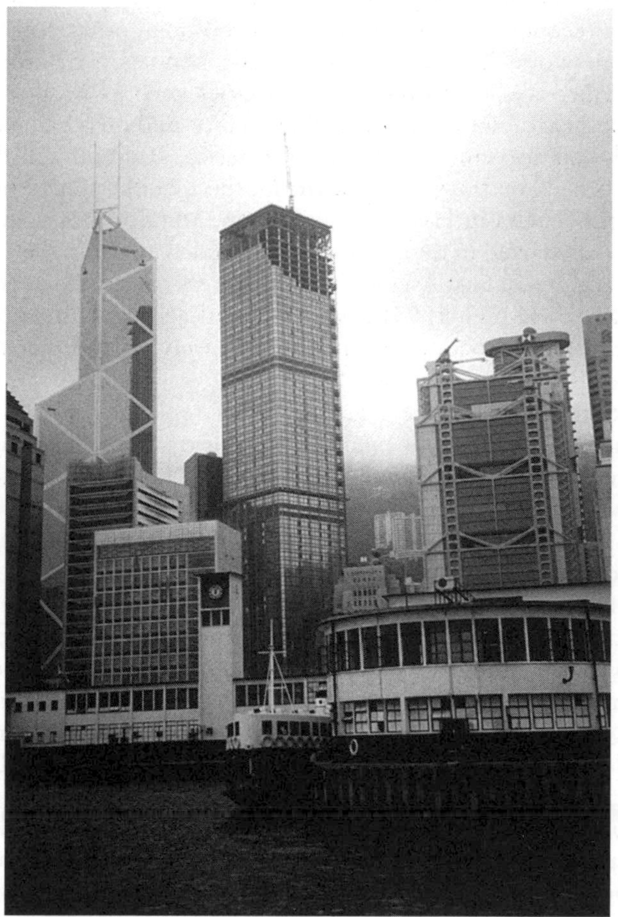

Figure 18.2 Hong Kong Island (© Sophie Watson)

There is a large literature about ethnic Chinese business networks in various Asian countries (Hamilton 1991; Kunio 1988; Wu and Wu 1980; Jesudason 1989; Hsing 1998). A very brief summary is provided here as background. The significant role of ethnic Chinese businesses in Southeast Asia is considered to be largely the result of exclusion from other avenues of advancement (in politics and in the military). Many migrants from China regarded themselves as sojourners who would one day accumulate sufficient savings to return to their home village with wealth and status. The 1949 revolution in China changed all that.

Arrighi and others (1996) placed the current discussions about Chinese business networks in a historical context. They argue that the present trade network has its antecedent in the historic "tribute and trade" network that developed when the Chinese Empire was hegemonic in Asia. When the Chinese Empire's power was eclipsed first by colonial powers and later by Japan in the nineteenth century, that trade network continued to develop as the tried and trusted method that overseas Chinese merchants used to conduct business with each other. In the second half of the nineteenth century, the export of Chinese labor, especially from the impoverished south, to fuel the economic activities of the new colonial powers in Southeast Asia, reinforced this network. The network provided channels for remittances back to China and entwined itself with the new port cities such as Malacca, Penang, and Singapore in Southeast Asia where the Chinese labor and merchants congregated. A similar network had also emerged in North America. Beginning in the 1950s, with China turning its back on the rest of the world, the foci of the network shifted from China to multiple centers in Hong Kong, Taiwan, and Southeast Asia. The globalization process that started in the 1970s and proceeded apace in the 1980s coincided with the rise of regions in East Asia as the new centers of manufacturing and exports to the rest of the world (Wu 1994). Asian regional economic integration, which is part and parcel of this process, was aided immensely by the preexisting overseas Chinese network (Chen and Drysdale 1995).

The networks that ensured the safe transfer of remittances back to China over time transformed into banks and financial institutions that aided business growth among the ethnic Chinese in Southeast Asia. In Hong Kong and Taiwan, the economic growth of the 1970s and early 1980s was based on manufacturing. As manufacturing labor costs became too expensive and shifted to southern China, the economy of Hong Kong restructured towards one that is based on finance, trade, and tourism. Much of the wealth was made in property development catering to the housing needs of the burgeoning middle class. While in general most of the wealth of the Southeast Asian Chinese was based on resource extraction and commodities (such as tin mining, timber, and oil palms) and trade, the wealth of the Hong Kong entrepreneurs was based on entrepôt trade, small and medium-scale manufacturing, and property development. On the other hand, manufacturing is still the backbone of wealth creation in Taiwan (Gereffi and Wyman 1990). Banking and finance was always in the background as the base on which the business networks flourished.

The significance of Asian economic growth can be gleaned by the large fiscal reserves held by Hong Kong, Singapore, and Taiwan. Together they have amassed fiscal reserves of US$237 billion; some four times that of the United States in 1998 (*Asia Week*, July 3, 1998 and *The Economist*, June 27 to July 3, 1998). Consequently, these countries have, by the mid-1980s, become significant exporters of capital to other nations, especially in the Asia Pacific region (Chen and Kwan 1997). Hong Kong and Singapore are also considered havens for much of the Southeast Asian ethnic Chinese capital. This capital-exporting role spilled over from investments in manufacturing to urban development.

Migration and Urban Development

During the last two decades, global migration streams have shifted from an Atlantic-based to a Pacific-based movement. In the major destination countries such as Australia, Canada, and the United States, and even minor destinations such as New Zealand, the origins of the majority of the migrant settlers have shifted from Europe to Asia (Table 18.1) (Ho and Farmer 1994). This sea change is also remarkable for the corresponding shifts in the characteristics of the immigrants. Whereas historically migration was largely the avenue by which the poor sought better fortunes in the lands of opportunities, giving rise to the characterization of the

Table 18.1 Ten major source countries of Australian and Canadian immigrants 1981–96 (percentage of total)

Australia				Canada			
1981–82		1995–96		1990		1996*	
UK	31.3	NZ	12.4	UK	14.7	Hong Kong	10.5
NZ	9.9	UK	11.4	China	7.6	China	8.5
Vietnam	9.4	China	11.3	India	7.3	India	6.9
Poland	4.9	USA	6.8	Lebanon	6.0	Philippines	6.9
S. Africa	2.8	India	3.7	Vietnam	6.3	Sri Lanka	4.3
Philippines	2.8	Vietnam	3.6	Philippines	4.6	Poland	3.6
Germany	2.6	Philippines	3.3	Poland	3.2	Taiwan	3.1
Netherlands	2.0	S. Africa	3.2	Portugal	3.6	Vietnam	3.1
Malaysia	2.0	Sri Lanka	2.0	Haiti	2.9	USA	2.8
Cambodia	1.8	Indonesia	1.8				
Other	30.5	Other	42.9	Other	40.8	Other	50.3

* for the period between 1991 and the first 4 months of 1996

Source: Adapted from Inglis et al. (1994) pp. 10–11; Statistics Canada; Department of Immigration and Multicultural Affairs Australia, 1997.

United States as the "Gold Mountain" or Australia as the "New Gold Mountain" among the poor Chinese immigrants, this is no longer necessarily the case (Ip et al. 1998). The new migrants are predominantly from the middle and upper-middle classes, many are highly trained professionals and some are entrepreneurs with capital to invest (Inglis and Wu 1990) (Kurin and Larry 1997). Not all migrants are wealthy or entrepreneurs with capital, but there is a significant shift in the characteristics of the new migrants compared to those who migrated prior to the 1960s. Large-scale migration and the concentration of the new migrants in a few Asia Pacific cities have created new opportunities.

Immigration flows to North America and Australia bring with them significant urban development impacts. Similar impacts can be observed from the investments attracted to new growth frontiers such as China. Some of the impacts have to do with new business practices that have direct bearing on urban development, but most can be summarized under the following categories: economic and financial composition, social and spatial distribution, urban community politics, and business practices (see Table 18.2).

Economic impacts

The diaspora Chinese bring with them capital for investment or at the least a demand for housing in the destinations where they settle. For those who migrated to Australia and Canada under the "business migration" category, setting up a business or showing proof of bona fide investment is an essential requirement for obtaining an entry visa (Woo 1998; Smart 1994). There are also those who seek investment opportunities in areas either close to home or in areas where new demands can be expected. Attention tends to be focused on cities where large

Table 18.2 Summary of impacts

Impacts	Forms of Impact	Characteristics	Examples
Economic	a. commercial i. enclaves ii. suburbanization	– special development or concentration of commercial enterprises catering to specific ethnic groups	Asian Malls (Vancouver and Cupertino, California) Chatswood, Sydney
	b. residential i. high-end housing ii. speculative residential estates	– residential development aimed at specific group of potential purchasers (Hong Kong immigrants or overseas Chinese)	Vancouver Guangdong province, China
Social and spatial	a. composition and size of immigration b. characteristics of migrants c. dialect/regional backgrounds a. recreating enclaves b. suburban nodes c. overseas Chinese estates	– shift to majority of immigrants from Asia – concentration of Asian immigrants settling in a few select cities – concentration of ethnic Chinese and dialect groups in the metropolitan area – shift of ethnic Chinese population over time to suburban locations	Canada and Australia "Little Taipei," Los Angeles San Francisco Sydney Guangdong province, China
Urban community politics	a. planning issues i. neighborhood design ii. signage b. mainstream political participation	– conflicts over neighborhood conservation – conflicts over physical design and compatibility issues – ethnic groups participation in mainstream political activities	Vancouver Cabramatta, Sydney Quebec Monterey Park and Cupertino, California
Business practices	a. off-the-plan sales b. strata-titled shopping malls c. infrastructure project d. land banking	– marketing strategies aimed at potential immigrants or Asia-based purchasers – use of property development strategies to fulfill immigration requirements – global capital and long-term investments in growth frontier	Sydney, Vancouver Guanding Province, China

numbers of immigrants congregate. In Canada and Australia, for example, the large influx of immigrants from Hong Kong, Taiwan, and the mainland stimulated many businesses such as grocery stores, restaurants, and other ethnic-owned businesses largely catering to specific ethnic or dialect groups. Scholars differ in their interpretation of these economic enclaves. Zhou argues that Chinatowns are "incubators" for ethnic businesses and provide economic opportunities for the next generations (Zhou 1992). Others point to the exploitation of new immigrant workers by Chinatown businesses (Kwong 1987; Loo 1992). These tend, however, to be studies of traditional enclaves of Chinatown in the United States, and not the new developments stimulated by the more recent waves of immigrants in countries such as Australia, Canada, or even the newly suburbanized parts of the United States.

Chinatowns or other ethnic enclaves are districts dominated by ethnic businesses and some residential congregations of the same ethnic group. Two new variations have emerged through the suburbanization of the ethnic population. The first are known as "Asian malls" and the other as satellite Chinatowns. In Vancouver, what are known as "Asian malls" signify medium-sized multistoreyed shopping-center developments aimed almost exclusively at businesses catering to Asian migrants (Wu 1996). The Richmond district of Vancouver is a prime example with several malls established by overseas capital and often managed by firms established by individuals from Hong Kong. Some of the malls are configured as strata-titled units for sale to potential investors. Not only was this way of configuring shopping malls new in Canada, it was also new in that investments in such strata-titled shop spaces qualified as approved investments for business migrants. In these shopping malls, the businesses are run by migrants from Hong Kong and the patrons are largely from Hong Kong so that the lingua franca in the shopping mall is Cantonese.

The suburban or satellite Chinatowns are often misnomers in that they have little in common with the popular image of traditional Chinatowns, those old enclaves tarted up with traditional Chinese arches and motifs, often found on the edge of the Central Business District in cities such as New York, Vancouver, and Sydney. They differ from the first type by largely arising from much broader processes of suburbanization of the ethnic population and businesses springing up to serve their needs. Such development could range from the highly concentrated quasi-suburban neighborhood shopping areas in the Richmond district of San Francisco (Wong 1994), the quasi-suburban shopping nodes of Chatswood and Ashfield in Sydney, to the borough of Queens in New York City. The additional key characteristics are that they are firmly urban based, vary in their degree of mixture with other mainstream or ethnic businesses, and one dialect group tends to dominate.

At least three types of residential developments can be identified as a result of Chinese migration. First, inner-city and Central Business District (CBD) developments catering to investors or settlers from Asia. This pattern can be observed in cities such as Vancouver and Sydney where locally based developers, possibly financed with investments from Asia, cater to a perceived market niche of newly migrated Asians and potential Asian investors. In the process, new marketing strategies and sales methods have been adopted (Olds 1997). Second are the developers who seek out sites in desirable neighborhoods and redevelop or build new houses to cater to those new immigrants or investors who can afford such high-end housing. The most obvious example are the so-called Monster Houses in Vancouver. New owners who bought an existing modest house in a highly desirable neighborhood sought to redevelop and build a larger house to accommodate their needs and their sense of style. In turn, this motivated developers to start speculative investments in the same neighborhoods to cater to the perceived taste and demands of certain segments of the new immigrant population (Hutton 1998). Third, in areas such as southern Guangdong in China, where land is relatively inexpensive, housing estates have been developed to cater to the demands of overseas Chinese as housing for their relatives in China or as a "second" home for retirement or investment (Wu 1993).

New immigrants brought with them economic opportunities that many, both local businesses and newly established businesses, sought to exploit. By catering to these needs, they have created new forms of development and stimulated new political debates. Analysis of new immigrants in San Francisco and Los Angeles impact on the

Figure 18.3 Cabramatta – Chinese-Vietnamese locality, Sydney (© Steve Pile)

established Chinatown community have all pointed to class conflicts within the diaspora Chinese community (Kwong 1987; Chen 1992). Recent immigrants with capital to invest often stimulate new developments that may be detrimental to the interest of the less well-off Chinese whose inexpensive housing or places of work are often redeveloped for very different purposes and higher price ranges. This type of analysis has not been carried out in locations such as Sydney and Vancouver, making comparisons difficult.

Social and spatial changes

While not all new immigrants necessarily wish to congregate in the same location in their new destinations, there are those who do. For some, especially those with poor English language skills, the social support of a community with similar background, language, or dialect, and immigration experience is highly desirable. For those families where one or both of the parents commute between the new location and place of origin, such a community represents a source of potential and perceived social support in an alien land. The Hong Kong and Chinese press call these men who constantly travel across the Pacific without their wives "astronauts," which aptly describes the sense of "rootlessness" many have experienced.

Ethnic enclaves in large metropolitan areas conjure up stereotypical images of the traditional Chinatowns. While this can be observed in many of the older metropolises such as New York City, San Francisco (Wong 1994), Vancouver (Anderson 1991), and Sydney, other examples of suburbanization are emerging. Well-documented recent examples are "Little Taipei" in the Los Angeles area (Fong 1994;

Waldinger and Tseng 1992; Tseng 1994) and the largely ethnic Chinese-Vietnamese enclave of Cabramatta in the western suburbs of metropolitan Sydney (Murphy and Watson 1997). Though these are both examples of suburban ethnic enclaves, there are marked differences. "Little Taipei" is settled mainly by upwardly mobile middle-class migrants from Taiwan who sought housing and a lifestyle which differed from their experience in Taiwan. Cabramatta in Sydney is more akin to the bootstrap effort of a community of boat people seeking to establish a new life in a new land. Both of these examples illustrate the suburbanization of ethnic communities as new immigrants have sought areas to establish themselves. In the case of "Little Taipei" it was more a deliberate effort to create a new enclave for a subgroup of ethnic Chinese immigrants who have the same regional culture and dialect (Fong 1994); while Cabramatta is an example of an economically disadvantaged group seeking a low-cost location to establish itself.

Yet not all immigrants wish to live in ethnic enclaves and many have the means to make the choice. Whether in Los Angeles, Vancouver, or Sydney, the socially upward mobile professionals, and those with capital, often seek to purchase in the sought-after residential neighborhoods seen as more befitting their own socioeconomic status and residential preferences. Not all of their new neighbours welcome them with open arms, with some local residents objecting to the ostentatious style of housing as not fitting into the existing neighborhood (Mitchell 1996; Ley 1998; Smart and Smart 1996). Mitchell has characterized part of these reactions as the original residents' fear of loss of identity and traditional culture. There are few comparable studies in other cities, though anecdotal evidence from Sydney and "Little Taipei" suggests this type of conflict is not isolated.

The influx of Asian immigrants into the large metropolitan areas of the Asia Pacific has also stimulated new developments in the central and inner city aimed at attracting overseas buyers (Seek and Wu 1994). Such housing established a new way of marketing real estate which brought a new practice of "selling off the plan." This was evident in Vancouver (Olds 1997; Mitchell 1996) and the same practice, allowed by local legislation, is rife in Sydney, Perth, and other major destinations of Asian immigrants. Just as immigrants have changed the physical landscape, so also they have stimulated innovations in the sales and marketing practice in the property market. The same is true in the commercial market.

One of the more blatant forays of Chinese diaspora capital is the rampant development of housing in China aimed at the overseas Chinese market. Thus it is now common, in a large number of cities and towns in China, to find housing estates or apartment complexes that are priced well beyond the affordability of the local population and unabashedly touted as housing for overseas investors. The development of these housing estates is the direct consequence of the Open Policies of China that, among other reforms, allow non-Chinese nationals to lease land. All land in China is state owned. Land is leased on the basis of the usage on the land. For example, agricultural land may carry a lease term of 50 to 80 years whereas land for hotels may be for a period of 35 years. Residential development usually carries a lease of 50 to 60 years. The demand side of the equation, in the case of Hong Kong, is fueled by two major factors: first, the high cost of housing in Hong Kong, therefore Hong Kong Chinese search for alternative property investment opportunities, and second, the desire of some overseas Chinese to make provisions for their relatives in China.

The context of development is the lax controls that local officials have over urban development in their locality. The surge of industrial development allowed by the Open Policies and facilitated by the move of manufacturing from the high labor-cost areas of Hong Kong and Taiwan to southern coastal China have made the same areas attractive to other development, notably residential.

The height of speculative property development in southern China, especially in the areas immediately north of Hong Kong, coincided with the peak of property price rises in Hong Kong. At least two groups of individuals were attracted to invest in property in China. The first was those who made gains during the property boom in Hong Kong and elsewhere, looking for new opportunities to reap new windfalls. The second group consisted of those who were unable to capitalize on the property boom in Hong Kong because they did not have the substantial capital required to break into the expensive market of Hong Kong, but who nonetheless had sufficient capital to speculate or invest in a market where prices were well below those of Hong Kong. Some among the first and second groups, looking beyond the return of Hong Kong to China, regarded the possibilities of retiring or having a second home in China.

During the period around the height of the speculative fervor, in one six-month period alone in 1993, some 15,000 residential units located in ten small towns within a two-hour drive from Hong Kong were available for sale to Hong Kong or other overseas Chinese residents (Wu 1993). These developments are sold off the plan to potential purchasers based in Hong Kong, often through real-estate fairs held in Hong Kong to inform and sign up potential purchasers. This area is perhaps special in that the concentration of such development is visible. Similar developments, but of a lesser concentration, can be found across the major coastal cities and towns of China. In the province of Fujian, many of the real-estate development projects are aimed at Taiwanese compatriots. In Shanghai and Beijing the estates are aimed especially at those who work for multinational or foreign companies.

The significance of such developments is complex. First, such housing estates are often not developed according to the overall development plans of the jurisdiction in which they are constructed. Thus the developments often destroy valuable arable land, or are developed in areas unsuitable for housing, or are developed with little or no improvements to the overall urban infrastructure of the area. The consequences are environmental impacts from the loss of arable land, soil erosion, the lack of facilities to supply clean water or to treat the wastewater generated. From the perspective of the purchasers, the lack of adequate water supply is the first of many potential problems that they could face.

A second, but much more important issue as far as urban development is concerned is the emergence of an urban structure in Chinese cities and towns that begins to resemble that of capitalist cities. The past five decades of urban development in China have created an urban structure that does not have the same degree of residential segregation by socioeconomic status as major Western cities. This was partly because until recently, the differences in the wage levels were not that great, but mostly it was due to the way housing was provided or assigned to the individual. Until the recent housing reforms starting in the 1990s, an individual was assigned housing based on his or her work unit. A factory worker was likely to be assigned housing in the compound of the factory or in the housing estate owned by the factory, while an academic would be housed within or close by the campus.

The new housing developments and the July 1998 housing reforms by which the Chinese government no longer assigns housing to the population, introduced a new element. Desirable housing – therefore more expensive housing – is likely to be located in the better locations of the city, by virtue of its transportation, convenience, views or other positive attributes. Gradually but surely, a new urban residential structure is emerging which will be based on affordability and the ability of overseas developers to purchase prime sites. This will lead to socioeconomic segregation much like most Western cities. In short, one of the consequences of diaspora Chinese capital investing in real-estate development is fundamental changes to the spatial structure of cities and towns in China, in both the distribution of land uses and in the spatial distribution of socioeconomic groups within the urban area.

Urban community politics

The best-documented cases of conflicts that have arisen from the urban development stimulated by recent migrants are the Monster Houses in Vancouver. The community political action generated by these new developments or redevelopments of existing residential sites has created a number of divergent responses and interpretations. Some argue that this is merely part of the changing dynamics of any urban neighborhood (Hutton 1998), while others have studied the rhetoric used to describe or explain the development (Smart and Smart 1996; Ley 1998). Observers have pointed out that large residences are not really new in many of these neighborhoods. Some of the older-style houses are indeed very large and are referred to as "mansions." The term "Monster Houses" is therefore considered by some to be deliberately pejorative. Still others have noted that similar issues are raised in controls over matters such as signage (Canadian Press 1998).

These points and the resultant community political debates are not confined to Vancouver or Canada. The same concerns were raised in Monterey Park, Los Angeles when the first inklings of "Little Taipei" were formed (Fong 1994). Further recent examples in Silicon Valley reflect more positive community reactions (Miller and Steinberger 1998). In both of the cases in California, the debates have led to active participation by the new immigrants in mainstream politics to have their voices heard. In these ways, not only do the diaspora Chinese stimulate community reactions and political actions, they themselves become involved.

Enclaves and satellite Chinatowns are not the only expressions of Asian investments in commercial properties nor do such developments always generate virulent opposition. In Brisbane, Australia, a much more sophisticated form of investments has been identified. Ip and Wu (1996) called this "cosmopolitanization" to refer to the fact that the immigrants have managed to introduce new international elements into the existing or redeveloped shopping centers to cater to the needs of the local population, by expanding the range of goods and services available while at the same time introducing new elements that serve the new immigrants. Not only is this form of new development less confronting to the existing population, it also offers genuine expansions of the range and diversity of shopping and entertainment possibilities. While the new proprietors may be Asian, they operate coffee shops that serve the latest coffee blends as well as shops that present more traditional Asian choices such as specialist restaurants that serve regional cuisines, noodles, or snacks. In the process, they challenge the local officials to deal with new activities (such as karaoke bars) in suburban locations.

Business practices and investment targets

The physical forms of development are but one aspect of the impacts of diaspora capital. Equally important are the changes in business practices adopted by local entrepreneurs who wish to capture the new investments. Property developers have used a variety of means to access the pool of potential investors. For the potential investors from Hong Kong and other parts of Southeast Asia, sales off the plan is an accepted sales method though this may not be widely practiced locally – such as in Vancouver. In the late 1980s and early 1990s, when such investments were common, property fairs in Hong Kong, Singapore, and other Southeast Asian cities were common occurrences to attract potential investors to real-estate projects in Australia, Canada, and China. Some investors purchased properties sight unseen and encountered unscrupulous developers who promised a great deal but delivered little. A common complaint is misrepresentation of the location of the property, its proximity to the center of the city and to amenities. Where local regulations are available, such misrepresentations are quickly brought to account but where such regulations are lax or nonexisting, then it is a case of "buyers beware."

Another of the consequences of the business migration program in Canada is the response of local developers (who may themselves have migrated earlier) to the potential market of business migrants. One innovation was that of developing shopping malls in which shop spaces are sold as strata-titled units. Investors in such spaces satisfied the Canadian Immigration Department's requirements that the "business migrant" show proof of investment and a new business initiative. Hence part of the impetus of the Asian malls in Vancouver has been investment driven. The commercial and social consequences are often secondary to the developers and investors. Diaspora Chinese investments in North America and Australia have tended to be limited to real-estate and business investments. This is not the case in China where very large projects such as toll roads, electricity generation, and even railways have attracted overseas investors, many of whom are diaspora Chinese. The first superhighway in the province of Guangdong linking Shenzhen (the city next to Hong Kong) to the provincial capital and other towns in the Pearl River Delta is an investment spearheaded by a large investor and contractor in Hong Kong. The significance of such investments is more than changing transportation access. Equally profound is the transformation of the countryside along the route to potential urban uses. By changing accessibility, new areas become potential sites for urban development thus transforming a whole region's urban future. Diaspora Chinese investments in infrastructure projects bring with them significant international investment since the projects are usually multimillion and require long-term financing of the kind that real-estate projects do not command. Through these involvements, the diaspora Chinese have brought with them the international finance community. The same is found in Thailand and the Philippines where Hong Kong engineering and developer firms had toll road and electricity plant projects.

The substantial investments for infrastructure sometimes pale in relation to the investments spent on amassing huge tracts of land with the main purpose of capturing future growth and appreciation in values. In many small towns all across southern China, Chinese overseas have selected choice real estate for future development. This is especially true in areas where the diaspora Chinese investors have a network of kin and dialect advantages. Land banking of this scale is unprecedented in China. The local government officials welcome it because it generates income immediately through the payments for leasehold right and land tax. The investors are pleased because they can capture the spillover effects of the investments they bring to the region and will have significant control over what development will occur and in what sequence.

One of the many uses of the remittances back to China from those who migrated in the late nineteenth century and early twentieth century was for the purchase of land. Those who worked overseas wanted to create a nest egg to return to, and the purchase of land back in the home village was preferred. In the late twentieth century, land banking is appearing in a different form. Diaspora Chinese investors, reacting to the rapid growth experienced by China during much of the last decade, are positioning themselves for even greater future growth. One of the strategies is to amass privately held land banks in areas considered to have great growth potential. While this phenomenon can be observed in the large cities, it is more evident in the smaller centers and major towns.

During the first years of Open Policies and especially after the Tiananmen incident, the overseas Chinese were one group who were wooed by the Chinese government to invest in China – to help the "motherland." Many investors obliged (Kohut and Cheng 1996). Some took the view that the best way to proceed was to examine opportunities in areas near their home village – where their ancestors originated, providing the dual advantages of similar dialects and kinship ties (Hsing 1996). Local officials, until then, were not familiar with international business or investments. They were however, attuned to the possibility of overseas kin who made good coming back to invest or to provide donations for worthy causes – such as new schools or hospitals – for the locality. By the same token, those overseas Chinese investors who did not have a great deal of experience investing in China considered it easier to deal with those who spoke the same dialect and who were kin. They found the local officials obliging and willing to cooperate, especially when certain advantages were placed in their way.

Many of the diaspora Chinese investors found themselves treated as a privileged class, fawned over by the local and provincial officials and often given latitudes impossible to obtain elsewhere. Land would be offered at very attractive prices, probably a small fraction of the prices associated with land back in their places of origin. Planning and building regulations were waived or made to fit the investment plans of the investors. The astute diaspora Chinese investors not only took advantage of the possibilities for themselves, but they would often turn to their fellow kin back in their places of origin and offer them a chance to join the consortium to invest in China. Not only were business risks minimized through sharing, but they themselves gained a great deal of prestige among their peers and among the Chinese officials – for introducing their kin to investment opportunities and for introducing a wider range of investors to the locality (Wu 1997).

Conclusions

The flow of new migrants to the large metropolitan areas of the Asia Pacific brought new developments, ranging from new enclaves, new housing forms and sales methods, and new shopping districts that both challenged and expanded the range in the existing community. To the extent that flows of new immigrants are part of globalization processes, these new immigrants have made significant impacts on urban development that are more than additional demand for housing and commercial areas, but are ones that have changed the physical form, have added to the complexity of the urban economy and have introduced new methods of retailing real estate.

Diaspora Chinese capital has impacted on urban development around Asia Pacific in a number of ways. Studies of these cities need to take into account the special impacts and ripples generated by diaspora Chinese capital. These impacts are diverse and the cultural expressions are equally varied. The traditional studies of Chinatowns are no longer geographically or analytically adequate. This brief review points to at least three major dimensions: the variety of impacts, the diversity of regional backgrounds, and the importance of the local context.

At least four major types of impacts can be identified: the variety of forms of the developments, the different ways of merchandizing the developments, the impacts on urban structures, and impacts on the commercial landscape. Suburban Chinatowns, satellite Chinatowns and suburban Asian malls found in a number of Asia Pacific cities are the physical manifestations of the new investments. Depending on the community where the new developments have taken place, they can represent a "cosmopolitanizing" influence by introducing both international and ethnic specific varieties serving the local and the new immigrant population. In many Chinese coastal cities where housing estates (aimed exclusively at overseas purchasers) have developed, long-term fundamental changes to the urban structure are emerging. These new developments also stimulate new approaches to merchandizing the development through off-the-plan sales and strata-titled shopping mall spaces.

The examples cited in this chapter have referred to specific regional cultures and/or dialect groups and their impact on developments. For example, it is important to note the congregation of regional cultural and dialect groupings that have emerged in the satellite Chinatowns across the Asia Pacific region. Cantonese-speaking ethnic Chinese, largely from Hong Kong, dominate the Richmond district of San Francisco and Chatswood in Sydney. Ashfield in Sydney is known as "Little Shanghai," with businesses predominantly owned and operated by those who have migrated from the Shanghai region of China. Queens Borough in New York is, on the other hand, Taiwanese, similar to "Little Taipei" in Los Angeles.

The same would be true of any studies of the major land banking and developments in a variety of smaller cities and towns in China, reflecting the importance of recognizing kinship ties and business networks back in the places of origin. Any study of diaspora Chinese capital around the Asia Pacific needs to be cognizant of the significance of regional culture and dialects and their influence on spatial concentrations as well as the business and other networks they represent. Also underlying this discussion is the local context in which the new developments have taken place. There is as yet insufficient research to comment extensively or compare the local context in which the variety of developments occurs. The land-banking activities reported in various small towns and cities in China are unlikely to be accommodated in other Asian Pacific cities. In Vancouver, important questions were raised about the government's open-arm approach to diaspora Chinese capital (Mitchell 1996), while Waldinger and Tseng have speculated on the local politics that help shape "Little Taipei" in Los Angeles (Waldinger and Tseng 1992).

What this brief review has attempted to show is that at the turn of the millennium, one set of important forces that is having considerable impacts on urban development in Asia and the Pacific is diaspora capital. While this review has dealt with diaspora Chinese capital, the same questions could be raised about the impacts, for example, of diaspora Korean and Indian capital. Comparative studies of these diasporas and the different ways they impact on urban development would enrich our understanding of urban development in a globalized world where boundaries are less and less important to capital, while at the same time impacts on urban development are localized.

REFERENCES

Adelman, H. et al. (eds.) 1994: *Immigration and Refugee Policy: Australia and Canada*. Melbourne: Melbourne University Press.

Anderson, K. 1991: *Vancouver's Chinatown: Racial Discourse in Canada, 1875–1980*. Montreal: McGill-Queen's University Press.

Arrighi, G. et al. 1996: *The Rise of East Asia in World Historical Perspective*. Planning Workshop, Binghamton: Fernand Braudel Center, State University of New York at Binghamton.

Borrus, M. 1997: *Left for Dead: Asian Production Networks and the Revival of US Electronics*. Berkeley: Berkeley Roundtable on the International Economy.

Canadian Press 1998: Quebec eases stand on Chinatown signs. *Vancouver Sun*, AlO.

Chen, E. and Kwan, C. H. (eds.) 1997: *Asia's Borderless Economy: The Emergence of Subregional Zones*. Sydney: Allen and Unwin.

Chen, E. K. Y. and Drysdale, P. (eds.) 1995: *Corporate Links and Foreign Dire Investment in Asia and the Pacific*. Pymble: Harper Educational.

Chen, H.-S. 1992: *Chinatown No More*. Ithaca, NY: Cornell University Press.

Fong, T. P. 1994: *The First Suburban Chinatown: The Remaking of Monterey Park, California*. Philadelphia: Temple University Press.

Gereffi, G. and Wyman, D. L. (eds.) 1990: *Manufacturing Miracles: Paths of Industrialization in Latin America and East Asia*. Princeton, NJ: Princeton University Press.

Goldberg, M. 1985: *The Chinese Connection: Getting Plugged in to Pacific Rim Real Estate*. Vancouver: University of British Columbia Press.

Goldberg, M. 1996: The integration of Asia and Pacific Rim real estate markets. *Canadian Chamber of Commerce in Hong Kong Papers (Nov./Dec.)*.

Hamilton, G., (ed.) 1991: *Business Networks and Economic Development in East and Southeast Asia*. Hong Kong: Centre of Asian Studies, University of Hong Kong.

Ho, E. S. and Farmer, R. 1994: The Hong Kong Chinese in Auckland. In R. Skeldon (ed.), *Reluctant Exiles*. New York: M. E. Sharpe, 215–34.

Hsing, Y. A. 1996: Blood thicker than water: interpersonal relations and Taiwanese investment in southern China. *Environment and Planning*, 28, 2241–61.

Hsing, Y.-T. 1998: *Making Capitalism in China: The Taiwan Connection*. New York: Oxford University Press.

Hutton, T. 1998: International immigration as a dynamic of metropolitan transformation: the case of Vancouver. In E. Laquian, A. Laquian, and T. McGee (eds.), *The Silent Debate: Asian Immigration and Racism in Canada*, Vancouve: Institute for Asian Research, University of British Columbia, 285–314.

Inglis, C. et al. (eds.) 1992: *Asians in Australia: The Dynamics of Migration and Settlement*. Sydney: Allen and Unwin.

Inglis, C. and C.-T. Wu 1990: The "new" migration of Asian skills and capital in the Asia Pacific region: its implications for new directions in theory and research. In R. Reed (ed.), *Patterns of Migration in Southeast Asia*. Berkeley, center for South and Southeast Asian Studies. Occasional Paper, 16, 282–302.

Ip, D. et al. 1998: Cosmopolitanizing Australian suburbia: Asian investments in Sunnybank. *Journal of Population Studies*, 19, 53–79.

Ip, D. F. et al. 1998: Gold mountain no more: impressions of Australian society among recent Asian immigrants. In E. Sinn (ed.), *The Last Half Century of Chinese Overseas*. Hong Kong: University of Hong Kong Press.

Jesudason, J. V. 1989: *Ethnicity and the Economy: The State, Chinese Business and Multinationals in Malaysia*. Singapore: Oxford University Press.

Kohut, J. and Cheng, A. T. 1996: *Return of the Merchant Mandarins*. Asia, Inc.

Kotkin, J. 1993: *Tribes: How Race, Religion and Identity Determine Success in the New Global Economy*. New York: Random House.

Kunio, Y. 1988: *The Rise of Ersatz Capitalism in South-East Asia*. Singapore: Oxford University Press.

Kurin, R. and Larry, D. 1997: *Succeeding: Profiles of Chinese Canadian Entrepreneurs*. Vancouver: Asia Pacific Foundation of Canada.

Kwong, P. 1987: *The New Chinatown*. New York: Hill and Wang.

Lever-Tracy, C. et al. 1996: *The Chinese Diaspora and Mainland China: An Emerging Economic Synergy*. London: St. Martins Press.

Ley, D. 1998: The rhetoric of racism and the politics of explanation in the Vancouver housing market. In E. Laquian, A. Laquian and T. McGee (eds.), *The Silent Debate: Asian Immigration and Racism in Canada*. Vancouver: Institute for Asian Research, University of British Columbia, 331–48.

Loo, C. M. 1992: *Chinatown: Most Time, Hard Time*. New York: Praeger.

Miller M. and Steinberger, M. H. 1998: America's New Voice. *Far Eastern Economic Review*, 161, 29–32.

Mitchell, K. 1996: In whose interest? Transnational capital and the production of multiculturalism in Canada. In W. Rob and W. Dissanayake (eds.), *Global/Local*, Durham: Duke University Press, 219–51.

Murphy, P. and Watson, S. 1997: *Surface City: Sydney at the Millennium*. Sydney: Pluto Press.

Olds, K. 1997: *Developing the Trans-Pacific Property Market: Tales from Vancouver via Hong Kong*. Vancouver: Vancouver Centre of Excellence, University of British Columbia.

Read, R. *Patterns of Migration in Southeast Asia*. Berkeley: Center for South and Southeast Asian Studies. Occasional Paper No. 16, 282–302.

Sassen, S. 1991: *The Global City: New York, London, Tokyo*. Princeton: Princeton University Press.

Seek, N. H. and Wu, C. T. 1994: The impact of Asian migration on property investment. *Asian Migrant*, 7 (2), 52–7.

Skeldon, R. (ed.), (1994). *Reluctant Exiles? Migration from Hong Kong and the New Overseas Chinese*. New York: M. E. Sharp.

Skeldon, R. 1998: From multiculturalism to diaspora: changing identities in the context of Asian migration. In E. Laquian, A. Laquian, and T. McGee (eds.), *The Silent Debate: Asian Immigration and Racism in Canada*. Vancouver: Institute of Asian Research, University of British Columbia, 213–26.

Smart, A. and Smart, J. 1996: Monster homes: Hong Kong immigration to Canada, urban conflicts and contested representations of space. In J. Caulfield and L. Peake (eds.), *City Lives and City Forms: Critical Research and Canadian Urbanism*, 33–46.

Smart, J. 1994: Business immigration to Canada: deception and exploitation. In R. Skeldon (ed.), *Reluctant Exiles*. New York: M. E. Sharpe, 98–119.

Tseng, Y.-F. 1994: Chinese ethnic economy: San Gabriel Valley, Los Angeles County. *Journal of Urban Affairs*, 16 (2), 169–89.

Waldinger, R. and Tseng, Y. 1992: Divergent diasporas: the Chinese communities of New York and Los Angeles compared. *Revue Européenne des Migrations Internationales*, 8 (3), 91–114.

Wang, G. 1998: Upgrading the migrant: neither Huaqiao nor Huren. In E. Sinn (ed.), *The Last Half Century of Chinese Overseas*. Hong Kong: University of Hong Kong Press, pp. 15–33.

Wong, B. P. 1994: Hong Kong immigrants in San Francisco. In R. Skeldon (ed.), *Reluctant Exile*. New York: M. E. Sharpe, 235–54.

Woo, E. 1998: The new entrepreneurs and investors from Hong Kong: an assessment of the business program. In E. Laquian, A. Laquian, and T. McGee (eds.), *The Silent Debate: Asian Immigration and Racism in Canada*. Vancouver: Institute for Asian Research, University of British Columbia, 315–30.

World Bank 1993: *The East Asian Miracle*. New York: Oxford University Press.

Wu, C.-T. 1993: Hyper-growth and hyper-urbanization in Southern China. *Australian Development Bulletin*, 57, 30–4.

Wu, C.-T. 1994: *NIES and Their Cousins: Transnational Investments and Their Regional Impacts*. Fourth Asian Urbanization Conference, Taipei.

Wu, C.-T. 1997: Globalisation of the Chinese countryside: international capital and the transformation of the Pearl River Delta. In P. Rimmer (ed.), *Global-Local relations in Pacific Rim development*. Sydney: Allen and Unwin, 57–82.

Wu, C.-T. and Ip, D. 1996: Cosmopolitanizing Suburbia: Asian investments in Brisbane. Paper presented to the ACSP-AESOP Joint Conference, Toronto, Canada.

Wu, Y.-L. and Wu, C.-H. 1980: *Economic Development in Southeast Asia: The Chinese Dimension*. Stanford: Hoover Institution Press.

Zhou, M. 1992: *Chinatown: The Socioeconomic Potential of an Urban Enclave*. Philadelphia: Temple University Press.

Zysman, J. and Doherty, E. 1995: *The Evolving Role of the State in Asian Industrialization*. Berkeley: Berkeley Round Table on the International Economy.

Chapter 19

Capitalizing on Havana: The Return of the Repressed in a Late Socialist City

Charles Rutheiser

For much of the twentieth century, cities in socialist societies received a fraction of the attention devoted to examining the urban process under capitalism. Over the last 20 years, however, a growing body of international scholars have documented how centralized planning, the absence of market forces, and other features of a socialist "regime of urbanization" (Angotti 1993) created a variety of distinctive metropolitan forms (e.g. French and Hamilton 1979; Szelenyi 1983; D. M. Smith 1989; among others). In the 1990s the transition to postsocialist regimes intensified scholarly interest in the cities of the former Soviet Union and Eastern Europe (see Andrusz, Harloe, and Szelenyi 1996; Hegedüs and Tosics 1991). However, with the notable exception of a burgeoning literature on China (e.g. Chan 1994; Davis 1995; Gaubatz 1996; Wu 1997), the discourse of urbanization in the so-called socialist third world (Forbes and Thrift 1987) remains comparatively underdeveloped.

This chapter is intended as a modest contribution towards filling this discursive void by exploring the changing patterns of sociospatial organization in Havana, Cuba. Although in many respects a classic example of a primate city produced by the processes of dependent urbanization, in other aspects Havana resembles both the cosmopolitan cities of the American mainland and the erstwhile workers' paradises of the former Eastern bloc. Its built environment is the product of a syncretic blending of five centuries of European, North American, and Latin American urban forms, and the city's singularity is a dominant theme in the popular, scholarly, and artistic images generated by both native and foreigner alike. In short, Havana is characterized by an irreducible particularity that confounds simple generalization and classification.

The distinctive place-fullness of Havana's imagined and physical landscapes contrasts markedly with the increasing place-lessness of many contemporary urban environments (e.g. Zukin 1991; Sorkin 1992; Rutheiser 1996). Although by no means a command and control center of the regional, much less global economy, Havana is – if not a "world city" (Knox and Taylor 1995) – at least a city in the world-historical sense. In 1982, the historic center of Havana was designated a World Heritage Center by UNESCO. Since then, the Cuban government has made extensive efforts to restore and preserve what has been acknowledged to be part of the "cultural patrimony of humankind."

Given the internationally recognized importance of Habana Vieja, not to mention the limited resources of the Cuban state, it is perhaps not surprising that many of the current restoration efforts are financed from abroad. Foreign investment in tourism and urban redevelopment are part of the profound socioeconomic changes taking place during what Cubans refer to as "The Special Period in Time of Peace." Unlike other socialist societies that have withstood the demise of the Soviet bloc, such as China and Vietnam, Cuba has steadfastly resisted the turn towards large-scale market reforms of its centralized command economy. Instead, the Cuban state has sought to develop what it calls "islands of capitalism in a sea of socialism" (Eckstein 1994) through joint ventures with foreign corporate partners in select sectors of the economy, such as mining, manufacturing, and, above all, tourism, while at the same time discouraging private entrepreneurial activity by Cuban citizens. This new economic policy is known unofficially as *sociocapitalismo* or *socio-cap*.

Although foreign investment has been by no means limited to Havana – the touristic enclaves of Varadero Beach and Cayo Coco and the nickel works at Moa/Nicora are notable beneficiaries of the influx of foreign capital – sociocapitalist development has been most intensively concentrated in Havana, which remains home to one out of every five Cubans, and which continues to dominate the country's political, economic, and sociocultural life. By contrast, the effect of foreign investment on Cuba's secondary urban centers has been minimal.

This chapter looks at some of the effects that foreign investment and touristic-related development are having on the social and built form of Havana. Although current policies are viewed officially as a logical continuation of previous urban development strategies, sociocapitalism represents a sharp break from the urban policies and practices of the last four decades. In the argument that follows, I first briefly sketch the history of urban development in pre- and postrevolutionary Havana, before moving on to discuss some of the principal features and unintended consequences of this new regime of urbanization.

The Colonial Period, 1519–1898

For the first two and a half centuries of existence, *San Cristobal de la Habana* remained a relatively compact urban settlement oriented to maritime trade rather than its undeveloped hinterland. In the nineteenth century, trade and profits from the development of vast sugar and tobacco plantations in the interior stimulated the construction of new, extramural neighborhoods that resembled the contemporaneous urban environments then arising in Vienna, Paris, Barcelona, and other European cities (see Venegas 1990). The most characteristic features of this New Havana – celebrated by novelist Alejo Carpentier in his *Ciudad de las Columnas* (1970) – were the columned pedestrian arcades, or *portales*, that lined its major streets, as well as an architectural eclecticism that fused elements of Neoclassicism with Moorish, Baroque, Romanesque, Gothic, and even Art Nouveau (Venegas 1996). After 1868, however, Havana's growth was slowed by three decades of nearly continuous civil war, which ended with the establishment of a US protectorate in 1898 and a nominally independent Cuba in 1902.

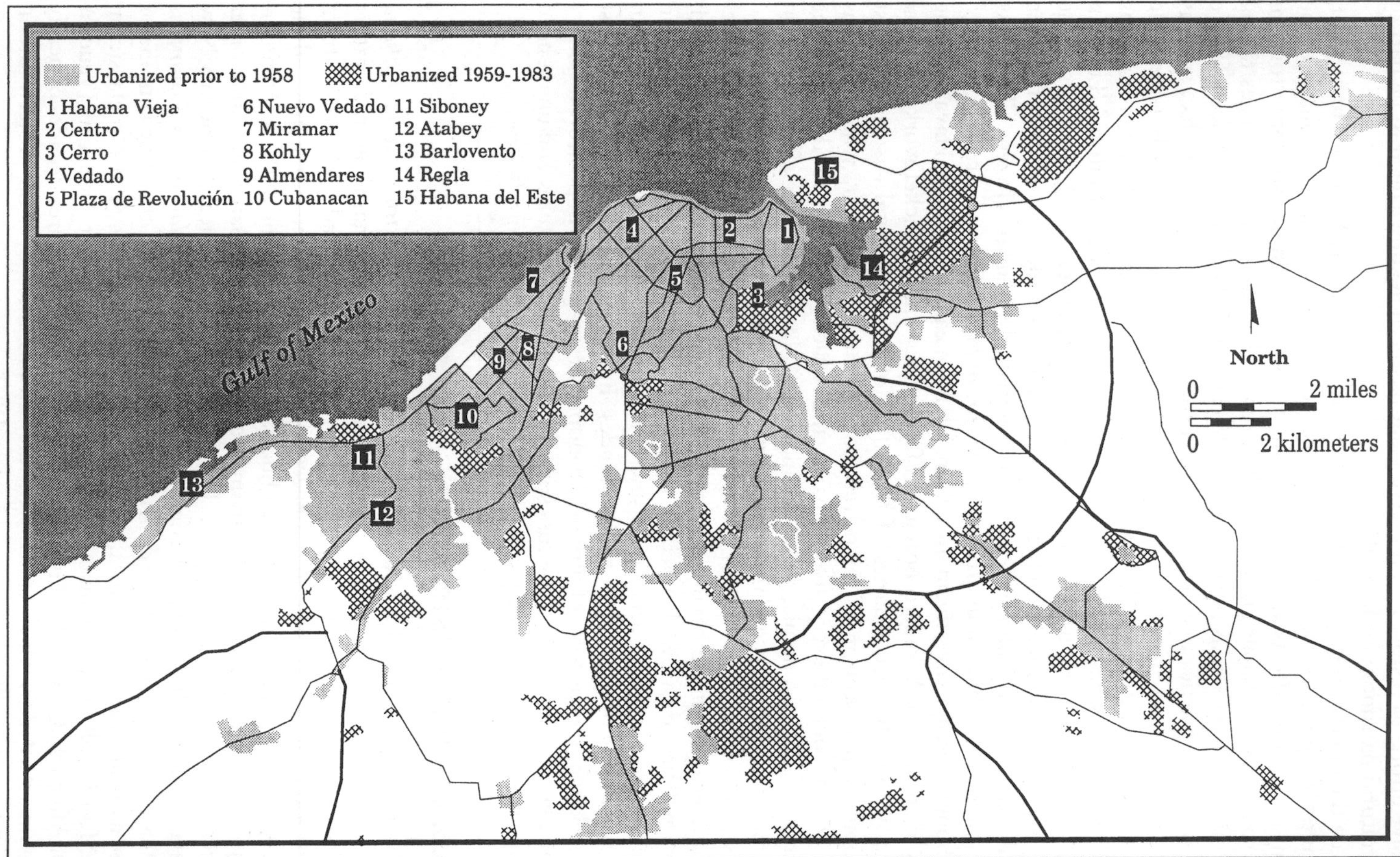

Figure 19.1 Havana and its neighborhoods

The Pseudo-Republic, 1898–1958

Havana's nineteenth-century growth was merely a harbinger of a more dramatic expansion during the first six decades of the twentieth century. Two distinct periods of frenzied development – the first between 1900 and 1929, the second, from 1940 to 1959 – triggered by windfall profits from the sugar industry and sustained by the complementary activities of local elites and foreign, mostly US, interests, stoked the construction of suburban subdivisions, high-rise office towers, and an extensive infrastructure to service the hundreds of thousands of US tourists that flocked annually to the island beginning in the 1920s.

With expansion came both a transformation in the use of urban space and an intensification of already existing patterns of socioeconomic specialization and segregation. As the city's more prosperous elements moved from the central districts of Habana, Centro, and Cerro to the peripheries, the former mansions of the elite and apartment buildings of the middle classes were intensively subdivided to house a growing influx of poor rural migrants, who by the 1950s arrived at a rate of more than 20,000 persons per year (Segre et al. 1997). During the latter part of the 1950s, commerce and government joined the exodus from the center. Domestic and foreign capital redeveloped the northern third of Vedado into a modernistic high-rise and high-status residential, commercial, and hotel district (see Lacey 1991: 281–301; Segre et al. 1997: 74–126), while just to the south, the Batista regime constructed a new ceremonial-administrative center around the Plaza Civica. Built in the grandiose "modern-monumental" style favored by authoritarian regimes (Segre 1989), the plaza was appropriated by the new government and was renamed the Plaza de Revolución in 1959.

On the eve of the Revolution, nearly one third of Havana's population lived in substandard, overcrowded, and aged dwellings located, for the most part, in the older parts of the urban core. The dense concentration of poverty in the center attracted the attention of the Batista regime, which commissioned plans to raze most of the depressed central area for a complex of high-modernist hotels, office buildings, and expressways that would connect the city to vast new speculative developments on the hitherto undeveloped lands in *Habana del Este* or East Havana (see Bastlund 1967; Segre 1989).

Enter the Revolution, 1959–1990

The advent of the Revolution halted the proposed refiguring of Havana and inadvertently preserved the historic core of the city from the uncreative destructions visited upon dozens of other American cities during the 1960s. However, the aims of the regime were not preservation, but transformation of the social order. Havana was viewed as a symbol of all that was wrong with Cuban society, and in keeping to Castro's maxim "a minimum of urbanism and a maximum of ruralism" (Gugler 1980), state investment during the 1960s focused on improving conditions in rural areas and secondary urban centers.

Within Havana itself numerous measures were taken to equalize conditions and erase class divides. The signature institutions of capitalist urbanity – real-estate speculation, landlordism, private commerce, gambling, and prostitution – were banned, although private home ownership was not. Under a series of urban reform laws, tens of thousands of renters received title to their residences. The city's most squalid squatter settlements were demolished and their inhabitants housed in new developments (see Butterworth 1980). Most residents, however, remained in place – there was no large-scale residential resettlement of the population. Private clubs and beaches were nationalized and the glitzy, modernist hotels and office buildings of Vedado were taken over by official mass organizations. In a move that symbolized the government's new priorities, the partially completed National Bank of Cuba tower was converted into the country's largest hospital.

By the end of the 1960s, nearly all of Havana's pre-Revolutionary elite had emigrated, along with many professional and middle-class families (Eckstein 1994: 152). The emigration led to the vacancy of thousands of homes and apartments, with the heaviest concentration in the posh neighborhoods west of the Almendares River. From the outset, the government decided that these areas would not be used to rehouse the city's poor. Instead, they declared these neighborhoods to be a "frozen zone" (*zona congelada*) that would be used instead by foreign embassies, government officials, schools, and cultural institutions. Despite the freezing out of formal residential uses, some areas of the frozen zone were thoroughly "de-bourgeoisified" (Eckstein 1977) through the conversion of housing stock into dormitories for students from the provinces. The Miramar neighborhood was perhaps the most radically affected. Prior to 1959 it had been an exclusive all-white neighbourhood, but by the mid-1960s it was inhabited by a mix of foreign technicians and Cubans from all ethno-racial and socioeconomic backgrounds, including thousands from what the older residents referred to as the "lower cultural levels" (see Lewis et al. 1978).

Still, not all parts of the frozen zone experienced such a dramatic cultural leveling. The most sumptuous of the pre-Revolutionary neighborhoods, such as El Country Club and Biltmore Estates, were renamed to honor the pre-Hispanic inhabitants of the island (Cubanacan and Siboney, respectively) and, symbolically cleansed of their former associations, were used to house high government officials and foreign dignitaries. In the 1980s and 1990s, these areas were further privileged by the construction of research facilities for Cuba's emergent biotechnology industry, an international convention center, and a series of luxury hotels for foreign visitors.

Although the anti-Havana ethos of the first years of the Revolution eased somewhat after the early 1970s, the city continued to atrophy on the greatly reduced resources allocated to it. As in many other socialist countries, the state's provision of housing lagged considerably behind demand (Hamberg 1986; Eckstein 1994). Even more importantly, the government also lacked the means to maintain old buildings and infrastructure. By the late 1980s the state reluctantly acknowledged that Havana suffered from many of the same problems that beset capitalist cities. According to official sources, 14 percent of the population lived in slums or unhealthy areas and no less than 20 percent of Havana's dwelling units lacked electricity or running water. In the mid-1980s, the Cuban government estimated the cost of needed repairs to the city's buildings, roads, sewers, and other infrastructure at between 10 billion and US$14 billion, or an amount almost equal to Cuba's annual GDP at that time (Segre et al. 1997: 181). More than a decade later, the total cost defies logical estimation.

The official recognition of Havana's problematic state during the late 1980s was part of a general campaign of "rectification of errors." Responsibility for land-use planning was partially decentralized and distributed among the planning and urban design directorates of the dozen municipalities that comprised the greater Havana Metropolitan Area. At the same time, a new entity, the Group for the Integrated Development of the Capital, or GDIC, was created to develop new ways of dealing with the problems created by three decades of neglect (GDIC 1990). These included developing a series of neighborhood workshops that would assist localities in designing and executing their own redevelopment activities, albeit within the general dictates of the state-sanctioned master plan (Coyula et al. 1995). The collapse of the Cuban economy in the early 1990s, however, radically transformed the scope and nature of the problems that urban planners had to deal with.

A Very Special Period, 1991–present

Following the dissolution of the Council for Mutual Economic Assistance (CMEA or Comecon) and the loss of massive subsidies to its economy, Cuba was obliged to slash state spending and court foreign investment. Between 1991 and 1997, Cuban state entities entered into more than 240 joint-venture agreements with corporate partners from Canada, Spain, Italy, France, Germany, Britain, and 37 other countries – even Israel. In 1993 the government legalized the possession of US dollars by Cuban citizens, and developed various means to "recapture" this much-needed hard currency from its population. Between 1994 and 1997, the Cuban economy grew at an average annual rate of 6 percent, with the most dramatic increases coming in tourism. In 1996, tourism was second only to remittances from abroad as a generator of hard currency, contributing more than US$1 billion to the Cuban economy (Martin 1997: 10).

The Cuban courting of foreign capital precedes the exigencies of the Special Period. The first decree law allowing for joint ventures between Cuban state corporations and foreign companies dates from 1982. Under this arrangement, the Cuban state entity would contribute land and guarantee access to low-cost labor and the ability to repatriate profits, while the foreign partner – which could own no more than 49 percent of the joint venture – would provide investment capital, technology, and managerial expertise (Eckstein 1994). In 1995 the law was amended to allow foreign partners majority ownership as well as the ability to participate in real-estate development ventures, provided that these projects were limited to hotels and other facilities for the sole use of tourists and foreigners.

Since 1995, the government has fielded hundreds of proposals for real-estate projects between foreign investors and the handful of corporate entities established by the state for that purpose (see GDIC, 1990). In the Miramar district, dozens of old mansions have been converted into offices for state corporations and joint ventures, in addition to restaurants and stores that recapture hard currency by selling scarce goods to those Cubans with access to dollars. Miramar is also the preferred locale for foreign investors seeking to build condominiums for foreigners. One recently completed luxury project sold all of its units at an average price of US$149 per square foot, which is comparable to real estate on Miami's Brickell Avenue (Reyes 1998). Two other projects with equivalent levels of amenity, totaling some 250 units, are under construction, and two new joint ventures have proposed to build several hundred more units nearby.

The Vedado district has also drawn the attention of foreign investors. Many of the Batista era luxury hotels have been extensively renovated and are managed by foreign corporations. In addition, more than a dozen new restaurants and nightclubs have opened up in recent years. In late 1997, one of the largest Cuban state entities opened a US-style shopping mall on the eastern edge of Vedado. Several other projects have been proposed, including a major renovation of the Focsa Building, once Havana's most luxurious apartment complex.

Although Miramar and Vedado are the choicest sites for new and future projects, the processes of sociocapitalist redevelopment have been so far most advanced in the *Casco Historico*, or Historic Center. Also referred to as *Habana Vieja*, the Historic Center is perceived to be something of a model for this new mode of urbanization, as it is the only area of the city that possesses a master plan to coordinate foreign investment and touristic projects with historic preservation and redevelopment of residential neighborhoods.

The Historic Center is home to some of Havana's most important civic monuments and places of touristic interest, as well as some of its most decayed and densely populated residential districts. By 1958, only 500 of the area's more than 4,000 buildings were considered to be in good repair. Since then, lack of maintenance and a shortage of housing has led to increased deterioration, especially in the southern part of the former walled city, such as the San Isidro neighborhood.

Preservation efforts in the Historic Center date from the early 1930s, although these were very modest in scope and only a few of the area's most significant monuments were partially restored. Hundreds of historic buildings were razed in subsequent decades and much of the area was slated for wholesale demolition in the late 1950s. Largely ignored for the first two decades of the Revolution, it was not until 1981 that the central government allocated major funds to the City Historian's Office for restoration purposes (see Argona 1981; Ministerio de Cultura 1983). In 1982, the area's designation as a World Heritage Site brought limited technical and financial aid from UNESCO and prompted an intensification of restoration efforts under the auspices of the National Center for Conservation, Restoration, and Museology, or CENCREM (Hernandez et al. 1990).

During the 1990s the economic crisis and the enhanced importance of tourism spurred a major reorganization of efforts in the Historic Center. Since 1994, redevelopment in the area has been overseen by a state corporation, Habaguanex, SA, an adjunct of the City Historian's Office. Although the Historian's Office receives a direct appropriation from state coffers, and must return some of its profit to the central government, the income generated by Habaguanex allows it to be a largely self-financed "island of capitalism." In 1996, Habaguanex grossed US$20 million in earnings (*Opciónes* 1997); the following year it grossed approximately $40 million. More than 70 rehabilitation projects are currently underway, or have been recently completed. Many of these projects were financed with capital from Spanish concerns. Spanish corporations and state agencies are so ubiquitous in redevelopment activities as to prompt many Cubans to speak of the *Re-conquista*, or Reconquest. However, a number of the most recent hotel projects have been funded by French, Dutch, and British firms.

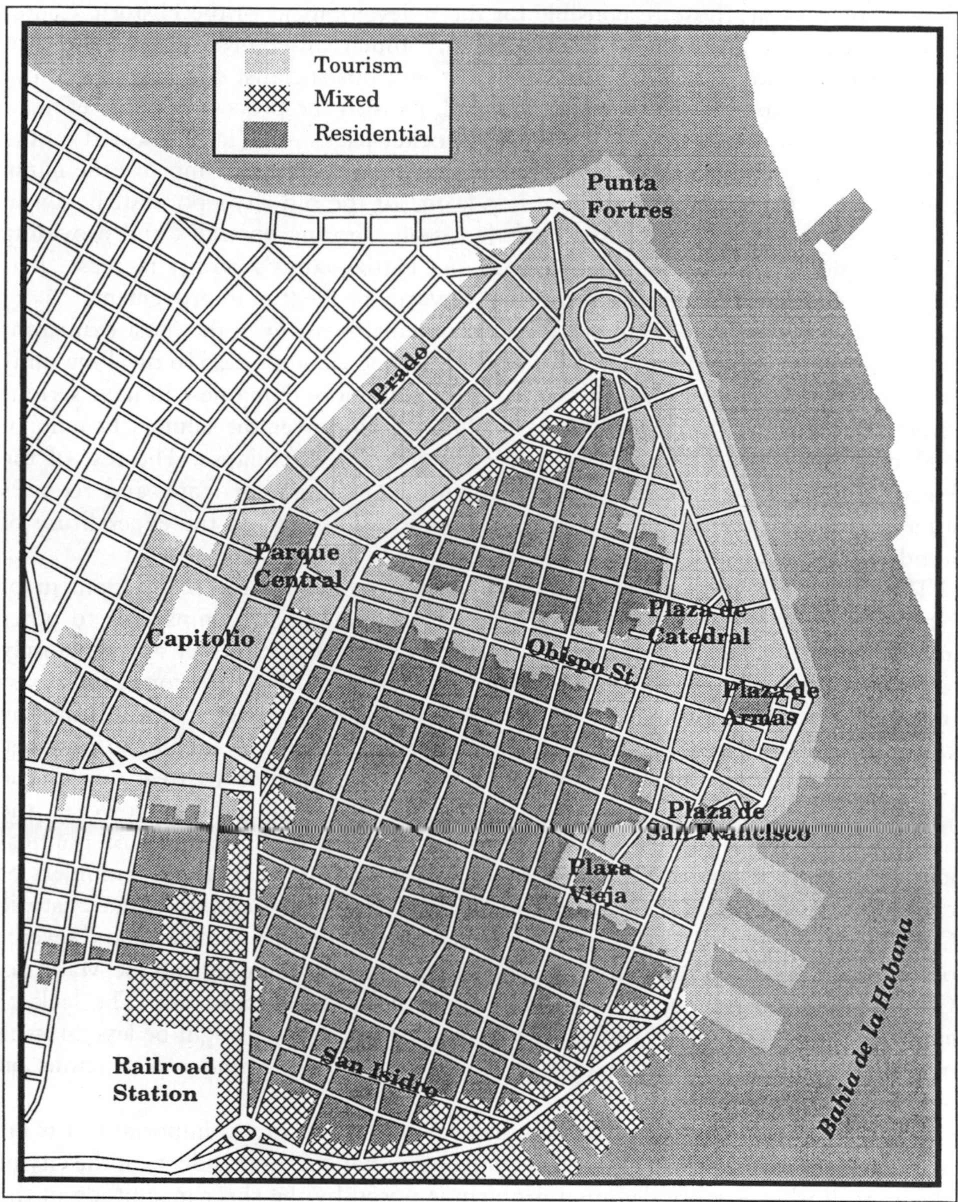

Figure 19.2 Historic Center of Havana

Under the direction of City Historian Eusebio Leal Spengler, Cuban and Spanish planners have devised a scheme to redevelop only certain areas for exclusively touristic purposes, while leaving much of the rest of the area in the hands of residents. More importantly, profits from the redevelopment of the touristic areas are to be used to rehabilitate substandard housing and build new community service facilities in other parts of Habana Vieja. Given the emphasis on improvement rather than displacement, those responsible for the redevelopment of the Historic Center have strenuously argued that their plans are much different from the rampant gentrification taking place in many capitalist and postsocialist cities (see N. Smith 1996). The Historian's Office has completed, or is in the process of completing, a library, a senior citizens home, and several pocket parks – the latter located on the sites of collapsed buildings. It has also started a pilot project to improve the living conditions in the San Isidro neighborhood, one of the old city's poorest. Begun in late 1996, the first phase focused on fixing roofs, shoring up walls, and providing proper toilets for one hundred dwellings. As Habaguanex's profits increase, it is expected that more funds will be directed towards residential improvements.

Still, the sheer scale of Habana Vieja's problems dwarf even the most exuberant profit estimates. More than one-third of the Historic Center's 22,516 dwelling units lack both running water and sanitary facilities, and more than one-half have serious structural problems (Rodriguez Aloma 1996: 29). Moreover, the salutary benefits of 100 new toilets are limited if the sewer system is near collapse. The rest of the Historic Center's – and city's – infrastructure is in a similar state, and requires intervention on greater than a neighborhood scale, as well as the expenditure of hundreds of millions of dollars.

The Historic Center is sometimes touted as a model for the redevelopment of Havana as a whole. However, the district is not completely comparable to other areas of the city. The redevelopment process in the Historic Center is both closely tied to, and limited by, concerns for historic preservation. No such constraints exist in other parts of the city which, while they have not been designated as historic by UNESCO, are characterized by a rich array of twentieth-century architectural styles. Critics claim that the reluctance to extend historical protection to areas outside the UNESCO-designated zone reflects the regime's anticapitalist bias. However, the limitation on historic preservation seems to be more than a matter of political ideology, of valorizing the colonial era while consigning the material reminders of capitalism to the rubbish tip of history. Indeed, the first building in the Historic Center to be restored with foreign funds was the former Stock Exchange, and several other structures slated for restoration such as the Bacardi Building and the Manzana Gomez shopping arcade, are key symbols of the arch-capitalist era. The lack of emphasis on historic preservation outside the Historic Center might be less an issue of socialist ideology than a matter of not wishing to place undue restrictions on investor prerogative.

While preservation of the city's unique architectural legacy is important, it is far from being the most pressing problem confronting *habaneros* (residents of the city of Havana). Rather, a more daunting problem is posed by the sheer magnitude of the deterioration of the city's physical infrastructure. In 1997, the government estimated that more than half of the city's buildings were in no better than poor condition and perhaps as many as 80,000 structures were too decayed to be rehabilitated (Lee 1997a). Between 1993 and 1996 alone, more than 5,300 structures experienced partial or total collapse, and many of the city's older sections resembled Beirut, Sarajevo, or London during the Blitz.

One of the ironies of *sociocapitalismo* is that it is leading to the revival of some of Havana's formerly most bourgeois neighborhoods, while promising to do very little for the remainder of the city. Unlike the Historic Center, there is at present no mechanism for leveraging foreign investment in Vedado and Miramar for the benefit of the residents of those neighborhoods, or any prospect of allowing significant foreign investment in projects for the end use of Cubans, rather than foreigners. While a number of foreign NGO-funded projects have been announced to rehabilitate tenements in the overcrowded Centro district, the amounts constitute a fraction of the sums being invested in touristic projects (*Granma International*, August 3, 1997). The prognosis is even bleaker for other areas of the city with little or no touristic interest.

Tourism and Socio-spatial Segregation

The separation between foreigners and residents is not just a matter of the touristic enclaves being set apart from the remainder of the city; it also characterizes life within the touristic zones themselves. Many recent travelers to Cuba have remarked on the "tourist apartheid" that is to be found there. That is, the only Cubans who may set foot in the new or newly renovated hotels, cafes, and restaurants are those who work there or those who are accompanied by a foreign guest. There is also a more insidious segregation at work, because even if Cubans are allowed unaccompanied entrance, most generally cannot afford to purchase even a soft drink at many of these establishments, which accept payment only in US dollars.

This double segregation has sparked considerable resentment from many Cubans. While government authorities have not gone to the extent of putting the streets of touristic areas off-limits to citizens, they have deployed a very visible security apparatus to ensure that the tourists are safe. Indeed, thanks to large numbers of police on the streets, Havana is easily the safest city in Latin America for tourists. However, crime, especially robbery, has increased considerably in recent years.

Despite the official separation between tourist and resident, the boundaries between citizen and guest are more permeable than not, and the "islands of capitalism in a sea of socialism" are merely the exposed promontories of a vast subterranean continent of un- and semisanctioned market activities. Although "la bolsa negra" (the informal economy) has existed for as long as the Revolution, the exigencies of the Special Period have stimulated creative survival strategies and an unprecedented amount of private entrepreneurial activity, especially in the provision of foodstuffs and services. Together with an estimated annual influx of more than $1 billion in remittances from abroad, the profits realized from dollar-denominated informal economic activities has led to increasing social divisions between those Cubans who have access to dollars and those who do not.

A good deal, although certainly not all, of the new informal economy is directly connected with the expansion of tourism. In the touristic zones of Vedado, Miramar, and the Historic Center, many households have turned their dining rooms into small restaurants called *paladares* and/or rent spare bedrooms to tourists at rates considerably below that charged by state and joint venture-owned operations (see Segre et al. 1997: 230–9). Faced with widespread evasion of the law prohibiting such illegal activities, in 1995 the government legalized and began to tax these unofficial purveyors of food and lodging. The legalization of these activities has in turn set in motion another kind of decidedly nonsocialist economic activity, as prospective entrepreneurs try to obtain space in prime touristic areas, such as Vedado, through swapping, rental, or outright but illegal purchase arrangements.

The most ubiquitous forms of entrepreneurial activity are still illegal. Those *habaneros* with access to cars and informal-sector gasoline have created an extensive fleet of taxis that compete with state-sanctioned operations, and often steer visitors to *paladares* and apartments for rent. Thousands of *jineteros* and *jineteras* (literally "jockeys") provide foreign visitors with black-market rum, cigars (usually counterfeit), and, especially, sex. Indeed, a revived sex trade is one of Havana's (and Cuba's) most compelling attractions in the eyes of many male visitors. While the traffic in sex is nowhere as large, complex, and organized as it was during the decadent extremes of the Batista era (see Greene 1980; Lacey 1991; Ragano et al. 1994), Havana has developed a well-earned reputation as the "Bangkok of the Caribbean." Frequent government crackdowns on taxis, prostitution, and hustling of goods have not succeeded in eradicating these activities, but have merely raised the prices charged to compensate for fines levied in dollars. While distasteful, the fines also provide the state with yet another means of recapturing hard currency.

Largely owing to the economic opportunities to be found there, the flow of migration to Havana has increased in recent years to the highest levels seen since the first years after the Revolution. In 1996, an estimated 28,000 persons migrated to the capital, a figure roughly equivalent to the latter years of the Batista regime (Lee 1997b). While the increase is partially offset by a significant out-migration (Segre et al. 1997), if this trend continues, it may begin to reverse one of the few accomplishments of the Revolution's urban policy, the reduction of Havana's rate of growth compared to other urban centers.

Conclusion

As the above-mentioned examples indicate, the Cuban government has not been successful in limiting capitalism to a handful of state-controlled enclaves. Rather, the growth of the informal economy and the success of tourist/foreigner-oriented enclaves has in turn stimulated the expansion of unsanctioned economic activities and the increasing social differentiation between those Cubans who possess dollars and those who lack access to them. Workers in the illegal tourist service trades can easily make more in one day, in dollars, than a highly trained professional earns in a month, in pesos. The social consequences of this inversion of status and income are only beginning to manifest themselves and demand further ethnographic investigation.

The further expansion of facilities for tourists and other foreigners promises only to intensify the social and spatial divide between the Historic Center, Vedado, Miramar, and the remainder of Greater Havana. The recommodification of land in the former three neighborhoods constitute dramatic eruptions of unequal value in an otherwise uniform land-rent surface. Without a comprehensive redevelopment plan and an entity to enforce it, as in the case of the Historic Center, the vast differential between current and potential land values constitutes a "rent gap" (N. Smith 1996) that will generate powerful pressures for the redevelopment of large areas of Miramar and Vedado for the exclusive use of foreigners and state entities. Despite the decentralization of land-use planning in the late 1980s, municipal and city authorities have played a very marginal role in the approval of joint-venture real-estate projects. The partial recommodification of land, the removal of certain areas from the control of local planning entities, and the creation of exclusive and exclusionary socio-spatial zones, all constitute serious breaks from the urban policies and practices of the last 40 years. Likewise, the reintegration of Cuba into the world economy as a purveyor of sun, sex, and cigars for foreigners stands in stark contrast to 40 years of revolutionary rhetoric. Despite the proliferation of billboards that boast: "We have, and will always have Socialism," this seems a questionable assertion. If current trends continue, the result is likely to be a city and national society as "dual" and unevenly developed as those found in other dependent societies in Latin America.

REFERENCES

Andruz, G., Harloe, M., and Szelenyi, I. (eds.) 1996: *Cities After Socialism.* Oxford: Blackwell Publishers.

Angotti, T. 1993: *Metropolis 2000: People, Poverty, and Planning.* London and New York: Routledge.

Argona, M. 1981: *La Habana Vieja: Restauración y revitalización.* La Habana: Departamento de Monumentos, Dirección de Patrimonio Cultural, Ministerio de Cultura.

Bastlund, K. 1967: *Jose Luis Sert: Architecture, City Planning, Urban Design.* London: Thames and Hudson.

Butterworth, D. 1980: *The People of Buena Ventura.* Urbana: University of Illinois Press.

Carpentier, A. 1970: *La ciudad de las columnas.* Barcelona: Editorial Lumen.

Chan, K. 1994: *Cities with Invisible Walls: Reinterpreting Urbanization in Post-1949 China.* Hong Kong and New York: Oxford University Press.

Coyula, M., Cabrera, M., and R. Oliveras. 1995: *Los Talleres de Transformacion Integral de los Barrios.* La Habana: Grupo para el Desarrollo Integral de la Capital.

Davis, D. (ed.) 1995: *Urban Spaces in Contemporary China.* Washington, DC: Woodrow Wilson Center Press; Cambridge: Cambridge University Press.

Eckstein, S. 1977: The debourgeoisment of Cuban cities. In I. Horowitz (ed.), *Cuban Communism,* New Brunswick, NJ: Transaction Books, pp. 443–75.

—— 1994: *Back From the Future: Cuba Under Castro.* Princeton: Princeton University Press.

Enyedl, G. 1996: Urbanization under socialism. In G. Andruzs et al., *Cities After Socialism,* Oxford: Basil Blackwell, pp. 100–18.

Forbes, D. and Thrift, N. (eds.) 1987: *The Socialist Third World.* Oxford: Basil Blackwell.

French, R., and Hamilton, F. (eds.) 1979: *The Socialist City Spatial Structure and Urban Policy.* Chicester and New York: John Wiley and Sons.

Gaubatz, P. 1996: *Beyond the Great Wall: Urban Form and Transformation on the Chinese Frontiers.* Stanford: Stanford University Press.

GDIC, 1990: Estudio urbano sobre el Tema Immobiliario en la ciudad de la Habana. Habana: Grupo para el Desarollo Integral de la Capital y la Dirección Provincial de Planamiento Física y Arquitectura.

Granma International. Agreement for Reconstruction of Tenements, August 3, 4.

Greene, G. 1980: *Ways of Escape.* New York: Simon and Schuster.

Gugler, J. 1980: A minimum of urbanism and a maximum of ruralism: the Cuban experience. *International Journal of Urban and Regional Research,* 4 (4), 516–35.

Hamberg, J. 1986: *Under Construction: Housing Policy in Revolutionary Cuba.* New York: Center for Cuban Studies.

Hegedüs, J., and Tosics, I. 1991: Gentrification in Eastern Europe: the case of Budapest. In J. van Weesep and S. Musterd (eds.), *Urban Housing for the Better-Off: Gentrification in Europe*. Utrecht: Stedelijke Netwerken.

Hernandez, T., Lores, R. and Mendez, L. 1990: *La Nueva Habana Vieja*. Lima: Camblo y Desarollo, Instituto de Investigaciónes.

Knox, P. and Taylor, P. (ed.) 1995: *World Cities in a World-System*. Cambridge: Cambridge University Press.

Lacey, R. 1991: *Little Man: Meyer Lansky and the Gangster Life*. New York: LB Books.

Lee, S. 1997a: Migraciones incontroladas hacia la capital (2). *Granma*, May 13, 6.

Lee, S. 1997b: Migraciones incontroladas hacia la capital (1). *Granma*, May 10, 8.

Lewis, O., Lewis, R., and Rigdon, S. 1978: *Neighbors: Living the Revolution: An Oral History of Contemporary Cuba*. Urbana: University of Illinois Press.

Martin, F. 1997: Foreign Real Estate Ventures and the Economy – 1996. *Negocios en Cuba*, July, 1 (1), 10.

Ministerio de Cultura 1983: *La Plaza Vieja*. La Habana: Plaza Vieja.

Opciónes. Resurge La Habana Vieja, April 6, 3.

Provincial de Planamiento Fisica y Arquitectura 1990: *Estrategia*. Habana: Groupo para el Desarollo Integral de la Capital.

Ragano, F., Ragano, N., and Raab, S. 1994: *Mob Lawyer*. New York: Scribner's.

Reyes, G. 1998: Luxury apartments rise in Havana, attract foreign investors. *Miami Herald*, October 4, A7.

Rodriguez Aloma, P. 1996: *Vieja en la memoria: apuntes para tin acercamiento a la habana vieja*. La Habana y Pamplona: Oficina de la Historador de la Ciudad de Habana y Colegio Oficial de Arquitectos Vasco Navarro.

Rutheiser, C. 1996: *Imagineering Atlanta: The Politics of Place in the City of Dreams*. London and New York: Verso.

Segre, R. 1989: *Arquitectura y urbanismo de la revolución cubana*. La Habana: Editorial Pueblo y Educación.

Segre, R., Coyula, M., and Scarpacl, J., 1997: *Havana: Two Faces of the Antillean Metropolis*. Chicester and New York: John Wiley and Sons.

Smith, D. M. 1989: *Urban Inequality Under State Socialism*. Cambridge: Cambridge University Press.

Smith, N. 1996: *The New Urban Frontier: Gentrification and the Revanchist City*. London and New York: Routledge.

Sorkin, M. (ed.) 1992: *Variations on a Theme Park*. New York: Hill and Wang.

Szelenyi, I. 1983: *Urban Inequalities Under State Socialism*. Oxford: Oxford University Press.

Venegas, C. 1990: *La Urbanización de las murallas: dependencia y modernidad*. La Habana: Editorial Letras Cubanas.

—— 1996: Havana between two centuries. Tr. N. Menocal and E. Shaw, *Journal of Decorative and Propaganda Arts*, 22, 12–34.

Wu, F. 1997: Urban restructuring in China's emerging market economy. *International Journal of Urban and Regional Research*, 14 (2), 218–42.

Zukin, S. 1991: *Landscapes of Power*. Berkeley: University of California Press.

Chapter 20

Urban Transformation in the Capitals of the Baltic States: Innovation, Culture and Finance

Philip Cooke, Erik Terk, Raite Karnite, Giedrius Blagnys

City governments everywhere are keen to ensure, as far as possible, that their economies replace lost jobs in declining industries as quickly and efficiently as possible. In that quest, new perspectives on the role and function of hitherto relatively passive elements in the urban fabric such as cultural facilities, banks, and universities have been projected. They are now, increasingly, seen as hubs of the microeconomy around which many other activities, all with economic value, coalesce. In what follows, this view will be explored from a number of angles. The main thrust is an analysis of the emergence of fast-growth industries in the three capital cities of the Baltic States which have undergone significant economic restructuring in recent years. In the original research, the Baltic cities were compared quantitatively and qualitatively with three regeneration cities of similar size in peripheral western Europe: Cardiff, Dublin, and Tampere.

The evolution of these cities in three key subeconomies centered upon cultural industries, financial services, and innovative, high-technology industry – all of which show fast employment and turnover growth – is described for the three Baltic capitals of Tallinn in Estonia, Riga in Latvia, and Vilnius in Lithuania. It is shown that the performance of the Baltic cities is highly variable but by no means as lagging as might be anticipated given their relatively recent liberation from state socialist management under the Soviet Union regime. All three show considerable strength in respect of cultural and innovative industry, though as yet relative stagnation in financial services. The empirical accounts are preceded by a review of key literature on fast-growth industries.

Review of Urban Growth Opportunities

Innovation activities

Recent research shows that some 80–90 percent of GDP growth is explained by the innovative activities of firms and other organizations with respect to product, process, and organizational innovation (Freeman 1994). Most of this activity occurs in or near urban settings and depends upon the capacity cities provide for interaction among diverse innovation actors and organizations within the large firm, between customer firms and suppliers, and among firms, research institutes, and university research laboratories. Writers such as Krugman (1995) have shown, theoretically, how urban concentration helps minimize knowledge imperfections and uncertainties among economic actors, and offers increasing returns to scale for those firms advantageously located in cities, where information intensities are highest. Thus cities and their nearby surroundings offer competitive advantage which, in turn, as Porter (1990) shows, derives fundamentally from spatial clustering of industries and the various support mechanisms, such as related input or output sectors, enterprise support services, and access to know-how, available in city or regional settings.

Competitive industries are, on the whole, innovative and likely to demonstrate a high capability for survival. It is widely believed that innovative firms in high performance or high technology sectors also tend to be associated with higher than average GDP and employment growth. Thus research conducted on employment growth in the world's leading high-technology complex at Silicon Valley in California showed that while total manufacturing employment grew from 131,000 in 1970 to 272,000 in 1985, high-technology employment grew (within those totals) from 52,000 to 215,000 over the same period. In other words, high-tech growth rates, measured in employment, were twice as high as already generally above-average growth in non high-technology sectors which were, nevertheless, secondarily associated with computing, communications, semiconductors, components, instruments, and software firms as input suppliers (Castells and Hall 1994).

The key sources of innovative firms are usually spin-offs from already existing firms and from university research laboratories (Dorfman 1983). The literature on the latter is extensive, that on the former less so. Four key points characterize the main argument regarding what Smilor et al. (1993) call the "entrepreneurial university." At a general level, first, the growth of a "knowledge society" means there is a greater valuation than hitherto of the importance of research results as a source of business opportunity. There is a rapidly growing market for scientific and technological knowledge. Second, universities and individual "academic entrepreneurs" are increasingly at the core of a cluster of local and global linkages through which knowledge is exploited. This ranges from industrial research contracts to consultancy and spin-off company management. Third, there is an accompanying growth in demand for secondary services associated with this process, including the expansion of industrial liaison functions, support for spin-off management training, patenting, and other intellectual property support and "campus company" foundation – the last as a means of managing business generated by academic enterprise (Dill 1995). A fourth, especially important element is the role of *science parks* in facilitating and promoting the formation of new-technology businesses. Modeled on the first successful one at Stanford University, these were supposed to be a key catalytic device for transferring abstract knowledge into commercial innovations. Left to the market, they tend to be relatively unsuccessful, but combined with support services like management training, business networking, and product marketing they have been shown to be highly successful (Jones-Evans and Klofsten 1997).

Culture industries

In a partly comparable way to that in which a long-established and traditional institution like a university may now be seen performing a catalytic economic role in the knowledge society, so there is now a wide recognition that traditional cultural facilities and activities have a catalytic economic role in the urban economy. Taking the three major US cities of New York, Los Angeles, and Chicago, Zukin (1995) showed that between 1980 and 1990 there had been a 34 percent increase in the employment of creative artists from 202,000 in 1980 to 270,000 in 1990, a phenomenon that has continued into the mid- and late 1990s. Among the larger categories of change in terms of creative occupation during that period were actors, directors, photographers, authors, designers, and architects. Of course, these aspects of the "symbolic economy" are responsible for a secondary employment impact upon demand for urban services such as accommodation, restaurants, transportation, and retailing. Given that it is widely accepted that there is a cultural industries multiplier of around 2 (Myerscough 1988), Zukin's estimate of a 68,000 employment increase for just the three major American metropolitan areas, in terms of core cultural industries employment, translates into an overall ascribable ten-year increase of 136,000. A rate of employment increase of over 13,000 per year compares favorably with the 11,000 per year increase in Silicon Valley's high-tech complex during the 1970–85 period.

Thus, culture, arts, and entertainment have come to be looked upon as a "new industry" with enormous growth potential. A study of Cologne showed that between 1985 and 1991 administrative budgets for the arts and culture grew by an average 34 percent while those for science and research declined by exactly the same percentage. This echoes a recognition by urban government of shifts in both latent and expressed demand for expenditure. The scale of urban governmental expenditure on cultural activities was, in 1991, some DM2 billion for cities of 500,000 or more in Germany (Friedrichs 1995). Cologne was by no means at the top of the ranking in terms of expenditure. Hamburg at some DM1,000 per inhabitant led the expenditure table, followed by Frankfurt (DM900), Stuttgart (DM395), Cologne (DM312) and Munich (DM237).

All of this points to the growth capability associated with "creative cities" (Landry et al. 1995). A keynote of this thinking is that "Historically, creativity and innovation have always been the lifeblood of our cities" (1995: 1). Cutbacks in expenditure of the kind suffered by German cities in the early 1990s also mean that artistically creative organizations have had to become more entrepreneurial in seeking to convince private financiers to invest in or sponsor their activities. The creative city is very much compatible with the innovative city, the latter perceived in terms of its incubator function regarding technology-intensive firms.

Financial services

The third growth industry of the 1980s–90s has been financial services. Although the boom of the 1980s has passed, to be followed by significant retrenchment in the early 1990s, there are signs that growing confidence following that recessionary period is, in cyclical terms, boosting the financial sector once again. Within financial services, the one important segment which has been growing despite the vicissitudes of financial services in general is "producer services." Producer services incorporate financial and other business services which act as inputs for other businesses. Output is frequently customized, nonroutine, and information-intensive and is provided by brokers, financial analysts, investment bankers, legal professionals, accountants, computer scientists, and specialist software analysts (Drennan 1996).

Key characteristics of such areas of the "symbolic economy" (Reich 1990) are that workforces are highly qualified, the industries involved are often creative and innovative, overlapping to some extent with the kind of innovative technology-intensive firms spinning out from universities or other research-based organizations. Employees receive higher than average incomes, a substantial proportion of the discretionary element of which is spent in the cultural economy of the arts, theater, and music and its secondary flotilla of activities in the nighttime economy. There is thus an interesting overlap at both the production and consumption end of the activities of the producer services economy with the spheres of the cultural economy in the creative city and the innovative economy in the "learning city." Like these two flanking economic spheres, the producer services economy-culture is one of highly developed social networks, highly attuned learning propensities, and high spatial clustering, facilitating the moderation of transaction costs by the trustful exchange of tacit knowledge as well as the more normal arm's-length exchange of contract-based market transactions in codified knowledge.

As Drennan makes clear, and is in any case well known, producer services activities are most highly concentrated in the very large global financial centers of London, New York, and Tokyo, though there is a hierarchy of lesser, though still major cities, specializing in particular markets. In each of these cities, producer services activities are key motors of their urban economies. Growth in producer services in London was 300,000 between 1971 and 1989, in New York also 300,000 from 1969 to 1994, while in Tokyo employment increased from 381,000 to 741,000 between 1969 and 1991. On average, therefore, the annual increment in producer services employment in the three key global cities over the decades of the 1970s and 1980s was 16,000 in London, 12,000 in New York, and 16,000 in Tokyo, a tri-city total per annum of 44,000 new jobs.

The Learning Economies: Tallinn, Riga, and Vilnius

It would be surprising if either the sources of information, the economic development processes, or the promotion policies of the urban or national governance bodies in the Baltic cities were to be of the same order as those, relatively sophisticated, action lines pursued in the West. The research approach adopted caused questions such as the ones explored thus far to be broached for the first time in each case. Nevertheless, it is clear that some elements, particularly with respect to cultural industries which bring discretionary tourist expenditure in their train, and the stimulation of innovative industries, are more pronounced than others. Thus, so underdeveloped were the financial services industries in all three countries and cities that there is relatively little of interest to report. However, this is far less the case for the other two sectors and this section will focus on them, with case illustrations, as appropriate.

Tallinn

Tallinn is blessed with a virtually intact medieval, Hanseatic Old Town within which much of its rich cultural infrastructure is located. This is planned to retain higher cultural activities, to evolve as a quiet haven with a revived café culture, art galleries, and residential conversions sympathetic to the historic character of the city. A more modern city center with contemporary arts, leisure, and entertainment centers is planned for the nearby waterfront area outside the medieval walls. All current projects are private ventures, the city government not yet having woken up to the economic dimension of culture. Thus, artists themselves, working through networks, have often been responsible for initiating and realizing projects with funding supplied through foreign foundations. Trade union statistics suggest as many as 5 percent of Tallinn's workforce may be directly and indirectly employed in cultural industries such as the performing arts, media, visual arts, and design, museums and libraries, and festivals. Some 41 percent are in the media sector, 24 percent in performing arts and 16 percent in visual arts and design (Võsa and Kuus 1997). Establishments such as the Estonian Drama Theater, Old Town Studio, State Puppet Theater, Russian Drama Theater and the Tallinn City Theater are among the most important of the city's nine theaters. The national opera theater – Estonia – is also in Tallinn. The City Theater is the subject of a major state investment involving adaptive reuse of medieval buildings. The main private, multicultural theater is Von Krahl, a focus for jazz, rock, dance, and an international music festival.

Tallinn's film production has suffered from the loss of Soviet subsidy. From 1993 to 1995, 6 full-length feature films, 49 documentaries and animated short features, and 36 newsreels were produced compared to 3 feature films, 48 documentaries, and 24 newsreels in 1985 alone under the old regime. Estonian classical music is of high international standard and Tallinn has four major companies, of which the Estonian Concert, the Estonian State Symphony Orchestra, and the Estonian Philharmonic Chamber Choir are examples; seven music festivals are also arranged in Tallinn each year. There is a buoyant press consisting of 17 weekly and 4 daily leading newspapers based in Tallinn out of a total for the city of some 90; books and periodicals are also published in substantial numbers. Estonian TV employs 728 people in Tallinn. There are seven cultural foundations in Tallinn, one, the Open Estonia Foundation funded by George Soros, the international financier and another, the Hereditas Foundation, by a combination of Nordic and American funds.

The Hereditas Foundation has supported one of Tallinn's most interesting cultural initiatives – the Old Town College and the Latin Quarter. This is a scheme to renovate not only the neglected Dominican monastic buildings (hence "Latin" quarter) in the heart of the Old Town, but the craft skills, folklore, music, heritage, and educational infrastructure associated with medieval Tallinn, to make it a lived rather than observed experience. The intention is to make the Latin Quarter a unique cultural tourism experience; the musical college exists, as do the craft workshops specializing in glass, custom-made clothing, ceramics, and leatherware. The key problem for the future is securing funding for further development.

Contrasting with this cultural emphasis upon a neomedieval revivalism aimed at cultural tourists is the emergence of a software industry in Estonia, and particularly in Tallinn. Terk and Võsa (1997) show that turnover was valued at $10 million in

1996 with employment of some 600, a third of the employees engaged in research and development. Practically all of the 120 companies involved are small, the largest employing a maximum of ten people. A handful are overseas owned, the whole industry being represented by the Association of Estonian Computing Companies. Two-thirds of firms operate in customized market niches, the rest as systems integrators and firms involved in standard package adaptation for the Estonian market. A considerable amount of subcontracting is conducted for Scandinavian and Finnish firms. Once again, investment finance is hindering the more rapid growth of the industry by its paucity.

Financial services have been performing well in Tallinn recently. Estonian banks experienced a large rise in profits and share prices in 1997. Hansabank, the largest with a net income of $13.5 million is now selling its banking software and consultancy services within the EU and to eastern Europe. Between them this bank and the next two largest, Union Bank and Savings Bank, contribute to total Estonian bank assets of $1,403 per capita compared with $951 in Latvia and $443 in Lithuania. Hansabank has opened 24 new branches and 90 cashpoints as well as offering telephone and Internet banking services. The sector, in general, sells on the quality of its service, innovation and marketing, but sees the need to restructure organizationally and to intensify its service development. More than a quarter of business is focused upon Tallinn and over half in Estonia. Ukraine and Russia are the main eastern markets.

Riga

Riga is a large city and 85 percent of Latvian industry – mainly still in large, Soviet-style enterprises – is concentrated there. There is a privatization policy in being, but most enterprises are close to bankruptcy. The city government has the political power but not the economic means to stimulate development until its property holdings are sold to raise capital. In terms of cultural industries' development, Karnite and Pocs (1997) point to the current absence of policy but the existence of quite a strong cultural infrastructure and, at national level, two key policy documents on cultural policy which assess future prospects, consider necessary laws, point to the strong state dependence of funding for culture (57% state, 6% private sector, 37% municipal) and the need for more private and associational participation. Like Tallinn, Riga has a fine medieval core and has prospects for developing its emergent tourist industry and enhancing its international potential as a congress and cultural center. The city is a member of the 61-member Baltic Cities network as well as seeking membership of the 72-member Eurocities partnership.

Riga's cultural infrastructure rests upon its 30 "culture houses," which sustain 340 amateur performing troupes, 28 museums with attendances at 722,000 in 1994, 7 theaters with attendances of 630,000, and a film-production industry which, with 5 feature-length films, 31 shorter films and 16 newsreels in 1994, was operating at less than half the capacity of 1980. As in Tallinn, there is a vast range of musical and other performance disciplines with Academies of Music, Arts and Culture which both perform and train artists. Large numbers of books, periodicals, and newspapers are produced, though there is as yet only the single state-run TV station. Virtually all this activity is centered in Riga. Tourist arrivals declined from 100,000 in 1991 to 43,000 in 1994, international arrivals going down from 79,000 to 36,000 over the period, suggesting the market suffered from an initially very high increase in prices for a relatively poor quality of service.

As in Tallinn, Riga has been developing an indigenous software industry. This is the most developed growth sector in Riga. There is considerable interaction among small and medium enterprises (10–50 employees) and integration with the computer hardware sector. There are 176 firms, of which 40 are pure software firms and the others both hardware and software specialists; all were established after 1991 by computer staff from former state enterprises. The industry is wholly private and receives no subsidies; few firms have foreign contracts or joint-ventures partners. In general, it appears from comparative analyses conducted by the European Union statistical service, Eurostat, that Latvia is one of the more laggard economies in the Central and Eastern European bloc in respect of levels of "economically active" enterprises, largely due to slow privatization and low levels of foreign investment. A possible model for future development of innovative industry lies in the Latvian Technological Centre (LTC) in Riga. This is a partnership between the city, the Latvian Academy of Sciences, the Institute of Physical Energy Studies, and the Association of Science and Technology Societies. It supports some 30 start-up firms in an incubator environment, specializing in IT, biotechnology, and environmental technologies, with support from the EU Copernicus programme.

In Latvia, as noted, the asset base is smaller at $951 per capita, loans, too, at $244 per capita (compared with $769 in Estonia and $238 per capita in Lithuania), and deposits $577 per capita compared to $847 (Estonia) and $318 (Lithuania). GDP is lower in Latvia at $487 per capita than either Lithuania ($550 per capita) or Estonia ($641). Growth in the financial sector stabilized at around 5–7 percent per annum up to 1995 after a 40 percent increase in 1992. Employment in the sector grew from 7,000 in 1990 to 20,000 in 1995 when there was a financial crisis. By 1997 employment was 17,000. Most of this employment is in Riga and its environs. The banking system consists of the Latvian National Bank and at a second level, 12 main commercial banks. Between 1992 and 1997 the number of banks in total reduced from 67 to 34 due to the 1995 banking crisis caused by a weak deposit base and bankruptcies among new banks. Insurance, securities, and other financial services firms in reasonable numbers have also developed in Riga, serving the Latvian markets in the main.

Vilnius

Though a relatively large city Vilnius is not as dominant in Lithuania as the other cities are in their Baltic states. The population of 575,000 constitutes 16 percent of the national total of 3.7 million. The total number of enterprises is rising, there was an increase of 20 percent to 30,000 from 1995 to 1996, of which approximately 10 percent were foreign-owned on both occasions. Far more than Latvia, and perhaps even Tallinn in Estonia, Lithuania has been open to significant inward investment from the likes of KPMG, Price Waterhouse, and Arthur Andersen, management consultants and accountants which have been influential catalysts in the development of local enterprise. Tourism has developed successfully, generating at $150 million, some 4 percent of GDP, 87 percent of the activity associated with which is centered in Vilnius. This is helping stimulate the cultural sector which in Vilnius consists of 5 theaters, 4 concert halls, and 11 museums. In 1994 these generated 785,000 visits (Ecofin 1996). One of the most important organizations attracting international tourists is the Lithuanian Folk Culture Centre which is a research, educational and festival organizing institution. Like the other Baltic cities, Vilnius has an attractive historical center which houses many of its cultural assets. However, marketing, investment capital, and cultural tourism "know-how" are in need of substantial improvement.

Vilnius is, partly due to its relative openness to foreign investment, host to a number of international business and financial organizations such as the World Bank, European Bank for Reconstruction and Development, and credit lines such as the Lithuanian Development Bank, Vilnius Bank, Baltic American Enterprise Fund, Baltic Investment Fund, US-Baltic Foundation and the Open Society Fund. Seven million ecus were allocated by Phare, the EU development programme for SME business development for the 1993–9 period. By 1996 there were 11 commercial banks, a reduction from 26 in 1993 following a series of bankruptcies in 1995. Overall employment in the Vilnius banking sector is, nevertheless, relatively small at some 4,000 employees in 1995.

Developments in innovative industries in Vilnius and Lithuania more generally are hampered by limited investment finance and the lengthy lead-times for commercialization, but helped by the fact that Lithuania had a highly developed science and technology base under the Soviet system. Nevertheless, reductions in state funding have meant contractions in the R&D labor market since 1991 and this has stimulated entrepreneurship, especially in electronics and IT, and, to a lesser extent, biotechnology. Good links are retained with the university sector but the Soviet market for which Vilnius researchers and technologists were suppliers has, of course, disappeared. In 1994 all 29 Lithuanian research institutes were evaluated to establish their future viability and case for continued funding. The Institute of Semiconductor Physics at Vilnius received the top ranking. Here, considerable joint venturing between the institute and firms takes place, with commercialization of technologies the objective. Companies use institute equipment in return for a share in profits. Emergent SMEs (Small and Medium-sized Enterprises) in IT and other advanced-technology fields face barriers to growth based on capital shortages, inadequate management capability, unsatisfactory premises and lack of information about new markets. Technological capability is not seen as a problem, but rather an asset.

We may conclude this section of this study by judging, fairly straightforwardly, that Tallinn, and Estonia in its train, has perhaps made the greatest progress in terms of its development of fast-growth industries and its acceptance for the next round of enlargement by the EU is testimony to its advance. Vilnius also has perhaps a more broad-based progress to report but there seem to be greater barriers to business expansion and fewer state or associational initiatives under development than in Tallinn. Riga, though the largest city, with considerable cultural and intellectual capital infrastructure, has progressed least in terms of strategic planning or associational or even entrepreneurial practices. This is because of severe financial difficulties, delays in privatization, and relatively unattractive former state enterprises with little obvious, future market attractiveness. Riga has the furthest to progress with, presently, the least fast-growth assets to sustain it.

Concluding Remarks and Policy Implications

An important part of this research involved eliciting assessments from the Baltic cities research teams of the policies being pursued in Western cities from the viewpoint of their possible relevance, suitably adapted, to their own cities of Tallinn, Riga, and Vilnius. Their collective responses give an indication of the kind of support needed, through Phare and other EU programs, the activities of foundations and investors, and the limited resources of the Baltic states themselves. There are four spheres in which there is widespread agreement on the lessons that could be learned from reviewing the experiences of the three research comparator cities of Dublin, Cardiff, and Tampere in dealing with processes of significant economic change and the need for economic regeneration.

Foremost, and plainly, finance is presently inadequate to enable city governments or their states to establish mechanisms for developing strategies or policies to take full advantage of opportunities associated with fast-growth industries. At a macro-level the Irish Industrial Development Authority and Welsh Development Agency were perceived to be crucial instruments for attracting overseas firms and helping build linkages with indigenous industry, but there was not the finance in any of the Baltic states to set up such organizations and staff them with appropriately trained personnel. Contrariwise, though, the ways in which policy networks operated across the public–private sector divide, enabling private risk-taking to be moderated by matching public funding for projects with clear objectives was widely admired. EU, state and city levels of governance could usefully extend matched-funding approaches for projects on which there is a clear consensus about wealth generation.

Second, there is a need for institution-building, learning, and training in urban governance. Presently most initiative comes from private individuals or groups, usually, in the latter case, working on a not-for-profit basis and dependent on limited foundation funds. City governments do not have strategic plans because they do not have clear goals or the means to fulfill them if they had them. Nevertheless actions can be taken in partnership with international, private, and voluntary organizations. However, there is widespread unfamiliarity with this approach to policy formation and only relatively limited capacity to evaluate innovative practices elsewhere. Training in urban leadership, funded through scholarship and study-visits for officials and politicians, is called for.

Third, there was recognition of the value of, first, understanding the economic worth to the city's economy of activities such as those associated with urban culture or university science. Such a perspective has been absent in the past and, while there are small indications of emergent university–industry or foundation–cultural industry relationships in Vilnius and Tallinn, the estimation of the Dublin approach to regenerating Temple Bar as an example for Old Town development with cultural sensitivity is palpable. Similarly, the great success of the Tampere Technology Park, and on a smaller scale, the Cardiff Medipark, in levering value from disinterested science were fully recognized. Once more, there is scope for enhancing emergent efforts with technical and financial support.

Fourth, Baltic city researchers were impressed with the capability of Western cities, firms, development agencies and others to *market* their goods and services, their image, and reputation. Such skills are in short supply in the Baltic cities, yet they have much in their built fabric, cultural, and scientific infrastructure of which to be proud. The problem, once again, is partly financial as the "quick buck" and poor quality of service experience revealed with the decline in foreign tourists to Riga, though this has not been so pronounced in Vilnius, or especially Tallinn. Being in a position to understand good practice, develop opportunity without killing the "golden goose" and formulate strategic, financial projects are among the most crucial learning processes that policymakers in the Baltic cities and the states to which they belong can usefully experience.

ACKNOWLEDGMENT

This research was undertaken with support from the European Commission's Phare-ACE Programme 1995.

REFERENCES

Bianchini, F. 1995: Night cultures, night economies. *Planning Practice and Research*, 10, 121–6.

Castells, M. and Hall, P. 1994: *Technopoles of the World*. London: Routledge.

Cooke, P. 1992: *Making a European City of the Future*. Cardiff: CASS.

Dill, D. 1995: University-industry entrepreneurship: the organization and management of American university technology. *Higher Education*, 29, 369–84.

Dorfman, N. 1983: Route 128: the development of a regional high technology economy. *Research Policy*, 12, 299–316.

Drennan, M. 1996: The dominance of international finance by London, New York and Tokyo. In P. Daniels and W. Lever (eds.), *The Global Economy in Transition*, London, Longman, 352–71.

Ecofin 1996: *Vilnius: Centre of Tourism and Business*. Vilnius (Phare-ACE Project Report).

Freeman, C. 1994: Innovation and growth. In M. Dodgson and R. Rothwell (eds.), *The Handbook of Industrial Innovation*, Cheltenham, Edward Elgar, 78–93.

Friedrichs, J. 1995: Cologne: a creative city. *European Planning Studies*, 3, 441–64.

Jones-Evans, D. and Klofsten, M. 1997: Universities and local economic development: the case of Linköping. *European Planning Studies*, 5, 1, 77–93.

Karnite, R. and Pocs, J. 1997: *Baltic Cities: Riga Study*. Riga, Latvian Academy of Sciences (Phare-ACE Project Report).

Krugman, P. 1995: *Development, Geography and Economic Theory*. Cambridge and London: MIT Press,

Landry, C., Bianchini, F., Ebert, R., Gnad, F., and Kunzmann, K. 1995: *The Creative City in Britain and Germany*. London, Anglo-German Foundation.

Myerscough, J. 1988: *The Economic Importance of the Arts in Britain*. London, Policy Studies Institute.

Organization for Economic Cooperation and Development 1994: *Jobs Survey*. Paris: OECD.

Porter, M. 1990: *The Competitive Advantage of Nations*. New York, The Free Press.

Reich, R. 1990: *The Work of Nations*. New York, Random House.

Smilor, R., Dietrich, G., and Gibson, D. 1993: The entrepreneurial university: the role of higher education in the United States in technology commercialization and economic development. *International Social Science Journal*, 45, 1–11.

Suzuki, P. 1996: The Upper Mills quarter of Bamberg: innovative, adaptive reuse. *European Planning Studies*, 4, 561–78.
Terk, E. and Võsa, E. 1997: *Software Sector in Tallinn*. Tallinn, Institute for Futures Studies (Phare-ACE Project Report).
Võsa, E. and Kuus, M. 1997: *Cultural Industries in Tallinn*. Tallinn, Institute for Futures Studies (Phare-ACE Project Report).
Zukin, S. 1995: *The Cultures of Cities*. Oxford: Blackwell.

Part III Cities of Division and Difference

Chapter 21

City Differences

Gary Bridge and Sophie Watson

Differences are constituted across many dimensions from race, class, and ethnicity to gender, sexuality, age, and able bodiedness, and none of these exists as a homogenous space or entity since they multiply and intersect with one another in complex, fluid, and diverse ways. Differences are constructed in, and themselves construct, city life and spaces. They are also constituted spatially, socially, and economically sometimes leading to polarization, inequality, zones of exclusion and fragmentation, and at other times constituting sites of power, resistance, and the celebration of identity. Difference is constituted in all spatial relations but the particularity of the city is that it concentrates differences through its density of

Figure 21.1 Aboriginal mural, Sydney (© Steve Pile)

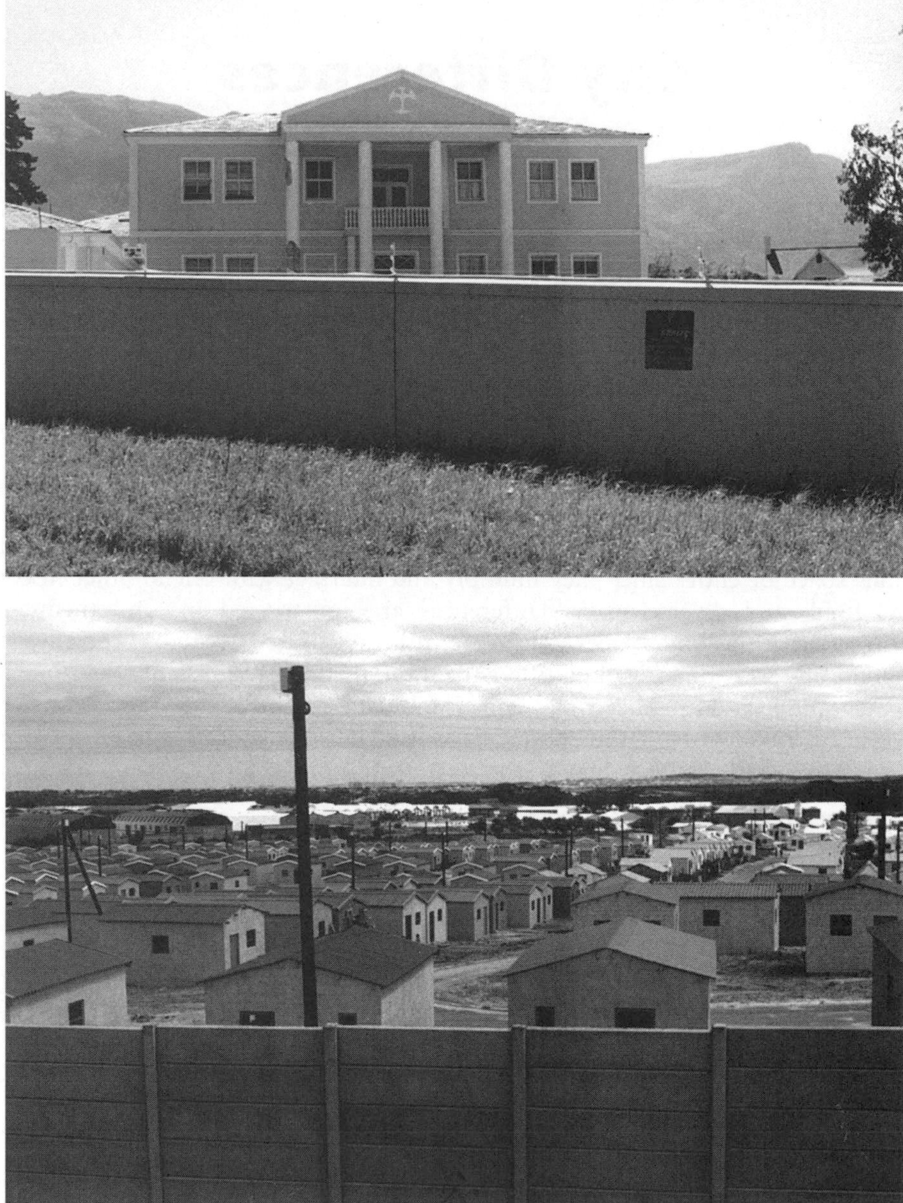

Figure 21.2 A tale of two cities? Cape Town (© Sophie Watson)

people and lived spaces, through the juxtaposition of different activities and land uses and through its intensities of interaction and interconnections (Massey, Allen, and Pile 1999).

Differences are not simply registered at the social, cultural, or economic level, they are also constituted symbolically with groups inscribing spaces and zones with particular meanings and discursive practices which may or may not be visible to outsiders. Different subjects and subjectivities are also constituted in the imagined spaces of the city and differential power relations are inscribed on urban bodies. There are thus no clear-cut boundaries and no simple divisions between groups which can easily be mapped on to city spaces, and these complexities are rarely represented in the statistical and census accounts on the basis of which much urban policy is formed.

Instead people inhabit multiple identities in multiple spaces and temporalities of the city, and these identities themselves constitute, shape, and create the very spaces and temporalities or the city. Thus the Central Business District of the large global city with its offices, smart restaurants, information networks and gyms, shapes the possibilities for social interaction, power, and control of the financier in the daylight, while the empty doorways or heating vents at night provide shelter for the homeless youth whose identities are constructed in these selfsame spaces which contain and make possible a whole different set of meanings and social practices. In turn these identities transform the very spaces they inhabit, shifting their appearance and atmosphere at different times of the day. Capturing this idea through the metaphor of city rhythms John Allen (Massey et al. 1999) describes the displacement of the early-morning vendors in São Paolo with the onset of the working day as the businessmen claim the space of their own at the same time as being forced to share it with the street children. While for Amin and Graham (1997) the divisions and differences enacted in these multiple spaces and times form the multiplex city.

There has been a sea change over the last two decades in how social/spatial divisions in cities are conceived with a shift from the notion of division to the idea of difference. In part this shift reflects changing social and economic processes, but just as importantly it reflects theoretical shifts which have provided new lenses through which to analyze cities. During the 1970s and early 1980s the dominance of Marxist thought meant that the focus of analysis was on economic rather than social divisions. Cities were analyzed as working in the interests of capital where the major cleavage was between the owners of the means of production (the capitalists) and the workers. Social divisions were thus predominantly seen as deriving from economic forces and organized around class with differing interpretations as to how class should be defined. Urban journals such as the International Journal of Urban and Regional Research (IJURR) and the work of David Harvey, Manuel Castells, Michael Harloe, and Enzo Mingione, to name just a handful of scholars among many, could be located in this paradigm.

Though seen as secondary to class in most analyses of cities – particularly in the West – the ways in which racial divisions were constituted in city spaces was also an important strand of work. In Birmingham – Rex and Moore (1967) analyzed the divisions within the housing sector in class terms, while William Julius Wilson (1987) investigated the causes, consequences, and extent of ghettoization in the United States. Feminist analyses of cities began to critique the dominance of class-based analyses towards the late 1970s and early 1980s arguing that gender divisions were spatially constructed in the city at the same time as themselves constructing a patriarchal city form and structure. These early writings are well illustrated by the volume of the *International Journal of Urban and Regional Research* in 1978 devoted solely to gender concerns. Though feminist perspectives challenged the emphasis on class as the major social/economic cleavage, they too tended to operate within fairly simple dualistic frameworks either drawing on Marxist ideas to establish a notion of patriarchal capitalism, where gender and class were worked together, or suggesting patriarchy as central with gender posited as the core social division.

One strand of urban analysis that can be located in this predominantly Marxist approach was one that mapped social and economic divisions on to cities in a fairly simplisitic and dualistic fashion. This paradigm was predicated on labor-market divisions and established the notion of the dual city or the divided city. This has drawn attention to growing social–spatial polarization in many cities in which the rich have got richer and the poor poorer, and the middle class has contracted (partly with the decline of the manufacturing sector and the massive expansion in service sector employment) leading to what is sometimes represented as an egg-timer-shaped occupational structure. Continuing a long tradition of urban inquiry which has examined inequality and processes of exclusion and ghettoization in the city, in this discourse social polarization was posited as an inevitable effect of global capitalist restructuring which was seen as an uneven process affecting cities and regions, and the people in them, in different ways, including some localities and groups while pushing others to the margins and spaces of exclusion. The economism of this discourse failed to recognize the heterogeneity of differences (Gibson 1998) and the differential access that people have to resources and networks from within an apparently homogenous community (Bridge 1997; Watson 1999). Others have seen globalization as tending instead towards greater homogeneity – the space of flows argument – where everywhere becomes the same and differences are ironed out as information and finance move at greater and greater speeds across the globe.

There is nevertheless ample evidence of strong polarizing tendencies in cities which are visible in the residential patterns of urban populations. For example, in some cities of the US, these tendencies have been particularly extreme where white people have fled to the suburbs, leaving the inner city to black and Hispanic minorities – what is sometimes referred to as the doughnut effect. The patterns though are usually more complex and fragmented than is sometimes suggested. For example, in Southeast Asian cities such as Bangkok extremely high-priced residences are juxtaposed with makeshift and often temporary dwellings. The picture in most cities is clearly too complicated to be captured by a dual model which inevitably homogenizes binary categories so that differences within groups such as the rich and the poor are rendered invisible.

The processes of globalization and social change, particularly in relation to gender relations and family structures, further make any straightforward account of the dual or divided city obsolete. One of the most significant impacts of globalization on cities has been the huge cultural changes which have occurred as a result of large numbers of migrants moving from one part of the world to another – and mostly into cities. As Sassen points out (1999) much of the analysis of global cities has focused on the economic sphere and on the infrastructure necessary for global cities to function – the large office blocks, the centrality of services, commercial centers, and central business districts. But there is another equally important story to tell, which until recently has been more invisible. This is the story of the analytic borderlands, the lives and spaces of the transnational communities who live in cities, whose work servicing the infrastructure of globalization is just as important as the more visible signs of corporate power (Sassen, chapter 15 of this volume).

The multicultural city is not a new phenomenon and cities have always been spaces of difference and complexity. As Anthony King (chapter 22 in this volume) points out, there are various non-European cities which were marked by racial and cultural diversity long before this was a characteristic of London or Paris. Nevertheless contemporary cities are increasingly affected by complex patterns of local/global interconnection and disconnection, and places are constructed in complex ways within diverse webs of social, economic, and cultural relations. In many cities – or parts of cities – the migrant populations equal or outnumber citizens born in that city. Thus in Fairfield, Sydney, non-English-speaking migrants constitute nearly half of the population, many of whom are Asian, reflecting the huge refugee migration from Vietnam and Cambodia over less than 20 years (Murphy and Watson 1997). In Melbourne the Greek population is greater than in any city in Greece apart from Athens, and similar stories can be told about the Salvadorean and Mexican communities in Los Angeles and many other cities of the world. This intersection of migrant cultures in the context of a particular place has produced a plethora of differentiated, hybrid, and heterogenous cultural geographies within cities.

The dual city model thus appears increasingly obsolete. As Sassen suggests (1996) it is less and less possible to accept the notion of a hierarchical ordering which has created the semblance of a unitary economic system in which individuals are clearly located. Though the center concentrates immense power, and potential global control, the margins, while less powerful in economic and political terms, can be powerful in other ways. The devalued sectors which rest largely on the labor of women, immigrants, and African-Americans in the cities of the US represent a terrain where battles are fought on many fronts and in many sites and these battles lack clear boundaries. Global cities are a result of transactions that fragment space, such that we can no longer talk about global cities as whole cities – instead what we have is bits of cities that are highly globalized – and bits juxtaposed that are completely cut out. In this sense some parts of cities can have more in common with parts of other global cities or cities in the same region than with the part of the city juxtaposed. This increasing valorization and devalorization of spaces goes hand in hand, and in many places is becoming more and more extreme (Sassen, chapter 15). This has led to the reconstruction of city space with growing contestation between different sections of the population – which is often highly spatialized.

It is clear then that the notion of simply polarized or dichotomized social/spatial divisions in cities does not take us far enough. Cities have always been, and will always be, places of heterogeneity. This is particularly evident in the changing social composition of households in the city. The last 30 years or so across the world have witnessed the collapse of the traditional nuclear family, despite its ideological force, and a growing diversity and fragmentation of households; which has occurred as a result of a number of factors. In the more Westernized cities the women's and gay liberation movements, an increase in educational and employment opportunities, and easier access to mortgages for women have had an impact on marriage patterns, with the result that fewer people are marrying, and if they do, at a later age, and more people are choosing to live alone or cohabit, with or without children, in heterosexual or gay relationships. At the same time, when relationships break down there is less and less stigma attached to divorce. In non-Western countries, patterns of rural–urban migration often associated with the search for a livelihood and work, have also served to disrupt more stable – often extended – family formations. Castells (1997) presents a compelling case for global shifts in household forms which he links not only with social movements but also with the rise of the informational global economy and technological changes in reproduction. One study estimated that one third of the world's households are headed by women, and in urban areas – particularly in Latin America and Africa – the figure exceeds 50 percent, while globally the phenomenon is on the increase (Moser 1993).

Any statistical mapping of differences inevitably ignores the more subtle forms of identification and construction of identities in the spaces of the city. In his early work Castells (1983) pointed to the importance of urban social movements as spaces of change, social organization, and resistance to the dominance of capitalist relations. More recently there has been a shift in his work to the notion of identities and an investigation as to how these are constructed in the network society as a result of globalization and information processes. At the same time feminist, postcolonial, poststructural, and queer theory have disrupted more traditional notions of difference, identity, and subjectivity and shifted the ways in which difference in the city can be thought and lived. A sustained critique of binaries and dualistic paradigms (where one term is privileged over – man over woman, white over black, heterosexual over homosexual) has given rise to an emphasis on the multiplicity of intersecting differences located in a multiplicity of sites. Rather than being seen as fixed, homogenous, immutable, identities are seen to be fluid and in a state of flux, as performed rather than given (Butler 1993), hybrid (Haraway 1991), and transgressive of norms. This postmodern subject is a decentred one which is partially formed and constituted within different discourses and sites at different times for different strategic purposes. The city is a key site here.

This "cultural turn" in urban theory has thus destabilized the importance of economic explanations of social/spatial divisions and drawn attention to the ways in which differences are constructed across a whole range of symbolic and cultural terrains. New cultural geographies map the ways different spaces in the city come to have different meanings and attachment for different groups. Thus a particular site can be ascribed meaning through codes which may be visible – to others in the case of, say, graffiti – or which may be hidden and only visible to those who "know." Such ascriptions of identity – often in the more interstitial spaces of the city – can represent powerful spaces of resistance and self-definition. The terrains and discourses which construct these identities can shift very rapidly as new strategies, such as new forms of communication, new styles or dress codes, are deployed by marginal groups. This is not to argue that economic and material conditions have become insignificant in constituting relations of exclusion and marginality; it is rather that the terrain of the economic intersects with other terrains producing new confluences of difference.

Living Differences

How differences are lived in the city cannot be read in any simple way. Concentrations of particular groups of people may in some instances represent a chosen and powerful space, a space where identities can be constituted or celebrated, or a minority may be concentrated in one place as a result of processes of exclusion. Darlinghurst in Sydney has developed over 20 years as a safe space where gay men have bought houses, established businesses and restaurants and where they can openly express their sexuality, following similar trends in the Castro area of San Francisco or Soho in London (Mort, chapter 26 of this volume). These areas have also been buoyant economically giving rise to the phenomenon of the pink dollar. Racial or ethnic areas can be more ambiguous. In some instances they may represent sites of power and possibilities in the form of community networks, business or employment opportunities, or cultural arenas – such as Chinatown in Vancouver, Lygon Street in Melbourne, or Little Italy in New York. In others they may be places of enclosure and lack of opportunity such as the classic ghetto.

Power is crucial here. Drawing on Foucault's (1991) notion that power is immanent in all social relations operating as a capillary network across the domain of the social, and intricately bound up with modes of resistance, then all city spaces are imbued with power. Different marginalities, such as race, gender, or sexuality, or other forms of exclusion, interrelate to concentrate sites of power disadvantage and are not simply a question of special needs or lifestyle but are embedded in power relations, whether these be symbolic or real. In Peter Marcuse's (1995) view, beneath the chaos and fragmentation of cities patterns are lurking. Thus he suggests that rather than thinking in terms of divisions it is useful to think in terms of quartered cities or five-parted ones where the parts are intricately linked, walled in, and walled out, hierarchical in power, material or imagined, and dependent on outside social forces. Foucault's (1991) panopticon as a metaphor for modern forms of surveillance has also proved helpful in understanding spaces of exclusion and regulation, notably through CCTV. In *City of Quartz*, Mike Davis (1992) analyzed the workings of power in Los Angeles through mechanisms of privatization and surveillance, coining the now well-used idea of the fortress city.

The forces that produce fragmented and divided cities are multifarious. In a capitalist land market accumulation of profit operates as a crucial economic force shaping the city. Neil Smith's work (1979, 1996) over two decades has seen the emergence of gentrification as the product of the urban land market and a growing "rent gap" between the current value of property on a site and the underlying value of the land. While not denying the significance of these forces, Chris Hamnett (chapter 28 of this volume) foregrounds instead the shift from an industrial to a postindustrial society and associated changes in class structure – in particular the expanded middle class and their consumer preferences. Whatever the forces in play, which may be several, the juxtaposition of rich and poor in city centers and the displacement of working-class households from the inner cities are now familiar consequences of gentrification in many cities over the last 30 years.

Planning has operated as another dividing force. Oren Yiftachel (1995) examines the practice of "planning as control" in Majd el Krum – an urbanizing Arab village in Israel's Galilee region – where the government has continuously attempted to contain, segregate, and dominate the process of Arab development, while Mabin (chapter 46 of this volume) makes a similar argument in the South African context. In this volume also, Robins and Aksoy (chapter 29) show how the modernizing agenda of urban planners in Istanbul, with their universalizing vision of rationality, inclusion, and order, has instead created communities in orbit on the edge of the city, thereby promoting greater segregation and division in Istanbul.

Symbolic and psychic attachments to space play another part in constituting social/spatial divisions in cities. Though homelessness, for example, results in part from economic forces and the failure of the housing market to provide accommodation to low-income groups – effectively an economic analysis – it can also be seen as a psychic space of resistance which involves the occupation of particular symbolic sites involving new spatial and social practices. David Sibley (1995) examines the more symbolic aspects of exclusion and spatial division where people are marginalized because they are feared and created as "other." Powerful groups "purify" and dominate space to create fear of minorities and ultimately exclude them from having a voice. Often in local conflicts in the city a community will represent itself as normal and is threatened by those who are perceived as different. Fears and anxieties are expressed in stereotypes which logically could be challenged by greater knowledge of, and interaction with, the unknown others though such a move could have limited success if done halfheartedly (Sibley 1995: 29).

Divergences in value systems also play a part in shaping and being shaped by particular urban forms. Lily Kong (chapter 30) shows how Singapore is inherently a city of division and difference, pulling particularly in two directions, between modernity and internationalism, built on economic processes and economic rationality, on the one hand, and heritage, culture, and tradition, premised on symbolic value systems, on the other. Whose values are inscribed in the spaces of the cities is also a question of contestation and is open to competing claims which are constituted in a field of power relations and not fixed. A typical example of clashing value systems in many Western cities has been in the construction of mosques in traditionally Christian or secular neighborhoods, where the mosque is seen as a symbolic site of otherness and difference and fiercely resisted (Murphy and Watson 1997).

The physical form of city spaces can also act to produce difference and consolidate marginality. This is particularly evident where disability is concerned. Brendan Gleeson (1998: 91) makes a forceful case for capitalist cities as disabling in their design in the sense that the physical layout of cities – both the land-use patterns and the internal design of buildings – discriminate against people with disabilities by not recognizing their mobility requirements. Feminists have made a similar point about city planning, where transport systems, which are focused on the transport needs of men commuting to the center from the suburbs for work, lock women into complicated and time-consuming travel patterns to carry out domestic and childrearing tasks in areas ill serviced by cross-suburb linkages. Age is similarly constructed as a dependence when city spaces such as ill-lit streets, blind alleys or underpasses, appear frightening or unsafe to the teenage girl or older woman, who fear assault. And, as Fincher (1998) suggests, lifestage assumptions are present in the understandings of urban spaces held by policymakers and urban analysts.

Differences are thus constituted within cities. But there are also differences between cities. Urban hierarchies are constructed in academic debate positioning cities in relation to one another along economic and political grids and criteria are established to designate some cities as global cities while excluding others. Notions of center or core/periphery, metropole/nonmetropole, colonial/ex-colonial, Western/non-Western implicitly construct hierarchies of power – and no easy terms, as we have discovered, can be deployed to distinguish city typologies which are not so imbued. The notion that there is some linearity of city development and progress from the premodern to the modern or postmodern, or from the undeveloped to the developed has come under increasing criticism. As Anthony King (chapter 22) points out, postcolonial criticism of dominant paradigms of urban studies are decentering the Eurocentric conceptions of the world in terms of society, space, and culture as well as in terms of temporality and history. John Connell and John Lea (1995), for example, argue that there were no premodern cities in Melanesian countries to be added to, replaced, or challenged by colonial order and discipline. Urbanization and the divisions thus engendered were a product of the colonial encounter.

In conclusion, differences and identities in cities are constituted in multiple and complex ways in multiple spaces of the city, and shift and change producing in turn different city spaces and new boundaries and borders. In chapter 42 we briefly consider some ideas about how difference can be productive or negotiated in the city, since difference is here to stay, always embedded in relations of power and potentially productive of new forms of politics in the city. Another interesting route is the recasting of notions of citizenship in the terrain of difference. Ali Rogers here suggests (chapter 24) that placing the city within citizenship debates loosens its connection with the state and nation and makes explicit its territorial or spatial foundations. Such an approach, he suggests, foregrounds the lived, material and representational practices of migrants and foreigners in the multicultural European city. As we have argued, and as chapters in this Companion explore, different spaces of the city constitute different identities and possibilities within a web of global/local connections which make every place unique whatever general patterns can also be drawn.

REFERENCES

Allen, J. 1999: Worlds within cities. In D. Massey, J. Allen, and S. Pile, *City Worlds*, London: Routledge.
Amin, A. and Graham, S. 1997: The ordinary city. *Transactions of the Institute of British Geographers*, NS 22 (4), 411–29.
Bridge, G. 1997: Mapping the terrain of time-space compression: power networks in everyday life. *Environment and planning D: Society and Space*, 15, 611–26.
Butler, J. 1993: *Bodies that Matter.* London: Routledge.
Castells, M. 1983: *The City and the Grassroots*. London: Edward Arnold.
Castells, M. 1997: *The Power of Identity.* Oxford: Blackwell.
Central Statistical Office 1996: *Social Trends 26*. London: HMSO.
Connell, J. and Lea, J. 1995: Distant places, other cities? Urban life in contemporary Papua New Guinea. In S. Watson and K. Gibson (eds.), *Postmodern Cities and Spaces*, Oxford: Blackwell, 165–83.
Davis, M. 1992: *City of Quartz*. London: Verso.
Fainstein, S., Gordon, I., and Harloe, M. 1992: *Divided Cities*. Oxford: Blackwell.
Fincher, R. 1998: In the right place at the right time? Life stages and urban spaces. In R. Fincher and J. Jacobs (eds.) 1998: *Cities of Difference*. New York: Guildford, 49–68.
Fincher, R. and Jacobs, J. (eds.) 1998: *Cities of Difference*. New York: Guildford.
Foucault, M. 1991: *Discipline and Punish: The Birth of the Prison*. Harmondsworth: Penguin.

Gibson, K. 1998: Social polarisation and the politics of difference: discourses in collision or collusion. In R. Fincher and J. Jacobs (eds.), *Cities of Difference*. New York: Guildford, 301–16.

Gleeson, B. 1998: Justice and the disabling city: In R. Fincher and J. Jacobs (eds.), *Cities of Difference*. New York: Guildford, 89–119.

Haraway, D. 1991: *Symians, Cyborgs and Women: The Reinvention of Nature*. London: Free Association Books.

Marcuse, P. 1995: Not chaos but walls: postmodernism and the partitioned city. In S. Watson, and K. Gibson (eds.), *Postmodern Cities and Spaces*. Oxford: Blackwell, 243–53.

Massey, D., Allen, J., and Pile, S. 1999: *City Worlds*. London: Routledge.

Moser, C. 1993: *Gender Planning and Development*. London: Routledge.

Murphy, P. and Watson, S. 1997: *Surface City: Sydney at the Millennium*. Bristol: Policy Press.

Rex, J. and Moore, R. 1967: *Race, Community and Conflict*. Oxford: Oxford University Press.

Sassen, S. 1996: Rebuilding the global city: economy, ethnicity and space. In A. King (ed.), *Re-Presenting the City*. London: Macmillan, 23–42.

Sassen, S. 1999: *Globalisation and its Discontents*. New York: The New Press.

Sennett, R. 1970: *The Uses of Disorder*. Harmondsworth: Penguin.

Sennett, R. 1990: *The Conscience of the Eye*. London: Faber and Faber.

Sibley, D. 1995: *Geographies of Exclusion*. London: Routledge.

Smith, N. 1979: Gentrification and capital: theory, practice and ideology in Society Hill. *Antipode*, 11 (3), 24–35.

Smith, N. 1996: *The New Urban Frontier: Gentrification and the Revanchist City*. London: Routledge.

Watson, S. 1999: Differences in cities in transition. In B. Blanke and R. Smith (eds.), *Cities in Transition: New Challenges, New Responsibilities*. London: Macmillan, 79–92.

Watson, S. and Gibson, K. (eds.) 1995: *Postmodern Cities and Spaces*. Oxford: Blackwell.

Wilson, W. J. 1987: *The Truly Disadvantaged: The Inner City, the Underclass and Public Policy*. Chicago: University of Chicago Press.

Yiftachel, O. 1995: The dark side of modernism: planning as control of an ethnic minority. In S. Watson and K. Gibson (eds.), *Postmodern Cities and Spaces*. Oxford: Blackwell, 216–42.

Chapter 22

Postcolonialism, Representation, and the City

Anthony D. King

Topicality, the essence of good journalism, is perhaps less important for the longer-term perspectives of academic writing. Nonetheless, I shall begin with two events dominating world headlines during the week I write this chapter (June 1998): the entry on to the world stage of India in the role of nuclear power, and the riots in Indonesia which have replaced Suharto, after 32 years in power as the dictatorial president of that country.

What these two events have in common is that both have been influenced by postcolonial states and conditions. Half a century after formal independence, the right wing, Hindu nationalist government of India has, with the widespread approval and "mass ecstacy" of its population (*India Today*, May 25, 1998), affirmed its independent status and consolidated the national imagination according to the most important criteria of state power and modernity laid down by other, predominantly Western nuclear states. Irrespective of "economic" indicators, this scientific, political, and military gesture is seen as the only equalizer that matters. In Indonesia, Suharto's "New Order" regime of modernization had followed two decades of fervent postcolonial nation-building under his equally nationalistic predecessor. In each case, regimes and nations have declared their own destiny, made their own history, irrespective of the views of world "others," and not least in response to the continued marginalizations of Western dominance and the slights and memories of older imperialisms. If these are topical events in the spring of 1998, they will be historical benchmarks by 2008.

Irrespective of these events, however, we might simply acknowledge (not least in regard to my argument below) that India (with one billion people) and Indonesia (with over 200 million) are two of the world's four largest populations (the latter, the largest Muslim population). Their major cities (Jakarta, Mumbai, Calcutta) number between nine and twelve million inhabitants.

Yet my main aim in this chapter is not to examine the *realpolitik* of the postcolonial state, let alone "the" postcolonial city itself. Nor will I attempt to counter a "Western" understanding of urban processes by counterposing an "Eastern" (or "non-Western") one, as the previous paragraph might suggest. Instead, I shall draw on a body of theory which, arguably, has developed out of the selective interaction between these two notional positions, a theory of hybridization (see Bhabha 1994) developed from the displacements of (urban) subjectivities and identities. I refer to the extensive literature on postcolonial theory and criticism generated in (and, I would argue, principally for) the Euro-American academy, especially since the late 1980s. I shall first say something briefly about the objectives of postcolonial theory and criticism, about the conditions governing its origins, and some of the critiques leveled against it. My aim is to see what it can tell us, not only about contemporary representations of "the city" but also, about some alternative ideas and directions for thinking about urban studies.

Interrogating the Postcolonial

Postcolonial criticism may be briefly described as an oppositional form of knowledge that critiques Eurocentric conceptions of the world. More fundamentally, in Mangin's words, "the term postcolonial refers not to a simple periodization but rather to a methodological revisionism which enables a wholesale critique of Western structures of knowledge and power, particularly those of the post-Enlightenment period"; it demands "a rethinking of the very terms by which knowledge has been constructed" (Mongin 1995: 2). For Achille Mbembe, postcoloniality is "the specific identity of a given historical trajectory, that of societies recently emerging from the experiences of colonization" (Mbembe 1992: 2). These two definitions neatly embody the idea of the postcolonial as an epoch, as a problematic, and as a form of expression and identity (Simon 1998: 230). Yet postcolonial criticism, as a new awareness or consciousness, is not just one thing; it can be distinguished from postcolonial theory as well as colonial discourse analysis, among others (Moore-Gilbert 1997, ch. 1). And for obvious reasons of continuing neocolonialism and imperialism, neither the term (McClintock 1992; Shohat 1992) nor the discourse (Dirlik 1997) go unchallenged. For Hall,

> In the re-staged narrative of the post-colonial, colonisation assumes the place and significance of a major, extended and ruptural world-historical event. By "colonisation", the "post-colonial" references something more than direct rule over certain areas of the world by the imperial powers. I think it is signifying the whole process of expansion, exploration, conquest, colonisation and imperial hegemonisation which constituted the "outer face", the constitutive outside, of European and then Western capitalist modernity after 1492 (Hall 1996: 249).

In the literature I am citing above, postcolonial criticism has principally emerged in anglo-phonic literary studies, and cultural studies more generally, especially from the mid- to late 1980s (Moore-Gilbert 1997; Williams and Chrisman 1994). Three questions may be asked. Given the existence of anticolonial nationalisms at least from the early twentieth century and the formal ending of most modern European colonial regimes in the two decades after 1947, why has a consciousness of colonialism in the making of the modern world and, not least, in the construction of its forms of academic knowledge, only fully surfaced in the Euro-American academy in the late 1980s and 1990s? Why has it emerged most prominently in regard to the humanities and not (or only later) in the social sciences? What is the connection, if any, between these (more recent) forms of postcolonial criticism and earlier studies of colonial space and urbanism?

As suggested elsewhere (King 1997) postcolonial criticism is an outcome of the new conditions of knowledge production that have emerged since the late 1970s and, in particular, in relation to the postcolonial diasporic transmigration of "Third World" intellectuals. By *trans*migration I refer both to the frequent movement of the transmigrant between being "abroad" and "back home," as well as the electronic/telematic connection between both places. It is these which enable postcolonial subjects (as well as others) to translate the social, political, and cultural capital gained in one setting into the social, political, cultural (and often economic) capital in another (after Schiller et al. 1995). Here, the capital is essentially intellectual as one-time "Third World" intellectuals have entered the Western (especially Euro-American) academy making, in the last decade, a significant impact on the cultural politics of knowledge creation, questioning traditional canons, and making space for diversity by developing new theoretical paradigms (McDowell 1995). Postcolonial scholars have not only challenged imperialism from the perspective of their previously marginalized positions in the "Third World" but also, in regard to discriminations of race, class, gender, sexuality, and ethnicity, from the position of internally colonized populations within the metropole. The real, as well as cultural racism of the Western academy, has also provided the context for the development of the discourse.

To summarize, therefore, critical perspectives in the humanities which draw on Foucault's insights into the "power/knowledge" relationship in the form of postcolonial studies have largely been developed in tandem with diasporic movements of postcolonial scholars to the metropole. In the social sciences, however, to oversimplify, somewhat comparable, though different, critical perspectives on the implications of imperialism in the construction of knowledge emerged some years earlier with the movement of scholars in the opposite direction (i.e. from the metropole to the postcolony). These would include (prior to Foucaultian influences), oppositional voices in "Development Studies" (for an overview, see Slater 1995), critiques in anthropology (Asad 1973; Cohn 1988) and in debates on the "the sociology of development and the underdevelopment of sociology" of Andre Gundar Frank, world-system perspective, and others in the late 1960s (see King 1995a). Though as Slater points out, the major weakness in the (mainly) Marxist accounts here was "the failure to theorize subjectivity and identity" (Slater 1995: 71).

Yet the failure of these various critical perspectives to fully interact must be accounted for not by the gaps between countries or languages but those that occur across the campus, *between* disciplines. For example, Moore-Gilbert writes in 1997 that "colonial discourse analysis now operates across an ever broader range of fields, including the history of law, anthropology, political economy, philosophy, historiography, art history, and psychoanalysis" (1997: 9), but makes no reference to studies in geography, planning, urbanism, or architecture. In his magisterial study of the impact of imperialism on the formation of knowledge and culture Edward Said does better in that, at least in passing, he refers to the impact of imperialism on metropolitan capitals and to the spatial transformations in colonial cities (Said 1994; see also King 1995a). There are, perhaps, other explanations to be offered.

The early exponents of postcolonial criticism focused on a critique of literary and historical writing and, as I have indicated, were located in the humanities of the

Western academy (this section is drawn from King 1995a). Subsequently, the objects of the deconstructive postcolonial critique expanded to include film, video, television, photography, painting – all examples of cultural praxis that are portable, mobile, and circulating in the West. Yet given that such literature, photography, or museum displays had existed for decades, if not centuries, why did this critique only get established in the late 1980s? And why did it not address, in any significant way, the impact of imperialism on the design and spatial disciplines of architecture, planning, and urban issues more generally, whether in the colony or, indeed, in the metropole (Home 1996; King 1976, 1990b)?

As suggested above, postcolonial criticism only developed in the West when a sufficient number of postcolonial intellectuals, and an audience for them, was established in the Western academy; as for the second question, the critique has not addressed issues in architecture and space, not only because they belong to different disciplines but because the cultural products on which imperial discourses are inscribed – the spaces of cities, landscapes, buildings – unlike literary texts, movies, and photography, are, for these postcolonial critics and their Western audiences, not only absent and distant, they are also not mobile. Critics have to take their own postcolonial subjectivities halfway round the world to experience them.

With perhaps the single exception of Fanon (1968), critical discourses on colonial urban culture, both in the colony and postcolony, positioned from a white, male, Western viewpoint, though generally also drawing on local indigenous postcolonial critiques, began in the 1950s and were usually the result of scholars in the social sciences, often working in "aid" or "development" roles in the colony or postcolony (See King 1976: 22, for early references). It was a discourse which spoke especially to the cultural politics of urban planning and issues of identity (1976, pp. 282–8). The renewed interest in these issues in the American academy in the late 1980s, also drawing to varying degrees on Foucault's "Power/Knowledge" paradigm (Metcalf 1989; Rabinow 1989), has as much to do with issues of theory in the Western academy (Wright 1991; AlSayyad 1991) as with urban policy and practice in the postcolony. Where the colonial city concept has been mobilized as a metaphor to represent the increasingly ethnically and spatially segregated situation of Western cities (King 1990a; Philo and Kearns 1993), revisionist discourses of "the global" (King 1990b) as well as poststructuralist approaches (Jacobs 1996) have led to studies on the imperial as well as the (technically) postimperial city (Driver and Gilbert 1998).

The more conscious application of the deconstructive methods of postcolonial criticism to the understanding of architecture, space, and urbanism have, with occasional exceptions (Noyes 1992) principally been the outcome of three conferences organized by a group of architects, academics and critics under the title of "Other Connections" and, in a deliberate attempt to avoid the influence of "Western hegemonies," located in Singapore (1993), Chandigarh (1995), and Melbourne (1997). In a selection of papers from the first two of these, *Postcolonial Space(s)*, the editors suggest that "Postcolonial space is a space of intervention into those architectural constructions that parade under a universalist guise and either exclude or repress differential spatialities or often disadvantaged ethnicities, communities or peoples." The essays, "located at the interstices of a number of disciplines including architecture, literary theory, cultural studies and philosophy" and informed by "poststructuralist theory, psychoanalytic interpretations and feminist studies" are seen as investigating "questions of representation and interpretation, issues of difference and identity" (Nalbantoglu and Wong 1997: 7).

Earlier studies on colonial urbanism provided a political, social, cultural, and behavioral interpretation of the physical and spatial forms of the colonial city, principally from the position of the colonizer, emphasizing their social and cultural effects, and in relation to symbolic values and issues of social and cultural identity (King 1976). In challenging universalist approaches, newer studies emphasize questions of representation, difference, and identity, including questions of race and gender. What seems to have been lost, however, is an acknowledgment of the real forces of *neo*colonialism, and with globalization, the exploitative relations of global capitalism with its gross inequities (see Dirlik 1997).

The major contribution of the more general postcolonial perspectives to the study of the city (and not only the so-called "postcolonial" city) is in the recognition of the essential reciprocity of colonial processes, in the questioning of simple binary dichotomies (between colonizer/colonized, East/West) and in acknowledging the uniqueness of particular colonial situations. To use Said's words, the colonial relationship is best understood in terms of "Overlapping Territories, Intertwined Histories"; it requires a questioning of those categories "presuming that the West and its culture are largely independent of other cultures" (Said 1994: 134). In specifically urban terms, these perspectives are illustrated in Yeoh's study of the "contested terrain" of colonial Singapore in which "the spaces of everyday life were developed, sustained, renegotiated, distorted, or countered by a Chinese counter-discourse in the everyday resistance of the colonized" (Yeoh 1996; see also Kusno 2000).

Decentering and Recentering Studies of the City

What are the implications of postcolonial criticism for urban studies more generally? The first would seem to be for a decentering of Eurocentric conceptions of the world, not only in terms of society, space, and culture but equally, in terms of temporality and history; to contest the view, in Chakrabarty's terms, that all histories tend to begin and end with Europe (Chakrabarty 1992). In this context, there are any number of reasons to challenge the taken-for-granted assumption that the "natural" study of contemporary urbanism should properly begin with the so-called "industrial capitalist, modernist city" in the West, an assumption probably made by urbanists since Adna Ferrin Weber in 1899. Without reference to the larger, often colonial space economies, markets and systems of urbanization and culture of which it was a part, there is no "autonomous" understanding of the "Euro-American" capitalist industrial city. Moreover, though not denying the global importance of the relationship between capitalism and industrial urbanism, there have been other systems of cities in the course of world history (Chase-Dunn 1985), not necessarily understood "economically," and more than one urban revolution. But such reasoning apart, we can also ask whose city, whose history is being privileged? Whose "global explanation" is being foisted on the world?

"Modern," "modernist," and "modernity" are equally ambiguous, nontransparent terms. The problem with "modernity" is to assume that it is an historical term, referencing time or history (without reference to space) rather than a cultural one that references a way of life. If modern means "now," "of the present," we need to know whose "now" and whose "where" is being privileged. As the English word "modern" has been around since the sixteenth century (King 1995b) it is evident that notions of modernity are ever-changing, inflected by such things as religion, politics, ideology. Different understandings of modernity exist simultaneously in different places, and under very different conditions. Colonial modernity is different from metropolitan modernity; Islamic modernity from Christian or "secular" modernity; postmodern modernity is different from premodern modernity. If one of the characteristics of the contemporary "modern" Western city is its ethnic, racial, and cultural diversity, this was characteristic of late eighteenth-century Batavia (Java) (Taylor 1983) long before it was characteristic of London or Paris.

In the words of McDowell, "Recognizing different ways of knowing does not mean abrogating responsibility for distinguishing between them" (1995: 281). We need to recognize where theories come from, the conditions that produce (and also circulate) them, how exclusive as well as inclusive they attempt to be, whose interests are advanced by them, and where. Forms of knowledge reflect the worlds and spaces of the powerful; they also reflect their own times.

Given the hegemony of Western forms of knowledge and the dominance of English-language publishing worldwide, it is not surprising, therefore, that if we read some of the most widely circulating urban studies in the last two decades, it seems that an apparent unity has descended over many of the world's cities in that they have been largely narrated through one or the other (interrelated) system of representation. On one hand, the concepts, discourses, and narratives of a disciplinary urban political economy (e.g. the *International Journal of Urban and Regional Research* in the 1980s) have had the effect of reducing the vast diversity of different topographies, politics, geographies, ethnicities, livelihoods, landscapes, peoples, memories, architectures, cultures, histories, religions, arts, languages, protests, identities, and differences of all kinds into a uniform collective whole, to be selectively understood as a series of urban social movements, cases of collective consumption, and instances of state intervention. On the other hand, with the invention of concepts of both the world and global city, stemming largely from a dominant American academy based either in Los Angeles or New York (with regional offices elsewhere) new paradigms have been launched the result of which, in prioritizing so-called "economic criteria," has focused (if not fixed) for a decade the attention of many urban scholars on perhaps 30 or 40 cities, all but three or four of them either in Europe or the United States (Knox and Taylor 1995; Knox 1995). As Duncan points out in relation to Burgess's "concentric zone" theory of the city in the infamous Chicago School of urban sociology, its effect was to ensure that all cities were made to defer to the form of Chicago (Duncan 1996: 259). Similarly, the effect of the "world" and "global city" paradigm has been to prompt scholars as well as municipal officials worldwide to ask, "Is this, or is this not a 'world city'?" Those that don't make the grade have, to some degree, dropped off the scholarly screen. The fixation on a particular socially constructed notion of "the economy" and "the accumulation of capital" without reference to the historical, cultural, and global conditions in which this has taken place and without reference to what, in other cities worldwide, gives meaning to people's lives leaves many questions unanswered.

I am not, of course, dismissing these two dominant paradigms offhand (not least as I have also been implicated in producing them). What I am saying is that such theories create particular social and cultural worlds that have meaning to those who use them. To imagine they are universally applicable, however, that they in any way give insight into the many different meanings of particular places, or can, without reference to the particular histories, politics, memories, or subjectivities, capture the highly diverse identities which exist in particular cities, is an illusion.

Here, perhaps the most striking absence in cross-cultural urban studies is reference to the institutions, power, and growing influence in many cities worldwide of religious movements, old and new. I refer here not simply to specific cities worldwide where the promotion or defense of particular religious identities has (for decades if not for centuries) been the defining force in the space and politics of the city – Belfast, Jerusalem, Beirut, Tehran, Varanasi, Rome, Istanbul – but also to the fact that, in a universe where worlds are shaped by particular religious *world*views, it might be worth asking why so-called "world cities" are overwhelmingly only in one of those worlds, conventionally understood as "Christian," and mostly in Protestant states.

Cities are not only sites of financial and economic activity, but also of symbolic and cultural capital. Particular sacred cities worldwide have, in recent years, become the sites for staging major religio-political struggles. In these, the essential element of the urban, namely, the building as symbolic signifier, as marker of sacred space, has become the preeminent site of religious and often violent political struggles – in India, Ayodhya, Amritsar, Mumbai; in the Middle East, Makka, Jerusalem; in Sri Lanka, Kandy, to say nothing of Waco in Texas, Jonesville, or the World Trade Center in New York. In Europe, new identities are inscribed, old ones violated, by the desecration of cemeteries or commemorative monuments. Sacred texts are stuck, like graffiti, on to one-time working-class walls. In the 1998 riots in Jakarta, shops of Indonesian ethnic Chinese were destroyed, except for those displaying Islamic signs. In India (and this is where I began) the city provides the stage for displays of Hindu nationalism. That I write here from an agnostic position should not inhibit the recognition that subjects live in worlds (and not least urban worlds) that are made and lived in through religious beliefs and worldviews or alternatively, as secular responses to them. New York's or London's trumpeting of being "global" (an inflated form of nationalism, or neo-imperialism) is not unconnected to many other cities being simply "national." If urban studies are to address issues of ethnicity, religion, nationalism, cultural identity, they need a language, and a set of concepts to do so. The question is not simply who is writing the city, or even where he or she is coming from. It is rather the positionality, and the theoretical language adopted.

ACKNOWLEDGMENTS

I am indebted to Abidin Kusno for his insightful comments on an earlier draft.

REFERENCES

AlSayyad, N. 1991: *Forms of Dominance: On the Architecture and Urbanism of the Colonial Enterprise*. Aldershot: Avebury.

Ahmad, Aijaz 1992: *In Theory: Classes, Nations, Literatures*. Delhi: Oxford University Press.

Asad, T. 1973: *Anthropology and the Colonial Encounter.* London: Ithaca Press.

Bhabha, H. 1994: *The Location of Culture*. London and New York: Routledge.

Chakrabarty, D. 1992: Postcoloniality and the artifice of history: who speaks for "Indian" pasts? *Representations*, 32 (winter), 1–27.

Chase-Dunn, C. K. 1985: The system of world-cities 800–1975. In M. Timberlake (ed.), *Urbanisation in the World-Economy*, New York: Academic Press, 269–92.

Cohn, B. S. 1988: *An Anthropologist Among the Historians and Other Essays*. Delhi: Oxford University Press.

Dirlik, A. 1997: *The Postcolonial Aura: Third World Criticism in the Age of Global Capitalism*. Boulder, CO: Westview Press.

Driver, F. and Gilbert, D. 1998: Heart of empire? Landscape, space and performance in imperial London. *Environment and Planning D: Society and Space*, 16 (1), 11–28.

Duncan, J. S. 1996: Me(trope)olis: or Hayden White among the urbanists. In A. D. King (ed.), *Re-Presenting the City: Ethnicity, Capital and Culture in the 21st Century Metropolis*. London and New York: Macmillan and New York University Press, 253–68.

Fanon, F. 1968: *The Wretched of the Earth*. New York: Grove Reprint. Originally published as *Les Damnes de la Terre*, ed. Francois Maspero, Paris, 1961.

Foucault, M. 1980: *Power/Knowledge*. New York: Pantheon Books.

Guha, R. 1988: Introduction to Cohn, op. cit.

Hall, S. 1996: When was the "post-colonial"? Thinking at the limit. In I. Chambers and L. Curti (eds.), *The Post-Colonial Question: Common Skies, Divided Horizons*, London and New York: Routledge, 242–60.

Home, R. 1996: *Of Planting and Planning: The Making of British Colonial Cities*. London: Spon.

India Today 1998: Editorial: nuclear afterglow, 23 (21) (May 25), 7.

Jacobs, Jane M. 1996: *Edge of Empire: Postcolonialism and the City.* London and New York: Routledge.

Johnston, R. J., Taylor, P. J., and Watts, M. J. (eds.), 1995: *Geographies of Global Change.* Oxford: Blackwell.

King, A. D. 1976: *Colonial Urban Development: Culture, Social Power and Environment.* London and Boston: Routledge and Kegan Paul.

King, A. D. 1990a: The new colonialism: global restructuring and the city. *Intersight* 1. Buffalo: School of Architecture: State University of New York at Buffalo.

King, A. D. 1990b: *Global Cities: Post-imperialism and the Internationalisation of London.* London and New York: Routledge.

King, A. D. 1995a: Writing colonial space: a review essay. *Comparative Studies in Society and History,* 37 (3), 541–54.

King, A. D. 1995b: The times and spaces of modernity (or Who needs postmodernism)? In S. Lash, M. Featherstone, and R. Robertson (eds.), *Global Modernities*, Newbury Park and London: Sage, 108–23.

King, A. D. 1997: Locution and location: positioning the postcolonial. In V. Prakash, op. cit., vol. 2, 295–310.

Knox, P. 1995: World cities and the organization of global space. In R. J. Johnston, P. J. Taylor, and M. J. Watts, op. cit. 232–47.

Knox, P. and Taylor P. J. (eds.), 1995: *World Cities in a World-System*. Cambridge: Cambridge University Press.
Kusno, A. 2000: *Behind the Postcolonial: Architecture, Urban Space and Political Cultures in Indonesia*. London and New York: Routledge.
Mangin, P. (ed.) 1996: *Contemporary Postcolonial Theory: A Reader.* London: Arnold.
Mbembe, A. 1992: The banality of power and the aesthetics of vulgarity in the postcolony, tr. J. Roitman, *Public Culture*, 4 (2) (spring), 1–30.
McDowell, L. 1995: Understanding diversity: the problem of/for theory. In R. J. Johnston, P. J. Taylor, and M. J. Watts, op. cit. 280–94.
McClintock, A. 1992: The angel of progress: pitfalls of the term "post-colonialism". *Social Text*, 31/32 (spring), 1–15.
Metcalf, T. R. 1989: *An Imperial Vision: Indian Architecture and Britain's Raj*. Berkeley: University of California Press.
Mongia, P. (ed.) 1996: Introduction to idem, *Contemporary Postcolonial Theory: A Reader.* London: Arnold, 1–15.
Moore-Gilbert, B. 1997: *Postcolonial Theory: Contexts, Practices, Politics*. London: Verso.
Nalbantoglu, G. B. and Wong, C. T. (eds.) 1997: *Postcolonial Space(s)*. Princeton: Princeton University Press.
Noyes, J. 1992: *Colonial Space: Spatiality in the Discourse of German Southwest Africa*. Philadelphia: Harwood Academic Publishing.
Philo, C. and Kearns, G. 1993: Culture, history, capital: a critical introduction to the selling of places. In G. Kearns and C. Philo (eds.), *Selling Places: The City as Cultural Capital, Past and Present*, Oxford: Pergamon, 1–32.
Prakash, V. (ed.) 1997: *Theatres of Decolonization: Architecture/Agency/Urbanism*. Seattle, WA: College of Architecture and Urban Planning, University of Washington, 2 vols.
Rabinow, P. 1989: *French Modern: Norms and Forms of the Social Environment*. Cambridge, MA: MIT Press.
Said, E. 1978: *Orientalism*. New York: Pantheon.
Said, E. 1994: *Culture and Imperialism*. London: Vintage.
Schiller, N., Basch, L., and Blanc-Szanton, C. 1995: From immigrant to transmigrant: theorising transnational migration. *Anthropological Quarterly*, 68 (1), 48–63.
Shohat, E. 1992: Notes on the postcolonial. *Social Text*, 31/32 (spring), 91–113.
Simon, D. 1998: Rethinking (post)modernism, postcolonialism, and posttraditionalism: south-north perspectives. *Environment and Planning D: Society and Space*, 16 (2), 219–45.
Slater, D. 1995: Trajectories of development theory: capitalism, socialism and beyond. In R. J. Johnston, P. J. Taylor, and M. J., Watts, op. cit., 63–76.
Taylor, J. G. 1983: *The Social World of Batavia*. Madison: University of Wisconsin Press.
Williams, P. and Chrisman, L. (eds.) 1994: *Colonial Discourse and Postcolonial Theory: A Reader.* New York: Columbia University Press.
Wright, G. 1991: *The Politics of Design in French Colonial Urbanism*. Chicago: University of Chicago Press.
Yeoh, B. S. A. 1996: *Contesting Space. Power Relations and the Urban Built Environment in Colonial Singapore*. Oxford: Oxford University Press.

Chapter 23

Cities in Quarters

Peter Marcuse

Everyone can see today, in any city in the world, that there are extremes of wealth and poverty, each concentrated in one or more sections of the city. The wealthy areas seem pretty well insulated from the city around them, sometimes in high-rise towers, sometimes at suburban-type remove. The poor areas, on the other hand, seem marginalized, unconnected to the economic and social life of the city around them. The concentration is voluntary for the rich, involuntary for the poor, it would seem. And there are other sections of each city that are neither very rich nor very poor; among them, differences can be perceived, not only of richness, but perhaps also of housing style, of culture, of language, of street pattern, of public spaces. Business areas are also very differentiated; factories are clearly different from office buildings, and their locations differ correspondingly. But some manufacturing is done in or near older business districts too. Commercial areas cater to buyers of different tastes and different incomes; they tend to cluster together in certain sections of town, often but not always near where their targeted customers live. Recreational areas, likewise, are used by different types of people for different purposes: the elderly want peace and quiet, toddlers need playgrounds, youth want fields for active sports – and different sports for different people, bocci for some, baseball for others, volleyball for a third type, with baseball even meaning different sports for different people.

All of these differences, these divisions of the city, seem quite natural and common-sensical to most of us, most of the time. But there are disturbing aspects to some of them, too. Poor areas seem to be getting poorer, rather than being in transition to improvement, and they seem, in many places, to be disproportionately occupied by members of minority groups, usually distinguishable by their color. They are more and more considered dangerous places to be in or to go. Ethnicity seems to be more and more a controversial issue, as the scale of immigration swells and debates about bilingualism, multiculturalism, self-segregation crowd newspaper columns and referendum ballots. Business areas seem more and more to be fencing themselves off, requiring permission and identification to even go in. Public places, like parks and streets and squares and plazas, seem to offer less and less opportunity for different people to meet people unlike themselves, to mix, to express themselves in a public arena. Cities today seem fragmented, partitioned – at the extreme, almost drawn and quartered, painfully pulled apart.

Are these perceptions correct? Are our cities becoming increasingly divided, polarized, fragmented?[1] If so, why? Is there a pattern to what is changed, a logic behind it? Who is responsible – is it simply a private sector phenomenon, reflecting changing individual preferences and behavior patterns, or is government involved, and if so, how? Is marginalization more than simply someone having to be at the bottom of the pile, and is it related to ghettoization? Should anything be done about these developments? Can anything be done?

These questions have been central to much of the debate about urban policy around the world today, and not coincidentally have been major themes in urban research and writing over the last 30 years or so. Much of that discussion involves the relationship between these divisions and the effects of globalization on urban structure. Globalization is a broad and sometimes amorphous concept, but it is generally linked to a shift from manufacturing to services, from Fordist mass production to post-Fordist flexible production within manufacturing, to a heightened mobility of capital across national borders, partly in consequence of a reduced power of labor vis-à-vis capital, and thus also to a reduced welfare provision by national states. These developments have accentuated longer-term trends in the spatial structure of cities, in general leading to increased inequalities, increased social and economic divisions, and increased reflection of those divisions in space. This chapter traces some of those spatial consequences.[2]

The Nature of Divisions in Cities

To begin with, divisions in cities have always existed. It is not the fact that they are divided that is the particular characteristic of the partitioned city today; rather, it is the source and manner of their division. Some divisions arise of economic functionality, some are cultural, and some reflect and reinforce relationships of power; some are combinations of all three.

Division by economic function, broadly defined, is a generally accepted necessary division within a city. Zoning is today the accepted legal embodiment of such divisions. That zoning should be by function, generally defined as economic use (residential from heavy industrial from light industrial from retail from wholesaling from offices), is not as self-evident as it might seem; "performance zoning," for instance, attempts to define permitted uses of land not by their economic nature but by their environmental impact: traffic generated, shadows cast, air circulation impeded, green space occupied, etc. And, while "use" may separate manufacturing from retail from residential, it has never been quite clear why residential use for one family should be a different type of use than residential use by two or three families.[3] Be that as it may, separation by function, by use, is generally accepted today as in general an appropriate division within a city.

Other forms of division seem much more problematic, however. We may name four as of growing importance and concern today: divisions by

- class
- "race" or color
- ethnicity
- lifestyle.

These separate sources of division are often commingled, and even more often confused.[4] Walled or gated communities, for instance, are a growing feature of urban settlement patterns throughout the world, and reflect separation along each of these lines.[5] Only those living within them or their announced and welcomed visitors, are allowed in; usually private security is provided to enforce restrictions not only on entry but also on activities within. An estimated 4 million live in such communities in the United States, with the figure climbing to 15 million if all forms of privately regulated living communities are included.[6] If we add high-rise apartment buildings with security arrangements regulating entry, essentially vertical walled communities, the number grows even larger. If we were then to add the number of communities where restrictions on entry are enforced by effective social custom–racially discriminatory suburbs, developments limited to a narrow band of income-eligibles by price or law – we may almost describe many of our contemporary cities as entirely fragmented, composed only of a collection of separate areas of concentration of different people all desiring to stay apart from all others.

But the bases of separation between each of these parts of the contemporary city – ethnicity, lifestyle, class, and "race" – are not the same, and have very different impacts on the city. As a general rule:

- Divisions by class and "race" tend to be hierarchical, involuntary, socially determined, rigid, exclusionary, and incompatible with a democratic city life – although often legitimated as cultural divisions.
- Divisions by ethnicity and lifestyle tend to be cultural and voluntary, individually determined, fluid, non-exclusionary, and consistent with a democratic city life.

"Class" is a much-debated concept,[7] but for our purposes, the understanding of the division of space in cities, two characteristics are central: income, and power. Income, because much (not all!) of the allocation of land to different users is made in the market, in which those with higher incomes able to pay higher prices will prevail in their choices over those with lower incomes, and power, because that large part of land allocation not determined solely by the market, e.g. governed by zoning rules, owned or controlled by the state, subject to tax payments or entitled to subsidies, etc., is determined by relationships of power in the state and the economy. These two characteristics, which largely go together, are not bad indicators of class; they correlate quite consistently with "higher" and "lower " in almost any ranking of classes, but are somewhat more ambiguous in the exact lines of demarcation between them.[8]

Using these criteria, then, we may almost speak of separate cities within most cities today.

The Residential Cities

One may speak of separate residential cities. The *luxury areas of the city*, the residences of the wealthy, while located in clearly defined residential areas, are at the same time not spatially bound. The very rich, in terms of residential location, are not tied to any quarter of the city, just as the men that whipped the horses that pulled apart the quartered prisoner are not linked to any one of the resulting quarters. For the wealthy, the city is less important as a residential location than as a location of power and profit. The restructuring of cities has led to an increased profitability of real estate, from which the already wealthy disproportionately benefit. Joel Blau cites figures that indicate from 1973 to 1987 additional revenue from property constituted 45 percent of the income growth among the top 1 percent of the population.[9] It is for them first and foremost a profit-making machine. They profit from the activities conducted in the city, or (increasingly) from the real-estate values created by those activities; they may enjoy living in the city also, but have many other options. If they reside in the city, it is in a world insulated from contact with nonmembers of the class, with leisure time and satisfactions carefully placed and protected. If the city no longer offers profit or pleasure, they can abandon it; 75 percent of the chief executives of corporations having their headquarters in New York City lived outside the city in 1975.[10] It is a disposable city for them. Many years ago they were concerned to protect their separate space in the city by public instrumentalities such as zoning;[11] Seymour Toll vividly describes the interests of the wealthy residents of Fifth Avenue to protect their mansions from "inconsistent neighboring uses" through the adoption of New York City first zoning law in 1916. Today, each private high-rise condominium has its own security, and elsewhere walls protect the enclaves of the rich from intrusion. The new architecture of shopping malls, skywalks, and policed pedestrian malls is a striking physical mirror of the social separation. Downtown skywalks, for instance, both symbolically and physically, permit the men and women of business to walk over the heads of the poor and the menial.[12]

The *gentrified city*[13] serves the professionals, managers, technicians, yuppies in their twenties and college professors in their sixties: those who may be doing well themselves, yet work for and are ultimately at the mercy of others. The frustrated pseudo-creativity[14] of their actions leads to a quest for other satisfactions, found in consumption, in specific forms of culture, in "urbanity" devoid of its original historical content and more related to consumption than to intellectual productivity or political freedom.[15] The residential areas they occupy are chosen for environmental or social amenities, for their quiet or bustle, their history or fashion; gentrified working-class neighborhoods, older middle-class areas, new developments with modern and well-furnished apartments, all serve their needs. Locations close to work are important, because of long and unpredictable work schedules, the density of contacts, and the availability of services and contacts they permit.

The *suburban city* of the traditional family, suburban in tone if not in structures or location (see below) is sought out by better-paid workers, blue- and white-collar employees, the "lower middle class," the petit bourgeoisie. It provides stability, security, the comfortable world of consumption. Owner-occupancy of a single family house is preferred (depending on age, gender, household composition), but cooperative or condominium or rental apartments can be adequate, particularly if subsidized and/or well located to transportation. The home as symbol of self, exclusion of those of lower status, physical security against intrusion, political conservatism, comfort and escape from the work-a-day world (thus often substantial spatial separation from work) are characteristic. The protection of residential property values (the home functioning as financial security and inheritance as well as residence) are important. Archie Bunker is the pejorative stereotype; the proud and independent worker/citizen is the other side of the coin.[16]

The *tenement city* must do for lower-paid workers, workers earning the minimum wage or little more, often with irregular employment, few benefits, little job security, no chance of advancement. Their city is much less protective or insular. In earlier days their neighborhoods were called slums; when their residents were perceived as unruly and undisciplined, they were the victims of slum clearance and "up-grading" efforts; today they are shown their place by abandonment and/or by displacement, by service cuts, deterioration of public facilities, political neglect. Because they are needed for the functioning of the city as a whole, however, they have the ability to exert political pressure, to get public protections: rent regulation, public housing, were passed largely because of their activities, although often siphoned up to higher groups after the pressure went off. When their quarters were wanted for "higher uses," they were moved out, by urban renewal or by gentrification. The fight against displacement, under the banner of protecting their neighborhoods, has given rise to some of the most militant social movements of our time, particularly when coupled with the defense of the homes of their better-off neighbors.

The *abandoned city*, economic and, in the United States, racial, is the place for the very poor, the excluded, the never employed and permanently unemployed, the homeless and the shelter residents. A crumbling infrastructure, deteriorating housing, the domination of outside impersonal forces, direct street-level exploitation, racial and ethnic discrimination and segregation, the stereotyping of women, are everyday reality. The spatial concentration of the poor is reinforced by public policy; public (social, council) housing becomes more and more ghettoized housing of last resort (its better units being privatized as far as possible), drugs and crime are concentrated here, education and public services neglected.

The Multiple Cities of Business

In similar fashion, one may speak of different *cities of business and work*. The city of business and its divisions is not congruent in space with the residential city and its divisions. The dividing lines in the spatial patterns of economic activity define areas in which people of many occupations, classes, status, work in close proximity. Yet, if we define economic divisions by the primary activity taking place within them, one may again get a four- or five-part division.

The *controlling city*, the city of big decisions, includes a network of high-rise offices, brownstones or older mansions in prestigious locations, that is less and less locationally circumscribed. It includes yachts for some, the back seats of stretch limousines for others, airplanes and scattered residences for still others. But it is not spatially rooted. The controlling city is not spatially bounded, although the places where its activities at various times take place are of course located somewhere, and more secured by walls, barriers, conditions to entry, than any other part of the city.

Yet the controlling city tends to be located in (at the top of, physically and symbolically) the high-rise centers of advanced services, because those at the top of the chain of command wish to have at least those below them close at hand and responsive, and so it goes down the line. Our interviews with those responsible for planning the then new high-rise office tower for the Bank für Gemeinwirtschaft in

Frankfurt revealed professionals who had concluded that a separation of functions, with top executives downtown but all others in back-office locations, was the most efficient pattern for the bank, but who were overruled by their superiors, with only the advantage cited above as their reasoning. By the same token, Citibank in New York City wants its next level of professionals directly accessible to its top decision makers; credit card data entry operations may move to South Dakota, but not banking activities that require the exercise of discretion. Those locations, wherever they may be, are crucially tied together by communication and transportation channels which permit an existence insulated from all other parts of the city, if dependent on them.

The controlling city parallels in its occupancy and character, but is not congruent in time or space with, the luxury areas of the residential city. Its prototypical form is the citadel, the protectively defended high-rise complex in which business, refreshment, amusement, can be undertaken without threat of intrusion by anything unwanted, generally in "smart" buildings where communication with the world is possible without leaving the citadel, with either residential possibilities inside or direct access from luxury enclaves outside without touching the remainder of the everyday life of the city. Battery Park City in New York, Docklands in London, La Defense in Paris, Berinni in São Paulo, Lujiazui in Shanghai, all come close to the model.

The *city of advanced services*, of professional offices tightly clustered in downtowns, with many ancillary services internalized in high-rise office towers, is heavily enmeshed in a wide and technologically advanced communicative network. The skyscraper center is the stereotypical pattern, but not the only possibility. Locations may be at the edge of the center of the city, as in Frankfurt/Main, outside it, as in Paris at La Defense or outside Rome or the Docklands at London, or scattered around both inside and outside a city with good transportation and communications, as in Amsterdam. Social, "image," factors will also play a role; the "address" as well as the location is important for business. Whether in only one location or in several in a given city, however, there will be strong clustering, and the city of advanced services will be recognizable at a glance.

The city of advanced services parallels in the economic city the characteristics of the gentrified residential city.

The *city of direct production*, including not only manufacturing but also the lower-level production aspect of advanced services, government offices, the back offices of major firms, whether adjacent to their front offices or not, is located in clusters and with significant agglomerations but in varied locations within a metropolitan area. Varied, indeed, but not arbitrary or chaotic: where customers/clients (itself an interesting dichotomy!) wish to be in quick and easy contact, inner-city locations are preferred (as in the industrial valley between Midtown Manhattan and the Financial District for the printing industry, or Chinatown and the garment district for textile production, in New York City).

For mass production, locations will be different. Here the pattern has changed dramatically since the beginning of the industrial revolution. At first factories were near the center of the city; indeed, to a large extent they led to the growth of the city around them, as in the manufacturing cities of New England or the Midwest or the industrial cities of England. But more modern manufacturing methods require more single-story space, vastly more, with parking for automotive access rather than paths for workers coming on foot, and many more operations are internalized; so land costs become more important than local agglomeration economies, and suburban or rural locations are preferred. The city of direct production parallels but is clearly not congruent with, in either space or time, the residential suburban city. In a development pushing the suburb as a spatial form one step further, edge cities,[17] cities within the metropolitan area of major centers but largely self-contained in terms of residence and employment increasingly house both service and production functions, excluding only those relegated to the abandoned city in the center.

The *city of unskilled work* and the informal economy, small-scale manufacturing, warehousing, sweatshops, technically unskilled consumer services, immigrant industries, is closely intertwined with the cities of production and advanced services and thus located near them, but separately and in scattered clusters,[18] locations often determined in part by economic relations, in part by the patterns of the residential city. Because the nature of the labor supply determines the profitability of these activities, the residential location of workers willing to do low-paid and/or unskilled work has a major influence. Thus in New York City sweatshops located in Chinatown, or the Dominican areas of Washington Heights, in Miami in the Cuban enclave, or in the slums of cities throughout the world.

The economic city of unskilled work parallels the tenement city, although again in different times and places. In many developed countries, the city of unskilled work counts within it major ethnic enclaves, concentrations of immigrant communities whose recent arrival and sometimes fragile legal status makes them particularly vulnerable to the conditions of work at the lowest ends of the legal pay scale, and/or pushes them into subsistence activities within the informal labor market.

The *workless city*[19] (not because its residents do not work, but because their work is not rated or valued as "real" work in the prevailing view), the city of the less legal portions of the informal economy, the city of storage where otherwise undesired (NIMBY – Not In My Back Yard) facilities are located, the location of abandoned manufacturing buildings, generally is also congruent with the abandoned residential city. But for political protest many of the most polluting and environmentally detrimental components of the urban infrastructure, necessary for its economic survival but not directly tied to any one economic activity, are located here: sewage disposal plants, incinerators, bus garages, AIDS residences, housing for the homeless, juvenile detention centers, jails. New York City's recently adopted Fair Share regulations, aimed at distributing NIMBY facilities "equitably" among districts, are a reflection both of the extent of the problem and its political volatility.

The workless city largely parallels the abandoned city. And it is, in many places, also a ghetto to which a "racial," ethnic, or immigrant population is confined. We will return to this issue below.

Thus the cities of business. Divisions of commercial activity, of recreation, of entertainment, are likely to parallel these cities. For commercial activities, the sophisticated marketing analyses of modern merchandising define for us with operational precision the exact market a given retailer seeks. Income is the primary consideration: how up-scale a store is depends on the incomes of those it hopes to lure as its customers. Within the circle of wants of those at different income levels, appeal may further be narrowed to specific population groups, by lifestyle or demographic characteristic or, to a much lesser extent (except perhaps for foods) by ethnicity. Thus an up-scale department store near the coast may feature more shore-related sporting goods, near the mountains more goods related to skiing; a more down-scale store may feature bowling equipment here, gambling paraphernalia there. Mapping the location of Starbucks coffee bars, the latest craze in yuppie relaxation, provides a good map of the location of the gentrified city in New York. Malls will attract one class, boutiques another. And the location of each will be near the area in which it expects to find its customers.

The same divided distribution of recreational facilities can be easily traced: by looking at the kinds of facilities provided, one can judge quite accurately the class composition of the neighborhood in which it is located. Jockey clubs will be in the luxury city, country clubs in the gentrified city, baseball fields in the suburban city, basketball courts in the tenement city, fire hydrants in the abandoned city. And divided locational patterns similarly characterize religious institutions, from storefront evangelical sects in the abandoned city to high Episcopalian in the luxury city. None of these divisions is of course in complete congruence with the other; individual tastes can outweigh social conformity, historical locations are not so easily changed as population and class change, public efforts may or may not try to counteract the effect of distinctions by wealth.

"Racial", Ethnic, and Cultural Divisions

None of the foregoing can be understood, certainly not in the United States, and to a lesser extent not elsewhere either, without taking into account issues of "race," ethnicity, and culture.

The formation of the ghetto has been alluded to several times above. Ghettos are very different from enclaves; ghettos are involuntary spatial concentrations of those at the bottom of a hierarchy of power and wealth, usually confined on the basis of an ascribed characteristic such as color or "race"; enclaves are voluntary clusters, usually based on ethnicity, often coupled with immigrant status, in which solidarity provides strength and the opportunity for upward mobility.[20] Today's ghetto differs, not only from such enclaves, but also from older forms of the ghetto. It is new in that it has become what might be called an outcast ghetto, a ghetto of the excluded, the marginal, rather than only the isolated and "inferior." [21] It embodies a new relationship between the particular population group and the dominant society: one of economic as well as spatial exclusion.[22] The older integrationist hopes that the ghetto might disappear as an involuntary confinement in the face of an ever more open, democratic, and nonracist society, have largely disappeared.

The integrationist view of the ghetto is no longer shared by many in the United States deeply involved in the struggles of minority communities for justice.[23] They are responding, not only to the entrenched force of racism in the United States, but also to economic changes which broadly affect all major cities: a new situation in which capital is replacing labor and is shifting its locations for production at a rapid pace and on a worldwide basis, leaving an ever growing percentage of the population in the older industrial countries[24] not needed for production – no longer a "reserve army of the unemployed," because no reserve at home is any longer needed. Similarly, the opening of new markets worldwide has reduced the economic importance of maintaining an effective market at home with high wages and full employment, the old Keynsian strategy. Thus business interests see no use in ghetto residents for purposes of business; political leaders see more to lose than to gain in shaping public policies to benefit ghetto residents, and many in the majority, for complex reasons, continue to look down on ghetto residents. The ghetto is functional for "society" to the extent that it provides protection against the anger and the disorder that ghetto residents might cause if not limited to the space of the ghetto. Spatial isolation further gives employers, public officials, and agencies an easy way to identify the economic and social position of a given applicant for a job, for admission, or for benefits: by their address shall they be known. Ghetto residents are outcasts; hence an outcast ghetto, to "define, isolate, and contain" their victims.[25]

The developments that lead to ghettoization exist in many countries other than the United States as well. Events in Britain are similar enough to those in the United States to provoke an extensive debate as to whether there are "ghettos" in Britain;[26] major studies in continental Europe have raised similar questions about the concentration of Turks in Germany, Algerians in France, Indonesians in the Netherlands.[27] The conclusion of these studies generally has been to raise serious concern about tendencies moving in the direction of the pattern in the United States, but not yet comparable to it in scale.

In developing countries, while the impact of the factors that constitute globalization has been much more recent, current trends show a convergence of patterns, e.g. between São Paulo and New York City, or Shanghai and London. *Favelas* are the extreme example of abandoned cities – although abandonment is perhaps not the right word, since there was no prior period when they were better off. Early research focused, however, on precisely that characteristic that differentiated *favelas* from the outcast ghetto: their close relationship to the economy of the city in which, or around which, they developed. And in most developing countries race or color distinctions played a minor role. South Africa is of course the notable example of the exception, although the shantytowns that were much of the townships of apartheid South Africa were not, deliberately not, parts of the cities to which they related, and they were created well before the present phase of globalization of the world economy. Today, however, the pattern of ghettoization visible in the First World is also visible in the Third.[28] As unemployment increases in the industrial portions of the metropolitan region of São Paulo, the social "disorganization" characteristic of the ghettos of the United States, including the level and role of criminal activity, increases, and the overlapping of skin color and poverty becomes more visible.

Homelessness, both its extent and how it is treated, is a painful indicator of the strength of these processes of division in any given city. The homeless are essentially the diaspora of the abandoned city. The point is startlingly evident in the obsequiousness with which a city like New York rushes to evict the homeless from the streets or transportation centers that serve the citadels and the gentrified city, removing the homeless from the sight and sensibility of the rich to the distant ghettos of the poor, from washing down the floors of Grand Central Station with lye so no one would sleep on them to putting up "occupied look decals," posters of plants and venetian blinds pasted on the boarded-up windows of abandoned houses to create a Potemkin village for the rich to look at on their drive to work. Engels would have found the pattern familiar. But a new ingredient has been added to the historical picture: the homeless today, and the residents of the abandoned city in general, are permanent.

They have little hope of getting jobs, of joining the mainstream when conditions get better; in fact, the number of the homeless remains high through good times and bad, unlike in previous years, creating what is appropriately called the "new homeless."[29]

Conclusion

The criticism of the quartering of our cities does not imply a desire for cultural or social uniformity, or for the suppression of differences or the neglect of personal preferences and individual choices. Hierarchical differences, differences based on ascribed rather than achieved characteristics, differences that permit some to exercise power over others, are the problem, and it is a problem that is growing. What is called for then is not an egalitarian uniformity that wipes out all differences, but rather a careful structuring of public actions that will counteract the invidious pressures of hierarchical division and will solidify spaces of public openness, solidarity, and communication, so structured as to allow of a full expression of civic life and the activities of civil society without the distortions of power. The types of concrete public action such a policy would imply can only be briefly mentioned here: the constitution of public space, the attention to boundaries between groups and activities that promote positive contact and harmony, zoning that rewards social as well as physical diversity, public support for those organizations needing it to become full participants in city life, adequate subsidies (implying adequate redistribution) to provide an acceptable quality of life for all citizens.

The formulation of policies to deal with the harms revealed by the patterns of contemporary city life and structure is not hard; but the conflicts involved in putting such policies in place do not promise an easy success.

NOTES

1. For a criticism of the use of some of these terms, see Peter Marcuse, "'Dual city': a muddy metaphor for a quartered city," *International Journal of Urban and Regional Research*, 13, 4, (December 1989), pp. 697–708.
2. For a detailed discussion of the relationship between spatial structure within cities and globalization, see Peter Marcuse and Ronald van Kempen (eds.), *Globalizing Cities: A New Spatial Order?* (Blackwell, Oxford, 1999), and, more generally, Saskia Sassen, *Cities in a World Economy* (Pine Forge Press (Sage Publications), Thousand Oaks, CA, 1994).
3. The United States Supreme Court struggled with this issue in its landmark decision legitimating zoning under the United States Constitution, *Euclid v. Amber*, 272 US 365 (1926), and some commentators today consider it to have been mistaken in accepting this particular division. Even a separation between high-rise and low-rise buildings is today often questioned, as in new developments which deliberately mix sizes and configurations for variety and esthetic appeal.
4. The Chicago School, for instance, and the subsequent attempts to apply factorial analysis to the spatial structure of cities, their urban morphology, all share this weakness.
5. See Edward J. Blakely and Mary Gail Snyder, *Fortress America: Gated and Walled Communities in the United States* (Lincoln Institute of Land Policy, Cambridge, MA,

and Brookings Institution Press, Washington, DC, 1995); and Peter Marcuse, "Walls of fear and walls of Support," in *Architecture of Fear*, ed. Nan Ellin (Princeton University Press, Princeton, NJ, 1997), pp. 101–14, and Sophie Watson and Katherine Gibson (eds.), *Postmodern Cities and Spaces* (Blackwell, Oxford, 1994).

6. Evan McKenzie, *Privatopia: Homeowners Associations and the Rise of Residential Private Government.* (Yale University Press, New Haven, 1994).
7. See Erik Olin Wright, ed. *The Debate on Classes*, Verso, London, 1989. Classes used here are in any event not the same as Rex's "housing classes," because the basis for the distinction is economic, housing the result, rather than the reverse. John Rex, *Race, Community and Conflict* (Oxford University Press and Institute of Race Relations, London, 1967).
8. And they are of course not substantively defined by these indicators.
9. Joel Blau, *The Visible Poor: Homelessness in the United States* (Oxford University Press, New York, 1992), p. 85.
10. Steven Brint, in Mollenkopf and Castells, p. 155.
11. Toll, Seymor, 1969 *Zoned American*, Grossman, New York.
12. See Marcuse, Peter 1988. "Stadt – Ort der Entwicklung," in *Demokratische Gemeinde*, November, pp. 115–22; and Jonathan Barnett, "Redesigning the metropolis: the case for a new approach," *Journal of the American Planning Association*, 55, 2 (spring 1989), pp. 131–5.
13. I use the term here, not in its narrower sense, as a portion of the city in which higher-class groups have displaced lower class, see definitions in Peter Marcuse, "Gentrification, abandonment, and displacement: connections, causes, and policy responses in New York City," *Journal of Urban and Contemporary Law*, 28 (1985), pp. 195–240, but in the broader sense of areas occupied by, or intended for, professionals, managers, technicians, which may include newly constructed housing as well as housing "gentrified" in the narrower sense of the word.
14. The reference here is not to creative artists, to what in earlier days would have been called Bohemians, who cannot generally afford the prices of the gentrified city, and are more likely to live somewhere between the abandoned and the tenement city. To the extent that they tend to congregate in specific neighborhoods, they may serve as precursors of gentrification (see Damaris Rose. "Rethinking gentrification," *Environment and Planning D: Society and Space*, 2 (1984), pp. 47–74, who differentiates sharply among different categories of gentrifiers.
15. Hartmut Häusermann and Walter Siebel, 1987. *Neue Urbanität*. Suhrkamp, Frankfurt am Main. See also Marcuse, Peter, "Housing Markets and Labour Markets in the Quartered City," in *Housing and Labour Markets: Building the Connections*, ed. John Allen and Chris Hamnett (Unwin Hyman, London, 1991), pp. 118–35.
16. I still find Damaris Rose's "Toward a Re-evaluation of the Political Significance of Home-Ownership in Britain," in Political Economy of Housing Workshop, Conference of Socialist Economists, March 1980 *Housing Construction and the State*, London, pp. 71–6, one of the best pieces dealing with the very ambiguous relationships of home-ownership to political position.
17. The term comes from the quite uncritical but vivid discussion: Joel Garreau, *Edge City: Life on the New Frontier* (Doubleday, New York, 1991).
18. See, for instance Saskia Sassen, "New trends in the sociospatial organization of the New York City economy," in *Economic Restructuring and Political Response*, ed. Robert A. Beauregard (Sage, Newbury Park, CA, 1989), pp. 69–114, with brief but provocative comments on the intra-city spatial aspects of the trends she describes.
19. William Julius Wilson has been prominent among those pointing to the central position of the absence of work in shaping the lives of those in this division of the city; see

William Julius Wilson, *When Work Disappears: The World of the New Urban Poor* (Alfred A. Knopf, New York City, 1996).

20. I have suggested formal definitions in Peter Marcuse, "The enclave, the citadel, and the ghetto: what has changed in the post-Fordist US city," *Urban Affairs Review*, 33, 2, (November 1997), pp. 228–64.
21. Christian Kesteloot suggests, in an interesting paper, that "the growing importance of exclusion over marginalization" is a key characteristic of the present phase, Christian Kesteloot, "Three levels of socio-spatial polarization in Brussels." Paper presented at the ISA International Congress, Bielefeld, Germany, 1994.
22. "Institutionalized" is added to the definition by Van Amersfoort: a ghetto is "an institutionalized residential area in which all the inhabitants belong to a single ethnically, racially or religiously defined group and all members of this group live in this area... 'institutionalised' means that the inhabitants did not choose their dwelling or residential area themselves: they were to some degree coerced by society... by law or... by subtle discrimination." Quoted in Ronald Van Kempen, "Spatial segregation, spatial concentration, and social exclusion: theory and practice in Dutch cities." Paper presented at European Network for Housing Research Workshop, Copenhagen, May 1994, p. 3. It is thus apparently intended to be synonymous with "involuntary," and an important, if self-evident, addition to the definition. Were it to mean either "with its own institutions" or "created by formal institutions of the dominant society" it would raise other important questions.
23. See, for instance, Derrick Bell, *Faces at the Bottom of the Well: The Permanence of Racism* (Basic Books, New York, 1993).
24. And increasingly in newer ones also, witness the unemployment rate of 34% in São Paulo where 20 years ago it was in one of the fastest industrializing regions in the world.
25. The appropriate historical analogy for the outcast ghetto is more the leper colony than the medieval Jewish ghetto. For a detailed history of the United States ghetto, see Peter Marcuse, "Space over time: the changing position of the Black ghetto in the United States," *Netherlands Journal of Housing and the Built Environment*, 13, 1 (1998), pp. 7–24.
26. See Ceri Peach, "Does Britain have ghettos?" *Transactions of the Institute of British Geographers*, 22, 1 (1996), pp. 216–35.
27. For instance, John O'Loughlin and Jürgen Friedrichs, *Social Polarization in Post-Industrial Metropolises* (Walter de Gruyter, Berlin, 1996), H. Priemus, S. Musterd, and R. van Kempen, *Towards Undivided Cities in Western Europe: New Challenges for Urban Policy.* Part 7: comparative analysis (1998), pp. 5–20, and Marcuse and van Kempen, supra.
28. If indeed that distinction is still appropriate; major "Third World" cities could as easily be considered First World, from all points of view except the timing of their development and the nature of the national economies and states in which they exist.
29. See Peter Marcuse, "Space and race in the post-Fordist City: the outcast ghetto and advanced homelessness in the United States today," in *Urban Poverty and the Underclass*, ed. Enzo Mingione (Blackwell, Oxford, 1996), pp. 176–216.

Chapter 24

Citizenship, Multiculturalism, and the European City

Alisdair Rogers

This chapter aims to review recent theories of citizenship and attempts to relate them to the city. It focuses on the specific case of immigration and multiculturalism in the European city, mainly within the European Union. In recent years there has been much rethinking of citizenship, including the propagation of new concepts such as transnational, postnational, multicultural, and differentiated citizenship. Such debates have been generally associated with the national or state level, but some attention has also been given to the changing territorial conditions of citizenship. The European Union presents a particularly interesting situation, in which supranational cross-national and subnational territories can lay claim to political identity and cultural membership. If there is any substantial relationship between citizenship and non-national territories such as the city, then it is likely to be found within Europe.

Recent Theories of Citizenship

Citizenship is not what it used to be. Under the headline "Making a profit from portable patriotism," Mike Fritz in the *Los Angeles Times* (April 6, 1998) reports on a Denver broker who markets Belizean citizenship over the World Wide Web. Most of his clients are Russians, who are attracted to Belizean visas because they provide access to the British Commonwealth. The broker notes other advantages to possessing a second passport, including the avoidance of creditors and litigious spouses. He adds that, in Russia at least, additional citizenships have become a status symbol, one up on a Rolex or a Mercedes.

The "explosion of interest in the concept of citizenship" (Kymlicka and Norman 1994: 352) both within political theory and increasingly in other disciplines has been partly driven by the kinds of geopolitical changes suggested by this story. These include the future of the nation-state in the wake of globalization and regionalization; the role of civil society in the revolutions in former Communist-bloc countries; the weakening of the Keynesian and Fordist compacts at the heart of the welfare state; new social movements such as feminism and gay and lesbian rights; and, perhaps above all, the increase in immigration and asylum-seeking. It is no surprise therefore, that debates on citizenship have diffused beyond the domain of political philosophy. What remains less certain is whether this diffusion also dilutes the key normative and analytical insights of citizenship theory. Beyond rhetoric, is there any theoretical gain in linking cities and citizenship?

It is increasingly difficult to pin down a clear definition of citizenship. From a focus on the relationship between individuals, states, and rights, it has broadened to include more sociological questions such as the access to resources, inequality, membership in a political community, and identity. Under the influence of new social movements, citizenship has been extended from formal matters of belonging to some nation-state to more substantive ones of civil, political, social, economic and cultural rights and obligations (Garcia 1996; Holston and Appadurai 1996). Rather than define citizenship it is more constructive to describe the kinds of debates taking place within the theory. For the most part these share a common origin in seeking to go beyond the ideas of T. H. Marshall (Beiner 1995; Delanty 1997; Turner 1997). Marshall's idea of citizenship was that it was a status conferring full membership in society beyond the economic realm, which served to mitigate inequalities and conflicts founded on class. Taking the UK as his exemplar, he described the cumulative gain of citizenship rights, from legal (seventeenth to eighteenth centuries), to political (eighteenth to nineteenth centuries) and then, with the welfare state, social rights.

The limitations of Marshall's formulation have been explored by the several philosophies within political theory. These are well summarized by Kymlicka and Norman (1994), and can be briefly described as follows. Are there rights in other spheres, such as economic rights in the workplace, cultural rights of recognition or even animal rights? To what degree should rights be matched by responsibilities and obligations (conservative theory)? Should passive protections flowing from the state be accompanied by active engagement, making participation itself the purpose of citizenship (neorepublican theory)? Are rights cumulative, evolutionary, and progressive, or are there reversals and unevenness? Soysal (1994) argues that a new postnational citizenship based on the universal discourse of human rights has trumped older national forms and provided European migrants and foreigners with almost all the social and economic rights open to full citizens. Other commentators, for example Stasiulis (1997), detect a widespread retreat from inclusive forms of citizenship towards more hierarchical situations among North American and European countries. Finally, there are a series of questions arising from the fact that Marshall assumed a high degree of cultural homogeneity in society and did not allow for the plurality of cultures. This debate pits communitarians and nationalists on the one hand against certain liberals, postmodernists, and theorists of identity politics on the other. Do the benefits of citizenship only flow from prior and committed membership of a political community, for example through naturalization? Or, as Bauböck (1992) has argued, are they universal and egalitarian and so preceding membership? Can liberal states allow group rights for national minorities (Kymlicka 1995) or further, should they extend differentiated rights and special representation to oppressed groups (Young 1990)? Aside from who has it and how, how has citizenship itself been socially constructed through gender, class, race, and sexual differences (Kofman and England 1997)?

Running through all these debates, usually unnoticed, is the question of the relationship between citizenship and territory or space. Formally at least, a citizen is always a citizen of some*where*, perhaps one state or occasionally more than one. In substantive terms, the responsibilities, obligations, practices, and denials of citizenship are intimately connected with places and with spatially mediated forms of social inclusion and exclusion. As the story of the citizenship broker indicates, the relationships assumed to exist between identity, citizenship, and territory in the Westphalian system of states can no longer be so easily taken for granted.

The Multicultural European City

Estimates of the number of non-EU nationals resident in EU countries range between 15 and 17.5 million, or over 4 percent of the EU population. The foreign population therefore outnumbers ten of the fifteen EU members, without including a similar number of second- and third-generation migrant-origin individuals. In the early 1990s there were over a million immigrants a year into the EU, double the numbers of the 1980s (*Migration News*, April 1998). The flow declined in the second half of the decade. In 1996 immigrants accounted for three-quarters of the population growth of the EU, whose countries generally possess low birth rates. Aside from the unusual case of Luxembourg, EU countries can be divided into two main groups. In the first, generally northern and western countries with long-standing guestworker programs and/or migration from former colonies, between 4 and 10 percent of the population is enumerated as foreign in some sense. The second group, of Mediterranean and some Scandinavian countries, has foreign populations of fewer than 4 percent.

Migrants and their descendants are concentrated in cities. Moreover, they are overrepresented in large metropolitan areas and national capitals. For example, 55 percent of Portugal's foreigners are in Lisbon and over 40 percent of the Netherlands' minorities are found in the four largest urban centers. As a result, a number of European cities contain "foreign" communities of between a tenth and a third of their total inhabitants (see Table 24.1). These include increasingly cosmopolitan centers such as Brussels, Amsterdam, Stockholm, and London, where both EU and non-EU nationals are found. Although each city includes sizeable communities drawn from a few countries, they are also home to smaller communities from a much wider range of origins. For instance, in the Rinkeby district of Stockholm there are 127 different nationalities (Ålund 1997).

The problems faced by migrants and their descendants in these multicultural cities include employment, housing, education, services, racism and violence, segregation, religious freedom, etc. There is a substantial body of urban research on all these issues, albeit usually focusing on one at a time and continuing to rely heavily on concepts derived mainly from studies of the USA, such as assimilation, ghetto, and underclass. There is as yet no coherent and plausible European model. Citizenship theory may be an important component of any European approach to the multicultural city. To begin with, the legal status of citizenship, or nationality, is not universally available to migrants or, in some cases, to their children. Countries differ substantially in both their rules of naturalization and their ideologies of nationhood (Soysal 1994). France's civic republicanism stresses assimilation and nationality

Table 24.1 "Foreign" residents in selected West European cities in the 1990s

City	% "Foreign"	Main Nationalities
Brussels	28.5	Moroccan, French, Italian, Spanish
Amsterdam	32.2	Moroccan, Turkish, Surinamese
London	20.1	Irish, Indian, Caribbean, Bangladeshi
Paris	13.8	Algerian, Portuguese, Moroccan
Berlin (W.)	16.6	Turkish, Kurds, ex-Yugoslav, Polish
Frankfurt	29.2	ex-Yugoslav, Moroccan, Polish
Rotterdam	25.0	Turkish, Moroccan, Cape Verdean
Stockholm	17.0	Finn, Norwegian, ex-Yugoslav
Düsseldorf	16.3	Turkish, ex-Yugoslav
Oslo	15.8	Danish, Swedish, Pakistani
Liège	18.0	Italian, Moroccan, Spanish
Copenhagen	11.0	Turkish, Bosnian, Pakistani
Milan	5.0	Egyptian, Philippine, US
Lisbon	4.5	Cape Verdean, Angolan, Brazilian
Madrid	2.4	Argentine, English, French, Peruvian

Note: The figures in this table are taken from the city templates for the UNESCO MOST programme "Modes of Citizenship and Multicultural Policies in European Cities," available at www.unesco.org/most/p97city.htm. Different countries use different definitions of foreign, immigrant, and ethnic status. The table uses local definitions under the single description "foreign," which may therefore include individuals born or naturalized in the country in question.

based on residence in contrast to Germany's ethno-nationalistic ideology. The Netherlands retains some of the institutional structure of pillarization, the organization of social and political life around groupings founded on Catholicism, Protestantism, and secularism. Sweden practices a corporate form of multiculturalism, while the UK's citizenship and nationality laws remain a bewildering, if pragmatic, mess. Many countries are favorably inclined to dual citizenship but some, notoriously Germany, are not. There are up to 7.5 million resident noncitizens in Germany, including second and third generation individuals. The consequences of the liberalization of these laws by the new Schröder government in 1999 remain to be seen. Ireland, the Netherlands, Sweden, Denmark, and Norway grant local voting rights to noncitizens, as do some local states within Germany and Switzerland. EU nationals enjoy virtually full rights in whichever EU country they are resident. In Brussels for example, although the 135,000 EU expatriates working temporarily in the city will be able to vote, many of the 350,000 non-EU nationals making their lives there will not (*Reuters wire* March 21, 1998). Even given these hierarchies of formal citizenship, it is still an open question as to whether the possession of citizenship does in fact produce improved lives, more political participation, a greater sense of belonging and more social acceptance for migrants and their families.

Although, as Soysal has argued, noncitizens often enjoy many of the social and economic rights of citizens, these are mainly the property of guestworkers long resident in Europe. Since the 1980s, however, there has been a drastic increase in the number of marginalized migrants, seasonal and contract workers, street hawkers, women forced into the sex industry, female domestic workers, refugees, illegal immigrants and, at the other end of the spectrum, transient professionals and their families. What many of them share is that their lack of citizenship is functional in their exploitation. Moreover, even if residence were to become more widely accepted as the basis for formal citizenship, many marginal and transnational migrants are not, and may not intend being, permanently resident in any one country.

Since the Maastricht Treaty EU countries have moved towards a common citizenship (if only a residual one contingent upon prior citizenship in a member country) and a common immigration and asylum policy under the Schengen agreement (albeit unevenly applied in practice). These moves take place against a background of high unemployment, pressure on welfare services and the rise of new and strident nationalisms and racist politics. The spaces of citizenship across Europe are opening up, with both supranational and nationalistic/exclusionary alternatives already on the table. Is there also space for an inclusionary, tolerant, and just multicultural citizenship? Will it begin in the cities?

City and Citizenship

Holland is a country with some multicultural cities, rather than a multiethnic society.

Veenman 1995: 609

There has recently been an increasing connection made between the city and citizenship (for example in thematic special issues of *Public Culture*, *Urban Studies* and the *International Journal of Urban and Regional Research*, see Holston and Appadurai 1996; Garcia 1996; Imrie et al. 1996). There are five main reasons for the association. To begin with, revival of philosophical interest in citizenship often returns to its antecedents in Athens, Rome, the medieval borough and the many local sites of citizenship swept away by the emergence of the nation-state. Within some quarters there seems to be a nostalgia for the premodern European independent city-state and the leagues of mercantile cities (Castells 1994). The millet system governing the relations between religious groups under the Ottoman Empire and the Jewish ghetto provide alternative antecedents for the modern multicultural city.

Secondly, in the recomposition of territory and politics which Europe in particular is undergoing, some authors hold that neither the nation-state nor the supranational quasi-state are sufficient to exhaust the possibilities of citizenship or meet its challenges (Holston and Appadurai 1996). Into this democratic gap enters the city (Borja and Castells 1997). Forging new contracts with its residents, asserting political autonomy from its national and/or regional state and networking globally and locally, in this vision the city becomes a new political agent, capable of mediating between global and local processes, generating economic growth, securing the redistribution of resources and building a sustainable environment. Barcelona, Amsterdam, Berlin, Stockholm, and other cities have sought to produce their own strategic visions going beyond local economic development, often couched in the language of citizenship (see Vertovec 1996, on Berlin for example). Quite how meaningful or radical these strategies are remains to be seen. The evidence suggests that Western European cities are less autonomous from the state than their North

American counterparts (Harding 1997). An important line of inquiry will be how the transition from the stable and hierarchical structures of the Fordist local state to the more horizontal, project-specific and networked structure of the post-Fordist state will affect new migrants. In the US model, ethnic groups succeeded one another in a set of local political institutions. But what happens if this institutional structure itself changes?

Thirdly, insofar as current debates on citizenship raise questions about the relationship between membership in some form of community and the formal aspects of citizenship, cities are the sites of the most profound questions of belonging and identity. The assumption of shared community and culture as the basis for citizenship becomes most problematic in the city. Liberal and universalistic formulations face their strongest challenge from communitarian, neorepublican and identity politics formulations of citizenship. It is in the city that the contradictions between universal and differentiated conceptions of citizenship become most evident.

Cities are also the most productive sites of alternative citizenships, challenges from below (Holston and Appadurai 1996). Although the era of urban social movements has passed in Europe at least, there are signs of migrants and others negotiating new forms of citizenship. In some cases, these appear to have close connections with urban conditions. Perhaps the most notable is the Franco- Maghrebian struggle for citizenship in the French *banlieues* (Wihtol de Wenden 1995). Starting from a geographical and institutional base in the suburban trades unions and left-wing organizations, second-generation Maghrebians asserted *le droit à la différence* in the early 1980s and moved on to demand citizenship by participation independently of naturalization as French nationals. Cities can also be the site and medium of exclusionary discourses of citizenship, as found among the neo-Nazi campaigns for "foreigner-free" zones in former East Germany which began in the 1990s. The so-called liberation of bars, clubs, cafes, then streets and whole city quarters through violence and intimidation is described by neo-Nazis in terms of a counter-power, creating a space in which the state "remains outside" (*Guardian*, December 12, 1997).

Lastly, the focus upon the substance rather than the form of citizenship reveals significant local variations, both between states and within them. This is confirmed by the kinds of analyses provided by the European Commission COST program of Multiculturalism and Political Integration in European Cities. For example, Rex and Samad (1996) note significant differences between Bradford and Birmingham in their management of the needs and demands of visible minorities. It is also the assumption underlying the UNESCO-MOST program Modes of Citizenship and Multicultural Policies in European Cities. According to Soysal (1994) there are strong grounds for anticipating that different national "incorporation regimes" will encourage different degrees of local variation. Compared with corporatist or statist and centralized regimes such as Sweden or France, liberal and decentralized regimes such as Switzerland or the UK are likely to exhibit a more local level of incorporation. The absence of a central state organization of foreigners and migrants into groups for the purposes of representation, coupled with an adherence to liberal individualism, should allow more scope for the negotiation of substantial citizenship at the urban level. Whether or not there are such local differences and whether they are meaningful is a matter of empirical study. For example, in a comparison of Moroccan political mobilization in Lille and Utrecht, Bousetta (1997) discovered the anticipated contrast between nonethnic- and ethnic-based collective politics, but concluded that neither strategy was more successful than the other.

Holston and Appadurai (1996, p. 189) conclude that "cities are challenging, diverging from, and even replacing nations as the important space of citizenship – as the lived space not only of its uncertainties but also of its emergent forms." There is clearly sufficient ground for associating cities and citizenship, although it should be noted that the nation-state is far from finished and that national, supranational, and even transnational scales of analysis remain important. One can make two general observations about this association, especially as it concerns immigration. Firstly, European studies – perhaps in contrast with US writings – generally feature a division of labor between research on immigration and ethnicity on the one hand and on the city and urbanization on the other. Few scholars or research programs do anything other than hold one of these two terms constant while subjecting the other to scrutiny. Secondly, the city has usually (but not exclusively) appeared in the literature on citizenship as a taken-for-granted material space, not informed by the growing retheorization of space within political economy and interpretive approaches.

In the first instance, cities are the sites of research or the living laboratories of analysis. The complex processes of urbanization in the late twentieth century are generally contingent to the analysis. Research projects simply select from the range of European cities a series of naively given spaces. This can and does generate good research, for example Patrick Ireland's comparative study of four cities in two countries, France and Switzerland (Ireland 1994). For the most part it neglects many of the stock questions of political geography. These might include the impact of consolidated metropolitan government on minorities, as for example in Rotterdam, or the decentralization of public services in cities such as Stockholm. It could include the effect of the emergence of horizontal forms of governance within polynucleated city-regions such as Randstad, Lombardy, or the Lake Geneva cities. Whether representation is by citywide and group-specific consultative structures or by intraurban districts might also be expected to influence the political participation of migrants and minority ethnic groups.

The majority of studies hitherto remain wedded to conceptualizing the city in terms of absolute space, and have yet to fully engage with the range of theories which conceive of the urban in more relative or relational terms (Harvey 1996). They remain within what Agnew (1994) calls "a territorial trap," failing to examine the historical, geographical, and socially and politically constructed aspects of space and scale. A connection between approaches from a revived political economy and interpretive thinking and citizenship has yet to be made. There are some indications of what this might involve, for example in the call made by Painter and Philo (1995) to consider both material and immaterial spaces of citizenship through a closer attention to alternative or underground geographies that include interaction, organization, representation, and imagination. Recent work from North America has also hinted in this direction (for example D. Mitchell 1995; K. Mitchell 1997; Ruddick 1996; Staeheli and Thompson 1997). These studies combine a focus on the social and political construction of public space with a view that both identities and social boundaries are actively made through public spaces. A different tack is taken by Robinson (1997) in her use of Foucault's ideas on biopower, surveillance, and discipline to explore the spatial construction of differentiated citizenship in South Africa during and after apartheid.

What these and other studies share is a grounding of the questions of citizenship, particularly the dimensions of identity, community, and exclusion, in spaces, sites, and networks which are themselves part of the constitution of citizenship. Few of the current philosophies of citizenship have attempted such grounding to an adequate degree (with the exception of Young 1990). This reinforces the gap between theoretical speculations and empirical research and leaves many of the newer concepts of citizenship "floating" in an abstract realm. Thus the agora and the forum can remain unquestioned historical referents of citizenship, while "public space" often stays detached from any material basis in the lived experiences of cities. Amin and Graham have coined the term "the multiplex city" to describe the urban as "the co-presence of multiple spaces, multiple times and multiple webs of relations, tying local sites, subjects and fragments into globalizing networks of economic, social and cultural change" (Amin and Graham 1997: 417–18). Migrants and foreigners above all are implicated in this multiplex city and citizenship theory can be extended to address its many overlapping and intertwined features.

Conclusion

What can citizenship theory and urban theory do for one another? Based on an analysis of French politics between 1981 and 1995, Favell (1997) argues that there are times in which philosophical speculation can and does make a difference to policy outcomes. Even so, for the most part the abstract discussion is weak on translating terms into public policy. The time is certainly ripe for a reassessment of citizenship in Europe, both in its formal or legal status and in its broader substance. Citizenship theory provides urban analysts with a set of analytical and normative questions backed up by an increasingly rich philosophical debate. It can make links across the territorial scales of European governance, membership, and identity. For instance, are closed or exclusionary national borders a precondition for open or inclusive cities, as is often supposed by national politicians? By the same token, placing the city within citizenship theory loosens its connection with the nation and state and makes explicit its spatial or territorial foundations. Through good empirical and ethnographic studies of public spaces, of the kind referenced above, urban study can ground citizenship debate in the lived, material, and representational practices of migrants and foreigners in the multicultural European city.

ACKNOWLEDGMENTS

Much of the background for this article comes from a UNESCO Management of Social Transformation Program (MOST) program entitled Multicultural Policies and Modes of Citizenship in European Cities. Further details can be found at the website http://www.unesco.org/most/p97.htm.

REFERENCES

Agnew, J. 1994: The territorial trap: the geographical assumptions of International Relations Theory. *Review of International Political Economy*, 1 (1), 53–80.

Ålund, A. 1997: Co-operation for multi-ethnic inclusion: a project on local citizenship, participation and community integration in metropolitan Stockholm, Department of Sociology, University of Umeå.

Amin, A. and Graham, S. 1997: The ordinary city. *Transactions of the Institute of British Geographers*, NS 22 (4), 411–29.

Bauböck, R. 1992: *Immigration and the Boundaries of Citizenship*. Monographs in Ethnic Relations no. 4, Centre for Research in Ethnic Relations, University of Warwick, Coventry.

Beiner, R. 1995: Why citizenship constitutes a theoretical problem in the last decade of the twentieth century. In R. Beiner (ed.), *Theorizing Citizenship*, Albany, NY: State University of New York Press, 1–28.

Borja, J. and Castells, M. 1997: *Local and Global: Management of Cities in the Information Age*. London: Earthscan.

Bousetta, H. 1997: Citizenship and political participation in France and the Netherlands: reflections on two local cases. *New Community*, 23 (2), 215–31.

Castells, M. 1994: European cities, the informational society, and the global economy. *New Left Review*, 204, 18–32.

Delanty, G. 1997: Models of citizenship: defining european identity. Paper presented at the 2nd Convention of The European Association for the Advancement of Sciences, Europe: "Conflict and Cooperation," University of Nicosia, Cyprus, March.

Favell, A. 1997: Citizenship and immigration: pathologies of a progressive philosophy. *New Community*, 23 (2), 173–95.

Garcia, S. 1996: Cities and citizenship. *International Journal of Urban and Regional Research*, 20 (1), 7–21.

Harding, A. 1997: Urban regimes in a Europe of the cities? *European Urban and Regional Studies*, 4 (4), 291–314.

Harvey, D. 1996: *Justice, Nature and the Geography of Difference*. Oxford: Blackwell.

Holston, J. and Appadurai, A. 1996: Cities and citizenship. *Public Culture*, 8, 187–204.

Imrie, R., Pinch, S., and Boyle, M. 1996: Identities, citizenship and power in the cities. *Urban Studies*, 33 (8), 1255–61.

Ireland, P. 1994: *The Policy Challenge of Ethnic Diversity: Immigrant Politics in France and Switzerland*. Cambridge, MA: Harvard University Press.

Kofman, E. and England, K. 1997: Citizenship and international migration: taking account of gender, sexuality and "race." *Environment and Planning A*, 29 (2), 191–3.

Kymlicka, W. 1995: *Multicultural Citizenship*. Oxford: Oxford University Press.

Kymlicka, W. and Norman, W. 1994: The return of the citizen: a survey of recent work in citizenship theory. *Ethics*, 104 (2), 352–81.

Mitchell, D. 1995: "The end of public space?": People's Park, definitions of the public and democracy. *Annals of the Association of American Geographers*, 85, 108–33.

Mitchell, K. 1997: Transnational subjects: constituting the cultural citizen in an era of Pacific Rim capital. In A. Ong and D. Nonini (eds.), *Ungrounded Empires: The Cultural Politics of Modern Chinese Transnationalism*. London: Routledge, 228–56.

Painter, J. and Philo, C. 1995: Spaces of citizenship: an introduction. *Political Geography*, 14 (2), 107–20.

Rex, J. and Samad, Y. 1996: Multiculturalism and political integration in Birmingham and Bradford. *Innovation*, 9 (1), 11–31.

Robinson, J. 1997: The geopolitics of South African cities: states, citizens and territory. *Political Geography*, 16 (5), 365–86.

Ruddick, S. 1996: Constructing difference in public spaces: race, class and gender as interlocking systems. *Urban Geography*, 17 (2), 132–51.

Soysal, Y. N. 1994: *Limits of Citizenship: Migrants and Postnational Membership in Europe*. Chicago: University of Chicago Press.

Staeheli, L. and Thompson, A. 1997: Citizenship, community and struggles for public space. *Professional Geographer*, 49 (1), 28–38.

Stasiulis, D. K. 1997: International migration, rights, and the decline of "actually existing liberal democracy." *New Community*, 23 (2), 197–214.

Turner, B. S. 1997: Citizenship studies: a general theory. *Citizenship Studies*, 1 (1), 5–18.

Veenman, J. 1995: Ethnic minorities in the Netherlands. In K. McFate, R. Lawson, and W. J. Wilson (eds.), *Poverty, Inequality and the Future of Social Policy*. New York: Russell Sage Foundation, 607–28.

Vertovec, S. 1996: Berlin Multikulti: Germany, "foreigners" and "world-openness." *New Community*, 22 (3), 381–400.

Wihtol de Wenden, C. 1995: Generational change and political participation in French suburbs. *New Community*, 21 (1), 69–78.

Young, I. M. 1990: *Justice and the Politics of Difference*. Princeton, NJ: Princeton University Press.

Chapter 25

Working out the Urban: Gender Relations and the City

Liz Bondi and Hazel Christie

Working out the Urban: An Introduction

At the end of the twentieth century urban social relations are vastly different from those found in the cities of a hundred years ago. In advanced Western societies it is clear that the old central cities, many of which lend their names to major metropolitan hinterlands, contain a shrinking proportion of wealth and population (Fainstein and Campbell 1996: 2). We have also learnt that the old decays unevenly and that rapid shifts in the patterning of uneven development between both sectors of the economy and geographical regions have rendered some cities command centers of the global economy or nests of technological innovation, while others have experienced deindustrialization and stagnation even while they encompass large populations (Castells 1989; King 1990).

At the same time, intraurban variations have remained marked, and the reshaping of physical and social space has brought inequalities of urban living into starker relief. Concentrations of impoverishment, racial and ethnic discrimination, together with areas where the homeless wander or disaffected youth congregate, are part and parcel of the new urban condition entailed in the transition to a post-Fordist era. But in contrast to this "universal tale of urban woe" (Harvey 1996: 405) other parts of cities have experienced revival and reinvestment. Flows of population and affluence into gentrified neighborhoods, often adjacent to areas of great poverty, have produced a landscape of privilege and wealth, demarcated from poorer areas by walls and gates, which sharpen the distinctions between the "haves" and the "have nots". The imprint of urbanization in the late 1990s is thus a checkerboard or mosaic of neighborhoods in which the wealthy attempt to keep the impoverished at bay despite their close proximity (Christopherson 1994).

Whatever the explanation for these divisions – and we locate these in transformations that have occurred in the nature of capitalist development in the twentieth century – it is widely accepted that changes in urban society affect people's everyday lives. While most emphasis has been placed on radical shifts in *class* composition and on the class characteristics of spatial practices (Massey 1984; Sayer and Walker

1992), we wish in this chapter to draw attention to research on gender identities and gender relations in the context of urban change in Western societies. In so doing we argue for an approach that highlights the nature and extent of gender divisions, especially as these intersect with other dimensions of social differentiation and identification in urban spaces. We advocate a materialist reading of urban conflict and change that highlights the gender configuring of practice: we do not in any way dismiss or downplay the significance of class (Connell 1995; see also Sharp 1996).

Feminist critiques of urban studies have argued that women's lives have remained either invisible or sorely misrepresented within a good deal of urban studies (see for example Bowlby, Lewis, McDowell, and Foord 1989; McDowell 1983; Mackenzie 1984). But in the last two decades these problems have begun to be corrected. In this chapter we are indebted to a tradition in feminist urban studies that understands gender to be a significant element in the unequal structuring of urban space, alongside class, race, ethnicity, and so on (for influential early examples see Mackenzie and Rose 1983; McDowell 1983). Like these accounts, we understand gender (together with class, race, and other axes of inequality) as a relational process through which social identities are forged, and through which material inequalities are sustained and challenged. Moreover, we understand gender, class, race, and so on to be inextricably interwoven and situated processes (compare Pratt and Hanson 1994). Identities and inequalities can therefore be understood as social practices. Following from this, our concern in this chapter is to understand the context in which particular groups of women and men "work out" their lives: how are their material conditions of life structured? We are especially interested in differences (and similarities) between women and men occupying different class positions.

We suggest that cities render the gender configuring of *social* practice particularly visible. It is in cities that we see the spatial imprint of women's differential position within structures of exploitation and within a segregated division of labor. And it is also in cities that the complex interplay of power relations, and the array of social institutions, which lie behind a given form of gender relations, are most graphically manifest. In short it is a space within which we can recognize different gender identities and from which we can analyze the different logics that are superimposed on and contribute to the creation of these multiple identities. The hallmark of urban identity in the late 1990s, we argue, is one of fragmented and contradictory experiences of gender.

To map different kinds of gender identities is only a first step, of course: we must also understand the relations between them. To keep the analysis dynamic, and to prevent multiple identities from being collapsed into one static typology of gender relations, we must unpack the milieux of class and race and scrutinize the gender relations operating within them. And we must also recognize that these differences are socially constructed in and across space. Geographers and urban theorists have recognized that processes in place give rise to diverse and sometimes fragmented ways of being and becoming in patriarchal, capitalist societies (Bondi 1998; Chouinard 1996; Pratt and Hanson 1994). This relational approach makes it easier to recognize the hard compulsions under which gender configurations are formed, the bitterness as well as the pleasure in gendered experiences. This is crucial at a time when capitalist economies are becoming more individualistic: it counters a widespread tendency to mistake new gender identities for alternative lifestyles, or for matters of consumer choice that are freely available to all women (Connell 1995).

So, in this chapter we adopt a dual focus in interpreting gender relations in advanced Western urban societies. We look first to the structural processes that have led to pressure to reorganize the interior spaces of cities, and which show the significance of gender differences within an interlocking matrix of power relations. And secondly, we link these changes in social structures and relationships to the lived experiences of women and men by comparing the life chances, opportunities, and identities of those who have benefited from new forms of capitalist accumulation with those who have been excluded from it. In so doing we suggest that attempts to evaluate general trends in gender relations are misplaced: we argue that convergences between the experiences of men and women, sometimes taken as evidence of greater gender equality, are inextricably bound up with deeply gendered forms of inequality that take particular spatial forms. While we illustrate our account with evidence drawn largely from cities in the UK, where both class and gender relations take specific forms, our general argument is applicable thoughout Western societies.

Gendering the Urban: A Theorization

It seems that capitalism is at a "crossroads" (Amin 1994: 1) in its historical development, as signaled by the emergence of forces – technological, social, spatial, and institutional – very different from those that dominated the economy after the Second World War. Inevitably there is much dispute about the precise magnitude and extent of the shifts involved but there is some consensus that the period from the mid-1970s represents a transition from one phase of capitalist development to another. Interpretations of this transition tend to hinge on assertions about the changing uses of labor (Peck 1996). Thus we hear much about the rationalization of manufacturing industry, about the emergence of new jobs in the service sector, and about developments in high-technology and knowledge-based industries (for example Castells 1994; Castells and Hall 1993; Sassen 1991). In short, we are now said to be living in a post-Fordist era, marked by flexibility and characterized by deepening social divisions of labor.

In contributing to and critiquing these debates, feminists have argued that the post-1970 period of capitalist restructuring has both speeded up the unraveling of an old gender order and has exposed the limitations of existing analyses of urbanization (McDowell 1991; Walby 1997). According to this argument, the idea and reality of cities as inherently divided cannot be understood without looking at realignments in gendered divisions of labor and in the structure of household organization. While much has been made of radical shifts in the nature of class relations, rather less has been said about how gender relations are built into the organization of the city and about how they continue to shape its development. Our starting point therefore is to broaden out some of these debates by looking at the gendered transformation of work practices, and so to read their implications for urban identities.

One way to capture the depth and complexity of the changes entailed in the emergence of a post-Fordist era is to ask a set of straightforward questions about who does what work and for what reward, through which broad shifts in sociospatial inequalities may be identified. In this context one major empirical trend cannot be overlooked – even by those who are not sympathetic to the feminist project – and that is the increase in the number of women in paid employment. Although in the UK as in other Western societies women have always worked for money, and have formed a significant component of the workforce without interruption since the 1830s (Hakim 1993), the postwar period has been characterized by a marked increase in the participation of women in paid employment. Data from the UK Population Census indicate that in 1951 some 43 percent of women were economically active while the corresponding figure for 1991 was over 70 percent. Another significant empirical trend – and one that has come under attack from opponents of the feminist project – is the decline in the number of men in full-time paid employment. In a post-Fordist economy, where manufacturing industry is no longer the main wealth-generating activity, opportunities for skilled manufacturing workers have been reduced to a low level. A combination of outdated skills, age, and lack of geographical mobility have rendered many men unemployable in the new economy, or at least unable to find jobs that bring benefits comparable to those they enjoyed previously.

The increase in female participation in the labor market gives the impression of considerable progress towards financial independence for women and towards more egalitarian lifestyles. However, an important theme to emerge from studies of socio-economic change in the UK contradicts this impression (Anderson, Bechhofer, and Gershuny 1994; Scott 1994). Evidence from national surveys about rewards for different kinds of jobs shows that women's average hourly pay rates, and, to an even greater extent, their average total incomes, are still markedly lower than men's, with little if any increase with age or duration in employment (Hutton 1994). This reflects the fact that the majority of the new employment opportunities taken up by women have been in part-time jobs, which bring limited employment-related rights or benefits, and which tend to be offered at relatively low rates of pay. Continuing sex segregation in the labor market is also significant: the majority of employees, whether male or female, work in occupations strongly dominated by members of their own sex, and industries dominated numerically by women tend to be less well remunerated. Thus, the failure of real income from part-time work to increase with the duration of employment, together with job segregation and labor market segmentation, have together resulted in the persistence of a substantial difference between women's and men's average earnings (Lindley 1994). While the predominance of part-time employment among women is more marked in the UK than in most other Western societies, these gender differences have proven to be equally persistent elsewhere (O'Reilly and Fagan 1998).

But this averaged picture hides more than it reveals about the recompositioning of the labor force and about the recasting of gender and class relations in the city. The old gender order, based on the model of the female caregiver and the male breadwinner, has given way to different alternatives, and for some women it is the best of times while for others it is the worst of times (Brenner 1993). Growing numbers of women with professional and vocational qualifications have moved into "core" jobs and are advancing up the career ladder particularly in the professions, public administration and management (Crompton and Sanderson 1990; Kay and Hagan 1995; Wills 1996). They are also making inroads into political office, and are changing cultural attitudes and images, albeit slowly (Casey 1995). The career paths and experiences of some of these female workers increasingly resemble those of their male counterparts, and illustrate a certain narrowing of gender divisions and inequalities. But such opportunities are not uniformly accessible to all women (or to all men). Increasing numbers of women are trapped in poorly paid jobs where occupational sex segregation persists and sexual harassment and violence against women remain entrenched (Beechey and Perkins 1987). Moreover an increasing number of men find themselves outside of "core" employment and many of them are subject to the same disadvantageous terms and conditions of employment previously associated strongly and specifically with women workers as well as racialized minorities. So among the less well paid too a narrowing of gender divisions in employment is apparent, accompanied by a widening of class differences among workers of the same sex. In this context greater gender parity is a Pyrrhic victory in which the majority have lost out. Thus a major characteristic of the post-Fordist era is that the insecurity engendered by a combination of poorly paid jobs, temporary contracts and limited employee protection is no longer limited to particular social groups previously positioned on the periphery of the labor market.

This restratification takes a particular spatial form. At the scale of households, an acute polarization is apparent between households with two professional salaries and those with low incomes or no incomes (Casey and McRae 1990; Jordan and Redley 1994). This has been exacerbated by characteristics of welfare provision, so that many households in the latter category are faced with a stark choice between two unattractive strategies: they can either attempt to maximize household income by adult members taking on double or triple working days, sequential shifts, and so on, or they face complete, long-term welfare dependency, which is often the only "choice" for lone-parent households (Glendinning 1991; McLaughlin 1994). As this indicates, improved wealth and status among one group of women has very limited "trickle down" effects: on the contrary, financial autonomy and independence for some is matched by economic insecurity and dependence (within the household or on the state) for others.

These two pictures, one of women's economic success and prosperity and the other of their poverty and marginalization, coexist and reflect the contradictions and tensions of the post-Fordist regime of accumulation. Moreover, this deepening of socioeconomic inequalities is not the result of structural variations in rates of economic growth, that is from there being more economic success in one place or part of the economy than another. Rather these inequalities operate at the very heart of contemporary economic processes (Massey and Allen 1995: 123–4). One of the consequences of this generates another aspect of the spatiality of restratification in the form of the close juxtaposition of poverty and affluence within urban areas to which we have already drawn attention.

The significance of the new interlocking divisions and spatialities of gender and class that we have described extends well beyond the world of work to encompass relations within the household unit and domestic politics, as well as the expression of new identities in the urban arena. Indeed, as Connell has suggested, we find "the gender configuring of practice however we slice the social world, whatever unit of analysis we choose" (1995: 71). It is to experiences of, and identities forged through, these practices to which we now turn.

Different Worlds of Work, Different Experiences of the City

Questions about the formation of new gender identities in the urban arena have vexed many feminist geographers (Bondi 1991; Ruddick 1996). The development of fragmented and contradictory experiences of gender in contemporary urban life, and their impact on gender identities, have attracted a good deal of attention (Collins 1991; Marshall 1994). That the feminization of the economy is a key factor in the everyday lives of women and men is also widely acknowledged. However, less attention has been paid to the connections between gender identities and post-Fordist economic relations. This neglect is explained, at least in part, by the claims of some poststructuralists that work can no longer be regarded as the primary basis for social organization or self-identity (Casey 1995). However we would suggest that there is a compelling case to be made for retaining the primacy of work and work relations in explaining the formation of new gender identities. This case is vested in the power differentials created between those who have been central to and benefited from the most recent rounds of capitalist accumulation and those who have been excluded from it.

In asserting the continued significance of work and work relations, we do not understand "work" in any prescriptive (or normative) sense as being based on full-time paid employment (see Gorz 1989). Rather we are arguing that the positions women and men occupy in relation to the (very uneven) distribution of economic opportunities and economic rewards apparent in post-Fordist regimes frame experiences in a manner that is fundamental to the forging of gender identities. We illustrate the working out of this with reference to two different groups of urban residents.

The best of times for some: gender, gentrification and urban affluence

The material significance of the distribution of work and work relations relates closely to other aspects of urban culture. A growing literature on city cultures and urban lifestyles points to new architectural, artistic, and cultural styles, which are sometimes described in terms of a postmodern shift (Featherstone 1991; Watson and Gibson 1995). Whether postmodern esthetic and cultural movements resist or endorse the logic of post-Fordist capitalist accumulation, the refashionings of urban space that result are intimately connected to the emergence of new urban sensibilities (Harvey 1989; Jameson 1991; Soja 1989, 1996). And it is within these urban spaces that cultural identities, including gender identities, are forged and maintained. So gender identities, work relations, cultural styles, and the meanings of urban space are constructed together in the late twentieth-century urban arena (Ruddick 1996).

Gentrifiers in particular, are often considered to be in the vanguard of these trends in their search for quality in urban living, whether through proximity to consumption palaces and sophisticated entertainment, or through the creation and exploitation of distinctively stylized ways of life (see for example Bridge 1994; Butler 1995; Jager 1986; Ley 1994; Ley and Mills 1993; Mills 1988; Smith 1996; Zukin 1982). Several dimensions of these experiences emerge from debates about the relative importance of, and the relationship between, class and gender in processes of gentrification (Bondi 1991; Butler and Hamnett 1994; Rose 1989; Smith 1987; Warde 1991). In the various ways in which inner-urban neighborhoods have been transformed to accommodate particular strands of the middle classes of the late twentieth century a close interweaving between work relations, household form, urban culture, and gender identities is apparent.

A number of studies draw attention to career orientation and career success among women gentrifers, including female members of heterosexual dual-career households, women living alone, lone parents, and women living in lesbian partnerships (see for example Bondi 1999; Butler and Hamnett 1994; Rose 1989; Rothenberg 1995). While occurring predominantly in public sector professions strongly dominated by women, this at least suggests some shifts in contemporary constructions of femininity. Small inroads into previously male preserves such as the finance sector provide sharper evidence of ways in which gender identities and gender relations at work are being renegotiated (McDowell and Court 1994). Higher educational qualifications are crucial to this advancement and an intergenerational class dimension is apparent: for example in the UK the daughters of men in professional employment are considerably more likely than other women to move into a professional career themselves (Savage, Barlow, Dickens, and Fielding 1992).

Women and men in service-class employment exercise a good deal of choice in their housing and household conditions. While salaries in the female-dominated public sector professions in particular are modest compared to most male-dominated service-sector occupations, in many cities access to gentrified housing on one such income is a real possibility. The opportunities of dual-career households, particularly where both partners are in prestigious service sector occupations, are often much wider and consequently it is hardly surprising that the class transformations associated with gentrification vary considerably between different localities at both interurban and intraurban scales (see Beauregard 1990; Butler and Hamnett 1994; Lees 1994; Smith 1996). Nor is it surprising that gentrifiers adopt a wide range of household forms, including substantial numbers that appear "conventional" in the sense of containing a heterosexual couple plus children with the man in higher-status employment than the woman (see Butler and Hamnett 1994) as well as many that do not conform to this pattern (see Bondi 1999; Rose 1989; Rothenberg 1995). Thus, the phenomenon of gentrification fosters diverse experiences of urban living and a fragmentation of urban identities.

While the evidence available is limited, there is at least some indication that, even within the more "conventional" households in gentrified neighborhoods, attitudes to gender divisions are being formulated in ways that at least make space for egalitarian forms of gender identity (Bondi 1999; Butler and Hamnett 1994; Rose 1989; Rothenberg 1995). But the extent to which these trends are specific to gentrifiers remains in question: suburban lifestyles are changing too and even if rather fewer "non-traditional" households are to be found in suburban neighborhoods, it may be that this trend towards "lifestyle differentiation" within a discourse of equality operates throughout the late twentieth-century middle classes (Marsh 1990, 1994).

Perhaps the arena in which a reshaping of gender identities within the urban middle class is most evident is that of consumption practices. Relatively affluent inner-city neighborhoods with mixed land uses that incorporate both high-density residential accommodation and high-quality commercial outlets aimed at niche markets, including shops, restaurants, cinemas, and so on, have certainly attracted women (and men) who, through their sexual orientation, household form and career choices, are actively forging distinctive gender identities (Mort 1996; Wilson 1991). To a degree, these localities point to the emergence of a feminine urban identity. But the distinctiveness and potential of this identity, and the extent to which it is impressed upon urban space, are matters of dispute. While some suggest that it is prefigurative, serving to illustrate the possibility of more emancipatory forms of urban living (see especially Wilson 1991; Young 1990), we would advance a more cautious reading, emphasizing that it is a class-specific development contingent upon access to adequate resources, educational, cultural, and material (Bondi 1998; Ravetz 1996). Consequently it depends upon a restratification within the city and is constitutive of new forms of inequality, linked to very different urban experiences and forms of gender identity.

The worst of times for others: gender, exclusion and poverty

As we have indicated, this restratification is double edged and many women (and men) have lost out in the restructuring of work practices and work relations. Concentrations of poverty and deprivation in inner urban areas, as well as in peripheral housing estates, make for a very different urban world and a very different set of urban experiences from those of gentrifiers. Constraint, not choice, is the overwhelming experience of the housing market and many individuals and households are isolated from mainstream economic and social activities. Again, several dimensions of these experiences emerge from debates about the relative importance of, and the relationship between, class and gender in processes of exclusion (Green 1997; Jordan 1996). The revival of and reinvestment in inner-city neighborhoods has not been uniform and, if anything, the spatial link between the inner city and disadvantage has become more entrenched (Green 1994; McGregor and McConnachie 1995). As with the case of professional women, we can identify connections among work relations, household form, urban culture, and gender identities, but under very different socioeconomic circumstances.

Research shows that polarization of gender experiences is clearly and inextricably linked to change in the quantity and quality of employment. In contrast to the career orientation and success of women gentrifiers, research on impoverished women highlights the problematic aspects of new employment contracts in the late 1990s. Some of the main losers in the drive towards a low-wage economy have been the working-class women who cannot find full-time paid employment or who are not able to afford to go out to work because of the prohibitive costs of childcare (Harrop and Moss 1995; Ward, Dale, and Joshi 1996). Unlike the gentrifiers, these women have neither the educational qualifications needed to gain access to jobs in the core labor market nor the resources required to escape the physical decay and economic disadvantage found in their immediate environs.

Under these new employment conditions many of the poorest households survive by piecing together income from several poorly paid and/or insecure jobs. For those caught in the pernicious benefits traps and unable to afford to take work, long-term unemployment paves the road to exclusion and spatial restriction (Morris 1987, 1994). Again, an intergenerational class dimension is superimposed on this gender realignment: for example in the UK unemployment tends to run in families

(Payne 1987; Ward and Bird 1995). In the worst-case scenario a culture of poverty or an underclass develops which generates negative attitudes towards education, training, and employment (Brown 1995). In such circumstances it is not easy to find evidence of egalitarian shifts in contemporary constructions of femininity. Exploitative gender relations and gender segregation are more obvious, and are reflected in the careful policing of gender identities at work (Glucksmann 1990; Pringle 1989). Consequently, although the vast majority of women are positively orientated to work, and expect to spend most of their adult lives in productive employment, opportunities are curtailed. Thus, for the majority of people, employment restructuring has tended to shore up the ideology of motherhood and so perpetuated the disadvantageous positioning of women in the labor market (Adkins 1995; Pateman 1989).

The contestation of gender identities at work has been brought into sharper focus by the extent to which men have also lost out in the new kind of employment growth in the 1980s and 1990s. The normative (and masculinist) vision of work as full-time paid employment has been ruptured by high levels of male unemployment and by the extension of low-paid jobs, poor career prospects and precarious employment to substantial sections of the (white) male labor force. Although both sexes have lost out in the creation of "flexible" working practices, media attention has focused on the costs incurred by men. This is because masculine identity in particular has long been understood in relation to workplace culture in a manner that has persisted regardless of supposed shifts towards other bases of identity. The other side of this equation of course is that poverty and unemployment, and their association with lawlessness, crime, and fear of violence or intimidation in public places, have exposed working-class men to moral scrutiny, especially those who are young and/or unemployed (Campbell 1993; Valentine 1996). Women in similar employment circumstances have not generally been subjected to the same degree of public concern, whether sympathetic or vilificatory, although the debate about lone mothers is an important exception.

Women and men with limited employment opportunities cannot exercise much choice in their housing and household conditions. For many women living in poor households, including those with two earners, women living alone and single mothers, employment vulnerability reduces choice of residence, so that those who are disadvantaged in labor market terms tend to be found in the least desirable housing. This is true of both the public sector, where residualization of council housing has become more intense, and the private market where low households on low incomes are restricted to cheaper properties which are often in poor repair and in less desirable areas (Hills and Mullings 1991; Doling, Ford, and Stafford 1988). So evidence suggests that the operations of housing and labor markets interact so as to produce spatial concentrations of people with similar class and lifestyle characteristics.

Disadvantaged neighborhoods increasingly come to be seen as "problem areas" from which those with economic resources migrate. In these circumstances the most disadvantaged groups and communities become even more detached from the mainstream economy and the problems of long-term unemployment and welfare state dependence grow (Jordan, James, Kay, and Redley 1992; Lovering 1997). Gender identities in these impoverished urban neighborhoods are both an expression of new class relations and a statement about the connections among types of work, household dynamics, and neighborhood factors.

The costs of the new urban social relations embodied in these places are high. Women and men trapped in poverty suffer deleterious consequences – their health deteriorates, their skills decay, their aspirations decline and their self-confidence evaporates (Burchell 1994). An extensive literature shows that poverty and its side effects are not experienced equally by all household types or by all household members, and that hardship is borne disproportionately by women (Brannen and Wilson 1992; O'Brien 1995). Households headed by women, whether single mothers or the elderly living alone, are most vulnerable to poverty while in "conventional" nuclear families women surviving on low incomes are most likely to experience multiple disadvantage. Many women living under these restricted and restrictive economic conditions sacrifice the quest for more progressive gender relations to the need to ensure survival on a day-to-day basis. Women tend to undertake the extra mental labor involved in devising ways to reduce costs of living, and risk their own health, or sacrifice their own pleasures, by putting the needs of their partners and children above their own. Gender divisions may well be intensified by the consumption practices of the new urban poor. Here consumption is about "getting by" and the relentless grind of making ends meet in the midst of long-term adversity. The new class practices may shore up more traditional feminine roles; they have little to do with the search for style and good taste or the displays of social status often associated with the consumption practices of women in higher income categories. The trend towards "lifestyle differentiation" within a discourse of equality is not a luxury afforded to women in the lowest ranks of the income distribution.

These contrasts between the urban affluent and the urban poor illustrate our argument that the hallmark of urban identities in the late 1990s is one of fragmented or contradictory experiences of gender. Thus debates about the postmodern sensibility and the emancipatory nature of public space do not begin or end merely with accounts of the democratization or rehabilitation of urban space enjoyed by women gentrifiers. Indeed, not only are the freedoms of these spatial practices limited to a few, but the defence of this privileged lifestyle is translated into a proliferation of new repressions in space and movement (Davis 1990: 160; see also Christopherson 1994). Freedom for some is at the expense of control, manipulation, and ghettoization for "others" whose gendered or racialized identities constrain participation in the public sphere. Similarly the disenfranchised, the welfare dependent and the homeless, among others, are devalued and excluded, deliberately or otherwise, from the spaces of the urban elite. In short, social disintegration and increasing economic inequality have led to the commodification and privatization of urban space such that it is not universally accessible to a civic public.

Working out the Urban: A Conclusion and Prospectus

In this essay we have explored late twentieth-century forms of gender inequality and gendered identities from a materialist perspective. We have argued that post-Fordist economic relations have produced new and intense forms of social exclusion in

Western cities. We have identified convergences in at least some aspects of the experiences of women and men among both the urban affluent and the poor, and we have advanced an interpretation that does not marginalize gender domination in a tale of class oppression (Pratt 1991: 597). More specifically, we have drawn on research concerned with patterns of employment, the reorganization of housing markets and social polarization in cities to advance the feminist challenge to established ways of understanding processes of restructuring and their effects on the formation and experiences of various urban social groups. Our account also feeds into debates about the divided city, drawing attention to the gender configuring of class practices (Fainstein, Gordon, and Harloe 1992; Marcuse 1993).

We would suggest that our materialist reading of these complexities points towards several avenues for further research. While our account has engaged with issues of choice and constraint, there remains much scope to explore the strategies women and men use in planning and investing for their future needs. This would bring into the analysis consideration of life-courses in relation to paid employment, informal economic activities, family planning, childrearing, housing, and so on. It would also serve to illuminate intergenerational processes in the context of the gender configuring of class practices.

In this chapter we have drawn attention to ways in which class divisions are shaped by women's position within the income distribution. There is scope to examine more closely the nature of social relations between women earning higher incomes and those on lower incomes. Jordan (1994) has argued that exploitative employment relations are shaped by affluent women's preferences for "flexible" assistance with child-minding and domestic chores, and poor women's need to "fit in" employment with family responsibilities. This theme has been explored by Gregson and Lowe (1994) in relation to paid domestic work. Further research might explore other aspects of the decisions of dual-career households, including for example those pertaining to children's schooling (especially the use of private education and the exercise of parental choice within the state sector), to health-care (including the uptake of private health insurance and the use of private medical facilities), and so on. As well as illuminating the choices of the urban affluent, such research needs to explore the effects (unintended) on those excluded from the advantages their strategies are intended to capture. We also need to understand the dynamic relationship between the choices of the affluent, the shaping of social inequalities, and gender relations within households and communities.

The perspective we have adopted pays close attention to empirical evidence of gender inequalities and gendered experiences of urban life. In certain respects this contrasts with calls made a decade or so ago to go beyond empirical validation to more sophisticated theoretical understandings of gender divisions in urban society (Bowlby, Lewis, McDowell, and Foord 1989; Mackenzie 1984; Pratt 1991). Our argument can be understood as both a counterpoint to the influence of theoretically led (especially poststructuralist) approaches to questions of cultural identity in recent years, and as a response to the fragmentation of experience we have highlighted: we would argue that the multiplicity of differences that divide women in Western cities of the late twentieth century calls for research well grounded in the substantive complexities of life.

REFERENCES

Adkins, L. 1995: *Gendered Work: Sexuality, Family and the Labour Market*. Buckingham: Open University Press.

Amin, A. 1994: Post-Fordism: models, fantasies and phantoms of transition. In A. Amin (ed.), *Post-Fordism: A Reader*. Oxford: Basil Blackwell, pp. 1–40.

Anderson, M., Bechhofer, F., and Gershuny, J. (eds.) 1994: *The Social and Political Economy of the Household*. Oxford: Oxford University Press.

Beauregard, B. 1990: Trajectories of neighbourhood change: the case of gentrification. *Environment and Planning A*, 22, 855–74.

Beechey, V. and Perkins, T. 1987: *A Matter of Hours*. Cambridge: Polity.

Bondi, L. 1991: Gender divisions and gentrification: a critique. *Transactions of the Institute of British Geographers*, 16, 190–8.

Bondi, L. 1998: Gender, class and urban space: public and private space in contemporary urban landscapes. *Urban Geography*, 19, 160–85.

Bondi, L. 1999: Gender, class and gentrification: enriching the debate. *Environment and Planning D: Society and Space*.

Bowlby, S., Lewis, J., McDowell, L., and Foord, J. 1989: The geography of gender. In R. Peet and N. Thrift (eds.), *New Models in Geography*, 2. London: Unwin Hyman, 157–75.

Brannen, J. and Wilson, G. (eds.) 1992: *Give and Take in Families: Studies in Resource Distribution*. London: Allen and Unwin, 2nd ed.

Brenner, J. 1993: The best of times, the worst of times: US feminism today. *New Left Review*, 200, 101–60.

Bridge, G. 1994: Gentrification, class and residence: a reappraisal. *Environment and Planning D: Society and Space*, 12, 31–51.

Brown, P. 1995: Cultural capital and social exclusion: some observations on recent trends in education, employment and the labour market. *Work, Employment and Society*, 9, 29–51.

Burchell, B. 1994: The effects of labour market position, job insecurity and unemployment on psychological health. In D. Gallie, C. Marsh, and C. Vogler (eds.), *Social Change and the Experience of Unemployment*. Oxford: Oxford University Press, 188–212.

Butler, T. 1995: Gentrification and the urban middle classes. In T. Butler and M. Savage (eds.), *Social Change and the Middle Classes*. London: UCL Press, 188–204.

Butler, T. and Hamnett, C. 1994: Gentrification, class, and gender: some comments on Warde's "Gentrification as consumption". *Environment and Planning D: Society and Space*, 12, 477–94.

Campbell, B. 1993: *Goliath: Britian's Dangerous Places*. London: Methuen.

Casey, B. and McRae, S. 1990: Towards a more polarised labour market? *Policy Studies*, 11, 31–7.

Casey, C. 1995: *Work, Self and Society: After Industrialism*. London: Routledge.

Castells, M. 1989: *The Informational City: Information Technology, Economic Restructuring and the Urban-Regional Process*. Oxford: Basil Blackwell.

Castells, M. 1994: European cities, the informational society, and the global economy. *New Left Review*, 204, 18–32.

Castells, M. and Hall, P. 1993: *Technopoles of the World: The Making of 21st Century Industrial Complexes*. London: Routledge.

Chouinard, V. 1996: Gender and class identities in process and in place: the local state as a site of gender and class formation. *Environment and Planning A*, 28, 1485–1506.

Christopherson, S. 1994: The fortress city: privatised spaces, consumer citizenship. In A. Amin (ed.), *Post-Fordism: A Reader*. Oxford: Basil Blackwell, 409–27.

Collins, P. H. 1991: *Black Feminist Thought: Knowledge, Consciousness and the Politics of Empowerment*. London: Routledge.
Connell, R. W. 1995: *Masculinities*. Cambridge: Polity.
Crompton, R. and Sanderson, K. 1990: *Gendered Jobs and Social Change*. London: Unwin Hyman.
Davis, M. 1990: *City of Quartz*. London: Verso.
Doling, J., Ford, J., and Stafford, B. 1988: *A Property Owning Democracy*. Aldershot: Gower.
Fainstein, S. and Campbell, C. 1996: Introduction: Theories of Urban Development and their Implications for Policy and Planning. In S. Fainstein and C. Campbell (eds.), *Readings in Urban Theory*. Oxford: Basil Blackwell, 1–17.
Fainstein, S., Gordon, I., and Harloe, M. 1992: *Divided Cities*. Oxford: Blackwell.
Featherstone, M. 1991: *Consumer Culture and Postmodernism*. London: Sage.
Glendinning, C. 1991: Dependency and interdependency: the incomes of informal carers and the impact of social security. *Journal of Social Policy*, 19, 469–97.
Glucksmann, M. 1990: *Women Assemble*. London: Routledge.
Gorz, A. 1989: *Critique of Economic Reason*. London: Verso.
Green, A. 1994: *The Geography of Poverty and Wealth*. University of Warwick: Institute for Employment Research.
Green, A. 1997: Income and wealth. In M. Pacione (ed.), *Britian's Cities: Geographies of Division in Urban Britain*. London: Routledge, 179–202.
Gregson, N. and Lowe, M. 1994: *Servicing the Middle Classes: Class, Gender and Waged Domestic Work in Contemporary Britain*. London: Routledge.
Hakim, C. 1993: The myth of rising female employment. *Work, Employment and Society*, 7, 97–120.
Hanson, S. and Pratt, G. 1995: *Gender, Work and Space*. London: Routledge.
Harrop, A. and Moss, P. 1995: Trends in parental employment. *Work, Employment and Society*, 9, 421–44.
Harvey, D. 1989: *The Condition of Postmodernity*. Oxford: Basil Blackwell.
Harvey, D. 1996: *Justice, Nature and the Geography of Difference*. Oxford: Basil Blackwell.
Hills, J. and Mullings, B. 1991: Housing: A decent home for all at a price within their means? In J. Hills (ed.), *The State of Welfare: The Welfare State in Britain Since 1974*. Oxford: Clarendon Press, 135–205.
Hutton, S. 1994: Men's and women's incomes: evidence from survey data. *Journal of Social Policy*, 23, 21–40.
Jager, M. 1986: Class definition and the aesthetics of gentrification: Victoriana in Melbourne. In N. Smith and P. Williams (eds.), *Gentrification of the City*. Boston: Allen and Unwin, 78–91.
Jameson, F. 1991: *Postmodernism Or, The Cultural Logic of Late Capitalism*. London: Verso.
Jordan, B. 1994: *A Theory of Poverty and Social Exclusion*. Oxford: Polity.
Jordan, B., James, S., Kay, H., and Redley, M. 1992: *Trapped in Poverty? Labour Market Decisions in Low Income Families*. London: Routledge.
Jordan, B. and Redley, M. 1994: Polarization, underclass and the welfare state. *Work, Employment and Society*, 8, 153–76.
Kay, F. and Hagan, J. 1995: The persistent glass ceiling: gendered inequalities in the earnings of lawyers. *British Journal of Sociology*, 46, 279–310.
King, A. D. 1990: *Global Cities: Post-Imperialism and the Internationalization of London*. London: Routledge.
Lees, L. 1994: Rethinking gentrification: beyond the positions of economics or culture. *Progress in Human Geography*, 18, 137–50.
Ley, D. 1994: Gentrification and the politics of the new middle class. *Environment and Planning D: Society and Space*, 12, 53–74.

Ley, D. and Mills, C. 1993: Can there be a postmodernism of resistance in the urban landscape? In P. Knox (ed.), *The Restless Urban Landscape*. Englewood Cliffs, NJ: Prentice-Hall, 255–78.

Lindley, R. (ed.) 1994: *Labour Market Structures and Prospects for Women*. Manchester: Equal Opportunities Commission.

Lovering, J. 1997: Global restructuring and local impact. In M. Pacione (ed.) *Britain's Cities: Geographies of Division in Urban Britain*. London: Routledge, 63–87.

Mackenzie, S. 1984: Editorial introduction to special issue on women and environment. *Antipode*, 6, 3–10.

Mackenzie, S. and Rose, D. 1983: Industrial change, the domestic economy and home life. In J. Anderson, S. Duncan and R. Hudson (eds.), *Redundant Spaces in Cities and Regions*. London: Academic Press, 155–200.

Marcuse, P. 1993: What's so new about divided cities? *International Journal of Urban and Regional Research*, 17, 355–65.

Marsh, M. 1990: *Suburban Lives*. New Jersey: Rutgers University Press.

Marsh, M. 1994: (Ms)reading the suburbs. *American Quarterly*, 46, 40–8.

Marshall, B. 1994: *Engendering Modernity: Feminism, Social Theory and Social Change*. Cambridge: Polity.

Massey, D. 1984: *Spatial Divisions of Labour: Social Structures and the Geography of Production*. London: Macmillan.

Massey, D. and Allen, J. 1995: High-tech places: poverty in the midst of growth. In C. Philo (ed.), *Off the Map: The Social Geography of Poverty in the UK*. London: Child Poverty Action Group, 123–32.

McDowell, L. 1983: Towards an understanding of the gender division of urban space. *Environment and Planning D: Society and Space*, 1, 59–72.

McDowell, L. 1991: Life without father and Ford: the new gender order of post-Fordism. *Transactions, Institute of British Geographers*, 16, 400–19.

McDowell, L. 1995: Body work: Heterosexual gender performances in City workplaces. In D. Bell and G. Valentine (eds.), *Mapping Desire*. London: Routledge, 75–98.

McDowell, L. and Court, G. 1994: Missing subjects: gender, power and sexuality in merchant banking. *Economic Geography*, 70, 229–49.

McGregor, A. and McConnachie, M. 1995: Social exclusion, urban regeneration and economic reintegration. *Urban Studies*, 32, 1587–1600.

McLaughlin, E. 1994: Employment, unemployment and social security. In A. Glyn and D. Miliband (eds.), *Paying for Inequality*. London: IPPR/River Oram Press, 145–59.

Mills, C. 1988: "Life on the upslope": the postmodern landscape of gentrification. *Environment and Planning D: Society and Space*, 6, 169–89.

Morris, L. 1987: Constraints on gender. *Work, Employment and Society*, 1, 85–106.

Morris, L. 1994: Informal aspects of social divisions. *International Journal of Urban and Regional Research*, 18, 112–26.

Mort, F. 1996: *Cultures of Consumption*. London and New York: Routledge.

O'Brien, M. 1995: Allocation of resources within the household: children's perspectives. *The Sociological Review*, 43, 501–17.

O'Reilly, J. and Fagan, C. (eds.) 1998: Part-time prospects: An International Comparison of Part-time Work in Europe, North America and the Pacific Rim. London: Routledge.

Pateman, C. 1989: *The Disorder of Women: Democracy, Feminism and Political Theory*. Cambridge: Polity.

Payne, J. 1987: Does unemployment run in families? *Sociology*, 21, 199–214.

Peck, J. 1996: *Work Place: The Social Regulation of Labour Markets*. New York: Guilford.

Pratt, G. 1991: Feminist analyses of the restructuring of urban life. *Urban Geography*, 12, 594–605.

Pratt, G. and Hanson, S. 1994: Geography and the construction of difference. *Gender, Place and Culture*, 1, 5–29.

Pringle, R. 1989: *Secretaries Talk*. London: Verso.

Ravetz, A. 1996: Revaluations. "The Sphinx in the City." *City*, 1 (2), 155–61.

Rose, D. 1989: A feminist perspective of employment restructuring and gentrification: the case of Montréal. In J. Wolch and M. Dear (eds.), *The Power of Geography*. Boston: Unwin Hyman, 118–38.

Rothenberg, T. 1995: "And she told two friends": lesbians creating urban social space. In D. Bell and G. Valentine (eds.), *Mapping Desire*. London and New York: Routledge, 165–81.

Rubery, J. and Fagan. C. 1995: Gender segregation in societal context. *Work, Employment and Society*, 9, 213–40.

Ruddick, S. 1996: Constructing difference in public space: race, class and gender as interlocking systems. *Urban Geography*, 17, 132–51.

Sassen, S. 1991: *The Global City: New York, London, Tokyo*. Princeton, NJ: Princeton University Press.

Savage, M., Barlow, J., Dickens, P., and Fielding, A. 1992: *Property, Bureaucracy and Culture: Middle Class Formation in Contemporary Britain*. Andover, Hants: Routledge, Chapman and Hall.

Sayer, A. and Walker, R. 1992: *The New Social Economy: Reworking the Division of Labour*. Oxford: Basil Blackwell.

Scott, A. M. (ed.) 1994: *Gender Segregation and Social Change*. Oxford: Oxford University Press.

Sharp, J. P. 1996: Staking a claim to the high ground. *Scottish Geographical Magazine*, 112, 181–85.

Smith, N. 1987: Of yuppies and housing: gentrification, social restructuring, and the urban dream. *Environment and Planning D: Society and Space*, 5, 151–72.

Smith, N. 1996: *The New Urban Frontier*. London and New York: Routledge.

Soja, E. 1989: *Postmodern Geographies: The Reassertion of Space in Social Theory*. London: Verso.

Soja, E. 1996: *Thirdspace*. Oxford: Basil Blackwell.

Valentine, G. 1996: Children should be seen and not heard: the production and trangression of adults' public space. *Urban Geography*, 17, 205–20.

Walby, S. 1997: *Gender Transformation*. London: Routledge.

Ward, C., Dale, A., and Joshi, H. 1996: Combining employment with childcare: An escape from dependence? *Journal of Social Policy*, 25, 223–47.

Ward, H. and Bird, D. 1995: The JUVOS cohort: A longitudinal database of the claimant unemployed. *Employment Gazette*, 103, 345–50.

Warde, A. 1991: Gentrification as consumption: issues of class and gender. *Environment and Planning D: Society and Space*, 9, 223–32.

Watson, S. and Gibson, K. 1995: *Postmodern Cities and Spaces*. Oxford: Basil Blackwell.

Wills, J. 1996: Laboring for love? A comment on academics and their hours of work. *Antipode*, 28, 292–303.

Wilson, E. 1991: *The Sphinx in the City*. London: Virago.

Young, I. M. 1990: *Justice and the Politics of Difference*. Princeton, NJ: Princeton University Press.

Zukin, S. 1982: *Loft Living: Culture and Capital in Urban Change*. London: Century Hutchinson.

Chapter 26

The Sexual Geography of the City

Frank Mort

In the spring of 1953 London was the venue for the most extended display of official spectacle in Britain since the end of the Second World War. The Queen's coronation was the occasion for ritual display which reinforced the role of the capital not only as the focus for national celebration but also as the hub of a reformulated British Commonwealth. But coronation year also focused attention on more transgressive activities in the metropolis. In particular, it was the danger of sexuality, cut loose from its traditional moorings within marriage and the family and publicly flaunted on London's streets, which was the major anxiety. In a series of sensationalist exposés, the popular press told how the capital was in the grip of the twin vices of male homosexuality and female prostitution. These practices were flourishing in areas adjacent to the coronation route – for the center of depravity was given a specific setting. It was not London as a whole which was implicated in this geography of immorality, specific zones or quarters of the city were singled out. The most notorious of these was Soho in the heart of the capital's West End.

The moral state of London was viewed as sufficiently serious to warrant action by the Conservative government early the following year. The Home Office Committee on Homosexual Offences and Prostitution, usually known as the Wolfenden committee, after its chairman, John Wolfenden, is today best remembered as the body which recommended the partial decriminalization of male homosexuality (Hyde 1972; Weeks 1977; Jeffrey-Poulter 1991). Yet the scope of the inquiry was much more extensive. In the classic manner described by Michel Foucault, the committee sought to regulate homosexuality and prostitution by bringing these practices into greater visibility; by producing an extended discourse on the problems (Foucault 1978). As part of this strategy, central London was mapped – physically and symbolically – in terms of irregular sexualities. Much of the raw material for this process came from the police. The Metropolitan Police Commissioner submitted a document which was, in effect, a homosexual map of London. Spanning the whole of the greater West End, it ranged from Kensington Gardens, Knightsbridge and Hyde Park, through Victoria and across to Bloomsbury and the Strand. Circled in red ink were the places where police arrests for importuning and gross indecency were most frequently made. The familiar landmarks of London's central district had been redrawn to reveal the spaces of homosexual desire (Nott-Bower 1954, Appendix D).

My purpose in opening with this historical example is to highlight a number of themes which are important for exploring the relationship between sexuality and modern city life. This narrative about the sexual mapping of London in the 1950s raises more general questions about the ways in which sexual and moral identities have been formed – and transformed – through the regulation, occupation, and experience of urban space. In the work of the Wolfenden committee the streets, parks, and the more private places of the metropolis were understood to play an active part in the complex moral economy of the city. It is this relationship, between space, setting, and the representations and power relations of urban life, which concerns me here. The connection is well understood as a result of the recent work on the city by urban sociologists and cultural geographers, but its implications are far from accepted currency in studies of sexuality. The aim is to provide some guidelines for research into the sexual geography of the city.

Sexuality and Discourse

The past two decades have seen an explosion of writing on the historical and contemporary forms of sexuality. While such work has been driven by a wide variety of different concerns, a number of clearly identifiable agendas have predominated. Feminist, gay, and lesbian studies and the continuing impact of the work of Michel Foucault have been at the center of this expansion. Taken together, what is notable about this body of research is that it has profoundly revised historical and sociological understandings about the relationship between sexuality and modern life. Foucault's own major reassessment of the history of modern sexuality opened by challenging the whole evolutionary model of moral progress, in which nineteenth-century repression gave way to twentieth-century enlightenment. Foucault persuasively demonstrated that such a chronology was part of our own contemporary mythology as "the other Victorians" (Foucault 1978). In the 1970s and 1980s, feminist, gay, and lesbian historians were assembling their own critiques of sexual modernization (Weeks 1977; D'Emilio 1983: Faderman 1985). Linked to the lifestyle politics of the new social movements, and again challenging linear and developmental accounts, this research brought into focus the troubled and profoundly unstable history of modern sexuality. Highlighting the fact that freedom for some involved coercion and regulation for many others, these new studies revealed how access to knowledge and power about sex was shot through with ideologies of sexual and gender difference.

Linked to this critique of sexual modernism was the problematization of the very meaning and status of sexuality itself. This denaturalization of the object of research was at the heart of Foucault's interrogation of all forms of disciplinary power. The central issue was not whether societies say yes or no to sex, whether they permit or prohibit, but that both of these positions were part of the way in which sex was put into discourse. What mattered in consequence was how sexuality was represented: who writes, or speaks, and from what position. Foucault's insights into the representational quality of sexuality were anticipated by the postwar, Anglo-American traditions of labeling and role theory, with their emphasis on the constructed nature of sexual acts and values (McIntosh 1968; Gagnon and Simon 1974; Plummer 1975). But in the 1970s and 1980s Foucault's agenda was read in conjunction with the insights derived from poststructuralist linguistics in order to profoundly question the ways in which many social phenomena were understood. Together with the theories of Saussure and Derrida (Saussure 1983; Derrida 1967), Foucault's approach raised major doubts about a number of established research procedures. Above all, it was the emphasis on language and discourse which destabilized conventional methodologies. After Foucault and the other poststructuralists, the representational quality of all forms of knowledge – including that of sexuality – became a key concern.

Foucault's approach disturbed common-sense understandings of what a history of modern sexuality could be about. It uncovered sex in the most unlikely places, as well as in more familiar areas: within sanitary schemes for urban improvement, household manuals, statistical tables, medical dossiers and census returns. Sex intruded into the circuits of urban government, in addition to signifying bodily acts, identities, and desires. Modern sexuality was a *dispersed and decentered field*, and it was organized around multiple points of reference. Within this framework Foucault identified a number of nodal points which increasingly classified and regulated sex around the principles of reproductive and biological strength and around what he termed the "perverse implantations." The significance of these particular mechanisms of power nomination have been much argued over, but Foucault's basic insistence is worth reiterating; that sexuality is plural, rather than articulated around any single point of reference. One of the most significant consequences of this emphasis for research was that it opened up the space for an extremely productive exploration of the ways in which sex is *represented*, especially from cultural historians working on the construction of sexual knowledges and identities (Nead 1987; Jordanova 1989; Bland 1995). Recent work in this tradition has also been particularly adept at identifying the highly malleable and shifting dynamics of sexual desire across the nineteenth and twentieth centuries (Davidoff 1995; Bailey 1998). As a result, historians now know much more about the ways in which sexual regimes were lived at the level of specific relationships, liaisons, and encounters. If one implication of Foucault's analysis has been to suggest that sex is everywhere in modern societies, the other has been to identify the very particular networks through which it is produced. Foucault's studies, together with the subsequent work they have inspired, reveal that the field of sexuality is not simply an interesting but insignificant byway in the grander histories of modern life. This domain has formed part of the social project of modernity itself.

Sexual Geographies

It is all the more curious, then, that while recent cultural and historical studies have amply demonstrated the significance of language in generating sexual meanings, they have continued to underestimate the spatial dimensions of these practices. The neglect of social and symbolic geography remains a characteristic feature of research on sexuality, where the environment is usually treated as a relatively passive backdrop against which "real" social and cultural developments are enacted. The interrelationship between space and social processes has of course been extensively debated in the areas of cultural theory and human geography. Yet this research has either focused mainly on the contemporary features of urban space, or else it has pitched discussion at very high levels of abstraction, drawing on Marxist and poststructuralist traditions, which extend from Henri Lefebvre through to writers such as Michel de Certeau and David Harvey (de Certeau 1988; Harvey 1989; Lefebvre 1991). In accounts of this type the primary concern has been with theoretical exploration, in which space as well as time has been cast as a central part of the repertoire of capitalist development, modernity, postmodernity, or other similar global configurations. In contrast, the idea of a cultural history, which evaluates the spatial dimensions of social processes at particular points in time and in more limited settings, remains an underdeveloped project.

How might the idea of a geography of sexuality be conceived? Two recent books have pioneered studies of sexuality in the city, revealing how distinctive metropolitan environments have both regulated sexual subjects and provided the opportunities for human creativity and action. Judith Walkowitz's *City of Dreadful Delight*, 1992, traced the interrelationships between the politics and poetics of space and the multiple scripts of sexuality in late Victorian London. Reflecting the narrative challenges posed by the new agendas of cultural and literary history, Walkowitz explored the metropolis as a contested terrain, in which diverse groups of social actors were drawn into a series of overlapping narratives of sexual danger. One of the most significant aspects of her analysis was the insight that these sociosexual relationships were not only embedded in the physical geography of London, but were also present in a series of imaginary urban landscapes, which were shaped by the social scripts of melodrama, science, and masculine and feminine versions of cosmopolitanism (Walkowitz 1992). Walkowitz's account is a landmark study of urban culture in history, not only because of the wealth of its historical research, but also because it foregrounds the spatial relations of sexuality as a constitutive part of metropolitan modernity. George Chauncey's history of the making of the gay male world in New York in the first part of the twentieth century pioneered a different trajectory of sexuality in the city, centering on the social networks of homosociability created in the streets, private apartments, bathhouses, and saloons of Greenwich Village, Harlem, and Times Square (Chauncey 1995). Chauncey's research did not simply recover evidence about the extent of the early homosexual city, which was erased by a combination of cultural policing and political neglect, it also mapped an astonishingly diverse sexual geography at the heart of America's preeminent metropole. More often than not, this gay world existed in the same environments as African-American, Irish, and Italian immigrant neighborhoods. These were plural networks and liminal spaces, which were not structured according to the divisions between heterosexuality and homosexuality which became the dominant sexual regime within the United States during the postwar years. Chauncey's analysis points to the extremely porous nature of modern sexual identities, which are fluid and contingent partly because of their spatial proximity to other cultures and ways of life.

Two different projects emerge out of this research. Firstly, a concern with regulative space and with the spaces of regulation develops further Foucault's project of discipline and sexuality. Official maps of immorality have repeatedly worked to impose strategic order on the city, viewing urban sexuality as a major site of cultural disturbance. This bureaucratic and administrative geography has been pivotal in all forms of social policing. It was the impetus behind the police map of the city submitted to the Wolfenden committee, and it would be instantly recognizable to the magistrate and the sanitary engineer, as well as to the cartographer. Operating from on high, it mobilizes a panoptic vision of the city and its subjects, who are viewed as part of a landscape and an esthetics of discipline. The panoramic eye which maps the city in this way invariably offers the viewer mastery of its spaces through sight. The point of vision is invariably exterior to the practices it seeks to classify through processes of inclusion and exclusion. The weakness of this version of the urban landscape is that it refuses any invitation to come "down below" to the level of the street and its pedestrians. In that sense it remains a history of the city from above.

In contrast, the project advanced by the cultural geographer de Certeau has been one of antidiscipline (de Certeau 1985, 1988). In de Certeau's version of urban society, individuals and social groups in space resist the functionalist rationality of the city's grid-plan, drawn up by bureaucrats and administrators. His aim is not to illuminate the techniques of social regulation, but rather to bring to light the ways in which "the weak make use of the strong" (de Certeau 1988: xvii). That is to say, the terms on which resistances to discipline are part of the practices of everyday life. Here we are introduced to different types of spatial practices: the pedestrian rhetorics, the local networks and the wandering activities which produce a subtle logic of place as the site for individual and collective endeavors. This emphasis on what we might term "an ethnography of space" has proved extremely productive for identifying many of the manifestations of sexuality in the city. The prostitute's transactions with her clients, the wanderings of the gay *flâneur* and the machinations of other sexual bohemians are all conducted in specific environments and settings. De Certeau is not unique in defining space as part of the resistant practices of everyday life. In many respects his approach parallels the recent work of Anglo-American cultural studies, which has sought to rescue the urban cultures of subaltern groups from their banal and degraded status. Like some of that writing, de Certeau's efforts to define space as resistance at times traps him in a sentimental utopianism, whereby local cultures and small acts by their very definition constitute places of defiance to official geographies (Ross 1996; Rigby 1991). What is undoubtedly important about de Certeau's project is his emphasis on tracking subjects *in motion* as they move through the urban landscape.

Taken together, these insights provide an expanded vocabulary for analyzing the spectacle, performance, and regulation of sexuality in the city. Yet the emphasis should not be on urban sexualities in general, but on particular metropolitan environments, otherwise the specific relationships between culture and city space are lost. To return to the milieu with which we began – London. London's own distinctive moral geography has contributed to particular regimes of sexuality. In this and many other respects, London is decidedly not Paris, Berlin, or New York. The Danish architect and humanist Steen Eiler Rasmussen celebrated the cultural diversity of the English metropolis, as against the continental, planned city, in his influential history, *London, the Unique City* (Rasmussen 1937). The capital's characteristic administrative ad hocery, which has been visible repeatedly in its approaches to public health, hygiene, and sanitation, generated its own recognizable sexual atmosphere. The capital never experienced a *police des moeurs*, or moral police, on the Parisian or Prussian models, nor were its zones of respectable and disreputable behavior as strategically zoned as in some other European or American cities. Yet since the eighteenth century London has been shaped by a series of ongoing reforming initiatives, in which fears over disorder and disease have been linked to the moral state of its recalcitrant populations (Stedman Jones 1984; Mort 1987). Moreover, the capital's importance as the center of empire, and latterly of postcolonial migration, has thrown up a series of extraordinarily complex cultures of sexual otherness, which have repeatedly hybridized the city's existing populations. And unlike many Western metropoles in the twentieth century, London has continued in its traditional role as the site of royalty, the court, and aristocratic society, with their own elaborate displays of sexual ritual. The project for a spatial history of sexuality needs to address the making of these diverse sexual cultures as part of the fabric of modern metropolitan life (Mort and Nead 1999).

Speaking to Each Other

Yet the diversity of urban life is not only a matter for social analysis, it poses a profound question for civic politics – for how we live together in the city. Proliferating cultures of difference have weakened the bonds of civic participation; more often than not individuals and social groups are strangers to the destinies of each other – difference is frequently indifference. Richard Sennett, addressing the difficulties of the contemporary divided city, has suggested that it is the image of the body in pain which has the power to reach out and bridge these uncompassionate scenarios (Sennett 1994). Sexual bodies within city space present ambiguous and

Figure 26.1 Sydney gay and lesbian Mardi Gras parade (© Steve Pile)

contradictory cultural values, which in many ways epitomize both the difficulties and the possibilities of the present-day metropolis. The sexual body is at once marked by all of those forms of hyperindividualization – through dress and personal adornment, stylized forms of movement, display, and visual spectacle – which lie at the heart of urban self-presentation. While at the same time aficionados of the city's proliferating sexual cultures rely heavily on the marked and decorated body to recognize members of the same tribe. These localized collectivities are frequently lived as exclusive and exclusionary.

How in the contemporary city can individuals talk to those who are other than themselves? Forty years ago, in the Wolfenden committee's account of London, it was not necessary to discuss this; the center was still relatively secure as those who were cast as marginals were fixed as subordinate. Now the question is imperative. It haunts contemporary social policy and shadows the efforts of progressive politicians to put together a new language of social inclusion. The difficulty of balancing competing ways of living with a commitment to collective action is particularly pressing in all versions of the contemporary urban question. In other words, in all of those spheres of urban life where different ways of inhabiting the self have produced diverse value systems, rather than single certainties. The competing cultures of the postcolonial city, the divisions around differential access to and uses of space, sound, and movement are all manifestations of this problem. Sexuality features as part of this agenda, because sex has been cast both as an integral part of contemporary urban lifestyles and a core component of who we are as individuals.

By no means is all of this new. There is plenty of evidence to suggest that anxieties over social fragmentation and exclusion, together with the difficulties of reconciling the needs of individual self-determination to those of collective action, have been a marked feature of successive moments of urban modernity (Green 1990; Rifkin 1993). What is specific to our own time is that the political and social discourses which have been used to frame working solutions to these problems look increasingly bankrupt. If there is no consensus about endpoints, then there is a general acknowledgment that the present situation demands a resolution to the self–society equation which is different from those which dominated in the recent past.

Faced with the multiplication of urban problems, and with the clamor of voices who shout in the city, one response has been to recuperate traditions of civic communitarianism. Such an approach promotes the rebuilding of traditional forms of social solidarity as an antidote to disintegration (Etzione 1993). It is becoming the solution to the difficulties of living together in the city which is favored by politicians championing the "third way" in both Britain and the United States. What is problematic about this option is not simply its mild moral conservatism; it seeks to reinvent a language of communal values while ignoring the fact that large sections of the city's population no longer comprehend this discourse.

A different starting point is one which begins by acknowledging diversity and difference and the contingent nature of social and sexual value systems. The concept of radical pluralist democracy is differently nuanced according to differences of political interpretation, but all the advocates of this position return to reexamine the classic terrain of democratic liberalism (Laclau and Mouffe 1985; Rorty 1989; Sennett 1994; Weeks 1995). From this perspective the search is for flexible forms of collective association which can meet the late twentieth-century demand for individual self-determination. Such a project by its very nature cannot simply be pitched at the level of formal politics, it needs to recognize the cultural and personal dimensions of democratic communities. This is precisely the current terrain of many sexual cultures in the city. The Italian sociologist, Alberto Melucci, analyzing the phenomenon of contemporary social movements, has noted how these groupings consist of loose associations which are integral to the functioning of everyday life (Melucci 1989). These networks are notable for their stress on both individual needs and collective identities. Though membership is usually part-time, they constitute the laboratories in which new social experiences are invented and explored. Melucci insists that a necessary condition of contemporary democracy is the recognition of spaces of this kind, which are independent of government and political representation. They project forms of decision making in which "the signifying practices developed in everyday life can be heard independently from . . . political institutions" (Melucci 1989: 173). Many contemporary cultures of sexuality in the city project precisely these types of informal cultural initiative. Without lapsing into romanticism, we can characterize their operation as laboratory experiments in everyday living, where individual and collective needs jostle together for space. For the researcher the task remains both to map and to listen to these networks. This calls for an interdisciplinary project: for history, for ethnography, for cultural geography, and for all of those other genres which make meaning out of the landscapes of the city.

REFERENCES

Bailey, P. 1998: *Popular Culture and Performance in the Victorian City*. Cambridge: Cambridge University Press.

Bland, L. 1995: *Banishing the Beast: English Feminism and Sexual Morality 1885–1914*. London: Penguin.

Certeau, M. de 1985: Practices of space. In M. Blonsky (ed.), *On Signs*. Oxford: Blackwell, 122–45.

Certeau, M. de 1988: *The Practice of Everyday Life*, tr. S. Rendall. Berkeley: University of California Press.

Chauncey, G. 1995: *Gay New York: Gender, Urban Culture, and the Making of the Gay Male World, 1890–1940*. London: Flamingo.

Davidoff, L. 1995: *Worlds Between: Historical Perspectives on Gender and Class*. Cambridge: Polity.

D'Emilio, J. 1983: *Sexual Politics, Sexual Communities: The Making of a Homosexual Minority in the United States, 1940–70*. Chicago: University of Chicago Press.

Derrida, J. 1967: *De la Grammatologie*. Paris: Éditions de Minuit.

Etzione, A. 1993: *The Spirit of Community: Rights, Responsibilities and the Communitarian Agenda*. New York: Crown.

Faderman, L. 1985: *Surpassing the Love of Men: Romantic Friendship and Love Between Women from the Renaissance to the Present*. London: Women's Press.

Foucault, M. 1978: *The History of Sexuality*, vol. 1: *An Introduction*, tr. R. Hurley. New York: Pantheon.

Gagnon, J. and Simon, W. 1974: *Sexual Conduct: The Social Sources of Human Sexuality*. London: Hutchinson.

Green, N. 1990: *The Spectacle of Nature: Landscape and Bourgeois Culture in Nineteenth-Century France*. Manchester: Manchester University Press.

Harvey, D. 1989: *The Condition of Postmodernity: An Enquiry into the Origins of Cultural Change*. Oxford: Blackwell.

Hyde, H. M. 1972: *The Other Love: An Historical and Contemporary Survey of Homosexuality in Britain*. London: Mayflower.

Jeffrey-Poulter, S. 1991: *Peers, Queers and Commons: The Struggle for Gay Law Reform from 1950 to the Present*. London: Routledge.

Jordanova, L. 1989: *Sexual Visions: Images of Gender in Science and Medicine Between the Eighteenth and Twentieth Centuries*. London/ New York: Harvester Wheatsheaf.

Laclau E. and Mouffe C. 1985: *Hegemony and Socialist Strategy: Towards A Radical Democratic Politics*, tr. W. Moore and P. Commack. London: Verso.

Lefebvre, H. 1991: *The Production of Space*, tr. D. Nicolson-Smith. Oxford: Blackwell.

McIntosh, M. 1968: The homosexual role. *Social Problems*, 16 (2), 182–92.

Melucci, A. 1989: *Nomads of the Present: Social Movements and Individual Needs in Contemporary Society*. London: Hutchinson.

Mort, F. 1987: *Dangerous Sexualities: Medico-Moral Politics in England since 1830*. London: Routledge.

Mort, F. and Nead, L. (eds.) 1999: *New Formations: Sexual Geographies*. London: Lawrence and Wishart.

Nead, L. 1987: *Myths of Sexuality: Representations of Women in Victorian Britain*. Oxford: Blackwell.

Nott-Bower, Sir J. 1954: Memorandum of Sir John Nott-Bower to the Departmental Committee on Homosexual Offences and Prostitution. Public Record Office, HO 345/7.

Plummer, K. 1975: *Sexual Stigma: An Interactionist Account*. London: Routledge and Kegan Paul.

Rasmussen, S. E. 1937: *London, the Unique City*. London: Jonathan Cape.

Rifkin, A. 1993: *Street Noises: Parisian Pleasure, 1900–1940*. Manchester: Manchester University Press.

Rigby, B. 1991: *Popular Culture in Modern France*. London: Routledge.

Rorty, R. 1989. *Contingency, Irony and Solidarity*. Cambridge. Cambridge University Press.

Ross, K. 1996: Streetwise: the French invention of everyday life. *Parallax*, 2, 67–75.

Saussure, F. de 1983: *Course in General Linguistics*. London: Duckworth.

Sennett, R. 1994: *Flesh and Stone: The Body and the City in Western Civilization*. London/ Boston: Faber.

Stedman Jones, G. 1984: *Outcast London: A Study in the Relationship Between Classes in Victorian Society*. Harmondsworth: Penguin.

Walkowitz, J. 1992: *City of Dreadful Delight: Narratives of Sexual Danger in Late-Victorian London*. London: Virago.

Weeks, J. 1977: *Coming Out: Homosexual Politics in Britain from the Nineteenth Century to the Present*. London: Quartet.

Weeks, J. 1995: *Invented Moralities: Sexual Values in an Age of Uncertainty*. Cambridge: Polity.

Chapter 27

From the Other Side of the Tracks: Dual Cities, Third Spaces, and the Urban Uncanny in Contemporary Discourses of "Race" and Class

Phil Cohen

A sibyl, questioned about Marozia's fate said, "I see two cities, one of the rat and one of the swallow."

This was the interpretation of the oracle: today Marozia is a city where all run through leaden passages like packs of rats who tear from one another's teeth the leftovers which fall from the teeth of the most voracious one; but a new century is about to begin in which all the inhabitants of Marozia will fly like swallows, calling one another as in a game, showing off, their wings still, as they swoop, clearing the air of mosquitoes and gnats.

Was the oracle mistaken? Not necessarily. I interpret it in this way. Marozia consists of two cities, the rats and the swallows, both change over time, but their relationship does not change, the second is the one always about to free itself from the first.

Italo Calvino, *Invisible Cities*

The theme of the dual city, first popularized by the Victorian urban explorers, has not ceased to multiply its terms of reference in the twentieth century. To the cities of rich and poor, bourgeois and proletarian, indigenous and immigrant have been added cities of night and day, youth and age, established and outsiders; there are pink cities and black cities, global cities and mobile cities and cities where everyone with get-up-and-go has long since left town. Digital cities composed of virtual streets and neighborhoods where no one rules, OK, come up against analog cities where hopes and memories continue to stake out territorial claims over rival plots.

The spatializing of social difference of every kind proceeds apace, and the city as metaphor and matrix of this process has never been more to the forefront of the public imagination. And yet we are living at a time when hard and fast social divisions have supposedly weakened, cultural boundaries have become blurred, and third spaces proliferate on every side. Is this a new kind of contradiction, or an old one updated? Is there a subtle connection between these terms of polarization and their transcendence, a complicity between those who live on the other side of the class/race/sexuality line and those who take that line for a walk on the wild side in pursuit of less pedestrian forms of urban pleasure? In this chapter I am going to explore this conundrum with special reference to contemporary discourses of "race" and class.

Let us start with Calvino. He invites us to consider the question from the angle of modernity. He argues for the dual city as a constant if emergent property integral to modernity's powers of self-transformation. If we are still struggling to come to terms with the fact that the heroic attempt of modernist planners and architects to design a city of light and air fit for swallows resulted in the creation of so many urban rat runs, Calvino's little parable suggests that this is the beginning not the end of the story.

Some would argue that this is a somewhat overoptimistic view! The two cities of Morazia seem to approximate ever more closely to the split between the ideals of urban industrial living which inspired Corbusier et al. and the real cities we actually live in. The streamlined egalitarian city of the senses, where it retains its rhetorical power, is today largely confined to privatized utopias of urban flight encoded in domestic interiors, back gardens, or the home pages of the Internet. Otherwise the metropolitan sublime of the early urban romantics has given way to the public profanities of pollution, traffic gridlock, crime, poverty, and violence as distinguishing features of "the urban real."

In juxtaposing these two visions Calvino draws on a familiar distinction between an overview composed from a bird's (or a helicopter's) eye view of the city and an underview from those who are trapped in the urban rat race. This in turn rests on an equally familiar binarism: the invisible and visible city.

How the city has been visualized is inextricably bound up with strategies of civil governance. The Victorian explorers who pioneered the art of moral panic made that connection palpable through graphic descriptions – and photographs – of habits, habitats, and inhabitants whose appearance contradicted the official story of urban progress superintended by a philanthropic state. But since then the power of making a spectacle out of those who are visibly different has increasingly been complemented and even supplanted by the power to render invisible those whose faces do not fit the positive image being created for the promotion of the greater civic good (Smyth 1994).

Under the egis of high modernism it could be argued that these were two sides to the same story: the visibly deviant, and the invisibly disadvantaged were seen as a joint challenge – a test of modernity's transformative power. Today strategies for rendering visible and invisible are increasingly working at cross-purposes. The most obvious example is that we have moral panics about the emergence of an unemployed youth "underclass" with Blair, following Clinton, introducing zero tolerance policing and youth curfews in many frontline areas of metropolitan Britain. At the same time, these local "youth at risk" are entirely marginal to the global city view, taken with the proverbial wide-angled telephoto lens for glossy municipal brochures designed to promote inward investment. At best they are allowed to provide an ornamental backdrop to the happy-clappy service economy threading its way through the marinas and neoclassical piazza parlours; at worst they are simply airbrushed out of the picture because their presence – and in-your-face attitude – point up an embarrassing discrepancy between lived territory and official map.

Elsewhere, though, the marginalized and the outcast are recuperated as a site of exotic liminality through the intervention of a postmodernist style of urban imagineering; sensational scenarios of urban low life – hitherto carefully distanced through the screening devices of a historical or ethnographic discourse – are now rendered "transparent" and peopled with fresh young faces recruited to encourage the lifestyle tourist to sample the delights of a subterranean city that even the local inhabitants are not supposed to know. For this purpose youth subcultures are promoted as sexy signs of urban vitality and cosmopolitanism associated with the cultural industries that have increasingly come to dominate strategies of urban regeneration in these areas. In this way, the concentration of potentially dangerous difference, surrounded with the aura of something impenetrably Other, is used to generate a new kind of urban ethnoscape where poverty and powerlessness are dressed up in multicultural drag, and made to dance for their dinner to the latest megacity sounds.

Is it possible to understand this contemporary mise-en-scène as just the latest version of Calvino's two cities? Or do we need an altogether different kind of map? Perhaps by looking in a bit more detail at the provenance of the dualisms that have so profoundly shaped our view of the European city we may be able to get a better handle on the terms of a properly conjunctural analysis.

The Dual City as Body and Text

Richard Sennett has argued persuasively that as both motif and model, the dual city is an ancient device, as old as the Western idea of the city itself (Sennett 1990). According to Sennett, the greek *polis* was constructed primarily as a public realm of communicative possibility; in particular its boundaries were defined by the distance the sound of a human voice could carry from the central square or *agora*, so that if any citizen was in distress, their cry for help would not go unheeded. The spatial limits and conditions of direct vocal copresence thus defined a haptic sense of political community. The body thus articulated – the *demos* – was the collective voice of the citizenry in action. However not everyone who walked the streets of Athens, Thebes, or Sparta were citizens, or had a say in its affairs. Women, children, and slaves were not strictly speaking subjects at all, because their role was confined to the private or at least publicly invisible sphere of household – the *oike* and its governance. The household was here regarded as constituting the realm of necessity, of biological and social reproduction, of labor and what stayed the same, outside history. Those whose activities were confined to this sphere were by definition regarded as apolitical beings, denied access to the *agora*, without powers of articulation.

This split between a realm of material necessity – the realm of the *oekonomia* – and a realm of freedom and historical action – the realm of politics – was central to the Hellenic model of the *polis*. Sennett argues that it was reworked in terms of the Judaeo-Christian split between secular and spiritual to set in motion a long-standing quarrel between those who see the city as primarily a material infrastructure for accommodating a diversity of socially necessary functions, and those for whom it is essentially a space of representation for imagining and regulating the body politic and its cultural life. He cites Isodore of Seville as the first to explicitly make the distinction between *urbs/urban*, the stones laid for the practical purposes of shelter, commerce, and warfare, and *civitas*, the structures of feeling, ritual, custom, and belief that take form within it; this rests on a division between profane and sacred space which finds its contemporary academic resonance in what we might call the prosaics and poetics of sociospatial analysis: the first concentrating on the logistics of urban policy, planning, and administration, the second on the lived cultures and narratives through which the daily business of living, loving, working, traveling, and playing around in the city are conducted by different groups of citizens. Sennet argues that this conflict resumed but did not resolve the terms of the earlier distinction between the material and spiritual city. As such it can be traced right through to the modernist dialectic between the global heights of profane power commanded by state and capital, and local spaces of private or public retreat organized around purified identities and communities constructed "from below."

If such a line can be described, it would have to be a very broken and irregular one; the danger is that in drawing it, the historic shift from "haptic" cities, administered through bodily and vocal copresence to "cartographic" cities ruled by strategies of visual mapping and surveillance, is downplayed. Yet it is precisely through this shift that the project of modernity draws an invisible sightline under the feet of those who are included and excluded from its special dispensation (de Certeau 1995).

From the standpoint of governance, from which maps of every kind are drawn, the modern city has indeed come to be represented as a rational, ordered, visible whole (Harvey 1989). Especially when its superficial appearance is one of chaos and fragmentation the aim is to disclose the hidden organizing principles in order to subject them to conscious planning and control. The social sciences have played a key role in disseminating this model of urbanism throughout the West. Nevertheless there remain important national differences in the way large cities have been imagined, observed, written about, and governed. Metropolises in the USA and Germany have frequently been compared to gigantic engines of production and complex servo-mechanisms, melting pots and waste disposal systems, prisons and asylums (Sennett 1994). In all these cases the city is imagined to be a crucible or microcosm of the whole society, to contain all its disparate elements and hold them together in some kind of dynamic equilibrium.

Since at least the eighteenth century the Western metropolis has thus been assigned its own special chemistry, a more or less magical alchemy, in which different social elements (classes and ethnic groups) are transmuted into a new kind of urban fabric, where the streets, if not paved with gold, at least support the making of a common cosmopolitan culture. This imagination is, of course, haunted by the fear that the elements will prove too combustible to be contained in this way, that the melting pot will become a boiling cauldron. To stop it boiling over, however, requires the pouring of oil on troubled waters, and taking the matches away from anyone who might be tempted to fan the flames of resentment. This makes for a compelling urban soap opera which keeps us on the edge of suspense, for it is always a case of the fire next time.

This dramatic trope of a multicultural city has never been popular among the urban squirearchy in Britain. In the nineteenth century their anti-industrial temper drew them to other, safer analogies (Dyos 1985; Feldman and Stedman Jones 1991). The workings of cities were compared to those of bodies and texts, not primarily on account of any affinities of natural symbolism, but because the available disciplines which studied bodies and texts furnished strategies of urban and civic comprehension with which the elite felt more at home. Comparative anatomy, parasitology, epidemiology, on one side; classical philology, biblical exegesis and literary esthetics on the other provided the models and metaphors with which this stratum thought, felt, dreamt, and often disavowed, its relation to the city.

The first set of discourses made it possible to represent the city as Other, and then to isolate the Other in the city, to distinguish and classify the diseased habits, habitats, and happenings associated with the *race apart*; the second set of analogies made it possible to identify and celebrate those elements which might be assimilated into the body politic and strengthen the *backbone of the nation*. Here uniquely, and only for a time, the two cultures of Victorian science and humanities collaborated to common purpose and effect. We will look at each in turn.

Many commentators have been struck by the more obvious medical analogies: cities that are equipped with lungs, arteries, bloodstreams, bowels, hearts, and faces (Sennett 1994). Galen's theory of humors connects with Harvey's model of circulation to put flesh on the bare bones of bourgeois fears of social contagion and racial degeneration in the body politic. In keeping with the English propensity for advancing into the future looking over their shoulder towards the past, this backward-looking analogy was pressed into the service of modernity. The first rule of the capitalist city is, after all, the free circulation of commodities, both of labor and of goods. The role of the police in the Victorian city was to keep the wheels of industry turning as well as to keep the human traffic moving on the streets. Policing strategy was designed to prevent any blockage or disturbance to this circulation process; it thus applied not only to manifest forms of public disorder – riots, strikes, occupations, civil commotions of every kind – but also to the most elementary strategies through which groups of citizens colonized urban space, asserted their own proprietary rights over local amenity and resource and put a stop, however temporarily, to the remorseless logic of capital accumulation (Cohen 1998).

It is easy then to see the power of the body analogy; it furnished a naturalistic principle of circulation which in turn yielded an image of urban growth as a process of endless self-regeneration. It was more often used to represent its antithesis – processes of blight, and decay caused by parts that become dysfunctional, or parasitic, and disrupt the harmony of the whole.

However, to many Victorian observers there were numerous processes of urban growth which remained unrepresentable by these means. In particular the urban demographic seemed to have rendered the city into a foreign language or an illegible text (Walkovitz 1992). One of the main aims of the early urban explorers was to decipher its vernacular codes, parse its sentence structures, translate its idioms into a more familiar language and, if they were professional *flâneurs*, read the exotic signs between the lines of even the most pedestrian desires. This was an active methodology which permitted the working class and immigrant city to be read and written about in a way that rendered it both fascinating and a safe topic for conversation and concern in the middle-class drawing room. In this way organic images of urban health or disease were rendered into an intelligible and narratable text, with a story line which unfolded more or less teleologically, and featured heroes and villains, bearers of good news and bad.

The envisagement of the metropolis as a visual spectacle played an important part in this elaboration. As the metropolis grew in size and complexity, so totalizing perspectives of the urban panorama or diorama increasingly gave way to the synecdochal view – the choice of particular locations or perspectives as standing metonymically or metaphorically for the essence of the city. Inevitably these tended to be places associated with the exercise of various kinds of power – highly visible parts that exercised control over the now incomprehensible, invisible whole.

These two image repertoires could be – and were – combined to great effect. Bodies have invisible insides and visible outsides, texts legible surfaces and depths of meanings hidden "between the lines." Through their conjugation we arrive at the notions of a hidden urban underworld as an ultimate repository of inside stories and a socially transparent overworld where everything is on the surface, legible and light. It was through this moral economy that fluid hierarchies of wealth, status, skill, labor, and lifestyle were hardened into bitter binaries of rich and poor, native and immigrant, established and outsider (Stallybrass and White 1986).

The body/text code specialized in generating images of Otherness: certain visibly deviant features could now stand for a more general disreputability and a clear line could be drawn between those elements which were redeemable and those which were not (King 1995). The code held special implications for the way immigrants and ethnic minorities were treated – in particular for the dividing lines drawn between model minorities (i.e. those whose cultures were regarded as translatable and hence a suitable case for inclusion in programs of urban renewal) and those pariah minorities whose faces did not fit, whose cultures were regarded as too inscrutable to be read and whose presence was regarded as a threat to urban health and harmony. It is the latter, of course, who were made to represent the chaotic flux and flow of urban life, the anarchic vitality which is both subverting its rational organization, and yet from another standpoint is required by it. For after all they provide the local color that is otherwise lacking but which is so attractive to sociologists, filmmakers, bohemians, sex and lifestyle tourists and all those who want to experience how life is lived on the other side of the tracks (Jacobs 1996).

Today however the principles of urban circulation and inscription have moved on. The global city is constituted by the invisible circuitry of transnational capital and its space of information flows (Sassen 1991; Castells 1991, 1998). The powers of surveillance deployed by the nation-state have so far proved no match for the deregulation of markets and the Internet. International migrations of labor have generated diasporic information networks on a worldwide scale; at the same time the local social visibility of these communities has increased concomitantly to the point that they become the focus of concerted attack on the part of those who feel excluded from the global information flow. As one Bagladeshi leader in East London put it to me: "I can surf the internet, I can ring my family around the world, but I am afraid to go out of my own front door and across the street to the corner shop for a newspaper and loaf of bread in case I get attacked by some of the racist thugs who live down the end of the road" (quoted in Cohen 1996).

This dual city can no longer be visualized or understood by analogy to the body or the text. It no longer has an inside and an outside, there are no hidden messages waiting to be decoded (Soja 1989; Westwood and Williams 1996). Instead everything happens on the surface, with an impacted immediacy that is both bewildering and apparently beyond political redress. None of the customary graphologies – bio/ethno/historio/carto/topo – singly or in combination seem to provide a satisfactory "take" on what is happening.

It has been suggested that the postmodern frame merely glosses, where it does not actively celebrate, the systematic dislocation and randomized violence that prevails on many of our urban front lines (Harvey op cit). Certainly much of what passes for postmodernism can be seen as a search for new urban life-forms that reembody or recontextualize the lost dialectics of the visible and invisible city. But what if this dialectic is being worked through a more material and profane process of urban development?

Multicultural Capitalism, Third Spaces and the Invention of the "Postcolonial City"

Many recent commentators have pointed to the emergence of a new, multicultural, form of capitalism, in which the accumulation process requires not only an internationalized flow of information and ideas from a diversity of sources around the world but the presence of diasporic networks of labor drawn from non-European cultures. Let's briefly look at each side of this story in turn.

Multicultural capitalism – capitalism based on the re/production of cultural diversity and the marketing of exotic commodities – is at the cutting edge of globalization. It works by manufacturing local cultural goods and services and packaging them for global consumption as material signs of an authentic (sic) ethnicity (Appadurai 1997).

In contrast to the old "national" middle class still largely closeted in their local xenophobias, this operation works through a new cosmopolitan elite that both produces and consumes cultural diversity on a global scale, from world music to the latest in cross-over fashions in food and clothing. And unlike the homogenized business culture promoted by multinational companies with their rigid dress codes and concern for "corporate image," the lifestyles of this stratum advertise individuality, flair, difference – the same values they promote via their products.

The transnational middle class is no longer dominated, either demographically or ideologically, by more or less dead white men. Women, and members of ethnic and sexual minorities have been in the vanguard. And like any emergent social force they have constructed a view of the world in their own image, a world in which there is no reality outside its representation, where hybridity is celebrated and the pleasures of consumption are put at the cutting edge of change. En route, gender and race (but not class) have been transformed from topics of personal identity work into resources for consciously directed cultural production. Through the intervention of new rhetorics of entitlement, lifestyle innovation ceases to be merely a site of cultural labor, but a privileged means of accumulating cultural capital. And this in turn earns a return on personal investment that can be measured in strictly material terms.

This new fraction is a hybrid in another sense. It can be considered as a new aristocracy of labor insofar as it exercises a high degree of creative control over the technologies it operates. At the same time, it often merges the values of the premodern artisan with those of the postmodern entrepreneur. Unlike the old "self-made men" these do-it-yourself capitalists actively trade off their ethnicities or sexualities to give an added competitive edge to what is produced for the local/global market in "travelling ideas" (Wynne 1993).

But this is only one half of the story. The structures that produce this new multicultural middle class also throw up, as its necessary counterpart, a new kind of working class. Cultural industries require and actively promote a dual labor market, where a highly paid professional service class coexists with and sometimes directly employs a low-wage/low-skill servant class made up of women, young people, recent immigrants and refugees, and ethnic minorities. It is the preindustrial labor of these "hidden hands" that oils the postindustrial machineries of the cultural mass – from the bike couriers who deliver manuscripts or films to the seamstresses who sow the labels on designer jeans by hand, from the kitchen porters who staff the canteens of TV studios to the night cleaners who tidy the offices; as for the more visible economy it is students and unemployed cultural workers (actors, artists, writers) who are employed as front-of-house attractions in cafes, wine bars, and restaurants where their faces, and their arts of impression management, blend more acceptably into the middle-class mise-en-scène (Bianchini 1988; Zukin 1991).

This cultural labor force is more "flexible" than the historically sedimented sections of the old manual working class, less entrenched in a fixed habitus of customary work practice, and hence easier to hire and fire. Outside the workplace they are also major cultural innovators in their own right, continually introducing new topics of identity work, new hybridized styles of consumption which in turn provides the "raw material" for multicultural capitalism.

It is not the case that one "class" lives literally at the expense of the other. The exploitative nature of the classical capital/labor relation is not directly reproduced but takes on a more mediated form. Cultural labor – the work of inscribing collective meaning and personal identity on whatever materials are selected for this purpose (music, clothes, bodies, motorbikes, walls, etc.) – does not in itself create material value. It creates signs of authenticity and/or signatures of authorship. For these to function as marketable commodities they have first to be processed through a machinery of re-presentation. This is what cultural capital is and does: *it is the accumulated knowledge/power that intervenes to organize the commodification of cultural labor through its means of representation.* At the same time it transforms the topics of identity work into resources that can be traded off or bargained over.

It is possible in principle for the same individual or group to be on the side of cultural labor (for example as a local subject) and capital (as a global subject) at the same time, or to move continually between them. The imagined community of multicultural capitalism is, indeed, constituted by this constant to-ing and fro-ing, in which a kaleidoscope of signifying practices blurs the distinction between positions. Youth styles that trade off subcultural diversity provide a key currency of "free and equal exchange," or, if you prefer, mutual exploitation between the two "sides" in a way that turns structures of inequality into a kind of secret pact (Bourdieu 1995).

At another level the expanded role of design and communications technologies in every sphere of social production and consumption (Sassen 1991) and the growth of what Regis Debray has called, somewhat disparagingly, a mediocracy (Debray 1981), has thrown up an intelligentsia that straddles – and hence disrupts – established divisions between highbrow and lowbrow culture. A new kind of hybridized intellectual culture has emerged in which the invention of tradition, the profession of modernity, the cultivation of roots, and the embrace of liminality are no longer specialized strategies but can be combined in various permutations to compose a vibrant "postcolonial" intellectual mix.

Not surprisingly Black and Asian intellectuals and artists were in the vanguard of this movement. Many of them had graduated from the polyversities to join this new "cultural mass" and found themselves living and working through the digital revolution in information media and mass communications (Sharma, S. and A. 1997). It was not surprising (though not inevitable) that many of them saw issues of race and racism primarily through a cultural lens. Cultural racism was an apt enough description of the obstacles they faced in their struggle to assert autonomous spaces of creative activity in the artworld, the academy, and the mass media in a way that secured an adequate space of representation for the issues they wanted to address (Gupta 1993; Hall 1996).

Although its esthetic expression took many forms, the cultural fluidity associated with the "new ethnicities" movement also served to map out a cosmopolitan space, both real and imagined, of social mobility. Those who were on the move and "going places" now had a lexicon to describe their trajectory in other terms than those of the old class geographies which were in any case shifting their ground (Cannadine 1997). From this vantage point it was also possible to launch a swingeing attack on "middle brow" culture as a repository of a residual, but still imperial English parochialism, and to reclaim popular culture as the site of a dynamic and youthful urban multiculture (Back 1997).

All this helped to break thinking about race, nation, and ethnicity free from the essentializing discourses of Roots Radicalism and made the terms freshly exciting to work and play with. This take-up was facilitated by the promotion of another term which gave the notion of "new ethnicities" a spatial rather than a temporal dimension: diaspora.

Diaspora became "good to think with," as James Clifford put it, because it could be used to describe the global trajectory of traveling theory, a meeting place of postcolonial minds that was fully compatible with the digital age (Clifford 1994). En route, and through a process of projective identification that had little to do with their position in the real world, the refugee and the asylum seeker were "reinvented" as nomadic "postmodern" subjects (Cohen 1994).

The notion of cultural hybridity, wrested away from its racial problematic of miscegenation, served as a further resource for positively representing the processes of internal differentiation that were going on in second and third generation Black and Asian communities. In place of the pathologizing notion of young people caught "between cultures" there was the altogether more constructive vision of an inmixture of influence, where East met West on its own terms, and forged a dynamic "semiosphere" that put in question the cultural politics of both separatism and assimilationism (Werbner and Modood 1997).

Taken together these three terms (new ethnicities, hybridity, diaspora) thus worked to articulate the experience of those who were climbing out of the ethnic ghetto of "traditionalism" or communalism into the new multicultural middle class. They could now feel that their local climb up the social ladder of progress was part of a larger onwards march of ideas and populations across heterogeneous cultural space. The invention of the "postcolonial city" not only anchored these terms but gave Black and Asian cultural politics its own distinctive local/global habitation and a name, its own invented traditions, its own imagined history and geography, its own permeable – but still internally regulated – boundaries of belonging.

Once fluidity and floating signifiers became the esthetic trademark of a new multicultural intelligentsia, then by contrast, fixity and the failure to tolerate ambiguous or multiple identities were all too easily associated with an older generation stuck in their ways, or with a White and Black "underclass" immobilized at the bottom of the social ladder. A new moral binarism was established: between a progressive ethnoscape associated with the postcolonial city, celebrating a healthy, happy hybridity, and a reactionary landscape of "old ethnicities" mired in pathological purities or religious fundamentalisms belonging to the bad old colonial days. Underpinning the rhetoric of "third spaces" the familiar dualisms began to reemerge.

It could be argued that in this case the intervention of so-called "poststructuralist" modes of analysis, far from having broken with structuralism's obsessive concern with binary codes of race and class, simply reconfigured them in a rather more subtle form. But is there another way of understanding the relation between dual cities and third spaces which is less dependent on the art of deconstruction, while still putting the material phenomenology of the city back in touch with its cultural imagination?

The Urban Uncanny and Racism's Other Scene

In our traffic with everyday objects we move constantly between pure physics and pure landscape (Straus 1964). When we take the dog for a walk or go down the road to get the morning paper we unwittingly steer a course between the nonintuitive space of modern physics, the immediate sensory spaces which our bodies navigate, the private mental spaces of our dreams, memories, and fantasies, and the public geographical space that locates our journey within certain shared coordinates of social and cultural meaning.

Most people, including until recently most geographers, are not aware of how these different kinds of spatial orientation mesh in, how the stories we tell ourselves about where we have come from, where we are at, where we are going to in our lives, work to create a fictive concord between our positions in physical, psychological, cultural, and political space. Most people know nothing and care even less about the physical laws that govern the material environment, including the built environment; many have learnt to block out or defend themselves against the sights, sounds, smells, tastes, and touch of the city, because these sense impressions are felt intuitively to be ugly, or intrusive, or in some way bad and damaging to health; new technologies such as mobile phones, Walkmans, and pocket computers help create a second line of psychic defense by cocooning their users in a virtual space of communication that renders them impervious to their material and social surroundings; finally most uses of public space are part of taken-for-granted routines of shopping, traveling, gossiping, and hanging about, routines that are largely indifferent to the variously sedimented histories of architecture, urban economy, social regulation, and civic governance that make them more or less possible.

For all these reasons most of us for most of the time are on automatic pilot, dreaming in broad daylight with our eyes open as we move about the city. Whether we are stuck in traffic jams, or queuing for buses that never come, or milling about in crowds of shoppers, we learn to deal with the logistics of urban encounter by retreating into first person singular landscapes where these impedimenta function as symptomatic backdrops to the stories of progress (or lack of it) that we tell about our lives. But what are these urban daydreams about beyond this immediate and material self-reference? What ghosts from the past do they conjure up, what figures from the other scenes of city life emerge to remind us that in the midst of what is most familiar, we remain in some sense strangers to ourselves?

Freud was the first to provide us with a map of the urban *unheimlich*. In his famous paper on "The Uncanny" he writes:

> Once, as I was walking through the deserted streets of a provincial town which was strange to me, on a hot summer afternoon I found myself in a quarter whose character could not long remain in doubt. Nothing but painted women were to be seen at the windows of the small houses and I hastened to leave the narrow street at the next turning. But after having wandered about for a while without being directed, I suddenly found myself back in the same street, where my presence was now beginning to excite attention. I hurried away once more but only to arrive yet a third time by devious paths in the same place. Now however a feeling overcame me which I can only describe as uncanny and I was glad enough to abandon my exploratory walk and get straight back to the piazza I had left a short while before (Freud 1914).

How does the urban *unheimlich*, with its characteristic pattern of repeated interruption of social routine, described so clearly by Freud, emerge in the interstices of everyday encounters in the park, the subway, the shopping mall, the journey from home to school or work? We are dealing here with that special transferential relation to place though which an unfamiliar setting evokes the absence/presence of significant others, or invests the strange with a sense of déjà vu, and it directs our attention to a form of the dual city that is not much recognized or talked about.

As we have seen, the invisible city tends to have been defined purely negatively as everything that is excluded from the picture drawn by dominant strategies of graphic representation and surveillance. Yet the visible, ordered, rational city has as its necessary counterpoint a dreamcity where familiar landmarks are so transformed by fantasy and primary-process thinking that they can only be negotiated with the aid of a special map whose keys are only to be found in the subject's Unconscious (Cohen 1998; Vidler 1996). These two cities meet in sites of urban dereliction, tunnels that vanish into fog, labyrinthine streets that come to a dead end, industrial wastelands, shuttered houses, abandoned stations, deserted underpasses, cemeteries where ghost horses canter past the graves. In these holes in the urban fabric we come across the characteristic figures of the urban uncanny (Vidler op cit). Here dreaming with our eyes open we may run into our other more malevolent selves, have strange encounters with aliens posing as natives, meet robots, zombies, and other kinds of double trouble disguised in the form of our own flesh and blood. These "third spaces" in the urban fabric may be made by bulldozers or bazookas, zoning regulations or patterns of social segregation, but they are filled in by myths, legends, and popular fictions that are in no way reducible to their material effect.

The cultural landscaping of sites of urban/industrial dereliction over the last decades has insinuated a layer of symbolic distancing (and sometimes arch sentimentality) between these two cities so that they no longer engage in even the most coded kinds of conversation. Where kitsch or irony rules, OK, the raw material of the urban uncanny melts into the thin air of postmodernity (Soja 1989).

At the same time the demise of the crowded thoroughfare and street corner as a routine feature of working-class life and its replacement by more transient or simulated forms of social congregation has opened up many new sites for the figures of the urban uncanny to take hold. When the throng of familiar faces fades, along with the hubbub of gossip, when the routes that used to carry workers to and from the factories, mines, and docks become part of the postindustrial "scenery," then the "other scene" emerges into broad daylight, casting the shadow of "that which should have remained hidden" on to screen memories of place.

Finding the Way Home

Only those most at home in the local/global city are able to seize this opportunity to colonize the depopulated streets with figments of their sociological imagination; I've already suggested this is where the postcolonial intelligentsia likes to come out to play with difference. The theme of the alien and the stranger, the bogeyman, and even the thief, can here be safely appropriated and used to deconstruct the racist stereotypes in which they have historically been clothed.

Well-established Black cultures and communities that have to deal routinely with the daily residues of dangerous or difficult intercourse with the city have developed their own ways of immunizing themselves against the more traumatic effects of racism. Through a repertoire of precautionary tales, stories that forearm as well as forewarn about specific and hence actionable sites of threat, and through the construction of defensible spaces, they succeed in devising narrative landscapes in a way that reduces anxiety to predictable and tolerable levels. Urban fears can here be visualized, symbolized, narrated, worked through, and finally mastered. Thus distanced they could even, in some cases, lend a halo of enchantment to the experience of risk, yielding pleasurable adventure stories of dangers successfully negotiated, obstacles overcome, traps avoided, safe returns.

But what happens when this kind of normalization is no longer possible? For many people, living on the edge, on the permanent *qui vive* against unwelcome incursions by the powers that be into domains ruled by their own highly local prides of place, the themes of stranger danger tell a very different story. Here an untoward look, an unknown face, a remark made out of turn, a passing brush with the law, may be enough to break the fragile bond between what is loved and what is hated, what fascinates and what repels in the everyday attachment to place.

In collaboration with colleagues in Germany, I recently carried out a comparative ethnonarratological study into young people's landscapes of safety and danger in "urban frontline" areas of Hamburg and London's Docklands. We were interested in comparing the stories and mental maps constructed by young people living in areas of high racial polarization and violence, with those from areas where urban multi-cultures existed and hence "third spaces" might be easier to sustain.

One young man, Alan, who lived in a highly racialized part of the Isle of Dogs, told us that he thought the whole place might one day soon sink into the Thames under the weight of Canary Wharf and all the new building going on. He was worried that there might be a flood and he would be drowned in his sleep. In a subsequent discussion with his friends he told the following story:

> The other day we went across the water. It was "niggers galore," walking around, flash cars, flash clothes it's a Black's paradise over there. We went down the market and we saw this White geezer come up out of a manhole and he was speaking some foreign language. I dunno what it was – Russian I think. He didn't know where he was then just stumbled around like a zombie, bumping into people. Then he started talking to these Black muggers and they showed him where to go and they all went off together.

His friend backed up his story:

> Yeah, probably was Russian cos they had one of their warships out there in the river. They're probably working together with the Blacks in the sewers, you know. My dad says if Labour win the Russians are gonna take over Docklands and maybe the whole of London.

This conversation raises a number of important questions. Where do these zombies come from if not Russia? What connections do they make possible between Alan's anxiety, represented by the fear of being drowned in dreams, the sense that this community is being engulfed by a tide of structural change, and the racial panic about Black muggers?

The characterization of the zombie as someone who speaks in a foreign tongue understandable only by Blacks intimates that the Unconscious, as discourse of the Other, has here become directly racialized. At the same time the device furnishes a powerful trope of this boy's own sense of social alienation – stumbling around, bumping into people not knowing where he is, "a stranger in his own country." Of course he has ventured "over the water" (i.e. across the River Thames), and what he discovers on the other side, in the wake of earlier maritime adventurers, makes him feel even more at sea – a Black El Dorado, a land of Cockayne peopled by "niggers galore" who are clearly having a good time that by implication is denied to Whites. These pleasure principles, precisely because they have been appropriated by "the other" are only allowed to surface and make history by its "bad side" (Roediger 1991; Cohen 1996). The sewers, apart from the obvious associations with excreta and the disposal of human waste furnish a principle of "negative circulation" that connects all kinds of matter out of place: alien ideas, foreign bodies, unnatural alliances of every kind.

The Urban Uncanny provides a strategy of symbolic displacement and disavowal by means of which the racist discourse can plunder the sociological imagination for whatever material it needs to establish its "common sense." But not everyone has access to the *unheimlich*. People caught in the crossfire of racial and ethnic confrontation, in divided cities and nations, in Belfast and Sarajevo, Pristina, Jerusalem, or Beirut – where even the simplest act of crossing the street to buy a newspaper, or taking the dog for a walk can be a precipitator of disaster – do not have the luxury of such strategies of indirection. Instead they have to devise more immediate ways of staying on automatic pilot. Some become exhibitionists, hiding in the light of public attention, using techniques of mimicry or masquerade to flaunt their difference and turn the voyeur's gaze back upon itself; others turn inward, creating invisible, symbolic spaces of self-containment to protect memories, histories, hopes from further inspection and exploitation at the hands of outsiders whose concerns they do not trust; some mobilize to reclaim streets and communities from the grip of drug pushers or urban militia while others dream of returns or escapes to promised lands; perhaps the majority just get on with their everyday lives as best they can, concerned above all to secure their own immediate futures, indifferent to all the noise generated by politicians and cultural commentators.

Which brings us back to Italo Calvino, who, as it happens, has also given us a rather precise map of this process of negotiation, in a short story entitled "The Garden of Stubborn Cats":

> The city of cats and the city of men exist one inside the other, but they are not the same city. Few cats recall the time when there was no distinction: when the streets and squares of men were also the streets and squares of cats, and you lived in a broad and various space. But for several generations now domestic felines have been the prisoners of an uninhabitable city: the streets are uninterruptedly overrun by the mortal traffic of cat crushing automobiles, in every square foot of terrain where once a garden extended or a vacant lot, or the ruins of an old demolition now condominiums loom up, welfare housing, brand new skyscrapers.... But in this vertical city, in this compressed city where all voids tend to fill up and every block of cement tends to mingle with other blocks of cement, a kind of counter city opens, a negative city that consists of empty slices between wall and wall, a city of cavities, wells conduits, driveways, inner yards, like a network of dry canals on a planet of stucco and tar, and it is through this network, grazing the walls that the ancient cat population still scurries (Calvino 1976).

In these new catwalks, suspended between the virtual space of information flows, and the pedestrianism of contemporary politics Calvino suggests that we will find, if we know how and where and with whom to look, the elements of egalitarian community, at once residual and emergent, that the project of modernism invokes in principle, but in practice has overlooked.

It is here, if anywhere at all, that legendary cities might yet be built where Catholic and Protestant, Muslim and Serb, Jew, Christian, and Arab, Rat and Swallow might grow up learning the benefits of sharing the same approximate geography of risk. And here, instead of the fixed lines drawn by racism, between those who are human and those who are not, between those whose imagination takes flight only to rule the city, and those who are mired in the mundane, we may yet discover strategies of narration and navigation which lead us into a practical, sensuous engagement with what is truly "from the other side of the tracks."

REFERENCES

Appadurai, A. 1997: *Modernity at Large*. Chicago: University of Chicago Press.
Back, L. 1997: *New Ethnicities and Urban Multicultures*. London: UCL Press.

Bianchini, F. 1988: *City Centres, City Cultures*. Cambridge: Polity Press.
Bourdieu, P. 1995: *Free Exchange*. Cambridge: Polity Press.
Calvino, I. 1974: *Invisible Cities*. London: Paladin.
Calvino, I. 1976: *Marcovoldo*. London: Paladin.
Cannadine, D. 1997: *Class in Britain*. New Haven: Yale University Press.
Castells, M. 1991: *The Information City*. Oxford: Blackwell.
Castells, M. 1998: *The Rise of the Network Society*. Oxford: Blackwell.
Certeau, M. de 1994: *Strategies of Everyday Life*. London: Verso.
Clifford, J. 1994: *Travelling Culture*. Berkeley: University of California Press.
Cohen, P. 1994: Home Rules CNER/UEL. London: Centre for New Ethnicities Research.
Cohen, P. 1996: All white on the night. In Butler, T. and Rustin, M. (eds.) 1996: *Rising in the East*. London: Lawrence and Wishart.
Cohen, P. 1998: *Rethinking the Youth Question*. Basingstoke: Macmillan.
Debray, R. 1981: *Teachers, Writers, Celebrities*. London: Verso.
Dyos, H. J. (ed.) 1985: *Victorian Cities*. London: Routledge.
Feldman, D. and Stedman Jones, G. (eds.) 1991: *Metropolis*. London: Routledge.
Gupta, S. 1993: *Disrupted Borders*. London: Oram.
Harvey, D. 1989: *The Condition of Postmodernity*. Oxford: Blackwell.
Jacobs, J. 1996: *The Edge of Empire*. London: Routledge.
King, A. D. (ed.) 1995: *Representing the City*. Basingstoke: Macmillan.
Roediger, D. 1991: *Wages of Whiteness*. London: Verso.
Sassen, S. 1991: *The Global City*. Princeton, NJ: Princeton University Press.
Sennett, R. 1990: *The Conscience of the Eye*. London: Faber.
Sennett, R. 1994: *The Flesh and the Stone*. London: Faber.
Sharma, S. and Sharma, A. (eds.) 1997: *Disorienting Rhythms*. London: Zed Books.
Smyth, S. 1994: *Marketing the City*. London: Spon.
Soja, E. 1989: *Postmodern Geographies*. London: Verso.
Stallybrass, P. and White, A. 1986: *Politics and Poetics of Transgression*. London: Routledge.
Straus, E. 1964: *The Primacy of the Senses*. Chicago: University of Chicago Press.
Vidler, A. 1996: *The Architectural Uncanny*. London: MIT Press.
Walkovitz, J. 1992: *City of Dreadful Delight*. London: Virago.
Werbner, P. and Modood, T. (eds.) 1997: *Debating Cultural Hybridity*. London: Zed Books.
Westwood, S. and Williams, J. 1997: *Imagining Cities*. London: Routledge.
Wynne, D. 1993: *The Culture Industry*. Aldershot: Avebury.
Zukin, S. 1991: *Landscapes of Power*. Oxford: Oxford University Press.

Chapter 28

Gentrification, Postindustrialism, and Industrial and Occupational Restructuring in Global Cities

Chris Hamnett

Gentrification is now firmly established as a major phenomenon of Western cities and is established in both academic and popular discourse. It was first identified and labeled by Ruth Glass (1963) in London in the early 1960s. Her use of the term "gentrification" was ironic to point to the emergence of a new "urban gentry," paralleling the traditional eighteenth- and nineteenth-century rural gentry who comprised the class strata below the landed aristocracy. She identified gentrification as a complex process, or set of processes, involving physical improvement of the housing stock, housing tenure change from renting to owning, price rises, and the displacement or replacement of the existing working-class population by the middle classes.

> One by one, many of the working class quarters of London have been invaded by the middle-class – upper and lower – shabby modest mews and cottages... have been taken over when their leases expired, and have become elegant, expensive residences. Larger Victorian houses, downgraded in an earlier or recent period – which were used as lodging houses or were otherwise in multiple occupation – have been upgraded once again... Once this process of "gentrification" starts in a district it goes on rapidly until all or most of the original working class occupiers are displaced and the whole social character of the district is changed (Glass 1963: xviii).

In the years which followed, a growing body of literature appeared which revealed the emergence of gentrification in a wide range of cities from Vancouver (Ley 1978; Mills 1988), Philadelphia (Smith 1979), Washington (Gale 1979), New York (Schaffer and Smith 1986), Melbourne (Jager 1986), Toronto (Caulfield 1994), Sydney (Engels 1994), Adelaide (Badcock 1992), Paris (Savitch 1988; Carpenter and Lees 1995), and Montreal (Rose 1988). During this period the literature on gentrification has grown enormously and a large amount is now known about the characteristics of gentrifiers in different cities, their social background, cultural characteristics and proclivities and the nature of the processes of residential area transformation.

In 1996 and 1997 at least three major books on gentrification were published (Ley 1996; Smith 1996; Butler 1997). It therefore seems appropriate to briefly reflect on the current significance of gentrification, its scale, extent, causes, and consequences.

The Scale and Distribution of Gentrification

Gentrification is now widespread throughout many of the major cities of the Western world. It may still constitute "islands of renewal in seas of decay" as Berry suggested (1985) in the context of American cities, and it is outweighed in quantitative importance by large-scale suburbanization and exurbanization, but the islands are substantial and growing. There is little evidence for Bourne's (1993) suggestion that gentrification is essentially a historically specific product of the postwar baby boom generation and that, as this cohort ages and moves to the suburbs, so gentrification will gradually decline in importance (Badcock 1995). On the contrary, although there is a continued outward movement of professionals and managers from the inner cities to the suburbs, they appear to be replaced by an even larger flow of young professionals, managers, and workers in finance, business services, and the cultural and creative industries (Hamnett 1990).

As a result, the scale and extent of gentrified areas in cities such as New York, London, and Paris is gradually expanding, pushing steadily outwards into hitherto solidly working-class or minority areas such as Hackney in London (Butler 1997; May 1996), Bellville in Paris (Rhein 1998), and Harlem and the Lower East Side in New York (Schaffer and Smith 1986; Abu-Lughod 1994). Gentrification has been identified in a variety of different types of cities and contexts, and the idea of rural gentrification is now well established as the middle classes have moved into attractive rural villages or small towns, permanently or as second home owners (Cloke, Phillips, and Thrift 1995). It is clear, however that gentrification is a highly selective process: both at the interurban and the intraurban scale. Gentrification is most marked in a number of major cities with large and growing financial and business service sectors such as London, Paris, New York, Sydney, San Francisco, and Amsterdam, Toronto, or Vancouver. It is not widespread in cities with declining old industrial bases such as Pittsburgh, Buffalo, Detroit, the Ruhr, Liverpool, or Manchester. Nor is it very marked in cities which are largely twentieth-century creations such as Los Angeles, Phoenix, or Milton Keynes.

Explanations for Gentrification

The key question is why gentrification became significant when it did and where it did. There are two principal explanations for the emergence of gentrification. The first, supply-side explanation, put forward by Neil Smith (1979) sees gentrification as essentially a product of the urban land and property market. More specifically, he views it in terms of the emergence of a growing "rent gap" between the current value of property on a site and the underlying value of the land. In his view suburbanization and subsequent inner-city decline leads to the existence of devalued inner-city property on potentially valuable land which opens up the potential for profitable reinvestment. Thus Smith is extremely critical of explanations which stress the choices and preferences of gentrifiers, arguing that it is capital, and the institutions of the capitalist land market – developers, real-estate agents, mortgage lenders and the like – who hold the key to understanding gentrification, and that the culture and preferences of individual gentrifiers are largely irrelevant, or at most secondary aspects of the process which influence the specific manifestations of the process but not much else. As he puts it: "the needs of production – in particular the need to earn profit – are a more decisive initiative behind gentrification than consumer preference." He adds: "A theory of gentrification will need to explain the detailed historical mechanisms of capital depreciation in the inner-city and the precise way in which this depreciation produces the possibility of profitable reinvestment" (1979: 542).

The alternative view, which is argued here, is that while gentrification clearly involves changes in the structure of the land and property market, it is better seen as a product of the shift from an industrial to a postindustrial society in particular cities and associated changes in class structure, particularly the growth of an expanded middle class and their social relations, cultural tastes, and consumption practices. I see gentrification not as an inevitable consequence of the prior existence of a rent gap, but primarily as a result of the continuing economic transformation of major Western cities from manufacturing centers to centers of business services and the creative and cultural industries, with consequent changes in occupational structure, income distribution, gender relations, the housing market, and cultural tastes. In this respect, gentrification can be viewed as a major component of the transition from industrial to postindustrial cities, and it seems likely to be an important feature of urban life and structure for some time (Badcock 1995). To a significant extent, the expanded postindustrial middle class has replaced/displaced the industrial working class from desirable inner-city areas in cities where the financial and business and financial services sector has grown rapidly.

There is a third explanation, advanced by Redfern (1997), which argues that gentrification is best explained in terms of the availability and cost of domestic technology. More specifically, Redfern argues that it is existence of domestic technologies, and their falling real cost, which permits gentrification to occur: "you cannot have gentrification without being able to do up a house," as he puts it. Redfern claims that both the supply side and the demand side explanations share a common presumption: that "gentrifiers gentrify because they have to." He argues instead that "they gentrify because they can." I think Redfern has identifed an important issue here, but the falling real cost of domestic technologies which enable old houses to be modernized seems to be a necessary rather than a sufficient factor in explaining gentrification. If the supply of potential gentrifiable properties was not present, and the demand was not there, all the domestic technology in the world would be unlikely to lead to gentrification. Indeed, in many American inner cities the reality has been large-scale abandonment rather than gentrification (Dear 1976; Marcuse 1986).

In the declining industrial cities the class and income structure is not appropriate to support widespread gentrification, and in the latter there is not much in the way of gentrifiable, old inner-city property (though Smith would probably argue that a rent gap has not developed in such cities). There are small patches of gentrification in many old industrial or small provincial cities, but they are generally small scale.

Put simply, it is argued that gentrification is primarily a phenomenon of the late twentieth-century postindustrial service-based city. As the economic structure of these cities has evolved, so the social and occupational structure of the city has changed, and a new group of residents with different educational backgrounds, cultural values, preferences, and orientations has emerged (Ley 1980, 1996).

Cultural values, preferences, and orientations are necessary to underpin gentrification but they are not sufficient. If, hypothetically, members of the "new class," to use that term in a very loose way, working in central city financial, business, and creative and cultural industries, were not interested in living in inner-city properties (new or old) or inner-city neighborhoods, and were uninterested in what the city center had to offer in terms of culture, lifestyles, food, and entertainment, I see no reason why gentrification should emerge. Instead, the new urban elite would get on the train or in their cars and disappear into the suburbs every evening. In this respect, the cultural dimensions of gentrification are crucial and should not be downplayed or ignored. Gentrification is not simply a class or income phenomenon. It is also crucially linked to the creation of a new set of cultural and residential preferences. However, cultural factors alone are unlikely to bring gentrification into being on any significant scale. While it is true that Greenwich Village or Chelsea, London, were centers for artistic and bohemian culture in the 1950s, they were essentially small scale.

Gentrification and the Postindustrial City

What was required to underpin large-scale gentrification was a fundamental change in the economic base and occupational structure of cities: a shift from industrial to postindustrial or service-based economies. This only began to happen in the 1970s on a significant scale. The old, manufacturing-based cities of the nineteenth century and first half of the twentieth century had occupational class structures which were largely dominated by skilled, semi-skilled and unskilled manual workers. These workers were relatively poor and tended to live in relatively close proximity to their workplaces in the inner cities. The urban elite was small in size and although many of them lived in, or in close proximity to, the city center until the second half of the nineteenth century, at least in cities such as London, there was absolutely no pressure for expansion of the elite into surrounding working-class areas. On the contrary, there is some evidence that the middle classes left or were squeezed out of some parts of the inner-city as the industrial working class grew in the late nineteeth century. When the middle classes grew in size it was a relatively simple matter, using the new suburban railways, to construct new housing in what are now the nineteenth-century inner suburbs in areas such as Islington, North Kensington, or Brooklyn. It was still a relatively easy commute to work in the central city for the predominantly male office workers of that period (Prince 1964).

With the long decline of manufacturing industry and the growing importance of the service sector, particularly financial, business and professional services such as law, advertising, management consultancy, public relations, and public services such as health and education, the occupational structure of modern Western societes has changed dramatically. There has been a decline in the size of the manual working class and a sharp increase in the number and proportion of the professional, managerial, and technical groups: the so-called "new middle class" (Wright and Martin 1987; Myles 1988; Marshall and Rose 1985; Esping-Anderson 1993; Butler and Savage 1995) over the last 30 years. In addition, as Butler (1997) and others have pointed out, there has also been a sharp increase in the number and proportion of the workforce with higher educational qualifications.

It would seem that Bell (1973) was broadly right in asserting that postindustrialism has created a postindustrial society with a different occupational class structure and cultural characteristics and aspirations. This assertion has been strongly challenged by a number of Marxist commentators including Braverman (1974), Walker and Greenberg (1982), and Smith (1987) who instead argue that we are seeing a process of proletarianization and gradual deskilling of an expanded working class along with the shrinkage of the petit bourgeoisie. The evidence (Wright and Martin 1987) does not appear to support this view, however, even though the earnings evidence in the USA does clearly point to a fall in real earnings for a majority of the population in recent decades. There is also clear evidence of growing earnings and income inequality in a number of major global cities such as New York, London, and Paris (Hamnett and Cross 1998a and b).

Gentrification and Global Cities

As David Ley (1978) pointed out 20 years ago, the geography of postindustrial society is not even. Instead, the transition from industrialism to postindustrialism, at least in terms of industrial and occupational structure, has been most marked in a small number of major cities: the global or world cities. A number of commentators (Friedmann and Wolff 1982; Friedmann 1986; Sassen 1984, 1991) have argued that these cities are characterized by a new and distinctive class structure. Friedmann and Wolff (1982) suggested that "The primary social fact about world city formation is the polarisation of its social class divisions. Transnational elites are the dominant class in the world city and the city is arranged to suit their life styles and occupational necessities" (322). So too, Sassen (1991) argued that "New conditions of growth have contributed to elements of a new class alignment in global cities" (13).

The empirical evidence for this argument is strong and consistent. The changing socioeconomic structure of London over a period of years (Hamnett 1976, 1984, 1996) shows a clear picture of consistent upwards shift in occupational class structure of the economically active population. Similar evidence for the Netherlands (Hamnett 1994), Paris (Preteceille 1995), New York (Brint 1991) reveals the professional, managerial, and technical occupational groups have expanded considerably since the early 1960s, clerical and other junior white-collar workers have remained broadly stable, and skilled, semi-skilled and unskilled groups have shrunk. The result is a far more "professionalised" class structure than that of the traditional industrial city. At the same time, Burgers (1996) notes that there is a growing polarization in the Netherlands between an increasingly professionalized economically active workforce and the economically inactive and unemployed. Brughel (1996) also points to the downgrading of some occupations.

To argue for the importance of an expanded middle class is not, as Smith (1979) has suggested, an individualistic choice and preference-based explanation of gentrification. On the contrary, it is very firmly grounded in the changing industrial and occupational structure of advanced capitalist societies. In this respect, it is a strongly materialist explanation. Where it differs from Smith is in the relative emphasis it accords to the changing industrial and occupational structure of major cities rather than simply to changes in the structure of the property market and urban ground rents. I have argued elsewhere (Hamnett 1984, 1991) that a devalued inner urban property market is no guarantee of gentrification, as areas like Detroit and the Bronx readily testify (Deskins 1996). The link between an expanded middle class and gentrification is based, at least in part, on the fact that this new class is not only larger than hitherto but has a much higher income than the traditional inner-city working class. They are therefore able to systematically outbid existing residents for inner-city housing. But the changing industrial and occupational structure of Western cities does not automatically produce gentrification. As noted earlier, it is quite conceivable that the greatly expanded "new class" of managers and professionals could simply opt to live in the suburbs and, of course, many of them (and arguably the great majority) do precisely that. This is why the suburban areas of cities like Washington, DC, have continued to expand (Knox 1993) and why many potentially desirable inner-city areas have not been gentrified. If the whole, or even a majority, of the new class had opted for gentrification, the social and spatial structure of cities would be very different and prices in the inner cities would have spiralled out of sight. Indeed, there is an argument that, to some extent at least, a proportion of the new class have already been effectively priced out of desirable gentrified inner-city areas and forced to live further out where prices are more affordable. This argument would hold for London, Amsterdam, Paris, San Francisco, and much of Manhattan.

Gentrification, Education and Culture

But why do a significant proportion of the new class choose, and I use the term quite deliberately, to live in the inner-city rather than in the suburbs. This is where the role of education and culture become crucially important as Ley (1978, 1980, 1996), Mills (1988), Munt (1985), Lees (1994), Butler (1997), and others have pointed out. The principal argument is that gentrifiers constitute a specific fraction of the new middle class, distinguished by their generally high levels of education, high levels of cultural capital, and their cultural preferences and consumption norms. In addition to a prediliction for the cultural and entertainment facilities offered by the central city, they place a high esthetic value on the types of period property available in the inner-city, with their distinctive features. Ley terms this the estheticization of consumption. In addition, Butler (1997) argues that gentrifiers are frequently typified by relatively liberal social and political outlook and affiliations. They are disproportionately centre-left in political orientation and place a high value on interaction with those holding similar values or "people like us" as one of Butler's respondents put it. Jon May (1996) reached similar conclusions. While this is unlikely to be true of all gentrifiers in all areas, and Butler found sharp differences even within his study area of Hackney, it suggests that there is a high level of cultural and political self-selection among gentrifiers. Butler argues that gentrifiers constitute a specific fraction of the middle class characterized by high levels of cultural capital rather than financial capital (Butler and Savage 1996).

Butler also suggests, following Rose (1984), Bondi (1991), Warde (1991), and others that gentrifiers are also characterized by a distinctive structure of gender relations. Gentrifier households contain a disproportionate number of dual-career households characterized by high female economic activity rates and a disproportionate representation in city center service jobs which, it is argued, predispose them to locate within easy access of central city workplaces in order to both minimize commuting time and to make child-care arrangements more manageable. Warde argues that a change in gender relations is perhaps the central defining characteristic of gentrification and is more important than class. Butler and Hamnett (1994) argue, however, that while changes in gender relations associated with gentrification are important they have to be viewed in the context of a specific middle-class formation. Changes in gender relations within and without the home, or increases in the proportion of working women are unlikely to generate significant gentrification in their own right. However, allied to the increase in the number of women working in professional and managerial jobs and an increase in dual-career households they are of considerable significance. They are part and parcel of the transition from a male-dominated industrial society to a more feminized postindustrial society.

Conclusions

While there is no doubt that gentrification is consistently associated with a sharp increase in property prices in the areas where it occurs, I am dubious of the extent to which the rent gap is the principal driver of this process. There is no doubt that property prices in potentially gentrifiable areas are relatively low and that this is, or was, one of the key attractions for gentrifiers, but it is not a sufficient explanation. Without the demand from the expanding postindustrial urban service class, gentrification is unlikely to take place, however low property prices are. This is why there are large derelict inner-city areas in some American and European industrial cities. It may even be that there is no rent gap in these cities and that inner-city land and property prices are both depressed due to lack of effective demand. A developed rent gap may only be characteristic of cities which have a large, growing middle-class workforce (see Bourassa 1993; Badcock 1989: Clarke 1988 for discussion of the rent gap thesis.)

Smith developed the rent gap thesis as an alternative, materialist, explanation to what he viewed as excessively idealist explanations based on individual choice and preference (Smith 1979). It can be argued, however, that an explanation based on the structure of the urban property and rental market does not exhaust the range of possible materialist explanations. I would argue, on the contrary, that a focus on the changing industrial and occupational class and earning structures of capitalist cities, combined with an understanding of changes in the educational, gender, and cultural composition of the expanded urban middle class, is likely to prove equally productive. This said, it is important to link the analysis of changes in industrial and occupational structures and cultural change to analyses of changes in the structure of the residential and commercial property market in different cities if we are to achieve a comprehensive understanding of the processes producing gentrification.

REFERENCES

Abu-Lughod, J. (ed.) 1994: *From Urban Village to East Village: The Battle for New York's Lower East Side*. Oxford: Blackwell.

Badcock, B. 1989: An Australian view of the rent gap hypothesis. *Annals of the Association of American Geographers*, 79, 125–45.

Badcock, B. 1991: Neighbourhood change in inner Adelaide: an update. *Urban Studies*, 28, 553–8.

Badcock, B. 1992: Adelaide's heart transplant, 1970–88: the "transfer" of "value" within the built environment. *Environment and Planning A*, 24, 323–39.

Badcock, B. 1995: Notwithstanding the exaggerated claims, residential revitalization is changing the shape of some western cities: a response to Bourne. *Urban Studies*, 30, 191–5.

Beauregard, R. A. 1986: The chaos and complexity of gentrification. In N. Smith, P. R. Williams (eds.), *Gentrification of the City*. London: Allen and Unwin, 35–55.

Bell, D. 1973: *The Coming of Postindustrial Society*. New York: Basic Books.

Berry, B. 1985: Islands of renewal in seas of decay. In P. Peterson (ed.), *The New Urban Reality*, Washington, DC: Brookings Institute, 69–96.

Bondi, L. 1991: Gender divisions and gentrification: a critique. *Transactions of the Institute of British Geographers*, 16, 190–8.

Bourassa, S. 1993: The rent gap debunked. *Urban Studies*, 30, 1731–44.

Bourne, L. S. 1993: The demise of gentrification: a commentary and prospective view. *Urban Geography*, 14(1), 95–107.

Braverman, H. 1974: *Labor and Monopoly Capital: The Degregation of Work in the Twentieth Century*. New York: Monthly Review Press.

Bridge, G. 1994: Gentrification, class and residence. *Environment and Planning D*, 12, 31–51.

Brint, S. 1991: Upper professionals: a high command of commerce, culture and civic regulation. In J. Mollenkopf and M. Castells (eds.), *Dual City: Restructuring New York*. New York: Russell Sage, 155–76.

Brughel, I. 1996: Gendering the polarisation debate: comment on Hamnett's "Social Polarisation, Economic Restructuring and Welfare State Regimes". *Urban Studies*, 33 (8), 1431–40.

Burgers, J. 1996: No polarisation in Dutch cities? Inequality in a corporatist country. *Urban Studies*, 33(1), 99–105.

Butler, T. 1997: *Gentrification and the Middle Classes*. Aldershot: Ashgate.

Butler, T. and Hamnett, C. 1994: Gentrification, class and gender: some comments on Warde's gentrification as consumption. *Environment and Planning D*, 12, 477–93.

Butler, T. and Savage, M. (eds.) 1996: *Social Change and the Middle Classes*. London: UCL Press.

Carpenter, J. and Lees, L. 1995: Gentrification in New York, London and Paris: an international comparison. *International Journal of Urban and Regional Research*, 19, 285–302.

Caulfield, J. 1989: Gentrification and desire. *Canadian Review of Sociology and Anthropology*, 26, 617–32.

Caulfield, J. 1994: *City Form and Everyday Life: Toronto's Gentrification and Critical Social Theory*. Toronto: University of Toronto Press.

Clarke, E. 1988: The rent gap and the transformation of the built environment: case studies in Malmo 1860–1985. *Geografiska Annaler B*, 70, 241–54.

Cloke, P., Phillips, M., and Thrift, N. 1995: The new middle classes and the social construction of rural living. In T. Butler and M. Savage (eds.), *Social Change and the Middle Classes*. London: UCL Press, 220–38.

Dear, M. 1976: Abandoned housing. In J. S. Adams (ed.), *Urban Policy Making and Metropolitan Dynamics: A Comparative Geographical Analysis*. Cambridge, MA: Ballinger.

Deskins, D. 1996: Economic Restructuring, Job Opportunities and Black Social Dislocation in Detroit. In J. O'Loughlin and J. Friedrichs (eds.), *Social Polarization in Post-Industrial Metropolises*. Berlin and New York: Walter de Gryter.

Engels, B. 1994: Capital flows, redlining and gentrification: the pattern of mortgage lending and social change in Glebe, Sydney, 1960–1984. *International Journal of Urban and Regional Research*, 18 (4) 628–57.

Esping-Anderson, G. 1993: *Changing Classes: Stratification and Mobility in Post-Industrial Societies*. London: Sage.

Friedmann, J. 1986: The world city hypothesis. *Development and Change*, 17, 69–84.

Friedmann, J. and Wolff, G. 1982: World city formation: an agenda for research and action. *International Journal of Urban and Regional Research*, 309–43.

Gale, D. 1979: Middle class resettlement in older urban neighbourhoods. *Journal of the American Planning Association*, 45 (3), 293–304.

Glass, R. 1963: *London: Aspects of Change*. Centre for Urban Studies, London: University College London.

Hamnett, C. 1976: Social change and social segregation in inner London, 1961–71. *Urban Studies*, 13, 261–91.

Hamnett, C. 1984: Gentrification and residential location theory: a review and assessment. In D. T. Herbert and R. J. Johnston (eds.), *Geography and the Urban Environment*, vol. 6, London: John Wiley, 283–319.

Hamnett, C. and Cross, D. 1998a: Social polarisation and inequality in London: the earnings evidence, 1979–95. *Environment and Planning C*, 16, 659–80.

Hamnett, C. 1990: Migration and Residential social change: a longitudinal analysis of migration flows into, out of and within London, 1971–81. *Revue de Geographie de Lyon*, 65 (3), 155–63.

Hamnett, C. 1991: The blind men and the elephant: the explanation of gentrification. *Transactions of the Institute of British Geographers*, 16, 173–89.

Hamnett, C. 1994: Social polarisation in global cities: theory and evidence. *Urban Studies*, 31, 401–24.

Hamnett, C. 1996: Social polarisation, economic restructuring and welfare state regimes. *Urban Studies*, 33 (8), 1407–30.

Jager, M. 1986: Class definition and the aesthetics of gentrification. In N. Smith and P. R. Williams, (eds.), *Gentrification of the City*. London: Allen and Unwin, 78–91.

Knox, P. 1991: The restless urban landscape: economic and sociocultural change and the transformation of metropolitan Washington, DC. *Annals of the Association of American Geographers*, 81 (2), 181–209.

Knox, P. 1993: The restless urban landscape; economic and sociocultural change and the transformation of metropolitan Washington, DC. *Annals of the Association of American Geographers*, 81 (2), 181–209.

Lees, L. 1994: Rethinking gentrification: beyond the position of economics of culture. *Progress in Human Geography*, 18 (2), 137–50.

Ley, D. 1978: Inner city resurgence in its societal context. Mimeograph, paper presented at the AAG Annual Conference, New Orleans.

Ley, D. 1980: Liberal ideology and the post-industrial city. *Annals of the Association of American Geographers*, 70, 238–58.

Ley, D. 1986: Alternative explanations for inner-city gentrification: a Canadian assessment. *Annals of the Association of American Geographers*, 70, 238–58.

Ley, D. 1996: *The New Middle Class and the Remaking of the Central City*. Oxford: Oxford University Press.

Marcuse, P. 1986: Abandonment, gentrification and displacement: the linkages in New York City. In N. Smith and P. Williams (eds.), *Gentrification of the City.* London: Allen and Unwin, 153–77.

Marshall, G. and Rose, D. 1985: Proletarianisation in the British Class Structure? *British Journal of Sociology*, 24 (3), 377–96.

May, J. 1996: Globalisation and the politics of place: place and identity in an inner London neighbourhood. *Transactions of the Institute of British Geographers*, 21 (1), 194–215.

McDowell, L. 1997: The new service class: employment, gender and housing decisions among London bankers in the 1990s. *Environment and Planning A*, 29 (11), 2061–78.

Mills, C. 1988: Life on the upslope: the postmodern landscape of gentrification. *Environment and Planning D: Society and Space*, 6, 169–89.

Mollenkopf, J. and Castells, M. 1991: *Dual City: Restructuring New York*. New York: Russell Sage Foundation.

Munt, I. 1985: Economic restructuring, culture and gentrification: a case study of Battersea, London. *Environment and Planning A*, 19, 1175–97.

Murdie, R. A. 1996: Economic Restructuring and Social Polarization in Toronto. In J. O'Loughlin and J. Friedrichs (eds.), *Social Polarization in Post-Industrial Metropolises*, Berlin: Walter de Gruyter, 207–33.

Myles, J. 1988: The expanding middle: Canadian evidence on the de-skilling debate. *Canadian Review of Sociology and Anthropology*, 25, 247–67.

Preteceille, E. 1995: Division sociale de l'espace et globalisation: le case de la metropole parisienne. *Societies Contemporaines*, 22/23, 33–67.

Prince, H. C. 1964: North-West London 1864–1914. In Coppock, J. T. and Prince, H. C. (eds.), *Greater London*. London: Faber and Faber.

Redfern, P. 1997: A new look at gentrification: 1. Gentrification and domestic technologies. *Environment and Planning A*, 29 (7), 1275–96.

Rhein, C. 1998: Globalisation, social change and minorities in Metropolitan Paris, the emergence of new class patterns. *Urban Studies*, 35 (3), 429–48.

Rose, D. 1984: Rethinking gentrification: beyond the uneven development of Marxist urban theory. *Environment and Planning D: Society and Space*, 2, 47–74.

Rose, D. 1988: A feminist perspective on employment restructuring and gentrification: the case of Montreal. In J. Wolch and M. Dear (eds.), *The Power of Geography.* Winchester, MA: Unwin Hyman.

Sassen, S. 1991: *The Global City: London, New York and Tokyo*. Princeton, NJ: Princeton University Press.

Sassen, S. 1984: The new labor demand in global cities. In Smith, M. P. (ed.), Cities in Transformation, 26, *Urban Affairs Annual.* Beverley Hills: Sage.

Savitch, H. V. 1988: *Post-Industrial Cities: Politics and Planning in New York, Paris and London.* Princeton, NJ: Princeton University Press.

Schaffer, R. and Smith, N. 1986: The gentrification of Harlem? *Annals of the Association of American Geographers*, 76, 347–65.

Simmie, J. 1983: Beyond the industrial city. *Journal of the American Planning Association*, winter, 59–76.

Smith, N. 1979: Toward a theory of gentrification: a back to the city movement by capital not people. *Journal of the American Planning Association*, 45, 538–48.

Smith, N. 1987: Of yuppies and housing: gentrification, social restructuring and the urban dream. *Environment and Planning D: Society and Space*, 5, 151–72.

Smith, N. 1996: *The New Urban Frontier: Gentrification and the Revanchist City.* London: Routledge.

Walker, R. and Greenberg, D. 1982: Post-Industrialism and reform in the city: a critique. *Antipode*, 14, 17–32.

Warde, A. 1991: Gentrification as consumption: issues of class and gender. *Environment and Planning D: Society and Space*, 9, 223–32.
Wright, E. and Martin, B. 1987: The transformation of the American class structure, 1960–1980. *American Journal of Sociology*, 93, 1–29.

Chapter 29

Worlds Apart and Together: Trial by Space in Istanbul

Kevin Robins and Asu Aksoy

The rights of chaos, chaos too has rights.

Rosalind Belben, *Choosing Spectacles*

In his book *Vers la troisième ville?* Olivier Mongin (1995) reflects on what has been called the death of the city. It is in fact, he says, a question of two deaths: first, there has been the death of the urbanity associated with the "classic European city" (the "first age" of the city); and, then, that of twentieth-century urban modernism and its utopia of the Radiant City (the "second age"). Mongin's concern is with the possibilities for the rescue of urbanity, through the institution now of what he calls a "third age" of the city. This is our broad concern, too, and we want to give substance to our discussion by considering the urban question in one particular city, Istanbul. Istanbul's "first age" was different – it was as an Ottoman and Islamic city (Inalcık 1990) – but its "second age" was very much shaped by the modernist paradigm (involving, indeed, the conscious emulation of the European urbanist ideology). The city now is facing a fundamental challenge to its modernizing ethos, one that is associated with a growing polarization and politicization of space. In this context, we can perhaps identify some elements of what a new urbanism would have to be about, as well as what is blocking the institution of a "third age" urbanism.

We have to make a journey. It begins in Mecidiyeköy, a business district in the bustling center of Istanbul, where we take a minibus to Merter, located alongside the highway that goes out to the airport. Then we catch another minibus, and drive through district after working-class district – Şirinevler, Kocasinan, Küçükçekmece, Avcılar, old squatter areas that became peripheral municipalities in the 1960s and 1970s. The minibus travels on and on, constantly stopping to deposit passengers along the hectic highway and to hurriedly pick up new ones, until we have gone way past the airport, as if we were finally leaving the city behind, and then we skirt along the coastline of the Sea of Marmara. And after that we come to yet another expanse of urbanization, this one the consequence of the later migrations and settlements of the 1980s. At last, after one and a half hours on the hot and teeming road, we arrive at the minibus terminus and our final destination in the new municipality of

Esenyurt, 20 kilometres out of Istanbul. And what you see when you finally get to Esenyurt is really quite striking, not at all what you would expect if you weren't attuned to the unexpected developments that Istanbul always seems to throw up. It is a new kind of edge-city phenomenon, and one that in fact perfectly expresses the logic of end-of-century urbanization in this global metropolis. You can see it taking shape beside the massive new highway that now connects Istanbul to the Thracian city of Edirne.

On the left, if you are leaving the city, what occupies your field of vision is a vast expanse of *gecekondu*, or squatter settlements – dense and low-quality housing units, the earliest dating from the early 1980s, most of them in a permanent state of incompletion, with the vacant gaps of still unfinished floors and the antennae of concrete-encased construction metals sprouting from top storeys, in perpetual anticipation of future building activities, when the money comes in. This is the great squatter zone that grew up around, and quickly smothered, the old village of Esenyurt, to become, within a decade, virtually a city in its own right. For most established Istanbulians it is *terra incognita*, a place too far (effectively extraterrestrial). Like all the other squatter areas of Istanbul, it is generally regarded as a place of disorder, always a source of potential threat (as a breeding ground for religious fundamentalism or terrorism). For the most part, its social reality is disavowed, displaced by fearful images and fantasies of otherness. But, notwithstanding this resistance to its actuality, Esenyurt is most certainly part of the urban scene and reality of contemporary Istanbul, a very significant part of the late twentieth-century metropolis and its new kind of late twentieth-century urbanity.

And, if you turn your head towards the right-hand side of the Edirne highway, what you see is what seems, and in fact is, quite another world – a very different kind of urban development. What you confront is new and modern and purpose-built satellite towns (*uydu kentler*), and what you notice is a new world of seemingly luxurious apartment blocks with familiar, pattern-book postmodern design features, and of spacious and comfortable villas with large gardens and swimming pools. There are presently three such developments here. Bahçeşehir (which means Garden City) is the most established, with construction beginning in 1990, and also the largest, at around 13 million square metres; there are presently some 4,000 households living within its private and exclusive confines, and the number is projected to finally rise to 16,000. The other two developments, Esenkent and Boğazköy, encompassing 1 million and 2 million square metres of land respectively, are still in the early phase of construction, but will eventually contain around 13,000 housing units between them. Together, then, these three housing schemes will constitute a small city of a new kind, with a population rising to something like 120,000 people.

One way of making sense of what you see from the highway would be in terms of the contrast between old and new, in terms of a narrative of development from the apparent chaos of the *gecekondu* to the modern order of the new towns. Indeed, the new satellite districts are now being actively promoted as the prefigurative model for future housing and planning strategies in Istanbul – prototypes for the future city. In this particular Turkish context, one way of interpreting what is happening in Esenyurt might be in terms of the further extension and democratization of the long-term and "heroic" republican project for urban modernization (for a good account of the emergence and development of modernism in Turkish urban planning and architecture, see Bozdoğan 1997). What we will argue, however, is that this (predictable and complacent) narrative of progress in planning completely fails to address the significance of what is actually taking place on this edge of the city. For something extremely important is happening here, in the 1990s, to Istanbul's urban life and culture, but something that cannot be taken account of within the modernist conceptual grid. What we regard as remarkable is not the phenomenon of the satellite towns as such, but, rather, the logic that has conspired to produce this stark contrast between the new "modern" sites and the very different space of the squatter settlements. What is significant is the shocking juxtaposition of these opposed worlds of rich and poor, separated only by the *cordon sanitaire* of the main highway. Faraway, and yet so close.

How are we to make sense of this apparent fragmentation of urban space? In order to try to answer this question, we shall focus on the municipality of Esenyurt, and specifically on the relationship between its *gecekondu* area and its new zones of Esenkent and Boğazköy. We have chosen this particular area of the city because we think that it represents a microcosm of the kinds of change that are taking place more widely in Istanbul. The Esenyurt case demonstrates very well the way in which codes of spatial practice are moving towards an ever greater segregation of the urban scene, along class-based and identity-based lines. And, furthermore, it provides a valuable insight – valuable because it is counter-intuitive – into just how this logic of segregation has actually developed and progressed. Our central argument, grounded in what has happened in Esenyurt, is that the fracturing of the urban space has occurred, in large part, as an (unanticipated) consequence of the unfolding dynamic of the modernist-republican urban vision. We want to consider how it is that the policies and strategies of modern urban development and planning, which have always aspired to establish a coherent and integrated order in the urban environment, have actually and perversely come to be implicated in the process of fragmentation. We are concerned with the vicissitudes of urban modernism in Istanbul.

From a Village to a City

At the beginning of the 1980s, Esenyurt was no more than a village on the outskirts of Istanbul. During that decade, however, as more central locations ceased to be available, new migrants from Anatolia, and particularly, in this case, from the Kars region, increasingly began to settle at this great distance (20 kilometres) from the city. In 1989, the erstwhile village was made into a municipality, with a population of around 25,000 people. At that time there was no plan of any kind for the new urban settlement, and there was no urban infrastructure – no roads, no running water, no sewage system. The settlement was famous for its mud. More than anything else, the image of muddiness stuck to Esenyurt. It is said that when municipal officials went to the city center on business their shoes gave them away immediately, and that, out of embarrassment, they got into the habit of always carrying a spare pair of shoes with them. A promotional video – specially prepared by the Esenyurt municipality for the Habitat II conference, which was held in Istanbul in June 1996 – describes the district in its early days as being like a backward village, with new buildings being constructed one on top of another, according to the whims and desires of the new settlers, and with all the diseases that ensue as a consequence of such unregulated and unsanitary conditions. Esenyurt developed, then, as a typical *gecekondu* settlement, with all the problems associated with such settlements. And the problems could only escalate as, in the course of just a few years, through constant new waves of migration from the Anatolian countryside, the population of Esenyurt rose dramatically, reaching as much as 250,000 in 1996 (a 340–fold increase over 20 years).

Esenyurt was in many ways like all the other *gecekondu* zones, but, like them all of course, it has its own distinctive story, and it is this instructive story that we shall now recount. There is a key figure in the story of Esenyurt, and it has been his approach to urban planning that has brought the place into prominence. That figure has been Dr. Gürbüz Çapan, a medical doctor who has been the mayor of Esenyurt since the municipality was established in 1989. Çapan has a past history of involvement with radical leftist youth movements in the sixties and seventies, but now stands as an independent, and rather uncharacteristic, member of the centre-left Social Democratic Republican Party. As a former leftist, he had once actively encouraged the building of *gecekondu*s, adopting what was then conceived as a populist strategy for urban modernization. By the eighties, however, his views had changed significantly, reflecting a new and growing concern about what he perceived to be happening in these impoverished areas. Çapan was concerned about the throwing up of "ugly looking houses," coming to believe that the chaotic proliferation of squatter buildings was a sign that "the city ha[d] surrendered to the villager" (Öztürk 1997). And he was determined that Esenyurt should not fall into the disorderly confusion that was devastating other *gecekondu* areas – such as the notorious Ümraniye and Sultanbeyli "where rubbish tips had exploded, where people had been killed when they fell into potholes, and where mafias controlled the land market." The people were entitled, in his view, to more than just a shanty town – they were also entitled to a city.

Çapan and his team resolved "to bring a civilised way of life to a place with no urban culture" (*Cumhuriyet*, April 1, 1997). Esenyurt was described in one of the municipality's magazines "as a place with no architectural aesthetics, neither a city nor a village, lacking in trees, roads, water, infrastructure and social facilities." So, the bringing of civilization must, first of all, involve the very practical measure of building an adequate infrastructure to service the newly urbanized population, and then the drawing up of a rational development plan to ensure the coherent organization of the municipal space. But more was necessary. In the longer term, the new local authority came to believe, it was necessary to foster and sustain the very norms of a civilized urban culture. "Just imagine a place," Çapan is quoted as saying, "where there are goats, sheep, horses and cows... but where there is no respect for others, no culture of getting along together, and where everybody hangs on to their own village culture" (1997). He and his colleagues were putting forward a positive vision of urban life and culture, then, based on the integration and assimilation of the newly arrived populations into a common civic culture. The civilizing process must accordingly involve the imposition of a coherence and order on what was perceived as the unruly space of Esenyurt.

Now, it is important to be aware that this approach did not reflect a strategy that was new or that was particular to Çapan and his team. As we have already hinted, this kind of modernizing zeal already had strong roots in the culture, originating in the civilizing idealism of the nation-builders of the Turkish Republic. We may say that their approach to the modernization of Turkey, from the 1920s, involved the imposition of what they saw as a new rational order – based on the progressive values of European culture – over the disorderly remains of the Ottoman Empire (what has subsequently varied has only been the style in which the elites have gone about this reforming business – involving a difference between authoritarian and populist approaches). This reordering of the national space had to involve what Ayşe Kadıoğlu (1996: 86) describes as "an onslaught on the existing cultural practices . . . a process of estrangement of the people from some of their own cultural practices." Rationalization had to be achieved in spite of the people – and, more than that, in order to actually create the more civilized people who would then be fit to inhabit the newly civilized state. And this logic of rationalization had to extend to all forms of social management and administration. Thus, in the domain of architecture and urbanism, it became the imperative to create new rational spaces and places to accommodate the new model people. As Sibel Bozdoğan (1994: 46) puts it, "the mission of the new architecture in Turkey was narrating the modernity of the young nation as an idealised construct without conflicts and class antagonisms" (see also, Yavuz 1986). The modern city, like the modern nation, was imagined as a space that should be unitary, coherent, and ordered.

Çapan's approach was firmly grounded, then, in this modern, civilizing idealism. What it in fact represented, in the sphere of urban management, was a populist expression of the will to order, and one that was inspired by his leftist background. The aim was to bring about modernizing social reform by helping the people of Esenyurt to see what was in their best interests. In an interview with us, Çapan invoked the inspiring example of Fidel Castro, living with villagers in Cuba in the 1960s to show them how to improve their social conditions. In the same political mode, Çapan had believed that the only way of making the migrant villagers of Esenyurt understand anything new and modern was to show them how. So, he and his municipal team endeavored to teach the incoming squatters to build according to the new urban plan that had been instituted and, generally, to abide by the rules of city life. In essence, the new inhabitants of Esenyurt were expected to become assimilated into the modern space that they had now supposedly become part of.

To this end, it seemed vital to open up Esenyurt to the outside world and, thereby, to adapt it to the conditions of modern urban culture. A highly symbolic step in this direction was taken with the decision to construct a major new road linking Esenyurt to the main motorway network (when you approach the municipality the way we did, on the minibus through the older *gecekondu* areas, you are struck by the sight of what was an 8-meter-wide village road opening up into a 30-meter-wide, double-lane highway). When we spoke with Gürbüz Çapan, he put the point (using a medical analogy) that "if there was no main artery the city would die." He had anticipated that the highway would carry the lifeblood of commerce, communication, and culture to the community of Esenyurt. So adamant was he in this belief that he overrode any attempt by the locals to stop it, even going so far as to bulldoze through a site set aside by a group of religious activists for building a new mosque.

The reality of what eventually took place did not conform, however, to the master plan that the municipality was working to institute. The newly constructed road in fact turned out to be an exit route for what came to be an increasingly disillusioned modernizing vision. The municipality had succeeded in creating a new sewage and water system, and it had overseen the laying of a new communications network – as Çapan quite rightly observed, "no other municipality in Istanbul has done as much as we have." But what was becoming ever more apparent was that the recalcitrant citizens of Esenyurt could not be socially engineered into conformity with the municipality's program of urban rationalization. Çapan's well-laid plans were being thwarted by the very people who were supposed to benefit from them. "You couldn't intervene," he complained. "We came up with a plan in order to do this in an orderly fashion, but no one adheres to the plan." His modernizing aspirations, he acknowledged, "did not coincide with the realities of life." The migrants who came to Esenyurt brought with them their own culture, traditions and ways of living, and it seemed that these were resistant to the ordering zeal of the urban modernists. So, what Çapan then did was to use the new road to transport his vision beyond the intractable realities of Esenyurt.

From a City to a Satellite

Çapan's idealistic aspirations had been frustrated, but they were not diminished. The municipal team decided to tackle the problem of modernizing Esenyurt by means of a rather different strategy. It was proving impossible to introduce the kinds of changes that would turn Esenyurt into a "modern" city space. But perhaps it would be possible to institute the modern vision in an empty space – a space, that is to say, devoid of the established culture that was proving to be so inimical to rational ordering in Esenyurt. So, the road that Çapan had opened in Esenyurt became the means to transpose his urban project to the green field sites of Esenkent and Boğazköy. After three years in office, Gürbüz Çapan embarked on a huge project to build a modern satellite town at the edge of Esenyurt, on the other side of the Edirne highway, and adjacent to the already developing satellite development of Bahçeşehir. What he was now proposing to do was to take the people of Esenyurt away from the squatter conditions that seemed to stand in the way of their modernization, and to relocate them in a new and ordered environment that would, it was envisaged, facilitate their conversion finally to modern urban values. The new satellite towns of Esenkent and Boğazköy were envisaged as places in which it would be possible to create a new urban culture guided by the principles of modern civilization. "Muddled urbanisation is not our fate," declared Çapan (1994), "Low- and middle-class people can lead a civilised life in a city like Istanbul without having to bow to land speculators and without having to build illegal settlements." Esenkent was conceived as "not only a housing scheme, but also an alternative lifestyle." What was not possible in the actual space of the city would be achieved through the planned contrivance of a new synthetic space.

The way in which Gürbüz Çapan set about realizing his new project was really quite remarkable, and even heroic. What he did, in a move that was quite unprecedented, was to seize a vast tract of land (more than a million square metres) which was privately owned by a commercial holding company. "It is the first time," he defiantly claimed, "that private land has been appropriated and distributed to the people" (quoted in Öztürk 1997). One cannot but admire the nerve and audacity with which this Robin-Hood-style action was carried out. Even as acrimonious battles raged on, in and out of the courts, the Esenyurt municipality had set about transferring the land to housing cooperatives, which immediately began to construct the housing units that would constitute the new satellite colonies. When the legal situation was finally resolved, the land had been appropriated for significantly less than the going price (and the fact that this land was right next to Bahçeşehir, which was having great success in attracting the middle and upper classes of Istanbul, meant that its value continued to soar). What this act of public expropriation testified to was the persistence of the radical populist dimension in Çapan's urban political strategy.

But this populism was, for the most part, a gesture to the past, and now only constituted a residual element in Çapan's approach to the urban question. How the great land seizure was justified and its legality defended reveals what had come to prevail in his approach. Çapan and his lawyers made inventive use of an old law (Law 775) – passed in 1966 with the intention of halting the spread of *gecekondu* settlements and establishing so-called "prevention areas" – which had made it possible for state land that was deemed to be under threat from prospective squatters to pass into municipal ownership, along with funds to permit the rehabilitation of the land through new housing schemes for poor families. Their great and unprecedented coup was to draw on this law to legitimate the annexation of private property. What they argued was that this act of expropriation was entirely in conformity with the spirit of the law, in so far as it was intended to inhibit the development of illegal *gecekondu* settlements on the property and to provide shelter for the poor and deprived citizens of Esenyurt. Esenkent was intended, in Çapan's words, to be "a shanty town prevention district" (quoted in Öztürk 1997). It would demonstrate how a modern city for the people could be brought into existence, on land that had been returned to the people.

But, as we have said, Çapan was distancing himself from his former populism – he even suggested that the new housing projects of Esenkent and Boğazköy should be regarded as "an apology from the Turkish left to the people of Turkey" (Öztürk 1997). Esenkent came into existence out of a desire to create a contemporary urban space – a space like Bahçeşehir – for the less privileged inhabitants of Esenyurt. The slogan that drove the project forward was "contemporary living is everybody's right." Today's visitors to Esenkent are greeted by road signs that declare this to be "the route to contemporary life." Esenkent was to be both a modern and a model city, with green areas and parks, shopping centers, schools, and a hospital, and cultural and sporting facilities. The architecture of the new settlements was resolutely modern, though very dense, and intended to symbolize and sustain the lifestyles of contemporary urban culture. Shopping centers and social services were located in such a way as to provide easy access. Especially in the case of Boğazköy, the planners and architects sought to engineer every small aspect and detail of the urban environment so as to promote "the advancement of social relations" (this meant such features as public squares, cycling routes, pedestrian zones, pavements suitable for push chairs, facilities for the disabled, meeting places for women, and so on). What these satellite developments were seeking to create was spaces that could be characterized as "warm," "secure," and "human." The overriding ideal was that of order.

The objective was to bring into existence a newly ordered urban culture. If it was the case, in Esenyurt, that people had grouped according to their particular village identities, thereby contributing to fragmentation and insularity in urban culture, Çapan was resolved that, in Esenkent and Boğazköy, he would promote social interaction and integration. Culture was considered to be central to this project of creating a new and more convivial urbanity. Thus, an important and symbolic project was the construction of an open-air theatre: with a seating capacity of 4,000, it was the second largest in Istanbul, and was regarded as being a major cultural contribution from the periphery to the center of the city (it was said that Esenkent had "crowned Istanbul" with a major cultural institution). But, more than just a cultural project, Çapan's might also be regarded as a civilizational one, concerned to demonstrate how a new kind of urban living could be brought into existence in empty space. He has described it as a "social peace project" (see Ekinci 1996). The new development would constitute a melting pot and would promote social and cultural integration. No matter where they came from, the people who lived in this new urban space should learn to share and enjoy a common urban culture.

Two Kinds of People

The satellite project was in the heroic tradition, and driven by a great modernizing idealism. In its aspiration to reorder the city, or rather to constitute an alternative order beyond the imagined disorder of the old city, it constituted a utopian plan for the future of a part, at least, of Istanbul. The municipality's avowed intention was "to transform the migrant populations, who had become marginalised as a result of the damage they had inflicted on the city, into citizens who would take care of the trees, the roads and the green areas, and who would put pressure on the authorities with their democratic demands" (Esenyurt Municipality 1996). But again the project to institute a new urban order and model citizenship did not evolve as the municipal authority had anticipated (as with all such utopian projects it ran up against the human resistance to rationalization). In this instance, what happened was simply that the people of Esenyurt – the people in whose name the project had been undertaken – did not choose to come and live in the new districts.

Even though the cooperatives of Esenkent and Boğazköy would allow them to pay for new apartments in installments, it still seemed as if the costs of moving were beyond their means. But, far more crucially, it became apparent that they actually preferred to stay in Esenyurt and to hold on to their properties there. For these properties actually offered them far greater flexibility in managing their lives, with possibilities always to adapt or extend the structures that they had built, according to new circumstances. They were concerned, too, with making future provision, not just for themselves, but for extended families and dependents. For them, a house was not just a machine for living in, but the focus for a complex network of social relations, responsibilities, and obligations. Quite simply, in the environment of Esenyurt, which they themselves had built, and where they felt a sense of involvement, they could feel more in control of their destinies. There was simply too much to lose by moving to Esenkent and investing in Çapan's vision of the modern city and citizenship.

What then happened in Esenkent and Boğazköy was very significant, and also very much against the grain of the municipality's ideals and idealism. For the social vacuum was quickly filled by another population, and one that did find something very appealing about the new settlements. As advertisements and newspaper articles started to appear, praising Esenkent for its modern identity, its urban qualities, and its convenient facilities, so it began to attract the attention of a wider constituency, composed of mainly middle-class people from Istanbul. These new kinds of incomers to the periphery were in search of precisely what Esenkent did have to offer. For them, in spite of their density, the apartment blocks represented the possibility of acquiring an "ideal home." This ideal, as Ayşe Öncü points out, was all about enjoying the pleasures of a modern lifestyle – the apartment is, for the middle classes, a symbol of status and respectability, a place in which they can realize and express their newly acquired consumer identities – defined in absolute contrast to the chaos that they felt the rural migrants had brought into the city with them. Their modern space was a clean and orderly space, quiet and traffic-free, and with the clean air and unpolluted surroundings that an almost rural environment (located 20 kilometres from the center of the city) could promise. Such a space could accommodate a purified modern lifestyle, in retreat from everything that Istanbul had become as a consequence of its actual modernization.

What was bringing these respectable, modern migrants to satellite living was the cultural order that was associated with modern living in the marketing campaigns for Esenkent and Boğazköy. It was a question, not just of a safe physical environment, but also of a comfortable cultural environment. "What captured the imagination of Istanbul's middle classes, and became the focus of their desires, observes Ayşe Öncü (1997: 61), "was the homogeneity of a lifestyle cleansed of urban clutter – of poverty, of immigrants, of elbowing crowds . . . – a world of safe and antiseptic social spaces." They were drawn by the image of "a homogeneous, safe, orderly environment, distant both spatially and socially from the heterogeneous populations of Istanbul," a space in which they could sustain and enjoy together the "cherished purity of their own 'Westernised' way of life" (1997: 68–9). The appeal of the new satellite spaces would seem to lie in the clarity and homogeneity of their social order – which is, of course, utterly antithetical to any real ideal of urbanity. Esenkent and Boğazköy came to afford the middle classes the opportunity to shape their own social space, in seclusion.

Most discussions of contemporary urbanization in Istanbul conclude that its problems, maybe even its crisis, are a consequence of migration and the proliferation of unplanned and unruly *gecekondu* settlements. Now we must, indeed, accept that there is some truth in this judgment – and we should try to be lucid in analyzing what kind of truth it really is. But what we have been concerned to address in this discussion is the more counter-intuitive proposition that the modernizing agenda has also been implicated – and is perhaps now more than ever implicated – in what is wrong with Istanbul. We must recognize – as in the case of the Esenyurt municipality – that the program for urban modernization has been driven forward on the basis of altruism and social amelioration. And we should take note of the importance attached by the modernized or modernizing citizens of the city to a clean and safe quality of urban life. But we think it is absolutely necessary, nonetheless, to then go on to challenge the apparent self-evidence of the modernist vision and sensibility. We must be prepared to consider the awkward possibility that what presents itself in terms of being a solution to the contemporary urban question may, in fact, turn out to be making a significant contribution to the problems of the city now.

This – unintended and unacknowledged – contribution has largely been a consequence of the universalizing aspirations of the modernist project. The project has been all about imposing a comprehensive order on the perceived disorder of the urban space. Urban planners have assumed, and commonly insisted, that their own vision of the city is one that should be shared by all inhabitants of the city. Because they think of it as an enlightened vision, and seemingly cannot think of it in any other way, they make the assumption that acceptance of its premises is natural and, ultimately at least, ineluctable. And because they consider their own particular vision to be both rational and benign, they are likely to conclude that those who dissent from it are irrational and subversive. The dilemma is that the rationality of the plan is always fated to be at odds with the disorderly reality of actual urban conditions. This, as we saw, has been the perpetual bane of those who were seeking to impose their rational blueprint on the irregular lifeworld of Esenyurt. In Esenyurt, in the end, it became clear that the modernizing vision just could not accommodate the awkward disposition of migrant culture.

It is the growing recognition of this incapacity that is now bringing into prominence a second, and potentially more disturbing, problem with the modernizing agenda. The failure to recruit the others to their civilizing mission has begun to lead many who enjoy a modern lifestyle to rethink their approach to the city. And what they are deciding is that they will henceforth seek to realize their objectives, not at the scale of the city as a whole, but through the construction of small islands of modern urbanity. This new approach has become manifest through the proliferating development of housing schemes like Bahçesehir, Esenkent, and Boğazköy. Here we see how an ideal that once had universal and inclusive aspirations has come to express itself as no more than the survival strategy of a particular group of people. What they are seeking to create at the outer edges of Istanbul are new kinds of self-contained, self-sufficient, and self-regarding community. In these satellite colonies, it will be possible to sustain modern identities and modern lifestyles, in sequestration. Communities in orbit. This insular variant of modernism is choosing to turn its back on the city at large. In its new solipsistic form, we think that the modern vision threatens to promote greater segregation and consequently division in Istanbul.

We have heard it said that there are two kinds of people in Esenyurt: there are those who elect to live in comfortable and ordered conditions, in Esenkent; and there are those who prefer and choose to live in the conditions of squatter existence, in Esenyurt. What is implied is that there is one group that is urbane and civilized, and another that is primitive and uncivilized in its urban culture. Everything is in this implication. The former are constituted as the ones who must deal, in whatever way, with the problem that is created by the existence of the latter. And, in the very form in which the urban question is imagined and conceived, the very impossibility of its resolution is guaranteed.

Trial by Space

The modernist agenda dominated the discursive space of Istanbul even as the *gecekondu* culture came to prevail over the physical space of the city. But now, as circumstances have made their ideological supremacy seem increasingly vain, the proponents of the modernizing agenda are feeling the need to assert themselves through more than just words. Now there is a growing recognition that the control of real space is as important as – and perhaps more important than – the control of the city's intellectual and symbolic space. What we see in Istanbul at the century's end is an escalating struggle between competing social groups to register their existence on the urban scene – the growing politicization of urban space.

The middle classes, who suspect that they can no longer expect the city as a whole to develop in conformity with their own urban ideals and aspirations, are now choosing to invest both their resources and their identities in the new satellite developments at the edge of the city. And the poor and migrant populations of Istanbul continue with their illegal building activities on whatever land they can appropriate. What is consequently taking shape, through the ensuing frenzy of building activity, is an increasingly segmented and segregated urban landscape, a landscape of striking, often obscene, contrasts. Esenkent and the even more exclusive Bahçeşehir – which is selling luxury villas and even "intelligent houses" ("everything that a civilised person would aspire to") stand just across the road from, and in full view of, the poor and deprived *gecekondu* settlement of Esenyurt. The escape capsules of the affluent next to the survival zones of the urban poor. Worlds apart, but fated to be worlds together in space.

It is in space, said Henri Lefebvre, "that each idea of 'value' acquires or loses its distinctiveness through confrontation with the other values and ideas that it encounters there":

> Moreover – and more importantly – groups, classes or fractions of classes cannot constitute themselves, or recognise one another, as "subjects" unless they generate (or produce) a space. Ideas, representations or values which do not succeed in making their mark on space, and thus generating (or producing) an appropriate morphology, will lose all pith and become mere signs, resolve themselves into abstract descriptions, or mutate into fantasies (Lefebvre 1991: 416–17).

Today, Lefebvre maintained, no one can avoid "trial by space." Our discussion has precisely been concerned with how such contestation is pushing and pulling on the contemporary urban space. In the particular and distinctive circumstances of Istanbul, and more specifically of Esenyurt, we can see, all too clearly, how competing social groups, vigorously striving to make the presence of their end-of-century identities felt, are now dramatically recasting the morphology and texture of the city.

REFERENCES

Bozdoğan, S. 1994: Architecture, modernism and nation-building in Kemalist Turkey. *New Perspectives on Turkey*, 10, 37–55.

Bozdoğan, S. 1997: The predicament of modernism in Turkish architectural culture: an overview. In S. Bozdoğan and R. Kasaba (eds.), *Rethinking Modernity and National Identity in Turkey*. Seattle: University of Washington Press, 133–56.

Çapan, G. 1994: 1993 onur yılımız. *Çağdas Kent ve Yaşam*, 2 (3), 1–23.

Ekinci, O. 1996: Istanbul'u Esenket'te temize çektik, *Cumhuriyet*, April 15.

Esenyurt Municipality 1996: *Habitat II'ye doğru kentleşme, kooperatifleşme ve Esenkent-Boğazköy*. Istanbul: Esenyurt Municipality.

Inalcık, H. 1990: Istanbul: an Islamic city. *Journal of Islamic Studies*, 1, 3.

Kadıoğlu, A. 1996: The paradox of Turkish nationalism and the construction of official identity. *Middle Eastern Studies*, 32 (2), 177–93.

Lefebvre, H. 1991: *The Production of Space*. Oxford: Blackwell.

Mongin, O. 1995: *Vers la troisième ville?* Paris: Hachette.

Öncü, A. 1997: The myth of the "ideal home" travels across cultural borders to Istanbul. In A. Öncü and P. Weyland (eds.), *Space, Culture and Power: New Identities in Globalising Cities*. London: Zed Books, 56–72.

Öztürk, N. 1997: Esenkent, the Turkish left's apology to the people. *Turkish Daily News*, July 11.

Yavuz, Y. 1986: Turkish architecture during the Republican period. In G. Renda and C. M. Kortepeter (eds.), *The Transformation of Turkish Culture: The Atatürk Legacy*. Princeton, NJ: Kingston Press, 267–83.

Chapter 30

Value Conflicts, Identity Construction, and Urban Change

Lily L. Kong

In this chapter I argue that urban landscape changes are simultaneously the medium and outcome of the intersection of different sets of values. In other words, urban forms result from and contribute to the conflicts between different value systems, often represented by economic values privileging growth and redevelopment on one end of the spectrum, and more symbolic values giving prominence to, inter alia, the conservation of heritage and culture, on the other. Oftentimes, such value systems reflect the interests of different social, economic, and political groups, whose divergences take shape variously as contestation between state and civil society, for example, between urban planners and heritage groups, or tourism planners and local interest groups. Such value conflicts, it may be argued, shape the different identities that different groups (wish to) construct for their cities. At the risk of oversimplification, it may be said that pro-development groups are concerned with developing a city that is characterized by modernity while pro-heritage groups are more enamored by cities identified with history, culture, and other symbolic values. In this chapter I will illustrate these relationships between value conflicts, urban identities, and landscape changes using the example of Singapore. As a city-state, Singapore provides a unique case study for the analysis of how state policies at a national level impinge on the shaping of values, the construction of identities, and the development of urban form in a direct way, without mediation of local government. As a state with a strong central government bent on developing a "tropical city of excellence" (Urban Redevelopment Authority Annual Report 1991), and a multiracial and multireligious population that is becoming increasingly educated, the potential for conflict between different value systems is tremendous.

Singapore: A Developmental City-State

The city-state of Singapore has been described in many arenas as one of the world's economic miracles today. Indeed, Castells (1992: 56) argues that this achievement of economic success, with its concomitant high rates of economic growth and urban change, qualifies Singapore as a developmental state because the government calls upon these indices of development to legitimize itself. Yet, when the island-state first attained internal self-government in 1959 and then full independence in 1965, the government inherited a host of problems, chief of which were unemployment, housing shortages, unsanitary conditions, and poor economic performance. From the throes of Third World poverty and underdevelopment, the country has made the quantum leap to the status of newly industrialized country within two decades.

Many of these achievements are reflected in the tremendous urban change that has taken place over the last three decades. Slums and squatter settlements have been cleared, the housing landscape is now characterized mainly by high-rise public Housing and Development Board (HDB) flats, unhygienic roadside hawkers have been rehoused in modern hawker centers, and sanitary conditions have been vastly improved. All these have been made possible via a systematic urban planning process under the auspices of the Urban Redevelopment Authority (URA), with the cooperation of other state agencies such as the HDB. This urban planning process has, for a long time, been premised on the logic and rationality of economic planning, in which development goals have taken precedence over other symbolic values, be they historic, cultural, sacred, personal, social, or esthetic. It is only in recent years that there has been tangible evidence that parts of the urban fabric are being retained, a reflection perhaps of increasing appreciation of the cultural and historical values of these built forms. Indeed, in recent years, government leaders have called for the preservation of cultural forms and the values they embody as a way of "anchoring" Singaporeans in their "Asian identity" (URA Annual Report 1988/89: 21) which unfortunately had been systematically eroded with the large-scale demolition of parts of the city.

In what follows, I will explore the interconnections between symbolic values in the urban landscape on the one hand, and economic values, manifested in development imperatives, on the other. I argue that the urban conflicts that result are a reflection of a struggle over identity, involving the state, different groups of civil society, and the individual. The struggle involves finding a balance between developing a city that is plugged in to the global network, that is international in outlook, and carries a cosmopolitan identity, and a city that is simultaneously anchored in local heritage, retaining indigenous identities.

For heuristic reasons, I will polarize the possible interconnections between symbolic and economic values and their manifestations in the urban landscape. First, I will focus on the circumstances under which there are open contradictions between symbolic systems and economic values. I will do so by discussing the establishment, relocation, and demolition of religious buildings in Singapore, all of which follow pragmatic planning principles, and illustrate how they sometimes run counter to the sacred meanings and values that adherents invest in their religious buildings. Second, I will illustrate the situation when development openly harnesses history and culture, where they become part of the processes of production and consumption associated with capital accumulation. In other words, I will explore those situations where history and culture become commodified in heritage and culture industries, often anchored in tourism.

The Establishment, Relocation, and Demolition of Religious Buildings

One arena in which conflict arises between culture and capital is in the establishment, relocation, and demolition of religious buildings (see Kong 1992, 1993a and 1993b for further details). First, in the establishment of religious buildings, the state is guided by "rationality" and "pragmatic" planning. Specifically, the state sets aside parcels of land for tender by religious groups. These parcels of land are usually found in HDB new towns, allocated on the basis of the neighborhood principle, adapted from British and European town planning practices. The basic planning philosophy is maximum self-sufficiency in the satisfaction of basic community needs and so within each neighborhood there will be shopping facilities, community centers, recreation facilities, schools, medical care, and the like for residents. If there are more than three neighborhoods close together, then a town or district center will be built to provide higher-order goods and services, such as banks, theaters, cinemas, and department stores (Teh 1969: 175; Drakakis-Smith and Yeung 1977: 6). A strongly modernist stance is thus evident in town planning in which the successful formula is based on efficiency and functionalism (Ley 1989: 47–51). Urban planning, it would appear, is not primarily a matter of esthetics or meanings, but of economics, and the basic guiding principle is to increase the working efficiency of the city.

Given these underlying values, religious building sites are provided in new towns as another amenity which sections of the population require. Precise planning standards guiding the minimum provision of such sites are drawn up as they are for other amenities, as shown in Table 30.1. These guidelines take into consideration "demographic characteristics," "religious habits," as well as space requirements and architectural design for the different religious groups (Correspondence with Strategic Planning Branch, URA; and Systems and Research Department, HDB). These planning standards are reviewed periodically in the light of demographic and social changes. The precise sites are usually proposed by the HDB and submitted for consideration to the Master Plan Committee and approval of the Ministry of National Development.

While the state uses these openly economic principles and processes, for religious adherents the establishment of a place of worship should be guided by divine will and purpose. The following discussion, drawn from in-depth interviews with Christians, Hindus, Muslims, and Chinese religionists in 1989 and 1995 bears this out. As

Table 30.1 Planning standards for the provision of religious sites

Religious building	Approx. site area	Planning standard
Church	3,000 m^2 to 4,500 m^2	1 to 12,000 d.u.
Chinese temple	2,000 m^2 to 3,000 m^2	1 to 9,000 d.u.
Mosque	2,500 m^2	1 to 20,000 d.u.
Hindu temple	1,800 m^2 to 2,500 m^2	1 to 90,000 d.u.

d.u.: dwelling unit

Source: Systems and Research Department, Housing and Development Board, 1999

Cheng, a Methodist suggested, it is faith that underlies the setting up of churches and which "sweep[s] [people] to do as the Spirit leads them." The tension arises particularly when the two differing ideological systems embodied in pragmatic planning (championing economic values) and divine guidance (highlighting cultural meaning) pull in different directions. For example, in seeking to establish a building for worship, a group may feel that it is the divine will and that the community is ready for it and needs it. The rationality and pragmatism of planning principles, however, may suggest that such a group cannot be offered any site for use. In the case of the Mount Carmel group, for example, Wong (1986) chronicles the way in which the group felt divine guidance led them to set up a church building (today the Clementi Bible Centre), and how the "rational" and "pragmatic" planning procedures made it difficult for their efforts to be realized quickly. For instance, in the planning blueprints, there were "no designated religious sites available" where they requested one; when they tendered for a site in Pasir Panjang, they lost. Wong (1986) clearly illustrates the disappointments and frustrations that the group felt as a consequence of such conflict between their religious needs and the strictures of planning and developmental goals. Further evidence that economic imperatives are seen to be the overriding force in urban change is reflected in public conceptions that agencies and plans operating on principles of economic logic inevitably hold sway. Typical comments which illustrate such resigned acceptance include, for example, "HDB holds all the power. What right do we have?" Or, "If it is in the Master Plan, there is nothing we can do about it. We have to accept it."

This conflict between cultural and economic logic becomes more stark in situations involving relocation and/or demolition of religious buildings. I will elaborate on one of these situations, namely, when the sites of religious buildings are affected by public schemes. In 1973, a policy statement was made which asserted that "as people move out from old areas to be redeveloped, temples, mosques or churches will have to give way to urban renewal or new development, unless they are of historical and architectural value" (Press Statement, November 25, 1973). In other words, religious buildings will be treated like any other building which may come in the way of development. While there are religious buildings which have been preserved for architectural and historical reasons by the Preservation of Monuments Board (Kong and Yeoh 1994), there are none which are not historically and architecturally significant which have nevertheless been preserved because they are recognized as sacred space. Indeed, Dr. Tan Eng Liang (the then Senior Minister of State for National Development), further declared: "The resettlement policy is clear-cut, irrespective of religions, irrespective of owners and irrespective of organisations" (Parliamentary Debates, March 16, 1978, col. 978). In putting this policy into practice, the government acquired and cleared 23 mosques, 76 suraus (small mosques), 700 Chinese temples, 27 Hindu temples, and 19 churches for public development schemes between 1974 and 1987 (Press statement from Prime Minister's Office, October 3, 1987). Even though religious groups may be offered alternative sites, such sites are not offered on a one-to-one basis for "pragmatic," "economic" reasons: "It is not possible to have a temple for temple, a mosque for mosque, a church for church substitution. This is uneconomic, impractical and, in the limited land space of Singapore, impossible" (Press Statement, November 25, 1973). Instead, religious buildings affected by clearance (usually effected through the Land Acquisition Act) are primarily allocated land on a joint basis. In other words, one site is made available to two or more existing buildings of the same religion. In one instance, as many as eight Chinese temples were affected by clearance and because each could not afford a new place, all eight groups came together to build one temple (in 21 Tampines Street) to rehouse them all (*The Straits Times*, July 8, 1986).

Apart from religious buildings which have no choice but to leave under the force of the Land Acquisition Act, in some instances, the lease may have run out for the religious site just as redevelopment is about to take place. In such instances, the lease will not be extended, and those affected may not be allocated land. They will then have to tender and pay market value for sites set aside by the HDB for religious use, or sites put up for sale to religious groups and associations by the URA. This has caused some smaller religious buildings to close down completely because they could not find suitable alternative sites or because they could not afford the cost of new sites (*The Straits Times*, June 15, 1979).

While the development imperatives have taken precedence, many religious adherents in fact conceive of their religious places as sacred places that should not be destroyed, irrespective of their architectural or historical merit. This religious (cultural) symbolic value is manifested in a variety of ways. It is evident, for example, in those adherents who believe that religious places are intrinsically sacred, that is, the place is in and of itself spiritual because of its association with some form of divine manifestation or with some sacred event of tremendous significance (Tuan 1974: 146). For instance, Chandran, a devout elderly Hindu interviewee, cited the example of how a person may be told by a god (perhaps through a dream) that a temple is to be built on a particular piece of land, or that the god wants to reside there. The land and the temple thus constructed are therefore sacred. This, in fact, is believed to be the case for the Kaliamman temple at Old Toh Tuck Road, which was originally located at Lorong Ah Soo. Its founder had apparently been told in a dream by the deity of the new site and as a result, the temple had been moved to the new location. In such an instance, any attempt to demolish or relocate the temple for development purposes would not only represent the triumph of economic values over symbolic ones, it would be a serious defiance of divine will.

The conflicts between symbolic and economic values, as evidenced in the examples above, suggest divergences in identity construction. The identity that the state seeks to develop for Singapore is one premised on development, modernization, and growth. On the other hand, the values that are central to religious individuals suggest the importance of self-identities rooted in more symbolic and spiritual dimensions. To realize these self-identities requires that certain urban forms, namely, religious buildings, exist, following particular symbolic principles of existence. These tensions are constantly negotiated through the urban landscape, as the state renegotiates its own position on the importance of symbolic values (as evidenced in the next section) and as religious individuals themselves also renegotiate the centrality of urban forms in their spiritual identities (see Kong 1993b).

The Built Environment: Heritage and Conservation

Earlier, I indicated that parts of the urban fabric have been conserved in recent years. I also suggested that some of these include religious buildings which have been preserved for their historical and architectural value. Taken at face value, it may well appear that such conservation of the historic urban landscape is a distinctly "cultural" process, illustrating how cultural values have been given weight vis-à-vis the earlier dominance of economic imperatives. Yet, in what follows, I will show how culture and history are taken into the process of capital accumulation (see Kong and Yeoh 1994 for a more detailed discussion).

Despite the earlier priority given to demolition and redevelopment, conservation was given initial attention on the planning agenda in 1976 when the URA initiated studies involving the conservation and rehabilitation of whole areas. Chinatown was the most prominent among the large areas then under study (URA Annual Report 1976/77), and the guiding principle then was basically to retain the distinctive identity and character of the whole area. However, the study remained at the exploratory stage and little more was done for a long while. In 1984, the Emerald Hill area was converted into a landscaped pedestrian mall and the Peranakan Corner at the junction of Emerald Hill and Orchard Road was completed. These became the first tangible results of the URA's conservation of distinctive areas (URA Annual Report 1983/84: 22–3). This was quickly followed by detailed studies of Chinatown, Singapore River, Little India, and Kampong Glam in 1985 (URA Annual Report 1984/85: 3), which were presented to the public as the URA's Conservation Master Plan in 1986. The plan included the conservation of the city's historic district, named the Civic and Cultural District (MND Annual Report 1987: 35; Huang, Teo and Heng 1995). The area was given further attention in the form of a Master Plan released to the public in March 1988, with aims to develop the area into a major historical, cultural, and retail center, as well as a venue for national ceremonies and functions (URA Annual Report 1987/88: 2). In the same year, conservation manuals and guidelines for Chinatown, Kampong Glam, and Little India were also published, designed to help the public understand the historical character, planning, and architectural intentions in each district and assist them in conserving their properties. Ultimate recognition and acknowledgment were accorded to all these efforts in 1989 when the URA was made the national conservation authority. Their tasks were laid out in the Amended Planning Act of 1990, and included identifying buildings and areas of historical interest for conservation; preparing a conservation master plan; and guiding the implementation of conservation by the public and private sectors (Sections 10(6)(c), 13, 14 and 15, Planning Act, 1990). Since then, 20 areas have been officially designated "conservation areas."

What does the shift from the early preoccupation with redevelopment to the recent concern to conserve reveal of the place of cultural and historical values vis-à-vis economic ones? First, as intimated earlier, it signals a recognition of the value of Singapore's architectural and historical heritage (URA Annual Report 1986/87). Second, this change was precipitated by developments in the tourist industry. In the early 1980s there was a sharp fall in the rate of tourist arrivals. This led to the formation of a Tourism Task Force which was to identify the main problems and suggest solutions. One of their conclusions was that Singapore had "removed aspects of [its] Oriental mystique and charm . . . best symbolized in old buildings, traditional activities and bustling roadside activities" in its effort to construct a "modern metropolis" (Wong et al. 1984: 6). To woo tourists back to Singapore, it was recommended that Chinatown and other historical sites be conserved. That their recommendations were taken up reveals clearly the mutually constitutive relationship between capital and culture. Today, parts of Chinatown have already been conserved in accordance with stringent guidelines pertaining to the facade design, internal structure, signage, materials used, and any other forms of alteration or addition with a view to retaining historical continuity and the architectural distinctiveness of the place (URA Annual Report 1988: 52). Following these guidelines, property owners and developers have refurbished the visual and structural quality of shophouse units including their wall openings, five-foot ways, columns, pilasters, window shutters, balconies, and ornamentation. Yet, the fact that these are not purely "cultural" actions but economic ones as well is revealed in two ways: the ways in which shophouses are developed and marketed to businesses; and the ways in which the area as a whole is "imaged" and "sold" as a tourist spot.

Shophouses are sold on the market as "heritage" properties of particular interest to retailers wishing to "capture the shopping and gourmet traffic right in the traditional retail heart of Singapore" (*The Straits Times*, September 23, 1991). The URA has guided the process by encouraging certain types of building use and discouraging others. Approved trades include those usually identified as symbolic of Chinese tradition such as herbal tea shops, religious paraphernalia shops, Chinese medical halls, clog makers, mahjong makers, calligraphers, and fortune tellers. On the other hand, certain pollutive or incompatible trades are proscribed, such as engineering workshops, tire and battery shops, Western fast-food restaurants, supermarkets, and laundrettes (URA Annual Report 1988: 72–3). Within these broad parameters, however, URA's underlying philosophy is that the types of trades should be determined by market forces. This is because owners of conserved buildings must be economically viable in order to continue to restore and maintain them (*The Straits Times*, October 23, 1991). Thus, while meticulous attention is paid to preserving buildings and other structures, lifestyles and trades are left to the vagaries of free competition (*The Straits Times*, October 23, 1991). Yet, as many retailers rightly fear, such a system inevitably squeezes out the small, traditional businesses which cannot afford the postconservation rent hikes. It is in fact only the new upmarket services such as pubs (for example, Elvis in Tanjong Pagar), restaurants (for example, Blue Ginger in Neil Road) and businesses (such as Carrie Models in South Bridge Road) that can afford to operate in "new" Chinatown. In other words, the ostensibly "cultural" process of conservation is intimately embedded in processes of capital accumulation in which principles of profitability are prioritized.

As another example of how history and culture in Chinatown become embedded in processes of capital accumulation, I will focus on how conserved Chinatown caters to the tourist gaze. It is sold as the cradle of Singapore's early civilization and is identified in the Singapore Tourist Promotion Board literature with the pioneering spirit and enterprise of early Chinese immigrants to Singapore. It is showcased as a distinctively Chinese cultural area, what with the newly conserved shophouses, carefully adhering to preexisting architectural styles, "[brimming] over with life, capturing the essence of the old Chinese lifestyle in its temples and shophouses and nurturing a handful of traditional trades [such as] herbalists, temple idol carvers, calligraphers and effigy makers... in the face of progress" (Singapore Tourist Promotion Baord 1991: 28–9). Against a backcloth of shophouses and temples, large-scale festival activities, fairs, wayangs (operas), puppetry, and trishaw rides can be "staged" to provide both locals and tourists with "a different kind of experience" (URA Annual Report 1985: 15). No matter if these no longer provide the genuine pulse of everyday life and no matter if they are performances rather than quotidian experiences. They form a crucial part of a promotional image which upholds a heritage industry.

Yet, for many Singaporean Chinese who live and work in Chinatown, the cultural life of the place does not simply derive from the architectural form but in genuine longstanding trades and small businesses, and the concomitant familiar retailer–client relationships that do not exist any more with the new gentrified shops managed by new people. They are not convinced that conservation is for the locals. While they see the conserved shophouses as "nice and charming," they add that "they are not for us anymore," that "locals do not carry out purchases there but go simply to look," and that "the wares there are sold at tourist prices." While the spanking cleanliness and bright hues of the conserved rows of shophouses are generally seen as attractive, some feel that they "somehow don't look right," that they are "inauthentic," and that with the emphasis on the picturesque, they are suitably tailored to appeal to the "tourist's way of seeing" (Relph 1976: 85). That conserved Chinatown is a landscape made for tourist consumption is particularly evident when dusk approaches and tourists are bussed off: Chinatown residents assert that the place takes on the "silence of a ghost town without a soul in sight" compared to before when it "can be said to be a place with no night." Thus, Singaporeans interpret the Chinatown landscape as another promotional effort for the tourists, far removed from the practicalities of their own daily lives. Hence, the conserved Chinatown landscape ignores "the inner workings of culture" (Wagner and Mikesell 1962: 5). In being taken up in the process of capital accumulation, culture and history are harnessed in particular ways suitable to the imperatives of economic growth and development.

Another example of how culture and history are to be harnessed for economic ends is the case of the conservation of the Convent of the Holy Infant Jesus (CHIJ) in Victoria Street, which housed a convent, a Gothic chapel, and two Catholic schools. In 1981, a special area conservation working group was appointed under the auspices of the Urban Redevelopment Authority, comprising representatives from the URA and the then Singapore Tourism Promotion Board (STPB, now Singapore Tourism Board or STB). The final report put together by this working group was completed late that same year, in which several dozen sites were put up for consideration as conservation areas. The central quadrangle of CHIJ was one of them.

As a concrete step towards conservation, the STPB invited architectural firms to study the potential ways in which the buildings could be restored. The study was aimed at helping the board evaluate and shortlist a panel of architects able to undertake individual restoration projects. From late February 1987 onwards, 48 architectural firms were involved in the study, with the hope that about $260 million worth of restoration work would be bid for. An indication of what the STPB was hoping for was couched in the suggestions put forward by Mrs. Pamelia Lee, then STPB's Divisional Director for Product Development, to the Singapore Institute of Architects. These included the following: that any proposal would respect the architecture and former use of the premises; that the buildings could provide quality entertainment such as music and dance performances for audiences of "refined taste"; that the upper floors of the buildings could be leased to the performing arts for daytime operations; and that the ground floor and open spaces could be operated commercially for high-quality dining and entertainment, theme parties, and the like (*The Straits Times*, April 13, 1987). Up to this point, conservation of the CHIJ buildings were still understood to be the business of the state and its agencies (whether URA and/or STPB), with the understanding that there would be every effort to preserve the ambience of the chapel and its buildings against the commercialization of other like projects.

In March 1990, it was announced that the CHIJ site was to be tendered out, opening it to the vagaries of the commercial market. As many former students and other members of the public argued, private developers would not be able to maintain the character and mood of the place if they were too preoccupied with making it a commercial success. The URA on the other hand expressed the view that the government cannot finance all conservation projects; the private sector must be involved to ensure that conservation projects are economically feasible undertakings. The guiding principles in Singapore's conservation, as expounded by the then Chief Executive Officer and the Chief Planner of the URA, Mr. Liu Thai Ker, were that the private sector should be involved, particularly if no public sector use had been identified; that preservation must avoid wastage or duplication of efforts; and that buildings of architectural and historical significance should either be preserved or conserved. The decision to sell the site and hand over its conservation to commercial enterprises raised the ire of many. Public opinion focused on the view that by not undertaking the conservation exercise itself, the URA was in effect serving the complex on a platter to the forces of commercialization and all its concomitant ills of profit making. In response to such criticisms, the URA revealed that safeguards had been introduced to ensure that conservation objectives were met. For example, the project's plot ratio would be kept to under 0.8 as opposed to 9 or 10 in the surrounding commercial developments, that is, there would be no high-rise construction. The chapel was to be used only for cultural, religious or other uses that are "sensitive to the history of the building," for example, for classical concerts. For the rest of the complex, cultural, arts, and recreational activities were possible, including restaurants and shops, with trades, if they enhanced the image of the Civic District. The local consortium led by construction group Low Keng Huat (LKH), including jeweler Je Taime and restaurateur Lei Garden, won the bid on the basis of their "planning and design concept, proposed uses and trades," "the expertise of the developers and their consultants in developments of a similar nature" (*The Straits Times*, March 22, 1990).

Between their initial winning of the bid in February 1991 and 1994, the LKH consortium, first known as Cloisters Investment Pte Ltd, and subsequently Chijmes Investments Pte Ltd, has altered its marketing strategy – a reflection of its concern with economic viability and the changing retail scene in Singapore. The plans that were initially submitted included cultural and religious activities for the chapel, while the rest of the complex was given over to dining, retail, and exhibition activities. Their plans were to create an upmarket, exclusive image of the complex. It was envisaged that the chapel could be rented out for weddings or other celebrations or used as a center for cultural activities. Because of the superior acoustics, it could be used for music, dance, and drama performances. A courtyard of about

10 meters deep would be built in the basement, serving as a focal point for cultural activities such as musical performances. It would be surrounded by two levels of retail shops and a food court. The retail space would house upmarket boutiques, gift shops, and a jewelry centre. Indeed, a suggestion was made that the complex could be a one-stop place for a wedding celebration: after the ceremony in the chapel and reception in the courtyard, dinner could take place in the restaurant.

In early 1994, it was announced that the original concept of a retail complex with a food court would shift towards the establishment of an arts and lifestyle-based complex. The theme of fine food would still continue in the underground complex, together with an upscale flea market for art and antiques. The chapel would have its functions expanded from services and weddings (and Japanese going abroad for their weddings are also targeted) to include even company annual general meetings with state-of-the-art facilities (with rentals at about $5,000 a day). A permanent attraction would be negotiated in the form of a UK-based play, "Earth Child," for children aged between 8 and 12 (an acknowledgment of the fact that the site was always important as a school). The defining theme of the complex, it was said, would be a mix of the sense of the old as well as a sense of the upmarket. Hence, it would be possible to have a McDonald's if it looked old, while modern art would be totally acceptable if it was housed in a fine gallery. There were also plans for a brewery pub. Clearly, with unease about the continuing size and buying power of the market, Chijmes had chosen to broaden its clientele base from an exclusive upmarket one to a diversified base which would perhaps include the mass hamburger-eating public.

From the time of the decision to conserve the complex of buildings to Chijmes's mid-1990s marketing strategy ("Give the future of your business a glorious past"), all the changes reflect the constitutive relationship between historical and cultural values and economic principles. History and culture can be harnessed for economic goals, and history and culture have survived and been given a new lease of life precisely because of economic goals.

Once again, the urban form reflects and contributes to divergences in values and identities among different groups of Singaporeans. The state, as represented by its urban planners and tourism promoters, privilege economic values and give space to historical and cultural values only when they are handmaiden to developmental goals. Indeed, attempts are made to appropriate historical and cultural sites for economic ends. The identity to be constructed for Singapore is still one of an international city, but concomitantly, one with an "Asian" heritage as well. Capital, as represented by developers, retailers, and service providers, is driven by profit motives, and any identity to be evolved, whether international and modernist, or historical and heritage-based, is secondary to how well each may contribute to its ultimate goals. For individuals – especially former residents (including students) and former retailers of conserved districts and buildings – the "spirit" and identity of place, rooted in history and community life, are eroded with commercialization.

Conclusion

The identities that different groups seek to construct for their cities suggest divergences in value systems that simultaneously result in and are shaped by particular urban forms. Using the debates and operations surrounding urban (re)development, I have illustrated how a small city-state of no more than 640 square kilometres embodies multiple differences in values and identities. In attempting to achieve this aim, I have polarized the possible interconnections between different value systems by focusing on situations where there are conflicting symbolic systems and economic values; and situations where development openly harnesses history and culture, where they become part of the processes of production and consumption associated with capital accumulation, that is, when they become commodified.

What I have also sought to illustrate is how a global city such as Singapore is inherently a city of division and difference, pulling particularly in two directions: between modernity and internationalism, built on economic processes and economic rationality, on the one hand, and heritage, culture, and tradition, premised on symbolic value systems, on the other. And yet, the divergences are not simply clear-cut and separate. In fact, through conservation and adaptive reuse, history and heritage have been appropriated to play a constitutive role in urban transformation, and contribute to the sustenance of economic development. Not all histories and cultures are elevated, however. While histories and cultures of value (in economic terms) find their way onto the conservation agenda, others become ignored or marginalized. In other words, histories and cultures which are less challenging to development objectives are privileged while those which cannot be so readily appropriated into development goals are sidelined. This refraction of the past attests to a range of differently empowered ideologies that are constantly engaging one another in an apparently global city like Singapore, plugged as it is into global economies.

REFERENCES

Anderson, B. 1983: *Imagined Communities: Reflections on the Origin and Spread of Nationalism*. London: Verso.

Castells, M. 1992: Four Asian tigers with a dragon head: a comparative analysis of the state, economy and society in the Asian Pacific rim. In R. Appelbaum and J. Henderson (eds.), *States and Development in the Asian Pacific Rim*. Newbury Park: Sage, 33–70.

Drakakis-Smith, D. and Yeung, Y. M. 1977: Public housing in the city states of Hong Kong and Singapore. Occasional Paper 8, Development Studies Centre, Australian National University, Canberra.

Huang, S. et al. 1995: Conserving the civic and cultural district: state policies and public opinion. In B. S. A. Yeoh and L. Kong (eds.), *Portraits of places: History, Community and Identity in Singapore*. Singapore: Times Editions, 24–45.

Jacobs, J. 1992: Cultures of the past and urban transformation: the Spitalfields Market redevelopment in East London. In K. Anderson and F. Gale (eds.), *Inventing Places: Studies in Cultural Geography*. Melbourne: Longman Cheshire, 194–211.

Kong, L. 1992: The sacred and the secular: exploring contemporary meanings and values for religious buildings in Singapore. *Southeast Asian Journal of Social Science*, 20 (1), 18–42.

Kong, L. 1993a: Ideological hegemony and the political symbolism of religious buildings in Singapore. *Environment and Planning D: Society and Space*, 11 (1), 23–45.

Kong, L. 1993b: Negotiating conceptions of sacred space: a case study of religious buildings in Singapore. *Transactions of the Institute of British Geographers*, NS 18 (3), 342–58.

Kong, L. and Yeah, B. S. A. 1994: Urban conservation in Singapore: a survey of state policies and popular attitudes. *Urban Studies*, 31 (2), 247–65.

Ley, D. 1989: Modernism, post-modernism, and the struggle for place. In J. A. Agnew and J. S. Duncan (eds.), *The Power of Place: Bringing Together Geographical and Sociological Imaginations*. Winchester, MA: Unwin Hyman, 44–65.

MND Annual Report 1987: Singapore: Ministry of National Development.

Relph, E. 1976: *Place and Placelessness*. London: Pion.

STPB 1991: *Singapore: Official Guide*. Singapore: Singapore Tourist Promotion Board.

Teh, C. W. 1969: Public housing. In J. B. Ooi and H. D. Chiang (eds.), *Modern Singapore*. Singapore: University of Singapore Press, 171–80.

Tuan, Y. F. 1971: Man and nature, commission on college geography. Resource Paper No. 10, Association of American Geographers, Washington DC.

Tuan, Y. F. 1974: *Topophilia: A Study of Environmental Perception, Attitudes and Values*. Englewood Cliffs: Prentice-Hall.

URA 1985: *Conservation within the Central Area with the Plan for Chinatown*. Singapore: Urban Redevelopment Authority.

URA 1988: *Historic Districts in the Central Area: A Manual for Chinatown Conservation Area*. Singapore: Urban Redevelopment Authority.

Wagner, P. L. and Mikesell, M. W. 1962: General introduction: the themes of cultural geography. In P. L. Wagner and M. W. Mikesell (eds.), *Readings in Cultural Geography*. Chicago and London: University of Chicago Press, 1–24.

Wong, D. W. F. 1986: *The Building of a Dream*. Singapore: Christian Life Publishers.

Wong, K. C. et al. 1984: *Report of the Tourism Task Force*. Singapore: Ministry of Trade and Industry.

Wong, Poh Poh 1969: The surface configuration of Singapore Island: A quantitative description. *Journal of Tropical Geography*, 29, 64–74.

Wong, Poh Poh 1989: The transformation of the physical environment. In Kernial Singh Sandhu and Paul Wheatley (eds.), *The Management of Success: The Moulding of Modern Singapore*. Singapore: Institute of Southeast Asian Studies, 771–87.

Part IV Public Cultures and Everyday Space

Chapter 31

City Publics

Gary Bridge and Sophie Watson

The open, civilizing and democratic possibilities of cities have always fascinated urbanists. Here the dimensions of that literature are mapped out along three axes: the relationship between the notions of the public realm and city space, conceptions of "the public" and "the private," and the relationship between the "extraordinary" and the "everyday." Much of the existing literature on these issues assumes and is developed from, the experience of Western cities, a tendency we hope to avoid here. We explore these themes in terms of the relationships between conventional notions of the public realm – formal and institutional – alongside more informal, everyday practices through which the public is negotiated.

The social consequences of urbanization were a preoccupation of late nineteenth- and early twentieth-century Western writing on cities. Simmel ([1903] 1995) saw a blasé attitude to others developing as a response to the overstimulation of the city and from the pressure of capitalist markets to reduce all social encounters to the equivalent of exchange value. The industrial capitalist city became a place of suspicion, competition, and retreat into self. Tonnies ([1887] 1957) argued that cities separated out the multiple social ties of community (*gemeinschaft*) and made social exchanges specialized and one-dimensional in forms of urban association (*gesellschaft*). Wirth (1938) saw the size, density, and heterogeneity of cities resulting in a form of alienation or anomie. For some, the city of alienation and indifference meant being ignored and abandoned. For others who had command of the money economy and who benefited from living in a patriarchal society, it meant ease of movement and stimulation. Thus Walter Benjamin's figure of the *flâneur* (Benjamin 1969) was able to move through different spaces of the city and watch its activity but was not necessarily committed to, or embedded in, any of them.

Richard Sennett has long argued (Sennett 1974) that this sense of indifference and uncertainty in the city in Western culture changed the character of the public realm and encouraged a retreat into the private realm of the family and close friends. This public realm acquired a geography in the coffee houses and cafes of the seventeenth- and eighteenth-century city where the issues and the people discussing them were open to scrutiny. As cities grew and social relations were more influenced by industrial capitalism this urban arena broke down as people sought retreat in the private sphere. The public realm became one of studied impersonality, impartiality and rationality in the engagement with others. Yet for Sennett public urban spaces and the social heterogeneity of cities still offer more radically open and unpredictable encounters in ways which are socially progressive and civilizing. Unpredictability, spontaneity and a certain disorder (Sennett 1970) were at the core of Sennett's vision of a city that was based on encounter and performance in the public realm. Sennett (chapter 32 of this volume) opposes his view of the importance of performativity and the city as *teatro mundi* to the ideas of the city as impersonal rationality and self-repression that so preoccupied Simmel and others. Yet at the same time he concludes that the privatization of urban space and the separation of different groups has continued apace in the car-oriented, decentralized city. The problem is not one of overstimulation but understimulation and the loss of the public realm, a further restriction of the performative possibilities from which his analysis seeks to revivify the city.

For other writers urban public space is not so inclusive and potentially progressive. The unpredictability of encounter in cities may also result in conflict or a pervasive feeling of threat. Attacks, rapes, and mugging in certain spaces that are public in the sense that they are accessible to all, but are not safe for all (underpasses, concealed alleyways, nonresidential streets) have been of particular concern for women for example (Valentine 1989). Yet the streets are a contradictory site of the public for women. Victorian morality kept women off the streets (the prostitute or streetwalker was constructed as another category of woman) but the streets were also the spaces of freedom for women, away from the suffocation of the gendered space of the home and the private realm (Walkowitz 1992; Wilson 1992). Women who roamed the streets (the figure of the *flâneuse*) were unsettling for male society. What these contributions reveal is the contradictory nature of urban public space for women.

This contradiction has been encoded in urban planning. Notions of the public as open but impersonal became embedded in the physical design and planning of Western cities, and colonial cities. The building of, and access to, public space (parks, baths, libraries) was one of the great achievements of the municipal revolution in many Western cities. Yet at the same time it instilled an idea that space had to be ordered and rational and that in some senses space itself was neutral, in the Kantian sense, a container of activity. In contrast Sennett (1970) looks to heterogeneous spaces to bring different groups into performative encounter and this would work against the rationalizing and separating influences of urban planning and its tendencies to separate social groups and land uses. The links between a realm of encounter and the space of the city might not rely on the careful planning of public spaces but might be created through the encounters (chance or otherwise) in the everyday spaces of the city (streets, yards, stores). This is something that Jane Jacobs (1961) recognized in her analysis of movement, interruption, and encounter produced by the mixed activities of a New York street. Everyday spaces of the city can constitute a public realm.

In Western cities the idea of the "public" city and the "private" suburbs has strongly influenced planning regulations. These have essentially privatized women, leaving them confined to the domestic sphere in the suburbs or with an increasingly difficult mix of paid employment, child-care responsibilities, and domestic work in a city which separates all these features through planning and zoning regulations (McDowell 1983; Watson 1988). Feminist writers (e.g. Sandercock and Forsyth 1992; Hayden 1981) seek to influence design and planning to promote a nonsexist city. Other feminist negotiations seek to make the private public by publicizing activities that are normally confined to the private realm (such as childrearing and domestic tasks) or exposing private practices, such as domestic violence, to legal intervention.

City space is amibiguous for women not just because of the way certain parts of the city are occupied by men or the sexist nature of some social interaction in public but also because the "urban public realm" has been constituted as settled, predictable, rational, and monumental – and male. Other groups offer resistance to this dominant representation of public space. The significance of being identified with certain distinct parts of the city has been noted for some time in the case of the gay community (Chauncy 1995; Mort chapter 26 of this volume) and increasingly the lesbian community (Bell and Valentine 1995). It is also important to make an impression on public space both as an affirmation of identity and political statement – in bars and clubs and on the street, most famously in the form of the gay and lesbian Mardi Gras in Sydney (Murphy and Watson 1997).

The relationship between public space, access to that space and constructions of identity is a recurrent theme in writing on the city. Ambiguity, fluidity, and movement are metaphors that figure strongly in a number of the contributions in this section. As Jonathan Raban (1974) observed over a quarter of a century ago the "soft" areas of the city are the ones that are hard to define in any way and are often the most stimulating and challenging. The ambiguous nature of urban space for different groups is also problematic for the notion of a singular public realm. Fraser (1990) for instance suggests that these differences constitute distinct public realms rather than a singular public realm. She is concerned with the balance between a politics of representation and recognition. Exclusive public realms (what she calls "subaltern counter publics") might enable the disempowered to gain recognition.

We can see that "the public" is constituted in terms of recognition and interaction in city space. It is also constituted in the institutional realm, in forms of representative organizations and city governance. The attempt to fix the public realm in cities was often tied to certain spaces but also to a distinct form of "public" service provision. The period of rapid urbanization in Western cities led to all kinds of urban deprivation, poor housing, and health (graphically noted by Engels ([1844] 1993) in Manchester and the subject of philanthropic surveys of Booth and Rowntree in London). The great municipal reforms sought to counter this urban malaise. They resulted in the expansion of the public provision in municipal and city government policies to provide basic infrastructure such as drainage and street lighting but also the construction of public spaces in the form of parks, squares, libraries, and public baths. This reformist liberal conception of public provision had a profound influence on the built form and democratic realm and was most noticeable in large cities. It had the effect of interconnecting the notion of the public with the state and certain settled spaces in cities. Indeed Castells (1977) saw the provision of bundles of public goods as the primary role for cities in capitalism. Recent developments in the privatization, putting out, and marketization of public provision represent a rupture of the link forged in that earlier period between "public" service provision, the local state, and public spaces in cities.

A more important role for local government is now a feature of many non-Western cities. There has been a pervasive trend of decentralization of responsibilities for city governance away from the national state down to the regional and local level (Habitat 1996). For some, such as Castells (1997) this is an effort to sidestep the legitimation crises faced by many national governments and push the blame for lack of services down to localities. For others (such as Habitat) there is a suggestion that it results from elements of necessity – structural adjustment programs imposed by the World Bank and IMF have limited central government finances for welfare provision. But they also suggest an empowering element to this with increased democratization and links between an enhanced local state and grass-roots organization over service provision in cities. So it could be argued that such shifts represent the potential for a rejuvenated public realm in many non-Western cities.

It is instructive to think of conceptions of power and through what practices, institutions, and discourses the public is constituted. In many non-Western cities the formal public realm was something remote from the mass of the population, often tied to colonial interests and latterly to export markets and tourism. Indeed in thinking about the relations between the public and the private it is important to remember that most of the space of the cities worldwide and the majority of their activities are in private hands: not open to public scrutiny and secluded from areas of encounter. Most commercial and residential properties, and therefore land areas of the city, are held by private individuals. Although there are still tracts of land and monumental buildings, owned by the public, in terms of infrastructure, government, and other public buildings the privatization of urban space seems to be increasing. In many non-Western rapidly developing cities, the private ownership of land combines with the inability of governments to get access to it (either via the market because it is too expensive for cash-starved governments or because of the absence of legal mechanisms such as compulsory purchase, or through a lack of political will, or a prevailing regime of corruption).

Such land supply bottlenecks lead to massive shortfalls in housing provision resulting in homelessness or very poor accommodation for the mass of the cities' population who find their own solutions via squatting on unused land and self-provision of shelter. These "informal" organizations are significant not just for the provision of basic services but as a way of constructing a new public realm, a form of grass-roots representation. Although such social movements are generally targeted at specific issues it is clear that a number of them have had significant impacts on urban governance. Especially important are women's movements – such as those for political participation in Guadalajara, Mexico; neighborhood handicraft associations in Santiago, Chile; and struggles for health care in São Paulo, Brazil (Habitat 1996: 168). The growing importance of feminist movements in all their diversity in the cities of the world has been noted by Castells (1997, chapter 4). Despite the pervasive force of gender divisions, these movements represent a reconstitution of the public realm in relation to issues of work, health, and home; production and reproduction; and the toleration of difference.

The importance of women's movements points to a realm between the public and the private – that of civil society. For Gramsci civil society had a significant impact on the historic blocks of allegiance between groups in society. Castells (1997) sees civil society as an arena to perpetuate the state but also deeply rooted in the everyday lives of people. This implies that the arenas of the state might be seized without direct violent conflict. But civil blocks in society need not be active and progressive. Recently Maffesoli (1996) has argued that there has been a growth in tribal-like groupings based on niche markets for products, identity politics, and other loose associations, independent of government and political representation: neither private nor public. The significance of social networks and social capital in economic activity has been argued by Putnam (1995) and this civil arena has also received attention in Western nations as a resource in welfare economics – the so-called "third way". Here informal cultural and social networks are seen as economic and personal resources to assist in caring, job search, and skill enhancement. It is argued that this realm can provide welfare in ways not possible via the private market (capitalism) or public provision (socialism) thus throwing responsibility back on to groups who may be ill-equipped to respond.

Similar arguments about the significance of community are also being emphasized by communitarians against assumed universalizations of individualistic capitalism or remote state socialism (Etzioni 1993). However Young (1990ab) provides a useful warning that communities can be every bit as oppressive as individualism is alienating. They may also be imagined rather than constituted in material practices, or posited as homogeneous and cosy as opposed to fractured and constituted by power. And as Short reminds us (chapter 2 of this volume) they can be fascistic, prejudiced, and exclusionary.

Whatever the merits of the community as a sphere between the public and the private such connections are being made with great results under conditions of necessity rather than choice in many non-Western cities. The provision of credit, employment, housing, and some social services is made via grass-roots activity in informal social networks in the barrios and bustees. It is perhaps in non-Western examples that we find the realization of Castells' ideals in *The City and the Grassroots* (1983).

Against the efforts of urban social movements to open up the public realm, urban space is being increasingly privatized or savagely withdrawn, particularly in the downtown areas, to serve the interests of the growing middle classes and to sanitize the streets for the tourist gaze. Street traders, hawkers, and the homeless are purged from the streets to make way for a certain sort of public life that serves the interests of the wealthy and the "formal" economy. This goes for Western cities as well. At the extremes the privatization of public space becomes fortress-like and militaristic as private interests exert literal or symbolic violence on those urban dwellers whose presence unsettles economic interests. There are roll-top benches to prevent rough sleeping in Los Angeles (Davis 1990) for example, and militaristic sweeps of city streets in Yogyakarta to clean up the street children. Harriot Beazley (chapter 40) describes the violence and depredations that infuse the lives of the street boys of Yogyakarta whose grip on the city, and indeed life itself, is often very tenuous. Yet she goes on to show how the in-between spaces of the city also become a resource – for meeting and mutual aid, for work, for sleep, for escape from the city. Here we have the construction of a public and private life all within the public and liminal spaces of the city where public space is a place of temporary security with the constant threat of brutality.

There has been a significant literature in urban studies on "the end of public space" (Sorkin 1992; Mitchell 1995). This focuses on how the hitherto open and uncontrolled public spaces of the city, sites of unpredictable encounter, have been either made subject to controls and surveillance or have been made into semiprivatized spaces. The enclosed atrium replaces the courtyard, the shopping center replaces the street. The power of private capital to thematize and commodify these spaces as sites of consumption further degrades the opportunity for idling, casual mutual performance and display, and chance engagement. Urban spaces have been Disneyfied.

Yet such nostalgic formulations of a lost public space themselves construct an idealized perspective. If the new shopping centers and atria represent the end of democracy, public space must once have been open to participation, engagement, and control of the majority. Or to put this another way, who were the public of these lost public spaces, who was included and who was excluded, and for whom were these public spaces formerly more public (Deutsche 1996: 285)? In her discussions of public art Rosalyn Deutsche takes this further in asking how "images of public space create the public identities they seem merely to depict?" (1996: 286). What is important she suggests is how these images construct a public, what imagined identities are evoked for those that occupy the prescribed site, and whose identities are being reinforced.

The possibility of affirming identities in the public spaces of the city are inscribed in power relations and are thus conflictual. Rather than adopt Habermas's notion of the public sphere as a potential space for consensus, rationality, and implicit homogeneity, it may be more useful to imagine public space as constituted by difference and inherently unstable and fluid. Following Pringle and Watson's argument (1992) that interests do not exist as already fixed outside the state, but instead are formed within, and themselves form, the very arenas of the state, so identities are constituted by and constitute the public spaces of the city. Such a process can never be complete and as Mouffe (1992: 234–5) suggests, a democratic public sphere is predicated on difference, divisions, exclusions, and open contestation rather than on the imposition of unity, homogeneity, or consensus. Perhaps as Deutsche proposes, psychic anxiety lies beneath this mourning for a lost public sphere, when these responses may instead be read as "panicked reactions to the openness and indeterminacy of the democratic public as a phantom – a kind of agoraphobic behaviour adopted in the face of a public space that has a loss at its beginning" (1996: 325). In other words there never was a public sphere that included everyone, and maybe these new privatized/ public spaces of the city simply include a different public.

Disputes over the assumptions behind constructions of the public and the private are not confined to Western scholarship on Western cities. They also mark the boundaries of assumptions from a Western experience and the contrasts (as well as similarities) in non-Western urban realms. Non-Western cities disrupt many assumptions about the relationship between the public and the private even further. What in the West is treated as the domestic realm is lived out in public in many cities. In Hanoi for example men are shaved on the street – see Figure 31.1. The domestic realm is also often the site of production for the public economy. Homes are sites of economic production and often exchange of goods. At the same time some urban homeless create spaces of privacy through marking territory when all they have is public space – now more clearly a feature of Western cities also.

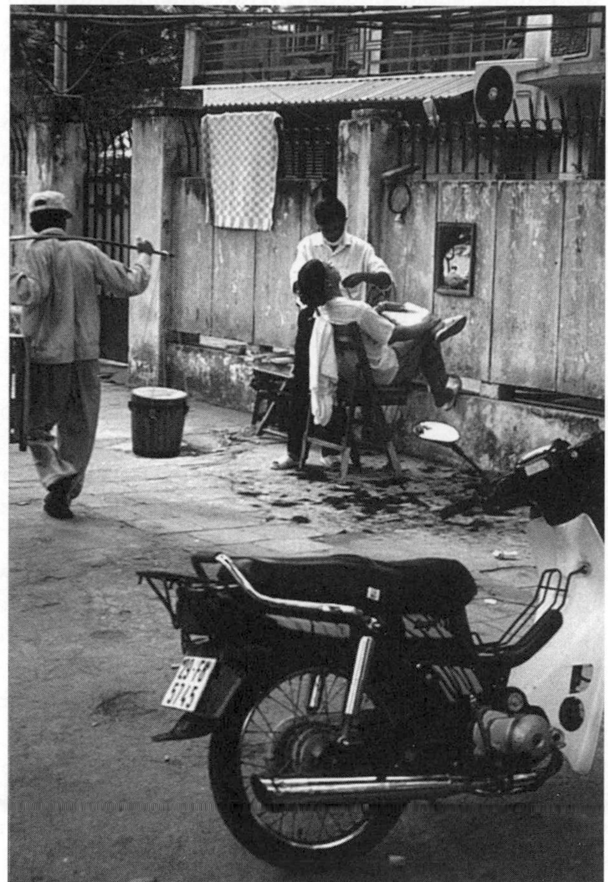

Figure 31.1 Street barber in Hanoi (© Sophie Watson)

Studies of public life in Western cities are secular. Whereas the public in Western cities is infused with impartiality and rationality, in many non-Western cities it is experienced through the partiality of the figure of the monarch or through religious observance. As Annette Hamilton (chapter 39) describes, in Bangkok much of the public life of the city is expressed through the personage of the King. At most times separate and secluded from the public the King's person becomes important at certain ceremonies (such as the annual Ploughing Ceremony to celebrate the beginning of the agricultural season) or in certain spaces, such as Sanam Luang, a public open space and royal cremation ground. The vertical city represents the cosmology of merit. These sacred/personified meanings of the public demand a reexamination of the public and the city.

This interweaving of the public and the private indicates the degree to which much of the prior discussion of the public realm and everyday life has been based on Western cities. It also shows how those prior assumptions are being questioned and discussion raised about the ambiguity of the public and the private, the monumental and the everyday in critical readings of Western cities as well.

This transgression of the public and the private, the intimate and the abstract, is felt in other ways. The separation of public and private so long pursued in Western cities has also been a highly visual act (Benjamin 1969; Sennett 1990) which has led to the representation of conceived space in the planning imaginaries as a visual act, an act of putting at a distance and separating out. As Urry (chapter 33) argues other senses might enhance the sense of leakage between these realms as the city is experienced in everyday life. Smell cannot be so easily controlled as the gaze and can lead to a blurring of the public and the private as intimate smells leak into the public arena and public smells invade private spaces. The politics and technology of the control of smells says a great deal about the more subconscious governmentality of the city and the separation of public and private.

The dimensions of the relationship between the public realm and urban space have brought into question the notion of the everyday and everyday life. There has been a rapidly burgeoning literature adapting notions of the "everyday" to city life. For Lefebvre (1991) the everyday was the arena where capitalist alienation was greatest (or constant) and yet was also an escape route via the extraordinariness of the mundane (a Sunday in the country as a form of resistance and celebration). The everyday is set up against the systemic oppressions of capitalism or bureaucracy or commodification. For Habermas (1984; 1987) the everyday lifeworld has been separated out and made provincial by "the system" – but it still retains the possibilities for communicative action and the reconstitution of the degraded public realm via communicative rationality and discourse ethics. For de Certeau (1984) it is the repository of an array of tactics of resistance. Many of these themes are explicitly spatial breaking down the quotidian violence of rational planning – in a form of "pedestrian rhetoric," a different way of inscribing the city through walking. By following the critical signposts, Gibson and Rossiter (chapter 37) reflect, on walking through the city one can draw in different experiences of the city. Gibson and Rossiter discuss how a supremely commodified space (a department store window) is transformed through perfomativity into a domestic space, and the renewed sense of encounter between the performers living in the space and the audience on the street and the expressions of care this encourages. The ordinary becomes extra-ordinary and the street perfomativities can become a new space for politics and a public realm. More traditional forms of protest can also be made significant almost by their ordinariness and occupation of public space – witness John Paul Jones's inspiring description of the street politics of Jackie Smith (chapter 38).

As we have seen, much of the discussion of the public has been constituted in terms of the oppressive practices of the state (in the form of rational bureaucratic planning for example), or the economy resulting in the decline of the public realm. Alternatively, it might be constituted as a hyperpublic realm of surveillance and control in this totally administered and panoptic world (Foucault 1991). Equally the conceived spaces of planners and the preoccupations of urban scholars have rested with noticeable public space, of monumental public space. Recent writing on the city asks us to look elsewhere for the public. Thrift (chapter 34) begins by quoting Musil that there is nothing so inconspicuous as a monument; we must have other sensitivities to the city, in the mundane practices of everyday life. Sennett has argued that productive urban encounter will not be the impartiality of rationality but the performance of the *teatro mundi*, while Thrift takes hold of the performative turn in social theory to look at the positive elements of contemporary city life. This is not about the center and the public, nor the private and periphery, but the liberating aspects of the gesture and the hitherto unnoticed. Gibson and Rossiter see public performance from within the commodified space of the department store window. Democracy might be relational and dialogic rather than representational and institutional. The street politics of Jackie Smith is a deadly serious performance to reactivate and animate (rather than simply make public) the memory of Martin Luther King. But as John Paul Jones acknowledges, perhaps King lives through the activities of both the King museum and the street protest of Jackie Smith, and the street that separates these two activities is the key zone of engagement – the public realm.

These developments represent a decentralizing of public space. They build on the ambiguity about public spaces in the city first advanced by feminist scholars, and open up possibilities in the interstices of everyday life. But everyday life need not mean copresence. There are new public spaces that have nothing to do with physical copresence. The openness of cyberspace is one possibility for unpredictable encounter (taking full account of the social selectiveness of global unevenness of access to this medium). There is a transformation of the intimate. Cyberspace also presents us with the possibilities of a spaceless public realm. Paradoxically it also has the potential to open up new spaces for "the public" in particular cities. Graham and Aurigi contrast global cybercities and virtual cities. The local participatory possibilities of virtual cities open up the possibilities for non-copresent participatory democracy.

Mediated interactions and the nature of a tolerant public realm also preoccupied Iris Young. She sees the city as a type of relationship and one that might lead to a new conception of the public. It is a coming together of strangers but one which posits tolerance and a civilized engagement – "the acknowledgement of unassimilated otherness." Here the public is a climate of mutual civility that is respectful of others in all their aspects. This seems to be a long way from where we started with the rough and tumble of encounter and discomfort that Sennett advocated. And this is one of the key elements on which contemporary discussions of the public realm and everyday space turn. Is the public a realm of encounter and activity (through traditional notions of politics and collective action and social movements) or is it one of inaction, mutual regard and understanding, a "letting be" as Heidegger calls it. Is the public realm discursively constituted as Habermas would have it or socially constituted and constitutive of the physical spaces of the city?

What are generally assumed to be more distant mediations of memory are now more present phenomena in our understanding of the meaning of public cultures and everyday spaces of cities. Christine Boyer's work has pointed to the importance of collective memory in the constitution of the city (Boyer 1994) but as Steve Pile has pointed out (chapter 8) our relation to cities is partly about phantoms and traces of the past and the subconscious. The repression and manifestation of desire in the city (see Walkowitz 1992) have been opposed to the rational and the phenomenal and the public. Now even these borderlands are open for inspection. All these questions are now very much on the agenda in thinking about cities. How they are resolved will have a profound effect not just on thinking about cities themselves but also on how we think about future urban democracy.

REFERENCES

Bell, D. and Valentine, G. (eds.) 1995: *Mapping Desire: The Geographies of Sexualities*. London: Routledge.

Benjamin, W. 1969: *Illuminations*. New York: Schocken.

Boyer, C. 1994: *The City of Collective Memory: Its Historical Imagery and Architectural Entertainment*. Cambridge, MA: MIT Press.

Castells, M. 1977: *The Urban Question*. London: Edward Arnold.

Castells, M. 1983: *The City and the Grassroots: A Cross-Cultural Theory of Urban Social Movements*. London: Edward Arnold.

Castells, M. 1997: *The Information Age: Economy Society and Culture*, vol. 2: *The Power of Identity*. Oxford: Blackwell.

Certeau, M. de 1984: *The Practice of Everyday Life*. Berkeley: University of California Press.

Chauncey, G. 1995: *Gay New York: Gender, Urban Culture and the Making of the Gay Male World 1890–1940*. London: Flamingo.

Davis, M. 1990: *City of Quartz: Excavating the Future in Los Angeles*. London: Verso.

Deutsche, R. 1996: *Evictions: Art and Spatial Politics*. Cambridge, MA: MIT Press.

Engels, F. [1844] 1993: *The Condition of the Working Class in England*, ed. with an introduction by D. McLellan. Oxford: Oxford University Press.

Etzioni, A. 1993: *The Spirit of Community: Rights, Responsibilities and the Communitarian Agenda*. New York: Crown.

Foucault, M. 1991: *Discipline and Punish: The Birth of the Prison*. Tr. from the French by Alan Sheridan. London: Penguin.

Fraser, N. 1990: Rethinking the public sphere: a contribution to the critique of actually existing democracy. *Social Text*, 25 (6), 56–80.

Habermas, J. 1984: *The Theory of Communicative Action*, vol. 1: *Reason and the Rationalisation of Society*, tr T. McCarthy. London: Heinemann.

Habermas, J. 1987: *The Theory of Communicative Action*, vol. 2: *Lifeworld and System – a Critique of Functionalist Reason*, tr. T. McCarthy. Cambridge: Polity.

Habitat – United Nations Centre for Human Settlements 1996: *An Urbanizing World: Global report on Human Settlements 1996*. Oxford: Oxford University Press.

Hayden, D. 1980: What would a non-sexist city be like? Speculations on housing, urban design, and human work. *Signs* 5(3) supplement S170–S187.

Jacobs, J. 1961: *The Death and Life of Great American Cities*. Harmondsworth: Penguin.

Lefebvre, H. 1991: *Critique of Everyday Life*, tr. J. Moore. London: Verso.

McDowell, L. 1983: Towards an understanding of the gender division of urban space. *Environment and Planning D: Society and Space*, 1, 59–72.

Maffesoli, M. 1996: *The Time of Tribes: The Decline of Individualism in Mass Society*, tr. D. Smith. London: Sage.

Mitchell, D. 1995: The end of public space? People's Park, definitions of the public and democracy. *Annals of the Association of American Geographers*, 85, 108–33.

Mouffe, C. 1992: Democratic citizenship and political community. In C. Mouffe (ed.), *Dimensions in Radical Democracy: Pluralism, Citizenship, Community*. London: Verso, 229–58.

Murphy, P. and Watson, S. 1997: *Surface City: Sydney at the Millennium*. Bristol: Policy.

Pringle, R. and Watson, S. 1992: Constructing interests: feminisms and the post-structural state. In M. Barrett and A. Phillips (eds.), *Destabilising Theory*. Oxford: Policy Press, 53–73.

Putnam, R. 1995: Bowling alone: America's declining social capital. *Journal of Democracy*, 6, 65–78.

Raban, J. 1974: *Soft City*. London: Hamilton.
Sandercock, L. and Forsyth, A. 1992: A gender agenda: New directions for planning theory. *Journal of the American Planning Association*, 58 , 49–59.
Sennett, R. 1970: *The Uses of Disorder*. Harmondsworth: Penguin.
Sennett, R. 1974: *The Fall of Public Man*. New York: Norton.
Sennett, R. 1990: *The Conscience of the Eye: The Design and Social Life of Cities*. London: Faber and Faber.
Simmel, G. [1903] 1995: Metropolis and mental life. In P. Kasinitz (ed.), *Metropolis: Centre and Symbol of our Times*. Basingstoke: Macmillan, 30–45.
Sorkin, M. 1992: *Variations on a Theme Park: The New American City and the End of Public Space*. New York: Hill and Wong.
Tonnies, F. [1887] 1957: *Community and Society*. East Lancing, MI: Michigan State University.
Valentine, G. 1989: The geography of women's fear. *Area* 21, 385–90.
Walkowitz, J. 1992: *City of Dreadful Delight*. London: Virago.
Watson, S. 1988: *Accommodating Inequality*. Sydney: Allen and Unwin.
Wilson, E. 1992: *The Sphinx and the City*. London: Virago.
Wirth, L. 1938: Urbanism as a way of life. *American Journal of Sociology*, 44, 1–24.
Young, I. 1990a: The ideal of community and the politics of difference. In L. Nicholson (ed.), *Feminism/Postmodernism*. London: Verso, 300–23.
Young I. 1990b: *Justice and the Politics of Difference*. Princeton: Princeton University Press.

Chapter 32

Reflections on the Public Realm[1]

Richard Sennett

What I would like to lay out is several ways in which in the last century concepts of public life have changed and now need to change again, including my own concepts of the public realm. At the time of the French Revolution when political philosophers used the word public they tended to try to get hold of what it meant for a society to shift from court-based power to urban power, from court to city. And "le publique" would no longer be a public that referred to the workings of royal power but was instead something that was self-constituting. Probably the most significant moves made to understand that shift in political philosophy were made by Kant and Hegel in terms of equating the public with the impersonal. And the problematic, for Hegel in particular, was "how could an impersonal realm be self-constituting?"

Hegel's answer to this dominated most of nineteenth-century thinking about the public realm. He tried to give an account of the self-constituting impersonal public by making an equation between the impersonal and the rational. Basically what it meant was that the public realm was a realm of political action bordering on state power and the citizen's participation was in the realm of the state rather than civil society. That is, he made a distinction between the public and the civil, where civil society is the realm of partial interests. It is also the realm of face-to-face associations which, Hegel argued, are inherently irrational because they lack the properties of having a universalizable law. Civil society is one of fractures and partialities. And that equation of the impersonal to the rational in terms of laws which apply to everyone was not a useful way of trying to understand the public realm from the nineteenth century – it permeates Mill, it permeates Marx. It makes a separation between the public and civil society.

Simmel's Mask of Rationality

In our century the story I want to begin to pick up is the way in which in thinking about the public realm this separation of the public and the civil was eroded. We owe this in particular to Simmel 90 years ago both in his *Philosophy of Money* and various Berlin lectures, and the one we all know (and his earliest), *The Metropolis and Mental life*. What Simmel tried to do was to drag the issue of impersonal rationality back into civil society, and specifically to the city, as the fundamental institution of civil society. And you may remember the peculiar way this occurs. Looking around the Berlin of his time what Simmel observed in others, and certainly felt in himself, was the fact that this enormous, dense city provoked in people at the bottom level a sense of psychic overstimulation. At the physical level people living in the city were threatened with a kind of chaos of multiple stimulations. Nobody, he said, could live as an animal in the city, meaning by that that no one could live by his or her senses in the city. In order to deal with this psychic overstimulation, the intensity of urban life he observed in Berlin at that time, Simmel formulated the notion of the mask of rationality. That is, he redefined the issue of rationality not as a question of law, but as the kind of qualities of behavior which would lead people to be able to manage their physical sense impressions. What he means by "rational" is rather neutral exchanges between people in a state of equilibrium among strangers.

Simmel argued that the impulse to trade using money for instance was not at the heart of urban life – something that had to do with the accumulation of profit, but had to do with a way of balancing out relations between strangers in public so that they did not have to deal with each other face-to-face emotionally and so on. Money and all kinds of rational trades based on money stood for Simmel as a medium for ironing out this terrible chaos of stimulation in the city. He looked at money as a psychological transaction rather than as an economic one, which seems very bizarre to us now. But the notion more largely with Simmel is that when people are faced with the condition of density and diversity they have to take refuge from it, they cannot live in it. And they take refuge from it by forms of impersonal relations in which the players know the value of what they are doing (as it were), in which there is very little room for interpretation and in which the relations are equilibrated. So that people for instance will see on the street somebody who has had a heart attack and they will know to walk around that person rather than to try to ask the person what has happened. It is that kind of notion of indifference as a defense mechanism that Simmel argued had a rationality to it, which is the rationality of equilibrating impersonal exchange.

On the positive side what Simmel did was to show that rationality was a social construct in everyday life and that that begins to distinguish a man of our time rather than a man of Hegel's time. That rationality is a reaction to something else – it is a social construction. It is not a property of state law – urban rationality as in Hegel – nor even, as in Weber, is rationality a property of civic action. It is something that is rooted in the inability of people to live in cities openly as animals. The negative of this Simmelian notion of the mask of rationality is that information is exchanged in this way but communication is lowered, particularly communication that transcends self-interest as well as communication of an emotional sort. The way in which you create an impersonal public realm is by lowering, as it were, the amount of information given. What this mask does is restrict the amount that people can know about you. It is reduced to information that can be codified and exchanged like money.

Importantly what is missing in this notion of the urban mask is that people never get beyond self-representations to each other. By that I mean that when Simmel looked on the streets of Berlin, what he saw his fellow urbanites doing in public was identifying themselves to others in such a way that the others would know that they were not going to be invaded. For example, people would never come up to a stranger and begin talking in a wild way or without introducing why they were saying what they were saying. The notion would be that in the public realm you would always identify yourself in such a way that the anxiety about the other was damped down by giving them clues about who you are. Probably the most brilliant of all Simmel's insights in this regard was his notion that this kind of city rationality would be more effective if it operated by the eye than if by the mouth. That is, that this is a visual order rather than an oral one. You can create that sense of exchange on the street more easily if you do not speak but take clues from each other about how to look. So it is a privileging of the visual over the verbal in the name of this peculiar thing that he called urban rationality that I am calling the mask of rationality. And that is how, in my reading of Simmel, what we think of as the modern problem of public order, of the public realm, takes shape.

What Simmel gave to us as urbanists was a notion of impersonal life as being caught between the bodily experience which was unmanageable, and a kind of self-repression through rationality which gradually constricted the urban realm so that it was a realm of neutral information rather than full self-exposure which operated by more visual than verbal cues. To give you just a practical idea of what he meant by the notion of strangers meeting on the street: they know what to do to pass each other. They know how to manage their eyes so that they do not stare into each other. All of these are codes for managing the insanity of overstimulation, an irrational that is their exchange relationship.

Getting Beyond the Mask of Rationality: Notions of the Public for Arendt and Habermas

So there, in my view, is where our problem in thinking about what is the public realm began – with this very particular theory. The problem in the twentieth century that theorists of the public realm have had to deal with is not the first or positive part of Simmel's achievement – that is the notion that rationality is an essential construct – but the second or more negative part of this theory, which is that rationality in this form is repressive. It is in general a problem that appears in Freud for instance, and it appears in all the permutations of negative dialectics that inform the Frankfurt School. For urbanists it has inspired two very different responses particularly after the Second World War. One of them is a trajectory that is embodied in the writings of Hannah Arendt and Habermas. The other is a trajectory that is much more social-scientific embodied in the writings of people like Erving Goffman, Clifford Geertz, and some of my own writing. I would like to give you a brief account of how each of these two schools have tried to deal with Simmel's negative – that is the problem of the public realm being a realm of repression.

Arendt interestingly was a very close reader of Simmel, and what she tried to argue was that the public realm need not fall into this kind of Simmelian self-repression. What it meant for Arendt is that there is a kind of space, a metaphoric space in society, which transcends self-interest. Arendt went back to some of the Hegelian notions about the refusal of civil society as the location for the public realm. Particularly she refused the notion that labor constitutes anything that we can call public life. The argument that is made in *The Human Condition* is that there has to be a space in society where people no longer have to speak in the name of their labor, most of which she found to be labor which was oppressed, where they were free from representing themselves as economic animals and where they were free from fear of speaking. When that could happen and people were freed from the fear of speaking, they entered the public realm. That is, she reversed the Simmelian notion of sight and speech and argued that the public realm was a realm in which we had to privilege speech over sight.

That is what this idealized agora and the idealization of Athens itself is about in Arendt. It is a space that is no longer a visual space but a place for speech. The notion of it is quite humane in a way, in that if what we have is spaces of self-representation à la Simmel, then of course in a capitalist society the people who have the most power will be the ones who colonize the public realm. It is an idealization of entering and leaving civil society in order to empower everybody with speech, and this is why Arendt insists that the public realm has to be founded above all on equal rights of discourse. It is also why the whole constitutionalism in Arendt is founded on the notion of free speech. That is the public realm.

In some ways the Habermasian picture of the public realm is richer than Arendt's because he does not want to particularly exclude questions of labor and economy from the public. The whole trajectory of Habermas's project is to try to find a way to bring that aspect of civil society back into the discussion of what is the public realm, and also to look at impersonality in a slightly different way from Arendt. For Arendt the impersonal meant, as it does to John Rawls, the fact that you cannot identify how rich somebody is and what they do for a living. In other words, there is a veil of ignorance which is cast over the conventional means of categorizing people in the public realm. For Habermas the impersonal means much more that the conditions of talking about interest, fully revealing oneself to other people, gradually means that people begin talking about what interest is, rather than about defending their own interest. There is a kind of idealization in Habermas's work, that the more interactive one's discourse becomes the more the very process of speaking to others begins to work against the simple representation of self-interest. This is what the theory of communicative interaction is all about in regard to the public realm, which then begins to make people separate or objectify the nature of interests from their own interests. Thus public space for Habermas is a realm which forces people to discuss what the objects of interests are, rather than simply say, "I am your employer – do as I say." That is why he put so much emphasis on newspapers, for instance, and letters to the editor in newspapers – these kinds of things are terribly important to him. It is why when the Internet first began Habermas was wildly excited about it because this looked to him like a public realm of the sort that fits this theory of communicative interaction. What he most liked about it was that people could talk to each other in different ways, like the possibility of altering their own identities, and so on. There was some capacity not simply to be classified by speech. But the assumption that is rather different from Arendt's is that the more diversity there is in the public realm, and the more there is a mixture of interests, the more objectifying the process of discourse is going to be. Thus it is a way of recovering the notion of rationality in another form, where in this case, diversity leads to rationality via its objectification of interests.

Now what I would say about both Hannah Arendt and Habermas is that when they use the term "public realm" what they are talking about is an activity, which is first, an activity that is clarified by communication with strangers, and second, it is purified of self-interest through the effort to speak and hear clearly. That may seem like a nice nostrum but what it means, and I think the edge that it has, is that it supposes that discourse among strangers is more complete and objective than discourse among intimates. That is, you do not think as rationally and you do not speak as rationally to those whom you love as to those who are strangers to you – that is the cutting edge of this. This is why Hanneh Arendt rejected psychoanalysis and why she thought that politics and psychology could never be reconciled, because the moment that one speaks to a stranger with whom one has no affective relationship is the moment in which one can also leave oneself. So that it is a privileging of the public over the private. That is how Simmel's negative is dealt with, by arguing that impersonality is a fuller system of meaning than private life. The public person is fuller, more rational, more complete, and more liberated than the person in private life.

Putting Aside the Mask of Rationality: Performativity in the Public Realm

The second response to Simmel – in thinking about the public realm – has a very old name to it; it could be called a school of *teatro mundi* or theater of the world and, as I said, it is represented variously in my writings and in those of Erving Goffman and Clifford Geertz. What it tries to do on the one hand is cut free discussions of public life from questions about rationality – to push this whole issue to the side. Instead it tries to focus on the problem of how strangers express themselves to each other, that is, how they communicate emotionally with people whom they do not know. It is the parallel problem between the way in which an actor or an actress comes on stage and moves strangers to believe he or she is about to die of sickness or is just about to murder his or her mother or whatever, and enacts the problems which people face in everyday life – of making themselves credible speakers to people they do not know. This is not about communicating information but about communicating something that, we might say, has a rhetorical force, but even more that there is a credible scene in which what is spoken is something that the other has to take in and respond to.

One way to think about this – and that is what Goffman's theory of role playing, and my, or Geertz's, notions of theatricality are about – is the idea that other people can act information so that it becomes believable, moving and arousing to other people. To give you a specific example of this, you will remember something many people quote who have read Habermas's work on the public sphere – the discussion of newspapers and coffee houses. What he focuses on is the fact that in these newspapers which are read in coffee houses for the first time during the eighteenth century you have cheap mass-produced instruments of communication among strangers. A different way of looking at that as a public activity is the kind of thing I tried to do in *The Fall of Public Man*, which is to understand what happened when people discussed with each other what they read in the papers – how did they go about doing that? And what I found is that these places – these coffee houses – are the origins of our modern insurance companies. For example, Lloyds of London began as a coffee house and maybe it has stayed that way. For information to be freely exchanged and for people to believe what they heard, even though they might be of very different classes – you had a kind of theatrical activity – which was that people spoke in these coffee houses in imitation of what they heard in theatres, so that they had powers of eloquence which they literally borrowed from theatrical speech as a way to convince others that the information they were giving them was credible. It is a realm in which there is the privileging of speech over the eye – and of course where this is between somebody who is a tailor and somebody who might be a baronet looking at each other, then they obviously know that they are not in the same realm. But by using this highly artificial language that is similar, this highly theatrical language, they have a kind of common speech which creates an "as if" as though they are in the same realm – and this is literally a suspension of disbelief.

This kind of analysis of role playing in public is what this other tradition of public life is about. In terms of cities this kind of approach to the public domain is much more tied to the material conditions of daily life, which we can understand if we think back to Renaissance practitioners of *teatro mundi* like Inigo Jones, for instance, in London. Inigo Jones would try out architectural designs on stage that he thought about in terms of "is this a space in which people can move around in believably, and does it work as an architectural space?" This long tradition of thinking about whether the kinds of spaces in which people are noticing others who are different and are reacting to them, which has strangers paying attention to them and so on, is part of what this tradition of *teatro mundi* has been about. So it is a much more visually orientated way of thinking about the public realm à la Habermas and Arendt.

In my own work I argue that the spaces which are most possessed of these powers – provoking role playing and this *teatro* of public life – are multifunctional rather than monofunctional – an argument I made in *The Uses of Disorder.* That is to say, that disorder in public is something that provokes the impulse, the freedom to be disorderly in public, and provokes more vivacity in public spaces. Thus the privatization of space occurs by making it monofunctional. What I have argued is that there is a very complex relation between convention and disorder of public space and that the more that that play between the disorder of public spaces and conventional behavior can be exploited and encouraged, the more public life is enhanced.

The second thing I would say about this tradition of *teatro mundi* is that by design it is more attuned to engage with the question of difference and make the question of difference concrete – certainly more than Arendt, and I also think, Habermas have done. In Arendt, the whole notion of the public realm is one that transcends difference by design. That is to say when you enter into the public, you take off the particularities of being black, a woman, or poor and you enter into the community of equalization of speech in which self-reference is seen as a violation of the norms of politics. Habermas's notion is that with fuller communicative interaction the differences do not go away, but they do not matter to people, so it does not have that Arendtian fiction of the agora. For Habermas, if you have a vivid public realm, eventually if there is enough interaction, a poor black will feel himself/herself entitled to speak openly to a rich white. So for Habermas the whole politics of the public realm is to make that kind of entitlement, that kind of growing together so that one thinks about what race is or class is without self-reference, occur more and more.

By contrast other writers, and in this regard I think of Erving Goffman and Clifford Geertz most, tried to emphasize the ways in which the conventions of behavior with others in public depend on people dealing with and acknowledging the differences of others in terms of age, race, class, sexual preference, and so on. In this case, the notion is that people are self-dramatizing with respect to their differences in the public realm. That is what they mean by public behavior – it is a kind of self-dramatization which they think is good.

I have taken a rather different tack on this question of difference in public life. What I have been interested in with regard to this question of difference is how people portray themselves to others not, as it were, in the centers of places, but at the edges. This is why my analysis is focused not on the hub of communities, on central business districts or places like Trafalgar Square but on all those seemingly dead edges where one community, one difference, meets another. And as a practicing urbanist what I try to do is bring those spaces where the differences touch alive. That is, for me, if you take the dramatization of difference seriously, the place where it really matters – not where you meet a whole lot of people like yourself but where you are reluctant to meet those who are *unlike* you. The deficit about this *teatro mundi* is that it has contained within it nevertheless a certain kind of political indifference, for example as in the work of Albert Speer. What Goffman, Geertz, and I have failed to address in our work is what a liberated politics is – what is a liberating theatricality in the city and what is a repressive one?

I lay all this out to say that this, I think, represents so far how a modern conception can resume a public realm that is composed of people looking on each other, who are strangers and who are impersonal. What is interesting is the fact that the seemingly self-repressive qualities of the public realm that Simmel perceived, and that Freud perceived in another way, (or that Horkheimer and Adorno perceived after the Second World War) took two very different paths. One of them, focused on *the public realm as an action* (the Arendtian, Habermasian approach), tended to try and look to recover once again the Hegelian notion (but in very different ways) that the public and civil society were at least separable. And the other – the *teatro mundi* way of looking at the public realm – focused on civil society to be sure, but tried to throw out the whole preoccupation with rationality and impersonality which marked most of the century, and tried to discover a kind of self-dramatization as a principle of creating a public life. My own approach was to focus on territory – on the issue of boundaries rather than centers and to focus on the peculiar balance between theatricality and disorder in public space itself.

Now we have to take a different tack I think because a century after Simmel two rather different questions about conceiving the public realm have come into being. As discussed earlier, for Simmel the problem was psychic overstimulation, yet it would be very difficult to argue that most modern cities are psychically overstimulating places. In contrast the problem is precisely creating the stimulus of being in the public. And it seems to me that this is going to require a whole different set of thoughts about what the logic is of getting people together who are stimulated by the presence of others, because of the very practical things like the fact that automobiles are probably the ultimate piece of technology for isolating people from the stimulation of difference – you die if you get too stimulated by it. Similarly the cities we know now tend to be much more outward than inward – differences tend to separate and they are not edges between communities which can be made interactive because there is too much space between them.

A whole range of questions arise as to how to create a public realm in which people will tolerate being stimulated by the other, and this is not just a matter of capitalist domination. The destimulation of the city is something that has also tapped that Simmelian fear of being overwhelmed by difference and there is a confluence of causes between power and desire. So that issue of stimulation, rather than overstimulation, needs to be faced. And the other issue for a new public realm does not concern politics alone, as much as political economy, and the need to focus not on global markets but on the transformation of bureaucracy that has occurred in the last 20 years – both in work and the welfare state, because that transformation of bureaucracy is intensely privatizing and individualizing. The body politic has been rent asunder by the way in which people work, by the relationship to their needs and political economy. There is a long discussion we could have about what these changes in the bureaucracy of work and the changing bureaucracy of the welfare state mean, but the essential point is that the effect on individuals is intensely privatizing. So in thinking about a strong public realm the question is to think about how to countervail this, and the question for us as urbanists is, can powers of place of the public do that work? That is, is place a really meaningful element in countervailing the individualizing effects of these great changes in the work and welfare bureaucracies? For me the issue that now faces us is how this impersonal realm of the public can be conceived in collective terms rather than in terms of issues of rationality. That is ultimately a more political project and also a more open-ended one.

This is a summary of the main currents in thinking about public life in this and the last century. Maybe now the things that have occupied me and earlier generations have come to an end and something else more addressed to the conditions of contemporary capitalism has to grow up as a sense of what public life is.

NOTE

1. This lecture was delivered as a plenary session of the "Cities at the Millennium" conference in London at RIBA, December 1998.

Chapter 33

City Life and the Senses

John Urry

Introduction

In this chapter I develop an issue interestingly expressed by Popper when he characterizes "closed societies" as a "concrete group of individuals, related to one another...by concrete physical relationships such as *touch*, *smell*, and *sight*" (1962: 173; emphasis added). In the following I explore, not the senses powerful within closed societies, but how such senses operate in "open societies" and especially in what we might call "open cities." Which senses dominate and what role do they play in producing the spatializations of city life within the "West" (for an alternative account of sensing nature, see Macnaghten and Urry 1998: ch. 4)?

Rodaway usefully elaborates a "sensuous geography" which connects together analyses of body, sense, and space (1994). As well as the *social* character of the senses emphasized by Simmel (Frisby and Featherstone 1997), Rodaway shows that the senses are also spatial. Each sense contributes to people's orientation in space; to their awareness of spatial relationships; and to the appreciation of the qualities of particular micro- and macro-spatial environments. Moreover, each sense gives rise to metaphors which attest to the relative importance of each within everyday life. With regard to sight, it is often said that "we see" something when we understand it; someone who does not understand a topic is said to be "blind"; farsighted leaders are said to be "visionary"; while intellectuals may be able to "illuminate" or "shed light on" a particular topic. By contrast those who cannot understand some issue remain "in the dark" (and see Hibbitts 1994: 240–1).

Rodaway further suggests that there are five distinct ways in which different senses are interconnected with each other to produce a sensed environment: *co-operation* between the senses; a *hierarchy* between different senses, as with the visual sense during much of the recent history of the West; a *sequencing* of one sense which has to follow on from another sense; a *threshold* of effect of a particular sense which has to be met before another sense is operative; and *reciprocal* relations of a certain sense with the object which appears to "afford" it an appropriate response (1994: 36–7).

Visuality

The hierarchy of the senses within Western culture over the past few centuries has placed the visual at the top (Rorty 1980). This was the outcome of various developments. These included new ecclesiastical styles of architecture of the Middle Ages which allowed increasingly large amounts of light to filter through the brightly colored stained-glass windows. The medieval fascination with light and color was also to be seen in the growth of heraldry as a complex visual code denoting chivalric identification and allegiance (Hibbitts 1994: 251). In the fifteenth-century linear perspectivism enabled three-dimensional space to be represented on a two-dimensional plane. There was also the development of the science of optics and the fascination with the mirror as a popular object found in grand houses and later in urban shops. Also there was the growth of an increasingly "spectacular" urban legal system with colourful robes and elaborate courtrooms.

Most significant was the invention of the printing press which reduced the relative power of the oral/aural sense and enhanced the seeing of the written word, as well as pictures and maps (Hibbitts 1994: 255). Jay summarizes the significance of this visual sense within the broad sweep of Western culture: "with the rise of modern science, the Gutenberg revolution in printing and the Albertian emphasis on perspective in painting, vision was given an especially powerful role in the modern era" (1986: 179). Marshall McLuhan similarly argues that "as our age slips back into the oral and auditory modes . . . we become sharply aware of the uncritical acceptance of visual metaphors and models by many past centuries"; to be real a thing must, he says, be visible (1962: 238).

Simmel makes two important points about this visual sense. First, the eye is a unique "sociological achievement" (Frisby and Featherstone 1997: 111). Looking at one another effects the connections and interactions of individuals. Simmel terms this the most direct and "purest" interaction. It is the look between people (what we now call "eye-contact") which produces extraordinary moments of intimacy. This is because "[o]ne cannot take through the eye without at the same time giving"; this produces the "most complete reciprocity" of person to person, face to face (Frisby and Featherstone 1997: 112). The look is returned, and this results from the expressive meaning of the face. What we see in the person is the lasting part of them, "the history of their life and . . . the timeless dowry of nature" (Frisby and Featherstone 1997: 115). By contrast the ear and the nose do not reciprocate – they only take but do not give.

This intimacy of eye contact was initially given urban expression in nineteenth-century Paris, with its sidewalk cafes in which lovers could be "private in public" (Berman 1983). This intimacy was enhanced by the streams of anonymous city-dwellers and visitors, none of whom would return the look of the lovers. They remained wrapped in the intimacy of their particular face-to-faceness, surrounded by the rush, pace, and anonymity of the city life going on all around them.

Second, Simmel notes that only the visual sense enables possession and property; while that which we hear is already past and provides no property to possess (Frisby and Featherstone 1997: 116). The visual sense enables people to take possession, not only of other people, but also of diverse environments. It enables the world to be controlled at a distance, combining detachment and mastery (see Robins 1996: 20). By seeking distance a proper "view" is gained, abstracted from the hustle and bustle of everyday city life (see Hibbitts 1994: 293).

This power of possession is best seen in the development of photography. Adam summarizes: "The eye of the camera can be seen as the ultimate realisation of that vision: monocular, neutral, detached and disembodied, it views the world at a distance, fixes it with its nature, and separates observer from observed in an absolute way" (1995: 8). Photography is thus a particularly powerful signifying practice which reproduces a dominant set of images and, at the very same time, conceals its constructed character (see Berger 1972; Sontag 1979; Albers and James 1988; Urry 1990). It also gives shape to the very processes of movement around the city (see Urry 1990: 137–40). Photographic practices thus reinforce the dominance of the visual gaze, including that of the male over the bodyscape of women within the city. By contrast, Irigaray argues that for women "investment in the look is not as privileged in women as in men. More than other senses, the eye objectifies and masters. It sets at a distance, and maintains a distance" (1979: 50; and see Heidegger on the "modern world picture" 1979: 134).

This visual sense is moreover increasingly mediatized, as it shifts from the printing press to electronic modes of representation, and from the camera to the circulation of digital images. Such transformations stem from the nineteenth-century process by which there was a "separation of the senses" and especially the visual sense from touch and hearing (see Crawshaw and Urry 1997, on such a sequencing of the senses). The autonomization of sight enabled the quantification and homogenization of visual experience. Many new objects of the visual began to circulate in the city – including commodities, mirrors, plate-glass windows, postcards, photographs and so on. These objects displayed a visual enchantment in which magic and spirituality were displaced by visual appearances and surface features, reflecting in the city the mass of consumers passing by.

In the twentieth-century city, most powerful systems of modern incarceration involve the complicity of sight in their routine operations of power. "Distancing, mastering, objectifying – the voyeuristic look exercises control through a visualization which merges with a victimization of its object" (Deutsche 1991: 11). It is argued that we live in a "surveillance society," even when we are apparently roaming freely through a shopping center or the countryside (Lyon 1994). Virilio has particularly emphasized the novel importance of video surveillance techniques to changing the morphology of the contemporary city and hence of the trust that the public now have to invest in such institutions of surveillance (1988). It has been calculated that one is "captured" on film 20 times during a walk through a major shopping center. What is striking about such CCTV techniques is their ordinariness, much akin to the child playing video games in an arcade or on a home computer (Robins 1996: 20–1; and see the film *Sliver*).

Thus the city both is fascinated with, and hugely denigrates, the visual. This ambivalence is reflected in the diverse discourses surrounding travel. On the one hand, we live in a society of spectacle as cities have been transformed into diverse and collectable spectacles. But on the other hand, there is denigration of the mere sightseer to different towns and cities. The person who only lets the sense of sight have free rein is ridiculed. Such sightseers are taken to be superficial in their appreciation of environments, peoples, and places. Many people are often embarrassed about mere sightseeing. Sight is not seen as the noblest of the senses but as the most superficial, as getting in the way of real experiences that should involve other senses and necessitate much longer periods of time in order to be immersed in the site/sight (see Crawshaw and Urry 1997, for further detail).

The critique of the sightseer is taken to the extreme in the analysis of "hyper-reality," forms of simulated experience which have the appearance of being more "real" than the original (Baudrillard 1981; Eco 1986). The sense of vision is reduced to a limited array of features, it is then exaggerated and it comes to dominate the other senses. Hyper-real places are characterized by surface which does not respond to or welcome the viewer. The sense of sight is seduced by the most immediate and visible aspects of the scene, such as the facades of Main Street in Disneyland. What is not experienced in such hyper-real places is a different visual sense, the baroque (Jay 1992; Buci-Glucksmann 1984). This involves the fascination for opacity, unreadability, and indecipherability. Jay seeks to celebrate "the dazzling, disorientating, ecstatic surplus of images in baroque visual experience... [the] rejection of the monocular geometricalization of the Cartesian tradition... the baroque self-consciously revels in the contradictions between surface and depth, disparaging as a result any attempt to reduce the multiplicity of visual spaces into any one coherent essence" (1992: 187). He talks of baroque planning seeking to engage all the senses as found in some carnivals and festivals (1992: 192). This partly parallels Sennett's critique of the blandness of the "neutralised city" which is based upon fear of social contact with the stranger involving the various senses (1991). Sennett advocates the positive uses of disorder, contradiction, and ambiguity in the development of contemporary cities (and see Robins 1996: 100–1).

Likewise feminists have argued that the concentration upon the visual sense overemphasizes appearance, image, and surface. Iragaray argues that in Western cultures "the preponderance of the look over the smell, taste, touch and hearing has brought about an impoverishment of bodily relations. The moment the look dominates, the body loses its materiality" (1978: 123; Mulvey 1989). This emphasis upon the visual reduces the body to surface, marginalizes the multiple sensuousness of the body and impoverishes the relationship of the body to its environment. And at the same time the visual overemphasizes masculinist efforts to exert mastery over the female body, particularly through the voyeurism effected via the pornographic picture (Taylor 1994: 268). By contrast a feminist consciousness emphasizes the dominant visual sense less and seeks to integrate all of the senses in a more rounded way, which does not seek to exert mastery over the "other" (Rodaway 1994: 123). Other writers have particularly emphasized the significance of aural traditions in women's lives – especially within socially dense urban areas – to talking and listening, telling stories, engaging in intimate detailed dialog or gossip and the use of the metaphor of "giving voice" (Hibbitts 1994: 271–3).

Smell and Touch

I turn now to these other senses and their complex relationships with visuality. I begin with nineteenth-century urban England. In 1838 the House of Commons Select Committee argued that, because there were whole areas of London through which no thoroughfares passed, the lowest class of person was secluded from the observation and the influence of "better educated neighbours" (Stallybrass and White 1986: 134). Engels noted how the social ecology of the industrial city had the effect of "hiding from the eyes of wealthy gentlemen and ladies . . . the misery and squalor that . . . complement . . . their riches and luxury" (cited Marcus 1973: 259). It was claimed that the "lower" classes would be greatly improved if they became visible to the middle and upper classes. There are parallels here with the rebuilding of Paris and its hugely enhanced visibility which resulted from replacing the medieval street plan with the grand boulevards of the Second Empire (see Berman 1983).

In Britain visibility was increasingly viewed as central to the regulation of the lower classes within the new cities. As the "other" class were now seen in the massive cities of nineteenth-century Britain, the upper class desperately tried not to touch them (unless of course they were prostitutes or domestic servants who were deemed available for touching by upper-class men). The concepts of "contagion" and "contamination" were the tropes through which the upper class apprehended nineteenth-century city life (Stallybrass and White 1986). As the "promiscuity" of the public space became increasingly unavoidable, so the upper and middle classes sought to avoid touching the potentially contaminating "other," the "dangerous classes."

This was in turn reflected in the development of Victorian domestic architecture which was designed to regulate the flows of bodies, keeping servants apart from the family "below stairs," adults apart from children who were in the nursey, and male children apart from female children. As a contemporary argued, there were: "two currents of 'circulation' in a family dwelling . . . There is the activity of the master and his friends, which occurs on the most visible, genteel and accessible routes, and there is the 'circulation' of the servants, tradesmen and everyone else who provides the home with services, and this should take place in the least conspicuous and most discreet way possible" (quoted in Roderick 1997: 116).

More generally, the upper class mainly sought to gaze upon the other, while standing on their balconies. The balcony took on special significance in nineteenth-century life and literature as the place from which one could gaze but not be touched, could participate in the crowd yet be separate from it. It was one of the earliest examples of replacing the city of touch with the city of visibility (see Robins 1996: 20). According to Benjamin the balcony demonstrates superiority over the crowd, as the observer "scrutinizes the throng" (1969: 173). The later development of the skyscraper, beginning in 1880s Chicago, also enabled those inside to gaze down and across the crowd, while being insulated from the smells and the potential touch of those who were below. In Chicago the avoidance of the smells of the meat processing industry was a particularly important spur to building skyscrapers up into the light.

And there are parallels with the way in which the contemporary tourist bus gives a bird's eye view, in but not of the crowd, gazing down on the crowd in safety, without the heat, the smells, and the touch. It is as though the scene is being viewed on a screen, and sounds, noises, and the contaminating touch are all precluded because of the empire of the gaze effected through the windows of the bus. Thus the dominance of sight over the dangerous sense of smell has been effected through a number of physical objects and technologies, such as the balcony, the skyscraper and the air-conditioned bus.

Smell was thus significant in the cultural construction of the nineteenth-century Western city. It demarcated the unnaturalness of the city. Stallybrass and White argue that in the mid-nineteenth-century "the city... still continued to invade the privatised body and household of the bourgeoisie as smell. It was, primarily, the sense of smell which enraged social reformers, since smell, whilst, like touch, encoding revulsion, had a pervasive and invisible presence difficult to regulate" (1986: 139). Smells, sewers, rats, and the mad played key roles in the nineteenth-century construction of class relations within the large cities. Later, in the 1930s, George Orwell noted powerful odors along the road to Wigan Pier (1937: 159).

As the nineteenth-century upper class repressed reference to their own lower bodily functions, they increasingly referred to the simultaneous dangers *and* fascinations of the lowlife of the "other," including the smells of the slum, the ragpicker, the prostitute, the sewer, the dangers of the rat, below stairs, the kneeling maid and so on (Shields 1991 on lowlife in nineteenth-century Brighton). The upper class in nineteenth-century British cities experienced a particular "way of sensing" such cities, in which smell played a pivotal role. The odors of death, madness, and decay were thought to be ever-present in the industrial city (Tuan 1993: 61–2; Classen, Howes, and Synnott 1994: 165–9, on the class and ethnic structuring of such smellscapes). There was thought to be a distinctive "stench of the poor" in Paris (Corbin 1986: ch. 9). There was a pronounced rhetoric of the delights of the "open air," that is air that did not smell of the city, for those apparently confined to living within nineteenth-century cities.

Lefebvre more generally argues that the production of different spaces is crucially bound up with smell. He says that "where an intimacy occurs between 'subject' and 'object', it must surely be the world of smell and the places where they reside" (1991: 197). Olfaction seems to provide a more direct and less premeditated encounter with the environment; and one which cannot be turned on and off. It provokes an unmediated sense of the surrounding townscapes. Tuan argues that the directness and immediacy of smell provides a sharp contrast with the abstractive and compositional characteristics of sight (1993: 57).

One way of examining smell is in terms of the diverse "smellscapes" which organize and mobilize people's feelings about particular places (including what one might also call the "tastescapes" of different gastronomic regimes). This concept brings out how smells are spatially ordered and place-related. (Porteous 1990: 369). In particular, the olfactory sense is important in evoking memories of specific places, normally because of certain physical objects and their characteristic smells which are thought to inhabit certain places (see Tuan 1993: 57). And even if we cannot name the particular smell it can still be important in helping to create and sustain one's sense of a particular place or experience. It can generate both revulsion and attraction; as such it can play a major role in constructing and sustaining major distinctions of social taste.

Rodaway summarizes the power of smell in relationship to place as "the perception of an odour in or across a given space, perhaps with varying intensities, which will linger for a while and then fade, and a differentiation of one smell from another and the association of odours with particular things, organisms, situations and emotions which all contribute to a sense of place and the character places" (1994: 68). Toni Morrison writes in the *Song of Solomon* of how

> On autumn nights, in some parts of the city, the wind from the lake [Superior] brings a sweetish smell to shore. An odo[u]r like crystallized ginger, or sweet iced tea with a dark clove floating in it . . . there was this heavy spice-sweet smell that made you think of the East and striped tents . . . The two men . . . could smell the air, but they didn't think of ginger. Each thought it was the way freedom smelled, or justice, or luxury, or vengeance (1989: 184–5).

Simmel argues that the sense of smell is a particularly "dissociating sense," transmitting more repulsions than attractions (Frisby and Featherstone 1997: 119). He talks of "olfactory intolerance," suggesting for example that hostility between Germans and Jews has been particularly generated by distinctions of smell (see Guérer 1993: 27). More generally he thought that the "effluvia" of the working class posed a threat to social solidarity (Frisby and Featherstone 1997: 118). This became more pronounced during the twentieth-century as domestic hygiene has been very unevenly introduced, so reinforcing class attitudes of social and moral superiority based upon smell. The stigma of odor has provided a constant basis of stratification, resulting from what Simmel terms the "invincible disgust inspired by the sense of smell" (cited Guérer 1993: 34).

Modern societies have apparently reduced the sense of smell by comparison with the other senses (Lefebvre 1991). Premodern societies had been very much characterized by distinctions of smell (see Classen, Howes, and Synnott 1994, on the significance of aroma within the classical world). In modern societies there is an apparent dislike of strong odors and the emergence of various technologies, objects, and manuals which seek to purify smells out of everyday life. These include the development of public health systems which separate water from sewerage and which involve channeling sewage underground away from both the nose and the eye (Roderick 1997). Corporeal functions and processes came to occupy a "proper place" within the home; they were increasingly spatially differentiated from each other and based upon the control and regulation of various bodily and piped fluids. In particular as water came to be piped separately from sewage so it was possible to wash the whole body much more frequently; bath and shower technology were developed and also came to be given a "proper place" within the home. A lack of smell came to indicate personal and public cleanliness. Domestic design develops so as to exclude animal and related smells.

More generally, Bauman argues that "Modernity declared war on smells. Scents had no room in the shiny temple of perfect order modernity set out to erect" (1993: 24). For Bauman modernity sought to neutralize smells by creating zones of control in which the senses would not be offended. Zoning became an element of public policy in which planners accepted that repugnant smells are in fact an inevitable by-product of urban-industrial society. Refuse dumps, sewage plants, meat processing factories, industrial plants and so on are all spaces in which bad smells are concentrated, and are typically screened off by being situated on the periphery of cities. Domestic architecture developed which confined smells to particular areas of the home, to the backyard, and the water closet. This war of smell within modernity was carried to the extreme in the Nazi period, where the Jews were routinely referred to as "stinking" and their supposed smell was associated with physical and moral corruption (Classen, Howes, and Synnott 1994: 170–5).

But smell is a subversive sense since it cannot be wholly banished (Bauman 1993). Smell reveals the artificiality of modernity; it shows following Latour that we have never been really modern (1993). The modern project to create a pure, rational order of things is undermined by the sweet smell of decomposition which continuously escapes control and regulation. Thus the "stench of Auschwitz" could not be eliminated even when at the end of the war the Nazis desperately tried to conceal what had happened through ridding the camps of the stench of death (Classen, Howes, and Synnott 1994: 175). Bauman submits that decomposition has "a sweet smell," exerting its revenge upon a modern world which cannot be subject to complete purification and control (1993).

The ways in which smells emanate from diverse objects, including especially the human body, results in the social significance and power of diverse hybrids such as sewage systems, notions of hygiene, and new discourses and technologies of domestic architecture. More generally Roderick argues that, although there are all sorts of *smelly* substances within houses and apartments (such as sewage, dirty water, and gas, as well as the *dangerous* flows of electricity and boiling water), modernity has sought to confine their flows to various channels. But of course these flowing substances are always threatening to seep through the walls of these channels and to enter the "home," analogous to the way that blood does not stay within its own vessels (Roderick 1997: 128). Much women's work within the home has been based upon taking a special responsibility for these dirty fluids, somewhat paralleling Grosz's characterization of the female body as "a leaking, uncontrollable, seeping liquid; as formless flow; as viscosity, entrapping, secreting" (1994: 203). Men only enter the scene when the seepage gets out of hand and it is they who climb along the vessels of the house, to clean and repair the pipes that flow above the ceilings and behind the walls, which confine the dirty and the dangerous.

Conclusion

Thus I have considered some of the ways that vision and smell form and reform themselves to constitute the evolving spatiality of the nineteenth- and twentieth-century city (I have not considered the non-Western city, see Edensor 1998). With more time I would have developed similar analyses of the acoustic sense, which like smell cannot be turned on and off. According to Simmel "the ear is the egoistic organ pure and simple, which only takes but does not give" (Frisby and Featherstone 1997: 115). Within the contemporary city there appears to be a reinvigorated oral culture reflected in musak, loudspeakers, ghetto blasters, telephone bells, traffic, mobile phones, sex chat lines, and so on (see Hibbitts 1994: 302–3). I would also have considered further the sense of touch. I noted how cities have been transformed so as to avoid what Canetti terms "the touch of the unknown" (1973), to replace the city of touch with the radiant city. But it should also be noted that people necessarily move among bodies which continuously touch and are touched, in a kind of reciprocity of contact (see Robins 1996: 33). Unlike the seeer who can look without being seen, the toucher is always touched (see Grosz 1994: 45).

Invoking the senses challenges much of our understanding of city life. On the basis of an account of the microspatiality of those in a city confined to a wheelchair, Massey points to the significance of the diverse senses: "there are local landscapes of sense other than vision. Try imagining – and designing – a city of sound and touch, a city that plays to all the senses" (and we might add, a city that plays to taste and smell; see Massey forthcoming).

REFERENCES

Adam, B. 1995a: Radiated Identities: In Pursuit of the Temporal Complexity of Conceptual Cultural Practices. Theory, Culture and Society Conference, Berlin, August.

Albers, P. and James, W. 1988: Travel photography: a methodological approach. *Annals of Tourism Research*, 15, 134–58.

Baudrillard, J. 1981: *For a Critique of the Economy of the Sign*. St Louis: Telos.

Bauman, Z. 1993: The sweet smell of decomposition. In C. Rojek and B. Turner (eds.), *Forget Baudrillard*? London: Routledge, 22–46.

Benjamin, W. 1969: *Illuminations*. New York: Schocken.

Berger, J. 1972: *Ways of Seeing*. Harmondsworth: Penguin.

Berman, M. 1983: *All That Is Solid Melts Into Air*. London: Verso.

Buci-Glucksmann, C. 1984: *Baroque Reason: The Aesthetics of Modernity*. London: Sage.

Canetti, E. 1973: *Crowds and Power*. Harmondsworth: Penguin.

Classen, C., Howes, D., and Synnott, A. 1994. *Aroma: The Cultural History of Smell*. London: Routledge.

Corbin, A. 1986: *The Frail and the Fragrant*. Leamington Spa: Berg.

Crawshaw, C. and Urry, J. 1997: Tourism and the photographic eye. In C. Rojek and J. Urry (eds.), *Touring Cultures*. London: Routledge, 176–95.

Deutsche, R. 1991: Boys town. *Environment and Planning D: Society and Space*, 9, 5–30.

Eco, U. 1986: *Travels in Hyper-Reality*. London: Picador.

Edensor, T. 1998: *Tourists at the Taj*. London: Routledge.

Frisby, D. and Featherstone, M. (eds.) 1997. *Simmel on Culture*. London: Sage.

Grosz, E. 1994: *Volatile Bodies: Towards a Corporeal Feminism*. Sydney: Allen and Unwin.

Guérer, A. le 1993: *Scent: The Mysterious and Essential Powers of Smell*. London: Chatto and Windus.

Heidegger, M. 1979: *One-Way Street and Other Writings*. London: New Left.

Hibbitts, B. 1994: Making sense of metaphors: visuality, aurality, and the reconfiguration of American legal discourse. *Cardozo Law Review*, 16, 229–356.

Iragaray, L. 1978: Interview with L. Iragaray. In M.-F. Hans and G. Lapouge (eds.), *Les Femmes, La Pornographie et L'Erotisme*. Paris: Minuit.

Jay, M. 1986: In the empire of the gaze: Foucault and the denigration of vision in twentieth-century French thought. In D. Hoy (ed.), *Foucault: A Critical Reader*. Oxford: Blackwell, 175–204.

Jay, M. 1992: Scopic regimes of modernity. In S. Lash and J. Friedman (eds.), *Modernity and Identity*. Oxford: Blackwell, 178–95.

Latour, B. 1993: *We Have Never Been Modern*. Hemel Hempstead: Harvester Wheatsheaf.

Lefebvre, H. 1991: *The Production of Space*. Oxford: Blackwell.

Lyon, D. 1994: *The Electronic Eye: The Rise of the Surveillance Society*. Cambridge: Polity.

Macnaghten, P. and Urry, J. 1998: *Contested Natures*. London: Sage.

Marcus, S. 1973: Reading the illegible. In H. Dyos and M. Wolff (eds.), *The Victorian City: Images and Reality*, vol 1. London: Routledge and Kegan Paul.

Massey, D. forthcoming. *Living in Wythenshawe*. Mimeo: Social Sciences, Open University.

McLuhan, M. 1962: *The Gutenberg Galaxy*. London: Routledge.

Morrison, T. 1989: *Song of Solomon*. London: Picador.

Mulvey, L. 1989: *Visual and Other Pleasures*. London: Macmillan.
Orwell, G. 1937: *The Road to Wigan Pier*. London: Victor Gollancz.
Popper, K. 1962: *The Open Society and its Enemies*. London: Routledge and Kegan Paul.
Porteous, J. 1990: *Landscapes of the Mind: Worlds of Sense and Metaphor*. Toronto: Toronto University Press.
Robins, K. 1996: *Into the Image*. London: Routledge.
Rodaway, P. 1994: *Sensuous Geographies*. London: Routledge.
Roderick, I. 1997: Household sanitation and the flows of domestic space. *Space and Culture*, 1, 105–32.
Rorty, R. 1980: *Philosophy and the Mirror of Nature*. Oxford: Blackwell.
Sennett, R. 1991: *The Conscience of the Eye*. London: Faber.
Shields, R. 1991: *Places on the Margin*. London: Routledge.
Sontag, S. 1979: *On Photography*. Harmondsworth: Penguin.
Stallybrass, P. and White, A. 1986: *The Politics and Poetics of Transgression*. London: Methuen.
Taylor, J. 1994: *A Dream of England*. Manchester: Manchester University Press.
Tuan, Y.-F. 1993: *Passing Strange and Wonderful*. Washington, DC: Island.
Urry, J. 1990: *The Tourist Gaze*. London: Sage.
Virilio, P. 1988. The work of art in the age of electronic reproduction. Interview in *Block*, 14, 4–7.

Chapter 34

With Child to See any Strange Thing: Everyday Life in the City

Nigel J. Thrift

The question is not so much do we notice (attend to) the city? No doubt we do. Rather the point is, how do we notice it? For long periods of time, I suspect we notice very little at all, at least in the accepted sense of the term. Rather "we" are very small parts of a "transhuman" field of activity which ebbs and flows. Our urban world, in other words, is rather like Musil's monuments, there and not there, only fitfully attended to.

There is nothing in the world as invisible as a monument. They are no doubt erected to be seen – indeed to attract attention. But at the same time they are impregnated with something that repels attention, causing the glance to roll right off, like water droplets off an oil cloth, without even pausing for a moment. You can walk down the street for months, know every address, every shop window, every policeman along the way, and you would even miss a coin that someone dropped on the sidewalk; but you are very surprised when, one day, staring up at a pretty chambermaid on the first floor of a building, you notice a not-at-all tiny plaque on which, engraved in indelible letters, you read that from eighteen hundred and a little more the unforgettable so-and-so lived and created here. Many people have the same experience even with larger than life-sized statues... You never look at them, and do not usually have the slightest notion of whom they are supposed to represent, except that maybe you know if it's a man or a woman (Musil cited in Anderson 1998: 61).

Over the years, one literature has tried to understand how we notice the city – and, I might add, how it notices us – and it is this literature that I aim to summarize in this chapter. It is a strange literature, attempting to bring something into the light yet well aware of the shadowy necessity of dreams and superstitions, deeply intellectual yet desperate to capture the sensuous bend and sway of bodies in motion, cleaving to the notion of the chance encounter yet just as strongly attached to notions of predestination. It is a literature about the city as experienced – the murmurs, the glances, the song, and the dance – yet the nature of that experience, and how, and even if it can be represented, is precisely what is at issue.

This mainly twentieth-century literature is usually referred to as a literature on "everyday life" in the city and it takes in tangled surrealist authors like Breton (e.g. Cohen 1993), lonely visionaries like Benjamin (e.g. Buck-Morss 1989; Gilloch 1997; Caygill 1998), perpetual revolutionaries like Debord and the other situationists (Sadler 1998), forensic romantics like de Certeau (Ahearne 1996), and Marxists becoming something else like Henri Lefebvre (Shields 1998). For this motley crew, the city is more than just a "pragmatic disruption of singularities" (Benjamin 1915: 37, cited in Caygill 1998: 9). Rather, it is a place in which it is possible to press the bounds of experience, find redemption, make new dreams. It is a lost and found place which, rather like Peter Ackroyd's sequence of London novels, always contains something hidden which we can just touch, if we but try.

For those writers, the city makes philosophically inclined theory into a new political site within which conduct can gather and be transformed. Nice work, if you can get it. But can you? In this short chapter, I want to provide a synthetic account of these writers' work which is sympathetic but also critical. I will suggest that they are engaged in an analysis of the city which is double-edged and that this tension in their works is never resolved.

But I will argue that this work can be used to produce new and productive readings of the city. Therefore, in what follows, I will begin to clear the ground by attending to the side of these writers' urban encounters which has not stood the test of time. Then I will attend to that side of these writers' work that has continued to resonate. In the third part of the chapter I will consider the new work which has taken up the challenge that these writers offer.

The Case for the Prosecution

There is a dark side to these authors' urban writings which seems to elide precisely the object of their sympathy: ongoing practices of going on. Thus an account of the city is too often produced which is as exclusionary as the forces these writers intend to combat. Why might this be? There are, I think, three reasons. The first is, quite simply, location. The cities that these writers consider are doubly centered. They are nearly all important urban centers – pivots of the world – and, more than that, their writing nearly all concerns the central cores of such cities. It is difficult to think of the situationists in Stevenage, de Certeau in Catford, or Lefebvre in Lewisham – though it is a beguiling prospect. In particular, where suburbs exist in their writings – if they exist at all – they are rejected as inert, conformist, and oppressive, the haunts of the intellectually challenged (Silverstone 1997).

The second and more complex reason is that these writers want to pull in cities – or at least the parts of cities that count – as their prime exemplars of the commodification of everyday life in modernity. According to most of these accounts there has been a remorseless drive to commodification which leaves precious little room for anything but a homogenized conformity. Consumption is but a mirror of mass production, valuing objects simply because they are new. Consumption therefore becomes conformist drudgery. Contact between people is swallowed up by commodities which become animated as a result. But this Old Testament depiction, and its corresponding desire for complete historical immanence, has become harder to bear as a New Testament of commodities and consumption has been written over the last 20 years or so which understands the process of commodification in rather different and more variegated ways which can grasp hold of the "thinginess" of things. Developments like actor-network theory have recoded the object world, producing an account which points to the sheer density of practices in which objects and humans are involved and which regards objects as conditions of possibility for thinking the world, even as means of authentication, just as much as a means of the erasure of "humanity."

The third reason is what we might call a snobbish romanticism about the city and its inhabitants. These authors want to believe that the city is an all-consuming capitalist machine, a space of superordinate strategies, and, at the same time, a treasure trove of chance encounters which allow us to see round the dominant system, a subordinate space of tactics. Following nineteenth-century writers like Baudelaire, the city is therefore able to function as a means of administering shocks which can disrupt situated forms of perception and affect the subject's ability to represent her- or himself. The city therefore promises precious moments of epiphany. At its worst, this stance can become a kind of macho heroism; the *flâneur* wanders the streets "au hasard, allowing the eye to roam randomly across the urban scene" (Prendergast 1992: 149), sometimes feeling a frisson of fear, but essentially safe to experience what may turn up. Or such a stance may be generalized out, as in the work of de Certeau, into an esthetic of resistance which writes the city as a "forest" of marginalized (and unexplained), "unplanned and unconnected," acts of resistance that conjure up "a migrational or metaphorical city" which "eludes discipline without being outside the field in which it is exercised" (de Certeau 1984: 96). But, as Bennett (1998: 75) puts it, in taking this tack de Certeau manages to make "nothing out of something," by producing an account of everyday urban life which resolutely opposes the systematic spaces of strategy to the timely acts of the weak, the visual register of survey from afar to the tactile register of feeling near to and the legitimated to the illegitimate. He erases all spaces outside the spaces of power and is therefore left to plaintively conjure up an outside to the dominant urban text without the aid of the sociological spaces – with their political hum – which have been obliterated by this move.

In other words, de Certeau illustrates the chief problem with so many accounts of everyday life in the city; they seek – often while proclaiming the exact opposite – a ground, a legitimate space of legitimate being which can be opposed to a "larger" illegitimate system. Everyday life becomes a kind of authentic "second nature," the thing itself – alive, real, immediate – which can be both celebrated and can become an object of acute nostalgia (Thrift 1996; Crook 1998). Of course, these are hardly the first accounts in social theory to do this, but they seem to be particularly prone to this vice. It is as if the very size and complexity of the modern city defeats them and they are only able to function by portraying everyday life as a kind of wonderful defeat.

To summarize, too often in work on everyday life in cities, the inhabitants of the city became ciphers caught in the swirl of modernity, condemned to endlessly repeat "new time" (Osborne 1995) by a more or less enveloping historical force – capitalism – which transforms time into "a dynamic and historical force in its own right" (Koselleck 1985: 246, cited in Osborne 1995: 11). The city is simultaneously open to the future and closed. The city is in permanent transition but to only one end.

No wonder, then, that these writers tended to fix on the particular registers of urban experience which confirmed this vision, and, indeed, in the nineteenth-century were used to create it: speed, shock, chance, bustle, noise, unsettling encounters. The city becomes a blur.

Yet, at the same time, it would be foolish to argue that these writers embody only an impulse "to reduce every order of reality to a unique vocabulary" (Hennion and Latour 1997: 4). In their desire to make the city come alive they also provide a case for their defense, to which I now turn.

The Case for the Defense

It doesn't have to be like this and in these authors' writings one can find another world than the command performance I have so briefly sketched above. This world is based, I think, on three principles.

Thus, first of all, there is the notion of experience. What each of these writers attempts to do is to understand the city as possibility. Cities shine with the light of possibility and happenstance. Granted this light may be blotted out but the resources are there. This sense of the city as a field of possibility, borne out of chance encounters, new forms of experience based, for example, on new technologies, and on the production of new more open subjectivities can be found in all these authors to at least some degree. For example, Benjamin's recasting of Kant's category of experience as a notion of speculative experience – though it might well "be judged a cautionary failure" (Caygill 1998: 3) – provides a means of opening up a new kind of reading of the city which by redefining reading more broadly also redefined what could be read. Thus

> configuration is regarded as the condition of legibility: to be legible (ie to conform to the conditions of possible reading as experience) is not the congruence of an intended meaning, but is rather the discovery of a "non sensuous similarity" between confined patterns. As the example of the dance suggests, these patterns are not exclusively spatial – for space in itself is but a particular form of "non sensuous similarity" or patterning – but can also be temporal, emphasised in accent, metre and rhythm. Indeed it is crucial for Benjamin's argument that space and time (Kant's forms of intuition) be regarded as modes of configuration whose plasticity, or openness to other forms of patterning, can "decay" or be "transformed". Space and time will feature as the givens of transcendental philosophy become modes of configuration which can be understood as providing the contours of but one among many possible configurations of experience (Caygill 1998: 5).

It follows that, on such a reading of reading, experience is constantly being redefined by modes of perambulation through the city (walking, driving, phoning, e-mailing, and so on) and by the new microclimates of movement and communication (the airport, the highway, and so on) that these perambulations demand and supply. These are the new highways and byways of experience which in turn provide all manner of expressive potentials (in the media, art and so on) which seep gradually into the general culture (Cubitt 1998).

Another way to consider the constant generation of new forms of experience is as new apprehensions of time, which the city both manifests and generates. In the work of the surrealists Benjamin and Lefebvre this is a constant theme. In Lefebvre's later work on rhythmanalysis, experience of the city depends upon attention to rhythms whose "characteristic features are really temporal and rhythmical, not visual" (Lefebvre 1996: 223). The city is a symphony of rhythms, a perpetual renewal.

Whatever the means, the attempt is quite clear: to acknowledge the expressive potential of the city arising out of the play of possibility. These authors want to speak to the bubbling urban imaginary.

Second, this sense of how the city is experienced privileges different kinds of knowledge, and most specifically, the practical knowledges which provide the means by which cities keep going. These are the "great underground" (Taussig 1992: 26) of habitual and yet improvisational knowledges which produce most of the city's daily routine. Yet these are also the minor knowledges which have been least examined.[1] What each of these authors provides – each in their different ways – is the beginnings of a gazetteer of these knowledges based upon some clearly interconnected principles. One of these is the immense importance of embodiment, of the power of bodies to get a hold of the world through their ability to conjure up virtual "as-if" worlds and so make possibilities possible. Here, in particular, we can point to Benjamin's emphasis on mimesis, on getting hold of something by means of its likeness. But, in turn, this emphasis on the tactile appropriation of embodiment generates two further impulses. Thus, embodiment articulates and is articulated by a whole range of senses. Its tactility operates in the many registers of sensate life which can combine in many different ways. In Benjamin's terms, embodiment is "chromatic" and excessive in that as a medium it provides an almost infinite number of definitions, a constantly multiplying multiplicity. And cities both amplify and arrest the sensory load. Take sight and sound.

> Below, towards the right, a traffic light: on red, the cars stop, pedestrians cross, soft hummings, a babble of voices. One does not converse while crossing a dangerous intersection, threatened by wild animals and elephants about to leap, taxis, buses, trucks and various cars. So there is a relative silence in this crowd. A kind of soft murmur and sometimes a cry, a call.
>
> Therefore, when the cars stop, people produce a completely different sound: feet and words. From left to right and vice versa and on the pavements along the perpendicular street. At the green light, step and voices stop. A second of silence and its the surge, the burst of speed of tens of cars accelerating as fast as possible (Lefebvre 1996: 220).

Then embodiment makes no sense taken apart from the "object world." Things are such a vital part of the world that they cannot be separated: they are a vital part of embodied perception. There is "a palpable, sensuous connection between the very body of the perceiver and the perceived" (Taussig 1992: 21). Objects are not inanimate; they are a part of what it is to be animate and this process is an "unstoppable merging" (Taussig 1992: 25). Thus, to quote the early Benjamin, "they perceive us; their gaze propels us into the future, since we do not respond to them but instead step among them" (Benjamin 1914, cited in Caygill 1998: 8). In other words, "the passage from the subject to the object requires neither a leap of analysis, nor the crossing of the desert" (Lefebvre 1996: 227). Close to practice such distinctions became all but meaningless. Indeed in Lefebvre's notion of rhythm, the idea is clearly to produce a term which passes between such distinctions. It gives a positive role to the material presence of objects and, in doing so, it does not allow them to become just commodities.

Continue and you will see this [courtyard] garden and the objects (which have nothing to do with things) polyrhythmically, or, if you prefer, symphonically. Instead of a collection of congealed things, you will follow each being, each body, as having above all, its time. Each therefore having its place, its rhythms, with its immediate past, a near future and hereafter (Lefebvre 1996: 223–4).

Then, third, each of these writers wants to write the city in new ways. Most particularly they want to write the city in such a way as to make it clear that the city is not only about writing. And writing is not just about the mechanics of capturing the city in print. The ambition goes much farther than that. To begin with, it is an attempt to make the city legible in a whole series of registers. Benjamin's agonized organization and reorganization of the *Passagen Werk*, de Certeau's poetics, Lefebvre's rhythmanalysis – these are all attempts to free the city to perform across the spectrum of possibilities. Then, the inclination is to write the city as a complex entity, able to hold many different and ongoing projects in tension, able to encompass numerous spaces and times in continual transformation, able to admit of other possible features. Thus, for Lefebvre (1985: 110), for example:

To think about the city is to hold and maintain its conflictual aspects: constraints and possibilities, peacefulness and violence, meetings and solitude, gatherings and separation, the trivial and the poetic, brutal fundamentalism and surprising improvisation... One can hope that it will turn out well but the urban can become the centre of barbarity, domination, dependence, and exploitation... In thinking about these perspectives, let us leave a place for events, initiatives, decisions. All the hands have not been played. The sense of history does not suppose any historic determinism, any destiny.

Expressing this complexity may involve metaphors, such as Benjamin's notion of porosity, crucial to the rendering of Naples; or it may involve an understanding of the different rhythms which punctuate daily life, as in Lefebvre's rhythmanalysis of Mediterranean cities. The point is that the ambition to write complexity complexly, means that it is not possible to either "meticulously [describe] a privileged and known place, or throw ourselves into a lyricism aroused by the splendour of the cities evoked" (Lefebvre 1996: 240). Something else is needed. Then, the desire to write the city may often involve capturing the role, the ache, of speculative moments, of situations, by attempting to produce situations. Thus writing becomes something ever wider, something theatrical, and performative. What is clear, then, is that writing the city can be approached in many ways, through poetry, through novels, through theater, through situationist setups. Writing, becomes, in other words, a more general practice of inscription and citation.

Coda

The theorists of everyday life in the city have continued to provide stimulation for those studying the city. But, increasingly, these ideas now form a platform from which their work has been taken in other directions, directions which they may or may not have dreamed of. In this third section, I want to argue that the intellectual and practical boost given by the theorists of everyday life has now become general across the social sciences and promises – in the fullness of time – to produce new senses of how the city can be noticed.

In particular, I will argue that a whole brew of new ideas on the three most positive elements of the work of theorists of everyday life in the city – from the vitalist pragmatics of writers like Deleuze, through feminist accounts of poiesis, through actor-network theory, to so-called discursive psychology, all of which stress the nonrepresentational – has put a powerful spin on these ideas.

Thus, to begin with, the emphasis on the city as a field of possibility has been invigorated by chance encounters with other theoretical traditions – for example, the social psychology of Bakhtin, Voloshinov and others – which have extended our understanding of the city as a skilled accomplishment, based on the improvisatory "fictions" of practical knowledges which constitute the lore of the city. These fictions are dialogical phenomena which

> constitute a third sphere of events, distant from both action and behaviour: (i) they cannot be accounted simply as actions (for they are not done by individuals, thus they cannot be explained by giving a person's reasons); neither (ii) can they be treated as simply "just happening" behaviour (to be explained by discovering their causes); (iii) they occur in a chaotic zone of indeterminacy or uncertainty in between the other two spheres. And as such, although continuing aspects of each, occurrence in this sphere do not seem amenable to any clear characterisations at all. Indeed, although not wholly unspecified, it is their very lack of any final specificity, their lack of a completely predetermined structure, and thus their openness to being determined further by those involved in them, in practice ... that is their central defining feature (Shotter and Billig 1998: 27).

In particular, this open sense of possibility has led to a consideration of embodied activity which is intent on understanding bodies' ability to conjure up "virtual" urban worlds – play, dreams, daydreams, and the like – which through their own imaginary mutability are able to both confirm and extend the city's own constant metamorphosis (Bowlby 1998; Steedman 1998). Thus it is that the city finds expression; "streets in perpetual motions as in dreams, where it's the city which dreams itself, navigating in all directions through the strata of rock, life and meaning which make up its layers, progressively re-inventing the laws of its unstable gravitation" (Réda 1986, cited in Sheringham 1996: 105). Thus, as Sheringham (1996) so nicely puts it, there is a shift from the imaginary city to the imaginative city, actively caught up in self-invention. In Réda's (1977, 1987, 1982) works for example, the subject is absorbed into the city, like one of the leaves on a tree shivering in the breeze, or what Réda (1987) calls a "reflective antenna," becoming a small part of spaces which possess sufficient practical resemblances – "emptiness, theatricality, darkness, alternatives of frenetic activity and quiescence, noise and silence, endless repetitions and series – of gestures (in the theatre), objects (in the library), financial transactions (in the Bourse), messages (at the post offices)" (Sheringham 1996: 109) – to provide a kind of imaginative resonance which is itself a crucial urban resource. The cities' practices echo through each other producing ghostly lines of interference.

Of course, none of this is to suggest that practices of oppression don't exist in the city: this is not a naive or a utopian vision. Rather it is to suggest two things. One is that practices of oppression are themselves created by skilled improvisations. They are as anthropologically charged and as dialogical as any other aspect of culture: they too are a part of everyday life. Then, much of the power of practices to dictate the course of events comes from the remorseless buildup of small and fleeting detail in speech and objects which "points" towards certain conclusions without requiring conscious articulation, what Shotter and Billig (1998) have argued operates as a "dialogic unconscious." For example, "in the gaps between and within words, involving the dialogic gaps filled by the little unnoticed words, ideology inserts itself and so is reproduced while speakers direct their consciousness on to matters where the dialectics of justification and altruism can be safely limited" (Shotter and Billig 1998: 21).

Then, to pass on to the second important element of the work of the theorists of everyday life, cities must be seen as repositories of practical knowledge but this practical knowledge is constantly transmuting. One of these transmutations is that cities have become repositories of "objectivity"; they are – increasingly – crowded with objects which – increasingly – "speak back." Objects become more "person"-like, just as persons have become more "object"-like (Gell 1998; Boyne 1998). However, cities are not therefore assuming a "posthuman" character, as argued in some of the more fraught and exaggerated interpretations of information technologies now current, such as Virilio's writings on the city (e.g. Virilio 1991), but rather a transhuman one, in which we dwell among badly analyzed composites – networks of flesh and machines – and are ourselves badly analyzed composites, to paraphrase Deleuze (1994). What is clear is that in this world of weak subjectivity (Guattari 1997),

> It is not a question of humanizing the universe of machines so that everywhere one sees only the mirror image of our own desire for control, influence, design, and mastery. Human thought clearly plays a major role in the evolution of a machinic phylogenesis, but it is hubris which leads them to the positioning of the human, all too human as the meaning and telos of this machinism. For the greater part of evolution human thought has relied on the mediation of technical machines – an ongoing mnemotechnics is constitutive of human thinking – but this cannot mean that the thought that is generated can be characterised as solely or strictly "human" in terms of some ethic of possessive individualism. Thought is "transhuman" in all the senses of the word one cares to think of. The music which these machines speak does not provide access to a single, unsocial truth of Being, as if *techne* possessed an essence available only to humans as part of their supposed unique and privileged residency in the cosmos; rather, machines provide pathic and cartographic access to a plurality of beings and of worlds (Ansell-Pearson 1998: 6).

In turn this transhuman order is constantly multiplying time and spaces[2]. The city becomes a series of silhouettes of silhouettes which "overlook" each other, an "oligopticon" (Latour and Hermant 1998).

Another transmutation is that practical knowledges have thus become increasingly concerned, as a result of the general expansion of these transhuman actor-networks (or actant-rhizomes, to use the Deleuzian nomenclature), with the oblique, the transparent, and the haunted; the latent, if you like. Practical knowledge of cities is haunted by apparitions which are the unintended consequences of the complexity of modern cities, cities in which multiple time-spaces are being produced, which overlap, interact, and interfere, producing hybrids which change the structure of urban experience as they are gathered in by practical knowledges.

These are knowledges of what is permitted and prohibited, present and absent, surprising and unsurprising. These are the knowledges of the gaps and the in and betweens. These are the "flashing half-signs" (Gordon 1997: 204) which prefigure new urban topologies.

> The way of the ghost is haunting, and haunting is a very particular way of knowing what has happened or is happening. Being haunted draws us affectively, sometimes against our will and always a bit marginally, into the structure of feeling of a reality we come to experience, not as cold knowledge, but as transformative recognition (Gordon 1997: 8).

Or, to put it another way,

> A structure of feeling "actualises presence" (Williams 1977: 135) as the tangled exchange of noisy silences and seething absences. Such a tangle – of object and experience – is haunting. And haunting describes a practical consciousness that is "always more than a handling of fixed forms and units." Haunting describes just those "experiences to which the fixed forms do not speak at all, they do not recognise" (p. 130).

Or, to put it one more way, cities do not add up. Rather, they accumulate[3].

There is, then, one more positive element of the work of theorists of everyday life to build upon. That is the matter of writing. Writing cities has become an endeavor which is manifold. There has been an explosion of means of communicating the city which, nowadays, is concentrated around the term "performance." The current "performative turn" across the social sciences and humanities has provided those who are trying to communicate cities with a whole reservoir full of practices of production and disclosure of situations which have heretofore been neglected (cf. Thrift 2000). Various forms of theater, opera, concert and dance, performance art, multimedia, all have something important to contribute to an understanding of the precarious emptiness of the "now" in which practical knowledges must operate. They are, if you like, a means of conjuring up the imaginary edge of cities, both in terms of the risks all cities involve and the representations that every now and then break through and become a part of the common cultural hoard (Finnegan 1998).

Of course, performance is still irrefutably bound up with the written word. Certainly, many who are interested in performance have tried to work towards a model of "performative writing" which can capture some of the travails of performance and can constitute a performance in its own right, often taking models from poetry. But again, much performance is written in different scripts which can better capture embodied practices. For example, in television and movies there are elaborate forms of movement notation based in the mechanics of production. Similarly in dance there are movement scripts like Labanotation. But, fundamentally, much performance cannot be written down. It is unwritable, and unsayable and has to be communicated in other registers. And that is its fascination so far as the study of everyday life in the city goes; it is a living demonstration of those skills we have but cannot firmly cultivate in the linguistic domain, and it can – in the best work – provide a sense of new styles of urban living which might simultaneously produce new senses of how the world is. Indeed, in that performance is orientated towards relationally responsive events rather than referential representative forms of rationality, it can furnish us with methodologies which can banish the urge to mastery and control. After all, "only if we are prepared to change our hierarchically ordered centripetal ways, and to dialogically balance them with ones of a more centrifugal and relational kind, can we ever hope to arrive at a psychology properly respectful of the 'little details' of people's 'inner lives', and to overcome some of the seemingly basic ideological methods of our time" (Shotter and Billig 1998: 27). In other words, the performative turn can help to plumb the meanings of democracy in ways which can be written into practice (Spinosa, Flores, and Dreyfus 1997).

Let me, then, conclude. The magical but wounded power of the city does not lie in great theatrical urban landscapes, but in the slow accumulation of skill and intuition that is the best means of coping with the elusive, phantasmic, emergent and often only just there fabric of everyday life. This "problematic" rather than "theorematic" (Deleuze and Guattari 1987) knowledge of practice provides a different means of knowing and writing the social world, one which makes common cause with the subjects and objects of its analysis by "understanding... the representation as contiguous with that being represented and not as suspended above and distant from the represented" (Taussig 1992: 10). Perhaps the most heartening aspect, then, of current work on everyday life in the city is its commitment to democratic methods of exploring the urban, from the detailed exigencies of relational pedagogy (e.g. McNamee and Gergen 1998; Newman and Holzman 1997) through to the grander projects of legislative theater and the like (e.g. Boal 1998). Such developments are a means of satisfying the longing for a riper, less diminished urban future by boosting the horizons of what is possible – through noticing the city in new ways.

NOTES

1. These practical knowledges have numerous minor elements, especially of gender and ethnicity, but, as I point out later, they cannot be seen as simply or even mainly transgressive (cf. Butler 1993). But, for example, women are relatively often associated with the nonvisual senses that characterize much of the literature on everyday life in the city (Classen 1998).
2. Information technology is clearly producing new times and spaces (see Cubitt 1998), but it is unwise to assume that these times and spaces are in some way transcendental. Most of them are still ad hoc assemblages.
3. Georges Perec's urban writing is a wonderful example of these kinds of insights (e.g. Perec 1987). Perec was, for a time, associated with Henri Lefebvre (Ed Soja, personal communication).

REFERENCES

Ahearne, J. 1996: *Michel de Certeau*. Cambridge: Polity Press.
Ansell-Pearson, K. 1998: *Viroid Life: Perspectives on Nietzsche and the Transhuman Condition*. London: Routledge.
Bennett, T. 1998: *Culture: A Reformer's Science*. London: Sage.
Boal, A. 1998: *Legislative Theatre: Using Performance to Make Politics*. London: Routledge.
Bowlby, R. 1998: The other day: the interpretation of daydreams. *New Formations*, 34, 9–26.
Boyne, R. 1998: Angels in the archive: lines into the future in the work of Jacques Derrida and Michael Serres. In S. Lash, A. Quick, and R. Roberts (eds.), *Time and Value*. Oxford: Blackwell, 48–64.

Buck-Morss, S. 1989: *The Dialectics of Seeing: Walter Benjamin and the Arcades Project*. Cambridge, MA: MIT Press.
Butler, J. 1993: *Bodies that Matter: On the Discursive Limits of Sex*. New York: Routledge.
Caygill, H. 1998: *Walter Benjamin: The Colour of Experience*. London: Routledge.
Certeau, M. de 1984: *The Practice of Everyday Life*. Berkeley: University of California Press.
Classen, C. 1998: *The Colour of Angels: Cosmology, Gender and the Aesthetic Imagination*. London: Routledge.
Cohen, M. 1993: *Profane Illumination: Walter Benjamin and the Paris of Surrealist Revolution*. Berkeley: University of California Press.
Crook, S. 1998: Minotaurs and other monsters. "Everyday life" in recent social theory. *Sociology*, 32, 523–40.
Cubitt, J. 1998: *Digital Aesthetics*. London: Sage.
Deleuze, G. 1994: *Difference and Repitition*. New York: Columbia University Press.
Deleuze, G. and Guattari, F. 1987: *A Thousand Plateaus*. Minneapolis: University of Minnesota Press.
Finnegan, R. 1998: *Tales From a City*. Cambridge: Cambridge University Press.
Gell, A. 1998: *Art and Agency*. Oxford: Oxford University Press.
Gilloch, G. 1997: *Myth and Metropolis: Walter Benjamin and the City*. Cambridge: Polity Press.
Gordon, A. 1997: *Ghostly Matters: Haunting and the Social Imagination*. Minneapolis: University of Minnesota Press.
Guattari, F. 1997: *Chaosmosis: An Ethico-Aesthetic Paradigm*. Sydney: Power Publications.
Hennion, A. and Latour, B. 1997: How to Make Mistakes on so Many Things at Once – and Become Famous for This. At http://www.ensmp.fr/~latour/p art/p51.htm1
Latour, B. and Hermant, E. 1998: *Paris: Ville Invisible*. Paris: Institut Synthelabo/La Découverte.
Lefebvre, H. 1985: *Qu'est ce que Penser?* Paris: Publisud.
Lefebvre, H. 1991: *The Production of Space*. Oxford: Blackwell.
Lefebvre, H. 1996: *Writings on Cities*. Oxford: Blackwell.
McNamee, F. and Gergen, T. 1998: *Relational Pyschology*. London: Sage.
Musil, R. in Anderson, B. 1998: *The Spectre of Comparisons: Nationalism, South East Asia and the World*. London: Verso.
Newman, F. and Holzman, L. 1997: *The End of Knowing: A New Developmental Way of Learning*. London: Routledge.
Osborne, P. 1995: *The Politics of Time: Modernity and Avant-Garde*. London: Verso.
Perec, G. 1987: *Life: A User's Manual*. London: Harvill Press.
Prendergast, C. 1992: *Paris and the Nineteenth Century*. Oxford: Blackwell.
Réda, J. 1977: *Les Ruines de Paris*. Paris: Galliniard.
Réda, J. 1987: *Hors les Murs*. Paris: Galliniard.
Réda, J. 1992: *Le Sens de la Marche*. Paris: Galliniard.
Sadler, S. 1998: *The Situationist City*. Cambridge, MA: MIT Press.
Sheringham, M. 1996: City space, mental space, poetic space: Paris in Breton, Benjamin and Réda. In M. Sheringham (ed.), *Parisian Fields*. London: Reaktion, 85–114.
Shields, R. 1998: *Love and Struggle*. London: Routledge.
Shotter, J. and Billig, M. 1998: A Bakhtinian psychology: from out of the heads of individuals, and into the dialogues between them. In M. Bell and M. Gardiner (eds.), *Bakhtin and the Human Sciences*. London: Sage, 13–29.
Silverstone, R. (ed.) 1997: *Visions of Suburbia*. London: Routledge.

Spinosa C., Flores F., and Dreyfus H. 1997: *Disclosing New Worlds: Entrepreneurship, Democratic Action and the Cultivation of Solidarity.* Cambridge, MA: MIT Press.

Steedman, C. 1998: What a rag rug really means. *Journal of Material Culture*, 3, 259–81.

Taussig, M. 1992: *The Nervous System*. New York: Routledge.

Taussig, M. 1993: *Mimesis and Alterity: A Particular History of the Senses*. New York: Routledge.

Thrift, N. J. 2000: Afterwords. *Environment and Planning D, Society and Space* (forthcoming).

Thrift, N. J. 1996: *Spatial Formations*. London: Sage.

Virilio, P. 1991: *The Lost Dimension*. New York: Semiotext (e).

Williams, R. 1977: *Marxism and Literature*. Oxford: Oxford University Press.

Chapter 35

Walter Benjamin, Urban Studies and the Narratives of City Life

Michael Keith

But for me to descend into what is truly the mind's lower depths, where it is no longer a question of the night's falling and rising again (and is that the day?), means to follow the Rue Fontaine back to the Theatre des Deux Masques, which has now been replaced by a cabaret.

Breton 1960: 39

Introduction

In trying to tell the story of how people have attempted to theorize the economic and social life of cities the name of Walter Benjamin is commonly absent from what we might loosely refer to as the canon of urban studies.[1] This should not be so. In part this chapter points towards an intellectual project that might reinscribe such a history and reinstate Benjamin as a significant character in the castlist of urban social theory. But only in part. There is only limited value in the relay race metaphor of intellectual influence, the carriers of truth passing on the baton of progress in the steady accumulation of scientific knowledge. And if the value of such an Enlightenment metaphor is moot it also cuts against the very grain of Benjamin's own rather less optimistic version of the relationship between the intellectual and the social and political world.

And so there are two complementary purposes to this chapter. One is to focus upon some of the constellatory themes that Benjamin treated upon in his descriptions of the nature of city life and the other is to illustrate how some of these thematics continue to have both analytical and political value in the present. The argument of the former is to suggest that Benjamin's work conveys a sense of an individual of the past working in analytical territory that defies ready categorization but resonates in the problems and issues of a present that confronts the hyper-real excesses of today's sprawling metropolises and the polyphonous exercises that take the city as an organizing theme or a significant focus of contemporary social theory.

The second argument is that at the heart of Benjamin's conceptual framework is a simple analytical move that finesses many of the more stale debates that have plagued mainstream urban studies for several years. Because the observer and the observed are continually problematized within Benjamin's work the relationship between subject and object disrupts any simplistic invocations of theorizing the city. In short Benjamin's work is as much about the manner in which an urban sensibility structures our narratives of the real as it is about the manner in which the city itself is an object of scrutiny. The proper function of a social theory of cities never was and never could be a chimeric search for the essence of the urban. It always needed to occupy a more complex and more ambivalent relationship between the production of time and space and the realization of city form, both as represented and as a crucible of representation.

Genealogies: The Beatification of Walter B. and Alternative Histories of Urban Thought[2]

Benjamin confounds easy categorization in part because his personal failure to receive academic recognition prohibits ready disciplinary labels and in part because of the manner in which he resolutely refused to distinguish between some of the more conventional oppositions in academic debate. His writing crosses traditional genres: much of his work, including the portraits of the cities of Naples, Paris, Moscow, and Berlin, was repeatedly reworked as radio broadcast, journalistic text, and theoretical prose. Culture intertwines with economy, discursive prose alternates with analytical theory, and the anecdotal continually infests narratives of generalization, a set of tensions that are more often than not resolved through the genre of the axiomatic ambiguities that sometimes seem more characteristic of an early-day Borges than the programmatic certainties of friends and sometime colleagues of his in the Frankfurt School of critical theory.

Benjamin's work has come to the attention of Anglophone audiences principally through the translations of two collections of his writing: *Illuminations* (1973) and *One Way Street and Other Writings* (1979) and through a disciplinary focus that derives mostly from his thinking about the relationship between culture and technology that influences the thinking of late 1970s and early 1980s debates in cultural and social theory (e.g. Arendt 1972; Eagleton 1981; Buck-Morss 1989).[3] Such discussion impinged little on the ferment of debate around social theory and the city that characterized approximately the same time period and was most visible in successive Urban Change and Conflict biennial conferences and in journals such as the *International Journal of Urban and Regional Research*. Consequently, the more recent flush of interest in the work of Benjamin might loosely be identified with the cultural turn in mainstream writing about contemporary cities. Yet while such a link is historically plausible it would be intellectually simplistic. While it is easy to suggest that Benjamin's work offers few insights on the manner in which the debate of the 1970s and 1980s attempted to "theorize" the nature of the city as variously a crucible of economic production, social reproduction, mass consumption, or political mobilization, it is also the case that to reduce his contribution to the domain of the cultural would be equally misleading.[4] Instead it is possible both to historicize Benjamin's writing as an exploration of modernity experienced through the new urbanism that emerged at the end of the nineteenth and beginning of the twentieth-century, and also to trace the contours of his thought in the writings of individuals that succeeded him.

Such an exercise most obviously looks at those writers who followed Benjamin chronologically. But we might also consider a reassessment of some of the explorations of the problematic urban that predated Benjamin's work. Though there is no space to do so here, it is possible to look again at exercises such as those of Engels, Booth, and Mayhew that in confronting urban life were struggling to come to terms with precisely the same phenomena of capitalist modernity that Benjamin himself confronted. Such a culturally sensitive reading of what appears to be nineteenth-century reportage or economism has in recent years led to a much more nuanced understanding of matters as diverse as the use of statistical measurement of health and mortality (Hacking 1990), the metropolitan roots of a colonial sensibility (Stallybrass and White 1986), the rhetorical rendering visible of the economy in Engels (Marcus 1973), and the governmental problematics of the nineteenth-century city. Benjamin's own work is usefully read alongside such recent contributions and consequently offers as much to the cultural focus of a new economic sociology as it does to a cultural rendering of the contemporary city.

In so many ways ahead of contemporary thinking about the urban condition, Benjamin resolutely tied the economic to the cultural, the theoretical to the empirical, technology to sensibility; identified the modern city as the cumulative realities of fabricated time and space. The city was a rebus through which a social totality might be read but any such totality was also a social construction of particular modes of representation. In this sense it is at times the sheer overload of information in the early twentieth-century city that distinguishes it for Benjamin. In the face of such confusion how is it possible to knit together a narrative that makes sense of the urban experience to the urban dweller? There is a hidden, rarely told genealogy of stories of the urban that would involve a reassessment of Benjamin's place in the canon of urban studies. The future of the past is invariably uncertain. But if Benjamin's comment that "even the dead will not be safe from the enemy if he wins" has any degree of truth it is possible to summarize such influence, albeit too briefly. So although any such typology is in part arbitrary it might be worth highlighting five strands of work that remain influential and can plausibly be related to Benjamin's own thinking.

1. The culture of money and the cultural production of economic value
2. Problematizing the real and the production of space and time
3. The city as text and emblem
4. Aura, distance, and closeness and the problem of the city view
5. Authenticity and urbanism as corporeal experience

The culture of money and the cultural production of economic value

In 1912 Benjamin attended the lectures of Georg Simmel in Berlin and in all of his work subsequently rarely failed to stress the cultural dimensions of the nature of economic life.[5] Just as Marx argued metonymically from the circulation of the smallest commodity to the structure of capitalism, Benjamin stresses the culture of commodification that cannot divorce materialist economy from an estheticized sense of a changing present.

This is most easily illustrated from two of his most well-known pieces. In the *One Way Street* a montage of lists, theses, aphorisms, and observations on the nature of everyday life cluster around the "Imperial Panorama Tour of German Inflation." Likewise, Benjamin's invocation of the *flâneur* is commonly cast as a particular city character but less often seen in his final destination; seduced by the commodities of the department store, hypnotized by the culture of money.

Both the *flâneur* and *One Way Street* have received attention in mainstream cultural studies but Benjamin's influence should also be recognized in contemporary economic sociology. The affinity with Bourdieu is self-evident and his attempts to render visible the artifice of urban change and the spectacular if hallucinatory economism at the heart of grand projects of urban regeneration prefigures more recent demonstrations of the imagineering of cities (Boyer 1994; Sorkin 1992; Harvey 1990; Jacobs 1996; Kearns and Philo 1993), while the fascination with the social production of the technologies of the relations of production sits easily alongside a focus on the social aspects of economic life (Thrift 1996; Lash and Urry 1994) and the political and cultural construction of Adam Smith's hidden hand of the marketplace.

Problematizing the real and the production of space and time

There are times when Benjamin has been celebrated as reasserting or "reactivating" the value of space in relation to time (Soja 1996: 71). However, perhaps it is more useful to think of Benjamin's significance in terms of an analytical problematization of naive notions of the real, his interest lying in the manner in which temporalities and spatialities become not just media of truth but narrative constructions of modernist realities.

Benjamin does not reject a notion of the real but instead renders visible the modes of fabrication through which the real is constructed as an object of representation. The outright rejection of Whiggish ordering of historical progression is never more clearly and prophetically stated than when in *One Way Street* Benjamin comments that "the assumption that things cannot go on like this will one day find itself apprised of the fact that for the suffering of individuals as of communities there is only one limit beyond which things cannot go: annihilation" (Benjamin 1979: 55).

Benjamin's suspicion of history was most readily described in his purchase of Klee's painting "Angelus Novus":

> His eyes are staring, his mouth is open, his wings are spread. This is how one pictures the angel of history. His face is turned towards the past. Where we perceive a chain of events, he sees one single catastrophe which keeps piling wreckage upon wreckage and hurls it in front of his feet. The angel would like to stay, awaken the dead and make whole what has been smashed. But a storm has been blowing from Paradise; it has got caught in his wings with such violence that the angel can no longer close them. This storm irresistibly propels him into the future to which his back is turned, while the pile of debris before him grows skyward. This storm is what we call progress (Benjamin 1968: 249; also quoted by Buck-Morss 1989: 95).

His fascination with the manner in which places and spaces, histories and memories are socially constructed and technologically mediated compounds this pessimism but makes both the textual strategies of the city observer and the confusing multiple realities of the urban condition a legitimate subject matter for his multimedia collections of prose, cuttings and artifacts. Again such concerns with the nature of the shock in the urban sensibility link directly to those of latter-day theorists such as Lefebvre and Virilio (Der Derian 1998: 3).

There is consequently in Benjamin's work a problematization of the real but not a discounting of it. More importantly, as simultaneously both real and imagined (Soja 1996; Keith and Pile 1993) the city was the outcome of a variety of technologies of representation; an accumulation of statistical constructs, panoramic views and appropriated places, objects of government and moments of both fascination and fear, all held together by a narrative that foregrounded the fairy tales of capitalism. Such a multiplicity again can be read both against the fascinating but at times naive engagements of Chicago School ethnographies and also in advance of the urban theorists of the 1990s such as Neil Smith, Rosalyn Deutsche, Sharon Zukin, and Ed Soja who have focused in the wake of Lefebvre on the production of space. Benjamin's project also demanded both theoretical sophistication and also a resolutely empirical engagement that confounds some of the more simplistic invocations of postmodern urbanism and potentially provides an exemplary case of how the dirty reality of everyday city life can be confronted with the never innocent labor of academic investigation. The refusal of history is a refusal of a particular kind of ordering that characterizes both Benjamin's work and its own afterlife. There is no compensatory celebration of the spatial. Spatiality too for Benjamin is artifactual.

The city as text and emblem

Although his appropriation of landscape was explicitly textual Benjamin did not merely read the landscapes of the modern city, he confronted the urban with all of his senses and in the texts of both the city portraits and *One Way Street* the visual is only one of many forms of production of knowledge.[6]

In reading the city Benjamin's fascination with the minute and the mundane served "to build up the major constructions out of the smallest clearly and precisely manufactured building blocks. Indeed to discover in the analysis of the smallest individual elements of the crystal the totality of what exists" (Benjamin, quoted by Frisby 1985: 190). Benjamin's work will seize on the marginal detail of everyday life and read it through metonymy and metaphor to render the ephemeral emblematic of urban culture as a whole. Particular historical moments and characters are likewise rendered visible in order to describe through allegory the political present.[7]

This manner in which his exercises in city semiotics were both nuanced and multifaceted has been sensitively and beautifully explored in the work of Gilloch (1996) and Buck-Morss (1989). Confronted by the "abortions of urban architectonics" "Benjamin regards the marginalia of the city as the most important clues for its decipherment" (Gilloch 1996: 30).[8] The relationship between meaning, reader, and environment creates a precedent that works through the process of the dialectical image: "Dialectical images are a modern form of emblematics.... The crumbling of the monuments that were built to signify the immortality of civilisation becomes proof rather of its transiency" (Buck-Morss 1989: 170).

Benjamin was clearly both influenced by surrealism and also influential in bringing its insights to bear on the modern city. In his own words "no face is as surrealistic in the same degree as the true face of the city" (Benjamin [1929] 1985: 230). There is a legacy here that is self-evident. Through his interest in allegory, metaphor, and metonymy there is no Barthes without Benjamin, Italo Calvino's *Invisible Cities* (1977) could have been written by Benjamin on opium playing de Quincey in Marseilles, and the miniature emblematic portrayals of contemporary urbanity seen in the narratives of Iain Chambers, Elizabeth Wilson, Patrick Wright, Iain Sinclair, and Jonathan Raban in London or Mike Davis in Los Angeles all draw their inspiration, even if occasionally unknowingly, from a genre of writing that bears a close relation to Benjamin's pioneering confrontation with the cities of his autobiography.

In a related manner Benjamin's city portraits are fascinated by the relationship between empirical experience, theoretical knowledges, authority, and the spatial practices of knowing a city. In "Berlin Chronicle" (Benjamin 1932) the city of Benjamin's childhood is introduced through the five guides to the city that figure as alternative modes of authority, each betraying the juxtaposition between the prosaic, the mundane, and the mythological that creates a caste of mind that places the body in the city, that makes psychogeographies plausible, psychoanalysis defensible, and the symbolic centrality of what is socially marginal comprehensible (Pile 1996; Stallybrass and White 1986).

Aura, distance, and closeness and the problem of the city view

The unclouded, innocent eye has become a lie, perhaps the whole naive mode of expression sheer incompetence. Today the most real, the mercantile gaze into the heart of things is the advertisement. It abolishes the space where contemplation moved.

One Way Street, p. 89

It is the notion of the collection and the questioning of the self-evidence of both history and/or geography as particular forms of storytelling that led Benjamin to think seriously about the problematics of the view, exemplified in his discussions around the panorama and the kaleidoscope as organizing technologies of the eye: "The aeroplane passenger sees only how the road pushes through the landscape, how it unfolds according to the same laws as the terrain surrounding it. Only he who walks the road on foot learns of the power it commands, and of how, from the very scenery that for the flier is only the unfurled plain, it calls forth distances, belvederes, clearings, prospects at each of its turns like a commander deploying soldiers at a front" (*One Way Street*, p. 50).

Benjamin was expert in deciphering the manner in which the smallest changes in ways of being produced such major ruptures in ways of knowing and such changes were overwhelmingly flowing through and from the cities of twentieth-century modernity. From whether or not people looked at each other on new forms of public transport to the visual ordering of newspaper print perhaps Benjamin's most influential work focused on the relationship between technology and cultural reproduction.

It was after all Benjamin who in the "Photography" essay problematized the nature of the view from on high as opposed to the view from the street. But it was de Certeau, Lefebvre, and others who drew on this problematic erroneously to privilege the everyday and the mundane in a form of romanticism that unnecessarily renders the view from high stigmatized. Analysts should not forget that Benjamin was fascinated by the beguiling totalities of the panorama as well as, rather than in preference to, the sensorium of the street.

Hence it was not a valorization of a particular perspective that Benjamin sought as much as an understanding of the optical unconscious that perspective invoked and the consequent need for "a salutory estrangement between man and his surroundings" and "a politically educated eye under whose gaze all intimacies are sacrificed to the illumination of detail" (Benjamin [1931] 1985: 251).

The implications of such work have perhaps been most perceptively explored in the work of Christine Boyer, particularly in the groundbreaking "City of Collective Memory" (1994), but the implications of the meditations on closeness and distance have, with some honorable exceptions (Savage and Warde 1993), been largely ignored in any urban studies attempt to reconcile economic spaces with the culture of cities.

Authenticity and urbanism as corporeal experience

Benjamin's esthetic sensibility, anecdotal prose, and the foregrounding of the individual within the matrix of knowledge production may appear to offer one account for his absence in the canon of urban studies. His work has been at times characterized as exceptional to a tradition of social investigation and thus can be divorced from both orthodox Marxist histories of the capitalist city (Katznelson 1992) and a more culturalist genealogy that links nineteenth-century explorers of the city to Chicago School ethnography through community studies literature to Birmingham School Cultural Studies.

George Steiner has even hardened this distinction between an esthetic domain and the scrutiny of the world of the social, using it almost to explain Benjamin's academic failure and lamenting his posthumous (mis)appropriation by the "new left." He has suggested that this fascination with the nature of allegory and emblem meant that "It is the Aby Warburg group, first in Germany and later in the Warburg Institute in London which would have afforded Benjamin a genuine intellectual, psychological home, not the Horkheimer-Adorno Institute for Social Research in the Social Sciences with which his relations were to prove so ambivalent and, during his life time, sterile" (Steiner 1985: 19). Such a categorization both traduces the work of Adorno in particular and more importantly undervalues the true nature of Benjamin's approach. For it is precisely his refusal to separate esthetics from politics and from political economy that makes his writing so insightful, even if the price of such insight makes the work so difficult to categorize. It is also such categorical bleeding that evokes a set of thematics that resonate in the contemporary city.

Thematics: The Social Rendered Visible through Stories of the City

Benjamin was fascinated by *The Entry of Christ into Brussels* painted by the Belgian/English artist James Ensor in 1889. Emblematically, the picture is now hung in the exact replica of a Pompeii villa in Malibu, California, that serves as the Getty Museum. Allegorically there is a sense in which it is possible to use this image as a frame through which we can identify thematics within Benjamin's work that speak to the present and exemplify the continuing significance of his work.

Figure 35.1 *Christ's Entry into Brussels in 1889* (oil on canvas, 1888, 252×430.5 cm. The J. Paul Getty Museum, Los Angeles)

In Benjamin's writing in and about city life the immediacy of the new was confronted in the relics of the old; modernity for Benjamin is at least in part about the writhing transformations of social form that occupy the built fabric of the preindustrial polis: the crowd in the city, the transmogrified urban scenery, the shocking impact of new technologies, the piling up of catastrophic changes in the name of history that was fossilized in the relics of everyday city life. But what is equally significant for Benjamin is the manner in which these realities are made comprehensible; through technologies of representation, methodologies of apprehension, and narratives that both organize time and space and use temporality and spatiality to organize their rationality. This focus on the relation between the plural and contradictory realities of city life and the plural and sometimes incommensurable ways of knowing the city emerges at the end of the nineteenth-century in a variety of representative genres but speaks to the sensory overload of the urban that makes the link between Simmel and Benjamin already discussed explicit, and between Benjamin and Ensor revealing.

Ensor described himself as fascinated by the phantasmagoria of the city and in this image the loaded metaphor of the mask, the self-conscious deployment of the carnivalesque in a "visual equivalent to Bakhtin's text" (Hyman 1997: 78), and the Palm Sunday celebration that precedes by five days the humiliation of the crucifixion are paralleled in Benjamin's fascination with authenticity, identity, allegory, and the baroque; his historical pessimism and his deployment of iconic figures to carry the weight of representation.

Benjamin likened Ensor's esthetic to that of Edgar Allen Poe and used the work in his exploration of the nature of the *flâneur*: "Fear, revulsion and horror were the emotions which the big city crowd aroused in those who first observed it. For Poe it has something barbaric; discipline just manages to tame it. Later James Ensor tirelessly confronted its discipline with its wildness; he liked to put military groups in his carnival mobs, and both got along splendidly – as the prototype of totalitarian states, in which the police make common cause with the looters" ([1939] 1973: 170).

Benjamin goes on to castigate Poe for saddling the faces in the crowd with an "absurd" kind of uniformity. The politics of the imagery is moot.[9] However, the placard that reads "Fanfares Doctrinaires: Toujours reussi" invokes a fear of ideology but more significantly the image as a whole exemplifies the problematic sociological act of observation. Benjamin draws on Baudelaire's notion of the man shocked by immersion in the city crowd as "a kaleidoscope equipped with consciousness" attempting to know the city through technologies of representation that privilege the visual (Benjamin 1973: 187). But while the technologies of seeing and the perspectival exercises in observation qualify our ability to know the city, "the social" is made visible by a crowd of exemplary characters. Under the banner "Vive La Sociale" that acts as legend or caption at the top of the painting the crowd and the street become realizations of Brussels society; as a theater of the grotesque the whole can only be known through its carnivalesque parts.

In a precisely similar vein Benjamin's work is littered with a series of iconic characters who simultaneously are figures through which the urban is rendered comprehensible and also display the limits of such totalized tales of the city.

Pierre Missac has characterized Benjamin's methodology as "moving like a knight in chess" (1995: 61) and for him Benjamin's city is known via the senses through which it is experienced, the guides through which it is mapped and the technologies of representation through which it is exhibited. Consequently, the urban world is inhabited by a "gallery of types" (Missac 1995: 76) who personify the modalities through which the city is apprehended, experienced, explored, narrated, and rendered visible in alternative versions of reality and truth. In this way Benjamin opens his narrative of "Berlin Chronicle" with explicit reference to the five guides which allowed him to know the city, including "Paris itself [as] the fourth in the series of voluntary or involuntary guides that began with my nursemaids." Elsewhere, at various times the storyteller, the collector, the archeologist, the *flâneur*, the child, the ragpicker, the stamp collector, the statistician, the detective, the sandwich board man and the gambler are among the many characters who exemplify metaphorically different ways of knowing the city and who invoke metonymically different cities that can be known.[10]

Such "types" are not unproblematic. Indeed the continual play between observer and the observed makes the weaknesses in Benjamin's work all too visible. The notion of the opening up of feminized space brings with it a particular resonance of the urban explorer (Boyer 1996; Heron 1993), commonly identified in other forms of phallocentric city narrative: traced in Blake's and Dickens's London of the past, Chandler's Los Angeles of past and present, and in Iain Sinclair's psychogeographies of London. In the figure of the whore as well as in the extended debates about the gendering of the *flâneuse* (Tester 1994; Wilson 1992; Wolff 1985) the sexualization of the street is clearly problematic: "There is no doubt, at any rate, that a feeling of crossing the threshold of one's class for the first time had a part in the almost unequalled fascination of publicly accosting a whore in the street. At the beginning, however, this was a crossing of frontiers not only social but topographical, in the sense that whole networks of streets were opened up under the auspices of prostitution" (Missac 1995: 106).

However these types are quite deliberately unfinished and imperfect narrative devices. In an insightful passage in the essay on Kafka Benjamin evokes a parallel: "In Indian mythology there are the gandharvas, celestial creatures, beings in an unfinished state. Kafka's assistants are of that kind: neither members of nor strangers to, any of the other groups of figures, but, rather, messengers from one to the other. . . . They have not yet been completely released from the womb of nature" (Benjamin 1973: 113).

His way of moving like a knight in chess through narrative figures that are consciously "unfinished" points to a different sort of interdisciplinarity in the study of the city than that most conventionally understood. Benjamin's thinking escapes disciplinary categorization precisely because disciplinary categorization is the object of its study. City types become the organizing tropes which mediate knowledges of the city but they imply a diverse range of forms of presentation. Hence there is a complementary fascination in Benjamin with the ethical, esthetic, and technological mechanisms through which such knowledges are collected, organized, narrated, exhibited, and displayed.

Ways of studying the city imply cognate technologies through which meaning is rendered comprehensible: the story and the novel, the newspaper and the photograph, the museum and the exhibition – all render visible particular forms of the truth marked by their conditions of production and characterized by ethical as well as epistemological traces. It is the artifice of the rendition that seems to fascinate Benjamin, an artifice that in concealing itself displaces narrative and subsumes the psychoanalytic moment; that through the shocks of the surreal is rendered visible as the hidden machinations of the powerful and the seductive logics of the commodity. When Benjamin opts for literary montage and suggests that he has "nothing to say, only to show" it is precisely because of his preference for such "profane illuminations" of the world in which we live."[11] In part the city's totality is confounded by this kaleidoscopic dimension of what he describes as a constellatory epistemology. In this way we should not look to Benjamin for a handbook for social investigation but as a form of stage lighting for particular forms of intellectual inquiry in the city. But what is surely more interesting is to turn Benjamin's investigations back on themselves; to expose the connections between *flâneurie*, journalism, and the sociological gaze; to expose the construction of temporalities and spatialities within particular narrative forms and to use his continual bleeding of one context into another to help to provide an ethical compass for social research in the cities of difference that are diminished by conventional genres of urban studies.

At present the cities of social policy, sociology, geography, anthropology, and history seem to bear little resemblance to each other and at a subdisciplinary level the similarities may be even weaker, divided by methodological, paradigmatic, and ideological competition. The argument here is that a kaleidoscopic framing of such competition might be helpful. Consequently, Benjamin's work points towards a contextualization rather than a relativization of knowledges of the urban, a move that on one level may appear mundane yet at another level is more complex. Such a notion explicitly does not echo a return to the empirical or equate with the urban studies variant of E. P. Thompson's Poverty of Theory diatribe that emerges in the introductory chapters of Peter Hall's (1998) curiously Eurocentric recent volume *Cities in Civilization*. Such a notion of contextualization has been explored elsewhere (Keith and Pile 1993) but commonly involves a reconsidering of the relationship between the empirical and the theoretical through the blurring of conventional boundaries between the esthetic, the ethical, and the epistemological and is particularly germane to contemporary cities characterized by the production of multiple temporalities and spatialities, estheticized commodities, and an ethical vacuum that is endangered by humanistic excess.

Time and Space and Technology in the City of Many Perspectives

The plurality of the urban confounds attempts to define the essence of the city. Any attempt to turn knowledges into a visible form reveals the artifice of cartography. Benjamin plays with this polysemy; he muses on the idea of plotting his life on a map (Benjamin [1932] 1985: 295), is fascinated by the prospect that "The map is almost as close to becoming the centre of the new Russian iconic cult as Lenin's portrait" (Benjamin [1928] 1985: 196), and variously considers the city as labyrinth, statistical artifact, exhibition, collage, panorama, and sensorium.

Consequently, the interplay between closeness and distance which is at the heart of Benjamin's "Work of Art" essay and informs the representational variations in most of the city writing is clearly not about the valorization of a particular perspective. Time is mediated through the production of histories and autobiographies, exemplified through iconic figures such as the child who sees the city with a strange gaze. Space, through different framings of the visible, different kinds of view and different technologies of representation mediates the multiplicity of spatialities that are realized through iconic figures such as the stranger and the *flâneur*. As Gilloch puts it: "Benjamin offers a subtle, intricate interplay of perspectives in which closeness is paradoxically achieved through distance. The city is rendered strange not so much through a simple effect of distance but rather through the continual movement or fluctuation of vantage points. There is flux between the minutely detailed close-up and the distant observation. Benjamin's images of the city are not static but dialectical in character" (1996: 62).

Hence the plastic construction of the relations between time and space (Bullock and Jennings 1996: 499) draw an analytical focus towards the construction of both temporality and spatiality as structures of sensibility that can only be disrupted and revealed through juxtaposition, sudden (surreal) ruptures of the narrative imperatives of geographies and histories of the subject. Any disciplinary celebration of the collapse of the tyrannies of privileged time and the end of history is consequently mistaken (Soja 1996). If Benjamin teaches us anything it is that the artifice subsumed in such narratives caution against such ordering – whether it is through privileging either temporal or spatial. The order of things disguises as much as it reveals, can be disrupted through juxtaposition but this does not render analysis ethically rudderless by their composition.

"The commodity as poetic object"[12]

If Marx and Engels display the material conditions of production through which the very fabric of social life becomes commodified then Benjamin exposes the manner in which this process of commodification not only permeates all cultural forms but is also mediated through practices of cultural representation. He is effectively a pioneering cartographer of the nexus between culture and capital. Studies of the new industrial sectors, cultural industries, and cultural quarters in contemporary cities, and designer economies that are as much about signs as spaces all need to draw on a substantive understanding of the estheticization of the commodity. In this sense for contemporary urban studies Benjamin is invaluable and timely for his pioneering understanding of what he described as the commodity as poetic object, an analytical path that points towards a bringing together of cultural studies approaches to the city with political economies of the urban.

Conventional political economies of the city have focused on an analysis of the changing forces of production that generate the specifics of the contingent relations of production at particular times and places. In contrast Benjamin foregrounds the narrative forms through which the process of commodification is rendered visible, the commodity fetish, and the emergence of specifically capitalist forms of time and space.

Commodification and the nature of the fetishism of consumption can only be understood through the manner in which "commodities . . . store the fantasy energy social transformation in reified form" (Buck-Morss 1989: 29). Although Benjamin abandoned plans to title the Arcades Project as "A dialectical Fairy Scene" because it was too poetic (Buck-Morss 1989: 49) the process of estheticization remains central throughout all of his writing on cities: "Methodologically, one should begin by investigating the links between myth and money throughout the course of history, to the point where money had drawn so many elements from Christianity that it could establish its own myth" (Benjamin 1921: 290).

In Terry Eagleton's terms "In this kind of microanalysis, the individual phenomenon is grasped in all of its overdetermined complexity as a kind of cryptic code or riddling rebus to be deciphered, a drastically abbreviated image of social processes which the discerning eye will persuade it to yield up. . . . What this method then delivers is a kind of poetic or novelistic sociology in which the whole seems to consist of nothing but a dense tessellation of graphic images; and to this extent it represents an estheticized model of social inquiry" (1990: 329–30).

Benjamin develops a "constellatory epistemology" where "Ideas are to objects as constellations are to stars. This means, in the first place, that they are neither their concepts nor their laws" (Benjamin, quoted by Eagleton 1990: 328). Esthetics, epistemology, and ethics are thus simultaneously realized through such constellatory themes, for "Just as philosophy makes use of symbolic concepts to draw ethics and language into the realm of theory, in the same way it is possible for theory (logic) to be incorporated into ethics and language in symbolic form. We then see the emergence of ethical and aesthetic critique" (Benjamin 1919: 219).

Yet this inquiry, in taking the esthetic dimension seriously does not lose sight of the practice of signification of the ever more obscure relationships between use value and exchange value that lie at the heart of increasingly estheticized forms of commodification. Again for Eagleton "It is a matter, rather, of constructing a stringent economy of the object which nevertheless refuses the allure of identity, allowing its constituents to light each other up in all their contradictoriness" (1990: 330).

Antihumanism and narrative

One Way Street and Other Writings was one of only two books both completed and published in Benjamin's lifetime. It is a meditation on the nature of the contemporary condition, one of Benjamin's most experimental and self-consciously avant gardeist investigations of modernity. Throughout this and other work the city works as the organizing theme through which Benjamin's thoughts are expressed.

Perhaps *One Way Street* is most readily rendered accessible if read alongside the essay on Surrealism. The apparently random and frequently winsome nature of the prose should not disguise the attempt to develop a very specific political program within the rhetoric of the shock, that follows on from the significance of constellation and juxtaposition. As Buck-Morss has cataloged, the engagement with Surrealism was a productive one but not one exclusively celebratory. The exposure of the fabricated nature of normal history and natural geography was supposed to awaken alternative ways of thinking about time and space.[13]

In this sense the instrumental political fabrication of alternative ways of thinking about the political was precisely the target of some of Benjamin's methodological tropes. As Buck-Morss has commented: "Fascism reversed the avant-garde practice of putting reality onto the stage, staging not only political spectacles but historical events, and thereby making 'reality' itself theatre" (Buck-Morss 1989: 36). The attention that is paid to narrative shape, the construction and artifice of the story, the mediating role of an iconography of landscape all points to an interweaving of esthetics, epistemic, and ethics within a specific notion of freedom: "Since Bakunin, Europe has lacked a radical concept of freedom. The Surrealists have one. They are the first to liquidate the sclerotic-liberal-moral-humanistic ideal of freedom because they are convinced that 'freedom which on this earth can only be bought with a thousand of the hardest sacrifices, must be enjoyed unrestrictedly in its fullness without any kind of pragmatic calculation as long as it lasts'" (Benjamin 1929: 136).

Exemplifications: Debates in Need of Walter

In thinking through the interplay between the city as a whole and the parts of the city it is possible to suggest, albeit too briefly, the sorts of urban studies problematics that Benjamin might speak to today. Most obviously, this implies a rejection of both an epistemology and a politics that privilege the everyday and valorize the street as the residue of a particular kind of humanistic city. More specifically, there is a generic take on de Certeau's (1984) spatial practices that ignores the Photography essay meditations of Benjamin and instead valorizes the poets of the streets and decries the phallocentric will to power implicit in the representations of the panorama city. At times this has emerged as a lucid and powerful critique of a particular kind of masculinist urban studies (Boyer 1996; Deutsche 1996). But the critique of boys' stories that render the city visible in particular kinds of ways should not obscure an engagement with the manner in which the urban becomes the subject of discourse and the object of technological control in other representations of the whole city.

As Barth has put it: "The Practice of Everyday Life, it seems to me, misjudges the scale, temporality and technology by which visibility can be attached to power in the dominating way it describes. In thinking that visibility operates over the space of the city, de Certeau is imagining that a city is more disciplined than governed, and this confuses the space and the technology of disciplinary visibility with the fact that domination is, unfortunately, very much consistent with the liberal government of cities and states" (1996: 474).

Benjamin reveals the impossibility of the viewer moving outside the scopic regime without denigrating the process of empirical scrutiny and observation.[14] This circumscribes the politics of the gaze but does not decry a speculative analysis of the urban: "From within this space there is no place from which to gain an inclusive experience of the city, or to represent it, since every box is also a stage, every viewer a viewed. In this understanding of spatial experience (which may be described as 'speculative') every position is in a process of negotiating its relations with other positions; there is no fixed or spatial form which governs the location of participants in the way of Hausmann's boulevards in Paris" (Caygill 1998: 122).

In a sense George Steiner captures this in his suggestion that "It is not only that Benjamin is trapped in the hermeneutic cycle – the use of the part to define the whole whose own definition governs the status of the part – but, like Heidegger, he welcomes this circularity, perceiving in it the characteristic intimacy which binds object to interpretation and interpretation to object in the humanities" (Steiner 1985: 21).

There is consequently a plurality of contemporary debates where the tension between the part and the whole are rendered visible in the cities of urban studies and where Benjamin's contribution remains germane. To reveal the city as an object of government, a modality through which the conduct of conduct will be mediated (Foucault 1991), suggests a line of investigation of the technologies through which the temporalities and the spatialities of the whole city are represented. The signs of the city from graffiti tag (Hebdige 1993; Back, Keith, and Solomos 1999) to virtual realities of the inscriptions of Sim City (Soja 1999) demand a reflection on the interplay of technology, representation, and the urban.

The auratic artifice of tales of contemporary urban regeneration draw on the exhibitionism that was at the heart of Benjamin's Arcades Project. The analogous city, "not quite a real city nor entirely a fictitious one" (Boyer 1994: 175), that emerges in the United Kingdom in 1999 through an Urban Task Force headed by the architect Richard Rogers that works through a highly estheticized urbanism invokes an intertextual bleeding that would be taken for granted by Benjamin.

A fascination with psychoanalytic readings of the city are similarly indebted (Pile 1996). Notions of landscape as the outcome of visual organization point towards a study of the relationship between perspectivalism and urban life (Jay 1992, 1994). By questioning the philosophy of experience Benjamin directs us towards a sensorium of knowledges of the urban that play off the aural, oral, felt, and always real and imagined realities: "It forces philosophy to recognise that the experience of the city perpetually challenges and undermines the categories that are applied to it – even those of porosity and transitivity" (Caygill 1998: 124)

The democratic whole that is represented in debates on London government needs to be scrutinized for the polis that it narrates and the objects of representative democracy that emerge and range from the reinvented king as putative mayor down to the newly accountable definitions of police.

Reading the tragic history of the racist murder of Stephen Lawrence through the mapping of white supremacist suburbs of London echoes a transatlantic dialog on the iconography of the burbs and the hood, that speaks to a sophisticated rendition of the interplay between myth and metropolis and demands a response to Richard Wright's suggestion that Black and White writers are always struggling over the capture of reality in prose.

The new industrial sectors that emerge in in Seoul and Lagos as much as the new cultural industries and the cultural quarters of Chicago and Los Angeles demand a political economy of globalization that builds on a sophisticated notion of culture (Robins and Webster 1999). The city of bits, the city of flows, the informational city, and the divided city all cry out for a specific contextualization of the urban through the narratives of time and space that they organize (Castells 1996, 1997, 1998).

Conclusion

In this chapter Benjamin is not offered up as the source of some alternative paradigm of urban studies.[15] His work is helpful in avoiding both the mirage of a defining theoretical essence of the city and a Luddism that can render the city invisible in contemporary social theory. Chimeric searches for the identity of the city plagued the urban studies literature of the Anglophone world throughout the 1970s and the early 1980s. Yet at the heart of this chapter is a suggestion that both the empirical utility of the urban and the theoretical value of the city are in no way jeopardized by the failure of this longing for the pure definition of the urban condition. Benjamin is one social theorist who makes it possible for us to invert the conventional problematic; to ask instead about the stories through which cities are rendered visible as comprehensible elements of different modes of thoughts, genres of writing, regimes of the visual, modalities of government, and rationalizations of the economic.

He points towards a more modest theoretical ambition, the notion of thought and explanation that is focused on the close scrutiny of individual objects in their broader sociological context; the inspection from up close and from a distance, simultaneously and in turn. If this at times intimates further small-scale victories and large-scale defeats, then it might also point to a reconsideration of the manner in which theoretical and empirical labors are respectively valorized and credentialized in the cities of everyday life.

NOTES

1. It is interesting to note that the name of Walter Benjamin remains resolutely absent from both the bibliography and the index of first and second editions of Peter Saunders' influential volume on *Social Theory and the Urban Question* (1981, 1986).
2. With apologies to J. P. Dunleavy.
3. There is however a vast and rapidly growing secondary literature on the work of Benjamin. The two volumes of most direct relevance for an understanding of Benjamin's work on the city are those of Buck-Morss 1989, and Gilloch 1996; but other useful sources include A. Benjamin 1989; Caygill 1998; Eagleton 1981; Frisby 1985; Missac 1995; Smith 1983; Smith 1995; Steinberg 1996; Weigel 1996.

4. Indeed Peter Hall's recent dismissal of the "Marxist highway and the Postmodernist byway," for which he oddly appears to hold Benjamin almost principally responsible, caricatures Benjamin's contribution in precisely this way (Hall 1998: 12–13).
5. See a fuller description in Momme Broderson's biography (1996: 46) which describes the manner in which Benjamin was "fascinated by Simmel's absolute precision in speech and writings, the diversity of topics in his lectures, his eye for detail, his reference to marginal cultural and historical phenomena, his inquiring scepticism: in short his ability to promote independent thought and a growing awareness rather than induce numb astonishment at the monuments of history and philosophy."
6. In his explorations of the urban Benjamin suggests that "the city became a book in my hands" (Benjamin [1935–73]: 1985: 91).
7. For an extremely rich analysis of the typology of such a method divided into the thematics of fossil, ruin, wish-image, and the fetish of mythic history see Buck-Morss (1989); and for a description of the resonance of this typology for an understanding of contemporary culture see McRobbie (1994).
8. Benjamin comments in *One Way Street* "Great cities – whose incompatibly sustaining and reassuring power encloses those at work within them in the peace of a fortress and lifts from them, with a view of the horizon, awareness of the ever vigilant elemental forces – are seen to be breached at all points by the invading countryside.... The insecurity of even the busy areas puts the city dweller in the opaque and truly dreadful situation in which he must assimilate, along with the isolated monstrosities from the open country, the abortions of urban architectonics" (Benjamin [1935–73] 1985: 59).
9. It is interesting to compare Robert Hughes' suggestion that "In 1888 the Belgian artist James Ensor had depicted the crowd greeting the Entry of Christ into Brussels as a mass of bobbing, grinning and stupefied heads, using it to convey the idea that society – or, to be exact, the proletariat which Ensor hated with a paranoid passion – was not merely unreal but a sort of daemonic carnival, a collective of threatening masks (Hughes 1980: 283) with Ensor's role as a founding member of the socialist society Les XX, his critique of the conservative establishment in Belgium, and Susan Canning's suggestion that a thematic that runs through his work is one of "social critique" which commonly emerges as "the victory of marginalised individuals... over the ruling class" (Canning 1997: 58–9).
10. "Note that the figures of the collector, the ragpicker, and the detective wander trough the fields of the fossil and the ruin, while the fields of action of the prostitute, the gambler and the flâneur are those of wish-images, and of the fetish as their phantasmagoric form" (Buck-Morss 1991: 212).
11. See the Surealism essay, p. 227.
12. Buck-Morss points out that the third section of the planned essay on Baudelaire commissioned by the Institute of Social Research was to be called "The Commodity as Poetic Object" (Buck-Morss 1991: 209).
13. In Buck-Morss's terms "Benjamin's essay [on Surrealism] also criticizes the nihilistic anarchism of Surrealism, the lack of a constructive, dictatorial, and disciplined side to its thinking that could 'bind revolt to the revolution'. The Surrealists recognized reality as a dream; the Passagen-Werk was to evoke history in order to awaken its readers from it. Hence the title for the Arcades Project in this early stage: 'a dialectical Fairy Scene'. Benjamin was intending to tell the story of Sleeping Beauty once again" (Buck-Morss 1989: 34).
14. The organization of the gaze is significant but this does not negate the value of observation – only contextualizes it: "One technical feature is significant here, especially with regard to newsreels, the propagandist element of which can hardly be overestimated. Mass reproduction is aided especially by the reproduction of masses. In big

parades and monster rallies, in sports events and in war, all of which nowadays are captured by camera and sound recording, the masses are brought face to face with themselves. This process whose significance need not be stressed, is intimately connected with the development of the techniques of reproduction and photography. Mass movements are usually discerned more clearly by a camera than by a naked eye. A bird's eye view best captures gatherings of hundreds of thousands. And even though such a view may be as accessible to the human eye as to the camera, the image received by the eye cannot be enlarged the way that a negative is enlarged. This means that mass movements, including war, constitute a form of human behaviour which particularly favours mechanical equipment" (The Work of Art in the Age of Mechanical Reproduction, Benjamin 1973).

15. Again Buck-Morss is useful in her suggestion that "His legacy to readers that come after him is a nonauthoritarian system of inheritance, which compares less to the bourgeois mode of passing down cultural teasures as the spoils of conquering forces, than to the utopian tradition of fairy tales, which instruct without dominating, and so many of which 'are the traditional stories about victory over those forces'" (Buck-Morss 1991: 337).

REFERENCES

Aragon, L. [1926] 1994: *Paris Peasant*. Boston, MA: Exact Change.

Arendt, H. 1972: Walter Benjamin: 1892–1940. Introduction to W. Benjamin, *Illuminations*. London: Fontana, pp. 7–58.

Back, L. Keith, M., and Solomos, J. 1999: Reading the writing on the wall. In D. Slayden and R. K. Whillock (eds.), *Soundbite Culture: The Death of Discourse in a Wired World*. London: Sage, pp. 69–102.

Barth, L. 1996: Immemorial visibilities: seeing the city's difference. *Environment and Planning A*, 28 (3), 471–93.

Barthes, R. 1973: *Mythologies*. London: Granada.

Benjamin, A. 1989: *The Problems of Modernity: Adorno and Benjamin*, ch. 7. London: Routledge.

Benjamin, W. 1919: The theory of criticism. In M. Bullock and M. W. Jennings (eds.), *Walter Benjamin: Selected Writings*, vol. 1, 1913–26. Cambridge, MA: Harvard University Press, 1996, pp. 217–19.

Benjamin, W. 1921: Capitalism as religion. In M. Bullock and M. W. Jennings (eds.), *Walter Benjamin: Selected Writings*, vol. 1, 1913–26. Cambridge, MA: Harvard University Press, 1996, pp. 288–91.

Benjamin, W. [1925–26] 1979: One way street. In W. Benjamin, *One Way Street and Other Writings*. London: Verso.

Benjamin, W. [1928] 1985: Marseilles. In W. Benjamin, *One Way Street and Other Writings*. London: Verso.

Benjamin, W. [1929] 1985: Surrealism: the last snapshot of the European intelligentsia. In W. Benjamin, *One Way Street and Other Writings*. London: Verso, pp. 225–40.

Benjamin, W. [1931] 1985: A small history of photography. In W. Benjamin, *One Way Street and Other Writings*. London: Verso.

Benjamin, W. [1932] 1979: Berlin chronicle. In W. Benjamin, *One Way Street and Other Writings*. London: Verso.

Benjamin, W. [1939] 1973: On some motifs in Baudelaire. In W. Benjamin, *Illuminations*. London: Fontana.

Benjamin, W. [1935–73] 1973: The work of Art in the Age of Mechanical Reproduction. In W. Benjamin (ed.) *Illuminations*. London: Fontana.
Benjamin, W. 1973: *Illuminations*. London: Fontana.
Benjamin, W. 1977: *The Origin of German Tragic Drama*. London: Verso.
Benjamin, W. 1985: *One Way Street and Other Writings*. London: Verso.
Benjamin, W. and Lacis, A. [1924] 1985: Naples. In W. Benjamin, *One Way Street and Other Writings*. London: Verso, pp. 167–76.
Boyer, C. 1994: *The City of Collective Memory: Its Historical Imagery and Architectural Entertainments*. Cambridge, MA: MIT Press.
Boyer, C. 1996: Electronic disruptions and black holes of the city: the issues of gender and urbanism in the age of electronic communication. In C. Boyer, *Cybercities*. New York. Princeton Architectural Press, pp. 183–240.
Breton, A. 1960: *Nadja*. New York: Grove Press.
Broderson, M. 1996: *Walter Benjamin: A Biography*. London: Verso.
Brown, C. (ed.) 1997: *James Ensor 1860–1949 Theatre of Masks*. London: Lund Humphries.
Buck-Morss, S. 1989: *The Dialectics of Seeing: Walter Benjamin and the Arcades Project*. London: MIT Press.
Bullock, M. and Jennings, A. 1996: *The Collected Work of Walter Benjamin*, vol. 1. Harvard, MA: Harvard University Press.
Calvino, I. 1977: *Invisible Cities*. London: Vintage.
Canning, S. M. 1997: Visionary politics: the social subtext of James Ensor's religious imagery. In C. Brown (ed.), *James Ensor 1860–1949 Theatre of Masks*. London: Lund Humphries.
Castells, M. 1996: The rise of the network society. *The Information Age: Economy, Society, Culture*, vol. 1. Oxford: Blackwell.
Castells, M. 1997: The power of identity. *The Information Age: Economy, Society, Culture*, vol. 2. Oxford: Blackwell.
Castells, M. 1998: End of millennium. *The Information Age: Economy, Society, Culture*, vol. 3. Oxford: Blackwell.
Caygill, H. 1998: *Walter Benjamin: The Colour of Experience*. London: Routledge.
Certeau, M. de 1984: *The Practice of Everyday Life*. Berkeley, CA: University of California Press.
Debord, G. 1983: *Society of the Spectacle*. Detroit, MI: Black and Red.
Der Derian, J. 1998: *The Virilio Reader*. Oxford: Blackwell.
Deutsche, R. 1996: *Evictions*. Cambridge, MA: MIT Press.
Eagleton, T. 1981: *Walter Benjamin or Towards a Revolutionary Criticism*. London: Verso.
Eagleton, T. 1990: *The Ideology Of The Aesthetic*. Oxford: Blackwell.
Eco, U. 1994: Fakes and forgeries. In U. Eco (ed.), *In The Limits of Interpretation*. Bloomington: Indiana University Press, pp. 174–202.
Foucault, M. 1991: Governmentality. In G. Burchell, C. Gordon, and P. Miller (eds), *The Foucault Effect: Studies in Governmentality*. Hemel Hempstead: Harvester and Wheatsheaf, pp. 87–104.
Frisby, D. 1985: *Fragments of Modernity*, ch. 4. Oxford: Polity.
Gilloch, G. 1996: *Myth and Metropolis: Walter Benjamin and The City*. Oxford: Polity.
Hacking, I. 1990: *The Taming of Chance*. Cambridge: Cambridge University Press.
Hall, P. 1998: *Cities in Civilization*. London: Weidenfeld and Nicholson.
Harvey, 1990: *The Condition of Postmodernity*. Oxford: Blackwell.
Hayden, Dolores 1995: *The Power of Place*. Cambridge, MA: MIT Press.
Hebdige, D. 1993: Welcome to the Terrordome: Jean Michel Basquiat and the Dark Side of Hybridity. In R. Marshall (ed.) *Jean Michel Basquiat*. New York: Whitney.

Heron, L. 1993: *Women Writing the City: In Streets of Desire*. London: Virago.
Hughes, R. 1980: *The Shock of the New*. London: BBC Books.
Hyman, T. 1997: A Carnival Sense of the World. In C. Brown (ed.), *James Ensor 1860–1949 Theatre of Masks*. London: Lund Humphries, pp. 76–99.
Jacobs, J. M. 1996: *Edge of Empire: Postcolonialism and the City*. London: Routledge.
Jay, M. 1992: Scopic regimes of modernity. In S. Lash and J. Friedmann (eds.), *Modernity and Identity*. Oxford: Blackwell, pp. 178–95.
Jay, M. 1994: *Downcast Eyes*. Berkeley, CA: University of California Press.
Katznelson, I. 1992: *Marxism and the City*. Oxford: Clarendon.
Kearns, G. and Philo, C. 1993: *Selling Places: The City as Cultural Capital*. Oxford: Pergamon.
Keith, M. and Pile, S. (eds.) 1993: *Place and the Politics of Identity*. London: Routledge.
Lash, S. and Urry, J. 1994: *Economies of Signs and Space*. London: Sage.
Marcus, S. 1973: Reading the illegible. In H. J. Dyos and M. Wolff (eds.), *The Victorian City*. London: Routledge and Kegan Paul, pp. 257–76.
McRobbie, A. 1994: The *Passagenwerk* and the place of Walter Benjamin in cultural studies. In A. McRobbie (ed.) *Postmodernism and Popular Culture*. London: Routledge, pp. 96–120.
Missac, P. 1995: *Walter Benjamin's Passages*. Cambridge, MA: MIT Press.
Moriarty, M. 1991: *Roland Barthes*. Oxford: Polity.
Pile, S. 1996: *The Body and the City: Psychoanalysis, Space and Subjectivity*. London: Routledge.
Raban, J. 1974: *Soft City*. London: Collins.
Robins, K. and Webster, F. 1999: *Times of the Technoculture: From the Information Society to the Virtual Life*. London: Routledge.
Rushdie, S. 1995: *The Moor's Last Sigh*. London: Jonathan Cape.
Saunders, P. 1981: *Social Theory and The Urban Question*. London: Hutchinson.
Saunders, P. 1986: *Social Theory and The Urban Question*. London: Hutchinson, 2nd edn.
Savage, M. and Warde, A. 1993: *Urban Sociology, Capitalism and Modernity*, chs. 5, 6. Basingstoke: Macmillan.
Smith, G. (ed.) 1983: Walter Benjamin: Philosophy, History and Aesthetics. *The Philosophical Forum*, 15, 1–2. Chicago, Ill: University of Chicago Press.
Smith, G. (ed.) 1995: *On Walter Benjamin: Critical Essays and Recollections*. Cambridge, MA: MIT Press.
Soja, E. 1989: *Postmodern Geographies*. London and New York: Verso.
Soja, E. 1996: *Thirdspace: Journeys to Los Angeles and other Real-and-Imagined Places*. Oxford: Blackwell.
Soja, E. 1999: *Postmetropolis: Critical Studies of Cities and Regions*. Oxford: Blackwell.
Sorkin, M. (ed.) 1992: *Variations on a Theme Park: The New American City and The End of Public Space*. New York: Hill and Wang.
Stallybrass, P. and White, A. 1986: *The Politics and Poetics of Transgression*. London: Methuen.
Steinberg 1996: *Walter Benjamin and the Demands of History*. Ithaca, New York: Cornell University Press.
Steiner, G. 1985: Introduction. In W. Benjamin *The Origin of German Tragic Drama*. London: Verso.
Szondi, P. [1962] 1995: Walter Benjamin's city portraits. In G. Smith (ed.) *On Walter Benjamin: Critical Essays and Recollections*. Cambridge, MA: MIT Press.
Tester, K. (ed.) 1994: *The Flâneur*. London: Routledge.
Thrift, N. 1996: *Spatial Formations*. London: Sage.

Weigel, S. 1996: *Body and Image-Space*. London: Routledge.
Wilson, E. 1992: The invisible flâneur. *New Left Review*, 191, 90–110.
Wolff, J. 1985: The invisible flâneuse: women and the literature of modernity. *Theory, Culture and Society* 2 (3), 37–48.
Wright, P. 1992: *A Journey Through Ruins: The Last Days of London*. London: Radius.

Chapter 36

"X Marks the Spot: Times Square Dead or Alive?"

M. Christine Boyer

Times Square/42nd Street is a place-name on the map of Manhattan as well as a representational space. Defined as the meeting of two triangles forming an "X" at 42nd Street where Broadway crosses Seventh Avenue, it was once the popular entertainment district of vaudeville and the legendary Broadway theater. Since the early twentieth century this rowdy playground has been the central public place where New Yorkers celebrate New Year's Eve. Frequented by thousands of daily commuters who arrive via its labyrinthine subway system, Times Square/42nd Street is linked directly to the entire metropolitan region. As its name designates, it used to be the location of great newspaper and radio headquarters. But at this very moment in time, the place has been rendered by Disney and turned into a wax museum with the likes of Madame Tussaud. This neon-encrusted "X" is regulated by design guidelines that call for a requisite number of Lutses [Light Units in Times Square] and controlled by urban designers who have planned its spontaneous unplannedness. Times Square/42nd Street has become "New York Land," a themed shopping district where Disney competes with Warner Brothers, and Virgin Megastore confronts the live music studio of MTV. Times Square/42nd Street promises to be a mega-entertainment complex trimmed with a 25-screen cinema complex, a Planet Hollywood movie-star hotel, restored historic theaters, and as many themed restaurants as the area can hold. Patrolled by private policemen, its garbage picked up by private collectors, and its signage refurbished by private donations – under the general guidelines set down by its Business Investment District (BID) – it is as clean as a whistle. Times Square/42nd Street has become the tourist epicenter of Manhattan.

Many New Yorkers wonder how this has happened to such an iconic place of popular culture. Will Times Square/42nd Street survive, will its competitive chaos and tough-guy allure be able to hold out against the latest onslaught of improvement schemes? Or has a grand mistake been made – and this dysfunction junction been mauled by disimprovement policies amending its authentic nature instead of its corruption? Has Times Square/42nd Street become another nonplace instantly recognizable from the images that circulate on television and cinema screens but a space that is never experienced directly (Auge 1995)? Is it in danger of extinction or disappearance – reduced to an any-space-whatever? Gilles Deleuze claimed that "any-space-whatever is not an abstract universal.... It is a perfectly singular space, which has merely lost its homogeneity, that is, the principle of its metric relations or the connections of its own parts, so that the linkages can be made in an infinite number of ways. It is a space of virtual conjunction, grasped as pure locus of the possible" (Delueze 1986). Indeed, Times Square/42nd Street appears to juxtapose in a single real place several different types of spaces. This open-ended disjunctive set of sites coexists simultaneously as a retrotheater district, a media center, a Disneyland, a suburban-style shopping mall, an advertising zone, a corporate office park, a movie but also a song, a novel, a play, a street, and a way of life. Will it also be called a center for the visual arts, a place for emerging electronic industries, a truly plugged-in space connected to the rest of the world?

Once upon a time, Times Square/42nd Street was a place where prostitutes, pimps, or hucksters rubbed shoulders with out-of-town conventioneers, theater audiences, corporate executive secretaries, tourists, and families. But now Times Square's vice zone, which reached its zenith in the 1970s when more than a hundred X-rated adult bookstores, peep shows and topless clubs concentrated there, has been broken up by a 1995 zoning order that allows only eight such establishments to remain. But spiralling real-estate prices and exorbitant rents have done more damage to the old Times Square than any zoning regulation or design guideline ever could have wrought. The last pieces of this remodeled media center are just now falling into place. Sixteen years ago, when the city and state decided to clean up Times Square they offered developers of the four giant office towers located at the heart of the "X" and known as Times Square Center – a center designed several times by Philip Johnson and John Burgee in the early 1980s – unbelievably large tax abatements if they would turn Times Square into a new headquarters for financial corporations. The collapse of New York's real-estate market and an array of law suits put an end to that dream. Meantime, the public and architects were given time to rethink the importance of Times Square as the crossroads where consumers and producers of popular culture inevitably meet.

Hopes for a new financial district to rival Wall Street gave way to a new reality that Times Square/42nd Street would soon become the media center of the world. As the idea developed, the four giant towers have been replaced piecemeal: a tower already under construction for Conde Nast Publications is rising on the northeast corner of Broadway and Times Square; across from this site on the western side of the Square, Reuters news and information services will build a 30-story headquarters. Two more towers – yet to be designed – will be built on the southside of 42nd Street, east and west of Seventh Avenue, whose tenants are likely to be Disney and Home Box Office. Following the special zoning requirements, the Conde Nast structure contains a ten-story cylinder cantilevered over the northwest corner and outfitted with neon signs. A metal grid on its other corner facade will permit a mixture of advertising gimmicks including video and electronic screens. Crowned at the top of its tower by four huge square panels looming out over the cityscape, these will house satellite dishes or other high-technology equipment. The design for the new 30-story Reuters Building contains similar gestures such as a fourth-floor newsroom visible from the street and a news zipper extending down to the sidewalk, all of which make the pedestrian aware that media art is the required adornment for all commercial architecture in Times Square. Some believe the revival of Times Square/42nd Street began in 1993 when Disney decided to make a modest investment in what was then considered to be a dead and dreary center of Manhattan by agreeing to renovate the New Amsterdam Theater on 42nd Street south. The city was more than willing to offer this entertainment giant both subsidies and guarantees that it would not risk its brand name, feeling secure that Disney would lure others to follow in its powerful wake. Perhaps Mr. Eisner, The Walt Disney Company's CEO since 1987, needed no such assurance for he proclaimed: "I know what 42nd Street can be, and it is going to completely rejuvenate New York. I want to be part of that, and I want to be part of that as an executive of the Disney Company and I want to be part of that as a former New Yorker." Five years later, the entire 13 acres of Times Square/42nd Street contains the hottest real-estate property in the world. The overall cleanup of Times Square/42nd Street has generated spin-off effects enlarging its theatrical tableaux: the "Stardust Dine-O-Mat" on 43rd Street appears to be a 1940s blue-plate restaurant with waitresses attired as if they were the Andrews Sisters, a Hansen's Times Square Brewery Restaurant has opened, as has a Ferrara's delicatessen, O'Lunney's Tavern, and a virtual-reality emporium called "Cinema Ride." Besides the Virgin Megastore, Live Entertainment of Toronto, and AMC Entertainment Inc., other communications and media have already arrived in Times Square or made commitments to do so. AMC Entertainment Inc. has even moved to an old burlesque house on the south side of 42nd Street, The Empire Theater, 70 feet down the street where it will form the entrance to its much proclaimed 25-screen movie theater complex.

None of the acts in this revival show, however, has been accomplished without a great deal of anxiety and fear that Times Square/42nd Street has been mauled, sanitized, Disneyfied (see Berman 1995; Elany 1997; Huxtable 1997; Koolhaas 1996). It arouses a general fear that no one will ever experience in this commodified place the unique reality of New York. Some blame Mickey Mouse as the virtuoso in charge of a marketing show that offers token images of the city laced with saccharine cheer in preference to the dirty real thing. Others fear the burning heat of a cultural meltdown where popular art and the mainstream commandeer the show. They believe that the exotic, the overcomplex, the unique can still be used to oppose the commonplace, the banal, and the widely available and thus they maintain a snobbish contempt for Disney, Warner Brothers, and the Ford Motor Company, all of whom are making their architectural debut on the reinvigorated stage of Times Square. Others believe that seedy old Times Square was utterly authentic, ablaze with stroboscopic liveliness and vibrating energy sustaining a tempo of desire both pleasurable and degenerate. They wish that Disney could be banished to the South Bronx, to an invisible rather than animated presence. Still others point out that the advertising war of signs taking place around the square has raised the entry stakes to billions of dollars in the competition to obtain mediaspace in this preeminently televisual place. At such a level, it is guaranteed that only megacorporations can play in the real-estate game. When merged or woven together the visual prejudices of these architectural critics and judges of place take the elite road to culture – relying on all the binary polarities that pit High Art against the Popular Arts, the pure against the devalued, the oppositional against the affirmative.

While acknowledging the dangers of global capitalism and its strategy of cultural appropriation, it is time to erect a monument to the old Times Square in order to resist the seductions of regressive nostalgia. There is something melancholy in the repetitive refrain that Times Square has died, been Disneyfied, reduced to another middle-class mall. There is a tendency to reify the authentic – or idealize the has-been – that used to hover about the place. Something paradoxical and pessimistic occurs in the outpourings of regrets remarking on the ruination of Times Square as a site of collective gathering because this special iconic place has been transformed into a mediascape where mass entertainment pacifies the spectator, where consumers are lulled to sleep, and passers-by are enticed by yet more blazing advertisements. What this outpouring of moralistic laments implicitly confirms is that cultural critics are tired of Pop Art – its promise has become classical, refined, even pleasurable. There is nothing to "learn from 42nd Street" when the symbolic expressions and semantic codes of commercial art no longer shock, when the manipulations of city images and signs are taken for granted as the visual vocabulary that spells out a place. Lawrence Alloway has been credited with coining the expression "pop art" in the mid-1950s. It was a term he used to approve of mass-produced objects and mass media imagery and to banish for ever the outmoded concepts of eternal value and artistic creativity. In the 1990s the abundance of mass communication and the esthetics of plenty are no longer an embarrassment to the custodians of art and the curators of taste. Like a good advertising campaign, Pop Art has saturated the market with its name and presence and become the fully accepted icon of the new Times Square.

It is assumed by those who market the new Times Square, as well as by the cultural critics who lament its demise, that the place once contained a unique, even authentic, experience (Losell 1997). Both promoters and critics appeal to history as the stable source from which contemporary representations should draw. The sole reason that tourists visit Times Square – or any other historic site – is to stand on the spot where something took place, to see and experience the pleasures of a world-famous location. Critics make the same connection: the new Times Square ought to represent a deeper historical encounter with place. They blame consumers and tourists for corrupting the real experience of Times Square and trivializing the place for they have emptied it of meaning and settled too easily for stereotypical replacements and illusionary simulations. Yet it is difficult to determine what more authentic experience would correct its false illusions and what deeper historical meaning its signs and symbols should reference.

An appeal to Times Square's history is troublesome because the death of this famous place did not happen overnight. Legitimate theater along 42nd Street has been threatened with extinction at least since the 1930s when most of its theaters were turned into movie houses. The last legitimate stage production closed its doors in 1937. Of the 13 fabled theaters on 42nd Street, all built between 1899 and 1920, there are only 5 survivors. Furthermore, Times Square has been in trouble and its image in need of repair at least since 1961 when the 24-story triangular Times Tower built in 1904 was sold, remodeled and rechristened the Allied Chemical Tower. Damaging blows to Times Square's historic imagery have been delivered by New York City's real-estate market: a midtown zoning district was in force between 1982 and 1987 and allowed taller and bulkier skyscrapers from Times Square to Columbus Circle along the Broadway spine, plus a competitive war with the Wall Street area favored Times

Square as an office park because it is the city's most densely populated mass transit hub and lies in close proximity to commuter rail lines at Grand Central Station and Penn Station. In addition, there is the city's economic development policies pushing family-style entertainment for the masses as a tourist incentive and demanding that the gutter sordidness and notorious vice zone of Times Square be erased by reallocating sex to zones on the periphery of the city and almost outlawing its appearance along 42nd Street. Even "the Great White Way," the razzle-dazzle electronic wizardry of great neon signs that have turned the night lights of Times Square into a midtown Coney Island since the 1920s has been tampered with. A 1987 ordinance mandates the amount of illuminated signage and the degree of brilliance that new buildings must carry. The city wants these new signs to be as flashy as possible, and advertising is clearly allowed, in an attempt to eradicate the fact that most of Times Square already has become a dull and dark canyon of overlarge skyscraper office towers.

But there is nothing novel about the peculiarly American event of advertising to be seen in Times Square. When Le Corbusier visited New York in the 1930s, he surmised that the origin of American advertising lay in the great size of the country. Millions of citizens stretched over vast open spaces had constantly to be informed that this or that existed. He found advertising to be banal and without plastic quality, it should be banned from the streets of the city But the lights of Broadway were seductive, and Le Corbusier admitted that he could not

> pass by the luminous advertising on Broadway. Everyone has heard about that incandescent path cutting diagonally across Manhattan in which the mob of idlers and patrons of motion pictures, burlesque shows and theaters moves. Electricity reigns, but it is dynamic here, exploding, moving, sparkling, with lights turning white, blue, red, green, yellow. The things behind it are disappointing. These close-range constellations, this Milky Way in which you are carried along, lead to objects of enjoyment which are often mediocre. So much the worst for advertising! . . . And on Broadway, divided by feelings of melancholy and lively gaiety, I wander along in a hopeless search for an intelligent burlesque show in which the nude white bodies of beautiful women will spring up in witty flashes under the paradisiac illumination of the spotlights (Le Corbusier 1947: 101).

Le Corbusier, like the cultural critics of contemporary times who oppose the illusions of tourism to the authenticity of history, pits a naive American culture without profundity against a deeper sense of history that only a European would know.

This opposition is repeated and embellished by another traveler to America, Erich Mendelsohn, who published a book of his photographs taken in 1924. Under a section entitled "The Grotesque" he underlined a photograph of "New York: Broadway at Night" with the following caption: "Uncanny. The contours of the buildings are erased. But in one's consciousness they still rise, chase one another, trample one another./ This is the foil for the flaming scripts, the rocket fire of the moving illuminated ads, emerging and submerging, disappearing and breaking out again over the thousands of autos and the maelstrom of pleasure-seeking people./ Still disordered, because exaggerated, but all the same already full of imaginative beauty, which will one day be complete." Mendelsohn labeled another "Grotesque" photograph "Broadway by Daylight" and gave it the following caption: "[it] loses the mystery, intoxication, the glitter of the night./ Is nothing more than unbridled, wild, shouts itself hoarse. Grandiose tomfoolery of a universal fair: collars, sugar, Orpheum, toothbrushes, tobacco, and 'Vote for Charles E. Gehring'" (Mendelsohn 1993: 52–4). Mendelsohn's reference to "uncanny" displays the pull of contradictory forces, the love/hate relationship of cultural critics when they come in contact with the commercial art that America so blatantly represents. It is animalistic, trampling underfoot more refined culture; and it is pure spectacle, reducing everything to frivolity and fun. The critic must build a defense against American levelings, but it is a defense that is ambivalent, displaying both dread of the grotesque, the chaotic, the seductive, yet revealing a curiosity to look behind first appearances, to probe into the depths, to discover more profound meaning. Thus is set up a movement back and forth between averting one's eyes and desiring to see more, between admiration and dislike.

Oppositions that set real against false attractions, that seek profound instead of superficial experiences, do not allow the critic to move beyond repetitious and pessimistic refrains when they encounter contemporary Times Square. They fail to recognize that neither Disney nor Mickey Mouse is the problem, but their bagful of technological tricks is. Americans have always been more interested in the medium than the message, and wondrous technology seems to fascinate the most. The animated world of Disney, beyond anything else, promises the dream that technology can conquer nature, can control the physical world. Furthermore, it is technology, the animation apparatus (consisting of frames and cuts, the speed, tempo and rhythm of movement, the method of caricature and drawing – in fact everything that makes possible the dissolution of the photographic and the realistic into each other) that enables the characters to transform themselves and to assume any form.

When shifts in technology are taken into account, it is not the loss of Times Square as an emblematic space of industrial capital that critics should mourn, but the passing of a mechanized industrial art into that of the electronic. When Jean Charlot celebrated Disney's new art of motion in 1939, he described it as an art that "could be multiplied by mechanical means" so that "the world might rid itself of the idolatry of the 'original' and resuscitate ancient collective traditions, Gothic and Egyptian" (Charlot 1939: 269–70). Because animated drawings were manipulated by so many hands from the birth of the plot to the inking of the line, they smashed the idea of an "original." By eradicating any idiosyncratic traces of an artist's individuality through homogenizing technical procedures, Disney cartoons simulated a unified whole and produced an art that could be enjoyed by everyone. When the Museum of Modern Art held an exhibit in the summer of 1942 entitled "Walt Disney's 'Bambi': The Making of an Animated Sound Picture," they too considered Disney cartoons to be an industrial art. MOMA's press release described the production process step by step: Walt Disney was active only in the first step, that of "visualizing the story", but from then on the work was accomplished by artists, actors, musicians, background and layout men, animators and two hundred women as inkers and painters (MOMA material, cited in Mikulak 1996). MOMA went even further, describing how the Disney "factory" produced an industrial art: each task being specialized within separate departments and the entire production process organized into sequential units.

Times Square, and any other electronic space, is no longer reflective of the industrial ideology that assumed human mastery over the forces of nature and the physical world. This has now been replaced by notions of interface, interaction, and interchange. Perhaps it is through a deeper understanding of animation, the awareness that motion lies in between static poses, a constant coming into being that will open up to an exploration of electronic art. Innovations in telecommunications technology, distributed by many of the corporate giants who are seeking to reside in the refurbished Times Square, have ushered in a new era in which the recording, manipulation, and transmission of signs encourage a mixing of media – visual, verbal, and sound. Public space is being transformed into a mixture of signs, images, expressions both spatial and temporal, virtual and real – and this requires a new set of critical tools to evaluate change. It is no longer cars, machines, and technological tools but data, information, services, and entertainment that drive the economy. Space becomes an abstract computational space and representational forms mere algorithmic codes manipulated by a computer.

If there is to be a new geometry on which the city might be imagined, new space and time transformations that might enable us to envision creative potentialities – that something "new" pushing us toward experimentation and improvisation when we come in contact with the real – then it must be based not on the simulated displays and descriptive signs of our contemporary imagescapes – the result of a severed relationship between meaning and place – but instead on the open-ended display of virtual and actual images that allows for both a playful re-membering and an improvisational excess. This gesture aims to move beyond the melancholic opposition that decries tourism and praises authenticity, that criticizes illusion and seeks profundity. It requires a different map than the one we normally utilize as our conceptual tool to order and hierarchialize the actual territory of the city. Deleuze and Guatarri (1987: 12) have described such a map as "open and connectable in all of its dimensions; it is detachable, reversible, susceptible to constant modification. It can be torn, reversed, adapted to any kind of mounting, reworked by an individual, group, or social formation. It can be drawn on a wall, conceived of as a work of art, constructed as a political action or as a meditation.... it always has multiple entry-ways..."

REFERENCES

Auge, M. 1995: *Non-Places: Introduction to an Anthropology of Supermodernity*, tr. J. Howe. London: Verso.

Berman, M. 1995: Times Square, Times Square. *The Village Voice*, July 18, 23–26.

Charlot, J. 1939: But is it art? *American Scholar*, 8, 269–70.

Deleuze, G. 1986: *Cinema I The Movement Images*, tr. H. Tomlinson and B. Habberjam. Minneapolis: University of Minnesota Press.

Deleuze, G. and Guattari, F. 1987: *A Thousand Plateaus*, tr. B. Massumi. Minneapolis: University of Minnesota Press.

Elany, S. 1997: X-X-X marks the spot. *Out*, Dec./Jan., 115–16, 120, 172–3.

Huxtable, A. 1997: The ideal city. *Preservation*, March/April, 26–39, 95.

Koolhaas, R. 1996: Regrets. *Grand Street*, 57, 137–8.

Le Corbusier 1947: *When Cathedrals Were White*, tr. F. Hyslop, Jr. New York: MacGraw-Hill.

Losell, A. 1997: *History's Double: Cultural Tourism in Twentieth Century French Writing*. New York: St. Martin's Press.

Mendelsohn, E. 1993: *Erich Mendelsohn's "Amerika"*. New York: Dover Publications.

Mikulak, W. 1996: Disney and the art world: the early years. *Animation Journal*, 4, no. 2 spring, 18–42.

Chapter 37

Walking and Performing "the City": A Melbourne Chronicle

Benjamin Rossiter and Katherine Gibson

"The street level is dead space.... It is only a means of passage to the interior" – summed up Richard Sennet, two decades ago, his analysis of the most impressive and spectacular urban developments of his time, ushering in the new era of the post-modern metropolis.

Bauman 1994: 148–9

Today's action is, after all, different: it is, mostly, about *passing* from here to there, as fast as one can manage, preferably without stopping, better still without looking around. Beautiful passers-by hide inside automobiles with tinted windows. Those still on the pavement are waiters and sellers at best, but more often dangerous people pure and simple: layabouts, beggars, homeless conscience-soilers, drug pushers, pickpockets, muggers, child molesters and rapists waiting for the prey. To the innocent who had to leave for a moment the wheeled security of automobiles, or those others, still thinking of themselves as innocent, who cannot afford that security at all, street [sic] is more a jungle than the theater. One goes there because one must. A site fraught with risks, not chances; not meant for gentlemen of leisure, and certainly not for the faint-hearted among them. The street is the "out there" from which one hides, at home or inside the automobile, behind security locks and burglar alarms.

Bauman 1994: 148

Perhaps it's the fear that Richard Sennett and Zygmunt Bauman are right that drives the City of Melbourne to host a regular International Arts Festival in which all and sundry (and especially those who can't afford the ticket prices of the undercover shows) are enticed out on to the streets of the central city with the offer of free entertainment – street theater, food stalls, fireworks, and displays. The tinted glass is wound down, automobiles, security locks and burglar alarms abandoned, respectables and "deviants" intermix and the luxuriously wide (automobile, or was it cart, determined) streets of Batman's Melbourne are reclaimed and enlivened becoming home, for a brief few weeks, to *flâneurs* and *flâneuses* momentarily released from their otherwise largely suburban experience.

It was during this short burst of urban self-consciousness that I ventured out with family in tow to "take in the sights/sites." Not, of course, without the usual generational trade-off: walking the streets and enjoying the ambience with a specific look-in on the Urban Dream Capsule – a group of five male performance artists locked up in a department store window for the duration of the Arts Festival – in return for a visit to a city movie complex to see *Independence Day* – the latest Parental Guidance-rated Hollywood blockbuster with a prerelease hype that had captured the eight- and ten-year-olds' interest enough to motivate a tenuous companionability. So it was that through an afternoon and evening I walked in a city experiencing it from the street, from the theater seat and from the street again – materiality and representation jostling for priority.

In recollecting this day two different stories of the city stand out in stark contrast. One is the prevalent narrative of urban decay, immanent doom, and civic destruction told once again in the filmic representation of North American cities in *Independence Day*. Picking up on the apocalyptic tone adopted by many contemporary commentators of the "postmodern city," the movie shows civil disorder, hysterical masses, and sexuality gone awry as a shadow is cast over the cancerous, "sprawling giantism" of late twentieth-century urbanism by huge alien cities hovering in the sky (Mumford 1961: 618). One by one, each earthly metropolis is engulfed in a fiery blast emanating from the airborne monstrous craft. The city streets that for some, such as Bauman, have already become uninhabitable (except by the layabouts, beggars, homeless, drug pushers, etc.) or for others, such as Michael Sorkin (1992) and Paul Virilio (1991) have been rendered obsolete by the dominance of the screen interface and the fiber-optic superhighway, are finally erased, decimated, and consumed by the alien's fireballs. The modern city as a physical presence is rendered irrelevant and the technologically mediated "posturban" age is upon us. The central characters, a cast of souls who regain their masculinity and/or morality in an all-American way through violence and the exercise of force, abandon the cities and flee – not to the traditional anti-urban utopia of a lush green rural Eden, but to a secret hypertechnical military installation buried deep under the dry brown desert.

As each set of events necessary to the blockbuster genre was roughly welded together, laughs of incredulity burst forth from the teenagers sitting behind us indicating that even they could tell that this was a stupid (but not therefore unentertaining) movie. What was so compelling for this *flâneur/se* trapped in its web by a necessary familial transaction was the movie's resonance with the familiar modernist morality tale that underpins much cultural commentary and discourse upon postmodern urbanism. As it is told and retold in movie or in social theory the story of an urban/moral order under threat, of accelerating mayhem in the streets, ultimate physical destruction, and rebirth of a technologically mediated social order in which the street is invalidated as a social space repeatedly constitutes and reinforces the power of deep-seated anti-urban sentiments that in turn inform so much of our urban experience and practice.

So what a shock to return to the street and to resume walking in a city in the throes of celebrating the urban. It was early evening and people were everywhere, milling around, not seemingly going anywhere, but being sociable, entertained, and present. Here was another, very different city story – space occupied, not ceded to a narrative of despair or destruction. It is this other image that we want, in this chapter, to dwell upon and explore for its potential.

Walking (in) the City

The practice of walking and the reflection on urban walks contribute to a counter-discourse of the urban. This counter-discourse finds its power in relational opposition to those god's-eye conceptions of city form and changing structure that have been motivated by the modernist quest for lawful spatial order and captured by the organizing narrative of capitalist urbanization (Gibson-Graham 1996: ch. 4). Walter Benjamin, Roland Barthes, and Michel de Certeau among others have drawn upon this ambulatory counterpoint in their representations of the urban.

> The ordinary practitioners of the city live "down below," below the thresholds at which visibility begins. They walk – an elementary form of this experience of the city; they are walkers, *Wandersmanner*, whose bodies follow the thicks and thins of an urban "text" they write without being able to read it.... The networks of these moving, intersecting writings compose a manifold story that has neither author nor spectator, shaped by fragments of trajectories and alterations of spaces: in relation to representations, it remains daily and indefinitely other (de Certeau 1984: 93).

De Certeau invites us to walk in the city and to allow the "long poem of walking" to reveal and confuse what has been concealed and clarified by urban theory. Working against the "imaginary totalizations" produced by those who seek to render the city readable and therefore ultimately controllable, he encourages pedestrians to be producers of their own urban texts, to construct and occupy urban space inventively. Perhaps the metaphor of walking possesses the power to unsettle the narrative of (post)modern urban decay and civic disarray?

> This city can be known only by an activity of an ethnographic kind: you must orient yourself in it not by book, by address, but by walking, by sight, by habit, by experience; here every discovery is intense and fragile, it can be repeated or recovered only by memory of the trace it has left you: to visit a place for the first time is thereby to begin to write it: the address not being written, it must establish its own writing (Barthes 1982: 33–36).

As he meandered on foot through the (for him) "practically unclassified" streets of Tokyo guided only by impromptu drawings and gestures that elevated new ways of seeing and writing over old ways of speaking and reading, Barthes reflected that the "rational is merely one system among others" of knowing a place (1982: 33). His observations on Tokyo prompt us to challenge representations of a perceived coherence of the urban as embodied in the map, guide, telephone book, or indeed panopticon pronouncements on the "postmodern" (Western) city. Barthes writes of the trace left by the city in one's memories – of the feel of the pavement, the orientation of objects in space, the smells and tastes – its writing on/in you. And here he touches upon topics written about so lucidly by Benjamin: "autobiography has to do with time, with sequence and what makes up the continuous flow of life. Here, I am talking of a space, of moments and discontinuities. For even if months and years appear here, it is in the form they have at the moment of recollection" (Benjamin 1978: 28).

In "A Berlin Chronicle" Benjamin (1978) describes his own introduction to the city, recollecting street images and associated emotions, school spaces, friendships of his childhood and youth, buildings, and happenings in context. His urban writings represent a denarrativized city – a city temporarily released from the discursive structures imposed by history and rationality. He celebrates distracted thought and absent-minded strolling, straying, hovering, daydreaming, and idling as bodily/intellectual practices which are counter and subversive to the notion of productivity. Walking for Benjamin is a practice of remembrance. Memory is the "medium of past experience" just as the ground is the medium in which dead cities lie buried. Benjamin validates the power of imaginary maps and alerts us to the chance that "valuable things" left "lying around" the streets might be found, like objects long forgotten in an attic, and incorporated into the individual's experience of walking/knowing (in) the city (1978: 20). He places value on these discarded, little used or seemingly unimportant urban activities and spaces that are rarely seen to hold significance in conventional urban discourse. For Benjamin to dig and dig again in the same and new places reveals "hidden treasures" lying buried deep in one's memory (1978: 24–6). At the same time the "art of straying" and losing oneself in the city enables the mind to be more receptive to deceased experiences flashed into the present by involuntary memories. Walking might be seen as an invitation to allow sudden flashes of illumination and chance stumblings across hidden treasures to reshape urban knowledge, possibly invigorating pro-urban sentiments and writing different scripts for the "postmodern city."

We are interested in the enabling potentialities of re-presenting the city from the street – from the perspective of the walker and the street inhabitant. The trope of walking offers us ways of representing the city and constituting contemporary urban experience that might unsettle both the anti-urban apocalypticism of much contemporary urban thinking and the preoccupation with spatial ordering that has channelled urban representations and experience into the constricting binarisms of public/private, home/street, residential/non-residential. It allows new spatializations of the city to emerge and loosens the hold of historicist narratives of restructuring and postmodern decay. The body is reintroduced to the urban, but not in its capacity to occupy at various times private/residential space or public/industrial or commercial space, or to move between point A and point B as commuter or householder intimately linked to the functioning of capitalist production or reproduction. The body is introduced as a sensual being – smelling, remembering, rhythmically moving – jostling with other bodies and in the process constituting active, perhaps multiple, urban subjectivities. The walker becomes lost, allows the city – street signs, bars, cafes, billboards, passers-by – to "speak" to her as does a bird call in the wild or a twig crackling under foot in a forest (Benjamin 1978: 8–9). The speech act of walking creates stories, invents spaces, and opens up the city through its capacity to produce "anti-texts" within the text. The ambulatory occupation of urban space permits a myriad of unrealized possibilities to surface, triggering emotions and feelings that may lie dormant in many people.

The invitation to stroll, daydream, look about, and wander aimlessly through city space was offered to Melburnians during their International Arts Festival. Precisely because the city itself often appears in contemporary texts as an outmoded fragment or ruin of its former self, the strategy of enticing people on to the streets during the festival could be read as a recognition of the real abandonment of public civic space and therefore as a rearguard action by the City, or it could be seen as an intervention that operated completely outside this discourse of despair. We prefer the latter reading because on the day that our chronicle documents, flashes of illumination emanating from a boxed treasure suggested that walking in the city is an activity that turns up even greater possibilities for destabilization and reenchantment than at the time that Benjamin was writing.

Performing (in) the City

In a world where privacy is vanishing, come see your future. For sixteen days of the Festival, five of Melbourne's street performers will be hermetically sealed behind the glass walls of Myer's Bourke Street Windows!... these intrepid art-stronauts will translocate their entire lives to the heart of the city in a 24 hour a day, non-stop, incubation event. Without a curtain in sight. Watch them eat, sleep, entertain, perform – in our very own biosphere experiment that is at the cutting edge of performance art.

Melbourne Festival Guide 1996: 38

In a flash of recognition and then misrecognition it becomes clear that the Myer department store windows – home every Christmas to a wondrous scene of moving mechanical gnomes, fairies, elves and assorted fairy story characters – is occupied by grown living men! The crowd gathered in front of the windows is not mainly kids and their Christmas-shopping parents, but Melburnians of all ages and backgrounds gathered to observe the "Myersphere experiment." When we push our way to the front of the crowd it is "getting-ready-for-bed" time. Some of the five bald men are in their striped pyjamas – others are still in their day suits. One is in the window/room that contains the bathroom basin, shower (with partial screen) and exercise equipment, cleaning his teeth. He turns round to the crowd, my son bares his teeth and has them scrubbed – albeit through the "pane of separation" (Kermond 1996). The smudge of toothpaste on the inside surface remains in place all evening – a trace of the communicative act.

The Urban Dream Capsule (UDC) took the 1996 Melbourne Festival by surprise. By the time the art-stronauts (Andrew Morrish, Bruce Naylor, Nick Papas, Neil Thomas, and David Wells) emerged after 16 days of sealed isolation in the four adjoining shop windows, an estimated 200,000 people had viewed them for varying lengths of time. Even more had contacted them via fax, telephone, and email. At any time of day or night the crowd outside the windows never seemed to drop below 50. Sometimes it was cast in the subject position of "audience" to be "entertained" by the "elaborate synchronised ritualisation of everyday activities" (shaving heads in the morning, preparing meals, showering and preparing for bed). "People are transfixed by the spectacle, bonded by a sneaky sense of voyeurism coupled with outright fascination" (Scott-Norman 1996).

At other times members of the crowd actively communicated with the performers. On one occasion two people shouted through the glass to Neil Thomas (the mastermind of the performance), "We've got a house-warming present for you." They proceeded to attach a very small plant, perhaps a sweet pea, in a tiny square

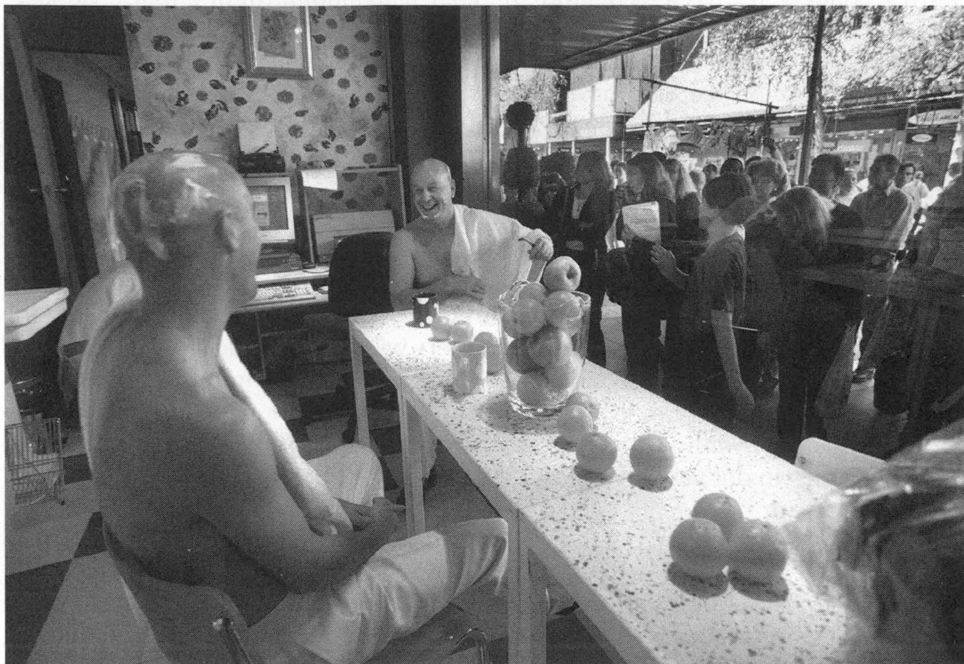

Figure 37.1 Art-stronaut Andrew Morrish has his daily headshave under the watchful eye of early morning shoppers (photo: Angela Wiley; from *The Age*, October 19, 1996)

pot about a metre from the ground. Thomas looked truly delighted. He wrote a sign which read "Please take care of our garden" and attached it to the inside of the window. Not long after someone else watered it. "The experience has been full of surprises, says Thomas. People turning up regularly with notepads to write messages on; people concerned about whether the capsulites were eating and sleeping enough; big burly guys, the type Thomas says don't usually go in for performance art, getting a charge out of the experience" (Schembri 1996b).

Partially conceived as an exposé of the increased technological surveillance of urban lives and the loss of privacy, the Myersphere experiment turned the disciplinary power of panopticon vision into a game. The UDC transformed a common tactic of the urban marginalized – occupation and performance – into an acceptable art form. Just as teenagers entertain themselves by acting up for the security cameras strategically placed in shopping malls and railroad stations, the capsulites acted up 24 hours a day under the constant gaze of countless Big Brothers. Out of harsh coldblooded scrutiny and visual invasion, those under surveillance generated love, humor, and identification.

Perhaps the potential for this inversion to take off as a model for urban interaction was infectious. When early the next year students of the city campus of RMIT University of Technology occupied the administration building for 19 days to protest the introduction of fee-paying courses, the television screen replaced the glass of the Myer store window. Media coverage of the sit-in produced images of recognition and resonance with the previous year's public occupation. The televised scenes of students on the second floor receiving food and supplies on a rope paralleled the UDC deliveries of food through their "backstage" door. Their window performances were more raucous and less polished, but nevertheless served to highlight issues of resources and survival for young people.

The languages of science and cyberspace were harnessed in the promotion of the UDC. The performers were scientific experimental subjects – their everyday life, the object of scientific observation by the crowd cast here as "researchers." They in turn cast themselves as scientific observers of the crowd: "There's a score where we imagine that we're in an alien bathysphere that has landed in Myer and we're there to observe. So it's like we're at the bottom of the sea – the sealife is floating by and we're taking notes" (cited in Schembri 1996a). And as experimental scientists testing out the usefulness of the Internet as a performance aid: "I don't know if this is good to say, but being honest, part of this thing was to check out whether the Internet was an interesting form of communication, and I just don't think it is. If you want to get real, come down and see the show. You can't beat that" (cited in Schembri 1996b).

As authentic scientists, the five bald men were open to discovery. In representational or naturalistic theater actors perform with a fictional "fourth wall" between them and the audience – while the audience sees the actors, the actors appear not to see the audience (McGaw 1980: 141; Whitmore 1994: 60). Street performers, performance artists, and comedians often tilt at this convention moving through this fictional wall to variously shock and engage. In accordance with their exploratory mission, the UDC placed themselves behind an actual fourth wall and discovered that it proved to be quite porous. They found that the plate-glass window, described by Richard Sennett in terms of its "strong power of isolation" and its ability to divide the "physical senses" through the way it insulates those inside "from sound and touch and other human beings" outside (1990: 109), was indeed permeable. Sociality could cross the boundary, it could osmose through the tinted glass and transform scientific practice into playful intercourse. And in this experiment, even this paneful communication was more compelling than the cyberspace variety.

For many, the UDC was a treasure to be stumbled over, providing a fleeting interchange and welcome laugh in an otherwise impersonal space. For us it provides inspiration for thinking the city outside the hegemonic frames of inherited urban theory. We are not only interested in the ways in which it worked to unsettle prevalent urban "stories" such as that of the diminished privacy and increased technological surveillance of contemporary urban life. We are also intrigued with the way in which it destabilized binary modes of thinking the city and in the process helped to interpellate and constitute very different urban subjects. In bringing the private, domestic realm on to the streets this "public exposition of the mundane" (*The Age*, Nov 5, 1996, editorial) took just a little step further than do TV soapies, docudramas like *Sylvania Waters*, and infotainment shows such as *Burke's Backyard* and *The Home Show* toward demystifying the private and rendering the practice of individual self-management a public "entertainment." The "audience" admired the apartment's decor and were concerned that the art-stronauts were getting enough to eat, enough sleep, and were cleaning their teeth before they went to bed.

At the same time the very act of living on the street in Melbourne's Central Business District in an environment that dripped of affluence (a brightly lit interior with all the mod-cons, comfortable beds, paintings on the wall, a well-stacked

Figure 37.2 In their "living room" the Urban Dream Capsule art-stronauts perform for a Festival audience (photo: Penny Stephens; from *Sunday Age*, November 3, 1996)

refrigerator) spoke to two current political concerns – the homeless and the Postcode 3000 invasion. Among the audience were, indeed, real street inhabitors, people who through force of circumstance and sometimes inclination actually do live on the streets of Melbourne. And rubbing shoulders with them, no doubt, were the new residents of modern apartment blocks and office conversions who have been actively recruited by the City to move into Postcode 3000 to "revitalize" the urban center (and perhaps constitute a force to agitate for the clean-up of street people in the area). For the homeless and homed to comfortably share the same space and stand, for a nanosecond at least, as one in a space that is usually premised on the exclusion of "undesirables" is a rare experience. For a moment, imaginary battle lines between "illegitimate" occupants and the "legitimate" residents might have been forgotten in the interpellation of all concerned as a heterogeneous "we." Perhaps such a collective positioning of the performers and crowd would have stirred the question as to why the ethic of care that was being actively generated for the UDC dwellers might not extend to those who actually live on the streets?

Certainly we need not ignore the extent to which the UDC inhabitants, unlike people living on the streets, were permitted to dwell in city space *because* they were performers. Nor need we overlook the ways in which elements of the performance appeared as a spectacle of consumption that worked to advertise the store and its wares – particularly as, following the UDC's success, the window space continued to be used as a live advertising space exhibiting anything from models in underwear to cooking demonstrations. But to recognize the existence of these forces does not annul the alternative power and challenging nature of the performance.

In some small way the UDC enabled a degree of sustained interaction over 16 days that had the capacity to alter the way the city is experienced and thought. In observing this interaction, many people appeared to possess a sense of contentment in being involved, even if it was simply watching others in their communication with members of the UDC. People owned the UDC, participated in the performance, and permeated its glassed boundary. As they became attached to the UDC, the city became more inhabitable. By openly inhabiting the uninhabitable, the UDC challenged the imagined fixed spatiality of the domicile upon which the city is dependent. It troubled the perceived solidity of public/private and home/street boundaries. Perhaps as a consequence of the performance, the city appeared less of a place to be wary and more of a place to belong or occupy.

"Street theater and freak shows, [Thomas] said, have strong parallels" (Kermond 1996). Certainly the UDC was a freak occurrence, a flash of intense brilliance in an already full-with-brilliance International Arts Festival. For any one of the 200,000 visitors to the site an illumination of very ordinary acts rendered extraordinary was produced. Straying past this city site people were captured and drawn into its excess, energy, and unknowability. By the end of the third day the performers also stumbled across this secret: "Yesterday we had our first serious meeting, expressing concerns about burn-out, over-excitement, disorganisation. Then all promptly performed like maniacs for eight hours without stop. It's not really tiring. It's inspiring. The audience fuels our energies as we fuel theirs. Behind the window, it's performer's heaven" (Thomas 1996).

The overexcitement and stimulation of the city is something that urban commentators from Simmel on have observed and been wary of. In the quest for order, control, and a homogeneous conception of civility such subversive emotions and affects have often been deemed dangerous. Perhaps now, however, this (feminized) energy is less threatening? As political theorists cast around for new postmodern models of citizenship such as Iris Marion Young's "the being together of strangers" (1990: 232) and Alphonso Lingis's "the community of those who have nothing in common" (1994) we can see here a glimpse of a new civility of excess. Interpellated as communicators across technology, physical barriers, social and cultural difference, the crowd and the UDC modelled new forms of address and care: "And the biggest surprise? 'What this show has done is put people in a space where they're very beautiful,' Thomas says in the draped-off area behind the capsule (where the toilet is). 'People are really smiling and they're very loving. It's just brought out that side'" (Schembri 1996b: B10). "'People come along and do the most amazing drawings for us,' he says. 'There's this incredible sense of comradeship and love and care that comes through the windows, and also through the e-mail and the fax – and that's like 'Wow! I don't mind seeing that'" (Schembri 1996b).

Conclusion

The poetics of walking permits encounters with city fragments and seemingly "unimportant" urban activities – the practices of urbanism that are not neatly folded into forceful stories of capitalist urbanization, social polarization, urban consolidation, and dead city syndrome. How are we to think of these entertaining but ultimately "unimportant" experiences? One way is to critically address the discourse which discursively "discards" these urban treasures placing them in a position of marginality on the urban terrain. In the face of the alien spaceships in *Independence Day* urban street performances appear quixotic, small, and ineffectual. Similarly, in the face of apocalyptic pronouncements on the state of cities and city life "under late or postmodern capitalism" the transformative potential of walking and performing appears weak, powerless, and foolish. But these are representations all.

In the distracted state of watching and interacting with the UDC perhaps the shock defense of urban fear and alienation produced by dominant urban narratives was pierced in many of the UDC's diverse audience? Perhaps the "rhetoric of walking" allowed new conversations to begin between urban subjects and a rewriting of the urban text to commence? It was not only the speech/performance acts of the UDC that confronted and sidestepped dominant images of the city, but also the feelings and speech that flowed on the footpath between the walkers momentarily arrested by the brilliance of what caught their eyes. Straying in city space exposed walkers to the things that are concealed by the concept city of urban planning and theory. Stories such as those that can be composed around the UDC have the power to rewrite the city. They can contribute to a vision of the city as a site of potentiality, not imminent destruction; of civic sensibility as caring of others, not competitively self-interested; of urban structures as permeable and diverse, not rigid and limited and of urban narratives that lean toward enabling futures, not nostalgic pasts.

REFERENCES

Barthes, R. 1982: *Empire of Signs*, tr. Richard Howard. New York: Hill and Wang.

Bauman, Z. 1994: Desert spectacular. In K. Tester (ed.), *The Flâneur.* London/New York: Routledge, 138–57.

Benjamin, W. 1978: A Berlin chronicle. In P. Demetz (ed.), tr. E. Jephcott. *Reflections: Essays, Aphorisms, Autobiographical Writings*, New York: Schocken Books, 3–60.

Certeau, M. de 1984: *The Practice of Everyday Life*, tr. S. Rendell. Berkeley: University of California Press.

Felski, R. 1995: *The Gender of Modernity.* Cambridge, MA: Harvard University Press.

Gibson-Graham, J. K. 1996: *The End of Capitalism (As We Knew It): A Feminist Critique of Political Economy.* Cambridge, MA: Blackwell.

Kermond, C. 1996: Suffering the pane of separation. *The Age* (Melbourne), Oct. 19, A5.

Lingis, A. 1994: *The Community of Those Who Have Nothing in Common.* Bloomington: Indiana University Press.

McGraw, C. 1980: *Acting is Believing: A Basic Method.* New York: Rinehart and Winston.

Morris, M. 1998: *Too Little Too Late.* Bloomington: Indiana University Press.

Mumford, L. 1961: *The City in History.* Harmondsworth/Ringwood: Penguin.

Rose G. 1993: *Feminism and Geography.* London: Polity Press.

Schembri, J. 1996a: The window of opportunities. *The Age* (Melbourne), Oct. 11, 5.

Schembri, J. 1996b: Opening the urban dream (time) capsule. *The Age* (Melbourne), Nov. 1, B10.

Scott-Norman, F. 1996: Bald, bold and an act with more front than Myer. *The Age* (Melbourne), Oct. 26, A31.

Sennett, R. 1990: *The Conscience of the Eye: The Design and Social Life of Cities*. New York: Alfred A. Knopf.

Sorkin, M. (ed.) 1992: Introduction. In *Variations on a Theme Park: The New American City and the End of Public Space*. New York: Hill and Wang, xi-xv.

Swanson, G. 1995: "Drunk with glitter": Consuming spaces and sexual geographies. In S. Watson and K. Gibson (eds.), *Postmodern Cities and Spaces*, Oxford/Cambridge: Blackwell, 80–98.

Thomas, N. 1996: Behind life's window, tired means inspired. *The Age* (Melbourne), Oct. 21, B3.

Valentine, G. 1993: (Hetero)sexing space: lesbian perceptions and experiences of everyday spaces. *Environment and Planning D: Society and Space*, 11, 395–413.

Virilio, P. 1991: The overexposed city. In *The Lost Dimension*, tr. D. Moshenberg. New York: Semiotext(e).

Whitmore, J. 1994: *Directing Postmodern Theater: Shaping Signification in Performance*. Ann Arbor: University of Michigan Press.

Wilson, E. 1991: *The Sphinx in the City*. London: Virago.

Wilson, E. 1995: The Invisible Flâneur. In S. Watson and K. Gibson (eds.), *Postmodern Cities and Spaces*. Oxford Cambridge: Blackwell, 59–79.

Young, I. M. 1990: *Justice and the Politics of Difference*. Princeton: Princeton University Press.

Chapter 38

The Street Politics of Jackie Smith

John Paul Jones III

...geneaological practice transforms history from a judgment on the past in the name of a present truth to a "counter-memory" that combats our current modes of truth and justice, helping us to understand and change the present by placing it in a new relation to the past.

Jonathan Arac, *Postmodernism and Politics*, p. xviii

On April 3, 1968, Martin Luther King, Jr., together with Jesse Jackson and Ralph Albernathy, arrived in Memphis, Tennessee to lend their support for striking garbage workers. They stayed at the historically Black Lorraine Motel, located adjacent to the city's Black business district on the outskirts of downtown Memphis (Figure 38.1). The next day, while standing on the balcony outside his room, King was shot down by a bullet fired from across the street. The instant was captured in a famous Joseph Louw photograph (Figure 38.2), an image that immediately became an emblem of the 1960s. Today, the Lorraine is both a shrine to the fallen civil rights leader (Figure 38.3) and the site of the nation's first civil rights museum.

The transformation of the Lorraine took many years. Following King's death, it continued to operate as a motel, but not surprisingly, it drew more curiosity seekers than guests. By the 1970s it was a run-down building badly in need of repair, an embarrassment for the city of Memphis not unlike Dealy Plaza was for Dallas. In the early 1980s, a local Black official, D'Army Bailey, and the mayor of Memphis, Dick Hackett, put into place a fundraising project to save the Lorraine. By the late 1980s, the nonprofit Lorraine Civil Rights Museum Foundation had assembled some nine million dollars from the City of Memphis, Shelby County, and the State of Tennessee, as well as from various private sources. The renovation project involved removing one wing of the old motel to create a portion of the museum (Figure 38.4), while preserving the wing containing King's room, number 306.

Inside the main area visitors are treated to a short introductory film, to traveling galleries celebrating African-American contributions to art, education, and science,

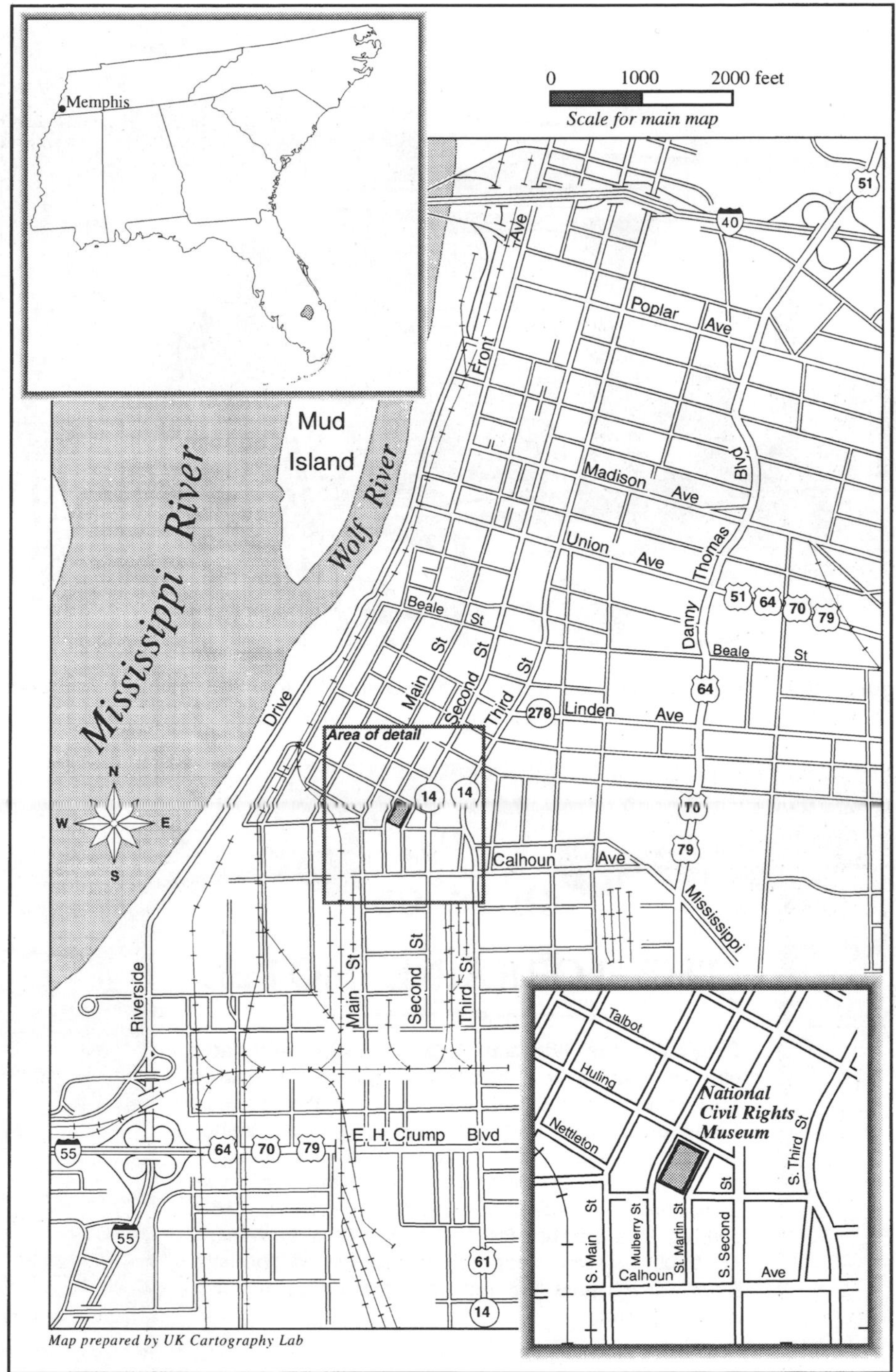

Figure 38.1 Location of the Lorraine Motel, site of the National Civil Rights Museum in Memphis, Tennessee

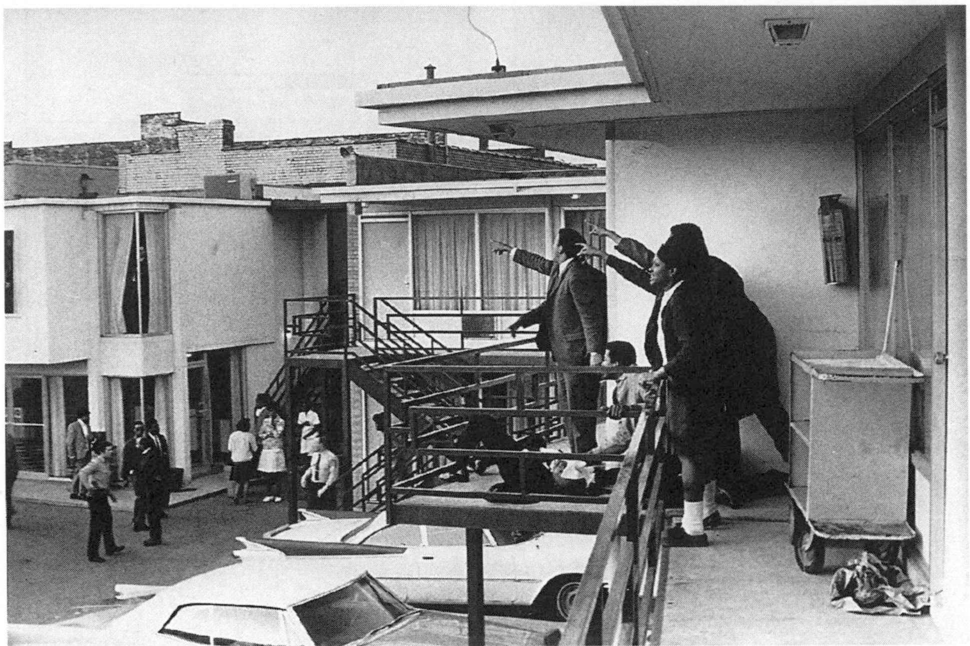

Figure 38.2 King's assassination at the Lorraine. Photo by Joseph Louw/LIFE Magazine © TIME Inc. Used with permission

Figure 38.3 Historical marker describing the significance of the Lorraine Motel

Figure 38.4 The National Civil Rights Museum. At left is the entrance to the museum

and to displays recounting the history of the US civil rights movement. The showcase of the museum is a series of hands-on exhibits combining audio, video, and interactive audience participation. These cover the Montgomery bus boycott, the court case, *Brown* vs. *Board of Education*, the desegregation of Little Rock's Central High School, the March on Washington, and the Memphis garbage strike. Visitors can also view the site of King's death, either from the brick-inlay courtyard below the balcony, complete with historic automobiles of King's era (Figure 38.5), or from room 306, faithfully redecorated to represent the way it was when King spent his last night in the Lorraine.

The National Civil Rights Museum attracts some 100,000 visitors annually. One year, while on a visit to Memphis, I too planned a visit. Rounding the back of the Lorraine on foot from downtown Memphis, I suddenly and unpreparedly confronted the balcony, a site intertextually linked to Louw's famous photograph. In the stillness of that moment I noticed a woman (Figure 38.6), Jacqueline Smith. She struck a discomforting presence across the street from the museum, sitting on a tattered old couch, with handmade placards in protest of what she called the "Civil Wrong Museum." Rather than continue into the museum, I crossed the street to talk to her, asking about her protest. Thus began a series of visits I have made to the Lorraine over several years, never once violating her request that I boycott the museum. This chapter is about her story.

Figure 38.5 The balcony outside the preserved wing of the motel. The automobiles reference the cars captured in Joseph Louw's photograph (Figure 38.2)

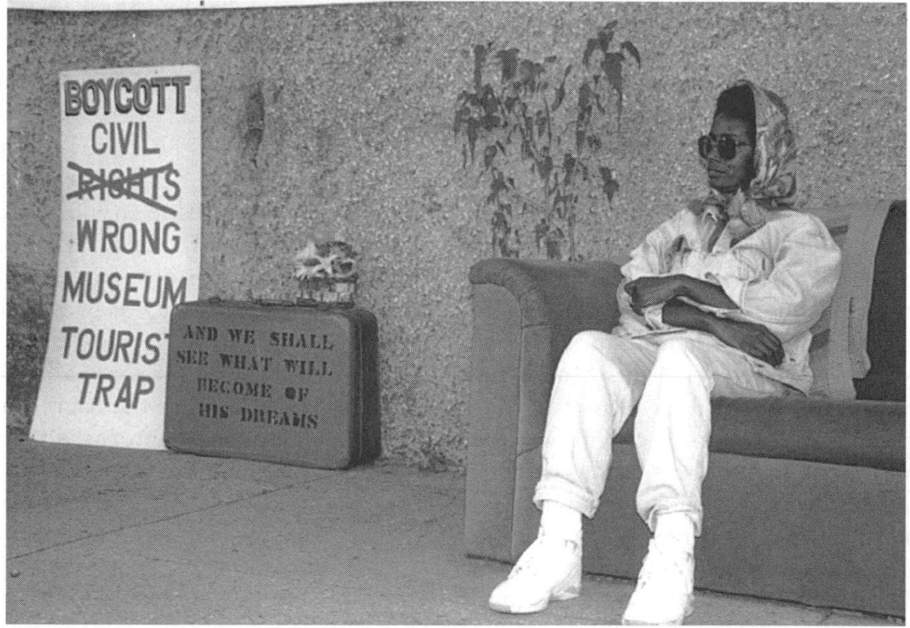

Figure 38.6 Jacqueline "Jackie" Smith protests the Lorraine's transformation into a museum

Jackie's Protest

Jackie's protest operates at several levels. Listeners – at least those who cross the street to talk to her, for she is under a court injunction not to disrupt the museum's operations – will first learn that she is against the use of the site as a civil rights museum. For her, civil rights is an ongoing, everyday struggle that must be practiced (Figure 38.7); it should not be petrified, canonized, and memorialized in a series of interactive exhibits. Jackie believes that a civil rights museum is an all-too-comforting experience for visitors, implying that civil rights were won with desegregated buses, schools, and lunch counters. Among his other writings, as a rationale for her protest, Jackie points to King's final sermon, in which he rejects eulogies and awards, affirming instead actions such as feeding the hungry, clothing the naked, and counseling those in prison. Jackie maintains that the Lorraine should be used in ways consistent with King's philosophy, particularly by helping those living in the deteriorated community in which it is located, which she notes is characterized by unemployment, poor housing, drugs, and crime. Accordingly, Jackie maintains that the Lorraine should house a homeless shelter, a medical clinic, a job-training center, and a drug rehabilitation facility. Jackie goes on to record the rationale for her protest:

> That's why I'm protesting . . . that would be the main reason and the fact that the way King said he wanted to be remembered is simply being ignored in favor of bricks and mortar, lifeless, been set up and done for appearances, does not solve the social problems, does not get

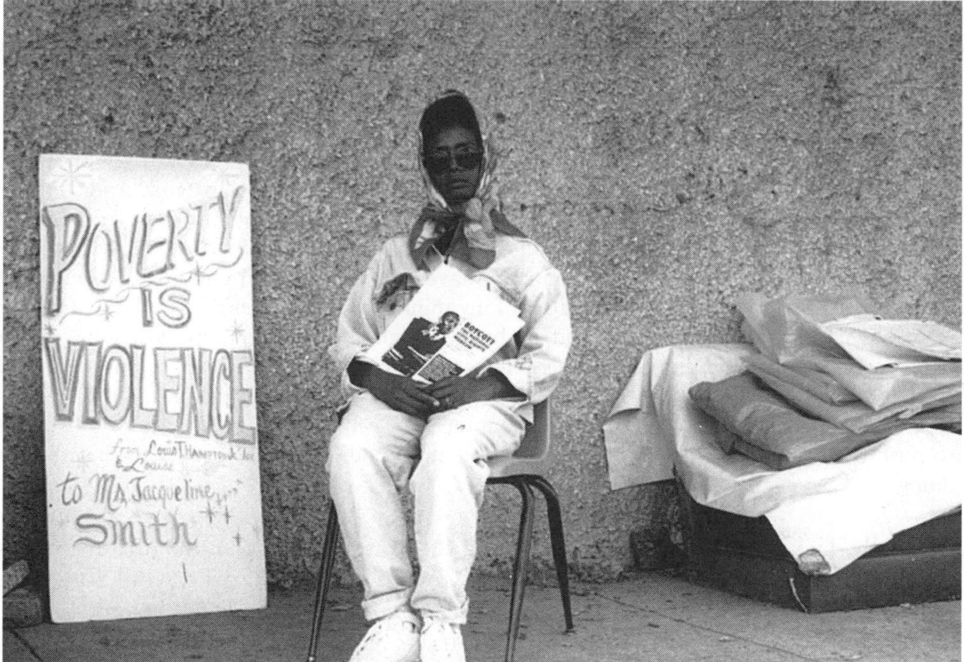

Figure 38.7 Jackie asks Memphis residents and visitors to boycott the museum

to the root of our problems, and that's what King was all about, he was about serving humanity, and helping, that was his basic philosophy and I don't see that being focused on. All I see being focused on is how many tourists did we get, how much money did we make, what is the tally, that's what I see, the bottom line, somebody sitting back trying to make a dollar.... I just think the reason for having a museum at the site of Dr. King's death for educational purposes lacks substance because we have a run-down neighborhood, poverty, homelessness, crime, drug abuse, all these ills that plague our society. I just feel that those problems are more important because we need to be trying to eradicate them.

Those who linger to speak with Jackie can also hear her offer a detailed political-economy critique of land development in the area around the Lorraine. She cites explicit and de facto redlining, castigates the nearby gated communities alongside the Mississippi river that house such luminaries as Memphis's favorite daughter, actress Cybil Sheppard, and laments the use of the Lorraine by the city's White establishment as a stimulant for gentrification. As Jackie notes, "Blacks have lived and operated business in this area for years. Now they want to tear the buildings down and replace them with high-rent apartments they know we can't afford." "Where are we supposed to go?" she asks. Tracing a story common to many US cities, Jackie offers that the Lorraine's development "is just a ploy to get the Blacks out of the neighborhood. It's one of the biggest landgrabbing conspiracies. It's urban renewal, all over again, but now it goes by the name of gentrification." Jackie will also hold forth about the 1979 strategic plan that still guides changes in the built environment around the hotel. The plan predicted that rising rents would substantially alter the neighborhood's racial composition:

They [urban planners] predicted that by year 2000 there would be only 21 percent of African-Americans in the area even though at the time that they wrote the report there were 79 percent African-Americans in the area. And within that report they had the number of condominiums and townhouses they had planned on building and they had how much they would cost, and so the report was broken down to income levels, and see by that they made their prediction that there would be only 21 percent African-Americans in this area, because they know we can't afford the apartments and townhouses and condominiums that they built. And so that's how they came up with the figures, and I'm telling you, you've probably gone around and looked around for yourself and you see all the new apartments that have sprung up and they look like they've been here for years but they have not, they've been building on them now since the early eighties. So it's not a matter of my thinking, it's a matter that we know for sure what has taken place in this area, and we had... neighborhood meetings with some of the planners of this area and they just simply told us what was going to transpire in this area. And so that's when I began to speak out against what was going on because, hey, Dr. King was assassinated here. I mean you going to mistreat the poor people that live down here, you going to push them aside in order to gentrify the neighborhood? And that's exactly what they're doing.

Finally, Jackie offers a cultural critique of the museum. She protests turning King's death site into a "partyhouse" by the city of Memphis. Who, she asks, would organize champagne brunches and courtyard dancing (Figure 38.8) in such a sacred space? She protests using the Lorraine to attract tourists to Memphis, and its emergence as an obligatory stop for conventioneers (Figure 38.9), some of whom are treated to black-tie galas under the balcony of room 306. She critiques the interactive exhibits

Figure 38.8 The museum is a site for some of the city's cultural events

as a form of entertainment inappropriate for the Lorraine; she argues that everything one could learn in the museum – and more – is already contained in the public library; and, noting the lack of historical authenticity of the museum's exhibits, she laughs at the pilgrims who throw themselves in a fit of emotion on the automobiles under the balcony, cars in which King never actually rode:

> Well one thing I see is that the Lorraine is being separated from its history. They are trying to turn it into something that it was not and I think that's a mistake. I think the Lorraine should be set up to deal with today's problems, to deal with today's discrimination, crime, poverty and that sort of thing. But they have turned the Lorraine into just another place for entertainment, parties. I don't think it's right to turn the death site of Dr. King into a place to party. I really think that that's wrong. He didn't come here to die, so why should somebody take death and capitalize off of it and turn that site where he died into a place to party? To me that is totally wrong, distasteful, and I don't think that is the proper way to honor the memory of a man like Dr. King.

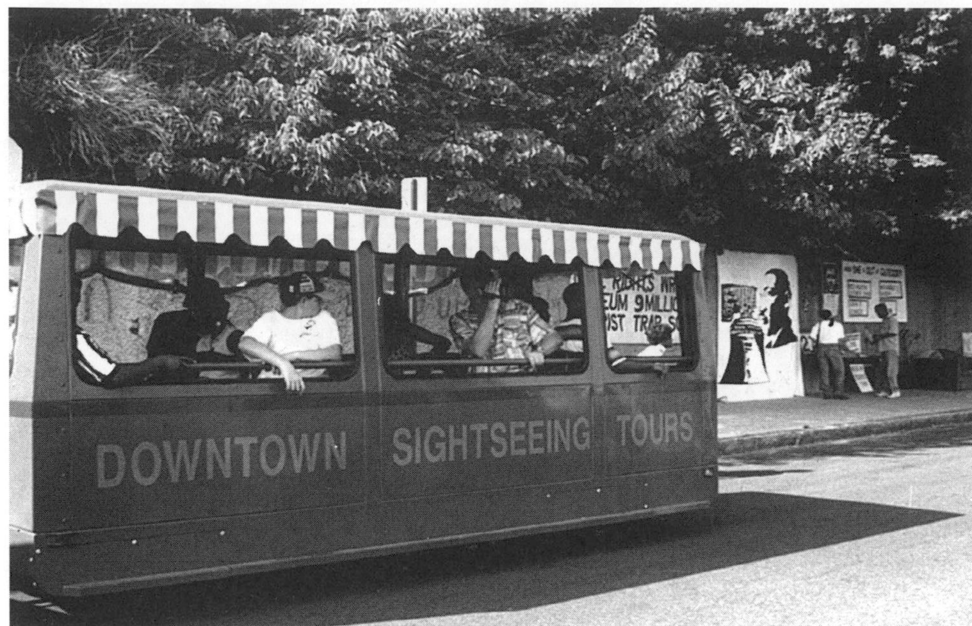

Figure 38.9 The street between Jackie and the museum is regularly traversed by vehicles, such as this one, carrying tourists

What is most remarkable about Jackie's protest is its duration. Jackie was the night manager and the last resident of the old Lorraine Motel. In January 1988, the building was condemned for the museum project, but she locked herself in her room and refused to leave, even after the water and electricity had been turned off. She and the local government entered into a 50-day siege that ended when Jackie was forcibly evicted from the building on March 2, 1988. She was deposited on the sidewalk outside the Lorraine, and from that moment forward, day and night, she has been living in protest outside the museum, a large sign recording the number of days (Figure 38.10). Not the weather, harassment by local officials, nor racist acts against her life, have deterred her. She turned 47 years old when the protest entered its eleventh year, but through my various visits I have never heard her express any doubt about her actions; as she puts it, "I am too stubborn to give up."

As a result of her everyday presence, Jackie has herself become an institution, even, a tourist attraction in her own right (Figure 38.11). Some visitors will stop to hear her story for the first time, but summer in Memphis is the site of scores of reunions among African-Americans whose families extend from Chicago to the lower Mississippi delta, and both the museum and Jackie have become an annual affair for many of these families. Local friends and neighbors will also drop by frequently.

Street Politics

Jackie's protest encourages a range of reflections relevant to the nature of politics, space, and memory. Traditionally conceived by urban researchers in electoral and

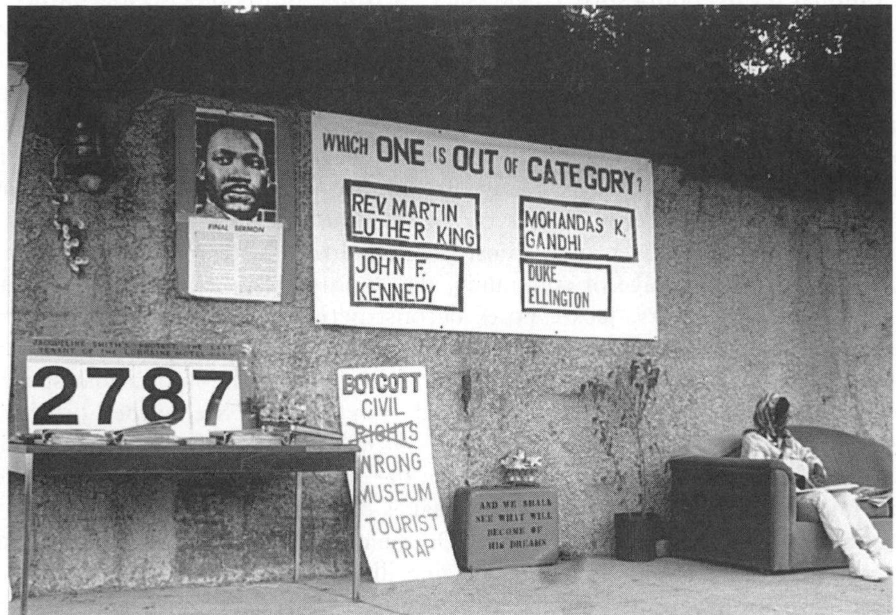

Figure 38.10 The sign records the number of consecutive days Jackie has protested. This photograph was taken in 1995. As of this writing, she is still there

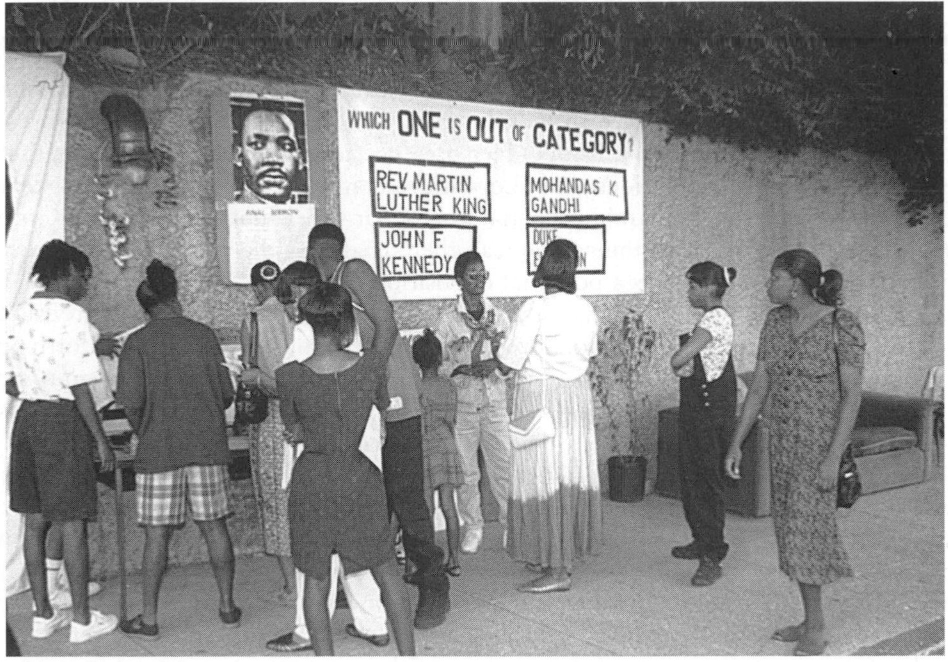

Figure 38.11 Memphis visitors inquire about the protest

institutional terms, politics for Jackie emerges from, and is practiced at, a deeply personal level. Her vigil sharply contrasts civic and personal politics, effectively demonstrating how the strategies of capital and state institutions can be countermanded, if not overturned, by the persistent, everyday tactics of those located on the margin. Jackie thus reminds us of other "bottom up" urban politics, including the protestations of graffiti artists, parade and carnival demonstrators, and alternative media activists. And yet, unlike many of these forms of protest – but like King himself – she explicitly taps a reservoir of religious discourse, demonstrating its critical resourcefulness over and against the secularized discourses of the state. In opposition to the language of community development espoused by city officials, planners, and developers, Jackie poses deconstructive-style questions: What precisely is meant by "community," or by "development"? Defined by and for whom?

In another vein, Jackie reminds us of Henri Lefebvre's admonition that space is never neutral, but is a product literally filled with ideology. Seeing the Lorraine in these terms enables us to understand Jackie's protest as "spatial praxis" – a specifically geographic form of political action. On the one hand, the target of her protest is the Lorraine, and through this site she makes connections to the wider spaces of Memphis that the museum fails to serve. On the other hand, her continuous spatial presence across the street from the Lorraine illustrates that her chosen forms of protest – witnessing, testifying, and vigilance – are themselves deeply geographic practices; in other words, the "eye of power" has location and direction. Jackie's protest also tells a story about the "social construction" of history, by which is not meant that history is in the mind, but that it is only available to us through socially mediated forms of experience and interpretation. In this space in particular we learn that the social authority to determine what will be history, and how it will be honored, is typically bound to the state apparatus, as it is with so many memorials, museums, and state-sanctioned parades. But through Jackie we equally learn that no commemoration is ever fully sealed, since no history is ever without subjects who experience, interpret, and learn from it differently. Jackie shows us, in other words, that the Lorraine is not a tombstone. Her presence taps a surplus of meaning that exceeds the authorial intentionality of Lorraine's creators. It is in fact this excess that enables and makes meaningful her spatial praxis, for she demonstrates that for both space and history, as in all things political, there is always the potential for reinterpretation, and hence always a potential oppositional moment.

Finally, in asking Memphis visitors to make a choice between her activist vision for the Lorraine and the institutionalized memorialization of civil rights put forth by the museum's curators, she implicitly poses the question: "what does it mean to be political?" I have listened as scores of visitors have interacted with her, with this question just below the surface. Some will side with the museum, and encourage Jackie to find more productive pursuits for her energies. Others will applaud her vision and offer both moral and, occasionally, material support. And I have struggled with both responses: how can one measure Jackie's vision for the museum over and against its arguable educational benefits, which include the visits of as many as 50,000 school-age visitors each year? One answer to this question is to conceive of the productive politics of this space as located in the street that separates Jackie from the museum, that interstitial space that juxtaposes and puts into sharp relief one version of African-American history to another. On the one hand is an attempt to preserve the memory of civil rights so that the struggle is not forgotten; on the other hand is Jackie's effort to activate that memory for the unfinished project of civil rights. Seen in this way, perhaps visitors like me return to Memphis because of the dialectical and co-constitutive tensions produced by the structure of the Lorraine and Jackie's critical presence. And, perhaps Jackie's legacy will be, if not the transformation of the Lorraine, more critical reflection on the politics that reside in this and other spaces of memory.

ACKNOWLEDGMENTS

This paper was presented at the Inaugural International Conference in Critical Geography (Vancouver), the Association of American Geographers (Boston), the Southeastern Division of the Association of American Geographers (Memphis), and the Cities at the Millennium Conference (London), as well as at the University of Wisconsin, the University of Toledo, Clarion University, University of Wales at Aberystwyth, Southwest Texas State University, and the University of Kentucky's African American Studies and Research Program. My thanks to Nick Blomley, Gary Bridge, Bernadette Caldwell, Tim Cresswell, Margo Kleinfeld, Geraldine Pratt, Tobie Saad, Gerald Smith, Gerald Thomas, Sent Visser, and Sophie Watson for these invitations. I also want to thank Deborah Dixon, Owen Dwyer, Wolfgang Natter, and the audiences at these presentations for offering insights and comments. I am of course most of all indebted to Jackie. Readers may contact her by writing to PO Box 3482, Memphis TN 38173-0482.

SUGGESTED READINGS

Certeau, M. de 1984: *The Practice of Everyday Life*. Berkeley: University of California Press.
Cresswell, T. 1996: *In Place/Out of Place*. Minneapolis: University of Minnesota Press.
Foucault, M. 1980: *Power/Knowledge*, ed. Colin Godon. New York: Pantheon.
Keith, M., and Pile, S. (eds.) 1993: *Place and the Politics of Identity*. London: Routledge.
Lefebvre, H. 1996: *Writings on Cities*, tr. Eleonore Kofman and Elizabeth Lebas. Oxford: Blackwell.
Pile, S. and Keith, M. (eds.) 1997: *Geographies of Resistance*. London: Routledge.
Scott, J. C. 1990: *Domination and the Arts of Resistance: Hidden Transcripts*. New Haven: Yale University Press.
Smith, N. 1996: *The New Urban Frontier: Gentrification and the Revanchist City*. London: Routledge.
Soja, E. W. 1996: *Thirdspace: Journeys to Los Angeles and other Real-and-Imagined Places*. Oxford: Blackwell.

Chapter 39

Wonderful, Terrible: Everyday Life in Bangkok

Annette Hamilton

The cities of the South have been generally absent from recent urban theory. For a time, at the height of modernist social theory in the 1960s, the "Third World City" received attention as constituted by its "problems" – problems of poverty, over-population, crowding, environmental degradation. This was accounted for by the decomposition of premodern agricultural societies, whose primary living site was thought to be "the village," fading in importance as the engines of industrialization and urbanization began to dominate in the new landscapes of modernity. In a broad sense, this was (and is) true enough. But the city in the non-West is often disregarded as a phenomenon in its own right, with its own distinctive history, traditions, rhythms, meanings and senses of place. It is as if the city as a space of human life belongs properly to the West. Non-Western cities are seen as the epiphenomena of social change rather than as integral to their own society's history and culture.

In this chapter I want to write about Bangkok, one of the largest and most complex cities of the Southeast Asian region. In doing so, I want to situate the city as a site having its own meanings and forms, not as an ersatz Western city but as the central node in the processes of transformation under late global modernity for all the peoples of Thailand, wherever they live. I take my inspiration from Walter Benjamin's "dialectics of seeing," or rather, of experiencing, presenting spaces and images drawn from the everyday-life world at a moment when the structurations of modern capitalism have taken an uncertain, uneven hold. Such an enterprise could fill a book, or multiple volumes. Here, only a sketch is presented, in order to pose Bangkok against its still-meaningful past, one which is implicit within its future.

There are many kinds of everyday in Bangkok, shared spaces, pulsions from the past, a memorialized present which feels like the future, already. An outstanding example of indigenous urbanism in Southeast Asia, three centuries of Royal presence are imprinted upon the city, creating a "discursive culture of place" (O'Connor 1990: 61). The people know the city by its signifying sites: palaces, statues, monuments, temples, shrines, markets, and waterways. Ancient though they may be, they are not "heritage," but zones constantly reinvested with desire and meaning, where people make offerings to spirits and images known to answer prayers, to provide winning lottery numbers or ensure success in examinations. These are small, intimate spaces, but equally important are the vast public areas where collective affirmations or contestations take place, in events refracting past and present. Around the base of the Democracy Monument, and in the surrounding streets, vast crowds have gathered during this half-century, most recently in May 1992, when protests against corruption and unrepresentative government resulted in many tragic deaths but also substantial political change. This time, though, the protestors arrived in expensive cars carrying mobile phones; a "middle-class revolution" was said to be underway in the heart of the city (Sunghsidh and Pasuk 1993: 27).

Other shared spaces are sites of pleasure: the open "wet" markets where rich and poor mingle over the catfish and eels squirming in basins, sparkling fruits and vegetables just in from the countryside, sacks of rice of ten varieties, orchids and roses, chicken-feet, chili pastes, strips of still-bloody meats, honeys from the distant forests, possibly traded by mountain people who have never seen a city. Or at Chatuchak Park where hundreds of thousands visit the weekend market, circulating, perambulating, gazing: at giant spiders, monkeys, poodles, vegetables, amulets, cutlasses, kitchenware, military surplus, every conceivable thing which can be bought and sold.

Bangkok is the capital of Thailand (once known as Siam). The only nation of Southeast Asia never to have been colonized, Thailand has been in the forefront of the "Asian Economic Miracle," until recently exhibiting massive annual rises in Gross Domestic Product (8–10%+) and forging a new identity as a primary participant in the globalization of the region. The city, known formally as Krung Thep Maha Nakorn (The Great City of Angels), lies on a flat floodplain along the Chao Phraya River, which debouches into the Gulf of Thailand not far to the south. A classic example of the primate city, Bangkok dominates the economy and the imagination of the nation. With a population of around eight million (or more, considering illegal immigrants and circular migrants) it is more than 20 times larger than any other urban settlement in the country. Virtually all major transport links go through the city, shuttling thousands in and out every single day. Capital is concentrated in the capital: 95 percent of all goods, import and export, pass through Bangkok. The major Western and Japanese trading companies and banks and a large proportion of manufacturing industry are located in the Greater Metropolitan Region. Nearby provinces are now dormitory suburbs. Economic, social, and political power – and cultural capital – are to be found only in the city. Families on the road to wealth must move there: many prominent Sino-Thai business empires, for instance, were founded on agricultural activities in the provinces but as their wealth grew they inevitably moved to the city and consolidated their business links, diversifying into the vast family-based conglomerates which have been so strongly identified with the "Asian economic miracle" (Krikkiat and Yoshihara 1983: 20–21).

Baan-kok (village of native plums) was originally the site of a French fort in the mid-seventeenth century and a largely Chinese trading and customs post until the late eighteenth century (Smithies 1986: 4–5). The Royal City with its new name was founded by King Rama I, first of the present Chakri Dynasty, in the aftermath of the destruction of the former capital Ayutthaya by the Burmese in 1767. Urbanism is deeply implicated in the traditional political and social structures of Southeast Asia. The ancient kingdoms have been described as "galactic polities" – zones of power with a king and his city at the center, from which influence, protection, and authority radiate outwards and to which duty, tribute, and subordination are drawn. Complex principles of Hindu-Buddhist cosmology underlie the idea of the city, and its layout. Each dynasty has its own capital and the capital city is above all the space of the King, who is the fulcrum around which the entire social order turns, embodying sacred and superordinate powers, which extend their influence to all those who live within his city. Bangkok today is said to have no "center," in a geographical urban sense. But the city, as it was three hundred years ago, is centered by the presence of the King.

The Royal City contains an immensely complex network of buildings, including the Grand Palace, the Throne Hall, and the Temple of the Emerald Buddha. The Royal Family today resides to the north in Chitralada Palace, not accessible to the public, but regular ceremonies are still held in the Grand Palace and its precincts, most notably the changing of the robes of the Emerald Buddha by the King in person, three times a year. Nearby, Sanam Luang, the great public open space which is the traditional royal cremation ground, provides a site for enormous public gatherings which spectacularize the relation between monarch and people. The annual Ploughing Ceremony, marking the beginning of the agricultural season, is presided over by the Royal Family, reenacting a ritual which goes back to the thirteenth century (Gerson 1996: 22–3). Other public events include celebrations of the King's birthday, significant anniversaries of the present reign, and in 1996 the cremation of the King's late mother, a daylong ritual attended by over half a million people wearing black, a huge crowd in respectful, uncanny silence. The event was televised nationally on all channels, and "the people" brought together in symbolic unity magnified by the new technologies of inclusion.

In public spaces, including the thousands of streets and lanes of the city where people mingle, stop, shop, sit side by side, and eat a bowl of noodles, difference is canceled, or put into abeyance. But, in most other respects, the lives of the rich and the poor, the foreign and the local, the immigrant and the householder, the ethnically marked and the "genuine Thai," the Muslim and the Buddhist, scarcely touch on each other. Bangkok has been a diverse, multicultural city since its inception: in the 1880s almost half the 500,000 inhabitants were of Chinese origin, with substantial numbers of Indians, Persians, Javanese, Malays, Burmese, Khmer, Lao, Mon, and Vietnamese, as well as *farang* (white Westerners), mostly English, Dutch, French, German, Portuguese and Swedish (Wilson 1989: 54).

One hundred years ago the city began to reflect the modernizing policies of the great King Chulalongkorn (1868–1910). This era created the preconditions for Bangkok's contemporary modernity. Canals were filled in to make roads upon which carriages could pass, the network of alleyways and floating houses and markets edging the river was removed and replaced by brick buildings. Many grand new buildings were constructed which reflected a blending of European and Thai sensibilities. The West became fashionable; the Thai elite learned English, French, and German; many traveled and studied abroad. The Royal Family patronized sciences, medicine, and learning, and introduced Western architects, sculptors, and painters to teach their craft to local people.

As Thailand became increasingly aware of the West, the question of "Thai identity" asserted itself. The position of the Chinese was especially important, given their dominance in the economy. At times respected, at other times rejected, the Chinese became increasingly assimilated, marrying Thai women, taking Thai names, speaking Thai in everyday life. Nevertheless the patriarchal structure of the Chinese family remained strong, providing one of the basic elements of the Sino-Thai business class which has been so strongly identified with the "economic miracle" (Pasuk and Baker 1996).

Today, the question of "identity" has come into prominence once again, precisely as the effects of globalization have been most strongly felt. As the new middle classes, academics, and commentators express angst over the loss of "authentic Thai culture" the distinctions of wealth and poverty in the country multiply exponentially. Bangkok, like most Asian cities, does little to disguise social inequality. The legless beggar who rents his square meter of pavement outside the entry to the new shopping mall, the filthy children asleep on the overhead walkway, the thousands crowded into jerry-built slums along the city railway lines, serve as constant reminders that poverty and suffering are ever-present. Thailand has until recently had no social security system. Thai culture stresses the individual, the role of destiny or *karma* in life's outcomes, the obligation not to interfere in the destinies of others. The very poor and the very rich are believed to be in their respective conditions for good reason. There is no such thing as an "accident of birth."

A kind of laissez faire at the level of philosophy is reflected in a similar condition in public life which creates strange contradictions in modernity. These attitudes ensure an endless supply of the cheap human labor essential to the late capitalist economy, yet the necessary rationalization of the life-world (Habermas 1984) which it also requires is constantly being undermined. This tension marks the city, producing endless shifting negotiations at the level of public policy as multiple arms of an immensely complex bureaucracy struggle over the same issues, most notably the chronic crisis of traffic, transport and city amenities, public health, air pollution. The prime purpose of each agency seems to be to maintain its own continued existence. Rather than overall coherence or cooperation, each is in opposition to the other, trying to outdo the other, promoting different resolutions to the city's problems (here a monorail, there an overhead expressway, here another road system), all under the control of separate bureaucratic agencies. The overall political structure, with the complex relations between the military, government, and business (cf. Pasuk and Baker 1996) means also that personal enrichment for "persons of influence" is often more important than any apparent functional purpose of the agency or organization. The citizens, meanwhile, make the best of their situation, surviving, enjoying, suffering, in wonder and terror at life in Bangkok.

Material

Bangkok is an intensely physical city. The smell of carbon monoxide mixed with garlic and spices, fetid drains, a hint of sewer; heat radiating from the road and glass-fronted buildings, above all the noise, the traffic ceaselessly throbbing, the whine of motorcycles, the perils of walking, of crossing a road, of breathing, the delirium after three hours in an open bus in a traffic jam, the sheer impossibility of everyday life.

The city decomposes and rebuilds itself every day. In the 1960s, four- or five-story "rowhouses" were built for a population beginning to burgeon: now damp eats into the cement, old paint peels, timber rots. Thousands live in the interstices between vast high-rise glistening offices and apartment buildings fronting the main roads. Inside, narrow laneways and alleys wind in accordance with the accidents of building-time, something built here, demolished there, leaving a space and a new passageway. On the top of many shophouses is a rooftop courtyard, often a carefully nurtured garden, an island of green on the roofline, where birds – black and white wrens – sometimes dance and flick their tails, and ravens sit on the forest of television antennas, the only nonhuman living creatures in the city apart of course from the cats, dogs, cockroaches, ants, rats, and occasional cobras.

The demolition of much of the low-rise central city is progressively replacing these dwellings with high-rise hotels, condominiuns, and office towers. In the remaining residential areas crowding is frequent; a random sample of Bangkok households found a level of household crowding four times that in Western societies (Edwards et al. 1994; Fuller et al. 1996). However Thai culture does not stress separation and privacy, and individuals tolerate far higher levels of shared space than any but the poorest in the West can tolerate. The Thai urban dweller's attitude cannot be predicated on Western planners' expectations. For example, it is clear that slum-dwellers often resist removal to state and private "low-cost housing," much of which remains vacant in Bangkok today (Yap 1996). Also in contradiction to Western understandings of "family values" a high proportion of Thai parents do not live with their children at all, leaving them to be raised by grandparents or other relatives in the provinces or elsewhere in Bangkok (Richter 1996). Husbands and wives, too, may live apart for long periods of time, depending on their employment opportunities. Thailand was among the first of the "developing nations" to drastically curtail fertility, in conjunction with women's widespread participation in the industrial labor force. As a result, "the family" as a co-resident domestic group is an increasingly tenuous entity. Women are choosing to have only one child (Richter et al. 1994) and informal marriage and divorce are so common as to be normative among the majority of the lower-paid population.

Although many are poor, the city promises much. The abundance of new Western-style material goods in every public space means people can hope to possess them, if not now, then in the future. So the city functions as a spectacle, a site of desire, pulling towards it thousands and thousands from the countryside who come to work, to labour, to hope, to obtain money to send home to their families, and, in the narrative dreams of the city, to go back home a rich person, buy a rice farm, rehouse the elderly parents. The city guarantees nothing, but it provides hope, an escape from the certainty of provincial dullness, limited diets, backbreaking labour under a pitiless sun. It provides spaces and opportunities, but also threats and fears, fears of being robbed, of contracting terrible illnesses such as AIDS, of being unable to live in the material spaces, unable to endure the horrors the city can throw up in exchange for its pleasures.

For the wealthy, there is nothing which cannot be obtained in Bangkok. Automobiles, houses, clothing, jewelry, gold, every modern appliance, air conditioning, abundant supply of servants, ever more elaborate internal decor, access to world-class private hospitals full of the latest computerized tomographic scanners and magnetic resonance imaging machines (Nittayaramphong and Tangcharoensathien 1994) that ensure the smooth participation of the wealthy in the global flow of material goods and lifestyle desires. For over a decade, from the mid-eighties to the late nineties, this material plenty seemed limitless, and a new bourgeoisie expressed its tastes and preferences in an orgy of consumerism which sustained, and was sustained by, the endless demolition and rebuilding of the city itself, new shopping malls, international hotels, luxury condominiums and apartment buildings. During this decade the unifying aspects of public culture began to fray: the rich moved further and further away from the city, into suburban enclaves from which they excluded others, a fundamental shift in the interaction between material, space, and the social which hitherto had seen rich and poor living side by side in the city, in the same areas.

Vertical

Bangkok, now, is a vertical city. In traditional cosmological thought the vertical is the axis of merit, with superior above and inferior below. New construction techniques have permitted this axis to be expressed without restraint in the city. In the 1960s it was a vast horizontal plane glittering between water and sky, its highest point Wat Saket (the Golden Mount), site of the early cremation grounds for the poor (Smithies 1986). The first high-rise buildings appeared in the mid-1970s, and by the late 1980s and early 1990s the city was in a frenzy of the vertical. The heady eclectic architecture of the boom years rose as a result of several distinctive factors. Architecture as a profession has been limited since 1965 almost exclusively to Thai citizens. For complex reasons to do with landownership and entitlements there were no effective city planning ordinances or controls on either land clearance or building construction. Hence in the 1980s there was nothing to restrain development other than the available funds and the imaginations of clients and local architects. The *nouveaux riches* wanted every possible style of distinction in their new suburbs: a Roman villa, Spanish hacienda, Georgian manor. In the city, buildings sprouted Ionic, Doric, and Mock Tudor styles, as well as "Hollywood Gothic" (Hopkins and Hoskins 1995: 28–9). Young architects with six months' experience designed skyscrapers. Developers were their own planners and architectural anarchy reigned. Up, up, and up were the orders of the client: Baiyoke Tower One, in 1992, 60 stories high, was, by 1998, eclipsed by its neighbor Baiyoke Tower Two, at 90 stories. The Thai Wah Tower matched it. The sense of delirium experienced in this new built environment is hard to explain: the sky mirroring off vast glass spaces, window-cleaners perched with buckets and rags hundreds of feet above the city, laboriously washing down thousands of square meters of glass which will at once be dirty again in the city's murky air; the lavishness, absurdity, stunning beauty of it; a city composed of feral skychasers. What could be left of "Thai culture" in this modernist/postmodernist pastiche? Well, said the architects, not much... but there was at least the roof! Hence many of the dramatic vertical constructions are topped by little gestures towards the traditional steeply angled Thai roofline, creating the oddest sense of dislocation high in the sky.

Now much of the new cityscape is crossed by overhead transport systems, involving thousands of tonnes of concrete, giant stanchions lodged into the ground as far as they will go, creating a second level of streetscape so that the "below" world becomes dark, shaded, like a streetscape from Ridley Scott's film *Bladerunner.* The nerve of it! Skyscrapers multiplying enormous weights in steel, glass, and concrete, resting on a soft, unstable, muddy base. Bangkokians are pleased to tell you that the whole city is sinking – by some centimeters each year – into this sludge. And then it rains. Generally lasting from July to October, the rain falls in daily downpours and the city begins to fill. Pumping stations try to empty it out but particularly when the tide rises it is hopeless, the city is flooded, pedestrians wade through thigh-deep water their belongings in plastic bags on their heads, and tiny canoes like those plying the waterways of the city one hundred years ago creep along between the skyscrapers. Above all, traffic stops.

Immobile

The volume and density of Bangok traffic has become legendary, a media spectacle for Western documentaries, an evidence of irrationality and perversity, a failure of the project of modernity. Building up in the seventies, expanding in the eighties, finally exploding in the nineties beyond any management strategy, the traffic jams multiply. Peak hours last from 5 a.m. to 11 a.m. and 3 p.m. to 9 p.m. The richer people became, the more cars they bought, and the further they moved from the city into gated security estates. But the prestigious schools, colleges and universities, the banks, shopping centers, entertainment venues, offices and ministries and businesses remain in the city. Wealthy families need not one, but two or even three, cars with drivers. Families rise at 5.00, at 4.30 a.m. Children eat their breakfasts in the back of the car, tended by a maid, en route to their expensive private schools. At the end of the day, the same car has to go to get them home again. The parents likewise go in different cars to different parts of the city, and the driver drops them off and picks them up again. The density of traffic means that the slightest hitch in one part of the city quickly results in gridlock in others. Some days people sit in their cars for three or four hours at a time. People joke: you can be conceived, born, and die in your car. Portable toilets are called for along the street. Emergency vehicles cannot attend emergencies. A heart-attack victim in the city center at 5 p.m. is sure to die. Above the city, a helicopter flies, sending reports to a city radio station whose sole rationale is the giving and receiving of traffic reports. Trapped in their cars, motorists call up on their mobile phones "Accident at Patumwan intersection," or report "Traffic backed up to Soi 21."

The Bangkok Metropolitan Administration (BMA), governments, politicians, all claim they will resolve the traffic problem. Transportation plans multiply but no level of government can implement them (Daniere 1995). There is plenty of public transport (buses, taxis) but it all needs to use the same roads. Motorcycle taxis cluster at the intersections of main roads, providing the fastest and most perilous way of getting around the city. The cacophony at street level is deafening.

At major intersections, at peak hours, stand the traffic police, in tight boots and uniform, with masks over their noses and mouths. The fumes engulf them, the carbon monoxide eats their brains, their lungs collapse. In 1997 a traffic policeman began to hallucinate – instead of cars and buses, bikes and tuk-tuks, he saw a vast parade of spirits led by the long-dead King Chulalongkorn himself, proceeding up the thoroughfare. The policeman began to dance, gesturing to the oncoming manifestation of the spirits of modernity, holding up the traffic as the vast throng of supernaturals approached and passed slowly by.

By contrast, and miraculously, it is possible to experience the city when it is completely stilled. Suddenly all movement ceases, the noise abates. Pedestrians are alone on the street. And then, from a distance, motorcycle outriders swoop, followed by Rolls Royces and other "official" vehicles, flags of the kingdom fluttering. The Royal Family, perhaps even the King himself, traverses the city. When the King travels, all else is stilled. His route is opened before him: all roads leading to it are closed. Nothing impedes the royal movement. Pedestrians stand by the side of the road. The do not cheer or wave: they stand, heads bowed, subjects.

Just over 100 years ago, when the King traveled through his city, all were required to stay indoors. Bands of the King's archers and stave-carriers cleared the streets for the royal progress. Any person caught out of doors, in those days, had to prostrate himself, face down. Inside the houses, shutters were drawn. No commoner could look at the face of the King, but, if he did – peering through a chink in the wall, for example, or a glance upwards from the dust or mud – the offender was beaten, blinded, perhaps killed. Today, ordinary people are permitted to enter the King's presence, on certain very rare occasions: and they are permitted to watch his passage, behind the dark tinted windows of the royal vehicles, and share the spaces of the city. But, and here is a genuine transformation, even the most lowly person can look on the royal visage when it appears on television.

Mobile

For all the problems of vehicular movement, the streets, laneways, and alleys of the city are the sites of a continuous mobile commerce. Even though the Bangkok Metropolitan Administration has repeatedly tried to clear the sidewalks of vendors, selling and buying from mobile stands which take over the edges of the streets cannot, it seems, be prevented. Women with mobile kitchens set up restaurants, with folding tables, battered metal stools, condiments, utensils, the last word in fast food, providing noodles, soups, stir-fries, and omelettes in moments; diners perch at the edge of the traffic, chat, eat, drink, meet friends: for breakfast, a midmorning snack, lunch, anytime – anytime being a good time to eat (Yasmeen 1996). The dried-squid vendor pushes his cart along, ringing a bell. The pulse and nut vendors, migratory Indians from the subcontinent, carry trays of their wares on their heads. The hard-boiled-egg vendor wanders along, bearing a whole brazier full of hot charcoal on one side and eggs, chili, and sauces on the other. Glass-fronted cabinets on wheels contain fresh fruits on ice. As the day passes, crowds pulse in and out of the office buildings, the giant department stores and malls, wherever the business of the city takes place, and the swell of people eddies, pauses, stops, buys, eats. Further out along the residential streets, vendors push their carts and call out their wares: housewives and maids appear at their gates, haggle, purchase, take away the evening meal already cooked, in plastic bags. Others sell cane furniture, tables, chairs, cushions, pottery, plates, and glassware from their carts; others again come to buy: secondhand goods, empty cardboard boxes, wastepaper. Everything that can be bought and sold from a single person's pushcart will, sooner or later, appear at the gate.

Mall-time

There is also shopping to be done in the new spaces opened up by the consumptionist frenzy of boom-time. Since the mid-1980s, shopping centers and shopping malls have risen as among the most important signifying spaces of the city, paralleling the *wats* (Buddhist temples) as places around which life is oriented. Some are situated in glitzy mirrored spaces, multistoried, linked by escalators and atriums with displays, fountains, exhibitions. Department stores are often Asia-wide chains such as Robinson's, others are identified with Sino-Thai business families which began in an earlier phase of capitalist development, most famously the rice-milling dynasty now proprietors of the Central Department Store chain (cf. Pasuk and Baker 1996). In the Bangkok malls, the anchorstore is often Japanese: Sri Tokyu at Mah Boon Krong, Isetan at World Trade, Sogo at Sogo Centre. Malls are ranked in status, from the more "popular" to the most exclusive. There is a logic of display, of ambulation and bodily experience. In the majority of malls, small-scale independent vendors are located at the basement level; international fast-food outlets such as McDonald's, Kentucky Fried Chicken and Pizza Hut occupy higher levels, upmarket designer stores sell jewelry, CDs and videos, mobile phones and computers nearby. Homeware stores sell the latest in gadgets and furniture, and at or near the top, upmarket exclusive restaurants and bars, and perhaps a food court for the mass consumers, lead into the movie theaters and entertainment centers. These are perambulatory spaces cleared of vehicular traffic, where the movement of the body proceeds without the fear of machine-movement, a flâneurial space, air conditioned, a wandering environment and a space for looking, seeing, being seen, breathing, wanting. Outside, it might be storming, raining, fetid, desiccating: inside, it is comfortable, graspable, lookable – Benjamin's Arcades, revivified in today's Southeast Asia.

Big Market

The gobal capitalist market is knitted into the fabric of everyday life, although largely invisible. Global fluxes and flows, mostly symbols on computer screens, have somehow produced all this wealth and luxury in a small Southeast Asian nation. There are places in the city where the operation of this market is embodied: in Silom and Sathorn, where the minions of transnational capital wear their uniform of suits, and where the Western foreigner, the Chinese, Indian, African, and Thai wear Gucci and Armani, and drive BMWs and Mercedes. The head offices of the great banks, insurance, and finance companies are located along the streets of this area. But this is not a unified space, nothing like a Central Business District: in an adjacent street is a Hindu temple, a crowd of sidewalk vendors, and here, at a sudden intersection, the two notorious alleys which make up the places where that other district of desire is found: Patpong. Here is the primary space of the body-trade, flesh-trade which emerges after dark in a pulsation of disco, neon, bodies, sites of bizarre action – where play-and-pay is the rule, a dense network of bars and brothels with names harking back to imagined masculinist realms, some feudal, some merely inane: King's Castle, Pussy Galore, Vikings, Playskool, Long Gun.

Metastases

North, east, and south, networks of transportation spread out from the city. Countryside, rice fields, orchards, almost overnight become urban space. Cement, textiles, processed food, wood, and cork: name-brand international products, sports-shoes, clothing are churned out in makeshift factories along the new highways. The labour is provided by the streams of country girls and boys, most poorly educated and skilled only in farming. They arrive alone in the city, or have been hired by contractors, and are housed and fed on site. Many are paid below minimum wages, or not at all. Many are grateful anyway, for two meals a day and a place to shelter. Others, many of them young girls, feed the construction boom, carrying concrete and bricks up and down the high-rise buildings, earning $US2 a day, 12-hour days, seven days a week (Seabrook 1996).

Thousands of small communities, extended kinship networks of farmers, settlers, and traders, are obliterated. The city grows, expands, eats them all up. Where will they go? It doesn't matter. They stand in the way of the modern, they inhibit the development of housing estates, golf courses, factories, wholesale markets: they are human barriers to the logic of a globalized economy. They are sucked into the vortex, spat out, and they remove themselves, to sink or swim. There are no bodies to appeal to, or organs of the state to defend some idea of a right to a continued collective existence.

Resistance

Yet sometimes there is resistance. In old slum communities, such as those at Klong Toey near the port, residents of several generations' standing have refused to move. In spite of the poor conditions, crowding, damp, rats, people still want to stay in their place. Some who moved on later moved back again. Others resist removal in the name of history, culture, and religion. The old Muslim village of Baan Krua is probably the most famous. Right in the center of the city, surrounded by high-rise hotels and apartment blocks, it is a little oasis along a polluted canal, its mosque brightly painted and surrounded by waving palms. It stands in the way of one section of the new expressway, and in spite of the most vigorous efforts to force its removal and the relocation of its people, it has somehow managed to survive, notably with the support of academics, environmentalists, and historians. For how long? With the economic shock of the late 1990s maybe longer than anyone might have imagined.

IMF Terror

Thailand was declared an NIC (Newly Industrialized Country) by its own Prime Minister in the early 1990s. The heady mix of capital and consumption, rendered visible in every part of the city, seemed to have no end. It seemed that Bangkok, for all its woes, would grow and expand for ever, that new technological solutions, maybe even a subway, or magnetic railroads, or gigantic hoses pumping in fresh air – anything is possible – would rescue the city from its horrific aspects and reveal it as wondrous and magical at last. But the Asian Crisis of late 1997 called a dreadful halt to such imaginings. The wash of funds began to dry up; the irrationalities of the financial, business, and bureaucratic system were targeted for reform by what seemed to be, once again, a ruthless colonizing West. The outcome of the crisis became apparent at once on the face of the city. The overhead cranes dispersed, leaving buildings half-built, unfinished, unoccupied. The overhead train project paused, slowed, leaving whole sections built but joining to nothing. Thousands of illegal immigrants were deported; thousands more country people left the city, and returned home to swell the numbers of impoverished and near-subsistence rural folk. Banks folded; the middle classes could no longer be certain of employment; students studying abroad had to return home; sales of Mercedes automobiles dwindled. Bangkok, City of Angels, pauses, but its frantic pace is not visibly affected, swollen now with European tourists seeking the bargains to be wrested from a stumble in the rush to global integration. Bangkok could stand as a catastrophic example of modernity run mad; or it could yet unfold into one of the most astonishing cities anywhere in the world.

REFERENCES

Askew, Marc R. 1994: *Interpreting Bangkok: The Urban Question in Thai Studies*. Bangkok: Chulalongkorn University Press.

Daniere, A. G. 1995: Transportation planning and implementation in cities of the Third World: the case of Bangkok. *Environment and Planning C: Government and Policy*, 13 (1), 25–45.

Edwards, J. N. et al. 1994: Why people feel crowded: an examination of objective and subjective crowding. *Population and Environment*, 16 (2), 149–73.

Fuller, T. D., Edwards, J. N., Vorakitphokatorn, S., and Sermsri, S. 1996: Chronic stress and psychological well-being: evidence from Thailand on household crowding. *Social Science and Medicine*, 42 (2), 265–80.

Gerson, Ruth 1996: *Traditional Rituals in Thailand*. Kuala Lumpur and New York: Oxford University Press.

Habermas, Jurgen 1984: *The Theory of Communicative Action*, vol. 1: *Rationalization of Society*. Boston, MA: Beacon Press.

Hopkins, Allen W. and Hoskin, John 1995: *Bangkok by Design*. Bangkok: Post Books.

Krikkiat, Phipatseritham and Yoshihara, Kunio 1983: Business groups in Thailand. Institute of Southeast Asian Studies. Discussion Paper No. 41. Singapore.

Mills, Mary B. 1997: Contesting the margins of modernity: women, migration and consumption in Thailand. *American Ethnologist*, 24 (1), 37–61.

Nittayaramphong, S. and Tangcharoensathien, V. 1994: Thailand: private health care out of control. *Health Policy and Planning*, 9 (1), 31–40.

O'Connor, Richard A. 1990: Place, power and discourse in the Thai image of Bangkok. *Journal of the Siam Society*, 78 (2), 61–73.

Pasuk, Phongpaichit and Baker, Chris 1996: *Thailand's Boom!* St Leonards, NSW: Allen and Unwin.

Richter, K. 1996: Living separately as a child-care strategy: implications for women's work and family in urban Thailand. *Journal of Marriage and the Family*, 58 (2), 327–39.

Richter, K., Podhisita, C., Chamratrithirong, A., and Soonthorndhada, K. 1994: The impact of child-care on fertility in urban Thailand. *Demography*, 31 (4), 651–62.

Seabrook, Jeremy 1996: *In the Cities of the South*. London and New York: Verso.

Smithies, Michael 1986: *Old Bangkok*. Oxford University Press: Singapore.
Sungsidh, Piriyarangsan and Pasuk, Phongpaichit 1993: *The Middle Class and Thai Democracy*. Bangkok: Chulalongkorn University and Friedrich Ebert Stiftung.
Wilson, Constance O. 1989: Bangkok in 1883: an economic and social profile. *Journal of the Siam Society*, 77, (2) 49–58.
Yap, K. S. 1996: Low-income housing in a rapidly expanding urban economy: Bangkok 1985–1994. *Third World Planning Review*, 18 (3), 307–23.
Yasmeen, G. 1996: Plastic-bag housewives and postmodern restaurants: public and private in Bangkok's foodscape. *Urban Geography*, 17 (6), 526–44.

Chapter 40

Street Boys in Yogyakarta: Social and Spatial Exclusion in the Public Spaces of the City

Harriot Beazley

Control by dominating agents may be seen as complete, but there is always the possibility of subversion. We cannot understand the role of space in the reproduction of social relations without recognizing that the relatively powerless still have enough power to carve out spaces of control in respect of their day-to-day lives.

Sibley 1995: 76.

A familiar sight in Indonesia's cities is the number of children living and working on the streets and in other public places. The majority of children who are visible working on the streets are boys, between the ages of 7 and 17. There are also street girls, although they are not as visible or prolific as the boys.[1] This chapter examines the behavior patterns of homeless street boys in the city of Yogyakarta, Central Java.[2] By using the boys' survival strategies as an investigative device, it examines the ways in which their lives, experiences, earning opportunities, and identities are socially and spatially structured. The chapter begins by discussing who street children are in Indonesia, and the context in which they appear. It then describes the injustices which the children face from state and society, as well as the more physically coercive methods of domination which affect their daily lives.

The chapter then explores how, despite their subordination, street boys have developed a "repertoire of strategies" in order to survive (Clarke et al. 1976: 42–5). These strategies include the appropriation of public spaces which have contributed to the formation of a "cultural space": the *tekyan* subculture of Yogyakarta (Clarke et al. 1976). Such securing of space by subordinate groups has been described as the "carving out" or "chiseling away" of spaces of control from the margins of power (Sibley 1995; Clarke 1976; Scott 1990; White 1990; Yeoh and Huang 1996).

To understand the various settings of the *tekyan* subculture, I draw on selected spatial stories, or "mental maps," which were collected as a participatory research exercise in Yogyakarta (Gould and White 1974; Matthews 1980, 1986, 1992).[3]

These maps illustrate how the children's social marginality is reflected in the places they occupy and documents the images street boys have of the city, in the context of work and leisure. By exploring street children's production and use of space as "geographies of resistance" (Pile and Keith 1997), the chapter identifies some of the places the *tekyan* subculture have "won" for their own survival (Clarke et al. 1976: 45).

Victims of "Progress": Reasons for Street Children

The lives of street children cannot be fully explained without first understanding the context in which they appear. In Indonesia the presence of street children can partly be understood as a result of the country's economic growth strategy during President Soeharto's "development" ("*pembangunan*") and "progress" ("*kemajuan*") era (1966–98).[4] This strategy was aimed at integrating Indonesia into the global economy. It was based on a development ideology of industrialization, economic liberalism, foreign investment, low wages for "comparative advantage" over other countries, and the appropriation of public space by both global and local capital as commercial or leisure space. Such an approach caused Indonesia to experience radical social change, a widening gap between rich and poor, rapid urbanization, and the marginalization of millions excluded from the development process.

It was in this climate that many children drifted on to the streets in order to find alternative channels of income. Financial hardship, however, is not the only reason children start living on the streets. Quite often violence and physical abuse at home force a child to flee permanently, and some of the reasons given by children for leaving home included: being unloved and beaten; alcoholic fathers; pressure to do well at school; absent or separated parents; hostile stepparents; the influence of friends, and the attraction of street children's subcultures.

Survival activities

Once on the street, boys earn their money in various ways in different parts of the city, and all the children have different spaces in which they earn their living and establish friendships. Younger children usually shine shoes along the main street, Malioboro, scavenge for goods to recycle at the railroad station, or beg at traffic lights. Older boys busk with guitars on Malioboro, at bus stops and on bus routes across the city, and at various traffic-light intersections. They also make and sell handicrafts and "park" cars outside a nightclub on Malioboro. In Yogyakarta the different groups of homeless street boys name themselves collectively after the places where they work, sleep, and hang out in the city. They include: *anak Malioboro* (the Malioboro kids), after the main street; *anak Alun-Alun*, (the City Square boys); *anak stasiun* (the railroad station kids), *anak terminal* (the bus station kids); *anak shoping* (the Market kids); and *anak Surgawong* (the Surgawong kids), the children who live under a bridge in the north of the city (Figures 40.1, 40.2 and 40.3). These groups have constructed the symbolic walls of "home" which are invisible at first, but which can be understood as "symbolic cocoons in public space" (Arantes 1996: 86).

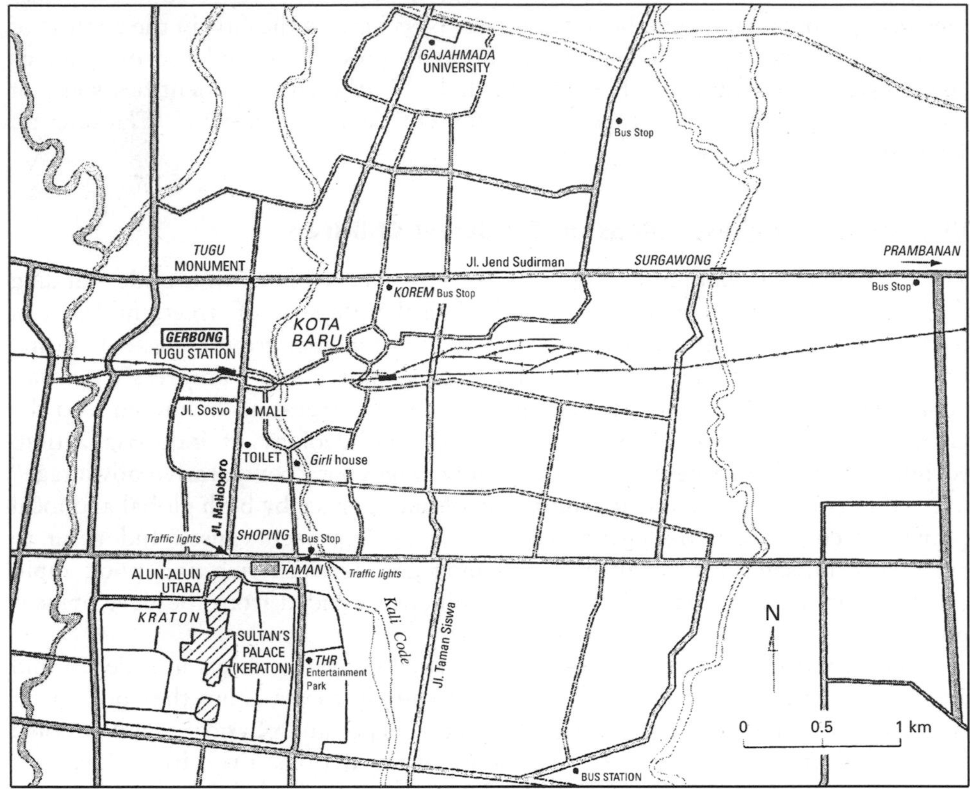

Figure 40.1 Yogykarta, central Java: population 472,000. Malioboro Street runs through the center of the city, from the railroad station towards the *Alun-Alun* (City Square) and *Keraton* (Sultan's Palace)

Social and Spatial Exclusion for Children "Out of Place"

> The social and the spatial are so thoroughly imbued with each other's presence . . . a sustained investigation of the "out of place" metaphor points to the fact that social power and social resistance are always already spatial. When an expression such as "out of place" is used it is impossible to clearly demarcate whether social or geographical place is denoted, place always means both.
>
> Cresswell 1996: 11

Street children in Indonesia are socially and spatially oppressed and the spaces they occupy are severely restricted by multiple forms of control. This is because street children are perceived as "out of place," even though it is often the processes of mainstream society that cause them to appropriate public spaces in the first place. Massey (1994: 269), conceives of space as being created out of social relations and as "social relations stretched out"; a complex web of relations of domination, subordination, solidarity and cooperation. In addition, "multiple identities . . . and margins . . . are all responses to the political inviability of absolute location"

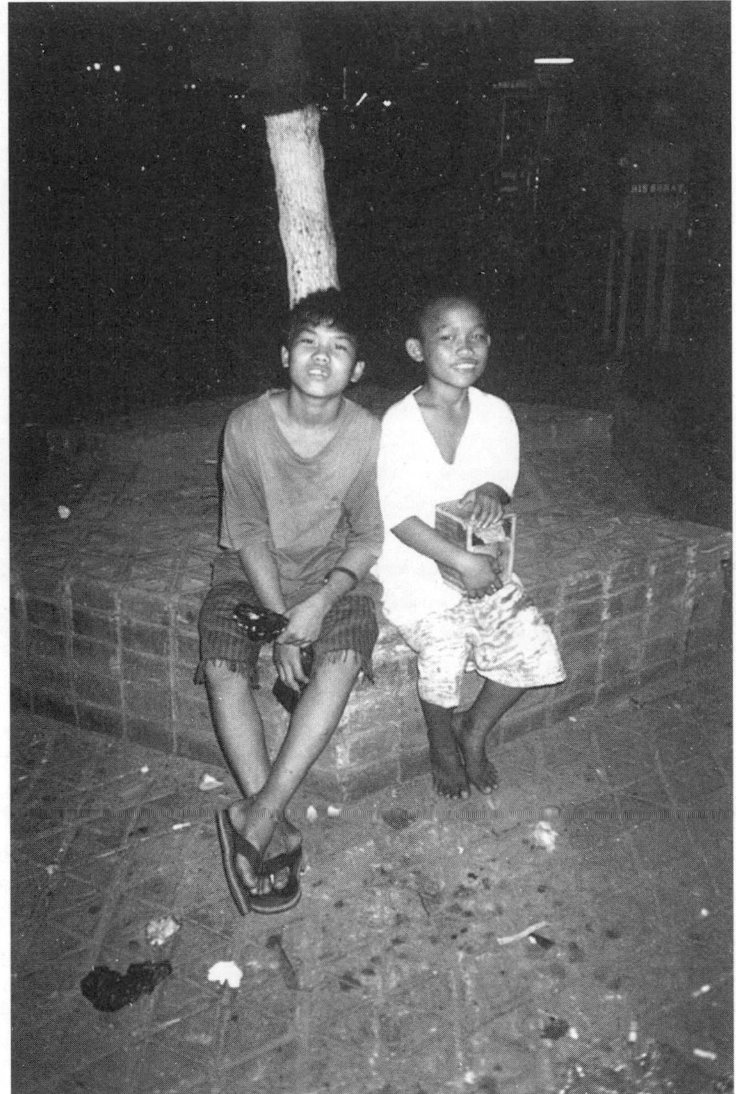

Figure 40.2 Shoe-shiners on Malioboro (© Harriot Beazley)

(Smith and Katz 1993). This describes well how the cultural spaces of street boys in Yogyakarta are created by their relations with authority (police, security guards, and army), and other groups on the street.

Social apartheid

In Indonesia social control and efforts to intervene in civil society can be detected in the operation of surveillance systems, such as the obligation to have an identity card (KTP). A KTP requires a birth certificate, a family register card and a family address which most homeless children do not have. Although children under the age of 17 do

Figure 40.3 City-square kids (© Harriot Beazley)

not need an identity card, they are supposed to be under the jurisdiction of their parents. When children have no parents or family registration card, they are outside the state-controlled system, and officially do not exist. There is no way for a child to get a KTP if they have no contact with their family. They are thus nonpeople for ever. As a result they cannot enjoy the benefits of state acceptance such as the right to an identity, an education, a home, healthcare, or any other basic rights specified by the United Nations Convention on the Rights of the Child (1989), and ratified by Indonesia in 1990 (Ertanto 1994).

In addition to this exclusion by the state, street children are also marginalized by the negative perceptions held by mainstream society, who view homeless street children as social pariahs infesting the city streets. This is because they are seen to be abandoned by their families, and to have lost their kinship ties which are the basis for locating people within Javanese society (Ertanto 1993). Further to this, public spaces such as shopping centers have been constructed as commercial spaces, where the new middle class does not wish to be confronted by poverty and dirty homeless children. Their presence is also perceived as a threat to national development, as it contradicts the desired image of a developing, modern nation, which the government and big businessmen wish to portray to potential foreign investors. Through a discourse of deviance street boys are consequently presented by the state and the media as a defilement of public space, an underclass which needs to be eradicated, and as "criminal." The construction of this criminal image is exemplified by the use of labels in the press such as *preman* (hoodlum), and GALI (*Gabungan Anak Liar*, "Gangs of Wild Children").

Spatial apartheid and social cleansing

Boys working on the streets are thus considered to be "out of place," and public spaces are controlled in a way that has been described by White (1996: 39) as "spatial apartheid based upon socioeconomic status." In Indonesia street boys are frequently evicted from public places and face the daily threat of violence and abuse by agencies of the state during their national "cleansing operations." These operations are used as a means to "discipline and educate" street social life, and to "eradicate street hooliganism and restore the public's sense of security" in major cities.[5] The children have their own word for these street raids: *garukan*. Police are responsible for confiscating and destroying street children's means of livelihood (musical instruments and goods to sell), for verbal abuse, severe beatings, torture in custody, and other mistreatment which street children repeatedly receive. "Cleansing" campaigns are often focused on bus terminals, shopping centers and other public areas, and as these are commonly occupied by street boys, they are often caught in the nets of the "sweep" operations. One reason for this is that everyone in Indonesia is supposed to carry their KTP at all times and face the possibility of on-the-spot checks. A child without any form of identification can be arrested.

Detentions by police after "cleansing operations" have sometimes resulted in death, and cases have been documented where "suspected criminals" have been shot attempting to flee from police, due to a *bahaya sikat* (shoot to kill) policy (Amnesty International 1994a).[6] In 1995 it was reported that the police shot and killed hundreds of *suspected* criminals in major cities, including Yogyakarta, during anticrime campaigns, and street children have been shot in such crusades (Amnesty International 1994b, Kusama 1995: 94).[7] Amnesty further reports that "those at greatest risk are individuals from marginalized groups, and those who . . . cannot get access to legal counsel" (Amnesty International 1996). Such groups include street children.

Tekyan: Subculture of Resistance

Street children are therefore both spatially and socially oppressed, and portrayed as a "problem" which needs to be solved. Public space, however, is an essential means of survival for street boys, as it is where they can access resources to alleviate their needs. In an attempt to find solidarity in the face of this persecution, homeless street boys in Yogyakarta have created their own distinctive social world: *tekyan*, a subculture with its own system of values, beliefs, hierarchies, and language. Meaning "just a little but enough," *tekyan* is a name used with pride in the boys' private language, and is a form of resistance to the names with negative connotations, such as *gelandangan* (vagrant), or *gembel* (poor, shabby and squalid), which are given to them by society (Berman and Beazley 1997).[8] The creation and maintenance of this street boy subculture can be seen not as a *problem*, but as a *solution* to the variety of problems children face in a world which is hostile to their very existence. Following Hebdige (1979: 81), "Each subcultural 'instance' represents a 'solution' to particular problems and contradictions." Through belonging to the *tekyan* street children are able to create positive self-identities for themselves and to escape feelings of shame. It is a way of "resisting and challenging the fraudulent claims of dominant groups" (Bondi 1993: 87).

Mental Maps

> The search for emancipation from social control instills the desire, the longing and in some cases even the practices of searching for a space "outside" of hegemonic social relations and valuations. Spaces "on the margin" become valued spaces, for those who seek to establish differences.
>
> Harvey 1996: 230

"Mental maps" drawn by the children were assembled to understand the street boys' production and use of space in the city, and their geographical responses to their marginalization (Gould and White 1974; Matthews 1980, 1986, 1992). Cognitive maps mark off space and indicate how the public space is managed, used, and experienced by different children in the same group. I asked the children to draw a map or picture of the parts of the city where they spent most of their time, the places which were important to them and which they knew best.

The mental images that the street boys built up of Yogyakarta reflected not only their surroundings but many aspects of their lives, with the patterns of information they used to define their environment varying with their age and length of time in the city. In parallel with Gould and White's (1974) study in Sweden, and Matthews' (1986) study in Britain, the geographical knowledge of the street boys in Yogyakarta appeared to grow outwards from the well-known places as the children got older, and a more complete mental image of the environment developed over time (Matthews 1986: 125; 1980: 172). For example, the majority of the younger Malioboro boys' maps suggested that they felt at home in restricted areas, as all the details were in the immediate vicinity of the toilet area, which is a meeting and hanging out place, and the center of gravity for many street boys (Figure 40.4). The younger boys' pictures also paid more attention to detail than the older boys' maps, and they personalized their accounts by drawing friends and particular features which they saw as significant, but which older boys did not include (Figure 40.5). This accords with Matthews' research which revealed the young child's concern with the minute and the incidental as compared to the adult world's perceptions (Matthews 1980: 172; 1992: 136).

As their experiences extended from the central area, the older boys indicated a much broader mental territory, and incorporated the bus stops and bus routes where they busked during the daytime, and also places where they went to hang out and to look for entertainment. Twelve-year-old Agus's map was particularly fascinating in its conception of space in the city as it was all related to the various bus routes he traveled along when he was busking (Figure 40.6).

As well as Malioboro Street, the older boys included places where they hung out, such as the toilet; *Rumah Girli* or *Cokro* (the NGO *Girli's* open house for street boys); the *THR* (the public entertainment park where live *Dangdut* music is played); the *Taman* (the city park where street girls, gay men, and transvestites hang out); and *gerbong* (the area where prostitutes and transvestites operate at night) (Figures 40.7 and 40.8). Sexual activity is an intrinsic part of street life, and street children have shifting sexual identities (Knopp 1995). This is because sex fulfills multiple needs for the children (including survival sex, comfort sex, and sex for protection), with multiple partners (transvestites, peers, street girls, adult men, tourists, and prostitutes), in different places in the city.

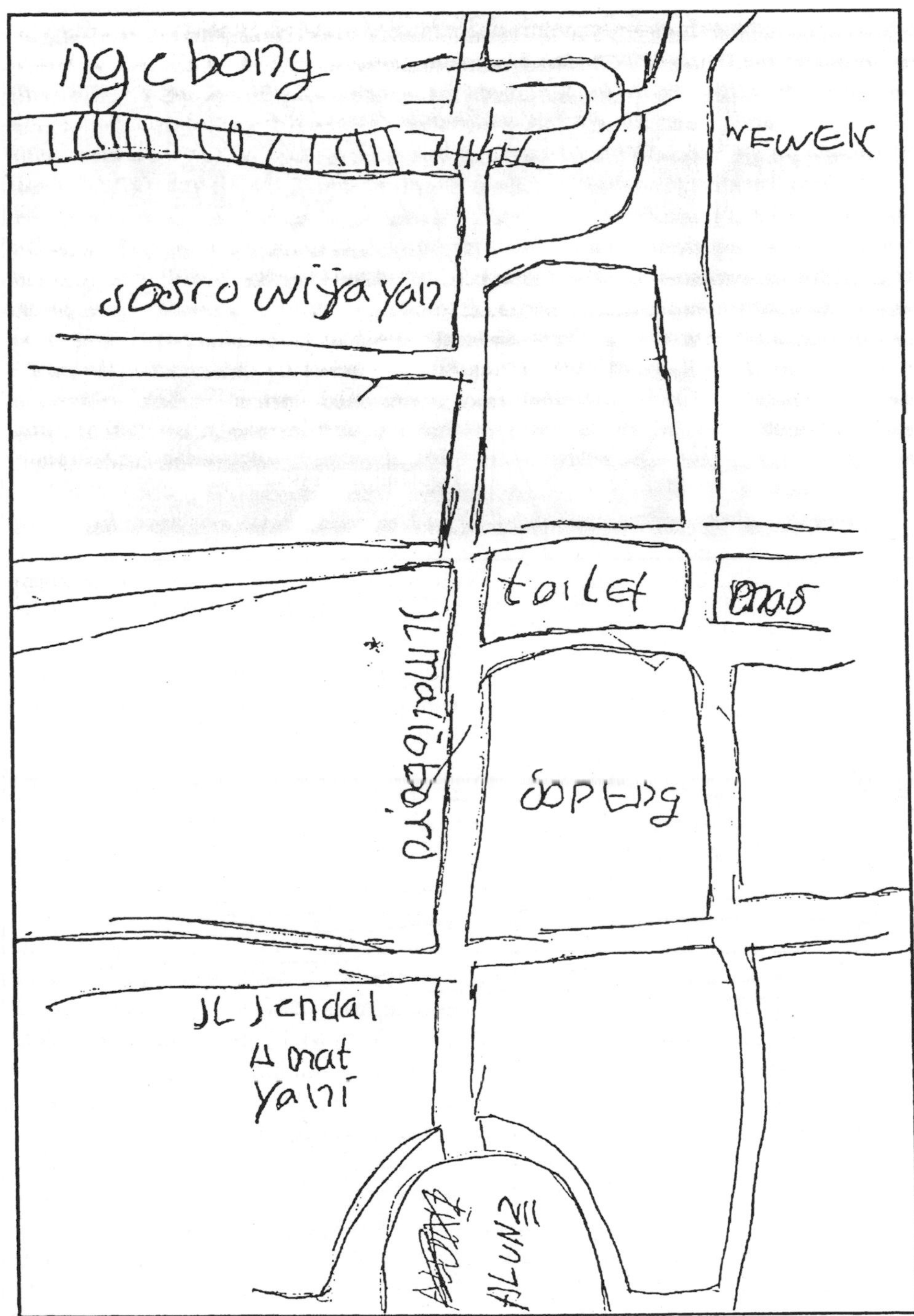

Figure 40.4 Bambang's (aged 11) map of Yogyakarta: Focus is on the Malioboro and toilet area, as well as *ngebong* (*Gerbong*), by the train tracks; Sosrowijayan street (where tourists and backpackers stay); *Sopeng* (the local market); and the *Alun-Alun* (City Square)

Figure 40.5 Sorio's (aged 10) map of Yogyakarta. Sorio has drawn the toilet area (top left of the map), the railroad station and railroad tracks. Malioboro Street runs through the center of the map. Sorio personalizes his account by drawing a train on to his map, as well as food stalls, a horse-drawn cart, and children playing under the tree outside the toilet on Malioboro (note that one of the children is carrying a tambourine for busking)

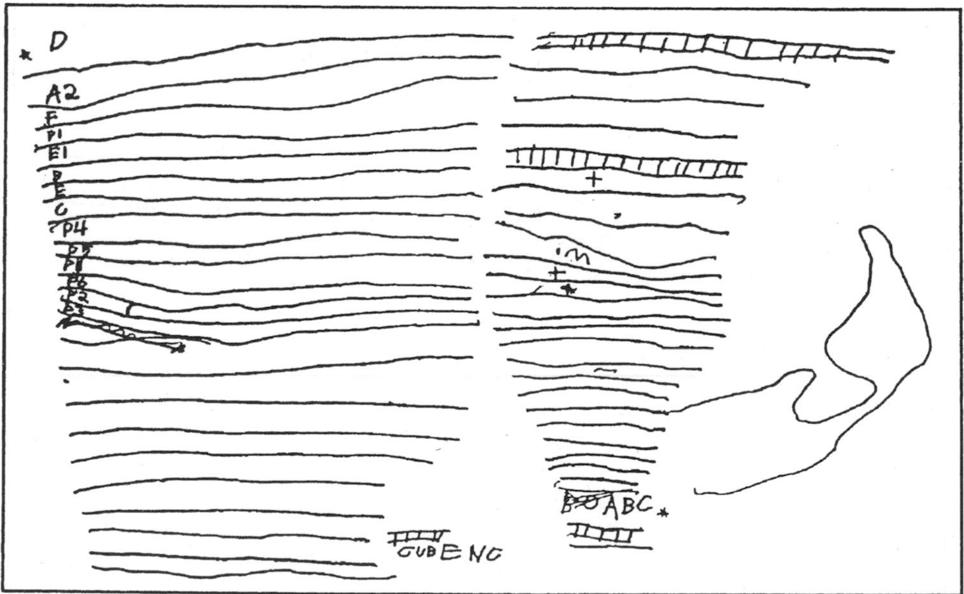

Figure 40.6 Agus's (aged 12) map of Yogyakarta. The letters and numbers relate to the numbered bays at the bus terminal, and the lines are the bus routes which branch out from the terminal and run through the city

Places as Pivotal Points

The maps show that the marginality of the places occupied by the children in Yogyakarta reflected their social marginality. The children appropriated these spaces for their own use, and the territories became their urban survival niches, where they could earn money, obtain food, and find enjoyment. People marginalized and stigmatized by rigid laws and attitudes claim and share spaces in the city which are available, even if it is a temporary use of space like the street (Murray 1993). These places are important for marginalized people to form a collective identity in opposition to oppression. The street can therefore be understood in terms of "specific territories which can be mapped according to specific activities carried out by specific groups" of street children (White 1996: 142).

In their maps the children developed a system of meaningful places which gave form and structure to their experiences in the world (Relph 1976: 1). There were two sites in particular which were meaningful for many street boys, and which all the children marked on their maps: the *stasiun* (the railroad station), and the toilet on Malioboro. These were pivotal points for the *tekyan* subculture, and were places which were essential for the children's survival and emotional well-being. They were what Matthews refers to as "mean centers of gravity" (1980: 174) or "beacons" (Matthews 1992).

Malioboro

Jalan Malioboro, or Malioboro Street, is the geographical and economic center of Yogyakarta. It is the main tourist and shopping avenue, and is all the more strategic due to Sosrowijayan Street, where many of the European tourists and backpackers stay. With its craft markets, food stalls, brand new shopping mall and shops, it is seen to play an important role in Indonesia's tourism business, for both foreign and domestic tourists. It is where diverse elements of the city are brought together in close, regular contact, and as indicated in the children's maps, it is at the center of many of the children's lives. The craft stalls are open all day until 9 p.m., and then the *lesehan* (food stalls) come out for the rest of the night. This is when the children work, until the early hours. Malioboro is a mass of "interconnected territories" of shoe-shiners, buskers, pickpockets, and vendors (Arantes 1996: 86). Along the mile-long stretch of road the younger boys shine shoes and older boys busk at the numerous *lesehan*, while people sit on rattan mats eating, chatting, and listening to the street musicians.

Toilet

The toilet is situated at the center of Malioboro, next to the tourist office, and forms a very definite image in the minds of all the children. It is a meeting place for Malioboro boys, a place to go to when not working, where the boys can relax, sleep, gamble, or hang out with friends. It represents a "cultural space" which has been "won" by the *tekyan* subculture for leisure and recreation (Hall and Jefferson 1993: 42). It is also a place where the boys hide their possessions, such as their shoeshine kits, guitars, and clothes. Outside the toilet there is a rattan mat which the boys put out to sit on. The mat serves to "mark" the place as a sign that it is an "owned" space.

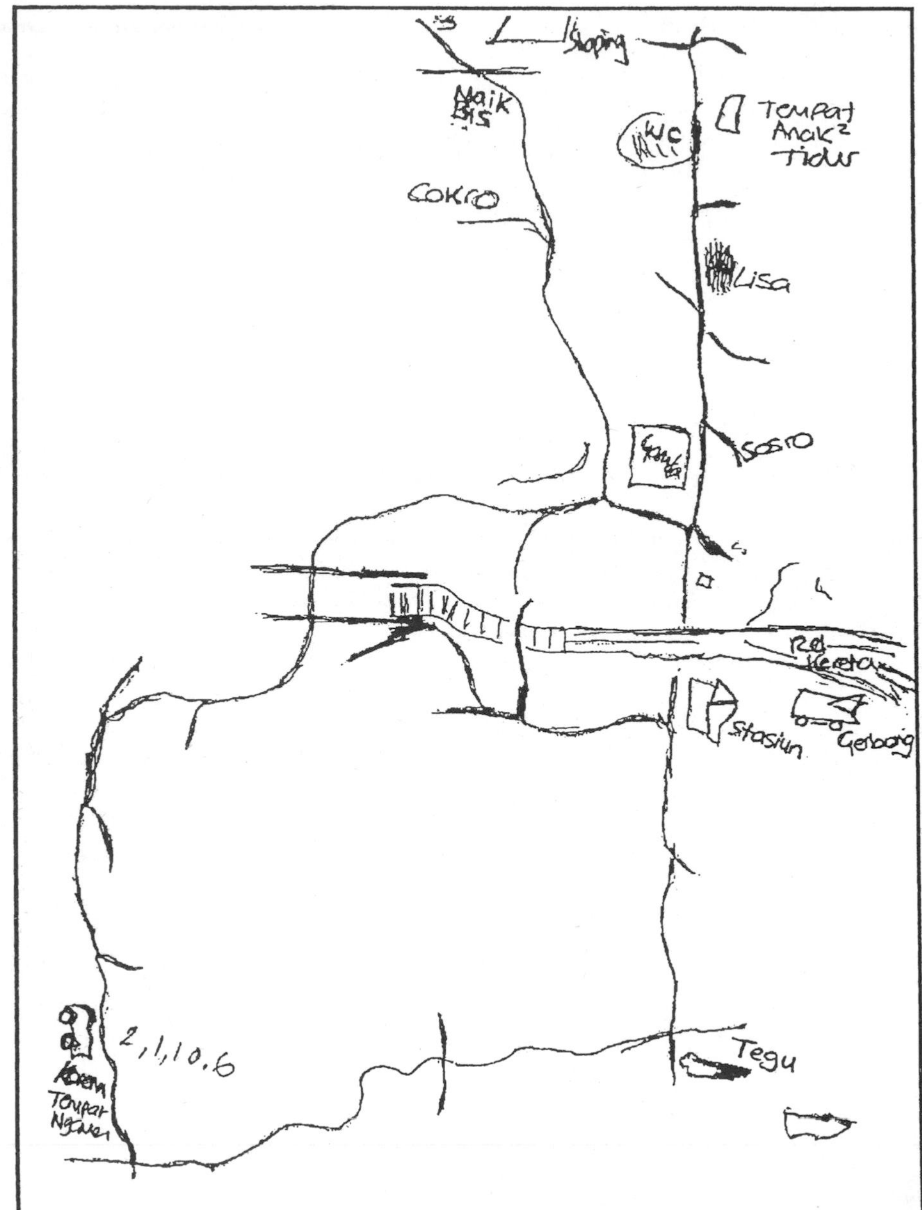

Figure 40.7 Hari's (aged 15) map of Yogyakarta. As well as *Shoping* (the local market) and the WC (toilet) on Malioboro, the map shows the bus stops and bus routes on which Hari worked: Korem/*Tempat Ngamen* (Korem/busking place, the numbers relate to the bus/route numbers); and Naik Bis. He also marks *Cokro* (the NGO *Girli's* open house); Lisa (a favourite food stall) and the *Tempat anak tidur* ("the place where the children sleep") on Malioboro; Sosro (the tourist street); the *stasiun* (railroad station) and *Gerbong* (depicted by a *gerbong*/ railroad car), and *Rel Kereta* (train tracks). (Note: the writing on the map is my own as Hari cannot read or write, and he asked me to mark the map as he instructed.)

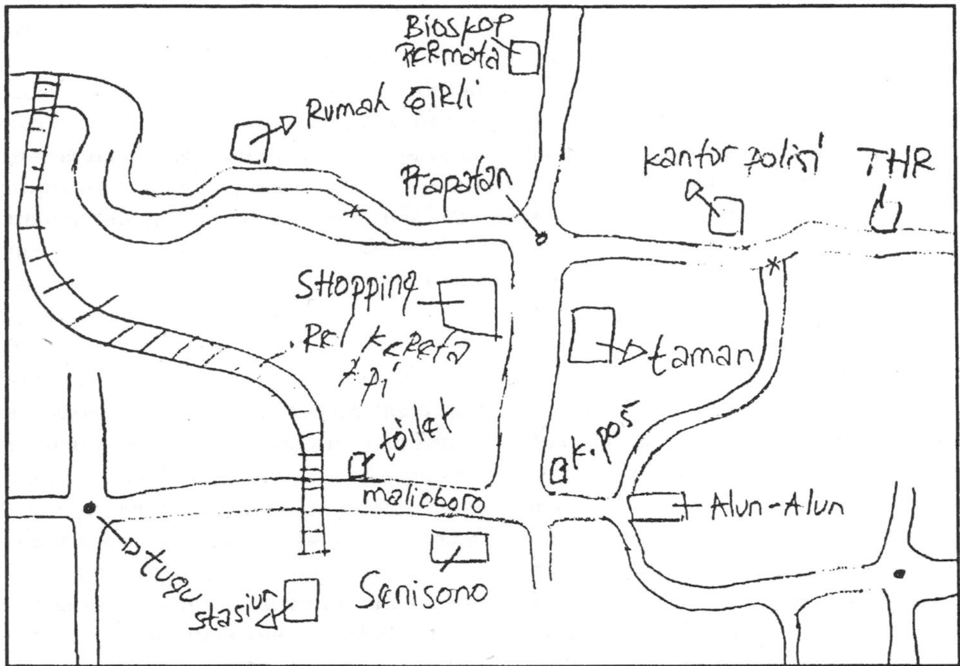

Figure 40.8 Edo's (aged 16) map of Yogyakarta. Edo has marked the Toilet on Malioboro, *Rumah Girli* (NGO open house); the *Alun-Alun* (City Square); *Shoping* (local market); *kantor polisi* (police station); Bioskop Permata (a cinema); two *prapatans* (traffic light intersections); the *Taman* (City Park); the THR (the People's Entertainment Park); and the *stasiun* (railroad station). Note the prominence of the *Rel Kereta Api*, "the railroad tracks" running through the city.

The toilet is a very masculine space, and a sense of belonging or not belonging contributes in an important way to the shaping of social space at the toilet. The boundaries around the toilet are policed by the older boys who are more dominant in the peer group. This power is superseded, however, by a more powerful force which occasionally visits the toilet area and is described by the boys as *penyakit* (the disease). This is the police or army who periodically arrive at the toilet to "clean up" the area, often kicking or beating the children who cannot get away. In a similar way to the "vigilante" off-duty police in Brazil, Colombia, and Guatemala, security forces sometimes take it upon themselves to "clean" the streets of these unsightly children after hours.[9]

The children at the toilet are not, therefore, safe from oppression and brutality. Many children told me, however, that they regarded it as a safe place, mainly because of their feelings of safety in numbers. The toilet is a meeting place for the *tekyan*, "a site of cultural resistance" and a "liberated zone," where street boys can feel a sense of safety, and relax. (Myslik 1996: 168). The safety they feel is an "emotional and psychological safety that comes from being in an area which has some sense of belonging or social control, even in the occasional absence of physical control" (Myslik 1996: 168).

Stasiun

The station and the railroad tracks running through the city featured in all of the children's maps. This was because high mobility is a particularly noticeable behavioral aspect of the *tekyan* subculture. They move across the country with considerable ease via Java's extensive rail system, riding on railroad cars which depart regularly from the station. The boys' high mobility and use of the railroads can be viewed as a form of geographical resistance, as they are a way of avoiding state authorities' control, enabling street boys to "jump scales" to other cities, away from oppression in one city to possible freedom in another (Smith 1994: 90).[10] The boys take up and leave a city if they are in trouble with the authorities, if the earning opportunities are bad, if there is a "clean-up operation" on the streets, if they have fallen out with someone, or if they just want to find adventure or follow friends. As a result, the railroad station is often a meeting point for street boys. It is a place for earning money, searching for leftover food, meeting other street kids, for spreading the *tekyan* subculture, and where newcomers are socialized to street life.

Conclusion

Street children in Indonesia face daily oppression through marginalization and violence from both state and society, which seeks to control unwanted groups through spatial ordering and public discourses. The exclusion of street boys from public spaces is often in the form of verbal abuse, evictions, arrests, beatings and torture while in police custody, and other excessive infringements of the children's basic human rights. It is such treatment which has contributed to their alienation, and led to the strengthening of a street boy subculture, the *tekyan*, as a group response of resistance, solidarity, and as a means of survival.

The *tekyan* of Yogyakarta contest their own exclusion by appropriating specific places in the city, and by constructing a network of entwined spaces for their everyday survival. This chapter has shown how these produced spaces reflect the street boys' social marginality, and describes these spaces as "urban niches" in which they can earn money, obtain food, feel safe, and find enjoyment, despite the hostility of outside forces. The boys in Yogyakarta marked these places on their maps: traffic lights, bus stops, the sides of roads and railroad tracks, outside a public toilet or an entertainment area, a city park, and other public spaces where access was not heavily controlled. The maps show that the children are not tied to any one place, and that they have numerous "symbolic cocoons," which they use in order to survive (Arantes 1996: 86). It is the "fluidity" of these spaces, and the flexibility of the children to shift from one place to another at a moment's notice, which ensures their survival (Massey 1994; Pile 1997). If, for example, one place becomes difficult to operate in, due to the threat of a *garukan*, then a child will quickly escape to another urban niche (a bus stop, traffic light, or even another city), in order to earn money.

In addition to "winning space" for their survival and existence, some of these appropriated spaces, such as the toilet and the railroad station, are also sites of interaction for street boys, and have become territories in which identities are constructed and where the *tekyan* subculture is formed. These places are what Scott (1990: 119) terms "off stage social sites in which resistance is developed and codified." Spaces such as the toilet create a strong sense of belonging and positive self-identity which allow the boys to look beyond the dangers of being homeless in the city, and to feel secure. In effect, certain spaces have become a "home *in* the public space," and help a boy to survive, and to feel as though he belongs and exists in a world which would rather he did not (Arantes 1996: 86).

In summary, street boys are not passive victims, but adopt various strategies of resistance to the marginalization imposed on them. They do this by occupying multiple and shifting sites around the city, and by employing an expansive range of survival strategies across diverse spatial relations. These actions can be understood as "geographies of resistance," and everyday forms of endurance (Pile and Keith 1997). Street boys' relationships with different places and their use of geographical spaces are, therefore, complex and multilayered, and their activities and behavior patterns change over time in response to their changing environment. Such adaptations are part of their survival.

ACKNOWLEDGMENTS

The research for this chapter was made possible with a CSFP award from the Association of Commonwealth Universities; a short-term ANU (Australian National University) Ph.D. scholarship; and a field research grant from the Department of Human Geography, in the Research School of Pacific and Asian Studies, ANU. I am indebted to the girls and boys who live and work on the streets of Yogyakarta, and to the children (and workers) of the NGO *Girli* for assisting me in my research. Without their friendship, support and acceptance, this account of their lives would not have been possible. Special thanks also to Alison Murray, Peter Rimmer and Lisa Law for their comments and suggestions on earlier drafts of this chapter. Of course, any shortcomings in the chapter are solely my responsibility, and should in no way be attributed to anyone else.

NOTES

1. One reason street girls are less visible is that they do not engage in the same income-earning activities as the boys (shining shoes, busking, selling goods, parking cars, scavenging, and begging). Usually, street girls survive by being looked after by their "boyfriends": their principle form of income and protection. Elsewhere I have written about the lives of street girls and how they live and operate in different parts of the city from street boys (Beazley 1998a; 1999).
2. UNICEF has defined street children into two broad categories: children *of* the street and children *on* the street, or the "homeless" and the "not homeless" (Balanan 1989: 60). Homeless children are those who live, work, and spend the majority of their time on the streets, and who have very little, if any, contact with their families.
3. Fieldwork was conducted over a period of 13 months, in 1995–7, as partial requirement for a Ph.D. in Human Geography at the Australian National University. I am grateful to the Commonwealth and State Fellowship Plan (CSFP), and the Australian National University for their funding. I am also indebted to the street children of Yogyakarta, and to all the workers and children of the street boy and *Rumah Girli* NGO (Non Governmental Organization) for their friendship and support while I was in Yogyakarta.

4. In May 1998 President Soeharto was forced to step down, after 32 years in power. He was revered as the "father of development" until the recent Asian monetary crisis which had severe socio-political repercussions in Indonesia and contributed to Soeharto's downfall.
5. War on preman declared. *Jakarta Post*, March 10, 14, 16 and 21, 1995.
6. For accounts and case studies of death in custody see Amnesty International 1996a. It should go without saying that extra judicial executions through the "shoot to kill" policy are a clear violation of the right to be presumed innocent until proved guilty, and the rights to personal liberty and a fair trial.
7. A street child, Rony Fardian, was shot down by security officers at the railroad station in Jakarta in 1994.
8. *Tekyan*, or *tikyan*, is derived from the Javanese *sithik ning lumayan*, meaning "just a little but enough."
9. In recent years there have been numerous documented accounts of death squads, police forces, business people, and vigilante groups murdering street children in South American cities. See for example Dimenstein (1991), *Amnesty International* (1994c:14–15; 1993: 6–7), and Swift (1996). In the past 20 years Indonesia, like Brazil, has experienced the lethal cocktail of capitalism, cronyism, and neoliberalism, which until recently, produced an "economic miracle" along with a huge disparity in the distribution of income.
10. Smith's (1994) account of the homeless in New York, examines the use of a "Homeless Vehicle" allowing homeless people to have greater spatial mobility, and thus enabling them to "jump scales." See also Cresswell (1993) who examines mobility as a form of resistance to ideals of family and home in the context of Kerouac's novel *On the Road* and established "norms" in 1950s America.

REFERENCES

Amnesty International. 1993: When Governments Get Away with Murder. *Amnesty International British Section Bulletin, Nov./Dec., 6–7.*

—— 1996a: *Working group for children newsletter*, Spring (Working Group for Children, Amnesty International, London).

—— 1996b: *Indonesia and East Timor: when will the Commission take action . . . ?* (Amnesty International Index: ASA 21/10/96), Feb. 1996.

—— 1994a. *Indonesia and East Timor: an Amnesty International briefing* (Amnesty International Index: ASA 21/16/94, London).

—— 1994b. *Operation Cleansing: human rights and APEC* (Amnesty International Index: ASA 21/50/94/Task Force Indonesia, London).

—— 1994c. Invited To Their Own Funerals. *Amnesty International British Section Bulletin*, Jan./Feb., 14–15.

Arantes, A. 1996: The war of places: symbolic boundaries and liminalities in urban space. *Theory, Culture and Society*, 13 (4), 81–92.

Balanon, L. G. 1989: Street Children: Strategies for Action. *Child Welfare*, 68, (1–3), 159–66.

Beazley, H. 1998a: Subcultures of resistance: street children's conception and use of space in Indonesia. *Malaysian Journal of Tropical Geography.*

—— 1999: "*'Just A Little But Enough': Street Children's Subcultures in Yogyakarta, Indonesia.*" Unpublished Ph.D. thesis, Australian National University, Canberra.

—— 1998b: Homeless street children in Yogyakarta, Indonesia. *Development Bulletin*, 44, 40–2.

Berman, L. and Beazley, H. 1997: The world's first street university. *Inside Indonesia*, 50, 11–12.

Bondi, L. 1993: Locating identity politics. In M. Keith, and S. Pile (eds.), *Place and the Politics of Identity*. London: Routledge, 84–101.

Clarke, J. , Hall, S. Jefferson, T., and Roberts, B. 1976: Subcultures, cultures and class. In S. Hall and T. Jefferson (eds.), *Resistance Through Rituals: Youth Subcultures in Post-war Britain*. London: Routledge.

Cresswell, T. 1992: The crucial "where" of graffiti: a geographical analysis of reactions to graffiti in New York. *Environment and Planning D: Society and Space*, 10, 329–44.

—— 1993: Mobility as resistance: a geographical reading of Kerouac's *On the Road. Transactions Of the Institute of British Geographers*, 18 (2), 249–62.

—— 1996: *In Place/Out of Place: Geography, Ideology and Transgression*. Minneapolis: University of Minnesota Press.

Davidson, G. 1996: The spaces of coping: women and poverty in Singapore. *Singapore Journal of Tropical Geography*, 17 (2), 113–131.

Dimenstein, G. 1991: *Brazil: War on Children*. London: Latin American Bureau.

Ertanto, B. 1993: Kere Ki Sah Mati. Yen Mati Ngrepoti: Studi Mengenai Anak Jalanan Dan Perubahan Sosial. (Vagrants should not die. Those that die create problems: A Study about Street Children and Social Change.) Paper presented to seminar The Social Position of Children in a Social Context, Gajah Mada University, Yogyakarta, Nov. 27).

—— 1994: Tak Ada KTP, Silahakan Pergi Dari Kampung: Studi Mengenai Politik Identitas Anak Jalanan di Kampung, Yogyakarta: Yayasan Humana.

Foucault, M. 1984: Space, knowledge, power. In P. Rabinow, (ed.), *The Foucault Reader*. New York: Pantheon Books, 239–56.

Gould, P. and White, R. 1974: *Mental Maps*. London: Penguin.

Guinness, P. 1994: Local society and culture. In H. Hill, (ed.), *Indonesia's New Order: The Dynamics of Socioeconomic Transformation*. Honolulu: University of Hawaii Press.

Hall, S. and Jefferson T. (eds.) [1976] 1993: *Resistance through Rituals: Youth subcultures in Post-war Britain*. London: Routledge.

Harvey, D. 1996: *Justice, Nature and the Geography of Difference*. Oxford: Blackwell.

Hebdige, D. 1979: *Subculture: The Meaning of Style*. London: Methuen.

Human Rights Watch Asia. 1994: *Tightening up in Indonesia Before the APEC Summit* October, 6 (12).

Keith, M. and Pile, S. (eds.) 1993: *Place and the Politics of Identity*. London: Routledge.

Knopp, L. 1995: Sexuality and urban space: a framework for analysis. In D. Bell and G. Valentine (eds.), *Mapping Desires: Geographies of Sexualities*. London: Routledge.

Kusuma, M. W. (ed.) 1995: *Tuhan Temani Aku: Rel Kehidupan Anak Jalanan*. (God is with Me: Street Children's lives) Jakarta: Institute Sosial Jakarta.

Massey, D. 1994: *Space, Place and Gender*. Oxford: Polity.

Mathews, M. H. 1980: The mental maps of children: images of Coventry's city center. *Geography*, 65, 1 (286).

—— 1986: Children as map-makers. *Geographical Magazine*, 58 (3), 124–6.

—— 1992: *Making Sense of Place: Children's Understanding of Large-Scale Environments*. Hemel Hempstead: Harvester Wheatsheaf.

Murray, A. 1993: City, subculture and sexuality: alternative spaces in Jakarta. *Development Bulletin*, 35–8.

Myslik, W. 1996: Renegotiating the social/ sexual identities of places: gay communities as safe havens or sites of resistance? In N. Duncan, (ed.), *Body Space: Destabilizing Geographies*. London: Routledge, 156–69.

Pile, S. 1997: Introduction. In S. Pile, and M. Keith, (eds.), *Geographies of Resistance.* London: Routledge, 1–32.

Pile, S. and Keith, M. (eds.) 1997: *Geographies of Resistance*. London: Routledge.

Relph, E. 1976: *Place and Placelessness*. London: Pion.

Scott, J. C. 1990: *Domination and the Arts of Resistance: Hidden Transcripts.* New Haven: Yale University Press.

Sibley, D. 1995: *Geographies of Exclusion: Society and Difference in the West.* London: Routledge.

Smith, N. 1994: Homeless/global: scaling places. In J. Bird, et al. (eds.), *Mapping the Futures: Local Cultures, Global change*. London: Routledge, 87–119.

Smith, N. and Katz, C. 1993: Grounding metaphor: towards a spatialized politics. In M. Keith, and S. Pile (eds.) *Place and The Politics of Idenlity.* London: Routledge.

Sullivan, J. 1986: Kampung and the state: the role of government in the development of urban community in Yogyakarta, *Indonesia*, 41, 63–8.

Swift, A. 1996: Scared of our own kids. *New Internationalist*, 276, 14–16.

UNICEF 1989: United Nations Convention On The Rights of The Child. UNICEF, New York.

US Department of State 1998: *Indonesia Report on Human Rights Practices for 1997.* Bureau of Democracy, Human Rights and Labor: New York.

White, R. 1990: *No Space of Their Own: Young people and Social Control in Australia.* Melbourne: Cambridge University Press.

—— 1996: No-go in the fortress city: young people, inequality and space. *Urban Policy and Research*, 14 (1), 37–50.

Yeoh, B. and Huang, S. 1996: Gender and urban space in the tropical third world. *Singapore Journal of Tropical Geography*, 17 (2), 105–12.

Chapter 41

Cyberspace and the City: The "Virtual City" in Europe

Alessandro Aurigi and Stephen Graham

Introduction: What is a "Virtual" City?

The Internet is a global grid of computer networks. It encompasses a burgeoning universe of transaction, exchange, representation, and communication. "Virtual communities" allow all sorts of groups to maintain interaction across distance. Electronic commerce supports online trading of a fast-growing range of goods and services. And complex combinations of images, sounds, and text, interconnected into the global hypertext labyrinth of the World Wide Web, provides, in a sense, a "parallel universe" (Benedikt 1991). The Internet is intimately interconnected with the social world while always being "one click away."

From *Wired* magazine to *The Economist*, we are constantly assailed these days by excited articles alleging that we are in the midst of some liberating "Digital Revolution" in which distance dies as a constraint on human life. With the rapid growth of "cyberspace," many such commentators have alleged that the online realm will grow to simply replace or transcend the material and social realms of the tangible urban world. All the rudiments of this world – the body, the book, physical transportation, place, and the city – have been alleged to be under threat from the pure, clean, dematerialized world of Internet-based existence (Negroponte 1995). As time and space barriers compress or collapse, human life, it is alleged, becomes less reliant on place in general, and urban place in particular. This global rush on-line, such commentators argue, heralds nothing less than global time-space omnipotence for the cyberspace *flâneurs* (Mitchell 1996). For the "terminal citizens" (Virilio 1993) of the planetary cyberspace realm, the "global village," rather than the city, is now the only meaningful community. Traditional notions of city life – the importance of propinquity, face-to-face interaction, street life, shopping and consumption, urban "community," neighborhoods, the particularities of urban culture and identities, etc. – are rendered extremely problematic, even anachronistic.

Clearly, electronic networks *can* substitute for some physical travel and face-to-face encounter, as phone banking and online shopping demonstrate. But it does not follow that cities will somehow "vanish" with the growth of the online realm. Rather, there is a complex *articulation* between cities, urban life, and the Internet

(Graham and Marvin 1996; Graham 1998). Metropolitan regions, in fact, dominate the physical infrastructure of host computers and telecoms links that make up the Internet; in the United States, moreover, this dominance may actually be growing (Moss and Townshend 1997). In fact, the global rush to urbanization and rising, although highly uneven, physical mobility is happening *at the same time* as the pervasive, although once again highly uneven, growth of electronic communications.

The extended, polycentric urban regions that are resulting from current urbanization trends are, essentially, giant *engines* of electronic communication of all types. Physical movement, face-to-face interactions, and urban life are, in fact, closely reliant on widening infrastructures of phones, mobile phones, electronic monitoring devices, Internet networks, TV and radio networks, electronic transaction and surveillance systems, and the like. New urbanization trends, based around electronic interaction, reflect this: "back-office" zones, multimedia districts, technopoles, "intelligent" buildings, "smart" communities, etc. (Graham and Marvin 1998). And, as well as global connections, the growth of the Internet is also powerfully fueled by local interconnections and transactions at the level at or below that of metropolitan regions, by representations of urban places, and by electronic communications that articulate closely with the dynamics of cities and urban regions. As with newsprint, the film theater, radio, and television before it, then, the Internet is, in essence, a medium of urban modernity which is closely bound up with the restructuring of old urban forms and the production of new ones.

But how, in detail, are cities articulating with IT-based exchanges and "cyberspace"? One particularly interesting phenomenon developing here is the so-called "virtual city." Through this phenomenon most European cities are, in effect, busily starting to construct electronic analogies of themselves, based on the Internet. A virtual city, such as the Amsterdam example in Figure 41.1, is an Internet site designed by urban agencies or Internet providers to directly represent, and articulate with, the dynamics of a specific "real" city. Virtual cities can be seen as a reaction to the fragmentary relationship betwen the Internet and particular cities caused by the fact that it is often as easy to interact with a computer on the other side of the world as with one in the next room. In the UK, for example, the US dominance of the Internet means that it is often easier to find weather information in Phoenix, Arizona, than in one's home city.

Virtual cities, then, are attempts to "ground" the globally interconnected online realm in real urban areas. In essence, they try to make the relationships between real places and online realms more clearly legible and comprehensible (in ways that are analogous to the efforts of urban designers to make urban spaces more legible and imageable in the minds of urban citizens). Thus, what we call "grounded" virtual cities attempt to provide a single, integrated Internet site through which some or all of the Internet services located in a particular city can be accessed. Again, *De Digitale Stad* (Figure 41.1) is the best-known example of a grounded virtual city which explicitly uses the "city" as a design metaphor for organizing services, chat rooms, debates, and information on the web site. In this case, the "map" of the virtual city is made up of themed city "squares," each of which contains all information and services related to its themes (politics, gay issues, transport, technology, sport, etc.). Thus, an explicit connection is made between the "virtual" with the

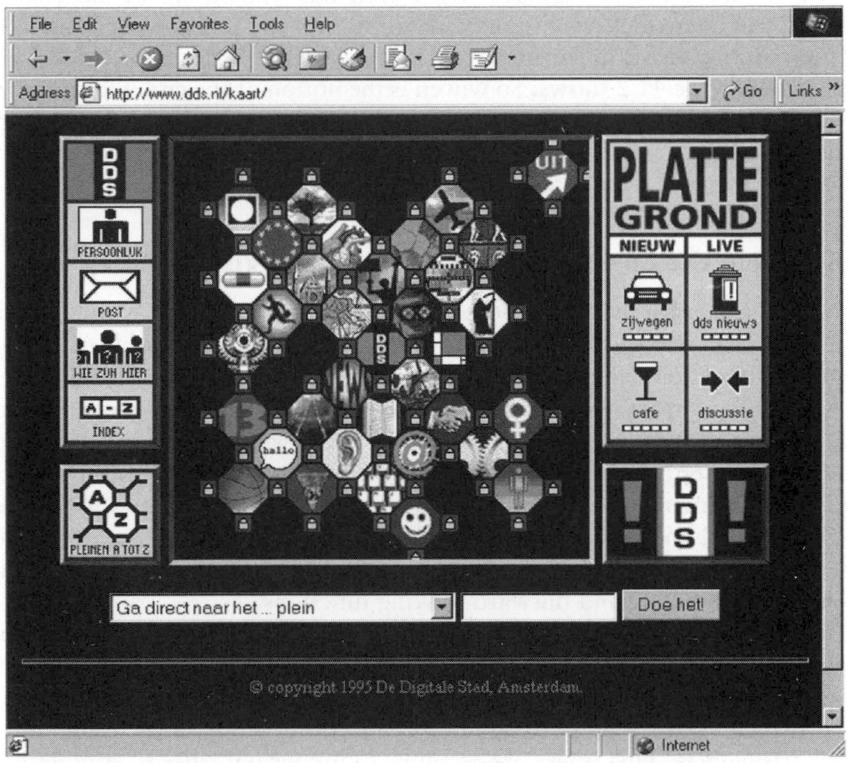

Figure 41.1 The Internet interface for *De Digitale Stadt*, Amsterdam, one of the best-known examples of a "grounded" virtual city which uses the urban metaphor of "town squares" to organize its services (at http://www.dds.nl/)

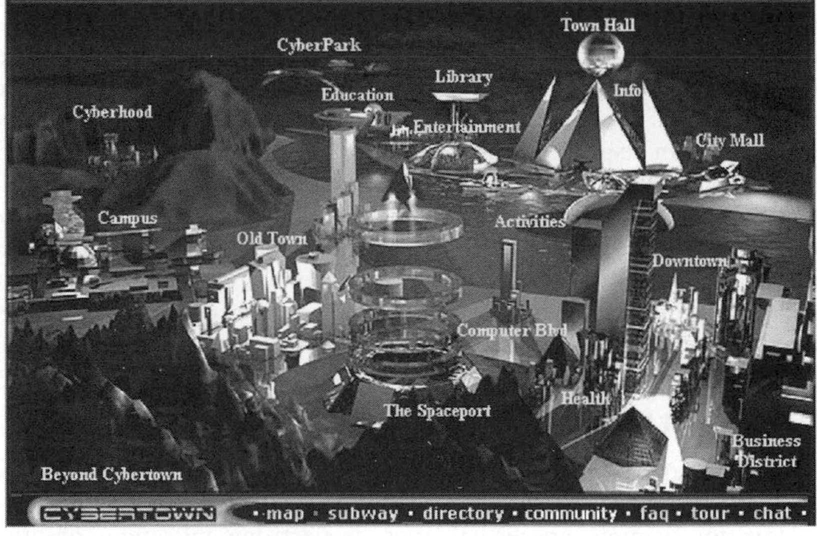

Figure 41.2 Cybertown, a "non-grounded" virtual city (at http://www.cybertown.com)

"real" city in the mind of the user (DDS even has 50,000 signed up electronic "residents" and its own electronic "city mayor").

In an interesting twist, however, virtual cities can also be "nongrounded," as the example from Figure 41.2 shows. So woven is the notion of the city into the mindset of the modern condition that the city can simply use some idealized urban metaphor as a legible interface for Internet services which are, in fact, scattered across host computers distributed right across the planet.

Forces Driving the Construction of "Grounded" Virtual Cities

Most often, "grounded" virtual cities signify the ambitions of innovative municipalities, keen to be seen to be "switched in" to the blossoming worlds of high-tech modernity centered on the Internet. They embody many ambitions, dreams, orientations, and configurations. In a sense, this is not surprising, as many key questions in contemporary urbanism can, in essence, be boiled down to questions of communication, information, and transaction. Thus, attempts to construct virtual cities necessarily have to engage with many of the key issues of social divisions, citizenship, civic culture, and urban policy and planning explored elsewhere in this book. And because of the globally interconnected nature of the Internet, they also tend to combine inward-looking and outward-looking functions.

On the one hand, as electronic versions of the classic discourse of place promotion, virtual cities can attempt to position cities within globalizing circuits of investment, tourism, conferences, and urban sports and cultural events. On the other, virtual cities can attempt to build up connections within cities. Many orientations are arising here. First, there are attempts to use virtual cities to stimulate local economic development, through the provision of incentives to high-tech innovation and "friction free" arenas within which linkages can be created between local firms, service providers, and consumers. Second, virtual cities can be "electronic democracy" initiatives, aiming both to widen social access to the Internet and improve relations between citizens, elected representatives, and public and private service providers. Third, they can be attempts to engineer a new "electronic public realm" for cities, supporting the development of online debates, discourses, and "communities" which feed back positively on the social dynamics of the "host" metropolis. And, finally, they can be purveyors of new practices of urban management, supporting the electronic delivery of public services and "intelligent" ways of managing urban services such as education, transport, waste, social services, and planning.

Some virtual cities attempt to address two or more of these interconnected areas. But there are clearly tensions here, as each orientation will suggest different practices of design, development, and management for the virtual city, different topologies of connection, and different criteria for evaluating success.

Surveying Virtual Urbanism

Such general aspects of virtual city innovation are now well documented (see, for example, Graham and Aurigi 1997). What is less clear, however, is the bigger picture. How, for example, are virtual cities, as electronic reflections of cities and systems of cites, developing across regions, nations, and continents? How can we understand the different types of virtual city that are emerging? And which actors and agencies are most active in shaping them?

In what remains of this brief chapter, we address these questions, looking in particular at the picture in Europe. We do this through the construction of a typology of virtual cities and an analysis of what types of virtual cities are developing where across Western Europe. This is based on an extensive web-based survey of the virtual cities directly related to major European cities of at least 200,000 inhabitants, completed during 1997 (a sample of 213 initiatives within 14 countries of the EU). Through it, we aimed to evaluate the scope and potential of virtual cities across Europe for achieving all the many objectives ascribed to them. Three essential principles, in particular, were the basis for this evaluation.

Informativeness

First, and most obviously, the richness of up-to-date information and the provision of useful services for citizens are fundamental features of virtual cities. The ability to overcome the barriers of space and time through the implementation of virtual city initiatives is seen as one of the crucial factors that can enhance the efficiency of the urban environment. In theory, highly effective services can also play an important role in the economic regeneration of a city, as well contributing to improving the relations between citizens and local administrations, both quantitatively and qualitatively.

Participation and social access

The need for urban IT initiatives to guarantee wider social participation and access in new technologies is a key issue from the current standpoint where elite social groups dominate access to computers and advanced telecommunications. Urban social polarization threatens to be deeply marked in access to new technologies. All studies about the demography of the Internet indicate that user groups are highly unrepresentative of the whole population. Usage of the Internet is still strongly polarized towards wealthy, relatively young, highly educated people. Moreover, many of the active users, by connecting from the workplace or the university, do not pay the bill for their "surfing." The idea of a wholesale diffusion of computers throughout our society is still more myth than reality; sales of personal computers tend to be targeted at customers who already own a PC and want to upgrade, rather than at beginners (Bannister 1995).

Social inclusiveness of urban citizens in virtual city initiatives is therefore our second key evaluation principle. It is also a point highlighted in the Interim Report of the High Level Experts Group of the European Union, titled "Building the European Information Society for Us All" (European Commission 1996). The authors recommend that particular care should be taken in including in the Information Society those groups that tend more often to be most marginalized, such as "the elderly, early and 'active' retired people, the unemployed and women" (p. 35).

Moreover, it must also be stressed that simply granting access to the Internet per se is not some ultimate answer to the problems of social inclusion, as is often implied. Some authors have noted that giving people the ability to retrieve information – however important this ability can be – is not enough to ensure real participation in the development of the "Information Society". Hoogvelt and Freeman (1996: 3), for example, note that "communities online grow from *communication* rather than information retrieval" (original emphasis). Being able to "read" information on your monitor does not equate with being visible and empowered in the vast electronic environment. Virtual cities therefore need to stress interactive communication (through e-mail etc.) rather than just passive information consumption (of web pages). Citizens, voluntary groups, and organizations therefore need to take an active part in the life of the virtual city, in the same way they should be able to do in the "real" city. This can be promoted through several forms of interactive communication, such as letting people publish their own information and contributions (one-to-many communication), or organizing virtual spaces for public discussion (many-to-many communication).

"Groundedness": the relationship with the host city

Our final principle is the degree to which virtual cities can demonstrate positive relationships with the city that host them, rather than merely operating as another Internet site geared towards global users. One of the main ideas stemming from the entire virtual cities movement is the claim that binding public cyberspace initiatives to precise places and communities is a great opportunity for social and economic regeneration, as well as for equality. This concept has been used to reaffirm the appropriateness of local IT developments as an alternative to utopian conceptions of cyberspace taking over reality as a nonplace inhabited by communities of interest that deny proximity, the meaning of urban places, and which imply that all human needs can now be met through a limitless, global electronic web which transcends the meaning of place. Dave Carter, a policymaker in Manchester and one of the initial promoters of virtual cities, argues that the ideas supporting a civic, localized cyberspace constitute "a critique of what might be termed the 'Utopian school' of future 'cyber-lifestyles' which sees cities becoming depopulated, 'instant electronic democracy' replacing the need for governmental structures and services and a dominant 'ruralist' lifestyle emerging" (Carter 1997: 139).

The concept of a "local" cyberspace, and that of a virtual city, thus stands as a vision of a collaborative and regenerative relationship between new technologies and the city. It asserts that positive articulations are possible betwen IT and the economic, social, and cultural fabric of cities which both benefit cities and make IT-based interactions more meaningful. To achieve this, of course, it is necessary to be as "grounded" as possible by primarily gearing toward local users. As Nina Wakeford suggests, "the advantage of community networks is in comparison to other forms of virtual community, which have only intermittent or an absence of shared geographic space" (Wakeford 1996).

Thus we need to assess how grounded Europe's virtual cities are. The presence of debate areas and forums, for example, can be a sign of an orientation towards inclusiveness and participation. But these forums must be dedicated to local problems or topics for virtual cities to be truly "grounded" experiments. Another example could be the choice of language to be used in the web pages. Multilanguage sites can be good for the inclusion of immigrant groups and for our increasingly multiethnic cities. But sometimes the opposite may happen, as local languages are neglected in an effort to attract the attention of global English-speaking business elites or tourists. A Spanish or Greek site that presents all of its information exclusively in English, without using the local language, inevitably establishes an extremely weak relationship with the local communities it is supposed to refer to.

The imperative of economically regenerating Western European cities adds another rationale for being as locally oriented as possible. Although the potential of the Internet as a mean of accessing global markets and arenas is an important aspect of the advent of the Information Society, a survey carried out in the US demonstrates that a great potential is embedded in the local markets. This probably stems from the people's natural need for a sense of place and proximity, even when they are purchasing goods or services. In fact, 80 percent of the purchases in the US are still carried out within a radius of 20 miles from home, primarily within the orbit of the metropolitan region (McElvogue 1997). Awareness of this trend is causing, if not a U-turn in the global orientation of electronic commerce services, at least a growing awareness of the potential of commercial Internet initiatives geared to local audiences. It is a fact that several well-known Internet directories, gateways, and search engines such as Yahoo, Lycos, or Infoseek – traditionally the symbols of the "global" Internet where information was available from any part of the world – have recently started providing local, national, or even "metropolitan" sets of information.

Virtual Cities: Mapping Ideal Types

Combining our discussion of these three dimensions of virtual city policy, it is possible to define a typology of "ideal types" of virtual city which we will use to inform our survey. This is shown in Figure 41.3.

● = Yes ○ = No	Informative	Participative	Grounded
"Brochure"	○	○	
"INFORMATION DESK"			
Tourists'/Investors' Kiosk	●	○	○
Civic Database	●	○	●
"ELECTRONIC PLACE"			
Cyber Mall	○	●	○
Cybersquare	○	●	●
"HOLISTIC–URBAN ANALOGY"			
Global Cybercity	●	●	○
Holistic Virtual City	●	●	●

Figure 41.3 "Ideal types" of virtual city

To define the six ideal types we have tried to relate our three principles to the content and orientation of the different types of virtual cities. For example, a "global cybercity" is a virtual city that is basically geared to a global audience. Such a site, while effectively exploiting the urban metaphor and providing a certain degree of complexity in information and communication, retains a very weak bond with the place it is supposed to belong to. On the other hand, a "holistic virtual city" tends to exploit the urban analogy primarily for a broad range of interrelated applications geared towards local purposes.

Virtual Cities in Europe

So what did our survey of 213 virtual cities, located within 167 European cities, reveal about the scope and orientation of digital urbanism in Europe? Three issues, in particular, are worthy of brief discussion here: the overall balance in Europe between different types of virtual cities, differences between the virtual cities, in different nations, and links between driving institutions and virtual city orientation.

The distribution of virtual city types in Europe

First, at the European level, it is clear that the percentage of the observed sites that can be included in the "holistic virtual cities" category is relatively small at around 10 percent (see Figure 41.4). This demonstrates that, despite all the hype, the use of the Internet for "civic" purposes is still quite limited and is used primarily as an electronic "brochure" or "data base" – a means for the one-way distribution of information to "consumers" of cities (citizens, businesses, tourists). Cities' use of the Internet is still overwhelmingly dominated by exploration of its potential as a cheap and innovative tool for information and, above all, promotion and place marketing. While this reflects the growing importance of city marketing to urban

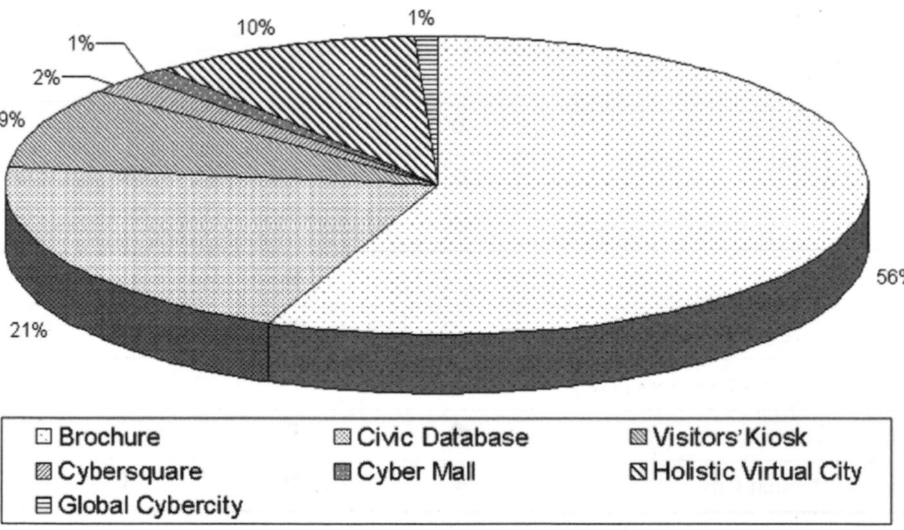

Figure 41.4 City-related Internet sites in the EU, 1997

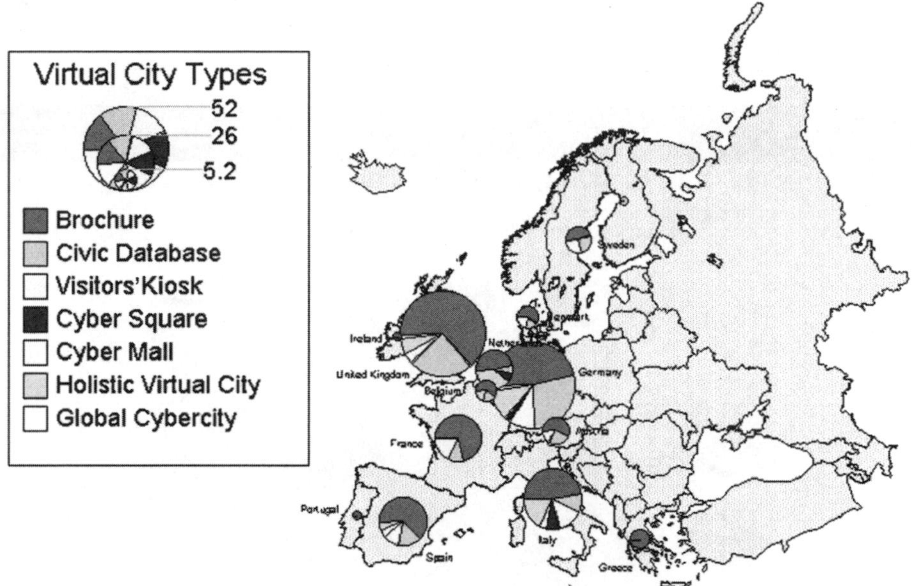

Figure 41.5 Distribution of virtual city types in the EU by nation, 1997

policy, the danger is that, in using the Internet to sell itself as convivial, clean, safe, well connected, and endowed with a high quality of life, every city offers a bland, similar, even standardized message.

Thus, paradoxically, virtual cities often become indistinguishable from each other, sanitized idealizations of postmodern consumption spaces which neglect or ignore real specificities of urban culture, politics, esthetics, or place. The point here is the way in which the dominance of virtual cities by urban marketing may effectively be contradictory. If, as many now argue, "cities are competing, and their edge is livability" (quoted in Boyer 1993: 125), virtual cities configured entirely to the serial repetition of "postmodern" urban icons for outside consumers prioritize the former but ignore the latter. From the point of view of technological innovation, a better urban "liveability" might be achieved through the provision of an effective public cyberspace that includes useful services and a democratic and participatory environment designed to address the needs of city populations and institutions.

National variations in virtual city orientation

Second, as we can see from Figure 41.5, there are clearly some notable differences in the development and orientation of virtual cities across the EU. These differences belie easy assumptions that a sharp divide exists in technological advancement between southern European and northern European countries. Italy, for example, has relatively advanced and sophisticated virtual cities, with a higher than average number of interactive and "holistic" virtual cities. The most well-known of these is the "Iperbole" initiative from Bologna city council (see Figure 41.6). Here, the relatively centralized power of Italian local authorities in determining local development policies is a key factor.

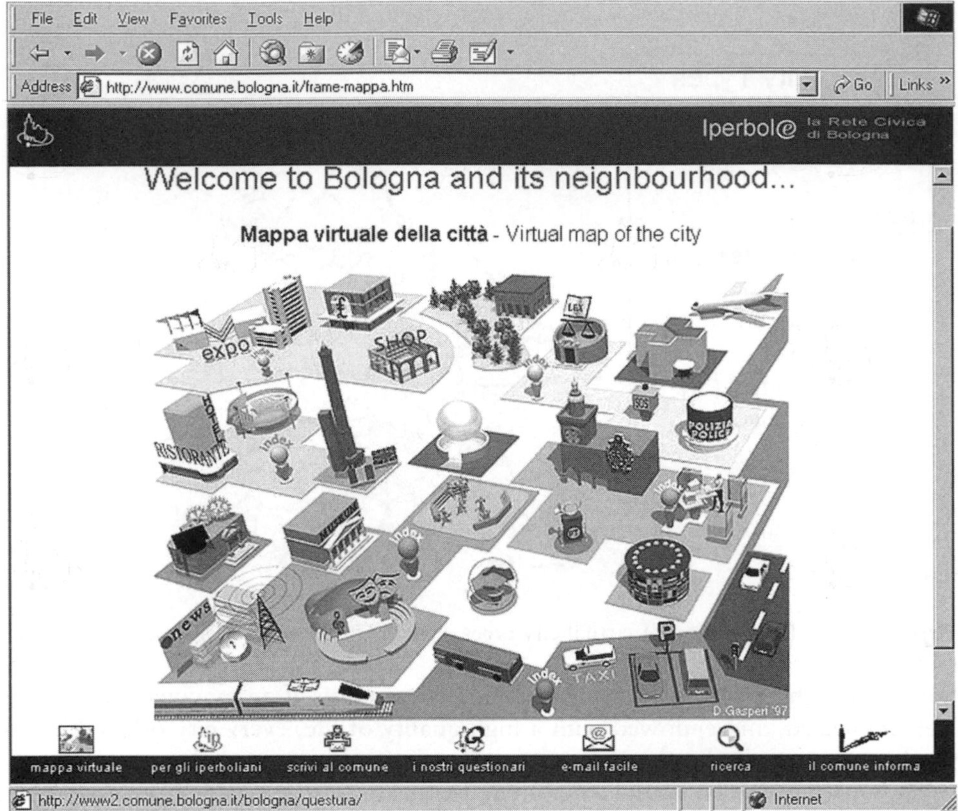

Figure 41.6 The *Iperbole* virtual city, Bologna, an example of an Italian "holistic" virtual city (at http://www.nettuno.it/bologna/MappaWelcome.html)

In France, meanwhile, virtual cities remain poorly developed. High-profile virtual city initiatives of the "holistic" kind are practically absent, in a nation that has recently been extremely sensitive towards the potential of new telecommunication technologies. The reason for this is the barrier presented by earlier IT technologies such as the Minitel systems, which have been widely adopted throughout France. The widespread use of city Minitelbased systems has prevented French municipalities from developing Internet-based initiatives.

The urban governance of virtual cities

Finally, it is interesting to analyze the links between the types of virtual cities under development and the institutions and sectors which instigate them. Not unsurprisingly, it seems that virtual cities present an interesting reflection on broader differences in practices and structures of urban governance as a whole across Europe (see Figure 41.7).

The contrast between Italy and the UK helps illustrate this point. The Italian chart shows quite clearly how local municipalism, and the role of the local councils, totally dominate local virtual city policies. In Italy, local authorities still tend to

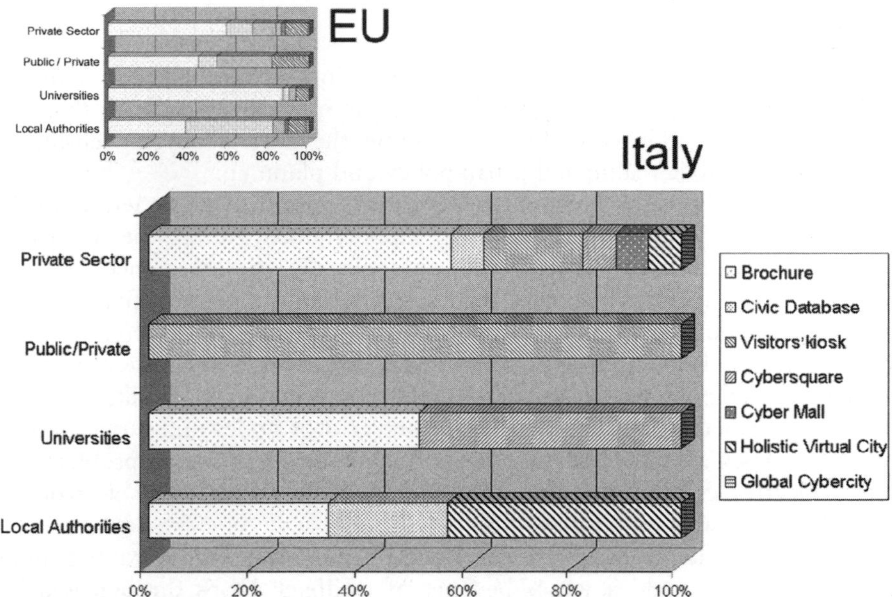

Figure 41.7 Relationships between originating institution and type of virtual city in Italy and the EU

identify themselves with the whole city, assuming a central, sometimes hegemonic, role in the management of the urban territory. Local councils remain the main actors and decision makers shaping the development of "public" cyberspace in Italian cities in the form of holistic virtual cities which tend to emphasize public service and links between municipality and citizenry. The participation of the private sector, while not completely absent from the picture, is often limited to the technical assistance from some IT firms. A precise and strict hierarchy maintains the role of the local council as the dominant force shaping all decisions about the design, content, and orientation of Italian virtual city initiatives.

The case of the UK is very different. Most of the relatively sophisticated virtual cities in the UK involve the establishment of "true" public–private partnerships with a good degree of collaboration among the different partners (local authorities, regeneration agencies, training organizations, universities, private firms, etc.) in shaping virtual cities. British virtual cities reflect the complex, competitive, and fragmented nature of urban governance in Britain. In British cities it is not uncommon for there to be several, competing, virtual analogies under development, arising from different partnership bodies, private sector agencies and universities. Each jostles for the attention of specialist audiences; the idea of a coherent "plan" to bring together all aspects of "local" cyberspace, as in the Italian model, might be seen to be as unrealistic as the idea that a single master plan may shape the physical development of a British metropolis in some dictatorial fashion. As Simon Davoudi notes, British "city governments are no longer the key locus for integration of urban relationships, but merely one of many actors competing for access to resources and control of agendas" (Davoudi 1995: 226).

Conclusion

The widening application of advanced information technologies, as a dramatic technological reconfiguration of urban society, is interwoven with all the aspects of city development addressed in this Companion: the material city; citizenship, civic culture and the public realm; and urban policy and planning.

Constantly at play in such city–IT relations is a central dynamic tension. On the one hand, there is the use of networks to support globalization, the collapsing of boundaries between urban spaces, and, consequently, the threatened loss of the notion that cities are anything more than arbitrary collections of activities within a physical space which are seamlessly integrated in a global space. Here, the citizen's urbanity transcends its reliance on a particular place; her experience of urban life, like that so often portrayed in the cyberpunk science fiction of the likes of William Gibson, becomes that of a limitless, planetary grid of nodes and services that are always "one click away." Here, the very notion of the city becomes problematic, as limitless electronic connections bind physical space into a pervasive electronic network space accessible from anywhere.

On the other hand, though, IT networks may rework the positive contributions of urbanity. They may add a whole new set of feedback loops through which the information, communications flows, representations, and transactions that bind us to city life become enlivened, coordinated, and supported. Electronic interactions reaffirm the complex fabric of city life, affording new potential for exchange, debate, inclusion, and dynamic mixture, improving the city in the process.

In essence, virtual city experimentation can be considered to be a small, although increasingly visible, attempt to maximize the latter while minimizing the former. At best, beyond the incessant hype about the Internet, it reflects real and concrete attempts to use IT in the search for positive articulations between urbanism and the "network society": what Manuel Castells has called "grassrooting the space of flows" (Castells 1996). Our research has shown how the electronic analogical world of virtual cities is blossoming across Europe; how a wide range of different virtual cities is being constructed; and how virtual cities reflect the particular styles of urban governance in different nations. We have seen that there is not some single "cyberspace" nor some single "virtual city movement"; rather, there is a contested terrain of differing models, orientations, and experiments. Information technologies, far from being some determining force in changing cities, are being woven into existing urban practices in complex and diverse ways that are only just starting to become apparent.

We have also shown, however, that attempts to genuinely harness IT as a new interactive public space at the urban level remain relatively insignificant. Much more powerful is the pervasive and hopeful flood of the one-way marketing of cities to the potential audience of elite Internet users across the planet – perhaps not surprisingly given current trends in urban development. The majority of the city-related Internet sites are configured almost entirely as glossy electronic brochures. In designing them, many decision makers are sticking to old, reassuring media paradigms based on the ideas behind TV broadcasting and paper-based publishing. These "models," which make alleged "virtual cities" extremely cheap to create and run, are being widely transferred and embedded into the new technology, to the extent of substantially limiting its potential for stimulating genuine local interaction and exchange.

It seems likely that this picture of virtual city innovation failing (so far) to live up to its hype extends beyond Europe. Recent evidence from the United States, for example, suggests that web cities there also tend to be much more prosaic than the excitedly transformative rhetoric of the Internet there suggests (Nunn and Rubleske 1997). In a detailed survey, numbers of towns and cities in the US actually using the web to deliver services and interactive spaces was far below that implied by national champions of urban IT innovation like the National League of Cities (1997: 72). US city governments were not found to be making the most of grants from Federal Government to develop community-oriented IT networks. And web services tend to be routine, unimaginative, and largely oriented, like those in Europe, towards one-way place promotion and information provision, rather than interactive communication (1997: 72–3).

To resort to an overcrude local–global distinction, there is clearly a danger that, within the virtual urbanism movement, the "global" notion that cities are merely products for international consumption is being emphasized at the expense of the "local" idea that cities are places of meaning, representation, politics, interaction, and experience. The virtual city, in short, is merely a high-tech and technologically modern embodiment of a very old tension.

REFERENCES

Bannister, N. 1995: Novelty of the Net wears off. *The Guardian On-line*, October 31.

Benedikt, M. 1991: Introduction. In M. Benedikt (ed.), *Cyberspace: First Steps*. Cambridge, MA: MIT Press, 1–25.

Boyer M. C. 1993: The city of illusion: New York's public places. In P. Knox, (ed.), *The Restless Urban Landscape*. Englewood Cliffs: Prentice-Hall, 111–23.

Carter D. 1997: Digital democracy or information aristocracy? In B. Loader (ed.), *The Governance of Cyberspace*. London: Routledge, 136–52.

Castells, M. 1996: *The Rise of the Network Society*. Oxford: Blackwell.

Davoudi S. 1995: Dilemmas of urban governance. In P. Healey et al. (eds.), *Managing Cities: the New Urban Context*. Chichester: Wiley and Sons, 225–30.

European Commission 1996: Building the European Information Society for Us All. First Reflections of the High Level Group of Experts, Interim Report.

Graham, S. 1998: The end of geography or the explosion of place? Conceptualising space, place and information technology. *Progress in Human Geography*, 22 (2), 165–85.

Graham, S. and Aurigi, A. 1997: Urbanising cyberspace? The scope and potential of the virtual cities movement. *City*, 7, 18–39.

Graham, S. and Marvin, S. 1996: *Telecommunications and the City: Electronic Spaces, Urban Places*. London: Routledge.

Graham, S. and Marvin, S. 1998: *Net Effects: Urban Planning and the Technological Future of Cities*. Working Paper 3 in The Richness of Cities Project, DEMOS/Comedia, London.

Hoogvelt, A. and Freeman, M. 1996: Community intranets. Mimeograph.

McElvogue L. 1997: Bright sites, big city. *The Guardian On-line*, February 20.

Mitchell, W. 1996: *City of Bits: Place, Space and the Infobahn*. Cambridge, MA: MIT Press.

Moss, M. and Townshend, A. 1997: Manhatten leads the Net nation. http://www.nyu.edu/urban/ny_affairs/telecom.html.

Negroponte, N. 1995: *Being Digital.* London: Hodder and Stoughton.

Nunn, S. and Rubleske, J. 1997: "Webbed" cities and development of national information highway: the creation of World Wide Web sites by US city governments. *Journal of Urban Technology*, 4 (1), 53–79.

Wakeford, N. 1996: Developing community intranets: key social issues and solutions. Mimeograph.

Virilio, P. 1993: The third interval: a critical transition. In V. Andermatt-Conley (ed.), *Rethinking Technologies*. London: University of Minnesota Press, 3–10.

Part V Urban Politics and Urban Interventions

Chapter 42

City Interventions

Gary Bridge and Sophie Watson

Any attempt to write a comprehensive overview of urban policy across the world, in an introduction of this kind, would undoubtedly fail. There is such a wide variation in cities, political systems, and forms of governance, specific cultures and national histories, on the one hand, and urban initiatives and responses to urban problems on the other. Instead in this chapter we briefly revisit the conceptual frameworks of this volume and consider at a broadbrush level the urban policies that have been constructed within these frames. What we are telling here is a metanarrative of policy possibilities and imagined and performed action, hinting where appropriate at more specific outcomes and approaches.

It could easily be argued that all urban policy is about imagining since in some sense policymaking inevitably involves imaginative leaps and visions of a better way to do things. However here the focus is on the terrain in which imagination has been translated into urban planning and design. Cities have been planned since their inception in the sense that the organization of space has been managed, while land, property rights, and the provision of urban services have all been organized in some form. But from a Western perspective – and one which subsequently had an influence on the formation of cities across the world, particularly the colonized world – the utopian visions of certain key players, rooted in Enlightenment thought, have had long-lasting effects on urban form and structure throughout the course of the twentieth century.

By the end of the nineteenth century the effects of industrialization on cities – the perceived disorder, pollution, ill health, chaos, and immorality – were increasingly erupting as a cause for public and moral concern. Discourses of cities as sites of moral degradation, unrest, and potential revolution were rife. In this context, the notions of progress, rationality, and order which were embedded in the project of modernity were translated into planning ideas and the desire to find a way of organizing social and economic activities in cities in a rational, predictable, and esthetically pleasing way (Boyer 1983). The aim was to improve the living conditions of urban populations without impeding economic progress and growth. Three visionaries define the utopian modernist tradition: Le Corbusier, Frank Lloyd

Wright, and Ebenezer Howard. Each of these had a profound influence on the way cities have been organized, even though none of them had his vision realized in a complete form.

Le Corbusier was born the son of a Swiss watchmaker. Order and precision were the very stuff of his childhood that arguably marked his later vision of the city as a machine for living. Corbusier developed several grand visions for cities: *La Ville Radieuse* (1933) and *La Ville Contemporaine* (1922), being the most fully developed and only partially realized in the planning of Chandigarh (Hall 1988). These modernist plans were large scale, interventionist, comprehensive, and embodied a belief in rationality and the possibility of order, easy mobility, the separation of home from work, and streamlined conditions of life.

Successful planning in Corbusier's view could iron out all of the chaotic city's ills. The model was based on a centralized bureaucracy with no notion of the populace being involved in the process. This was planning from above – neatly reflected in Le Corbusier's penchant for airplanes discussed by Antony Vidler in this Companion – where the organization of space implied the organization of people – the worker bees in an elaborate constructed hive where everyone knew their place. But as Alan Mabin (chapter 46 in this volume) points out, this was not the only tradition in modernist planning; rather there was another tradition which dated back to the Enlightenment and which incorporated much more explicit humanitarian objectives.

Frank Lloyd Wright is well known for his "Broadacre City" plan, which was conceived as a counterpoint to the traditional crowded and dense city, and was based around homesteads each set in an acre and connected by the private automobile which would effectively abolish distance and allow for a new community based on self-reliance and individualism (Le Gates and Stout 1996: 335). His vision, though, was never realized very successfully; instead what happened across the West was the persistence of compact core cities surrounded by urban sprawl where reliance on private transport created new forms dependency and privatized suburban family life, with all the problems that entailed – for women particularly (Watson 1988). Ebenezer Howard, with his idea of the garden city, probably had the greatest influence in Britain, though his ideas also took a material form in Australia and several other countries. This was a city form constituted by an anti-urban nostalgia for a rural idyll where the problems of the large metropolis were to be solved by building a number of small garden cities. These were economically independent, cooperatively owned, and surrounded by green belts to ensure their autonomy rather than a satellite relation to the city. Letchworth and Welwyn in Britain are two such experiments.

The comprehensive, rational, modernist plan Corbusier-style has played a dominant role in the planning imaginary of first Western cities, and subsequently colonized or Commonwealth countries to which it was imported, often by graduates from British planning schools. Embedded in these plans was an imagination of cities as ordered, well-functioning, streamlined spaces, where different land uses were clearly demarcated and separated out, and conflict between these was avoided. Underlying the modernist project were several assumptions: an ideology of progress and some notion of the better good, the notion that cities could be made better without necessarily changing the prevailing political economy, the idea that outcomes can be knowable in advance and that order and rationality were better than chaos and irrationality. Quotidian, messy, ordinary life was homogenized and regulated through these master plans where difference was denied and gendered assumptions prevailed. Its worst effects can be seen in the construction of huge monolithic housing estates in Britain, the USA, and Eastern Europe, some of which became such alienated, unpopular, and dangerous places, that the local authorities were forced to blow them up (famously, Pruitt Igoe in St. Louis, US, and Ronan Point in Britain).

In recent years there have been extensive critiques of modernist planning (Mabin chapter 46) as too homogenizing, insensitive to difference, and functionalist. Feminists and poststructuralists (see Hillier 1993; Watson and Gibson 1995) have criticized the inherent lack of recognition of cultural, racial, or gendered/sexed differences and embodiment, its masculinist assumptions, and the construction of universal principles which ignore the specificity and micropolitics of power/knowledge relations. They have stressed also the ways in which universal principles are imbued with normative social relations. In an earlier book Patsy Healey (1997) has attempted to construct a new kind of planning theory which addresses some of these issues which she defines as argumentative, communicative, or interpretive. Its key elements (pp. 29–30) are a recognition of the social construction of all forms of knowledge, its recognition of different forms of reasoning and communication, and of the diversity of interests and power relations in contemporary life. This is to be combined with a realization of the need to spread the ownership of public policies directed towards managing coexistence in shared spaces, and a recognition that this leads toward collaborative consensus-building practices and away from competitive interest bargaining. Here (chapter 43) Healey argues for a new planning imagination which recognizes the multiple relational webs transecting cities and which emphasizes that "making places" is not about technical rational solutions. Rather, it is about a strategic imagination, which addresses the specific attributes, which make a place matter to the different stakeholders of the city.

If we are to recognize that cities are complex and heterogeneous, and as such potentially fluid, productive, and enabling, then urban policies which address complexity rather than aim toward some kind of standardized rational solution could be the most useful. Comprehensive rational planning, embodied in the notion of the master plan can be critiqued on these grounds. These ideas connect with Sennett's earlier (1970) work on the uses of disorder. Sennett rails against the suburban neighborhood, socially homogeneous and enclosed. Such environments encourage the persistence of the myth of a purified community of neighborliness and security (although divisions may lurk under the surface). It also perpetuates a form of parochialism based on a naive childlike psychology about other communities in other areas that helps to hold together the internal community myth. Sennett argues that the only way to break down these purified notions, the only way to develop full maturity is to encounter other groups and situations. This happens in the inner city with its mixed communities in a form of politics of encounter. Indeed Sennett proposes a radical withdrawal of municipal support structures (bureaucracy, overall metropolitan planning, policing of local disputes) to heighten the encounter between and within groups. These anarchic survival communities avoid the isolation of their suburban counterparts. However this is a politics of encounter that is bought at the expense of any civic responsibility.

The imagined city in practice needs to be one where power is recognized, negotiated and shared and where frameworks are put in place to enable this. Such an imagination and its resultant practices are a long way from the notion of a solution imposed from above by those with knowledge, expertise, and power. Contemporary cities as we have seen are not homogeneous spaces that are readily amenable to planning solutions imposed from above. As cities are increasingly embedded in a complexity of networks and spaces of flows, where many of the assets of the cities are not fixed or even visible in the built environment, new planning imaginations become all the more urgent.

Division and Difference

Difference and diversity are crucially linked with polarization and divisions. In this sense difference implies a hierarchy of power by which some people are excluded and marginalized and others are not. But difference might also be constructed in a more positive vein. Individuals of different genders, age, race, ethnicity, sexuality, and so on, will usually value their specificity and not necessarily want to be subsumed under some homogenized notion of community for which certain urban policies, for example urban regeneration policies, are devised. The question then becomes both how, and what, are the crucial factors which marginalize and exclude a group or individual on the one hand, or empower them on the other. Urban policies can then be developed to address the underlying issues of exclusion and marginalization.

We have seen in Part III of this volume that cities are increasingly complex and complicated places where simple divisions, core and periphery, rich and poor, Blacks and Whites, and so on, tell only part of the story. What is important therefore in urban policy is to analyze these differences to see where they are productive and where they simply represent concentrations of disadvantage. What is also important is to recognize that economic, social, and cultural differences are persistent, and if notions of community and social justice are to be rethought and maintained in some form, then the tensions will need to be addressed. This means seeing individuals on their own, or individuals within households and communities as differently placed in terms of access to resources and opportunities depending on a range of crosscutting and interrelated factors such as race, age, gender, and social networks (Bridge 1994, 1997). It also means taking on the symbolic exclusions in city spaces that Sibley (1995) discusses as well as the more material and graphic exclusions of the gated suburbs in Mike Davis's Los Angeles (1990).

It could be argued that urban policy has played a crucial role itself in constructing difference. Feminist analysts have pointed out that cities have been structured around the patriarchal family and have been imbued with gendered assumptions (see McDowell 1983; Watson 1986, 1988). The separation of home from work implicit in many urban planning and policy initiatives has been based on the presumed unpaid labor of women maintaining domestic life and childcare and has further served to marginalize women in the suburbs. Housing policies in many countries have also assumed the traditional family both in terms of design and allocation, while transport systems are frequently organized around the male worker going from the suburb to the center of the city for work. In Tokyo the huge commuter times have led to the phenomenon of the fatherless home (as opposed to the single-parent family), where men live in the city center during the week and return to the suburbs for the weekend even though ostensibly they are commuting within one metropolitan area. But gendered patterns are becoming more complex and difficult to read. Bondi and Christie (chapter 25) highlight the fragmented and contradictory experiences of gender within post-Fordist relations where there is a growing social polarization in cities between women on class, income, and employment grounds where some women have experienced striking economic success while others have become increasingly poor and marginalized.

Discourses of race have also constructed, and been embedded in, urban policy. As Allan Cochrane argues (chapter 44), "race" has underpinned much British urban policy, though frequently as an unspoken presence. In Britain and the US race has been key to a discourse of the inner-city crisis or the problem of the ghetto from the 1960s particularly. The management of areas designated as dangerous has also effectively involved a racialization of those spaces and legitimated intervention by urban policymakers, social workers, and the police. Mike Davis (1990) provides some extreme illustrations of such police activity in the context of Los Angeles. Race has been a crucial element in urban policies in non-Western countries also, sometimes in a benign form, but more often urban policies have reinforced existing divisions. Alison Todes (chapter 52) shows how current South African urban policy is founded on intentions to reintegrate cities, though this has already been critiqued as yet another oppressive form of urban ordering based on a technocratic discourse as the solution (Robinson 1996). While in the context of Israel Oren Yiftachel (1995) has suggested that planning tools have often been used as a means of controlling and repressing minority groups.

Social-spatial divisions are most clearly mapped on the employment/unemployment axis. The single most determinant cause of poverty is unemployment from which other conditions such as homelessness, ill health, and crime can arise. In order to combat unemployment governments have deployed a whole range of national and regional strategies. Urban policy initiatives of this kind include local employment and economic development initiatives that can be variously successful. One of the problems with local area-based policies is that statistics of regional unemployment mask differences between and within households. Thus within one spatial community where unemployment is high the impact is strongly differentiated. For example, Pahl's (1984) study in the Isle of Sheppey nearly two decades ago illustrated the different resource-gathering abilities of different household members and their access to the self-provisioning of goods and services through informal sectors. Skill levels, local knowledges and contacts all have an effect. In many countries access to income and employment from the recycling of discarded goods can mean an escape from poverty and homelessness. Thus unemployment can mean different things to different people. Some individuals may be able to find other forms of income, while for others there is no such option. Unemployment is also crosscut by gender, race, and age, which makes it difficult to assess how different individuals within different households in areas of concentrated deprivation negotiate disadvantage.

Another terrain of social division in the city, which has been addressed by urban policy, is around gentrification. Smith (1996) sees the process of gentrification as an urban frontier, a frontier of capital and social division. The frontier of capital involves the movement of investment into hitherto devalorized neighborhoods, which leads to a social division as many working-class residents are displaced. An ideological scripting of the city through civic boosterism and notions of revitalization supports this process. This is a discourse that writes out the displaced poor. Smith argues that with the recession and degentrification in the late 1980s in the USA, this civic boosterism has been replaced by a neoconservative urban politics of the revanchist city. This is a politics of revenge where those most marginalized by the reconfigured community of money in the city (the poor and homeless) are scapegoated because of their visibility (e.g. with such policies as zero tolerance to beggars). In this sense difference is used as an ideological weapon. Policies to enable low-income residents to stay in gentrifying areas through the provision of various forms of secure low-rental social housing can maintain mixed neighborhoods. This happened, for example, in the inner cities of Australia in 1972–5 under Whitlam's progressive Department of Urban and Regional Development.

Social-spatial divisions have existed in extreme forms in cities like Johannesburg where apartheid separated whites from blacks. Many cities have similar versions. Here policies towards mixed developments of housing combined with a range of employment possibilities and services can form the basis of a more mixed local citizenry. Another terrain of division in cities which has provoked a whole gamut of urban policies across the world is the division between city centers and suburbs, edge cities, fringe developments, and squatter settlements. In many instances one area concentrates forms of privilege while othering the opposite space as impoverished, dangerous, uninteresting, or as wealthy and exciting. These homogeneous caricatures of city spaces invariably mask considerable complexity and difference.

Urban policies to address these spatial divisions have taken many forms. In some Western cities, attempts to contain the spread of cities and urban sprawl have included greenbelt policies, urban consolidation, land pricing strategies and planning regulations, as discussed by Patrick Troy (chapter 45) in the Australian context. Other policies have focused on decentralizing employment, infrastructure, and services to outer areas where disadvantage is concentrated. The provision of urban infrastructure and services is an issue of considerable urgency facing the megacities of Asia where the growth in areas like the Pearl River Delta has required rapid response to the needs of a fast-growing population.

Homelessness represents a further serious urban issue in many cities of the world, from the sidewalk dwellers of Bombay to the Pacific Islanders in Auckland. Again there are a range of possible urban policy approaches from the laissez faire inaction of neo-liberal city governments to a diversity of social/public housing initiatives from refuges and hostels to more permanent cooperative housing ventures. Urban policies will increasingly need to address the complexities of difference and forms of marginalization if cities are to be places where difference can be celebrated and enjoyed rather than forming the basis of exclusion.

Economy

The relationship between economic change and urban policy shows great differences across the globe. There are, however, a number of recurring themes that can be identified and these relate to conceptions of the public and the private and the scope of urban democracy. Here the connections between city economies and city publics and their relations to urban policy and politics are dealt with together.

As a general trend there has been a move from assumptions that the market should be regulated by policy to neoliberal arguments that unregulated markets are most beneficial. In the early days of industrial capitalism the market was seen as a source of growth and disorder. Adverse work conditions and social inequalities were most evident in the rapidly growing cities. The point of urban policy was to compensate for the inequalities caused by capitalist urbanization through the provision of welfare and infrastructure. From 1945 to the mid-1970s in the West this policy intervention in markets reached its high tide mark as government policy itself was seen as a form of macroeconomic regulation. In the Keynesian economy spending on public works was a way of overcoming the underconsumption and unemployment that came with slumps in the economy. Cities had a particular role in this. Their size and density of population represented a concentration of public works. In some cases city governments sought a direct role in regulating economic activity (such as the Economic Development Plan of the former Greater London Council in the 1980s).

City governments were more typically responsible for the provision of bundles of collective-consumption goods – the defining characteristic of the urban in the late 1970s according to Manuel Castells (Castells 1977). In an earlier phase of urbanization this activity had been seen in the great municipal revolutions providing basics such as street lighting and drainage through to libraries and public parks. This tradition was sustained in Western cities until the 1970s. Urban policy coped with collective demand for goods and services not provided by the market and attempted to deal with the excesses of market processes in the form of urban deprivation and division (see Cochrane, chapter 44). From an Australian perspective Patrick Troy (chapter 45) describes in detail the major elements of this state-led urban policy of compensation for market disorder. It involved the rational planning of infrastructure and the provision of services (housing, health, and education) to compensate for the depredations of the market.

World recession in the 1970s and the rise of supply-side economics resulted in the collapse of the Keynesian consensus and resulted in deregulation of markets and a different role for policy, particularly urban policy. From a conceptualization of the market economy as a source of disorder and damage, as well as growth, policy moved to regard the market as a solution to urban deprivation and social division. Rather than producing disorder the market was seen as a source of order, a mechanism for settling things in the most efficient way. The state on the other hand became the explanation for deprivation in new-right pronouncements, since it constrained the operation of free markets and therefore prosperity and encouraged sustained deprivation through welfare dependency (Murray 1994).

The neoliberal hegemony had a profound effect on urban policy. It meant the shift from a concern with the politics of consumption to one with the politics of production (analyzed by Alan Harding, chapter 48). The point of urban policy was to facilitate the operation of the market. There was a range of measures to attract new business to the city, from tax holidays and rent concessions on urban land through to a proliferation of place marketing techniques to catch the eye of would-be investors. The historic and recreational character of cities also became assets in the competition between cities for inward investment. The London Docklands development,

Battery Park City in New York, and Darling Harbor in Sydney are prime examples of this type of urban development. These broad shifts David Harvey characterized some time ago (Harvey 1989) as the transition from urban managerialism to urban entrepreneurialism.

At the same time as city governments were looking to attract capital investment their welfare functions were cut back. Urban services were increasingly privatized. Activities such as street cleaning and refuse collection were put out to private companies with the city government acting as a purchaser rather than provider of services. Privatization of public transport and state housing has occurred in many countries (although there are of course exceptions, such as Sweden and the Netherlands).

Whereas privatization of infrastructure has been a conscious policy shift in Western countries, in many non-Western cities the need to keep pace with demand and limited government resources means that the private sector has long been involved in certain service markets. For example private transport services became increasingly important in many African cities in the 1980s and 1990s as large public transport companies suffered in recession. Private minibus services, such as the dala-dalas of Dar Es Salaam and cent-cent in Brazzaville, became increasingly important for low-income groups. Nevertheless the primacy given to the private car in both Western and non-Western cities accounts for the logjam traffic conditions, loss of public space, and continued urban sprawl.

This privatization has extended to urban government itself. City government in the US has long been a coalition with private entrepreneurs, companies, and other powerful agents with a vested interest in the city. This model is increasingly true of other cities in the West as they become concerned with the politics of production. Urban growth coalitions and urban regimes increasingly account for urban policy in Western cities. Policy gets made and is implemented through public–private partnerships in which lines of accountability to the ordinary city dweller are not clearly drawn. They exist under the more nebulous term "urban governance," rather than government. There are democratizing tendencies in some cities. Many cities of continental Europe have had strong urban governments that have given them some independence and distinctiveness (e.g. communist or Red Bologna) and there is a move to follow the American model of strong mayors in English cities. Questions are raised here as to whether cities are the appropriate scale for participatory democracy such as discussions over city democracy and networks of cities in the European Union and the return to pan-city government in London. Nevertheless the degree to which these changes are supportive of democracy or urban economic boosterism remains an open question. It is noticeable that many of these changes to urban policy and government bear more resemblance to the premunicipal era in the early phase of capitalist urbanization.

Although characterized more by diversity than similarity non-Western cities do show parallels with the developments of urban policy in Western cities. In fact it is more and more the other way round as in certain characteristics Western cities come to resemble those of non-Western ones.

The deregulated city has been a long-standing characteristic of many non-Western cities. Untrammelled markets are undoubtedly a feature of the rapidly growing cities of East and Southeast Asian cities (at least until the economic crash of the late

1990s). Here urban interventions are about coping with the speed of growth and the necessity for housing and urban infrastructure. In order to keep pace with growth a whole range of policy mixes including private and public provision are pursued. In Singapore, as Chua Beng-Huat points out (chapter 51), the accommodation crisis has resulted in universal public provision of housing in order to support the demands of economic growth. In Beijing 92 percent, and in Hong Kong over 50 percent, of the population lives in public housing (reported in Habitat 1996). Many cities in Latin America, Africa, and South Asia had public housing programs from the 1950s to 1980s but shortage of funds meant that demand for dwellings could not be met. This resulted in an absence of accommodation or insecure shelter of very poor standard (there are over 1 billion people in these circumstances worldwide). Land supply problems also add to the difficulties that city governments have when it comes to housing. Much of the land is in private ownership and cannot be purchased by the state. In many countries building materials have to be imported thus adding to costs (more than 40 percent of the value of residential development in Accra and Dakar, for instance).

The response to the lack of state provisioning has been self-provisioning of accommodation, squatting on land and using any available local materials. In the face of exclusion from the public realm and from adequate support for local economic activity and forms of accommodation various forms of self-provisioning and grass-roots political organization sprang up. Diverse urban social movements represent significant forces for change in non-Western cities. Although such social movements are generally targeted at specific issues it is clear that many of them have had significant impacts on urban governance. Especially important are women's movements – such as those for political participation in Guadalajara, Mexico; neighborhood handicraft associations in Santiago, Chile; and struggles for health-care in São Paulo, Brazil (Habitat 1996: 168). These are political activities on the ground and in the barrios – often a million miles away from the concerns of their city governments and super-rich elites who look to international markets. Unlike the city and the grass roots of Castells' work this is the city separate from the grass roots. Public policy and public interests are often poles apart.

The growing importance of feminist movements in all their diversity in the cities of the world has been noted by Castells (1997, ch. 4). These movements are looking for practical improvements in the lives of city-dwellers but are also trying to redefine the public in noninstitutional, more radically open ways. In this they might confront more systematic forces of the state but their very openness – and the common themes of many of the issues they are concerned with – have implications and connections beyond the cities they are concerned with to other cities and groups. These forces (both progressive and regressive) are likely to become more prevalent in a more interconnected world. Social movements constitute the other side of globalization and offer the potential for a reconstituted public realm.

Self-provisioning has also taken on a discursive force in Western cities. Policy discussions of social capital (see Amin, chapter 11) hinge on the capacity of networks of disadvantaged individuals to become productive. Voluntary sector and grass roots organizations figure highly in policy manifestos for the social economy and the "third way" (between state socialism and free markets). There is also growing evidence of grass-roots self-provisioning in the form of credit unions in poor districts, local exchange trading systems (LETS) and the like. Whether valuable or not these community-based arguments bring the policy discourse about Western and non-Western cities closer together.

The wider forces of globalization beyond the cities are the context and the discipline for the formulation of urban policy – as are others. Swyngedouw and Kaika (chapter 47) develop the arguments on the city as natural (as in "nature-full") as well as a social and economic phenomenon. They critique the separation of nature and society – the city that was so prevalent in urban planning. Now planning and policy interventions are not simply local in provenance. Politics of the sustainable city tie urban policy decisions into wider biocultural processes and longer time horizons.

Environmental issues point up the differences between Western and non-Western policies over sustainability. In many non-Western cities sustainability is a matter of life and death and environmental problems are not just global but household issues (such as clean water and sanitation). Generally lower levels of consumption and sustainable practices, such as recycling, are already in place out of necessity. Tens of thousands of wastepickers scratch a living recycling rubbish in cities such as Manila. Environmental damage from pollution is a pressing concern for Western and non-Western cities alike. In Mexico City for example 11.2 million workdays a year are lost because of the bad health effects of pollution. Some measures for sustainable development are being attempted at the city level through the Agenda 21 program that came out of the 1992 Rio Earth Summit (now actively pursued by 1,200 local authorities in 33 countries – World Resources Institute 1996). In Western cities by contrast sustainability is concerned with the consequences of overconsumption.

The economies of many non-Western cities are divided between local production and consumption and global markets and the more "formal" economic sectors. For many this is a colonial legacy and one that is perpetuated in the neocolonial debt relations to which many countries of the south are subject. International financial organizations such as the IMF and the World Bank impose constraints on economies that essentially support the free market principle. This makes for sharp differences between the commercial globally oriented economic activity and local economic provisioning. Cities are divided between areas of affluence and extreme poverty. Although not as pronounced, the "move to the market" in Western cities has resulted in sharper contrasts of poverty and wealth and the divisions between cities and within particular cities between global and local activities (emphasized by Sassen, chapter 15).

Cities encompass different economies. The global/local split divides the attention of urban governments. Like their Western counterparts city authorities must get involved in place marketing for foreign business and tourist dollars, often at the expense of the needs of the local economy and the local population. The local state is often involved in ridding parts of cities of local enterprise and self-provisioning to create enclaves conducive for "global" activities. As Alison Todes (chapter 52) relates in the South African context this is a process of making cities safe for capital. The clearing of the street boys in Yogyakarta (Beazley, chapter 40) through to the revanchist politics of clearing out the homeless to ease the gentrification of the Lower East Side of New York City (Smith 1996) show the global nature of this form of city politics.

Making cities safe for capital results in the commercialization and commodification of urban space and this has impacts on the notion of the public and public space. The clearing of street markets and the homeless and their replacement with patrolled and protected tourist malls and business districts marks the "death of public space" in non-Western cities. In this sense many non-Western city governments are every bit as involved in creating suitable consumption landscapes for their middle classes and tourist markets. It also reveals the tendency for a local/global split in the public realm with formal institutions lacking the will, finances, or probity to truly represent their urban constituents.

All these issues raise questions about the nature of the public and the policymaking realm in contemporary urbanism. Any answer to Ray Pahl's original question "Whose city?" (1975) would now have to move beyond institutions of the elected state to take in the privatization of urban policymaking to include business and other nonelected interests. The purposes of urban policy have moved away from social-democratic notions of redistribution to the support of private capital investment. Widespread corruption and nepotism also make access to public institutions and public representation a problem in many cities.

In cases where there are interventions the worry is that they are based on outdated modernist and colonial solutions. Thus Alan Mabin writes of the sclerotic influence of the legacy of modernist planning and Alison Todes points to the inappropriateness of rational separation of land use and urban consolidation in Durban – separating out and disconnecting as it does the webs of indigenous economic networks and commercial strategies. What in a Western setting might be regarded as externalities to be countered by separation of different land uses, might well be necessary connections and an essential juxtaposition of the economy and the domestic sphere, and the public and the private in many non-Western cities. The reaction to modernist rationalism and the rigidities of planning are being felt particularly strongly in many rapidly developing cities as they present a set of kaleidoscopic conditions of formal/informal undocumented economic activity. Interestingly feminists have made similar arguments about the lack of flexibility in Western cities.

Again of course there are countervailing influences. In the years between the publication of the first and second UN reports on human settlements (1986–96) 30 countries moved to democratic political procedures. In many countries local governments have been made more responsible for urban affairs. This decentralization of responsibility is seen by some, such as Castells (1997), as a bid by national governments to avoid a crisis of legitimacy by pushing the blame for poor urban services down to the local level. For others (such as Habitat) there is a suggestion that structural adjustment programs force the hands of national governments to cut services. But they also suggest empowering possibilities through links between stronger local state and grass-roots organizations.

In conclusion, political and policy interventions in the urban arena have to face greater and greater complexities. No one policy is likely to be the solution for every city in the world, since policies need to be sensitive to the specificity of place and the global/local interconnections within which a city is situated. Following Healey, it is also important to stress the need for local communities – however these are defined – to be involved in the decisions that are going to affect their lives on a daily basis if exclusions and marginalities are to be addressed. Any urban intervention will produce conflicting outcomes and no one solution will suit all groups. Recognizing this, and refusing the idea that universal solutions are possible, means building into the processes of governance and government spaces for contestation and disagreement, so that politics can remain in play in the policy process rather than being cast to the sidelines in the drive for entrepreneurial advantage in the competitive market for cities.

REFERENCES

Boyer, M. C. 1983: *Dreaming the Rational City*. Princeton: MIT Press.

Bridge, G. 1994: Gentrification, class and residence: a reappraisal. *Environment and Planning D: Society and Space*, 12, 31–51.

Bridge, G. 1997: Mapping the terrain of time-space compression: power networks in everyday life. *Environment and Planning D: Society and Space*, 15, 611–26.

Castells, M. 1977: *The Urban Question*. London: Edward Arnold.

Castells, M. 1997: *The Information Age: Economy, Society and Culture*, vol. 2: *The Power of Identity*. Oxford: Blackwell.

Davis, M. 1990: *City of Quartz: Excavating the Future in Los Angeles*. London: Verso.

Habitat – United Nations Centre for Human Settlements 1996. *An Urbanizing World: Global Report on Human Settlements 1996*. Oxford: Oxford University Press.

Hall, P. 1988: *Cities of Tomorrow*. Oxford: Blackwell.

Harvey, D. 1989: From managerialism to entrepreneurialism: the transformation in urban governance in late capitalism. *Geografiska Annaler*, 71B, 3–17.

Healey, P. 1997: *Collaborative Planning: Shaping Places in Fragmented Societies*. London: Macmillan.

Hillier, J. 1993: To boldly go where no planners have ever... *Environment and Planning D: Society and Space*, 11, 89–113.

Le Gates, R. and Stout, F. (eds.) 1996: *The City Reader*. London: Routledge.

McDowell, L. 1983: Towards an understanding of the gender division of urban space. *Environment and Planning D: Society and Space*, 1, 59–72.

Murray, C. 1994: *Underclass: The Crisis Deepens*. Charles Murray with commentaries by Pete Alcock et al. London: IEA Health and Welfare Unit.

Pahl, R. 1975: *Whose City?* Harmondsworth: Penguin.

Pahl, R. 1984: *Divisions of Labour*. Oxford: Blackwell.

Robinson, J. 1996: *The Power of Apartheid: State Power and Space in South African Cities*. Oxford: Butterworth Heinemann.

Sennett, R. 1970: *The Uses of Disorder*. Harmondsworth: Penguin.

Sibley, D. 1995: *Geographies of Exclusion: Society and Difference in the West*. London: Routledge.

Smith, N. 1996: *The New Urban Frontier: Gentrification and the Revanchist City*. London: Routledge.

Watson, S. 1986: *Housing and Homelessness: A Feminist Perspective*. London: Routledge.

Watson, S. 1988: *Accommodating Inequality*. Sydney: Allen and Unwin.

Watson, S. and Gibson, K. (eds.) 1995: *Postmodern Cities and Spaces*. Oxford: Blackwell.

World Resources Institute 1996: *World Resources Report*. Washington, DC.

Yiftachel, O. 1995: The dark side of modernism: planning as control of an ethnic minority. In S. Watson and K. Gibson (eds.), *Postmodern Cities and Spaces*. Oxford: Blackwell, 216–42.

Chapter 43

Planning in Relational Space and Time: Responding to New Urban Realities

Patsy Healey

Urbanists and planners often tell a familiar story about cities in the modern age, to account for the rise of the twentieth-century planning idea. The appearance of big urban agglomerations, whether through the industrialization of nineteenth-century Western cities, or the explosive development of the cities of the developing world in the second part of the twentieth-century, generates images of chaotic disorder, characterized by appalling living conditions and damaging social, environmental, and economic conditions. The challenge for urban governance was to sort all this out, and produce a harmonious "order," smoothing out conflicts, and creating a framework for improved quality of life, business efficiency and conserving environmental assets. The "planning idea" seemed to provide the answer (Boyer 1983; Ward 1994). Planners brought to this task a conceptual equipment which mixed a designer's imagination with a regional geographer's conception of integrated spatial orders based on analyses of prevailing European settlement patterns of the early twentieth-century. Cities were relationally self-contained, pivoting around the city center, and spreading out across a rural region for which they acted as key markets and sites for relations with the outside world. Land uses in the city were to be separated, to reduce adverse impacts on each other. They were ordered hierarchically in terms of land value, in relation to access to the key location, the city center. Relations with the "outside world" were conducted through the industries which provided the "driver" for this integrated urban system (McLoughlin 1969; Forrester 1969) (see Figure 43.1).

These days, so the story goes, the conception of the self-contained, internally integrated, "uniplex" city is no longer believable, in a world of multiplex and globalized relationships. Cities are referred to as fragmented, in bits and pieces, divided, disorganized, chaotic (Mitchell 1995; Byrne 1996; Davis 1990). Urban governance capacity, once assumed to be located in the municipal office, has now been "distributed," undermined by competition with other sources of power (King and Stoker 1996). Municipalities and their planners have little leverage over the flow of events through which the sociospatial relations of cities are actively being constructed. The planning practices of the "ordering impetus" have become

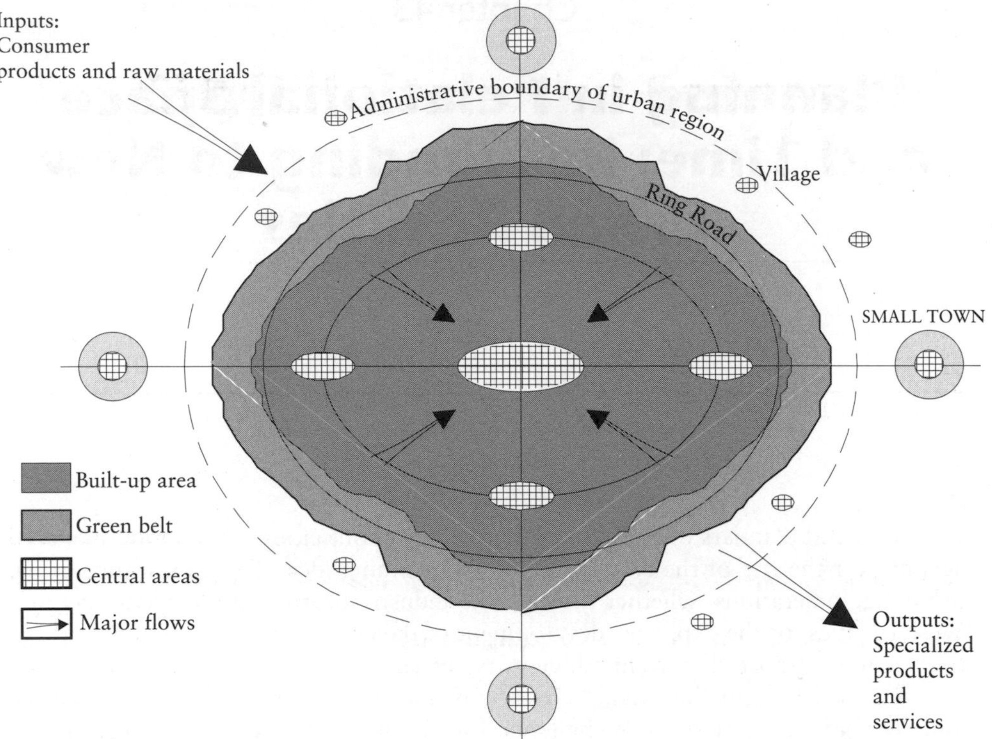

Figure 43.1 The "uniplex city"

part of the problem. Embedded in routine governance practices, planning has been criticized by analysts as class-driven, dominatory, the mode of action of a rationalizing social ordering project (Castells 1977; Boyer 1983; Yiftachel 1998). The planning idea, in one ending to this story, is a relic of the "command and control" welfare state, and of the modernist conceptual equipment of positivist science and utilitarian rationalism which went with it (Dear 1995). The analytical task is then to research urban governance practices, and "excavate" and critique these old ideas as they live on in governance routines (Huxley 1994; Healey 1999; Vigar et al. 2000).

Yet this ending does not seem to fit with another observable reality, the expanding public and political concern, with the quality and "sustainability" of urban conditions. Most people in the world now live in cities. Many of them take what opportunities become available to assert their concerns in public arenas. In some countries, and notably in Britain, the apparatus of planning systems has become a key institutional site for an increasingly complex dialectics of environmental contestation (Grove-White 1991; Owens 1997). The neoliberal strategy (as developed in, for example, Britain and New Zealand) is to seek to transform planning systems into quasi-market regulatory mechanisms for dealing with conflict mediation over complex spatially manifest environmental disputes (Healey 1998; Gleeson and

Grundy 1997). But this strategy fails to attend to the multiplicity of relationships which transect places and the complex ways they intersect in the assertion of place qualities. In particular, it "splits up" into separate issues people's daily life experiences and their sense of the qualities of particular places. Rejecting planners' conceptions of self-contained, integrated sociospatial systems, it assumes that the spatiality of relations and the meanings of places are unimportant dimensions in cities. It ignores the role of the assertion of "place identity" in counteracting the sense of explosive expansion and fragmentation of the relations which used to bind people and firms together in internally integrated urban systems. Places, to the exent that they are of any relevance to contemporary life, are in this conception made and unmade by the forces of market relations.

Such an approach privileges economic and material dimensions of existence over cultural, environmental, and political ones. But this is not the only story line for cities. There is another, arising from cultural studies, the "new" institutionalism, and the environmental movement, which emphasizes the importance of a politics of place-making. This other story line explicitly recognizes the multiple relationships which transect the space–time of cities and locales within them, a politics and governance practice which seeks to shape these relationships in order to cultivate their interrelationships, reduce the harm they cause to each other and actively shape place identities. Is there a new "planning imagination" which can be harnessed to this task, to help generate new practices and refurbish old ones?

In this chapter, I argue that there is such an emerging imagination. It is based in an explicit recognition of the multiple relational webs which transect cities, each with their own time horizons and spatial reach, each "creating," through their conceptions and activities, an imagined city and a socially and physically concrete one. It emphasizes that "making places" is achieved not by the imposition of a technical order by the state, but by the active social construction of place-focused frameworks and through efforts to cultivate a strategic imagination through which key attributes of a "place" can become identified and "owned" by the many stakeholders in the "place" of a city. In this way, "permanences" are created in the dynamic relational dialectics of urban life (Harvey 1996).

The planning idea emerges, in this story, as a form of governance, which is open, driven by inclusionary perspectives on what makes for human flourishing in the urban context, rather than the generalized ideologies of politicians or the self-interest of elites (Healey 1997; Sandercock 1998). Such a planning focuses on developing the qualities of "habitus," the places of daily life, of commercial endeavor, of social exchange, and the public realm. It involves asserting the qualities of places, to be promoted and maintained, against forces pushing in different directions. It involves practices which develop strategies, shape investment programs and frame regulatory judgments in open, visible forms, confronting the forces encouraging behind-the-scenes manipulation and subversion of publicly agreed policy directions. If successful in the struggle for power with competing governance forms, this kind of planning has the capacity to develop sufficient discursive strength to generate the political leverage to assert a broadly shared and "multiplex" "place identity." It then has the capacity to shape market opportunities and influence sociocultural evolutions.

Facing the Challenge of Multiplex Systems: Into the Finegrain of Practice[1]

I return to this normative planning idea at the end of the chapter. Some have argued that it is an ideal without any roots in contemporary planning practices from which it could grow and develop (Tewdwr-Jones and Allmendinger 1998). Certainly British planning practice has been heavily molded in recent years by neoliberal influences (Thornley 1991; Healey 1998). However, policy systems and practices are not static, but are pushed and pulled to respond to different situations. In this section, I illustrate such evolutions through an examination of two areas of English planning practice. Both cases are from the English context, with its distinctive governance and legal context for planning systems and their practices (CEC 1997). One shows the work of regulatory permitting, focusing on the negotiation of developers' contributions to ameliorating adverse impacts ("development control" and "planning gain/planning obligations" in British planning jargon). The other is of strategic spatial planmaking (the "structure plan" level of "development plans" in the British context). In both cases, models of integrated urban systems, with their two-dimensional "Euclidean" space and linear time, have decayed, to be replaced by conceptions of complex, open relations emerging in new discourses about impacts and about strategy. But these new ideas are developing hesitantly, without a coherent conceptual imagination and discourse to drive across the practice landscape. This creates a conceptual vacuum into which a despatialized neoliberal policy discourse has established itself. The dialectical struggle is now not merely between "uniplex" versus "multiplex" conceptions of urban sociospatial relations. It is overlain by another struggle between "place-blind" and "people-diminishing" urban policy versus "place-aware" and "people-sensitive" approaches.

The impacts of development projects

Many webs of relations are affected by development projects. These could potentially encompass the networks of, and relations between, landowners, developers, financiers, endusers, various third parties, different sectors of central and local government, local politics, national politics, pressure groups of all kinds. Some planning systems attempt to define the universe of potential impacts in advance and convert these into rules to apply to any development project that comes along. The British planning system, characterized by the exercise of administrative-political judgment in determining whether a permit should be given, in contrast provides a flexible formal structure in which new ideas about what impacts can emerge (Davies et al. 1989; Booth 1996; CEC 1997). The system structures the making of judgments so that planning officers pay attention to national statements of planning policy, local statements (primarily embodied in the "development plan"), and other considerations specific to the case (Cullingworth and Nadin 1994; Tewdwr-Jones 1997). Most discussion of the impacts of development traditionally focused on the qualities of the site, or on local impacts, and, in particular, on adjacent impacts. The primary concern was to "fit" a new project into the existing "jigsaw" landscape of buildings and open spaces and deal with the additional loads on infrastructure caused by a development (see Figure 43.2). Wider impacts were assumed to be addressed by the policy framework. The "development plan" was supposed to specify broadly the amounts of development which might be expected in an area, the general locations where such development might happen, and the time periods over which development might take place. But when a project actually arrives for the regulatory judgment, it comes with a whole nexus of potential relations of its own, which affect its viability and political acceptability. As it "lands" on a particular site at a particular time, it has impacts along all kinds of relations in which the site and the project have significance.

Until the 1980s, the implicit urban model used in assessing development impacts was the hierarchically integrated "uniplex" city. The land use pattern was taken as a proxy for the social processes. The relations of the activities were assumed to be structured by propinquity and utilitarian rationality. The city was presented as a kind of "jigsaw," the separate pieces making up a hierarchically ordered pattern. People went to work in the nearest business. They shopped at the nearest foodstore. They went to the city center for their durable shopping and cultural recreation. They were assumed to care most about what happened nearest to them. The focus of the assessment of development impacts was on "neighborhood" effects, adjacent to the site in question. Propinquity was the dominant principle and "planning gain" negotiations focused on honing the development project so it fitted better into its "jigsaw" space. By the 1980s, however, the conception of impacts widened out. For example, a large residential development project might generate complex drainage problems, as development upstream could damage downstream water flows. Agreements might be negotiated for actions and financial contributions which linked the stage of the building process and the state of the housing market to phased

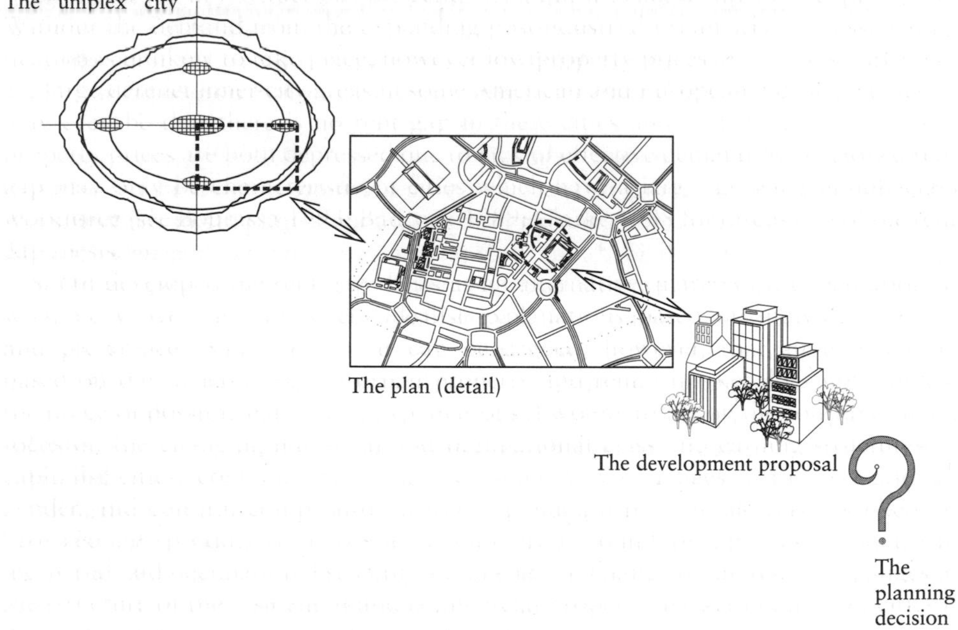

Figure 43.2 Fitting development projects into the "spatial jigsaw"

investment in a system of temporary and permanent balancing lakes and run-off channels across the drainage basin. In such a case, the flow dynamics of a hydrological system and the dynamic relations of a particular market supplement consideration of impacts were based on simple propinquity (Healey, Purdue, and Ennis 1995).

In some situations, local residents organize to demand some compensation for adverse impacts. This may lead to agreements not only for contributions to highway and drainage infrastructure, but to provision of schools and playing fields, recreational and amenity open space, and landscaping features. In one case, a developer of a project of 1,000 dwellings provided half a million pounds to a local parish council for recreational and community purposes. Here, propinquity gave special bargaining power to a particular and visible affected group.[2] This raises questions of legitimacy. Why do adjacent impacts get such consideration compared to more distant ones?

When disputes enter the legal arena, a more relational emphasis opens up, in the legal language of a "reasonable relationship" (Healey, Purdue, and Ennis 1995). In the division of labor between law and policy in the British planning system, it is left to planners to articulate what is a "reasonable" relationship. In principle, this allows the variable space–time linkages of a multiplex world to be brought into play. But these shifts are not underpinned by coherent conceptualizations. In the arenas of government policy, in local negotiations, in public inquiries, and the courts, planners struggle to articulate principles to govern the decisions they make. The pressures of local politics, and national pressure groups promoting conflicting objectives, are pushing them along. This privileges the circuitry of the vocal and powerful. Impacts on those without the power and resources to speak up, and on those distant in space and time, are neglected. This helps governance elites mediate conflicts in the short term. But many stakeholders and many relationships are not represented in these mediations. In a governance context where power is increasingly widely distributed, excluded considerations have a habit of popping up to disturb the apparent consensus and challenge the legitimacy of planning decisions and frameworks.

From development plans to local "visions"

Changing conceptualizations of space and time are more obvious in the arena of planmaking. British development plan practice in the second part of the twentieth-century may be crudely divided into three phases, reflecting the "master narrative" outlined above: the "blueprint" land use plans of the early postwar years, the strategic spatial plans grounded in conceptions of regional sociospatial systems, and the sectoralized policy plans of more recent years. The blueprint style arose in part from a conception that planners could control spatial change, rather than merely shape the flow of processes of change. The plan delineated what was to be built where, in five-year time periods, assuming that the complex relations of multiple development processes could be coordinated in a common time schedule. This managerial viewpoint was attached to a "uniplex" conception of the city, translated into a hierarchical spatial order. Activities and their relationships could be "read off" from the land use pattern. The classic British spatial plan associated with Patrick Abercrombie and others envisaged a city which combined the patterns of Isardian central place theory with the notions of self-contained *gemeinschaft* communities (Ravetz 1980; Hall et al. 1973).

This approach was heavily criticized in the 1960s for its failure to appreciate the dynamics of regional development. Drawing on a more sophisticated geography and ecology, and much influenced by Chapin (1965), British planning theorists sought to imagine the city in relational terms (e.g. McLoughlin 1969). The focus of attention shifted from spatial patterns per se, to the dynamics of the regional economic system and the urban communications system, both in terms of transport and information flows. Drawing heavily on economic base theory and the behavioral urban ecology of the Chicago sociologists, the ambition was to build dynamic "systems" models of the economic and social relations of settlements, and translate these into spatial patterns. Such models, it was hoped, would not only allow the exploration of alternative sociospatial scenarios (primarily to manage the relations between land needs for growth and infrastructure investment), they could also be used in regulatory practice, to allow the impacts of a development to be assessed by checking them out against the relational assumptions in the model, a kind of systematized environmental appraisal (Chapin 1965; McLoughlin 1969, 1973). These "systems models," which dominated the technical planning literature in Britain and the US in the late 1960s and early 1970s, underpinned early British attempts at producing the new kinds of "structure plan" introduced in the 1970s (Cowling and Steeley 1973). However, while more dynamic and relational than their predecessors, these models were still underpinned by hierarchically integrated, "uniplex," conceptions of the city.

A pioneering example in Britain was the South Hampshire Structure Plan (South Hampshire Structure Plan Advisory Committee 1972). This involved an elaborate exercise in modeling existing relationships, forecasting growth and then exploring different development location scenarios. The conceptions underlying the model were very simple: "Three activities and uses (i.e. land uses) are of particular strategic importance . . . – employment, homes and shopping" (para. 4.8, p. 19). Activities are seen to occur on sites connected by movement channels. Drawing on the classic Abercrombie tradition, the urban "structure" is set within a "rural framework" which provides resources of agriculture and recreation opportunities for the urban inhabitants (p. 21). This "largely self-contained city region" (para. 2.28, p. 10) is conceived in terms of a hierarchy of central places, but with a polynodal rather than a uninodal structure.

In the model, the dynamic of regional growth is perceived as largely internal to the area. External inputs are confined to migration flows from the rest of the South East Region. The language of analysis deals in aggregates rather than differentiated dynamics. There is no comment on the relational dynamics or locational preferences of the various firms which are "growing." The plan nevertheless presents a striking attempt to develop an overarching conception of the regional economy. The problem lies in its closure, and in the way it considers internal system relationships. It sets up the regional dynamics of the area as a closed system with internal feedback loops, on the lines of Forrester's conception of urban dynamics (Forrester 1969). This assumes equilibrium-seeking systems rather then evolutionary systems (Hwang 1996). It treats space as Euclidean and time as linear. In retrospect, the approach not only failed to identify the contingencies of the South Hampshire economy, which became obvious as recession and restructuring set in during the 1970s and 1980s. It also failed to consider the political, institutional, and resource context in which the regulation and promotion of development would take place. South Hampshire was treated as an "object" to which strategies were applied, rather than a dynamic mélange of social relations within which planning actions would be variously articulated and intertwined.

Despite serious economic difficulties in some sections of the regional economy, South Hampshire has continued to grow and the political problem of allocating sites for new development has become increasingly acute for both local and national politicians. By the 1990s, Hampshire County Council was locked in battles with central government over how much of the regional demand for housing in South East England as a whole would be accommodated in the county. Structure plan practice evolved in the 1980s to reflect the institutional context. The presentation of a spatial territory into which development would be fitted (the spatial "jigsaw") was replaced by an "institutional territory" in terms of which projects had to be legitimated (the institutional "jigsaw"). This recognized the power of agency in structuring space, but at the cost of losing the sense of space and place. The plan was no longer even a two-dimensional map. Instead, it became a record of sites and zones affected by particular policy considerations.

Hampshire County Council Structure Plan of 1994 was still concerned with accommodating growth and maintaining the discreteness of urban settlements. "A central theme of the Plan is to preserve the distinction between town and country as two different kinds of environment" (HCC 1994, para. 27, p. 10). "Strategic gaps" of landscape are to be retained between settlements, to sustain the illusion of self-contained settlements. Apart from these "inherited" spatial principles, the plan divides its material into a series of topics, each being discussed largely in isolation from the other. By 1996, however, a new concern with place and identity appears in the plan. The elements of the spatial order remain the same. However, "suburban development has tended to reduce local distinctiveness and sense of place in many parts of the County.... Community identity, a sense of place and belonging, which is part of this heritage, also needs to be defended" (HCC 1966, para. 21, p. 6).

The notion of community identity has political attractions in a county where the politics of the defense of place against further growth became acute in the 1990s. The 1996 Plan attempts a more coherent overview of the county as a place, using the marketing language of "vision" and the environmental language of "sustainability." The idea of a "Vision," borrowed from the business-marketing arena and from practices around urban regeneration projects, promotes the qualities of a place. It also potentially offers an "integrative conception" to bind the many, potentially conflicting parties, into a shared approach and/or program of actions (Neuman 1996; Healey et al. 1997; Stevenson 1998). But Hampshire's "Vision" is not developed into a reconception of the sociospatial dynamics of change in the subregion, nor is there any recognition of the multiplex times and places which are evolving in the county area. The topic chapters of the plan provide policy criteria, in the neoliberal mode, intended to be used in assessing actual development projects, at the point where the institutional and spatial "jigsaws" interact. This evolution of the Hampshire Structure Plans illustrates well how the uniplex strategic conception of the 1960s and 1970s decayed into a highly generalized conception of the "space" of the county, with the policy dynamic of the plan structured not by technical analyses of sociospatial dynamics, but by the politics of institutional interactions. In these interactions, multiplex space–time perspectives are consolidated through the voices

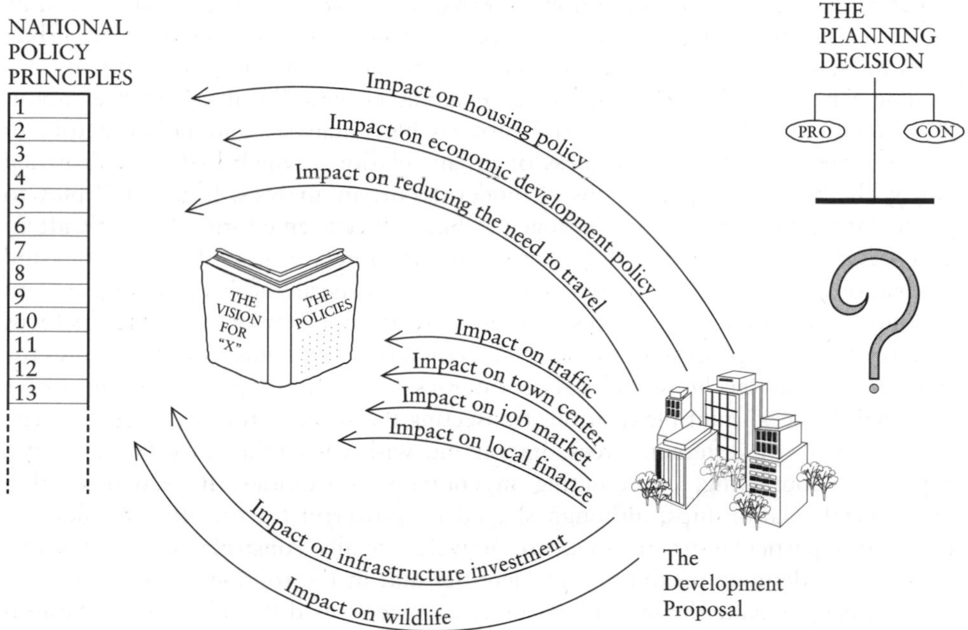

Figure 43.3 Fitting development projects into the "institutional jigsaw"

of powerful local players and the regulatory vocabulary of national planning policy (Tewdwr-Jones 1997; Healey 1998) (see Figure 43.3).

Reconceptualizing Planning in Relational Time and Space

In both these examples, simple models of sociospatial relations have been largely abandoned, though they live on in techniques (such as transport modeling and retail appraisal), in regulatory practices (the continued preoccupation with adjacent or site-based impacts), and in notions of "the local community" and its needs. But there is no coherent reconceptualization of the urban region in multiplex space and time. Instead, strands of understanding from contemporary urban and regional geography filter into analyses of economic issues, and ecosystemic ideas from the environmental sciences flow into policy with respect to the natural environment. Instead of being allowed to intertwine and develop innovatively, they are being forced into the straitjacket of despatialized policy criteria, which limit the relations which are considered and which ignore considerations of place identity. As a consequence, urban planning practice in Britain has become peculiarly unprepared for attention to the qualities of places.

Two evolutions are counteracting this narrowing of the thoughtworlds of English planning practice. The first focuses on developing a new "place imagination." The second emphasizes more inclusive practices for policy development and discussion, through which multiple perceptions can find voice and contribute to the active construction of new conceptions of "place identity."

The resources for new conceptions of urban dynamics and place qualities can be found in the exploding international social science literature on the city, urban economies, societies, environments, and governance – the subject matter of this volume. They can also be found in rich encounters with "local knowledge" about place relations.[3] The "postmodern" turn enabled analysts and policy actors to perceive the diversity and openness of urban relations, which had been drowned out by the holistic simplifications of modernist urban analysis. It gave full play to particularity, complexity, and contingency. But in its extreme forms, too little attention was given to relations and processes, and the interweaving of continuities and innovations in evolving urban dynamics. The new poststructuralist thinking, evident in many strands of analysis[4] takes a dynamic, relational view of urban life. Its focus is on relations and processes, not objects. It emphasizes dynamics not statics, and the complex interactions between local continuities and "social capital" and innovative potential. It "sees" multiple relations transecting the space of the city, each "driven" and "shaped" by different forces, interacting with each other in different ways, bypassing, conflicting, coordinating in complex trajectories. It recognizes that these social relationships, although shaped by powerful forces, often outside the space of a particular urban area, are actively socially constructed. In the social processes of defining meanings and identities and in the routine ways of living in the city, people make the multiplex times and places, its differentiations, cohesions and exclusions, and its power dynamics. The quality of the "places" of the urban lies in both the social resources – in the range and intersections of the relational resources available to people and firms, in the balance between security/stability and creative tension/innovation, in the capacity for collective development of "place quality" – and in the spatial manifestations of places: the key sites of public interaction, the symbolic reference points, the design of both "neighborhoods" and

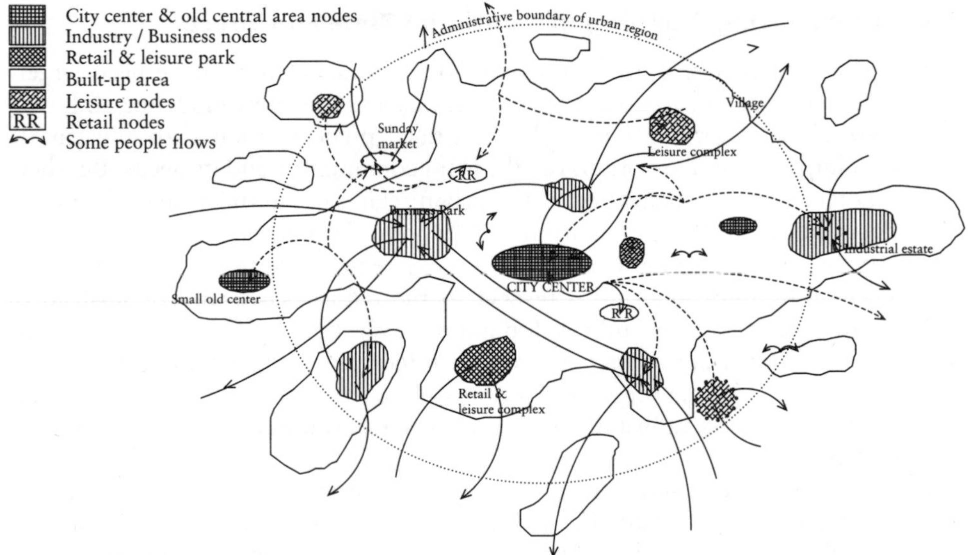

Figure 43.4 The "multiplex city"

"nodal areas" in the urban fabric (see Figure 43.4). The governance of "places" then has a key role in the development of these qualities, in the way governance processes intertwine with the complexity of intersecting relationships, helping to maintain and build meanings and relationships. Such governance can also help to "fix" and transmit place quality and identity in a multivocal context (see Sandercock 1998).[5]

This turns the spotlight on the quality of governance practices themselves. It is here that the alternative planning imagination outlined at the start of this chapter comes into play. It requires a governance dynamics and culture which encourages officials to move outside the city hall, to work interactively with the multiple relational webs which transect the urban. It involves combining formal analysis with "local knowledge" and popular imaginations, to identify the key qualities of places which people want to maintain, develop, enhance, and create. It draws on "conversations" between different relational worlds, through which some kind of shared ownership of strategies and regulatory and investment actions can develop, imbued with recognition of the inherent struggles, tensions, and conflicts which are manifest in any multivocal urban context. The developments within planning theory on communicative, collaborative planning processes provide rich resources for such a reconstruction of planning processes,[6] while the practice of partnership and "enabling governance" has generated an array of practical experience and "local knowledge" in many Western cities (see Douglass and Friedmann 1998).

But these practices also show that interactive governance and collaborative planning initiatives come in several forms. In some instances, such processes get hijacked as a way of reestablishing the hegemony of powerful groups. Specifically, they provide an opportunity for the reentry of local business elites into local governance in situations where they have been pushed aside by the ideological politics of the welfare state which set the "public" interest against "private" interests. This potential for takeover puts a premium on an inclusionary ethics, a commitment by those in governance positions to attend to the range of relations through which people and firms, in diverse ways, "inhabit" and give meaning to the urban. It demands that planners develop skills in facilitating encounters between different groups (Healey 1997) and bringing in voices currently on the margins of governance (Sandercock 1998). Such an inclusionary ethics needs to permeate the processes for building strategies and frameworks through which to promote particular place qualities. It needs to infuse not only the regulatory practices and investment programs through which material resources and opportunities are distributed, but also the way relational resources are developed. It needs to be grounded in broadly distributed rights to challenge governance actions on the grounds of inclusionary failures and in obligations to demonstrate inclusionary intentions (Healey 1997). Such an inclusionary ethics is not just needed to keep alive the idea of social justice in a world where the relations of injustice and domination are multiple and often invisible. They are also needed as a continual challenge to the embedding of a narrow and inflexible imagination as an inward-looking response to the dynamic dialectics of a multiplex world.

In many parts of the world, governance elites are trying to write new stories for their cities, to inscribe these stories in the identities of the key players upon whose actions the core relations of a city depend and to incorporate them into the practices of an urban governance which stretches beyond the town hall to a wide range of people involved in governance in one way or another.[7] The challenge for planners is to reconstruct their own ways of thinking and acting to provide creative resources for critiquing and facilitating this work of city story-writing. In this role, some of the evangelism of past generations of planners needs to be rediscovered. The planners of midcentury believed in their imagination for the city and what its values should be. This included a deep commitment to quality of life for "ordinary people," and to a more just distribution of life opportunities in the urban environment (Hall 1988, 1995; Ward 1994). Of course, their ideas about urban form, social organization and their power to influence events have all proved in retrospect erroneous and often damaging to these values. But it is not the values which were the problem. It was rather the belief that knowledge resides only with experts and that urban form is the prime determinant of the quality of urban life. A multiplex urban imagination among those who become the expert facilitators in urban governance, along with a commitment to an inclusionary ethic, could make a real difference to the future qualities of urban life. But this imagination needs to be informed by a rich and dynamic appreciation of the diverse everyday experiences and symbolic significances of our contemporary multiplex cities.

NOTES

1. This section is a substanially revised version of Graham and Healey 1999.
2. Such payments are actually very rare and much frowned on in British planning practice (Healey, Purdue, and Ennis 1995).
3. See, for example, Bishop 1998; Burton 1997.
4. Amin and Graham 1998; Healey 1997; Sandercock 1998; Thrift 1996; Amin and Thrift 1997; Castells 1996; Dematteis 1994; King 1996; Storper 1997; Friedmann 1993; Hwang 1996.
5. And thereby generating the kinds of stable meanings and "permanences" which are captured in notions of urban regimes (cf. Harvey 1996; Lauria 1997).
6. Forester 1993; Fischer and Forester 1993; Sager 1994; Innes 1995; Healey 1997; Healey, Hoch, Lauria, and Feldman 1997; Sandercock 1998.
7. The distinction between inscription and incorporation comes from Connerton 1989, but it parallels my own in between ways of thinking and ways of acting (Healey 1997).

REFERENCES

Amin, A. and Graham S. 1998: The ordinary city. *Transactions of the Institute of British Geographers*, 22, 411–29.

Amin, A. and Thrift N. 1997: Globalization, socioeconomics, territoriality. In R. Lee and J. Wills (eds.), *Geographies of Economies*. London: Arnold, 147–57.

Bishop, J. 1998: Reinventing planning 3: Collaboration and Consensus. *Town and Country Planning*, 67 (3), 111–13.

Booth, P. 1996: *Controlling Development*. London: UCL Press.

Boyer, C. 1983: *Dreaming the Rational City*. Boston: MIT Press.

Burton, P. 1997: *Community Visioning*. Bristol: Policy Press.

Byrne, D. 1996: Chaotic places of complex places. In S. Westwood and J. Williams (eds.), *Imagining Cities*. London: Routledge, 50–70.

Castells, M. 1977: *The Urban Question*. London: Edward Arnold.
Castells, M. 1996: *The Rise of the Network Society*. Oxford: Blackwell.
Chapin, S. J. 1965: *Urban Land Use Planning*. Urbana: University of Illinois Press.
Commission for the European Communities (CEC) 1997: *The EU Compendium of Spatial Planning Systems and Policies*. Brussels: European Communities.
Connerton, P. 1989: *How Societies Remember*. Cambridge: Cambridge University Press.
Cowling, T. and Steeley, G. 1973: *Sub-regional Planning Studies: An Evaluation*. Oxford: Pergamon Press.
Cullingworth, J. B. and Nadin, V. 1994: *Town and Country Planning in Britain*. London: Routledge.
Davies, H., Edwards, D., Hooper, A., and Punter, J. 1989: *Planning Control in Western Europe*. London: HMSO.
Davis, M. 1990: *Cities of Quartz*. London: Verso/Vintage.
Dear, M. 1995: Prolegomena for a post-modern urbanism. In P. Healey et al. (eds.), *Managing Cities*. London: Wiley, 27–44.
Dematteis, G. 1994: Global networks, local cities. *Flux*, 15, 17–24.
Douglass, M. and Friedmann, J. (eds.) 1998: *Cities for Citizens*. London: Wiley.
Fischer, F. and Forester, J. (eds.) 1993: *The Argumentative Turn in Policy Analysis and Planning*. London: UCL Press.
Flyvberg, B. 1998: Empowering civil society: Habermas, Foucault and the question of conflict. In M. Douglass and J. Friedmann, *Cities for Citizens*. London: Wiley, 185–212.
Forrester, J. 1969: *Urban Dynamics*. Boston: MIT Press.
Forester, J. 1993: *Critical Theory, Public Policy, and Planning Practice*. New York: State University of New York Press.
Friedmann, J. 1993: Towards a non-Euclidean mode of planning. *Journal of the American Planning Association*, 59 (4), 482–4.
Gleeson, B. and Grundy, K. J. 1997: New Zealand's planning revolution five years on: a preliminary assessment. *Journal of Environmental Planning and Management*, 40 (3), 293–314.
Graham, S. and Healey, P. 1999: Relational concepts of place and space: issues for planning theory and practice. *European Planning Studies*, 7 (15), 623–46.
Grove-White, R. 1991: Land, the law and environment. *Journal of Law and Society*, 18 (1), 32–47.
Hall, P. 1988: *Cities of Tomorrow*. Oxford: Blackwell.
Hall, P. 1995: Bringing Abercrombie back from the shades. *Town Planning Review*, 66 (3), 227–42.
Hall, P., Gracey, H., Drewett, R., and Thomas, R. 1973: *The Containment of Urban England*. London: George, Allen and Unwin.
Hampshire County Council (HCC) 1994: *Hampshire County Structure Plan (Approved)*. Winchester: Hampshire County Council.
Hampshire County Council (HCC) 1996: *Hampshire County Structure Plan 1996–2011 (Review): Deposit Version*. Winchester: Hampshire County Council.
Harvey, D. 1996: *Justice, Nature and the Geography of Difference*. Oxford, Blackwell.
Healey, P. 1997: *Collaborative Planning: Shaping Places in Fragmented Societies*. London: Macmillan.
Healey, P. 1998: Collaborative planning in a stakeholder society. *Town Planning Review*, 69 (1) 537–57.
Healey, P. 1999: Sites, jobs and portfolios: economic development discourses in the planning system. *Urban Studies*, 56 (1), 27–42.
Healey, P., Hoch, C., Lauria, M., and Feldman, M. 1997: Planning theory, political economy and the interpretive turn: the debate continues. *Planning Theory*, 17, summer (special issue).

Healey, P., Khakee, A., Motte, A., and Needham, B. 1997: *Making Strategic Spatial Plans: Innovation in Europe*. London: UCL Press.

Healey, P., Purdue, M., and Ennis, F. 1995: *Negotiating Development*. London: E. and F. N. Spon.

Huxley, M. 1994: Planning as a framework of power: utilitarian reform, Enlightenment logic and the control of space. In S. Ferber, C. Healey, and C. McAuliffe (eds.), *Beasts of Suburbs: Reinterpreting Culture in Australian Suburbs*. Melbourne: Melbourne University Press.

Hwang, S. W. 1996: The implications of the nonlinear paradigm for integrated environmental design and planning. *Journal of Planning Literature*, 11 (2), 167–80.

Innes, J. 1995: Planning Theory's emerging paradigm. *Journal of Planning Education and Research*, 14 (3), 183–90.

King, D. and Stoker, G. 1996: *Re-inventing Local Democracy*. London: Macmillan.

King, R. 1996: *Emancipating Space: Geography, Architecture, and Urban Design*. London: Guildford.

Lauria, M. (ed.) 1997: *Reconstructing Urban Regime Theory*. London: Sage.

McLoughlin, B. 1969: *Urban and Regional Planning: A Systems Approach*. London: Faber.

McLoughlin, B. 1973: *Control and Urban Planning*. London: Faber.

Mitchell, W. 1995: *City of Bits*. Cambridge, MA: MIT Press.

Neuman, M. 1996: Images as institution builders: metropolitan planning in Madrid. *European Planning Studies*, 4 (3), 293–312.

Owens, S. 1997: The Abercrombie Lecture: "Giants in the path": planning sustainability and environmental values. *Town Planning Review*, 68 (3), 293–304.

Ravetz, A. 1980: *Remaking Cities*. London: Croom Helm.

Sager, T. 1994: *Communicative Planning Theory*. Aldershot, Hants: Avebury.

Sandercock, L. 1998: *Towards Cosmopolis*. London: Wiley.

South Hampshire Structure Plan Advisory Committee 1972: South Hampshire Structure Plan. Winchester, Hampshire County Council.

Stevenson, D. 1998: Values, vision and governance in East London. *Rising East: The Journal of East London Studies*, 1(1), 15–35.

Storper, M. 1997: Regional economies as relational assets. In R. Lee and J. Wills (eds.), *Geographies of Economies*. London: Arnold, 248–58.

Tewdwr-Jones, M. 1997: Plans, policies and inter-governmental relations: assessing the role of national planning guidance in England and Wales. *Urban Studies*, 34 (10), 141–62.

Tewdwr-Jones, M. and Allmendinger, P. 1998: Deconstructing communicative rationality: a critique of Habermasian collaborative planning. *Environment and Planning A*, 30, 1979–89.

Thornley, A. 1991: *Urban Planning under Thatcherism*. London: Routledge.

Thrift, N. 1996: *Spatial Formations*. London: Sage.

Vigar, G., Healey, P., Hull, A., and Davoudi, S, 2000: *Planning, Governance and Spatial Strategy in Britain*. London: Macmillan.

Ward, S. 1994: *Planning and Urban Change*. London: Paul Chapman.

Yiftachel, O. 1998: Planning and social control: exploring the dark side. *Journal of Planning Literature*, 12 (4), 395–406.

Chapter 44

The Social Construction of Urban Policy

Allan D. Cochrane

There has been something commonly labeled "urban policy" since the early 1960s in the US and since the late 1960s in most European countries. The starting point of this chapter is a high degree of frustration about the ways in which debates about and around urban policy have generally been conducted. Even the academic literature is increasingly dominated by a "practical" or practice-oriented approach. The brief neo-Marxist fever associated with the writing of Harvey (1973) and Castells (1977) seems to have inoculated more recent writers against the dangers of recurrent infection. Authors generally either see themselves as reporting the ways of the experts to the wider public or as providing advice to the practitioners which will enable them to improve their practice.

A great deal of ink has been spilled at various times by people seeking to define what is meant by the "urban" to which one might expect urban policy to apply. An equal amount has probably been spilled on looking for definitions of "policy." Not so long ago Castells defined the "urban" through public policy – for him the "urban" was where collective consumption took place, and collective consumption was effectively understood to be the consumption services provided through the welfare state (Castells 1977).

Unfortunately such a circular definition – however elegant – is not very helpful for our purposes, since many of the policies that are not "urban" in this sense help to define the experience of urban life (including policing and economic development, as well as transfer payments through the social security and benefits systems). Equally important, spending on some programs (such as education and health) would qualify as collective consumption, but they are generally only seen as "urban" when specific area-based initiatives are launched. While it is tempting, as Blackman (1995) suggests, to try to capture all the initiatives that affect people living in cities as urban policy, there is a real danger that this will make the notion virtually meaningless. Since the vast majority of people in North America and Europe live in cities or urban areas – and most of the rest are dependent on cities for employment, income, and cultural activities – then almost every piece of social (and economic) policy could be reinterpreted as urban policy.

There is, however, at least one feature of urban policy that makes it highly distinctive. Other social policies are concerned with the delivery of services or the provision of support to "clients," "users," "consumers", or even "customers." Urban policy, by contrast, focuses on places and spatially delimited areas or the groups of people associated with them. Its problem definition starts from area rather than individual or even social group, although, of course, a concern with an area is often used as a coded way of referring to a concern about the particular groups which are believed to be concentrated in it. Instead of solving the difficulty of definition, however, this merely compounds it. It remains necessary to define the area – in practice different "urban" policies define their areas or territories differently. Although an area focus provides a useful starting point for analysis it also masks a very wide range of policy initiatives, concerned with dramatically different definitions of the problem faced either by urban areas or by those living in them.

Complexity and Coherence

It is possible to identify six main strands in the development of urban policy in Britain since the 1960s. Each of these also implies a different understanding of the "urban problem," yet it is the uneasy coexistence and changing balance between them that helps to define the nature of urban policy at any one time. Urban policy is the product of a complex interweaving of meanings, producing a changing pattern but with recognizable continuities.

Race

The issue of race has been like a thread running through urban policy in Britain (from Enoch Powell to Scarman and beyond). It underpins many of the specific understandings reflected in the other clusters, often as an unspoken subtext. Race has been a central element in the discourse that has defined the inner-city crisis or problem in British cities.

A racialized urban pathology was a crucial element in generating Britain's urban policy. The Urban Programme of the 1960s was an explicit response to fears about racial tensions in British cities. These fears were reinforced by the imagery of urban race riots – as usual in British policy discourse the US experience was presented as a frightening warning of what would follow unless action was taken. In a series of speeches in 1968 Enoch Powell prophesied that Britain's inner cities would be transformed into "alien territories." "Like the Roman," he said, "I seem to see the River Tiber foaming with blood" (Smithies and Fiddick 1969: 43). The response of Prime Minister Harold Wilson was to promise the introduction of an Urban Programme alongside increasingly tight immigration control. The very concentration of households with members whose origins were in the so-called New Commonwealth was identified as evidence of multiple deprivation.

The language of race was downplayed as urban policy developed through the 1970s into the 1980s. It only had a "walk-on part" in the 1977 White Paper, which emphasized economic regeneration, and was denounced as inherently "racist" by John Rex because it did not take the needs of Black communities into account. Rex (1988: 3) argued that by incorporating a strategy of "population replacement carried out in the name of 'dispersal and balance'" the new strategy effectively meant clearing the Black population out of the inner city, even if it was never directly expressed in those terms. The urban riots of 1981 and 1985 helped to force the issue of race explicitly back on to the agenda, particularly in the wake of the Scarman Report on the Brixton riots. But they only seem to have done so temporarily. The "traditional" elements of the Urban Programme (focused on voluntary/ community initiatives which were taken up by members of minority ethnic groups) were given a brief reprieve, only to disappear later in the decade. Spending on the "traditional" Urban Programme became a very small element in the overall inner-city program.

But "race" has not completely disappeared. It is still there as an important undercurrent. Even if formal urban policy programs are presented as color blind "everybody knows" that the inner city, the urban, equals Black (see, e.g., Faith in the City 1985). To some extent this has been translated into other aspects of social policy. Debates about the "underclass" have often been used to raise concerns about the parenting practices of members of some minority ethnic groups (particularly those from African-Caribbean backgrounds) (see, e.g., Murray 1990; Law 1996: 53–8). Similarly, although there has been an increasing reluctance to develop "racially" targeted initiatives, it is assumed that members of such communities are likely to benefit disproportionately from initiatives designed to improve access to training and education. Paradoxically, the construction of urban policy as color blind has helped (as in the US) to ensure that the label "urban" is widely understood to mean "Black." As Keith and Cross (1993: 8) notes in another context: "What appears at first glance to be missing, the centrality of race . . . turns out on closer inspection not to be missing at all, only unspoken."

Managing dangerous places

The "dangerous" nature of urban areas has been a recurrent theme of policy debates, and one of the key tasks of policymakers has historically been to deal with them, either by making them safer or by removing any threat to more "respectable" areas. Different forms of policing are also urban policies and the planning system can effectively operate to imprison some people in the dangerous places in which they live, while apparently "protecting" others.

Urban areas in the twentieth century have frequently been perceived as places of disorder, as threatening or dangerous places, both for those who live in them and for those who rely on them as places of production and consumption. The discovery of "mugging" as a specifically inner-city (and "Black") phenomenon in the early 1970s was simply one reflection of that (Hall et al. 1978). As Keith and Rogers (1991: 120) note, the inner city has effectively been "cast as alien normally via the stigmata of race or socialism, the locus of criminal delinquency, the site of disorder."

The language of race is an important element in the construction of urban areas as dangerous places, and the identification of dangerous places is also an important element in the construction of Black people as a problem. But the linkages between the urban, crime, and danger are not simply apparent in racialized discourses. The definition of young people – and particularly young men – as "out of control" has also fed into the recent imagery of cities as dangerous (see, e.g., Campbell's [1993] powerful description of young men on the rampage in her discussion of the disorders which seemed to spread across England in the early 1990s). Whatever the formulation or the location of the "problem" (inner or outer city) the message is clear enough: there are dangerous areas, and people from whom the respectable classes need to be protected (see Graham and Clarke 1996, for a review of the longer history of the relationship between cities and fears of crime). Although it is accepted that those living in such areas are the biggest victims, the main emphasis is placed on defining them as the "other" who need to be managed, if the rest of us are to retain a secure environment.

Policing of one sort or another has always been a key aspect of urban policy, but its profile has become increasingly significant since the early 1980s. Concerns about the policing of urban areas have led to legislation on criminal trespass as well as the launch of neighborhood watch initiatives, policies on street crime, dealing with young people, and the policing of racialized minority groups. In considering the role of policing strategies as a factor in the Brixton riots of 1981, the Scarman Report also confirmed the wider importance of policing as an urban policy (see also Keith 1993). The "Safer Cities" initiative launched in the late 1980s has explicitly highlighted the issue of urban crime, setting out to mobilize "communities" in the fight against crime (Walklate 1996). Resources are made available to protect and make safe, although this initiative itself confirms fear. So, for example, the use of CCTV and the development of private shopping malls help to create "safe" spaces, but they also help to establish the existence of other places as unsafe, as well as excluding certain behavior as unacceptable (see, e.g., Fyfe 1997: 257–8).

Urban planning (private as well as public) is used as a form of social control, for example through zoning and policies on housing density. At local level policies on lighting, traffic management, and protected space have all been developed in response to fears about crime. Private and public policies help to construct areas of protected/defended housing while marginalizing those who live in others. On the one hand large-scale redevelopment, sponsored by urban development corporations and other agencies, serves to renew and redefine some areas of the city, bringing them back into use (see, e.g., Byrne 1997), while others – the peripheral estates and other areas of social housing – become sinks for the poor and the delinquent, places to be managed and to be presented as terrible warnings to the middle classes and the respectable (disciplined and ordered) poor.

Community and social welfare

Many of the problems of contemporary society, from poverty to welfare seem to have been symbolically and practically consigned to the inner cities and peripheral estates. As a result urban policy has also been expected to take on the role of revitalizing the moral basis of British society.

Urban policy emerged in the context of an attempt to save the Keynesian welfare state, by redefining and restructuring it. In the British context, its origins can, perhaps, best be understood as one of the last gasps of a social-democratic project. The "modernization" strategy associated with the governments of the 1960s and early 1970s incorporated urban policy as one of its strands. In the late 1960s, urban regeneration, community work, and locally based provision were presented as alternatives to traditional forms of welfare and to traditional forms of planning and urban renewal. Notions of multiple deprivation drove understandings which stressed both the possibility of targeted provision and of self-help. The role of ideas which stressed "individual, family, and community malfunctioning" was clear alongside the almost religious fervor associated with the ambition to regenerate communities and encourage individual self-improvement (Higgins et al. 1983: 7, 14–19). This was later caricatured as the "social pathology" approach, that is, one which put the blame for inner-city problems on the behavior of those suffering from them (see, e.g., CDP 1997), but its significance as an alternative to traditional forms of welfare intervention is not so easily dismissed. The Blair government's "New Deal for Communities" announced in 1998 with its focus on revitalizing neighborhoods without effective local social and economic networks is merely the latest example of such an approach.

In the 1970s, academic analysis stressed the importance of collective or social consumption as defining urban policy, while community politics was understood as the politics of social reproduction (involving new social movements, often led by women; see, e.g., Cockburn 1977). Despite a shift in emphasis towards policies of economic regeneration and renewal at the end of the decade, the issue of community has continued to play its part in the language and sometimes in the practice of urban policy. It has increasingly been reintroduced as part of the process of redefining welfare in ways which highlight personal and collective (nonstate) responsibility. The report of the Commission on Social Justice (1994: 309) highlights the continued salience of such arguments in suggesting that "communities do not become strong because they are rich, rather they become rich because they are strong" (see also DETR 1997; Social Exclusion Unit 1998).

Notions of community have also been strongly mobilized around the community enterprise movement. Self-help through the market has been presented as a way forward, particularly for those areas unlikely to attract investment from the outside. The growth of community businesses in Scotland in the 1970s and 1980s has been widely documented and the Scottish example is the one which has been taken up to underpin the case for the development of community enterprise throughout the UK (see, e.g., Hayton 1996; Pearce 1993: 5–11). The more extreme claims for the success of community enterprise have increasingly been questioned and Hayton (1996) notes that it is difficult to discover the significance of "community" involvement and empowerment in practice. For our purposes, however, the point is not to make any judgment about the value of community businesses as the basis of a development strategy. It is rather to highlight the revival of forms of self-help in the field of local economic development, as well as in urban policy more generally. Much of this, of course, predates the election of a Labour government in 1997, but it is consistent with the approach increasingly being adopted towards welfare issues since then. This approach to urban policy is, in the words of the Commission on Social Justice (1994: 224), about finding ways of giving people and communities a "hand-up rather than a hand-out." It confirms that welfare is no longer about compensating for structural inequalities, but about helping people to operate more effectively in the labor market or in developing their own forms of social or community enterprise (see, e.g., Thake and Staubach 1993).

Developments in urban policy have often prefigured wider restructuring in the field of social welfare. It is in the urban arena, for example, that the increasingly close relationship between economic and social policy has been most apparent, in the move from "welfare" to "workfare," from a discourse of universal benefits to one of targeting, flexibility, and skills training (see also discussions of social and civic entrepreneurialism in Leadbetter 1997; Leadbetter and Goss 1998).

Coordination, partnership and multi-agency working

A belief in the importance of effective collaboration, partnership, and a comprehensive approach to urban problems, which cuts across traditional organizational divisions, runs through the history of urban policy in Britain, yet each new policy generation seems to be condemned to rediscover and identify this anew.

Urban policy incorporates an implicit and sometimes explicit critique of the organizational settlement associated with the Beveridge welfare state in the UK (Hughes and Lewis 1998, chs. 1 and 2). The "old" professional and departmental structures of the welfare state have regularly been dismissed as incapable of tackling urban problems. It is argued that more effective collaboration and a comprehensive and all-embracing approach will provide a way forward. In their report for the Department of the Environment, Robson et al. (1994: 52) approvingly note the comment that "Urban problems are multi-faceted: departments are not." They stress that more "interagency collaboration" is needed, pointing to what they see as the success of schemes "operating within defined areas," where "there has been scope to develop more integrated programs involving training, job creation, environmental and infrastructural improvements" (Robson et al. 1994: 52). This is not the place to question these conclusions, although it is worth recalling the sceptical comments of Edwards and Batley (1978: 245) who warn that an emphasis on comprehensive approaches and coordination may simply serve to mask the lack of an effective policy.

From the inception of the Urban Programme in the late 1960s to the introduction of the Single Regeneration Budget in the 1990s, the rhetoric of urban policy has consistently been couched in these terms. In the 1970s, the Community Development Projects were succeeded by the Comprehensive Community Programmes and those in turn were overtaken by the Inner City Partnerships spawned by the Inner Urban Areas Act. Each promised area-based coordination, albeit of a different sort and often at rather different spatial scales. One of the justifications for setting up the Urban Development Corporations in the 1990s (particularly in London's Docklands) was that the existing local authorities had proved unable to develop a coherent and comprehensive set of policies (see, e.g., Imrie and Thomas 1999). The Blair government's Social Exclusion Unit is only the latest in a long line of initiatives which promises the possibility of "joined-up thinking" in urban policy, expressed, for example, in the strategy proposed for neighborhood renewal (Social Exclusion Unit 1998). Because of the stress on areas (rather than "client" groups or service delivery) the practice of urban policy has always been characterized by an emphasis on coordination, multi-agency working and area-based teams. Not only have policy analysts consistently complained about a lack of coordination and stressed the need for a holistic approach, but initiative after initiative has been launched with the claim that this is what will be achieved.

Alongside an emphasis on coordination between agencies (and sometimes within them, across departmental and professional boundaries) there has been a stress on the importance of partnerships of one sort or another. The notion of partnerships is – of course – itself an elusive one, but it implies that no single agency is capable of

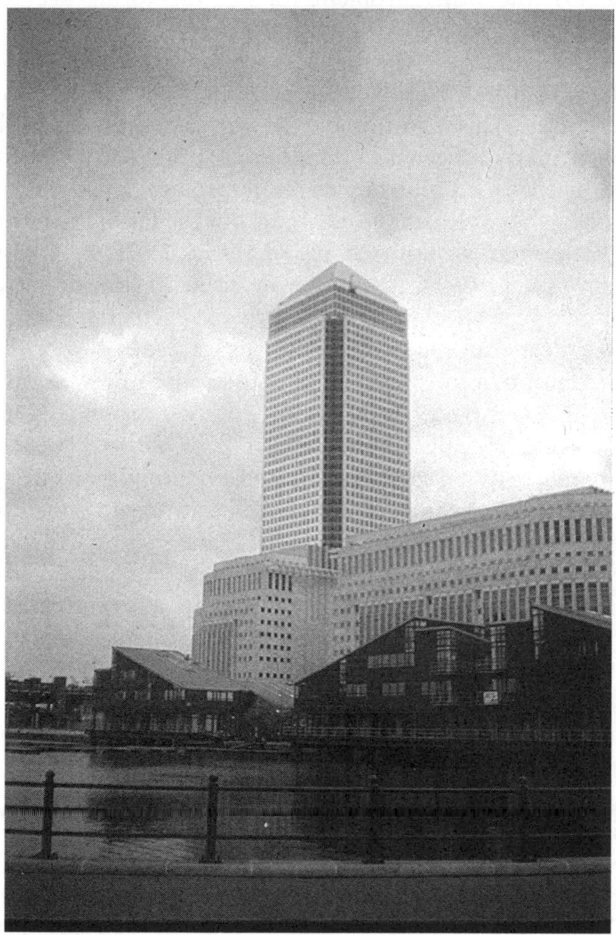

Figure 44.1 Heron Quay – London's Docklands (© Steve Pile)

tackling urban problems effectively. Partnership has been presented as a panacea – whether it is between statutory agencies of one sort or another, between statutory and voluntary agencies, between community and state, or between public and private sectors. So, for example, in the words of a Discussion Paper on regeneration programs prepared by the Department of the Environment, Transport and the Regions: "The advantage of partnerships is that if properly constituted and run they are more suited to implementing the bottom-up approach to regeneration than a single central or local government organisation. They can help to promote ownership of regeneration activity within local communities" (DETR 1997, para. 5.2.1).

Economic decline

Cities have frequently been used as metaphors for wider economic decline, and as a result urban policy has since the late 1970s increasingly been oriented toward economic regeneration – a model for the rest of society. Urban areas provided powerful symbols of the wider problems of manufacturing decline, with all the imagery of derelict land and empty buildings. The poverty of local residents could be more or less directly linked to factory closures and economic rationalization.

Since the mid-1970s Britain's problems have largely been described in terms which stress economic failure. This also found a powerful expression in the language of urban policy (particularly reflected in the notion of inner-city "regeneration"). The emphasis shifted, so that the problem was reinterpreted: not so much to do with the pathology of residents (or at least not only that) but the failure of cities as productive units, and as generators of wealth (see, e.g., Lawless 1981: 8; Atkinson and Moon 1994: 75). Urban policy was transformed to fit with a wider national political rhetoric of economic regeneration – public–private partnership and infrastructural investment (also reflected in muted form, for example, in the National Enterprise Board). Such a definition of the problem, of course, also allows for the possibility of subtle confusion in identifying the aims of policy, encouraging the building of alliances around vague slogans in which it is possible to believe that aims and ambitions are shared between government and community, local and national or global business, and business and community. The extent to which these ambitions are shared is perhaps less clear.

Elements of the economic analysis were taken up and reinterpreted with some glee by the Thatcher governments: the structural problem was reinterpreted as a lack of entrepreneurialism and the need to "free" enterprise from state restrictions (e.g. reflected in the launch of enterprise zones; see, e.g., Anderson 1990). Just as the Labour strategy for the late 1970s constructed urban areas in terms which fitted well with the government's broader understanding of the "British" problem (i.e. the need for economic modernization and regeneration) so the Conservative strategy of the 1980s constructed urban areas in terms which fitted well with their understanding of the "British" disease (i.e. broader dependency culture, lack of enterprise).

So urban policy also shifted towards a program of privatism (Barnekov et al. 1989), and the celebration of an enterprise culture. The state-led partnerships so beloved of the 1978 legislation were transformed into supposedly private-sector-led models. The role of urban policy was to assist with wealth creation, with emphasis being placed on the (re)creation of markets in inner urban areas – making those areas work productively again as sources of profitable production (see, e.g., Byrne 1997). Higgins et al. (1983: 83) quote the aims of Urban Programme circulars in the early 1980s to make "inner cities places where people wish to live and work." The implication was that those currently living in the inner cities might not be capable of leading the campaign for renewal. It is perhaps not surprising that the main emphasis of the urban development corporations (particularly the flagship London Docklands Development Corporation) was on property development and infrastructural spending rather than "community empowerment." Partnerships with business agencies were rather more significant than those with community organizations of local government (see, e.g., Imrie and Thomas 1999).

Cosmopolitan possibilities

Alongside a rhetoric of decline and disorder, there is also a continuing rhetoric which constructs cities as places of opportunity. Historically, of course, opportunity – particularly for those moving to cities – has often been seen as one of their key defining characteristics, but the economic and cultural vitality of urban areas has generally been underplayed as urban policy has developed since the 1960s. In the last decade, however, the balance has shifted. The cultural capital of cities is now frequently emphasized in the process of place marketing and the redefinition of urban policy as a form of entrepreneurialism.

There has been a dramatic explosion of global place marketing – every place wants to be someplace, and some places want to be world cities – although local authorities have been involved in forms of promotional activity over a much longer period. Urban politics has increasingly become a politics of growth. This has meant that the governance of cities has become more entrepreneurial and apparently more attuned to global market forces (see, e.g., Mayer 1995). The rise of urban entrepreneurialism can be seen in the intense interurban competition for high-profile events and feature developments, such as the Olympics or the European City of Culture, but this is just one reflection of the phenomenon. In the process of place marketing, the marketeers attempt to build on existing ("locally rooted") traditions and understandings to reposition places along lines which fit with the limited range of images preferred by managers, upmarket tourists and potential investors (Kearns and Philo 1993). In this context, the role of cities as cultural centers has now been widely recognized and strategies which seek to build on this recognition have now been developed in the most unlikely places (from Glasgow to Huddersfield). Cultural policy has been mobilized as a key element in the development of broad-based policies for urban regeneration throughout Europe (see, e.g., Bianchini and Parkinson 1993).

The urban development corporations of the late 1980s and early 1990s were also associated with a flood of image building and the commitment to prestige projects as symbols of renewal, what Edwards (1997: 826) has described as a "new urban glamour policy" – the London Docklands Development Corporation had Canary Wharf, Cardiff has plans for an Opera House, Liverpool had Albert Dock and the Tate Gallery. Place marketing has been institutionalized with the launch of initiatives such as City Pride. There has been a shift in emphasis away from dereliction, decline, and decay, towards one which stresses the cosmopolitan potential of urban areas.

Urban Policy and the Urban Experience

Although it is possible to identify these clusters of meaning separately, it is important to recognize the ways in which they interact in practice. They amount to a repertoire of urban polices which are utilized in different ways at different times, helping to generate fluid understandings of what makes places urban. In other words it is important not to follow those who argue for a more or less linear progression in the development of urban policy – from pathology to economic structure and (maybe) back again. Changes can be identified that reflect and shape the restructuring of the welfare state – with urban policy playing a key role in the making of a new (post-Beveridge, postwelfare) settlement (see, e.g., Hay 1996; Hughes and Lewis 1998).

The "progress" of urban policy has been crablike, moving first in one direction then in another, drawing on different elements of the repertoire at different times. Urban policy is a changing mix of initiatives, reflecting a changeable set of priorities and policy fashions, many of which owe little to the changing needs of urban areas and their residents. But shifts in approach within this ever changing policy field may also have dramatic effects on urban residents: they may be defined as pathological or victims of a dependency culture; criminals or victims of crime; as congenitally incapable of being entrepreneurial. Cities may be defined as economic failures (which may mean that moving out is the solution); as the homes of unskilled labor, and the unemployable or workshy (from lone parents through the long-term sick to young working class – or Black – men); or as the home of *flâneurs* and cafe society (which is not much fun if you are on the outside while the cultural elite has its fun); and so on. In other words, urban policy is not an innocent form of intervention, but itself helps to shape and define its object of intervention.

Urban policy is both socially produced and helps to make the urban problem seem natural, taken for granted. Dominant understandings of urban policy both reflect and influence the ways in which people experience urban living; urban policies help to define the urban "problem" or even the urban "crisis." They are not just responses to those problems but help to constitute them.

REFERENCES

Anderson, J. 1990: The new right, enterprise zones and urban development corporations. *International Journal of Urban and Regional Research*, 14 (3), 468–89.

Atkinson, R. and Moon, G. 1994: *Urban Policy in Britain: The City, the State and the Market*. Basingstoke and London: Macmillan.

Audit Commission 1991: *The Urban Regeneration Experience: Observations from Local Value for Money Audits*. London: HMSO.

Barnekov, T., Boyle, R., and Rich, D. 1989: *Privatism and Urban Policy in Britain and the United States* Oxford: Oxford University Press.

Bianchini, F. and Parkinson, M. (eds.) 1993: *Cultural Policy and Urban Regeneration: The West European Experience*. Manchester: Manchester University Press.

Blackman, T. 1995: *Urban Policy in Practice*. London: Routledge.

Burton, P. 1997: Urban policy and the myth of progress. *Policy and Politics*, 25 (4), 421–37.

Byrne, D. 1997: National social policy in the United Kingdom. In M. Pacione (ed.), *Britain's Cities: Geographies of Division in Urban Britain*. London: Routledge, 108–27.

Campbell, B. 1993: *Goliath: Britain's Dangerous Places*. London: Methuen.

Castells, M. 1977: *The Urban Question*. London: Edward Arnold.

CDP 1997: *Gilding the Ghetto*. London: National Community Development Project.

Clarke, J. and Cochrane, A. 1998: The social construction of social problems. In E. Saraga (ed.), *Embodying the Social: Constructions of Difference*. London: Routledge, 3–42.

Clarke, J., Cochrane, A., and McLaughlin, E. (eds.) 1994: *Managing Social Policy*. London: Sage.

Clarke, J. and Newman, J. 1997: *The Managerial State*. London: Sage.

Cockburn, C. 1977: *The Local State: The Management of Cities and People*. London: Pluto.

Commission on Social Justice 1994: *Social Justice: Strategies for National Renewal*. London: Vintage

DETR 1997: *Regeneration – The Way Forward*. London: Department of the Environment, Transport and the Regions.

Edwards, J. 1995: Social policy and the city. *Urban Studies*, 32 (4–5), 695–712.

Edwards, J. 1997: Urban policy: the victory of form over substance? *Urban Studies*, 34, 5–6, 825–43.

Edwards, J. and Batley, R. 1978: *The Politics of Positive Discrimination. An Evaluation of the Urban Programme 1967–77*. London: Tavistock.

Faith in the City 1985: *A Call for Action by Church and Nation: A Report of the Archbishop of Canterbury's Commission on Urban Priority Areas*. London: Church House Publishing.

Fyfe, N. 1997: Crime. In M. Pacione (ed.), *Britain's Cities: Geographies of Division in Urban Britain*. London: Routledge, 244–61.

Graham, P. and Clarke, J. 1996: Dangerous places. In J. Muncie and E. McLaughlin (eds.), *The Problem of Crime*. London: Sage, 143–81.

Hall, P. 1996: *Cities of Tomorrow: An Intellectual History of Urban Planning and Design in the Twentieth Century*. Updated edition. Oxford: Blackwell.

Hall, S., Critcher, C., Jefferson, T., Clarke, J., and Roberts, B. 1978: *Policing the Crisis*. London: Macmillan.

Harvey, D. 1973: *Social Justice and the City*. London: Edward Arnold.

Hay, C. 1996: *Re-Stating Social and Political Change*. Buckingham: Open University Press.

Hayton, K. 1996: A critical examination of the role of community business in urban regeneration. *Town Planning Review*, 67 (1), 1–20.

Higgins, J., Deakin, N., Edwards, J., and Wicks, M. 1983: *Government and Urban Poverty: Inside the Policy-making Process*. Oxford: Basil Blackwell.

Hughes, G. and Lewis, G. (eds.) 1998: *Unsettling Welfare: The Reconstruction of Social Policy*. London: Routledge.

Imrie, R. and Thomas, H. (eds.) 1999: *British Urban Policy and the Urban Development Corporations*. 2nd edition. London: Paul Chapman.

Kearns, G. and Philo, C. (eds.) 1993: *Selling Places: The City as Cultural Capital, Past and Present*. Oxford: Pergamon Press.

Keith, M. 1993: *Race, Riots and Policing*. London: UCL Press.

Keith, M. and Cross, M. 1993: Racism and the postmodern city. In M. Cross, and M. Keith, (eds.), *Racism, the City and the State*. London. Routledge, 1–30.

Keith, M. and Rogers, A. 1991: *Hollow Promises*. London: Mansell.

Law, I. 1996: *Racism, Ethnicity and Social Policy*. London: Prentice-Hall/Harvester Wheatsheaf.

Lawless, P. 1981: *Britain's Inner Cities: Problems and Policies*. London: Harper and Row.

Lawless, P. 1996: The inner cities: towards a new agenda. *Town Planning Review*, 67 (1), 21–43.

Leadbeater, C. 1997: *The Rise of Social Entrepreneurship*. London: Demos.

Leadbeater, C. and Goss, S. 1998: *Civic Entrepreneurship*. London: Demos.

Loftman, P. and Nevin, B. 1996: Going for growth: prestige projects in three British cities. *Urban Studies*, 33 (6), 991–1019.

Loney, M. 1983: *Community against Government: The British Community Development Project 1968–78. A Study of Government Incompetence*. London: Heinemann.

Marris, P. and Rein, M. 1971: *Dilemmas of Social Reform*. London: Routledge and Kegan Paul.

Mayer, M. 1995: Urban governance in the post-Fordist city. In P. Healey, S. Cameron, S. Davoudi, and A. Madani-Pour (eds.), *Managing Cities: The New Urban Context*, Chichester: John Wiley, 231–49.

Mooney, G. and Danson, M. 1995: Beyond "Culture City": Glasgow as dual city. Paper presented to the British Sociological Association Annual Conference on Contested Cities, University of Leicester.

Murray, C. 1990: *The Emerging British Underclass*. London: The IEA Health and Welfare Unit.

Pearce, J. 1993: *At the Heart of the Community Economy: Community Enterprise in a Changing World.* London: Calouste Gulbenkian Foundation.

Peck, J. 1997: *Work-Place: The Social Regulation of Labor Markets.* New York: Guilford.

Rex, J. 1988: *The Ghetto and the Underclass: Essays on Race and Social Policy.* Aldershot: Avebury.

Robson, B., Bradford, M., Deas, I., Hall, E., Harrison, E., Parkinson, M., Evans, R., Garde, P., Harding, A., and Robinson, F. 1994: *Assessing the Impact of Urban Policy.* London: HMSO.

Scarman, Lord 1981: *The Brixton Disorders 10–12 April 1981: The Scarman Inquiry.* London: HMSO.

Shaw, K. and Robinson, F. 1998: Learning from experience? Reflecting on two decades of British urban policy. *Town Planning Review,* 69 (1), 49–63.

Smithies, B. and Fiddick, P. 1969: *Enoch Powell on Immigration: An Analysis.* London: Sphere Books.

Social Exclusion Unit 1998: Bringing Britain together: a national strategy for neighborhood renewal. Cmnd 4045. London: The Stationery Office.

Stoker, G. 1995: Urban regime theory. In D. Judge, G. Stoker, and H. Wolman (eds.), *Theories of Urban Politics.* London: Sage, 54–71.

Thake, S. and Staubach, R. 1993: *Investing in People: Rescuing Communities from the Margins.* York: Joseph Rowntree Foundation.

Walklate, S. 1996: Community and crime prevention. In E. McLaughlin, and J. Muncie, (eds.), *Controlling Crime.* London: Sage, 293–331.

Wilks-Heeg, S. 1996: Urban experiments limited revisited: urban policy comes full circle. *Urban Studies,* 33 (8), 1263–97.

Chapter 45

Urban Planning in the Late Twentieth Century

Patrick Troy

Before we can discuss late twentieth-century urban planning we need to review the origins of urban planning and the forces which have shaped urban areas. We need to try to understand what happened to earlier attempts at planning urban areas and why planning in the late twentieth-century must differ from those earlier attempts.

This chapter is written largely with the experience of Australian cities in mind but illustrations and examples are chosen from cities which grew and flourished in the nineteenth-century. The implicit assumption is that the trajectory of cities was similar in all developed market economies in which most property was privately held. Much of the argument in Australia was influenced by conditions in European and North American cities. This account therefore makes reference to contributions to the general debate about urban issues and planning made by scholars in the Western context.

The Nineteenth-century City

Although there were earlier attempts to lay out towns in an ordered fashion urban development was not planned, and then regulated and controlled to achieve planning objectives until early in the twentieth-century (Mumford 1961). Nonetheless, the story starts with the recognition that contemporary urban planning has its roots in the nineteenth-century in which urbanization was uncoordinated, even chaotic, and led to living conditions which were very unequal (Ashworth 1954; Benevolo 1967; Cherry 1974; Cullingworth 1970, Hall 1988).

By the mid-nineteenth-century there was a perceived need for order and a strong view that emerging capitalist forms of production were under threat from popular discontent. A regulatory system was developed piecemeal to reduce chaos and some forms of inequality. Although the development of the regulatory system, especially in the English-speaking world, was devised largely to protect the institution of the common law (Sedley 1996), its evolution coincided with the rising discontent of the urban poor. There was increasing realization that the poor would have to be given healthier environments, better housing, safer buildings, and some share in the wealth of the community especially through access to collectively provided services and facilities such as schools, hospitals, and recreation facilities if the stability of the sociopolitical system was to be assured.

The demand for order led to the notion developed by social reformers that if we could only understand the "science" of the economic and political processes which were at play in society we could more equitably and efficiently arrange activities within the city. It was a highly political response to a situation in which some members of the powerful elites recognized that unless the poorer members of society shared some of the increase in wealth the new forces of democracy could lead to increased attempts at radical restructuring of society similar to that in the mid-nineteenth-century when the citizens of Paris made an attempt to overthrow their government and establish a commune (Rude 1980).

Simultaneously, and partly as a function of the stresses created by increasing concentrations of urban populations – including what we now call "environmental" stresses – demand grew for more assured supplies of potable water, for better, healthier ways of coping with the wastes of urban settlements and for better transport in and between human settlements.

By the end of the nineteenth-century the major industrial concentrations were strongly established as urban centers. Examples of such cities in Australia are Melbourne and Sydney which developed as major industrial cities as did Birmingham, Glasgow, London, Manchester, and Newcastle in Britain, and Chicago, New York, and Pittsburgh in the United States of America.

Apart from those which were traditional capitals these nineteenth-century cities were highly centralized. They had grown rapidly but incrementally, often at a key transport node. Their scale, nonetheless, permitted transport, manufacturing, warehousing, commerce, and the institutions of the state, including the administrative elements to be centrally colocated. The use of steam power for manufacturing processes and warehousing and the need to minimize energy transmission losses led to high-density factories and warehouses being clustered around railways and docks.

The scale of the cities also quickly exceeded the locally available water supplies and the capacity of the local environment to absorb the wastes generated by the population and the new industrial and commercial processes in which they were engaged. Water supplies became polluted and disease spread. Technological developments in hydraulic engineering made it feasible to respond to the demand for better water and sewerage services. Cities grew large enough and sufficient wealth was created within or "captured" by them to build the water supply and sewerage systems they required. In most cases water supply and sewerage systems were provided by publicly owned instrumentalities or statutory corporations to serve particular municipalities or cities. In Australia these local bodies were created with a degree of independence of government but answerable to Parliament (Dingle and Rasmussen 1991; Lloyd et al. 1992). This was done to ensure that the public "good" of improved health was experienced by all and to ensure an equitable supply of potable water to all residents. What we now call "big engineering" solutions were developed to meet these demands. By their nature these solutions were highly centralized and delivered by highly hierarchic institutions.

The concentration of jobs and services in the center of the city led to demand for increased access by increasing numbers of the population. Traffic congestion in city centers with narrow streets was a major source of inefficiency. The transport systems which had evolved to serve the urban populations were gradually supplemented by high-capacity fixed-rail systems.

The rise of the middle class and the general increase in the standard of living led to increased demand for housing. Working-class housing was notoriously poor (for England see Engels 1835) and was the subject of major campaigns based on extensive studies by social reformers who argued that the overcrowding and the lack of privacy should be tackled by increasing the size and comfort of dwellings. A number of enlightened industrialists and philanthropists established model housing estates for low-income families. Rowntree and Cadbury are two examples of nineteenth-century industrialist/philanthropist housing reformers in Britain. Governments were pressured to introduce minimum standards for housing and to accord tenants protection from some of the more egregious practices of landlords.

The demand was not only for increased and higher-quality space in the dwellings themselves but for increased private space in the form of private gardens (Howard 1902). It was also accompanied by an increased demand for public recreation space in the form of parks, gardens, and playing fields (Freestone 1989). Some part of this demand for increased recreational space resulted from the reduction in working hours and the consequential increase in leisure time. These pressures led to increased suburbanization of the cities (Jackson 1985). Some, especially colonial cities like Sydney and Melbourne, were suburban from their settlement (Davison 1993). Much of the explanation of the generally higher standard of living experienced by residents in these colonial cities compared with those in their European homelands came from the fact that they had the space around their dwellings to produce much of their own food and to make much of the furniture (Mullins 1981a, 1981b, 1987).

In the "New World" great interest was occasioned by proposals to build new national capitals. The planning and development of Washington stimulated debate over the ideal city (Reps 1967), and these ideas and arguments received a second fillip when the debate over the planning for the new national capital of Australia occurred early in the twentieth-century (Reps 1997).

As the world economy expanded, cities increased their populations but expanded in area faster and their population densities fell. Tramways and railroad systems were developed to meet the demands from the growing suburban populations. Public transport systems facilitated the further suburbanization and separation of residential areas from the noisy, crowded inner industrial areas with poor amenity.

The City in the Twentieth Century

By the early twentieth-century the scale of cities was causing a range of environmental problems. Their size meant they became large "point sources of pollution" as they discharged large volumes of sewage to the waterways including the open ocean. It had been assumed that the natural waterways would cope with the load of untreated sewage. For a while this was so as the sewage itself was relatively benign. But as its volume exceeded the capacity of the receiving waters, and its composition changed, it began to create major problems – especially in inland waterways.

The solution to the sewage "problem" was to develop large-scale treatment plants in which the sewage of whole cities was treated and the harmless (in terms of pathogenic organisms at least) effluent returned to the waterways. Many seaside cities, however, simply developed deep ocean outfalls which discharged the untreated sewage some distance out to sea where, it was assumed, the large volume of the receiving waters would be able to cope with the natural breakdown of the sewage.

Air pollution which had been a problem from earlier times now became a significant issue. Industrialization based on the combustion of coal produced major and seemingly intractable problems which were not resolved until the second half of the twentieth-century. The response to the air pollution was to introduce regulations governing the production of smoke and other exhaust gases and for city residents to seek to separate residential areas from industry and commerce, thus increasing the drive for suburbanization.

By the mid-twentieth-century the growth, inequalities, inefficiencies, and environmental stresses being experienced in the cities led to arguments for the introduction of city planning (Cullingworth 1970; Cherry 1996; Hall 1988). Strong town planning movements grew up in many countries. One after another cities in Australia adopted plans designed to minimize transport inefficiencies, to provide efficiency and order in the provision of infrastructure services generally, to separate residential from other incompatible uses, to protect the amenity of the city and to ensure in particular that the amenity of residents in poor areas was improved.

The end of the Second World War was followed by increased determination to improve the quality of urban life. Many of the English-speaking countries among the belligerents in the war promised programs to build "homes fit for heroes." The programs were not only devised to build better housing with greater security of tenure but also to ensure the provision of properly located employment, facilities, and services (Harloe 1995). In Australia the federal government conducted a major review of housing to determine how the housing system should be improved (CHC 1944). Part of the promise to give a greater stake in the country to its citizens was the undertaking to improve the quality of housing and the services available to residents as well as increased security of tenure. The commitment was reflected in the development of large public housing programs which offered low- to medium-income households better housing with greater security of tenure at affordable rents. Another lay in policies designed to increase home ownership. This mix of strategies varied between countries and it also had differential effects within them. In Australia most of the public housing was in the form of traditional single-family cottages and much of it was sold to eligible tenants. The home ownership policies of the Australian government succeeded in lifting owner occupation from about half in 1947 to over 70 percent in less than 15 years.

Postwar urban development was required to include a wider range of infrastructure services. There was widespread recognition that it was economically better to provide services as areas were developed than to try to insert them into existing developments later, which had been the traditional mode of progressive development in Australia. As a result of this change in policy the infrastructure authorities became powerful agents shaping urban growth as they set priorities in the development of their systems. One consequence of this was increases in the price of urban land because it meant that servicing authorities had to indicate where they would extend their systems next, thus conferring monopoly value on the land so designated.

The war itself had stimulated new industries using new technology. The subsequent peacetime industrial expansion employed much of that technology. Steam-powered factory machinery was rapidly replaced by reliable fractional horsepower electrical motors. The adoption of new quality control measures in industrial plants increased the quality and reliability of products. Materials handling technology in factories and warehouses, including the widespread use of forklift trucks, and the increasing use of internal combustion engine powered vehicles radically changed the transport of materials and finished products.

Industrial plants were released from the need to have rail sidings or a waterfront location and could locate to meet different site requirements. They needed large flat sites because manufacturing processes were now able to be laid out horizontally. The progressive move of industry from the older congested areas to new locations on the fringes of cities introduced new restructuring forces which were essentially centripetal in effect. That is, cities often had to make new investments in transport infrastructure, especially roads, to connect the new industrial locations into the rest of the metropolitan area. Although these new roads were part of the radial road system they led to the outward move of industrial employment.

The increased demand for private transport was met by rapid increases in the numbers of private cars in Australia. The increasing level of car ownership both was a response to and facilitated suburbanization. Increasing car ownership freed people to engage in the full range of activities available in the city. The road systems of cities were further centralized in their development, creating large levels of congestion. Investment in public transport, especially fixed-rail systems, was effectively held below replacement levels. The rise in car ownership was accompanied by a fall in public transport usage. A smaller proportion of trips were made as journeys to or from work. Shopping and recreational trips were more than half of all trips made. Central city interests managed to influence the investment in yet more centrally focused high-capacity roads even though it had become clear that the policy of constructing an extensive freeway system had not/could not diminish(ed) congestion. The proportion and, in some cases, the number of jobs in the city center fell. Increasing proportions of residents worked in or near the suburbs where they lived, yet the investment in roads and public transport, where it occurred, continued to assume and promote a highly centralized city structure.

The flight of the factories and warehouses from the city center was followed by a migration of retailing. The widespread takeup of domestic refrigerators after the war reduced the need for daily shopping for perishable goods. Changes in the organization of retailing and its adoption of new technology led to the development of "supermarkets" which offered volume purchases of food and household supplies at discounted prices which in turn led to the decline of traditional shopping centers. Further reorganization of the retailing sector led to the development of major "shopping malls" which further concentrated retailing, usually on large greenfield sites away from traditional shopping centers and away from the fixed-rail public transport systems. Traditional retailing centers identified in city plans withered and "unplanned" new ones sprang up. These major developments tended to change the structure of the city.

Two of the major developments which affected the structure of the Australian city over the last 30 years are transport related. The first is the development of air travel which has transformed the transport of people and high-value freight between cities nationally and internationally. The development of the airports and the industries to support them have resulted in major restructuring forces on the metropolitan areas of most large cities requiring new roads and, occasionally, new rail services to connect the city to its airports. These new investments in transport services have invariably been focused on the city center. In many cases the development of airports has been accompanied by massive public opposition from residents who are affected by the noise of airplane operation.

The second is the development of fast, reliable sea freight services for bulk and general cargo which led to major changes to the docks in most port cities. Because the old ports could not be redeveloped to meet the new demands of the new large-capacity vessels new ports were developed. They typically were some distance from the old centers and required massive reorganization of the road and rail systems to serve them. The new developments fractured all the traditional relationships between city and docks and the industries which supported them. New opportunities were opened to redevelop the "docklands" vacated and made derelict as shipping shifted its focus to the new sites.

Problems with the Rational Plan?

The postwar planning systems and plans were predicated on modernist or scientific notions of stability, consistency, predicability, and continuity. Although, with few exceptions, the plans were all drawn up for cities with private ownership of property few acknowledged the problems they would face in implementation. The plans were often "end state" plans which proved to be hard to adjust to the changing social mores, behavior, and attitudes of their residents or to accommodate the changes in industry, retailing, and commerce which occurred in them. They took little account of the fact that it was private owners of property who initiated land use change and development, so that the planning authority could only approve or disapprove development proposals. The planning process itself involved the traditional "survey – analysis – design" approach which had to be secretive and confidential to avoid individuals gaining advantage from premature or advanced knowledge of proposed planning changes, yet it also required a high degree of community consultation under which plans were exhibited and reviewed. It was extremely time-consuming and care had to be exercised because the zones ascribed to particular areas of land confirmed great value on them. Initially the process was designed to recover the "betterment" flowing from decisions to zone land to permit higher-value uses and to pay "compensation" to landowners deleteriously affected by zoning decisions. The dropping of the recovery of "betterment" basically destroyed the basis of planning and simultaneously opened the system to intense pressure from those who could benefit from zoning changes. The Australian planning system was heavily influenced by British writers, the most widely known exponent of the British system being Keeble (1959).

In Australia the planning authority was usually established as an independent statutory authority answerable to parliament, the planning scheme for Sydney being the most developed (Winston 1957). It had an "arm's length" relationship with ministers and attempted to establish its authority and create trust by establishing a regulatory framework based on technical criteria and widely accepted norms and conventions. It had no direct power over the investment decisions of servicing authorities, had few investment programs of its own, and relied on persuasion for its influence with other ministries in government. Unlike other agencies of government which set or influenced policy but which had no direct programs, such as the Treasury, it was not central to the setting of priorities. Moreover, the Treasuries State and Federal were ideologically opposed to planning, making it difficult for the planning authorities to gain support at the state level. In the Australian case although there was a strong degree of support for planning in the postwar period the decision to establish town planning was as much due to the need to comply with conditions laid down by the federal government which advanced funds for public housing but only if the states agreed to create town planning authorities.

By the early 1960s urban development pressures led to the recognition throughout the industrialized nations of a wide range of urban pathologies (Castells 1977). As in the USA and UK political concerns over urban and environmental issues became of central importance in Australia (Lloyd and Troy 1981). Public activism over environmental concerns found expression in a variety of ways including in local citizens' groups founded to fight a range of specific development proposals which residents felt would damage the environment or be injurious to their amenity. One of the most effective forms of protest was "Green Bans" under which industrial unions refused to allow development to occur on specific sites following community protest and representation (Burgman and Burgman 1998). The Australian Federal Government's initiatives included legislation modelled on USA initiatives requiring Environmental Impact Statements before developments were permitted to proceed. Although this raised the level of awareness of environmental issues it had the perverse effect of weakening the planning system. It would have been better to have included consideration of environmental issues as an integral part of the planning process.

Another problem with the rational plan was its inherently gendered conception of the city. Although women had always been important in the Australian workforce, as elsewhere, and were readily drafted into many occupations and industries during the Second World War it was nonetheless assumed that they would return to the more traditional home-centered life after the war. Increasing freedoms and recognition of their rights, however, together with the increasing economic need for them to work, facilitated by the development of labor-saving devices for the home, led to their continued and growing participation in paid employment. This was accompanied by later marriage and lower birthrates. By the early 1980s the fall in the number of school-age children per dwelling was being reflected in falling school enrolments. The "basic building block" of city planning had been "the neighborhood," which was based on the population needed to support a government-funded primary school. It had been assumed that this was a "given" and the hierarchy of school provision and, indeed, of shopping centers was based on this basic building block. The notion of the development of a sense of community was predicated on the assumption that the activities of households would be focused on the school and that this would provide the yeast for the development of a sense of engagement and commitment. For a while it served that function but was heavily dependent on the preparedness or ability of women to engage in supporting activities. But as the school enrolments fell due to cohort ageing and a fall in household size to the point where some schools were allegedly uneconomic and were closed, and as more women were working, this cohesive force weakened. The fall in the "apparent" school-age population in an area was also exacerbated by the "leakage" of children from the government school system to private schools. The cohesive community force was further weakened because the closure of the school was often accompanied by the failure of the traditional shopping centers which had been developed nearby.

The weakening of the neighborhood as a building block tended to accelerate the growth of the new unplanned metropolitan subcenters. Although this led to decentralization of retailing and some of the personal services, it was not tied to the existing fixed-rail public transport network and increased the demand for investment in roads which further enhanced the radial structure of the city.

The concurrent weakening of the political commitment to collective consumption led to a rise in the financial pressures under which the servicing authorities operated, making it more difficult for them to maintain or extend their coverage (Self 1993). The initial response of governments was to shift the burden for the provision of infrastructure to the private sector, for example, by requiring developers to provide services within new subdivisions (Neutze 1997). For a time this worked although it had marked inequitable effects because it redistributed wealth from poor to rich and from younger to older generations. Later, governments which had run down the reserves of the servicing agencies to fund their current operations were faced with large political pressures in part because, with the continued growth of the cities, they could not avoid the demands for services and partly because many of the services in the older cities were approaching the end of their "design lives" and were now in need of large-scale rehabilitation and renewal. Rather than explore new ways of providing the urban services which the residents expected, the government solution was to argue for a reduction in standards on the grounds that the old standards could no longer be afforded. By the early 1980s this was articulated as a drive for higher-density urban development on the assumption that changing the form of the city would reduce the demand for infrastructure investment (Troy 1996). A supplementary argument claimed that consolidated or compact cities would reduce the energy costs of their operation. It was also claimed that such cities would offer greater housing choice and that the stock of housing would more closely match the profile of household size. None of these claims was backed by empirical evidence. Similar arguments have been made in European and North American debates in favor of the compact city (Jenks et al. 1996).

The "really existing city" is highly decentralized yet its formal structure and the critical investment in transport continues to be made to support a highly centralized structure. The institutional structure of the city also remains powerfully centralized even though the great majority of residents live and focus their lives in urban subcentres and even though the mechanisms and processes of communication have undergone radical change. That is, in spite of the radical changes which have occurred in information technology few of the traditional institutions have used it to decentralize their operations and devolve decision making, making them more responsive and open to local participation. The technology and administrative structure of many servicing authorities remain focused on the nineteenth-century solutions which, while appropriate then, need to be reconsidered.

By the mid-1970s concerns over equity or social justice issues in the city again began to shape the demand for planning. Researchers and commentators again drew attention to the way the urban system itself exacerbated or created inequities (Badcock 1984; Harvey 1973; Troy 1981). For a period concern over social justice appeared to influence urban development policy but this was soon supplanted by preoccupation with issues of growth. The emerging evidence is that under these policies cities are becoming more segregated as lower-income households are forced into smaller dwellings at higher dwelling densities. The segregation becomes polarization, often being associated with groups who suffer multiple disadvantages or experience a variety of ethnic or religious discriminations. These effects have tended to confirm the view of critics that consolidation or compact city policies were thinly disguised attempts to reduce housing standards for lower-income groups.

Contemporary Trends

The planning system created in many countries after the Second World War is now in disarray. In Australia it proved incapable of anticipating the changes in mores, behavior, and attitudes of residents and corporations. More importantly it did not develop processes for responding to, shaping or managing them. Planning was seen as being too rigid and incapable of dynamic response. The professional planners themselves have been loath to enter into the debate over distributional aspects of city growth and operation. They have been reluctant to defend the ethical basis of their concerns and seem to have lost sight of their remit to defend the community interest. In many cases they have conducted little empirical research which might have improved their technical competence and enhanced their authority with a consequential increase in trust in their activities. Academic and professional planners have not offered a planning approach which could be more responsive and which relied less on the negative passive instruments employed in the early postwar planning schemes. The planning process has itself been politicized and used to achieve short-term objectives which are frequently the antithesis of planning (Stilwell 1993a, b).

Privatization made it difficult for governments to pursue social objectives including welfare and environmental targets. The terms of sale often make it extremely difficult for governments to improve standards or even to develop alternative technologies. Ownership of the services is often some distance from the city being served, making it even harder for the local community to exert pressure for improvement. In some cases the terms of privatization commit governments to guaranteeing profits for the service operators for decades to come, thus limiting future governments in their options for urban development. Some privatizations in Australia, especially in roads, are now the subject of legal challenge on the grounds that the prospectuses inviting investment in the infrastructure services are misleading or inaccurate. One of the serious consequences of the privatization of infrastructure services is that cities and their economies have become much more vulnerable. That is, they face increased risk of system failure and of the consequences of failure. The failure of the electricity supply to Auckland's CBD in 1998, the failure of the gas supply in Melbourne in 1998, the failure of the Sydney water supply to meet acceptable health standards for long periods in 1998, the failure of the sewage treatment plant in Adelaide in 1997/98 are all contemporary illustrations of the point.

More recently rising concern over environmental issues is forcing people to challenge the postmodernist explanation of urban development which is essentially defeatist in its conception. This renewed interest in a rational approach to urban development issues provides an opportunity for a renaissance of planning. The search for sustainable urban development under which cities develop and operate imposing minimum stress on the environment has led, in its first phase, to the acceptance of well-intentioned but empirically unsupported policies of containment. They have been buttressed by notions of "the urban" which are at variance with the aspirations and behavior of the great majority of the population. The policies were directed at changing urban form whereas the major inefficiencies of cities spring from their structure or the disposition of activities.

The second phase response is to return to fundamental questions about the size of the population and how it is distributed across the national system of cities. The response should also be to explore what services urban populations demand and how they might be met. This will inevitably mean that, given the limits to the supply of potable water, for example, new ways of meeting the demand for water will have to be developed. Similarly, we cannot continue to meet our energy needs from combustion of nonrenewable fuels and also meet international targets for the minimization of greenhouse gases. This must lead to the introduction of modes of production and operation of urban areas which minimize energy consumption. The exploration of ways of coping with the flow of wastes of urban living will also require a revised way of recovering and reusing resource from wastes and disposing of the remainder in ways which minimize environmental stress. The increasing polarization and segregation of cities will also need to be addressed if we are not to create the conditions which will destabilize the system as a whole.

Much has been written about the opportunities opened by the development of information technology (Castells 1996). The adoption of this technology has served to reinforce centralizing tendencies but it could equally be used to democratize the development and operation of the city. The paradox is that we have learned from our experience in managing relations between nations and, indeed, within them in the case of nations which are federations, how to organize, determine priorities and administer our affairs in a decentralized way yet we continue to approach the cities as though their affairs are naturally served by institutional structures which are highly centralized. A new form of planning which employs the new information technology could allow cities to be efficiently developed and operated as "federations" – more in the manner in which they actually operate now. This holds the promise of making it easier to achieve environmental targets while simultaneously making the city more accessible with lower levels of investment in urban systems, including transport, and avoiding the problems which flow from segregation. The cities could become more environmentally sustainable and more equitable but it will require a planning system which is at once more open and more interventionist (Healey 1997).

REFERENCES

Ashworth, W. 1954: *The Genesis of Modern British Town Planning*. London: Routledge and Kegan Paul.

Badcock, B. 1984: *Unfairly Structured Cities*. Oxford: Blackwell.
Benevolo, L. 1967: *The Origins of Modern Town Planning*. Translated from the Italian by Judith Landry. Cambridge, MA: MIT Press.
Burgman, M. and Burgman, V. 1998: *Green Bans, Red Unions: Environmental Activism and the New South Wales Builders Labourers' Federation*. Sydney: University of New South Wales Press.
Castells, M. 1977: *The Urban Question: A Marxist Approach*. London: Edward Arnold.
Castells, M. 1996: *The Rise of the Network Society*. Oxford: Blackwell.
Cherry, G. 1974: *The Evolution of British Town Planning*. Leighton Buzzard: Leonard Hill.
Cherry, G. 1996: *Town Planning in Britain since 1900: The Rise and Fall of the Planning Ideal*. Oxford: Blackwell.
Commonwealth Housing Commission (CHC) 1944: *Final Report*. Sydney: Ministry of Post-war Reconstruction.
Cullingworth, B. 1970: *Town and Country Planning in England and Wales*. 3rd edition. London: Allen and Unwin.
Davison, G. 1993: *The Past and Future of the Australian Suburb*. Canberra: Urban Research Program Working Paper 33.
Dingle, T. and Rasmussen, C. 1991: *Vital Connections: Melbourne and its Board of Works 1891–1991*. Melbourne: McPhee Gribble.
Engels, F. 1835: *The Housing Question*. New York: International Publishers.
Freestone, R. 1989: *Model Communities: The Garden City Movement in Australia*. Melbourne: Nelson.
Gleeson, B. 1999: *Geographies of Disability*. London: Routledge.
Hall, P. 1988: *Cities of Tomorrow: An Intellectual History of Urban Planning and Design in the Twentieth Century*. Oxford: Basil Blackwell.
Harloe, M. 1995: *The People's Home?* Oxford: Blackwell.
Harvey, D. 1973: *Social Justice and the City*. London: Edward Arnold.
Healey, P. 1997: *Collaborative Planning*. Basingstoke: Macmillan.
Howard, E. 1902: *Garden Cities of Tomorrow*. London: Faber and Faber.
Jackson, K. T. 1985: *Crabgrass Frontier: The Suburbanization of the United States*. New York: Oxford University Press.
Jenks, M., Burton, E., and Williams, K. 1996: *The Compact City: A Sustainable Urban Form?* London: E. and F. N. Spon.
Keeble, L. 1959: *Principles and Practices of Town and Country Planning*. London: The Estates Gazette.
Lloyd, C. and Troy, P. N. 1981: *Innovation and Reaction: The life and death of the Federal Department of Urban and Regional Development*. Sydney: George Allen and Unwin.
Lloyd, T., Troy, P., and Schreiner, S. 1992: *For the Public Health: The Hunter District Water Board 1892–1992*. Melbourne: Longman-Cheshire.
Merrifield, A. and Swyngedouw, E. 1995: *The Urbanisation of Injustice*. London: Lawrence and Wishart.
Mullins, P. 1981a: Theoretical perspectives on Australian urbanization: 1. material components in the reproduction of Australian labour power. *Australian and New Zealand Journal of Sociology*, 17 (1), 65–76.
—— 1981b: Theoretical perspectives on Australian urbanization: 2. Social components in the reproduction of labour power. *Australian and New Zealand Journal of Sociology*, 17 (3), 35–43.
—— 1987: Community and urban movements. *Sociological Review*, 35 (2), 347–69.
Mumford, L. 1961: *The City in History: Its origins, Its Transformations, and Its Prospects*. New York: Harcourt Brace.
Neutze, M. 1977: *Urban Development in Australia*. Sydney: George Allen and Unwin.

Neutze, M. 1997: *Funding Urban Services*. Sydney: Allen and Unwin.
Reps, J. 1967: *Monumental Washington: The Planning and Development of the Capital Center*. Princeton: Princeton University Press.
Reps, J. 1997: *Canberra 1912*. Melbourne University Press, Melbourne.
Rude, G. 1980: *Ideology and Popular Protest*. Chapel Hill: University of North Carolina Press.
Sedley, S. 1996: *The Common Law and the Constitution*. 1996 Radcliffe Lectures, University of Warwick.
Self, P. 1975: *Econocrats and the Policy Process: The Politics and Philosophy of Cost Benefit Analysis*. London: Macmillan.
Self, P. 1993: *Government by the Market? The Politics of Public Choice*. Basingstoke: Macmillan.
Stilwell, F. 1993a: *Beyond the Market*. Sydney: Pluto Press.
—— 1993b: *Economic Inequality: Who Gets What in Australia*. Sydney: Pluto Press.
Stretton, H. 1970: *Ideas for Australian Cities*. Adelaide: Orphan Books.
Troy, P. (ed.), 1981: *Equity in the City*. Sydney: George Allen and Unwin.
Troy, P. 1996: *The Perils of Urban Consolidation*. Sydney: Federation Press.
Winston, D. 1957: *Sydney's Great Experiment*. Sydney: Angus and Robertson.

Chapter 46

Varied Legacies of Modernism in Urban Planning

Alan Mabin

A few years ago, Sharon Zukin captured the essence of the intellectual challenge confronting present urban scholarship when she wrote of the "new spirit abroad in urban studies" (Zukin 1992: 489). Bob Beauregard has perhaps most forcefully brought this challenge to the attention of planners, especially in the United States, through his image of modernist planning as suspended precariously over the "post-modern abyss" (Beauregard 1989, 1991). In other parts of the English-reading world Goodchild (1990) has perhaps performed as significant a function. Beauregard conveys some of the sense of disruption which planners raised in the modernist discourses of planning schools perforce have felt in the circumstances of the nineties, when many of the props of the modernist worldview – even the very idea of *having* a worldview – have seemed knocked out. Moreover, the usual instruments of planning and their supports seem in disarray as everywhere and at every scale the state retreats, reducing budgets as it goes.

By now, however, the paragraph above repeats a familiar litany. Most urban planners know the song, and some love to sing it. Many *have* to write new refrains. All sorts of new directions in planning have been proposed, and many pursued with vigor – including Beauregard's "reestablishment of mediative roles between capital, labour and the state." On occasion the response has been still more planning activity, though almost certainly with further reduced effect (see, for example, Yiftachel and Alexander 1995: 280). But it seems to me that few are prepared to excavate the legacies bequeathed by the modernist past. Like all archaeologies, such excavation requires time and patience, and difficult decisions – to dig deeper in some areas than others, to lavish more attention on some artifacts than on their companions, and to choose which belong in museum displays, or in the basement, or in debate on their functions.

The first purpose of this chapter is to excavate some of the modernist planning past. Paths to modernist planning will be treated somewhat eclectically. At each point, the chapter attempts to emphasize the complexity and often contradictory nature of the evidence. This exercise leads on to the brief consideration of the questions: What can modern urban planning contribute to a post-modern era? What are its limitations?

Modernism and Planning

What modernist approaches to urban planning have had in common was (or is) a sense both of the scale of urban problems and of the necessity of major interventionist activity towards their solution. Lewis Mumford captured this sentiment clearly when, in reviewing Jose Luis Sert's *ABC of Urban Problems, Their Analysis, Their Solutions* (Sert 1944), he wrote in *The New Republic*: "Mr Sert believes that our cities can and should survive; but the condition for their survival is the application of large-scale town planning which will embrace the reorganization of regions and countrysides as well." Scale, intervention, comprehensiveness: all are present here. As important was the sense that intervention could actually accomplish improvement: "...it is possible to attack the prevailing waste and muddle..." (Yorke 1939: 132).

The grand scale and optimism of modernism in planning has not precluded a sense that the creation of the better "city tomorrow" would probably be slow (Fry 1944: 48ff) MARS (Modern Architecture Research Group, British affiliate of CIAM – Congrès Internationaux d'Architecture Moderne, founded in 1922) wanted to solve the perceived massive problems of London's urban form, but recognized that "We must find a solution that will allow us to deal with London, even if it is to be the work of several generations and we but its progenitors...spare time to prepare a plan for London... (Banham 1960: 86–7; Fry 1944: 94ff).

There is little sense that the future will overturn what seems to be appropriate now. One of the prominent members of MARS, Maxwell Fry, noted during the Second World War:

> Certain it is that the task to which we will turn so eagerly when peace comes does not lie within the power of a single generation to perform, but belongs more nearly to the century. Why therefore should we be deterred from the attempt to see the whole, and to frame principles which may help to govern the conduct of new generations. It were better to go only part of the way along a fine road than to reach the end of a blind alley (Fry 1944: 113–14).

It has often been noted how strongly modernism in planning represented a response to material conditions – what we might now call Fordism, machine production, the development of new building materials, "the new age of automobility" (Jackson 1985: title of chapter 9), and so on. Thus Le Corbusier in *Vers une Architecture* "extolled the achievements of engineers...and proclaimed the need for a more rational exploitation of the technique of modern engineering to provide on these foundations a solution to the problems of to-day..." (Yorke 1939: 45) – a paean to the *possibilities* to which modernist planning could respond, demonstrating a belief in the possibility of rationality.

Urban planning, of course, had to do with a response to *problems*; using new techniques to address and to solve those problems: in the view of CIAM in the early thirties, "It is the uncontrolled and disorderly development of the Machine Age which has produced the chaos of our cities" (Sert 1944: 246). Thus modernist planning can be apprehended as optimistic and grand in scale; but there is another feature of modernism which seems striking. The conditions to which it responded were not merely made more optimistic by the new material conditions available, but indeed were made more sombre by the "dislocations of the age" (James 1988: p. 600) – the wreckage, depression, even carnage and devastation to which modernist planning mostly responded in its formative phases. That modernist planning *became* a matter of centralized bureaucratic routine, remote from most citizens, does not mean that it always lacked a deeper and stirring response to appalling conditions – the powerful Burnham vision of making large plans to stir the blood (Moore 1921). After all, we usually learnt our planning history from texts which emphasized the origins of planning in the awful urban life of the late nineteenth and early twentieth-centuries in just those terms – Goodchild's (1990) "early modern" planning.

With roots in those earlier times, modernist planning took shapes and substances in the thirties and forties. It represented a broad school which understood, albeit in varying degrees, the sources of the "dislocations of the age" as "laissez-faire policies, free competition, present system of allotment of land (arbitrary and excessive degree of subdivision) . . . new factors have appeared – the economic crisis of our times, the chaos of our cities, the air-raid menace . . ." (Sert 1944: 152). This diagnosis (and the medical analogy is intriguing) was hardly confined to Europe. The city was chaotic, problematic, it degenerated the younger generation, in the eyes of Latin American planners of the period. Planning was necessary to control the growth of the city precisely to overcome these problems (Outtes 1994). If modernist planning showed some consensus on the sources of urban ills, and if its practitioners shared the same complex of optimism, scale, and time in solution of those ills, that nevertheless left plenty of room for divergent approaches to the spatial solutions which could be proposed and sometimes implemented. There was little dispute in the thirties on separating CIAM's "four urban functions" in space: indeed, part of the modernist ideas of adjusting urban form to cope with other modern developments lay in accepting that "Industrial districts should be independent of residential districts (indeed, of other districts as well), and should be isolated by means of green bands" and that "Certain industries [e.g. Ford] will require vast areas; others will need only small areas, with allowances for possible expansion (Sert 1944: 152, 154; also Athens Charter clause 5 on p. 248).

But as Fowler argues, especially in a chapter called "Why did we do it: explanations for the postwar urban environment," contest between garden city expansion and compact city concentration meant that modernist planning spoke with multiple voices on the subject of remaking urban form (Fowler 1992). From the early thirties some modernists protested what they saw as too dispersed a garden city solution to the contemporary urban problem. For example, Thomas Sharp attacked the evils of the "town-country" suburban ideal, anxious that modern housing development was "wastefully eating up the countryside" and pleading for a return to the planning of "real compact towns" (Sharp 1932; Richards 1940: 125). Modernism gave us both the "forms and ideologies of Wright and Le Corbusier . . . the clashing ideals of Broadacre City and Radiant City," with effects expressed in both "the physical design and politics of our cities . . ." (Fowler 1992: 173–5).

These clashing ideals intersected in various and noncongruent ways with political differences. Modernism of course contained contests, one of which lay between those who favored the "withering away of government" in the face of self-sufficiency and individualism (Wright) and those who saw a need for massive government or other hierarchical intervention to improve urban form (perhaps more Corbusian). For Le Corbusier "... a city for the machine age could never emerge from discussion and compromise: that was the path to chaos" (Fishman 1987: 239). And, of course, this contest sometimes appeared as a contradiction in the writing and practice of single individuals.

Authoritarian tendencies in *some* modernist approaches to city form have resonated most clearly in divided and segregated societies: thus "The experiment of Chandigarh... shows socially regressive traits. Especially symptomatic is Le Corbusier's cynically resigned acceptance of the caste system as a 'useful means of classification', the inhumanity of which he attempts to make more bearable by high architectural quality" (Lampugnani 1985: 130).

Such patrician attitudes are sometimes considered characteristic of many planners in the whole modern period, whatever their differences on matters such as urban form. To the (mostly) French example of Le Corbusier could be added the British example of Abercrombie – not only evidenced in his plans and approach to grand planning solutions but in his personal style, nowhere better illustrated than in the film of the 1944 London County Plan, *Proud City*. As Abercrombie handles his monocle at the fireside his patrician tones tell the public what is best for them (on the film, see Gold and Ward 1994). American, Brazilian, Canadian... and probably Yemeni or Zambian examples could be added. All would reveal what Docker calls a magisterial attitude – confidence in possession of the finest ideas, as judged by the leading exponents of modernism themselves (Docker 1994: 14, 22). And this confidence has survived the fact that, despite its apparently long-range view, there have been frequent changes in just what the finest ideas are considered to be. Nowhere is that facet of urbanist modernism more apparent than in the early history of "socialist" Eastern Europe: "Three times in little more than ten years, everything had begun all over again – at the end of the war, in 1949 and again in 1956" (Åman 1992: vii).

Of course, in Eastern Europe this arrogance combined well with degrees of authoritarian rule. Similarly, one thinks of South Africa, the development of apartheid and the evolution of its planning in the same period (cf. Mabin and Smit 1997). Outtes (1994) outlines similar phenomena in the increasingly dictator-ruled Latin America of the thirties and forties, where "representative institutions typical of democratic societies were seen as inefficient through the eyes of the planners." For example, an author in the leading Brazilian urban journal noted "Let us claim the convenience of the new mentality which cân see the benefits of single orientation" (Anon. 1940: 237). The culmination of such approaches may be found in Brasilia, "*the* modernist city" of Holston's (1989) account. And, of course, there is something eating away at these supremely confident and grandly assertive ideas. In Brasilia, it is the "Brasilianization" of the city as informality and popular alternatives cut into the grand plan of the earlier autocrats.

Alternative Modernisms

However, there is another tradition in modernist planning: a humanitarian (and sometimes socialist) one, with roots reaching back to the Enlightenment (Wolfe 1989: 62–77). In the quest to achieve humanitarian ends, urban planners are sometimes "considered to be socialist intruders on the rights of private property, and to some extent they are," as Fowler puts it. A socialist tradition in modernist planning can be traced back to Tony Garnier's *Cité Industrielle* of 1899–1904 – a contribution whose "principles of city planning were perfected by CIAM, and decisively influenced the *Charte d'Athènes*" if Lampugnani is to be believed (1985: 52–3). A variant on these ideas developed in Soviet planning in the thirties: for example, N. A. Milyutin's compact linear city quarter proposed for Stalingrad in 1930, imbued with good social intentions and attempted in highly authoritarian times. As with Le Corbusier's rather fatuous assertion, "The law of the land is that it shall support houses (the law of gravity) and not that it shall support the unmerited ascension of private fortunes" (Le Corbusier 1947: 100), such examples show how anticapitalist and authoritarian planning could variously mix or remain opposed throughout the modernist period in planning, producing the puzzles of Wright, Corb, and others (Yorke 1939: 34). For such reasons it is necessary to recognize that the legacies of modernism in planning are varied indeed.

Murray Bookchin argues that the significance of planners lies in the fact that they exist at all. Their existence shows market society's distrust that spontaneous economic and social activity can express itself in a beautiful city, let alone a habitable or efficient one (Fowler 1992: 171). But if we are to draw towards one tendency which would capture some coherence in modernism, it would surely lie in the discourses of control in modernist planning and urban policy: control to address the "dislocations of the age." These two facets – control and improvement – have been expressed in innumerable ways.

From the Barlow Commission on the distribution of industrial activity in England (which *The Economist* called the "Royal Commission on the Enormity of London," August 13, 1938, p. 313), through so many daily activities of urban planners in thousands of zoned cities, to such extremes as controlling the urbanization of rural people in Maoist China, apartheid South Africa or Soeharto Indonesia, instruments of control have been critical to modernist planning. Viewed from outside, all such planning can appear to turn the rationalist bases of modernism into the irrational (e.g. Norval 1993). Yiftachel has suggested that "The very same planning tools usually introduced to assist social reform and improvement in people's quality of life can be used as a means of controlling and repressing minority groups" (Yiftachel 1995: 218). Hoch puts a related point both more philosophically and more strongly, at least when "good modern planning" occurs in an uncertain environment: "Rational planning in the service of humane projects ends up producing effects far more perverse and destructive than the alleged problems such planning is supposed to solve... if planning inflames the illness it is supposed to cure, it would seem prudent to stop planning altogether" (Hoch 1992: 207, 212).

If one follows texts such as that of Åman (1992), such a comment strikes one as more than apposite in describing the kind of planning which characterized Eastern European cities in the fifties – and one could make similar points in relation to Argentina, Brazil, and South Africa.

Separations

It is easy to understand the reconstructionist thinking which preoccupied planners in so many parts of the world at the close of the Second World War. The great hopes of such planners – if they shared the aims of the Planning School at which Jacqueline Tyrwhitt, a prominent member of CIAM, taught, then there was an orientation to create a planning mindset:

> The School seeks to create . . . a corps of trained men [sic], possessing the necessary breadth of outlook and technical knowledge, whose collaboration with and ultimate succession to those who now perform similar tasks will, it is the Association's hope, ensure happy and ordered development in the place of the chaos which the nineteenth-century has left us (Association for Planning and Regional Reconstruction 1947: 4).

But these apparently laudable aims tied into some very specific ideas about the organization of urban space and society. Tyrwhitt concluded a textbook chapter of 1953 with a long quote from Giedion, clearly one of the moderns, which specifically thinks in terms of the distance there should be between residential and industrial sections . . . (the modern town planner) thinks no longer in terms of streets and axes, but in terms of population groupings (Tyrwhitt 1950: 145; the same points were made by MARS member Jane Drew, 1994).

This modernist thinking clearly lent itself to apartheid, in ways which Wilkinson and Japha have illustrated perhaps more clearly than any other authors (Wilkinson 1983; Japha 1986): a marriage of modernity and racism, something not dissimilar to what Bauman explores in *Modernity and the Holocaust* (1989). But more important, Baumann shows us that the holocaust – while not a predictable result of modernism – was rendered possible by modernism, and that such enormity fits easily with modernist "planning" in a variety of fields.

Does this urge to control disorder and create separations characterize *all* modernist planning? Or do some valuable artifacts lie in the modernist soil, awaiting exhumation, free or potentially free of the urge to control even though possessing the means? Reading the recent planning (and broader urban studies) literature raises images of the "terrifying landscape of postmodernism" (Dijink 1993). Authors such as Christopherson (1993), Davis (1990), and Judd (1994) certainly terrify with the awful prospect of increasing proportions of urban populations walled out of what a decreasing proportion is walled into. In some places, which may be the image of the future, the walled out already outnumber the walled in: in this sense the postmodern city "all comes together" in São Paulo, not in Los Angeles (*pace* Soja 1989). What effective future can possibly await those who now occupy the declining spaces, shrinking consumption patterns, and increasingly hideous images which may soon, if not now, form the lot of the world's urban majority? In cities like Johannesburg, Jakarta, or São Paulo, the collection of huge groups of people whom "the system of labour cannot or will not use" is not a marginal phenomenon: it is central to the politics of the future. Approaches to nonpaternalistic incorporation of the excluded are painful and take enormous amounts of resources, especially time, to develop.

The scale of the global urban problem is immense. There is a temptation to seize the initiative armed with the large-scale view of modernism. Behind the notion that urban life in much of the world is not environmentally "sustainable," lurks the probability that urban society is not politically sustainable unless "something" happens. Already new dislocations threaten the new age of privatized urban space, though such threats may seem more remote in midtown Manhattan than in Salvador do Bahia. Modernist ideas leap forward to address these dislocations, but they do so disjointedly and ineffectually. The acceleration of market and technological change seems to deny the modernist recognition that intended urban change may be slow. That recognition in any event is under attack whenever it can be accused of implying that the walled out should "wait on time," in Martin Luther King's still ringing phrase. Physical proposals put forward to relieve the conditions of the excluded seem destined to deepen that exclusion, as both low- and high-density urban forms, both mixed and single uses, appear to turn against them in the hands of the "city builders," to employ Fainstein's (1994) phrase. Greater democracy is welcomed, but weakened; it seems to have little effect on reducing the controls binding the lives of many.

But the great dislocations of this apparent *fin de siècle* seem to call for a grand drama. Can parts of the modernist legacy be exhumed to contribute heroic roles? If cities globally are descending into greater segregation, fragmentation, and control, in which large and even majority sections of populations suffer on the wrong side of the walls, what can the modernist tradition offer?

Democracy

In some cases, the very sweep of the modernist tradition has precipitated its rejection. It has become difficult to speak of planning without some embarrassment in many parts of central and eastern Europe (as reflected in papers and discussions, for example, at the Association of European Schools of Planning conference in Lodz, Poland, 1992). Despondency pervades the ranks of those who sought (or in some remaining cases seek) to bring planning ideas into practice elsewhere, particularly in North America, and probably more generally in the larger cities of Asia and Latin America, not to mention Africa. In the midst of the despondency, resignation, and ignorance which characterize the response, the arrival (or return) of democracy in Eastern Europe, Latin America, and South Africa suggests cases in which some of the older precepts may again be tested – and tested in the increasingly common circumstances of exclusion and control not merely of some minority groups, but of attempting to overcome the social, economic, and political exclusion of a majority (cf. Häussermann 1996: 222–30).

In a world of increasingly divided cities, suggested in phrases from recent publication titles such as "distorted cities" (Beauregard 1994), "fortress city" (Christopherson 1993), "urban control" (Judd 1994), "new walled cities" (Davis 1990), and "landscapes of power" (Zukin 1991), the reconstruction of cities after apartheid seems a beacon of hope to many planners worldwide. Discourses of progressive change confront the urban observer everywhere in South Africa, and indeed appear accepted if not hegemonic across the wide political spectrum. The modernist predilections of the ruling ANC are demonstrated in its election manifesto, the Reconstruction and Development Programme, which refers to "coherent vision," purposeful effort," "fundamental transformation," and "comprehensive redesign and reconstruction" among other examples of unequivocal modernist language. The difficulties of the project are rarely confronted, but any successes will be significant for the exploration of modernist planning in contemporary cities (Turok 1994, 1995; Harrison 1996).

Thus the Brazilian, Hungarian, and South African experiences at once attract and puzzle: for their cities are not the only ones "distorted" by modernist planning

(Beauregard 1994). These "non-northern/western" cases provide prisms (undoubtedly different from the prisms of Shanghai or Bangkok) through which to examine the varied impact of modernism on urban planning. Among the intentions of this chapter is the commencement of such an examination. To do so seems particularly apposite at a time when "segregation, fragmentation and surveillance" have become key features identified in the newer literature as characteristic of "post-modern" cities (Watson and Gibson 1995; Pagano 1993). If modernist planning approaches can now contribute to improving the lives of urban citizens in South Africa, their relevance can surely be considered elsewhere.

But the approaches to urban planning remain embedded in certain elements of modernism, despite the explicit rejection of "modernism" by some of the practitioners. For example, the key idea that urban form is *wrong* powerfully persists in South African planning discourse, where it is precisely the dislocations of apartheid which allow that persistence. Thus the first postapartheid planning law, called the Development Facilitation Act, sets out general principles which are intended to guide decision making on land development. They explicitly include such CIAM concepts as compacting the city and achieving order in various ways; but more fundamentally, they reflect the powerful modernist traditions – one that hopes to accomplish the better city through urban form, and one that believes the world can be guided through principles. The persistence of these modernist precepts in a country which has experienced radical democratization is an enigma until one recognizes the imperative to change the world, postapartheid, which can produce law similar to the Brazilian rhetoric of the forties: "The ideal, in a measure of this kind, is not wasting efforts in piece-meal activities but defining the general rules and following them inflexibly, during decades and decades" (Anon 1940: 237, cited in Outtes 1994).

Modernist Planning in a Postmodern Period?

Some have suggested that much planning thinking now "bears little resemblance to the positivist approaches that dominated a decade ago" – however we characterize the period, "there is certainly a different drumbeat" (Moore Milroy 1991: 187). Yet interrogation of the continuing legacies of modernism may defy that interpretation. And, again there is diversity, from near-total rejection of urban planning to the embrace of certain elements of the modernist tradition by new regimes. It is the South African example which is easiest to explore here, though others could be added.

South Africa's cities, and those of the rest of southern Africa, have been shaped in large and small ways by very modernist conceptions of planning – the achievement of structures which would support the society and economy of apartheid (Robinson 1990). Such an application of planning may be recognized as one designed, like that Yiftachel has described for Palestine/Israel (Yiftachel 1995), to promote social control and economic retardation – though its origins may be rather different. The opposition to apartheid planning based itself, of course, on an alternative but very much a modernist conception of planning – planning intended to redistribute power and comfort in a comprehensive and rationalist way, predicated on the notion of continued change in what seemed to be the relatively unilinear processes of economic development of the period. Thus conflict over the shape of the cities was essentially a conflict, heightened in the late seventies and early eighties, between two rationalist movements and planning approaches, despite their basis in conflicting "nationalisms." King notes that in "developing countries... it was thought that modernism would save cities from Europe's industrial-capitalist urban chaos" (1992: 146). Both the rationalist views of urban South Africa sought to do just that, one through planned oppression, the other through planned emancipation.

Meanwhile, the legacies of the modernist past in urban planning continue to weigh heavily on the conception of action. As Peter Marcuse (1993) points out, divided cities are nothing new. But there are new forces which promote division, and perhaps fewer which oppose. Globally, the roles of metropolitan governments and planning have weakened (Yiftachel and Alexander 1995: 280). Dramatic changes underway in urban space have more to do with Fainstein's (1994) city builders than with governments – and they tend to deepen the divides, not to overcome them by some magical "edge city" incantation (Beauregard 1995; Wilson 1995). Among the challenges will be to develop the certainty in planning which allows progressive planning to channel private development in socially useful ways (Christopherson 1993: 410, 419). These are lessons usefully learnt from São Paulo (Guedes 1992) to Santa Monica (Shearer in Krumholz and Clavel 1994). And in the most peripheral parts of the global community of divided cities, such fundamentals as class and gender relations remain little addressed. There is plenty of scope for new intellectual contributions to planning theory here – not to mention hearing the stories of planners from the South.

Some Conclusions

"City planning in Australia has failed to improve the welfare of our city dwellers..." wrote Leonie Sandercock (1976: 1) some years ago. Not only has urban planning failed to realize the dream of improved conditions of urban life, as Sandercock suggested of Australian planning, but in South Africa (and perhaps elsewhere) it has actually deepened patterns of oppression which it has taken decades to overthrow. However, the nature and impact of planning are much more textured, nuanced, and varied – some would say paradoxical or contradictory – than this contribution to racial and other forms of oppression would suggest. In most parts of the world planning has long included an ambition to improve urban life for less exalted parts of city populations, and these reformist, sometimes even revolutionary, sentiments have coexisted with less salubrious sentiments.

Modernist planning tried to remake the shape of cities to deal with the dislocations of its formative age. It fell on harder times as the dislocations became more complex and less obvious; indeed, it has fallen into some disrepute. We are now in a period when city form seems to be remade beyond the control of planning. Modernist planning has gone into retreat. But as city form is left to the private city builders, we end up with fortresses. Thus we hurtle towards new dislocations – where will we turn when movements arise which challenge those dislocations, which demand new city forms? In the South African case it is clear that we turn to elements of the modernist planning project to overcome the fragmentation and exclusion of apartheid; but this occurs because of the legacy of modernism within the liberation movement: perhaps also negatively, because other instruments do not yet present themselves.

The narrative of contemporary change in Johannesburg, São Paolo and Budapest is partly about the problems of "finding a means to handle, politically, waking up in a postmodern era while equipped only with the politics and planning practices of a modernist past" (Mabin 1995). The preliminary explorations reported here indicate merely how substantial some of the difficulties are, how some intersect with the experiences recounted from other parts of the world, and how some of the approaches to change which emancipatory movements find themselves adopting are full of difficulties and dangerous limitations. Attempts to confront some of the disabilities of the modernist forms under distinctly postmodern circumstances *with the aid of modernist planning ideas* are surely relevant to a wider frame.

The politics of urban emancipation in societies marked by massive unemployment, historically substantial but very incomplete proletarianization, disaffection, and industrial decline as well as particularly deeply etched patterns of social and spatial fragmentation are not matters of merely idiosyncratic interest. They certainly bear comparison with other societies in the South, and much greater similarity with cities in the global North can regrettably be anticipated in years to come.

Much of what has happened in social theory in the past 20 years or so has been about disempowering White, male, Western, and indeed modernist, figures, authors, theories – and the empowering of "other" voices. Does the "inclusion" of "voices from the borderlands" (Sandercock 1995) mean displacement of the modernist past? Or can some of its varied legacies survive in the new theories and practices of postmodern planning? Can we be postmodernists and still be planners when we grow up?

REFERENCES

Åman, Anders 1992: *Architecture and Ideology in Eastern Europe during the Stalin Era*. New York: Architectural History Foundation/CMMIT Press, second edition.

Anon. 1940: O plano da cidade. *Urbanismo e Viao*, 3 (8), 237.

Association for Planning and Regional Reconstruction 1947: *Information Bulletin*, 1947, 46/47.

Banham, Reyner 1960: *Theory and Design in the First Machine Age*. London: The Architectural Press, 1960.

Bauman, Z. 1989: *Modernity and the Holocaust*. Oxford: Polity Press.

Beauregard, Robert 1989: Between modernity and postmodernity: the ambiguous position of US planning. *Environment and Planning D: Society and Space*, 7 (4), 381–95.

Beauregard, Robert 1991: Without a net: modernist planning and the postmodern abyss. *Journal of Planning Education and Research*, 10 (3), 189–94.

Beauregard, Robert 1994: *Distorted Cities: Harvey S. Perloff Lecture*. Los Angeles: UCLA School of Architecture and Urban Planning.

Beauregard, Robert 1995: Edge Cities: peripheralising the center. *Urban Geography*, 16 (8), 708–21.

Christopherson, Susan 1993: The fortress city: Privatized spaces, consumer citizenship. In A. Amin (ed.), *Post Fordism: A Reader*. Oxford: Blackwell, 189–94.

Davis, Mike 1990: *City of Quartz: Excavating the Future in Los Angeles*. London: Verso.

Dijink, G. 1993: Postmodernism, power, synergy. *Tijdschrift voor Economische en Sociale Geografie*, 84 (1), 178–80.

Docker, John 1994: *Postmodernism and Popular Culture: A Cultural History*. Cambridge: Cambridge University Press.

Drew, Jane 1994: Interview with Alan Mabin and Susan Parnell, Johannesburg (tape available on request).

Fainstein, Susan 1994: *The City Builders: Property, Politics and Planning in London and New York*. Oxford: Blackwell.

Fishman, Robert 1987: *Bourgeois Utopias: The Rise and Fall of Suburbia*. New York: Basic Books.

Fowler, E. P. 1992: *Building Cities that Work*. Montreal: McGill-Queens.

Fry, Maxwell 1944: *Fine Building*. London: Faber and Faber.

Gold, J. R. and Ward, S. V. 1994: "We're going to do it right this time": cinematic representations of urban planning and the British new towns. In S. C. Aitken and L. Zonn (eds.), *Place, Power, Situation and Spectacle: A Geography of Film*. Savage, MD: Roman and Littlefield.

Goodchild, B. 1990: Planning and the modern/postmodern debate. *Town Planning Review*, 61 (2), 119–35.

Guedes, Eliane 1992: Interview with Alan Mabin, São Paulo.

Harrison, P. 1996: Postmodernism confronts planning. *Town and Regional Planning*, 40, 26–34.

Häussermann, H. 1996: From the socialist to the capitalist city: experiences from Germany. In G. Andrusz, M. Harloe, and I. Szelenyi (eds.), *Cities after Socialism*. Oxford: Blackwell, 215–31.

Hoch, Charles 1992: The paradox of power in planning practice. *Journal of Planning Education and Research*, 11, 207–12.

Holston, James 1989: *The Modernist City: An Anthropological Critique of Brasilia*. Chicago: University of Chicago Press.

Jackson, K. T. 1985: *Crabgrass Frontier: The Suburbanization of the United States*. New York: Oxford.

James, T. 1988: Rhetoric and resistance: social science and community schools for Navajos in the 1930s. *History of Education Quarterly*, 28 (4), 599–626.

Japha, Derek 1986: The social programme of the South African Modern Movement in architecture. Paper presented to Africa Seminar, Centre for African Studies, University of Cape Town.

Judd, D. 1994: The rise of the new walled cities. In H. Liggett and D. Perry (eds.), *Representing the City*. Newberry Park: Sage.

King, Anthony 1992: Review of *The Modernist City: An Anthropological Critique of Brasilia* by James Holston. *International Journal of Urban and Regional Research*, 16 (1), 146.

Krumholz, N. and Clavel, P. 1994: *Reinventing Cities: Equity Planners Tell Their Stories*. Philadephia: Temple University Press.

Lampugnani, V. M. 1985: *Architecture and City Planning in the Twentieth Century*. New York: Van Nostrand.

Le Corbusier (Charles Edouard Jeanneret) 1947: *Concerning Town Planning*, tr. C. Entwhistle from the 1946 French *Propos d'Urbanisme*. London: The Architectural Press.

Mabin, Alan 1995: On the problems and prospects of overcoming segregation, fragmentation and surveillance in southern Africa's cities in the post-modern era. In S. Watson and K. Gibson (eds.), *Postmodern Cities and Spaces*. Oxford: Blackwell, 187–98.

Mabin, Alan and Smit, Dan 1997: "Reconstructing South Africa's cities: aspects of urban planning 1900–2000. *Planning Perspectives*, 12 (2), 193–223.

Marcuse, Peter 1993: What's so new about divided cities? *International Journal of Urban and Regional Research*, 17 (3), 355–65.

Marcuse, Peter 1996: Privatization and its discontents, property rights in land and housing in the transition in Eastern Europe. In G. Andrusz, M. Harloe, and I. Szelenyi (eds.), *Cities after Socialism*. Oxford: Blackwell, 119–91.

Moore, C. 1921: *Daniel H. Burnham: Architect, Planner of Cities*. Boston and New York: Houghton Mifflin.

Moore, Milroy, B. 1991: Into postmodern weightlessness. *Journal of Planning Education and Research*, 10 (3), 187–7.

Outtes, Joel 1994: Disciplining the society through the city: town planning genesis in Brazil and Argentina 1905–1945. Paper awarded Harold Blakemore Essay Prize 1994 and forthcoming in *Latin American Studies*.

Pagano, M. A. 1993: Book review essay: "Is the postmodern city different?" *Urban Affairs Quarterly*, 28 (4), 650–7.

Richards, J. M. 1940: *An Introduction to Modern Architecture*. Harmondsworth: Penguin.

Robinson, J. 1990: "A perfect system of control"? State power and "native locations" in South Africa. *Environment and Planning D: Society and Space*, 8, 135–62.

Sandercock, Leonie 1976: *Cities for Sale: Property, Politics and Urban Planning in Australia*. London: Heinemann.

Sandercock, Leonie 1995: Voices from the borderlands: a meditation on a metaphor. *Journal of Planning Education and Research*, 14 (1), 77–88.

Sert, J. L. 1944: *Can Our Cities Survive? An ABC of Urban Problems, Their Analysis, Their Solutions, Based on the Proposals Formulated by the Fourth and Fifth Congresses of the CIAM*. Cambridge, MA: Harvard University Press.

Sharpe, L. J. (ed.) 1995: *The Government of World Cities: The Future of the Metro Model*. New York: Wiley.

Sharp, T. 1932: *Town and Countryside*. Oxford: Oxford University Press.

Soja, Edward 1989: *Postmodern Geographies. The Reassertion of Space in Critical Social Theories*. New York: Verso.

Szelenyi, I. 1996: Cities under socialism – and after. In G. Andrusz, M. Harloe, and I. Szelenyi (eds.), *Cities after Socialism*. Oxford: Blackwell, 215–31.

Turok, Ivan 1994: Urban planning in the transition from apartheid: Part 2 – towards reconstruction. *Town Planning Review*, 65 (4), 355–74.

Turok, Ivan 1995: *Reconstruction and Development Programme IJURR*.

Tyrwhitt, J. 1950: *Town and Country Planning Textbook*, ed. Association for Planning and Regional Reconstruction with an introduction by William Holford. London: Architectural Press.

Watson, S. and Gibson, K. 1995: *Postmodern Cities and Spaces*. Oxford: Blackwell.

Wilkinson, P. 1983: Providing "adequate shelter": the South African state and the "resolution" of the African urban housing crisis, 1948–1954. In D. Hindson (ed.), *Working Papers in Southern African Studies Vol. 3*, Johannesburg: Ravan, 64–90.

Wilson, E. 1995: The rhetoric of urban space. *New Left Review*, 209, 146–60.

Wolfe, J. 1989: Theory, hypothesis, explanation and action: the example of urban planning. In A. Kobayashi and S. Mackenzie (eds.), *Remaking Human Geography*, Boston: Unwin Hyman.

Yiftachel, O. 1995: The dark side of modernism. In S. Watson and K. Gibson (eds.), *Postmodern Cities and Spaces*. Oxford: Blackwell.

Yiftachel, O. and Alexander, I. 1995: The state of metropolitan planning: decline or restructuring? *Environment and Planning C: Government and Policy*, 13 (2), 273–96.

Yorke, F. R. S. 1939: *A Key to Modern Architecture*. London: Blackie.

Zukin, S. 1991: *Landscapes of Power: From Detroit to Disneyworld*. Berkeley: University of California Press.

Zukin, S. 1992: The postmodern invasion: review essay. *International Journal of Urban and Regional Research*, 16 (3), 489.

Chapter 47

The Environment of the City...or the Urbanization of Nature

Erik Swyngedouw and Maria Kaïka

The question that now begins to gnaw at your mind is more anguished: outside Penthesilea does an outside exist? Or, no matter how far you go from the city, will you only pass from one limbo to another, never managing to leave it?

Italo Calvino ([1974] 1979: 122)

The exploitation of man and of nature, which takes place in the country, is realized and concentrated in the city.

Raymond Williams ([1973] 1993: 48)

It is in many ways astonishing that in the ballooning literature on the environment and among the innumerable environmental social movements, the city often figures in a rather marginal or, worse, antithetical manner. Even more surprising is the almost complete absence of a serious engagement with the environmental problematic in the prolific literature on the city.[1] At a time when the world is quickly approaching a situation in which more than half of its population dwells in big cities, the environmental question is generally often circumscribed to either rural or threatened "natural" environments or to "global" problems. Yet, the urbanization process is central to the momentous environmental changes and alleged problems that have inspired the emergence of environmental issues on the political agenda. Environmental movements are largely distinctly urban phenomena; environmental ideologies and discourses on the environment as well as the material transformation of nature generally originate in and radiate from the urban environment (Gottlieb 1993). In this chapter, we shall first consider ways of conceptualizing the relationship between nature and the city and argue that urbanization is a process of perpetual metabolic socioecological change that produces distinct (urban) environments or, in other words, the city is a process of urbanization of nature. We then revisit and critically assess the problematic character of the now popular notion of urban "sustainability." We shall subsequently discuss how the urbanization of nature has historically been infused by particular visions and ideologies about the "nature" of nature and of the city. In a final part, we shall make a case for a political-ecological perspective.

The Urbanization of Nature

In *Nature, Justice and the Geography of Difference*, David Harvey (1996) insists that there is nothing particularly "unnatural" about New York City or any other city. Cities are dense networks of interwoven sociospatial processes that are simultaneously human, material, natural, discursive, cultural, and organic. The myriad of transformations and metabolisms that support and maintain urban life, such as, for example, water, food, computers, or movies always combine environmental *and* social processes as infinitely interconnected (Swyngedouw 1999). Imagine, for example, standing on the corner of Piccadilly Circus and consider the socioenvironmental metabolic relations that come together and emanate from this global-local place: smells, tastes, and bodies from all nooks and crannies of the world are floating by, consumed, displayed, narrated, visualized, and transformed. The Rainforest shop and restaurant play to the tune of ecosensitive shopping and the multibillion pound eco-industry while competing with McDonald's burgers and Dunkin' Donuts; the sounds of world music vibrate from Towers Records and people, spices, clothes, foodstuffs, and materials from all over the world whirl by. The neon lights are fed by energy coming from nuclear power plants and from coal or gas burning electricity generators. The coffee I sip connects me to the conditions of peasants in Columbia or Tanzania and to the Thames River Basin as much as to climates and plants, pesticides and technologies, traders and merchants, shippers and bankers, bosses and workers. The cars burning fuels from oil-deposits and pumping CO_2 into the air, affecting forests and climates around the globe, further complete the global geographic mappings and traces that flow through the urban and "produce" London's cityscape as a palimpsest of densely layered bodily, local, national, and global – but geographically depressingly uneven – socioecological processes. This intermingling of things material and symbolic combines to produce a particular socioenvironmental milieu that welds nature, society, and the city together in a deeply heterogeneous, conflicting, and often disturbing whole (Swyngedouw 1996).

The socioecological footprint of the city has become global. There is no longer an outside or limit to the city and the urban process harbors social and ecological processes that have a myriad of local, regional, national, and global connections:

> The town exists only as a function of circulation and of circuits; it is a singular point on the circuits which create it and which it creates. It is defined by entries and exits: something must enter and exit from it. It imposes a frequency. It effects a polarisation of matter, inert, living or human.... It is a phenomenon of transconsistency, a network, because it is fundamentally in contact with other towns. It represents a threshold of deterritorialization because whatever the material involved, it must be deterritorialized enough to enter the network, to submit to polarisation, to follow the circuit of urban and road recoding. The maximum deterritorialization appears in the tendency...to separate from the backcountry, from the countryside (Deleuze and Guattari 1997: 313–16).

As Raymond Williams (1973) already pointed out in *The Country and the City*, the transformation of nature and the social relations inscribed therein are inextricably connected to the process of urbanization. The dialectic of the environment and urbanization consolidates a particular set of social relations through "an ecological transformation which requires the reproduction of those relations in order to sustain it" (Harvey 1996: 94). Those socioenvironmental changes result in the continuous production of new "natures," of new urban, social, and physical environmental conditions. All of these processes occur in the realms of power in which actors strive to defend and create their own environments in a context of class, ethnic, racial and/or gender conflicts, and power struggles. Of course, under capitalism, the commodity relation veils and hides the multiple socioecological processes of domination/subordination and exploitation/repression that feed the capitalist urbanization process and turn the city into a kaleidoscopic metabolic socioenvironmental process that stretches from the immediate environment to the remotest corners of the globe. Indeed, the apparently self-evident commodification of nature that fundamentally underpins a market-based society not only obscures the social relations of power inscribed therein, but also permits disconnecting the perpetual flows of transformed and commodified nature from its inevitable foundation, that is, the transformation of nature (Katz 1998).

In sum, the environment of the city (both social and physical) is the result of a historical-geographical process of the urbanization of nature. In the city, society and nature, representation and being, are inseparable, integral to each other, infinitely bound up, yet simultaneously, this hybrid socionatural "thing" called city is full of contradictions, tensions, and conflicts. The city becomes the palimpsest landscape that captures those proliferating objects that Donna Haraway calls "Cyborgs" or "Tricksters" (Haraway 1991, 1997) or that Bruno Latour refers to as "Quasi-Objects" (Latour 1993, 1996); they are intermediaries that embody and mediate nature and society and weave networks of infinite transgressions and liminal spaces. If I were to capture some of the metabolized flows that weave together the urban fabric and excavate the networks that brought them there, "I would pass with continuity from the local to the global, from the human to the non-human" (Latour 1993: 121). These flows would narrate many interrelated tales of the city: the story of its people and the powerful socioecological processes that produce the urban and its spaces of privilege and exclusion, of participation and marginality. These would-be stories of rats and bankers, of diseases and speculation in frozen pork bellies, or Nikkei-index futures and options, of chemical, physical, and biological reactions and transformations, of global warming and acid rain, of the capital, machinations, and strategies of city builders, of urban land developers, of the knowledges of the engineers, the scientists, and the economists. In sum, excavating the flows that constitute the urban would produce a political ecology of the urbanization of nature.

Yet, all this seems nevertheless very remote, if not antithetical, to "nature," to the "green and pleasant land" not tainted by humans and left to its own devices and fundamental laws of life as excavated by biologists, chemists, or physicists, and celebrated by many ecologists as the ultimate ecological frontier. In many of these accounts, the city figures as the antithesis of the assumed harmonious and equitable dynamics of "nature," and the "urban question" necessitates – so they argue – a decidedly anti-urban development trajectory (Trepl 1996).

(Un)thinking the Sustainable City

In the emerging literature on "the sustainable city," very little attention has been paid so far to the urban as a process of socioecological change,[2] while discussions about global environmental problems and the possibilities for a "sustainable" future customarily ignore the urban origin of many of the problems. Of course, "environmental" issues have been central to urban change and urban politics for at least a century if not more. As will be discussed below, visionaries of all sorts lamented the "unsustainable" character of early modern cities and proposed solutions and plans that would remedy the antinomies of urban life and produce a healthy "wholesome" urban living. Although the rhetoric has changed and new concepts like "sustainability" have become fashionable, the deep anti-urban sentiment combined with an idealized and romanticized invocation of a "superior" natural order has rarely been so loud. Much of these debates about restoring a more environmentally sound urban fabric ignore the very foundations on which the contemporary urbanization process rests.

Although Henri Lefebvre (1991) does not address the environment of the city directly, he does remind us of what the urban really is, i.e. something akin to a vast and variegated whirlpool replete with all the ambivalence of a space full of opportunity, playfulness, and liberating potential, while being entwined with spaces of oppression, exclusion, and marginalization. Cities seem to hold the promise of emancipation and freedom while skilfully mastering the whip of repression and domination. Ironically, relations of domination and power that infuse urban practices and which are contested and fought against in innumerable ways help create the differentiated environments that give cities their sweeping vitality. At the same time, these forms of resistance and subversion of dominant values tend only to perpetuate the conservative imagery of cities as places of chaos, social and environmental disintegration, and moral decay. Perpetual change and an ever shifting mosaic of environmentally and socioculturally distinct urban ecologies – varying from the manufactured landscaped gardens of gated communities and high-technology campuses to the ecological war zones of depressed neighborhoods with lead-painted walls and asbestos-covered ceilings, waste dumps and pollutant-infested areas – still shape the choreography of a capitalist urbanization process. The environment of the city is deeply caught up in this dialectical process and environmental ideologies, practices, and projects are part and parcel of this urbanization of nature process. Needless to say, the above constructionist perspective considers the process of urbanization to be an integral part of the production of new environments and new natures which sees both nature and society as fundamentally combined historical-geographical production processes (see, among others, Smith 1984, 1996, 1998; Castree 1995). This perspective has major consequences for political strategy. As Lewontin (1997: 137–8) insists:

> the constructionist view... is of some consequence to human action. A rational environmental movement cannot be built on the demand to save the environment, which, in any case, does not exist... Remaking the world is the universal property of living organisms and is inextricably bound up with their nature. Rather, we must decide what kind of world we want to live in and then try to manage the process of change as best we can approximate it.

In this sense, there is no such thing as an unsustainable city in general, but rather there are a series of urban and environmental processes that negatively affect some social groups while benefiting others. A just urban socioenvironmental perspective, therefore, always needs to consider the question of who gains and who pays and to ask serious questions about the multiple power relations through which deeply unjust socioenvironmental conditions are produced and maintained. This requires sensitivity to the political ecology of urbanization rather than invoking particular ideologies and views about the assumed qualities that inhere in nature itself. These ideologies have nevertheless permeated much of urban policies and practices over the past century or so. This is the theme we shall turn to next.

Tales of Nature and the City: Taming the Urban Wilderness and "Ecologizing" the City

To combat nature or to "enter into" it to the point of penetration; to grasp its dialectical aspects with respect to concentration; to order it geometrically, or to make of it, in cultivating one's garden, ideal nature, a chosen cosmological precinct (earthly paradise, nature propitious) to human living as against wild nature; or pedagogically to invoke it as mirror of truth and goodness of man – these are attitudes to which have corresponded, each in turn, precise and differentiated architectural responses.

Gregotti ([1966] 1993: 400)

Indeed, much of the history of modern urban planning has been infused and inspired by particular scriptings of the "nature" of nature. Gregotti's enquiry into the relationship between nature and the built environment captures very well the multiplicity of meanings and the variety of ideas, visions, and practices that emerge from each of these imaginings of nature. As Smith (1984) argues, capitalist societies hold a decidedly contradictory view of nature. On the one hand, nature is perceived as inherently "good," as possessing some innate superior moral code that has been subverted and perverted through "civilization" and "urbanization." The city, as the epitome of modern capitalist civilization, is often branded as "evil" and harboring the underbelly of modern society. Many urban planners and architects in the past (Howard, Olmsted, Proudhon, Unwin, or Geddes to name just a few) have invoked a romanticized notion of a lost and pristine "nature" as a means for sanitizing the city, both in literal terms of combating pollution, but also as "social sanitation" from urban crime, "deviance" and "undesirable" marginal urban groups. On the other hand, nature also stands for the "uncivilized," the dark and untamed wilderness that requires control and whose frontier has to be pushed outwards as "progress" accelerates. This ambivalence permeates the history of both environmental and urban theories and resulted in a quintessentially schizophrenic attitude towards both nature and the city.[3] These images of a wild and dangerous nature have been translated into the urban domain as well. The urban "wilderness" and the "concrete" jungle invoke images of an out-of-control urbanization process and an uncivilized "nature" which both need control and "mastering." At the same time, the city and a landscaped nature are heralded as the pinnacle of civilization, as "humanity's" triumph over the barbarism of uncivilized earlier times and as a sign of how the frontier of wild and untamed "nature" receded as "humanity" has progressed. This double "coding" (superior moral and ecological order on the one hand; barbarian, wild and uncivilized on the other) of both nature and of the city has prompted many of the environmental debates on and practices about the city today as much as in the past. Much of the urban "sustainability" literature and visions (such as, for example, Agenda 21) hark back to at least a century-old view that pictures the city as dystopian, bleak, horrid, and full of antinomies, tension and dehumanizing conditions.

Indeed, the very idea of "sustainability" in the sense of some sort of harmonious, non-destructive, quasi-organic, socioecologically relatively stable or – at least – equitable development is by no means new. The horrid environmental conditions in the West's nineteenth-century cities have been lamented and commented on by many contemporary commentators and have inspired generations of social engineers, philanthropists, philosophers, and planners. Charles Dickens, for example, gripped by a nostalgia that creeps up whenever the modernist process of "creative destruction" erases the imprint of the past and constructs a space and environment more "in tune" with its time, chronicled the life of London's underclass and lamented the loss of an allegedly superior, but increasingly lost, organic nonurban social order. Tönnies and Durkheim, founding fathers of modern sociology, were captivated by the rapid modernization process and the accompanying rise of an urban order, which they each described in contradistinction to an idealized and disappearing more rural, environmentally equitable and harmonious, inherently humane social order.

The socioenvironmental urban blight threatened not only the well-being of the elites but also began to challenge the bedrock of capitalist society as the marginalized and oppressed began to demand access to more "sustainable" and better environmental conditions (in terms of shelter, food, hygiene, medicine, and consumer commodities). The class character that underpinned socioenvironmental injustices was conveniently swept under the carpet. Instead, the nature of the city (not of society) needed change, by producing a city more in tune with the rhythms and rhymes of nature itself. It is not a surprise to find that visionary elites such as Lord Leverhulme began to experiment with new forms of urban living and organization. Port Sunlight, the paternalistically designed proletarian utopia at the rural side of the Mersey was an early attempt to sanitize the industrial city and combine nature with "healthy" living as a means to stem the rising tide of social unrest and to safeguard the esthetic and moral order of the elite. Ebenezer Howard's *Garden Cities of Tomorrow* (1898) incorporated the codes of this imagineered urban utopia in a rational and "scientific" plan for an inclusive, orderly, and frictionless quasi-urban form of spatial organization, based on a harmonious coexistence of urban and rural conditions: "But neither the town magnet nor the country magnet represents the full plan and purpose of nature. Human society and the beauty of nature are meant to be enjoyed together. The two magnets must be made one. As man and woman... supplement each other, so should town and country. The town is the symbol... town and country must be married" (p. 9).

British new towns breathe the spirit (but not necessarily the practice) of this, while Prince Charles's crusade for urban villages is one of its more recent expressions. At the other side of the Atlantic, Frederick Law Olmsted had already advocated a more symbiotic relation between nature and the city as a means to eliminate the evil emanating from the city and from "the pursuit of commerce" (Olmsted [1870] 1996). The sanitizing and purifying delights of "air and foliage" would, so he argues, turn parks and green havens into the new and true centers of the city. For both Le Corbusier and Frank Lloyd Wright – the gurus of twentieth-century modernism – entering nature into the city also became a means of restoring a healthy vitality to the city.[4] While Le Corbusier advocated a geometrical symmetry in which regimented green spaces would provide the setting for his "machines for living," Wright pursued a much more organic integration of nature and building. While both intended to take further the nineteenth-century ideas of marrying nature with the city as a means of restoring social harmony and achieving "wholesome" ideal living, their vision of nature was infused by a particular scripting of the "nature" of the urban. In fact, as LeGates and Stout (1996: 376–7) argue, the ideal living environment of Wright's or Le Corbusier's new cities would guarantee social harmony and avoid the tensions and (class) conflicts that characterized capitalist cities.

This idealized vision of how nature would sanitize, reodorize or otherwise cleanse the city – both materially and spiritually – celebrated a particular imagining of a manufactured "nature" as a healing force while condemning the "nature" of the capitalist city as dehumanizing. Socioenviromental degradation through urbanization could only be stopped by means of bringing "nature" back into the city. Without minimizing the heroic attempts of these great urban thinkers to humanize (and ecologize) the city by means of restoring a presumably lost natural order, most of the attempts to produce a "natural" fix to the ills and pains of modern urbanization dismally failed to achieve the harmonious urban order its advocates had hoped for. Smokestack industries and some other forms of industrial pollution disappeared from the city centers, not so much because of environmental concerns, but because of a combination of spatial displacements to the suburbs or the Third World and economic restructuring. Green spaces were introduced, but they often quickly became the dark spaces where crime thrived and women or children stayed away from them unless permanent supervision could be guaranteed. Ironically, of course, all this took place in an age when the sanitation movement strove to eliminate some forms of nature (rats, bacteria, faeces, etc.) by putting then underground or out of town (Corbin 1994; Goubert 1989; Gandy 1998).

While urban reformers revelled in the utopian idea of creating a wholesome urbanism by injecting the idealized virtues of a life closer to a particular imagined form of a balanced and harmonious "nature," a new generation of city-lovers came to the defense of the urban. Lewis Mumford (1938), for example, revelled in the contradictory nature of modern urbanization. For him, it was an opportunity for social disharmony and conflict, the breath of the new, the cracks and the meshes that enable new encounters and where the unexpected can turn up just around the corner, the dramas and joys that the city creates and the suburbs lack. The landscaped garden settlements of the suburban revolution became those places where nothing happened and nothing ever will (*dixit* Lefebvre). The intellectual critique of the stale managerial functionalism has also been voiced by Jane Jacobs in *Death and Life of Great American Cities* in which she lamented the loss of the finely grained intermingling of diverse activities in the city streets that characterized early modern cities. Equally strong were the voices of Murray Bookchin or Richard Sennett ([1970]

1996) in elevating the power of gentle disorder and soft anarchy as potentially liberating and emancipatory forces. Once again, particular images and understandings of nature are invoked here to argue for a more anarchic or chaotic form of urbanization. Christopher Alexander ([1965] 1996), for example, distinguishes between "natural" cities and "artificial" cities, the former arising "spontaneously, over many, many years," the latter "those cities and parts of cities which have been deliberately created by designers and planners" (p. 119). The soft disorder, the apparently gentle frictions associated with mixing, heterogeneity and difference, and the playful ease of everyday life that he identifies with "natural" cities are seen as the social equivalent to the benevolent disorder of nature itself. Urban "sustainability" resides in mimicking the evolutionary process of nature. It is not a surprise that these proto-environmentalists would find a receptive audience with the emerging environmental movement in the 1960s and early 1970s. As early as 1969, McHarg's seminal book *Design with Nature* proposed the first guidelines to "ecologize" the city, to bring nature squarely into the multiple relations that structure the urbanization process. For him, nature is a single interacting system and changes to any part of it will affect the operation of the whole. Ever since, attempts to define or create the "sustainable" city have been inspired by views about the "greening" of the city and reducing pollutants of all kind emanating from urban life.[5] Of course, the "nature" of pollutants changed with the times. In the eighteenth-century, it was miasmas and putrid air, in the nineteenth-century rats and manure and in the twentieth-century bacteria and later CO_2. They all shared a view that separated nature from the city, both conceptually and materially, as two distinct, yet interrelated, domains. The understanding of what "nature" is inspired views about what the city ought to be. Of course, the "nature" of nature could be marshaled flexibly. The absence of a clear view of what "nature" really is renders it open for all manners of interpretation and legitimization. The "flexibility" of the concept resides exactly in the process of separating things natural from things social which permits a discursive reading of what nature is to serve specific social ends, while ignoring the inevitable mediations between "nature" and "society."

Towards a Political Ecology of the Urban

While planners and urban scholars dwelled on the "nature" of the city, the urbanization process kept accelerating. In Europe today, more than 70 percent of the population lives in cities. On a world scale, we are rapidly approaching a situation in which more than half of the world's population lives in urban settings. Many postcolonial cities have become Malthusian battlegrounds in which a small elite enjoys a luxury beyond imagination, while so many others are engaged in a daily struggle for survival. In an environment in which sociospatial ordering by and for the market has become the dogma of the day, urban regions have become, more than ever before, landscapes of power where islands of extreme wealth and social power are interspersed with places of deprivation, exclusion, and decline. The powerful, for example, are now able to insulate themselves in hermetically sealed enclaves, where gated communities and sophisticated modes of surveillance are the order of the day. Controlled, manicured, and manufactured nature reinforces their sense of isolation while the environments of the underbelly of the city become dangerous ecological war zones (Davis 1990). Many of the subtropical gardens in permanently irrigated suburban gated communities display a genetic diversity and a combined gene pool that is only matched by the rainforest (Archer 1998). Unhealthy high ozone concentrations in our summertime city centers, the proliferation of asthmatic and other respiratory diseases (tuberculosis is now again endemic in the rat-infested poor Bengali neighborhoods of East London), HIV and spreading homelessness are reshaping urban landscapes and may claim more casualties than even the most pessimistic predictions of the human consequences of global warming. An environmental "fix" to urban problems may "restore" some form of nature in one place while accelerating socioecological disintegration elsewhere. Meanwhile, the bursting life of the city can only be sustained at the cost of unsustainable environmental degradation in other parts of the world. While companies in our cities and regions desperately try to instill an image and practice of environmental sensitivity, they continue to ransack the ecologies of less protected spaces in the postcolonial worlds. Shell, for example, boasts about the environmentally sensitive new production unit recently constructed in Rotterdam, while continuing to support the state-condoned genocide of the Ogoni-people in Nigeria and the socioecological destruction of their land. Surely, in less protected social spaces, the environmental risk to which workers (men, women, and children) are exposed still strike us as one of the prime environmental problems. In the proliferating "informal" urban economies of many cities, environmental conditions are truly unsustainable in terms of maintaining human life.

Of course, such a political-ecological perspective is not particularly new either. Over 150 years ago, Friedrich Engels (1844) wrote a devastating critique of the conditions of everyday life of the Mancunian working class and represented the choreography of capitalist urban modernization as a spatial flow of perpetual dis- and relocation, including a deeply uneven geography of environmental and sanitary conditions. For him, the city was at the same time the incarnation of progress, of a liberation from the toil and bonds that cuffed humans to the land, as well as offering the possibilities of resistance to the processes of the exploitation, domination, and socioecological disintegration that characterized capitalist urbanization. In one of the other great writings of the time, *The Communist Manifesto*, Marx and Engels (1848) suggested how modern (capitalist) life rests on a process of perpetual creative destruction and the relentless reshaping of social and environmental conditions. Harmony, cquilibrium, and an organic "natural" order are inimical to such restless reorganization of social and environmental conditions. For them, the transformation of nature and of society and the production of new forms, ideas, and environments operates through and is expressed by the contradictions engendered by the class character of capitalist society. The dystopian, putrid, and disintegrating cities reveal all the contradictions of capitalism, but they are also the harbinger of new social movements and of potentially emancipatory (socialist) politics that would bring both nature and the city under the egis of democratically controlled collective production process. While social Darwinists heralded a merciless and blind process of selection and competition, others – like Kropotkin (1901; [1914] 1955) and later Murray Bookchin – would insist on the possibility of remaking humanity and nature through cooperation, mutual aid, and the promotion of individual and collective freedom. Such perspectives insist that the environment is a collectively produced thing, the outcome of a process of socioecological change.

Over the past few years, a rapprochement has begun to assert itself between ecological thinking, political economy, urban studies, and critical social and cultural theory. William Cronon (1991), for example, in *Nature's Metropolis*, tells the story of Chicago from the vantage point of the socionatural processes that transformed both city and countryside and produced the particular political ecology that shaped the transformation of the Midwest as a particular American urbanized socionature. While symptomatically silent about the myriad of struggles that have infused this process (African-American, women's or workers' organizations and struggles are notoriously absent from or marginalized in his narrative), the book marks powerful pointers on the way of a political ecology of the urban. His masterly crafted rendition of the emergence of the Chicago Futures and Options Market on the basis of the socioecologically produced wheat landscape surrounding Chicago and the immense, but geographically uneven, time–space compression unleashed by the introduction of the telegraph, which disconnected the circulation time of information from that of the flow of commodities (in this case, wheat), provides a near-perfect analysis of how the nature and direction of ecological change intertwines with the dynamics of globalizing capital accumulation. This, in turn, fuses together in the emergence of particular institutions and practices that shape subsequent moments in the urbanization process.

Mike Davis (1990), from his part, in *City of Quartz* and other recent publications (Davis 1995, 1996) suggests how nature and society become materially and discursively constructed in and through the dialectics of Los Angeles' urbanization process and of the multiple social struggles that have infused and shaped this process in deeply uneven, exclusive and empowering/disempowering ways. For him, homelessness and racism combine with pollution, earthquakes, and water scarcity as the most acute socioecological problems that have been produced through the particular form of postindustrial capitalist development that has shaped LA's becoming the Third World Megalopolis. Indeed, the history of Los Angeles' urbanization process indicates how the socioecological transformation of desert lands, the manufacture of a socionature orchard, and subsequent construction of "silicon" landscapes is paralleled by urbanizing, capturing, and controlling ever larger and more distant watersheds, by speculatively pushing the frontier of "developable" land further outwards and by an ever changing, but immensely contested and socially significant (in terms of access and exclusion, empowerment/disempowerment) choreography of national laws, rules, and engineering projects (Worster 1985; Gottlieb and Fitzsimmons 1991; Fitzsimmons and Gottlieb 1996; Hundley 1992).

Of course, as the deserts bloomed, ecological and social disaster hit: water scarcity, pollution, congestion, and lack of sewage disposal combined with mounting economic and racial tension and a rising environmentalism (O'Connor 1998: 118; Gottlieb 1993; Keil and Desfor 1996). The rhetoric of disaster and scarcity often provided the discursive vehicles through which power brokers could continuously reinvent their boosterist dream. Picturing a simulacrum of drought, scarcity, and a return to the desert produced a spectacularized vision of the dystopian city whose fate is directly related to faith in the administrators, engineers, and technicians who make sure the tap keeps flowing and land is "developed." The hidden stories of pending socioecological disaster provide the ferment in which local, regional, and national socionatures are combined with engineering narratives, land speculation, and global flows of water, wine, and money.

Environmental change and urbanization thus become deeply caught up in the political ecology of the local and national state, the international divisions of labor and power, and local, regional, and global hydroclimatological cycles. Viewing the city as a process of continuous, but contested, socioecological change, which can be understood through the analysis of the circulation of socially and physically metabolized "nature," unlocks new arenas for thinking and acting on the city; arenas that are neither local nor global, but weave networks that are always simultaneously deeply localized and extend their reach over a certain scale, a certain spatial surface. The tensions, conflicts, and forces that flow with this process through the body, the city, the region, and the globe show the cracks in the lines, the meshes in the net, the spaces and plateaus of resistance and of power. As the twenty-first century will be the century of the urban megalopolises (to borrow Jean Gottman's [1971] famous phrase), the central question for an emancipatory urban politics revolves around how to construct a city that is sensitive to these myriad connections and turn the city into one of the pivotal arenas where class, gender, and ethnic issues combine with ecological and environmental questions.

NOTES

1. With some exceptions, such as Keil (1994; 1995; 1997), Gandy (1996), Harvey (1996), Swyngedouw (1996; 1997) Cronon (1991) and Davis (1990; 1995; 1996).
2. See, for example, Blowers (1993), Breheny (1992), Haughton and Hunter (1994) or, for a more critical perspective, Burgess, Carmona, and Kolstee (1997) or Baeten (forthcoming).
3. See, for example, Oelschlaeger (1991) or Wilson (1992).
4. See, among others, Le Corbusier ([1924] 1971); Lloyd Wright ([1935] 1996; 1958); Fishman (1982).
5. Pollution is, of course, also a strongly politicized concept whose meaning changes with time and place. For Mary Douglas (1984), for example, pollution is defined as "matter out of place."

REFERENCES

Alexander, C. [1965] 1996: A city is not a tree. In R. T. LeGates and F. Stout (eds.), *The City Reader*. London: Routledge, 119–31.

Archer, K. 1998: Imagineering nature: the post-industrial political ecology of Florida. Paper presented at RGS-IBG Annual Conference, Kingston, UK, January 5–8 (mimeographed). Copy available from K. Archer, Dpt of Geography, University of South Florida, Tampa, FL, USA.

Baeten, G. Forthcoming: Tragedy of the highway: Empowerment, disempowerment and the politics of sustainability discourses and practices. *European Planning Studies*, 7.

Blowers, A. (ed.) 1993: *Planning for a Sustainable Environment*. London: Earthscan.

Bookchin, M. [1974] 1986: *The Limits of the City*. New York: Black Rose Books.

Bookchin, M. 1991: *Urbanization without Cities*. New York: Black Rose Books.

Bookchin, M. 1996: *The Philosophy of Social Ecology*. New York: Black Rose Books.

Breheny, M. J. (ed.) 1992: *Sustainable Development and Urban Form*. London: Pion.
Burgess, R., Carmona, M., and Kolstee, T. (eds.) 1997: *The Challenge of Sustainable Cities*. London: Zed Books.
Calvino, I. [1974] 1979: *Invisible Cities*. London: Pan Books.
Castree, N. 1995: The nature of produced nature: materiality and knowledge construction in Marxism. *Antipode*, 27 (1), 12–48.
Corbin, A. 1994: *The Foul and the Fragrant*. London: Picador.
Cronon, W. 1991: *Nature's Metropolis*. New York: A. A. Norton.
Davis, M. 1990: *City of Quartz: Excavating the Future of Los Angeles*. London: Verso.
Davis, M. 1995: Los Angeles after the storm: the dialectic of ordinary disasters. *Antipode*, 37 (3), 221–41.
Davis, M. 1996: How Eden lost its garden: a political history of the Los Angeles landscape. In A. J. Scott and E. W. Soja (eds.), *The City: Los Angeles and Urban Theory at the End of the Twentieth Century*. Berkeley: University of California Press, 160–85
Deleuze, G. and Guattari, F. 1997: City/state. In N. Leich (ed.), *Rethinking Architecture*. London: Routledge, 313–16.
Douglas, M. 1984: *Purity and Danger: An Analysis of the Concepts of Pollution and Taboo*. Routledge: London.
Engels, F. [1845] 1987: *The Conditions of the Working Class in England in 1844*. Harmondsworth: Penguin.
Fishman, R. 1982: *Urban Utopias of the Twentieth Century*. Cambridge, MA: MIT Press.
Fitzsimmons, M. and Gottlieb, R. 1996: Bounding and binding metropolitan space: the ambiguous politics of nature in Los Angeles. In A. J. Scott and E. W. Soja (eds.), *The City – Los Angeles and Urban Theory at the End of the Twentieth Century*. Berkeley: University of California Press, 186–224.
Gandy, M. 1996: Crumbling land: the postmodernity debate and the analysis of environmental problems. *Progress in Human Geography*, 20 (1), 23–40.
Gandy, M. 1997: The making of a regulatory crisis: restructuring New York's water supply. *Transactions of the Institute of British Geographers*, NS, 22, 338–58.
Gandy, M. 1999: The Paris sewers and the rationalization of urban space. Transactions of the Institute of British Geographers 24, 23–44.
Gottlieb, R. 1993: *Forcing the Spring: The Transformation of the American Environmental Movement*. Washington, DC: Island Press.
Gottlieb, R. and Fitzsimmons, M. 1991: *Thirst for Growth*. Tucson: The University of Arizona Press.
Gottman, J. 1971: *Megalopolis*. Cambridge, MA: MIT Press.
Goubert, J. P. 1989: *The Conquest of Water*. Cambridge: Polity Press.
Gregotti, V. [1966] 1993: Architecture, environment, nature. In J. Ockman (ed.), *Architecture Culture 1943–1968*. New York: Rizzoli, 399–401.
Haraway, D. 1991: *Simians, Cyborgs and Women – The Reinvention of Nature*. London: Free Association Books.
Haraway, D. 1997: *Modest-Witness@Second-Millennium.FemaleMan©-Meets_ Onco Mouse™*. London: Routledge.
Harvey, D. 1996: *Nature, Justice and the Geography of Difference*. Oxford: Blackwell.
Haughton, G. and Hunter, C. 1994: *Sustainable Cities*. London: J. Kingsley.
Howard, E. 1898: *Garden Cities of Tomorrow*. London: Swan Sonnenschein.
Hundley, N. 1992: *The Great Thirst*. Berkeley: University of California Press.
Jacobs, J. 1961: *Death and Life of Great American Cities*. New York: Random House.
Katz, C. 1998: Whose nature, whose culture: private productions of space and the "preservation" of nature. In N. Castree and B. Willems-Braun (eds.), *Nature at the End of the*

Millennium: Remaking Reality at the End of the Twentieth Century. London: Routledge, 46–63.

Keil, R. 1994: *A World of Natures: Space, Perception and the Construction of Urban Environments*. Faculty of Environmental Studies, York University, Toronto (mimeographed).

Keil, R. 1995: The environmental problem in world cities. In P. L. Knox and P. J. Taylor (eds.). *World Cities in a World-System*. Cambridge: Cambridge University Press, 280–97.

Keil, R. 1997: Better natures – better cities? Urban environmental activism in Toronto and Los Angeles. Paper presented at the ISA-RC21 conference on "Cities in Transition," Humboldt University, Berlin, July 20–22 (mimeographed).

Keil, R., and Desfor, G. 1996: Making local environmental policy in Los Angeles. *Cities*, 13 (5), 303–13.

Kropotkin, P. 1901: *Fields, Factories and Workshops*. London: Swan Sonnenschein.

Kropotkin, P. [1914] 1955: *Mutual Aid*. Boston: Horizon.

Latour, B. 1993: *We Have Never Been Modern*. London: Harvester Wheatsheaf.

Latour, B. 1996: To modernize or to ecologize? That's the question. Mimeographed paper, Ecoles des Mines, Paris.

Le Corbusier, (Jeanneret, C.-E.) [1971] 1924: *The City of Tomorrow*, tr. F. Etchells. Cambridge, MA: MIT Press.

Lefebvre, H. 1991: *The Production of Space*. Oxford: Blackwell.

LeGates, R. T. and Stout, F. 1966: *The City Reader*. London: Routledge.

Lewontin, R. 1997: Genes, environment, and organisms. In R. B. Silvers (ed.), *Hidden Histories of Science*. London: Granta Books, 115–39.

Lloyd Wright, F. [1935] 1996: Broadacre City: a new community plan. In R. T. LeGates and F. Stout (eds.), *The City Reader*. London: Routledge, 377–81.

Lloyd Wright, F. 1958: *The Living City*. New York: Horizon.

Lukes, S. 1973: *Emile Durkheim, his Life and Work: A Historical and Critical Study*. London: Allen Lane.

Marx, K., and Engels, F. [1848] 1998: *The Communist Manifesto*. London: Verso.

McHarg, I. 1969: *Design with Nature*. Garden City, NY: Doubleday.

Mumford, L. 1938: *The Culture of Cities*. London: Secker and Warburg.

O'Connor, J. 1998: *Natural Causes: Essays in Ecological Marxism*. New York: Guilford Press.

Oelschlaeger, M. 1991: *The Idea of Wilderness*. New Haven and London: Yale University Press.

Olmsted, F. O. [1870] 1996: Public parks and the enlargement of towns. In R. T. LeGates and F. Stout (eds.), *The City Reader*. London: Routledge, 338–44.

Sennett, Richard [1970] 1996: *The Uses of Disorder: Personal Identity and City life*. London: Faber and Faber.

Smith, N. 1984: *Uneven Development: Nature, Capital and the Production of Space*. Oxford: Blackwell.

Smith, N. 1996: The production of nature. In G. Robertson, M. Mash, L. Tickner, J. Bird, B. Curtis and T. Putnam (eds.), *FutureNatural: Nature/Science/Culture*. London: Routledge, 35–54.

Smith, N. 1998: Antinomies of space and nature in Henri Lefebvre's The Production of Space. In A. Light, and J. M. Smith (eds.), *Philosophy and Geography*, vol. 2: *The Production of Public Space*. London/New York: Rowman and Littlefield, 49–70.

Swyngedouw, E. 1996: The city as a hybrid: on nature, society and cyborg urbanization. *Capitalism, Nature, Socialism*, 7(1), 65–80.

Swyngedouw, E. 1997: Power, nature and the city: the conquest of water and the political ecology of urbanization in Guayaquil, Ecuador: 1880–1980. *Environment and Planning A*, 29 (2), 311–32.

Swyngedouw, E. 1999: Modernity and hybridity: nature, regeneracionismo, and the production of the Spanish waterscape, 1890–1930. *Annals of the American Association of Geographers*, 89 (3), 443–65.

Tönnies, F. [1887] 1962: *Community and Society*, tr. C. P. Loomis. London: Harper Torchbook.

Trepl, L. 1996: City and ecology. *Capitalism, Nature, Socialism*, 7 (2), 85–94.

Williams, R. [1973] 1993: *The Country and the City*. London: The Hogarth Press.

Wilson, A. 1992: *The Culture of Nature: North American Landscape from Disney to Exxon Valdez*. Oxford: Blackwell.

Worster, D. (1985) *Rivers of Empire*. New York: Random House.

Chapter 48

Power and Urban Politics Revisited: The Uses and Abuses of North American Urban Political Economy

Alan Harding

Urban sociologists and political scientists in the United States have long been preoccupied with the politics of economic development in US cities and the extent to which business communities and business needs shape local policy agendas. These themes were strongly represented in the community power debate between pluralists (Dahl 1961; Banfield 1966; Polsby 1963), elite theorists (Hunter 1953) and neo-elite theorists (Bachrach and Baratz 1962) in the 1950s and 1960s. That debate, in essence, was about whether representative democracy in US cities ensured the diffusion of decision-making power across a broad range of interest groups or was simply a smokescreen behind which power was concentrated in the hands of a small, unrepresentative, business-dominated elite. While the community power debate has an established place in the international urban studies canon, the nature and forms of urban politics described by its various protagonists were generally regarded, outside the US, as highly country-specific.

Ever since the issues covered by that debate resurfaced, in a slightly different guise, in the writings of US urban political economists from the 1980s onward, however, US approaches have generated wider interest. A number of non-US commentators, having noticed more potential parallels between contemporary experiences in the US and elsewhere, have attempted, in particular, to use insights gleaned from two strands of the recent literature – the growth machine thesis (Logan and Molotch 1987) and urban regime theory (Stone and Sanders 1987; Elkin 1987; Stone 1989) – to underpin both non-US and cross-national analyses of the changing nature of urban politics and intervention (Harding 1999). This chapter asks why this reevaluation has occurred and examines the extent to which recent US approaches have been, and can be, useful to researchers in other national contexts. The first section outlines the two US approaches. A second section asks why they have been taken up by urban researchers outside the US and, focusing primarily upon UK work, illustrates both how they have been adapted for non-US study and the main problems that have arisen from attempts to do so. The final section asks what value remains in the two strands of US urban political economy once the major criticisms have been taken into consideration and outlines ways in which they might be made more useful for non-US urban political analysis.

Urban Regimes and Growth Machines: A Brief Summary

Both strands of recent US urban political economy emphasize the importance of coalition building, on one hand, and the urban politics of production – that is, attempts to strengthen local economies and promote employment growth – on the other. Their main focus is upon the way various "stakeholders," particularly from urban governments and local business communities, use their resources to support deliberate, strategic economic development initiatives. This distinguishes them from "structuralist" approaches – the dominant strands of urban theory immediately before and after the community power debate – which tended to ignore strategic decision making and made it appear that patterns of urban change were ordered by intangible mechanisms such as the "hidden hand of the market," the nature of capitalist social relations or quasi-biological "impersonal competition" (Logan and Molotch 1987: 4–12). Most important to the theorists themselves, though, it distinguishes their arguments from those advanced by Peterson in a book entitled *City Limits* (Peterson 1981; Logan and Swanstrom 1990).

Peterson saw the importance of the urban politics of production as being linked directly to US local authorities' limited capacity to engage in "redistributive politics"; that is, to use locally raised resources to support service provision which primarily benefits poorer urban residents. While not disputing the importance of local developmental politics and the fact that local administrations compete for firms and households, the new urban political economy rejected two features of Peterson's analysis. The first is his assertion that local politics hardly matters and that the environment in which city administrations operate determines all their significant choices. The second is his implication that cities have a single set of interests which can be understood without reference to preferences that are expressed, by city residents and users, through the political system or other channels.

Thus the advocates of the new urban political economy took issue with Peterson for the way he reached his conclusions (Sanders and Stone 1987a, 1987b; Peterson 1987), if not necessarily with the conclusions themselves. Their major goal was to put the politics back into urban political economy. Like the community power theorists they attempt to account for important aspects of urban change by examining the actions of the groups, individuals, and institutions that help produce them rather than assuming that people are swept along by larger forces over which they have no control. They insist that there is nothing automatic about the interactions between "urban elites" and the effects which flow from them. For them, cities and urban life are produced and reproduced, not by the playing out of some externally imposed logic, but by struggles and bargains between different groups and interests within (and beyond) cities. The outcomes of these struggles and bargains, they argue, far from serving the general "good of the city," reward some groups while disadvantaging others.

The way in which the two accounts approach the key issue of coalition building, however, is somewhat different. Urban regime theorists, drawing upon general neo-pluralist arguments about the interdependency of politics and markets (e.g. Lindblom 1977), accentuate the political. They focus upon the way in which urban local authorities, when seeking to achieve their aims, rely upon the support of external organizations and interests. The nature of the regimes those authorities seek to build depends upon the aims themselves, which in turn reflect the broader socioeconomic environments relevant to particular places and times, and the division of labor between various organizations and interests whose support is needed to realize them. The key to their analysis in all cases, however, is the observation that "successful electoral coalitions do not necessarily govern" (Stone and Sanders 1987: 286). In other words, in order to achieve anything beyond straightforward statutory tasks – particularly when their ambitions depend upon inducing market change – elected city leaders and their officials need the support of other powerful interests, especially within the business community.

Thus urban regimes bring together those who have access to, and can deliver, various resources, be they material, such as finance, personnel, and land and buildings, or intangibles such as political, regulatory, and informational resources. Since no single organization or group monopolizes these assets and there is no "conjoining structure of command" (Stone 1989: 5) to link asset-holders together, a regime is an informal mechanism for "civic cooperation," based upon mutual self-interest, "by which public bodies and private interests function together in order to be able to make and carry out governing decisions" (Stone 1989: 6). Regimes fuse what is otherwise a very fragmented capacity to act and enable independent social forces and organizations to coordinate their actions in a way they would not otherwise do over the range of issues upon which they can agree.

While it is intrinsic to the arguments of regime theorists that the needs and demands of business leaders will always tend to limit and help determine the options pursued by urban authorities, the channel of influence they identify runs from the public to the private sector. The growth machine thesis, by contrast, accentuates the economic and sees the flow of influence as running in the opposite direction. Logan and Molotch's arguments are founded upon the assertion (1987: 52) that "the activism of entrepreneurs is, and always has been, a critical force in shaping the urban system." They focus upon the way growth strategies are defined and promulgated by local business communities. The growth machine thesis offers finer-grained detail about who plays leading roles in growth strategies. For Logan and Molotch, the key to the growth machine is the way local land and property owners ("parochial capital") strive to maximize rental income by intensifying or changing the uses to which their geographically fixed assets are put. To do this successfully, they need the support of other business interests whose success depends upon local markets (e.g. local banks, media and utilities companies), nonlocal investors ("metropolitan capital"), and local authorities which, it is argued, are "primarily concerned with increasing growth" (Logan and Molotch 1987: 53).

Quite why this is seen as being so in most, but not all, cases is not satisfactorily resolved by Logan and Molotch. At certain points they, like other urban political economists (Clavel 1986; DeLeon 1992), suggest urban political leaderships can follow anti- or controlled-growth strategies. At others they argue, like the much-derided Peterson, that certain institutional features in the US system of local government predispose local authorities toward competitive, growth-orientated behavior.

And at yet other points it is implied that local public officials have some freedom of maneuver with respect to the politics of production but fail to use it. Like other interests, they can be seduced by the ideology of "value-free development" promulgated by core growth machine activists.

Urban regime theory, by contrast, sees little role for ideology in binding coalitions together. For Stone, in particular, the power of a regime lies in the fact that it can draw in a multitude of different, often ideologically incongruent, interests without there needing to be a meeting of minds on all issues. All that is required is for regime members to work together constructively on those issues upon which they can agree and not to let their disagreements threaten the integrity of the regime. Thus regime members support growth strategies because they calculate that the material benefits of having influence as a "supportive" insider are greater than those that might accrue from being a critical outsider. It is these material calculations, more than anything else, which Stone has in mind when he argues that the opponents of a broad-based, well-organized regime can win battles against particular development projects but rarely the war against growth politics in its broadest sense.

Regimes and Machines beyond the US

Urban regime theory and the growth coalition thesis attracted interest in other national contexts for two main reasons. First, an international process of economic restructuring and the dilemmas it posed for local economies and labor markets in the "advanced" economies resulted in the urban politics of production becoming more important irrespective of national boundaries. And second, there were patchy but internationally significant changes in the structures, forms, and aims of the primary agencies of local service delivery – local authorities – which resulted in processes of coalition formation becoming more salient. The scale and depth of these changes in the UK, in particular, posed problems for traditional approaches to urban political analysis which primarily focused upon local government politics and administration, relations between national and local governments, and the delivery of social and welfare services (i.e. the politics of consumption rather than production). These institutional and policy-based approaches addressed a crucial issue within postwar urban politics – the role of local government within the developing national welfare state – but by the late 1980s they were becoming untenable as a result of four factors.

The first was fragmentation in the institutional structures of local governance whose origins were found primarily, but not exclusively, in the "market-led" reforms of post-1979 Conservative governments (Stewart and Stoker 1989, 1994). These resulted in the delivery of local, publicly funded services by a growing range of unelected public agencies, voluntary organizations, and private firms. The second, as noted above, was the growing importance of the urban politics of production. This was best illustrated by the rapid growth in economic programs run by area-based agencies, be they local authorities, nonstatutory bodies, or government-appointed agencies (Eisenschitz and Gough 1994). The third change was the proliferation of public–private partnerships, notably as hybrid delivery agencies for local economic programs (Bailey et al. 1995). The fourth was the steady, government-induced metamorphosis of local authorities into enabling, rather than executive, bodies

(Wilson and Game 1994; Clarke and Stewart 1994) which inadvertently encouraged them to take a broader but less directive role across a range of local economic and social affairs.

The advantages of growth machine and urban regime approaches, then, were that they offered conceptual frameworks which linked together many aspects of the "new urban governance" while at the same time leaving a great deal open to empirical investigation. Thus US urban political economy approaches became more relevant beyond the US than their predecessors had been in an earlier period. That does not mean, however, that there has been much clarity about how the insights of US urban political economy could or should be applied in non-US contexts and what should be the primary focus of research. In fact the two approaches have been applied in very different ways.

Concentrating upon work within the UK, there are three clear differences from the sorts of approaches that might be expected from the original US sources. The first is the emphasis placed upon the actions of public sector agencies in general and local authorities in particular. For Bassett and Harloe, for example, the key to the Swindon growth machine was the way in which the local council took advantage of national policy shifts which supported economic and population expansion for much of the postwar period (Bassett 1990; Bassett and Harloe 1990). Similarly, Dunleavy et al. (1995) focus upon the degree to which council leaderships in London achieved backing for particular policy developments from national government and/or benefited, inadvertently or by design, from national policy change. In neither account is much reference made to the role of the private sector in coalition building or in influencing the nature and direction of local strategies. Neither do they examine the mechanics of coalition building between different parts of the public sector.

Second, even when UK research *has* adopted the American emphasis upon public–private sector relationships, it has focused upon institutionalized forms of collaboration. While urban America contains countless examples of public–private and nonprofit organizations, these rarely lie at the center of the analyses of US urban political economists. By contrast, in the UK, the dominant focus is upon public private partner*ships*, as institutions, rather than upon noninstitutionalized public private partner*ship*, as a process. As a result, a great deal of attention is paid to two kinds of institutionalized partnership: (1) what might be called "shotgun partnerships" (Harding 1998), that is, formalized public–private partnership machinery which is required by government at the national or European level in order to trigger the flow of various forms of discretionary funding, and (2) "bottom up partnerships" which, although they often rely on external government support, are more clearly driven by local interests (Ward 1996; Axford and Pinch 1994; Lloyd and Newlands 1988). Such analyses, although useful in their own terms, are much less wide-ranging in their scope and ambition than the better US regime studies (see, above all, Stone 1989).

A final difference concerns the question "When is a regime/machine not a regime/machine?" and, in particular, just how robust and long-lived a particular set of public–private, intergovernmental and/or interagency relationships need to be in order to be considered as a regime/growth machine. Sanders, Elkin, Logan, and Molotch – and Stone, in all but his most recent work (1997) – each imply that sustained relationships over a long period of time are defining features of regimes and growth machines. But the same criterion has not usually been adopted when interpreting the UK experience. Partly this is a reflection of the more institutional focus of much UK work and the fact that the institutional partnerships associated with particular public programs usually have a lifespan limited by that of the programs themselves. However, it also reflects a tendency to assume that regimes or growth machines can be found in all places at all times.

One extreme illustration of this tendency is Kantor et al.'s (1997) use of the label "radical regime" to describe the Trotsky-influenced Labour Party leadership of Liverpool City Council in the mid-1980s even though (1) its dominance within city politics lasted for barely a single electoral cycle of four years, and (2) during that time it alienated virtually every potential ally inside and outside the city whose support was needed to tackle the city's acute economic and social problem. Kantor et al. are not alone in using the term "regime" to describe internal political and executive leadership groups within local authorities rather than the broader, informal coalitions referred to by the likes of Stone, Sanders, and Elkin. However, such indiscriminate use of the term means there is a danger that it loses its precision and becomes "a new descriptive catchword...in place of an explanation of the phenomenon under question" (Stoker 1995: 62. See also Harding 1997; John and Cole 1998).

Reflections on the Uses and Abuses of American Urban Political Economy

It is clear, then, that researchers have found compelling reasons to adopt approaches associated with urban regime theory and the growth coalition thesis in analyzing the changing patterns and processes of urban governance in the UK, but that their efforts are associated with substantial problems. Whether the blame for this should lie with the theorists or those who apply the theories, though, is the subject of dispute between those who argue that US urban political economy does not provide researchers studying UK towns and cities – or indeed those in Europe more generally – with particularly useful analytic tools (Shaw 1994; Le Galès 1995; Wood 1996) and more sympathetic commentators who see potential in US approaches *if* they can be attuned more carefully to non-US circumstances (Keating 1991; Stoker and Mossberger 1994; Newman 1995; Stoker 1995; Ward 1996).

Central to both positions is the argument that US approaches are ethnocentric; in other words, that the economic, institutional, political, and cultural environment of the US is taken as a natural starting point for analysis. This is clearly a valid criticism. As Logan and Molotch (1987: 149) recognize, there are some key differences between the US and the UK – and Europe, more generally – which affect the importance of urban coalition formation and the degree of emphasis on local growth politics. Among the more important are the following:

1. The stronger role that business leaders play in US urban politics; either directly, as politicians, or indirectly, for example through the control of slating organizations which choose electoral candidates or the provision of campaign funds, particularly for city mayors.

2. The absence of a major nonbusiness political party in the US comparable to the social democratic, trades-union-based parties which tend to dominate urban politics in Europe.
3. A highly autonomous system of local land-use planning in the US compared to the European experience in which local planning tends to be regulated more heavily by higher levels of government.
4. A much weaker role for the public sector in the US in respect of the ownership, acquisition, servicing, and development of land.
5. A much greater reliance on the part of US local authorities on local funding sources, be they revenues raised from local businesses and residents or capital resources borrowed from private creditors through local bonds.

Taken together, these factors mean that the business voice in urban politics in the US is much stronger and there is a more direct trade-off between the ability of US local authorities to provide services and the buoyancy of local economies than there is in the UK/Europe, where the resources for urban service provision are redistributed at a national scale according to local needs. While it might be valid to question the extent to which some UK analyses based upon US urban political economy have failed to enquire into the development of public–private sector relationships, then, this criticism must be seen in context. Even those studies which have searched more carefully for regimes and growth machines of the type described in the US literature have ultimately argued that the public sector in Europe plays a much greater role in the urban politics of production than it does in the US. As a result, the roles of national and local governments, of other public and quasi-public sector bodies, and of intergovernmental relations invariably receive more attention outside the US. This is true not just in the UK context but in work on other European countries (see Strom 1996, on Germany; Terhorst and van de Ven 1995, on the Netherlands; and John and Cole 1998, on France).

It follows from this argument that, if more mileage is to be gained from the application of US urban political economy approaches in other national contexts, two things are needed. First, a more disciplined approach is needed to the testing of some of their key propositions. Second, more serious attempts are needed to grapple with their limitations, including the ethnocentricity of the literature. In other words, just as the work of Sanders, Stone, Elkin, Logan, and Molotch helped put the politics back into urban political economy, so the challenge for non-US researchers is to take the US out of US urban political economy and make best use of what remains.

In this regard, it is critical that future efforts put the "micro-diversity" of urban coalitions into a context of "macro-necessities" originating beyond the boundaries of any particular city or, indeed, nation (Jessop et al. 1996). One of the main limitations of the US literature when it comes to cross-national analysis is that while it encourages a focus upon the urban politics of production, it cannot explain its growing salience in different national contexts. This is unsurprising, given the unwritten assumption that urban growth politics is intrinsic to the American system of governance rather than an occasional feature which has recently become more important. The key issue outside the US, however, is not so much how enduring features of the institutional landscape generate growth politics but how recent changes have added to the momentum behind the urban politics of production.

A more holistic perspective is therefore needed to make sense of cross-national change. This, in turn, means drawing upon overarching theories of the state which can provide the basis for understanding common, cross-national changes in governmental structures and modes of operation.

Promising developments along these lines are already apparent in work which has attempted to link regulation theory – and the insights it provides into the processes of cross-national state restructuring and the growing importance of subnational economic development initiatives – to urban regime theory and its concern to explore the way in which local interests respond to changes in the urban economic and political environment (Jessop et al. 1996; Lauria 1997; Harding 1997). The value of such a link, however, would be demonstrated more clearly if the key propositions of both approaches were translated more rigorously into programs of empirical research. There is also a need to explore the way in which the urban politics of production, outside the US, is related to the urban politics of welfare and social provision. One line of argument that would repay further exploration, here, is that effective urban regimes or coalitions in Europe, rather than being associated primarily with the promotion of economic growth, are best defined as informal arrangements by which the pursuit of economic development is reconciled with the attainment of social and environmental goals. That agenda is clearly becoming more important as debates about the importance of social cohesion and environmental sustainability to long-term economic change are taken more seriously.

These concluding comments suggest that US urban political economy, as originally conceived, clearly has limitations for the purposes of non-US and/or cross-national analyses of urban politics and intervention. More positively, however, it has hopefully made two points in relation to this observation. First, that some of the core features of US urban political economy are worth retaining and building upon, even if they were not designed to be used cross-nationally. And second, that there is a realistic prospect of developing a political economy approach to urban coalition formation which can yield insights that commentators in the UK and the rest of Europe will find useful.

ACKNOWLEDGMENTS

The author is doubly indebted to the UK Economic and Social Research Council for the support which underpins this article. Much of the work on US urban political economy was undertaken as part of a project for its *Local Governance* program called "Coalition-formation and urban redevelopment: a cross-national study" (1993–5). The article also benefits from initial conceptual work carried out for a project entitled "Economic competitiveness, social cohesion and urban governance in Liverpool and Manchester," part of its *Cities: Competitiveness and Cohesion* program (1998–2000).

REFERENCES

Axford, N. and Pinch, S. 1994: Growth coalitions and local economic development strategy in southern England: A case study of the Hampshire Development Association. *Political Geography*, 13 (4), 344–60.

Bachrach, P. and Baratz, M. S. 1962: Two faces of power. *American Political Science Review*, 56, 947–52.

Bailey, N., Barker, A. and McDonald, K. 1995: *Partnership Agencies in British Urban Policy*. London: University College Press.

Banfield, Edward C. 1963: *City Politics*. Toronto: Vintage.

Bassett, K. 1990: Labour in the sunbelt: the politics of local economic development strategy in an "M4-corridor" town. *Political Geography Quarterly*, 9 (1), 67–83.

——1996: Partnerships, business elites and urban politics: new forms of governance in an English city. *Urban Studies*, 33, 539–55.

Bassett, K. and Harloe, M. 1990: Swindon: The rise and decline of a growth coalition. In M. Harloe, C. Pickvance, and J. Urry (eds.), *Place, Policy and Politics: Do Localities Matter?* London: Unwin Hyman, 42–61.

Clarke, M. and Stewart, J. 1994: The local authority and the new community governance. *Local Government Studies*, 20 (2), 163–76.

Clavel, P. 1986: *The Progressive City: Planning and Participation, 1969–1984*. New Brunswick, NJ: Rutgers University Press.

Dahl, R. A. 1961: *Who Governs?* New Haven: Yale University Press.

DeLeon, R. 1992: *Left Coast City: Progressive Politics in San Francisco 1975–91*. Lawrence, KS: University Press of Kansas.

Dunleavy, P., Dowding, K., King, D. and Margetts, H. 1995: Regime politics in London local government. Paper to the ESRC Local Governance Programme conference, Exeter, September.

Eisenschitz, A. and Gough, J. 1994: *The Politics of Local Economic Policy: The Problems and Possibilities of Local Initiative*. Basingstoke: Macmillan.

Elkin, S. L. 1987: *City and Regime in the American Republic*. Chicago: University of Chicago Press.

Harding, A. 1997: Urban regimes in the United States of Europe? *European Urban and Regional Studies*, 4 (4), 291–314.

——1998: Public–private partnerships in the UK. In J. Pierre (ed.), *Partnership in Urban Governance: European and American Experience*. London: Macmillan, 72–96.

——1999: North American urban political economy, urban theory, and UK research. *British Journal of Political Science*, 29 (3), 447–72.

Hunter, F. 1953: *Community Power Structure: A Study of Decision Makers*. Chapel Hill: University of North Carolina Press.

Jessop, B., Peck, J., and Tickell, A. 1996: Retooling the machine: economic crisis, state restructuring and urban politics. Paper to the Association of American Geographers meeting, Charlotte, NC, April.

John, P. and Cole, A. 1998: Urban regimes and local governance in Britain and France: policy adaption and coordination in Leeds and Lille. *Urban Affairs Review*, 33 (3), 382–404.

Kantor, P., Savitch, H. V., and Vicari Haddock, S. 1997: The political economy of urban regimes: a comparative perspective. *Urban Affairs Review*, 32, 348–77.

Keating, M. 1991: *Comparative Urban Politics: Power and the City in the United States, Canada, Britain and France*. Aldershot: Edward Elgar.

Lauria, M. (ed.), 1997: *Reconstructing Urban Regime Theory*. London: Sage.

Le Galès, P. 1995: Urban regimes and comparative urban politics. Paper to ECPR joint sessions workshop on "The changing local governance of Europe," Bordeaux, March.

Lindblom, C. E. 1977: *Politics and Markets: The World's Political-Economic Systems*. New York: Basic Books.

Lloyd, M. G. and Newlands, D. A. 1988: The "growth coalition" and urban economic development. *Local Economy*, 3 (1), 31–9.

Logan, J. R., and Molotch, H. 1987: *Urban Fortunes: The Political Economy of Place*. London: University of California Press.
Logan, J. R. and Swanstrom, T. (eds.), 1990: *Beyond the City Limits: Urban Policy and Economic Restructuring in Comparative Perspective*. Philadelphia, PA: Temple University Press.
Newman, P. 1995: The politics of urban redevelopment in London and Paris. *Planning Practice and Research*, 10, 15–23.
Peterson, P. 1981: *City Limits*. Chicago: University of Chicago Press.
—— 1987: Analyzing development politics: a response to Sanders and Stone. *Urban Affairs Quarterly*, 22, 540–7.
Polsby, N. W. 1963: *Community Power and Political Theory*. New Haven: Yale University Press.
Sanders, H. T and Stone, C. L. 1987a: Developmental politics reconsidered. *Urban Affairs Quarterly*, 22, 521–39.
—— 1987b: Competing paradigms: a rejoinder to Peterson. *Urban Affairs Quarterly*, 22, 548–51.
Shaw, K. 1994: The development of a new urban corporatism: the politics of urban regeneration in the North East of England. *Regional Studies*, 27 (3), 251–9.
Stewart, J. and Stoker, G. (eds.) 1989: *The Future of Local Government*. Basingstoke: Macmillan.
—— (ed.) 1994: *Local Government in the 1990s*. Basingstoke: Macmillan.
Stoker, G. 1995: Regime theory and urban politics. In D. Judge, G. Stoker, and H. Wolman (eds.), *Theories of Urban Politics*. London: Sage, 54–71.
Stoker, G. and Mossberger, K. 1994: Urban regime theory in comparative perspective. *Environment and Planning C: Government and Policy*, 12 (2), 195–212.
Stone, C. L. 1989: *Regime Politics: governing Atlanta 1946–1988*. Lawrence: University Press of Kansas.
—— 1997: Urban regime analysis: theory, service provision, and cross-national analysis. Paper to the ECPR workshop on Local Elites in a Comparative Perspective, Bern, February–March.
Stone, C. L. and Sanders, H. T. (eds.), 1987: *The Politics of Urban Development*. Lawrence, KS: University Press of Kansas.
Strom, E. 1996: In search of the growth coalition: American urban theories and the redevelopment of Berlin. *Urban Affairs Review*, 31 (4), 455–81.
Terhorst, P. and van de Ven, J. 1995: The national urban growth coalition in the Netherlands. *Political Geography Quarterly*, 14 (4), 343–61.
Ward, K. 1996: Rereading urban regime theory: a sympathetic critique. *Geoforum*, 27 (4), 427–38.
Wilson, D. and Game, C. (eds.), 1994: *Local Government in the United Kingdom*. Basingstoke: Macmillan.
Wood, A. 1996: Analysing the politics of local economic development: making sense of cross-national convergence. *Urban Studies*, 33 (8), 1281–95.

Chapter 49

Social Justice and the City: Equity, Cohesion, and the Politics of Space

Fran Tonkiss

The truth is that we cannot include as citizens all who are necessary for the city's existence.

Aristotle, *The Politics* III, v: 2

The city has been a primary context for thinking about questions of social justice, citizenship, and social cohesion. At a conceptual level, the public spaces of the city provide a stage for imagining larger conceptions of the social good. More substantively, cities as diverse social spaces and divided economic spaces raise issues of equality and inclusion in acute and often visible ways (Harvey 1973). In this discussion, I consider how concepts of social justice help to shape a politics of space, with particular reference to spatial initiatives within British government.

Social Justice, Equity and Cohesion

The discussion begins by briefly outlining a liberal conception of social justice in terms of objectives of equity and social cohesion. It goes on to sketch the relation between these social justice concerns and the development of urban policy in Britain. The main part of the discussion considers how questions of equity and cohesion have been spatialized within a framework of community, and in relation to processes of social exclusion and inclusion, within the politics of government under New Labour.

Notions of social justice within programs of liberal government draw heavily upon debates within liberal theory. In turn, these debates rest on a larger conception of citizenship in liberal societies. Citizenship, in a liberal context, is reflected in a set of conjoined political and civil rights. Political rights relate to the individual's participation within public life – in modern liberal democracies these include the right to join political parties and to stand for public office, as well as the principal right to vote. Civil rights, on the other hand, concern the rights of the individual in a free society; commonly taken to include freedom of speech, freedom of conscience, freedom of movement and association, the freedom to own and possess one's property, and justice before the law. Together, these primary rights establish the formal equality of citizens, at the same time marking the boundaries of a shared political and civil community.

A notion of social justice, however, goes beyond the formal rights of citizenship. At a further level, social justice is concerned with the fair distribution of economic and social goods (Rawls 1971). The necessary conditions for equal social membership, in this move, extend beyond civil and political rights to *social rights*. These include a degree of economic and social well-being, and rights to dignity and respect (Marshall 1950; Commission on Social Justice 1994). On this level, the concept of social justice is concerned not with the formal equality of citizens, but with the substantive inequalities between them. It proceeds on an understanding that the extent of meaningful social membership is shaped by people's material circumstances, and closed off by forms of prejudice and discrimination. If liberal rights of citizenship work to establish formal equality together with political and civil community, this second principle of social justice is based on a recognition of *actual* inequalities, and of the limits to social solidarity.

Against the formal equality of liberal citizenship, then, might be posited what John Rawls has called a "difference principle" (Rawls 1971: 74). Legal equality cannot in itself ensure an equitable share of social and economic advantages. Rawls proposes, therefore, that in a just society economic and social inequalities should be arranged so as to be of greatest benefit to its least advantaged members (1971: 83). This approach to social justice aims to realize principles of equity and fairness, at the same time as it assumes conditions of inequality and difference. As such it is central to a politics of social welfare that aims to redress the effects of inequality through the distribution of public goods, and the public redistribution of private goods.

There is a further point to be taken from Rawls's theory of social justice. In his account, shared conceptions of justice provide the basis for social cohesion: in a diverse society, he holds, "public agreement on questions of political and social justice supports ties of civic friendship and secures the bonds of association" (Rawls 1980: 540). Similarly, Marshall saw the provision of social rights as fundamentally linked to membership of a common culture (Marshall 1950); while more recently, Britain's Commission on Social Justice argued that economic and political legitimacy depended on a form of public support that people will very reasonably withhold unless they believe that the order under which they live has some concern for them and offers them chances that are, within the limits of the possible, fair (Commission on Social Justice 1994: 19).

Within these different accounts, notions of equity or fairness are closely tied to issues of social order and integration. Principles of social justice in this way translate the liberal ideal of equality and civic community into a more substantive commitment to equity and social inclusion.

How, then, might social justice objectives be realized in a policy context? For Rawls, political and economic arrangements invariably involve a version of the social good, and of how institutions and interventions might be designed in pursuit of this end (Rawls 1971: 259). In this sense, policy gives technical form to a broader ethos of government. In a recent British context, questions of social justice increasingly have been framed in terms of government efforts to "enable" individuals and communities to realize rather abstract "opportunities"; based on the assertion that what "government can do for people is limited, but there is no limit to what people and communities can be enabled to do for themselves" (Commission on Social Justice 1994: 22). The following discussion considers how this ethos of government is worked out in spatial terms.

Social Justice and Urban Policy

Issues of social justice were central to the development of urban policy in Britain. During the 1960s, a number of liberal capitalist governments undertook programs of policy intervention in response to the perceived urgency of an "urban problem." The precise nature of the "urban problem" was defined in various ways in different contexts, and commanded different kinds of policy response. In the British case, the urban was problematized in terms of two key factors: poverty and race. Informed by debates in the United States, the "inner city" came to be conceived as a new space of government, mapped along lines of severe deprivation and increasing racial tension (Blackman 1995: 43). Coordinated urban policy in large part responded to a series of studies – carried out by government researchers and by independent social scientists – that highlighted the concentration of poverty, entrenched male unemployment, low educational attainment and substandard housing in inner urban areas, frequently correlating these factors with the distribution of ethnic minority populations (Gibson and Langstaff 1982; Atkinson and Moon 1994).

The Urban Programme, introduced in 1968, was designed to provide a coherent framework for urban policy interventions. Bringing together a range of programs in education, social services, employment, industry, public order, and health, it marked out the inner city as a complex space of government. At the same time, it was based on a clear rationality of social justice: urban policies were to be directed towards areas of "special social need," identified on the basis of a number of indices of deprivation. The development of British urban policy in this way spatialized issues of social justice in terms of a social geography of need. Social and economic problems might be governed – and objectives of equity and social cohesion pursued – through the management of urban spaces. These twin objectives are especially evident in urban policy's orientation to problems of poverty and public order; problems which were understood in spatial and in racial terms.

While urban policy developed in Britain as a response to a set of social pathologies, by the end of the 1970s its central concerns had shifted towards issues of economic development. Urban deprivation increasingly came to be understood as an economic problem, with concomitant – although disputed – economic solutions. This conception of the "urban problem" was common to different political perspectives. Community Development Projects and Inner Urban Area Studies in the 1970s developed economic explanations for urban decline; albeit rather different ones from those which informed neoliberal urban policy in the 1980s and after (see CDP 1977; DoE 1977; DoE 1985). Under Conservative administrations after 1979, urban areas were conceived as sites of government in specific economic ways, and as amenable to certain economic forms of intervention, increasingly linked to market development (see Thornley 1992; Deakin and Edwards 1993). This is not to suggest, however, that economic initiatives wholly displaced social projects; rather, in a neoliberal context, economic objectives came to be seen as consonant with social and environmental concerns, and to be linked more broadly to the quality of urban life and the ambience of urban spaces.

An emphasis on economic development involved a reworking of the equity objectives of urban policy. By 1991, the minister with responsibility for urban policy was able to announce that the government was "turning the tide on the old idea that resources should flow towards needs, irrespective of how well they will be used" (Heseltine 1991: 11). In this move, neoliberal urban policy broke with a welfarist discourse of need, and articulated a new ethos for the government of the city. A social rationality of need was to give way to an economic rationality which directed resources to those areas with clear potential for development. This approach shaped urban policy initiatives in the 1990s, specifically within City Challenge schemes and through the operations of the Single Regeneration Budget. These programs provided funds to local agencies on a competitive basis, requiring them to attract private investment into urban development programs within a framework of public/private "partnership."

Such a shift from need to enterprise in the distribution of resources did not, however, entirely replace equity concerns within urban government. The targeting of local sites for development, rather, sought to meet equity objectives while rationalizing public budgets and allowing them to be steered more effectively in line with central government priorities. Strategies of targeting and competition might in this way be seen as instrumental solutions to larger problems of social justice and redistribution in the government of cities. Questions of distribution within urban policy – questions which had been located within a discourse of social need – became constructed as more narrowly economic problems. Area-targeting in this sense supported distinct, though not always separate, government rationalities – as a mechanism it was designed to ensure both equity *and* efficiency in the use of public resources. It produced a kind of mutuality between the social and economic government of the city – between a (rather weakened) concern with social justice, and objectives for local enterprise and market development. The sites of urban government in turn were understood as spaces of both deprivation and development; where social problems might be rendered amenable to economic solutions.

Social Justice as Social Inclusion: The Spatial Politics of New Labour

Changing approaches to the government of British cities have constituted the subjects of policy – the urban poor, ethnic minorities, the unemployed, the poorly housed – at the same time as they have marked out spaces of intervention. A politics of space in this way has been inseparable from the drawing of *social* boundaries. Such a link between the social and the spatial has helped to shape the politics of social justice developed under a New Labour government in Britain. This can be thought about in two ways. First, different urban spaces are identified as sites of social exclusion. Second, the space of "community" is seen as the basis of a politics of inclusion and civic solidarity.

A central project of the Labour government elected in Britain in 1997 has been to develop a "new politics" which goes beyond a form of social democracy centred on the state and a neoliberal politics oriented to the market (Blair 1998; Giddens 1998). While this opposition represents a rather simplistic understanding of an "old" politics of left and right, the New Labour agenda has been presented as a fundamental rethinking of the role and limits of government, and of its relation to the civil domain. Central to this idea is the view that government should act to promote individual and collective opportunities, and to foster a communitarian vision of civil society based on mutual rights and responsibilities (Blair 1998).

A notion of social justice is at the center of the new politics (Blair 1998: 1). This is based on a principle of the equal worth and dignity of citizens, which requires government to take a role in combating forms of discrimination that deny this fundamental equality (1998: 3). Beyond the principle of formal equality, however, lie issues of social and economic equity. This is understood, however, not in terms of a politics of distribution, but of the distribution of *opportunities* in society (see also Giddens 1998: 101). Equity objectives directed towards the effects of material inequalities are in this way translated into a (somewhat confused) notion of "opportunity for all." Blair contrasts such an approach to equity to the manner in which an "Old Left" too often had stifled opportunity in the name of abstract equality. Gross inequalities continue to be handed down from generation to generation, and the progressive Left should robustly tackle the obstacles to true equality of opportunity (Blair 1998: 3)

Welfarist principles of universalism are dismissed as a kind of "dull uniformity" in social provision, firmly associated with an outmoded, statist politics (1998: 3). At the same time, the new politics differentiates itself from a neoliberal position which identifies opportunity simply with individual freedoms, often based on an antipathy to the notion of "society" itself (1998: 1). Questions of equity, rather, extend beyond individual opportunity to a broader politics of social cohesion – as Blair notes, "without a fair distribution of the benefits of progress, societies risk falling apart in division, rancour and distrust" (1998: 20).

This second point opens on to a key dimension of the New Labour project. A chief register for New Labour's concern with social justice has been the language of social exclusion. In this way, issues of equity and social cohesion inform a particular approach to social space. Notions of inclusion and exclusion carry with them a conception of social boundaries and membership, marked out in part by acceptable forms of behavior and particular identities. As in Rawls's argument that shared conceptions of social justice secure the "ties of civic friendship," so New Labour's approach to social inclusion has been premised on a set of mutual rights and responsibilities; both among citizens and between citizens and government:

> For too long the demand for rights from the state was separated from the duties of citizenship and the imperative for mutual responsibility on the part of individuals and institutions. Unemployment benefits were often paid without strong reciprocal obligations; children were unsupported by absent parents (Blair 1998: 4).

Such a perspective outlines a communitarian vision of social rights and obligations, at the same time as it sets up particular individuals and groups as a problem for government.

The boundaries of social inclusion/exclusion are marked not only in terms of behavior and identities, but in terms of spaces. As well as targeting certain social groups (unemployed people, absent parents), a governmental concern with social exclusion centers on particular social spaces. Most notably, large public housing estates have been targeted as crucibles for processes of social exclusion. One of the initial objectives of the government's Social Exclusion Unit, a body designed to run across different policy domains in order to tackle issues of exclusion in a coordinated manner, was to address the condition of Britain's "worst" public housing estates, and the problems facing the three million people who live in these spaces. These problematic sites have been characterized in terms of multiple factors of social and economic deprivation – crime, unemployment, educational failure, poverty – in an approach that recalls with a very deep resonance the origins of urban policy in the identification of a complex "urban problem" in the 1960s. This spatial logic was reproduced in the form of various "Action Zones" – in education, health, and employment – that located socioeconomic problems firmly in physical sites.

The spatiality of social membership is particularly pronounced in respect of approaches to public order. In particular, public spaces have been identified with the activities of a law-abiding majority (Cooper 1998: 470–1). This has gone together with the problematization of certain activities, and of the presence of certain types of people, in public spaces. Problems of homelessness, for example, have frequently become translated into a question of the visible presence of homeless people on the streets; where too often an intolerable social condition has been collapsed into what are seen as unacceptable social activities – begging, public drinking, or forms of unauthorized street enterprise. One of the most striking spatial strategies developed by the New Labour government for the control of behavior in public space has been the provision for child curfews, designed with the aim both of protecting young people from potential public dangers, and of regulating their behavior in relation to appropriate times and spaces. They also invoke a strong notion of parental responsibility, based on the view that children's activities should be supervised within the space of the home.

These approaches to the politics of social exclusion, cohesion, and membership bring together spatial with social factors. Particular spaces, that is, are seen both to be shaped by and to reproduce certain kinds of behavior and social conditions. Such an approach to social space is evident in policies of regulation and public order, but also central to a politics of inclusion. A key domain within which a version of the social is integrated with a spatial politics is in New Labour's approach to "community." A language of "community" is both difficult to pin down and unvirtuous to reject: while it has been all-pervasive within the "new politics," it has not always been clearly defined. In broad terms, New Labour's approach to community might be thought about in two key ways. On one hand, notions of community refer to local social spaces as sites for policy intervention. Here, a politics of community provides a means of targeting areas of socioeconomic disadvantage in a concerted way. The government's New Deal for Communities was conceived as a means for realizing the rather notional version of community "partnership" that had characterized urban policy in the 1990s, in the form of more effective and inclusive local initiatives (see Blair 1998: 9). The politics of community, here, relates to a local scale of policy development that provides a means for distributing resources and directing initiatives towards specific sites. In this respect, it is consonant with an equity approach within government that seeks to address the effects of inequality through the distribution of public goods, and the public redistribution of private goods.

On the other hand, an extended sense of community has been invoked as an inclusive space of social membership. In this move, community refers not to the local spaces of social life, but to a larger collective of citizens – to an inclusive society itself. At different moments, then, "community" invokes a local politics of equity, and a broad politics of social cohesion. We might recall at this point the emphasis placed – within Blair's discourse as in the liberal theory of John Rawls – on social justice as a basis for social solidarity and order; for trust and "civic friendship." Through its recourse to notions of community, New Labour has sought a basis for general social order and cohesion in a vision of the local and affective. Similarly, its emphasis on interlocked rights and responsibilities – firmly grounded in a communitarian philosophy (see Etzioni 1995) – sets out a relation between citizens, and between citizens and government, which is highly immediate and even individualized. An inclusive politics of community underpins this effect:

> only a society small enough to permit trust is small enough to permit responsibility... Just as man's natural power of first hand knowledge, so his power of love or of active concern, is by nature limited, the limits of the city coincide with the range of man's active concern for nonanonymous individuals (Strauss 1973: 31).

A politics of community, then, might be seen as a means of extending the range of people's "active concern" for others by rendering them somehow *familiar;* brought together within relations of civic trust and mutual responsibility. The limits of the city, understood as a domain of social membership, in this way extend out from the local spaces of community to a notion of the larger public *as* community. In this approach "community" functions not as a euphemism for various social minorities or marginal groups, but as a container for the majority (see Cooper 1998: 470).

Conclusion

Principles of social justice invariably open on to a politics of space. Questions of equity and distribution are played out across physical spaces, while objectives of cohesion invoke a vision of an inclusive arena of citizenship. Since the late 1960s, British governments have undertaken urban initiatives on the basis of changing conceptions of the problems of the city – problems that have been variously understood in terms of need, deprivation, and development. By the beginning of the twenty-first century, a self-consciously "new politics" of government constructed the problem of social justice largely in terms of processes of social exclusion and inclusion. In this context, a politics of space referred both to the physical sites of exclusion – certain housing estates, on the streets, specific parts of the city – and to an inclusive space of community. In its approach to public space, further, the New Labour government marked out certain unacceptable forms of behavior, and consequently certain kinds of person such as the homeless or the juvenile, from the claims to public space of a responsible majority. As a place where social questions might be posed in spatial forms, the order of the city remained a primary way of imagining the basis for a cohesive and a good society.

REFERENCES

Aristotle 1995: *The Politics*, tr. E. Barker. Oxford: Oxford University Press.
Atkinson, R. and Moon, G. 1994: *Urban Policy in Britain: The City, the State and the Market*. Basingstoke: Macmillan.
Blackman, T. 1995: *Urban Policy in Britain*. London: Routledge.
Blair, T. 1998: *The Third Way: New Politics for the New Century*. London: The Fabian Society.
CDP 1977: *Gilding the Ghettos*. London: Community Development Project.
Commission on Social Justice 1994: *Social Justice: Strategies for National Renewal*. London: Vintage.
Cooper, D. 1998: Regard between strangers: diversity, equality and the reconstruction of public space. *Critical Social Policy*, 57, 18 (4), 465–92.
Deakin, N. and Edwards, J. 1993: *Enterprise and the Inner City*. London: Routledge.
DoE 1977: *Inner Urban Area Studies: Liverpool, Birmingham and Lambeth*. London: Department of the Environment.
DoE 1985: *Urban Programme Ministerial Guidelines*. London: Department of the Environment.
Etzioni, A. 1995: *The Spirit of Community: Rights, Responsibilities and the Communitarian Agenda*. London: Fontana.
Gibson, M. S. and Langstaff, M. J. 1982: *An Introduction to Urban Renewal*. London: Hutchinson.
Giddens, A. 1998: *The Third Way: The Renewal of Social Democracy*. Cambridge: Polity.
Harvey, D. 1973: *Social Justice and the City*. Oxford: Basil Blackwell.
Heseltine, M. 1991: The future of London. LWT London Lecture, December 12.
Marshall, T. H. 1950: *Citizenship and Social Class*. London: Routledge and Kegan Paul.
Rawls, J. 1971: *A Theory of Justice*. Oxford: Clarendon Press.
Rawls, J. 1980: Kantian constructivism in moral theory. *Journal of Philosophy*, 77 (9), 536–62.
Strauss, L. 1973: *Natural Rights and History*. Chicago: Chicago University Press.
Thornley, A. (ed.) 1992: *The Crisis in London*. London: Routledge.

Chapter 50

Property Markets and the Production of Inequality

Michael Edwards

The purpose of this chapter is to survey the way we analyze a number of familiar urban issues and to propose that a focus on the mediating role of land and property markets can offer an essential tool, both for better theorization (and linking) of urban issues and for considering the scope for action.

Modern Western societies are often described as "market" economies as though their defining characteristic is that exchange takes place in markets (rather than by gift or by barter). However this is simply untrue: market exchange was important in precapitalist societies and in the so-called "communist" countries and will no doubt have a role in any future society.

The central feature of modern societies is capitalism, and specifically the extension of market exchange to include labor power: it is the labor market which has been the defining feature of the modern world. Struggles about wages and conditions of work have been central to modern history and the exploitation of differences in wages is a driving force in globalization today. It is interesting to note that, since the collapse of the Soviet Union, the word "capitalism" has come to be used quite widely again to characterize the world system, even by those who – during the Cold War – would have distinguished the Western economies as "free-market," or "market," or even as "democratic." Within capitalism the central issue to be understood has always been the relationship between capital and labor, even though this relationship is interwoven with other kinds of relationship – gender, ethnicity, or local identity.

Markets are crucial within capitalism as key mechanisms through which social relations are implemented, enforced, and transmitted across boundaries. We keep seeing clear examples like the recent closure of a microchip factory in northern England because the Far Eastern economic crisis cheapened imports and meant that the English product could no longer compete in the European market. In the USA such episodes are frequent as the market competition from cheaper labor in NAFTA (the North American Free Trade Area) intensifies and factories in the north close down.

While market relationships like this are often brutally clear, they are also often misleading, essentially because an agreement between two people – to buy and to sell – has the superficial appearance of a voluntary and free exchange. As Adam Smith pointed out, the hidden hand of the market operates through individuals pursuing their own interests and making bargains that leave both parties better off. However this view of market exchange ignores the balance of power between buyer and seller (which can make the exchange anything but fair) and it ignores whatever determines the ruling market price: the overall balance of power between buyers and sellers. The worker has little choice about accepting a badly paid job if low wages are the only wages on offer. The farmer has to accept the market price for his animals if that is all the supermarket chains are offering.

Thus social relations operating through markets are often obscured – in the sense that market prices and market practices seem so "natural" and market exchanges, as instances of mutual consent, seem so "free" of coercion. The extension of market relations into ever more areas of urban life extends this obscuring of the underlying relationships: when the city council allocated housing sites the issues were clearly political; now that market criteria rule, the issues are the depoliticized ones of "viability" and "financial feasibility" and who are we to challenge these? The decision-making techniques for "feasibility testing" are now taught to students of planning as part of "technical" courses as though they were as value-neutral as forecasting heat loss through a wall.

The analysis of markets is subject to a major pitfall: bad abstraction. Conventional economics approaches markets from the starting point of an idealized abstraction: the textbook construct of the perfect market is defined by its numerous assumptions about perfect competition, perfect information, divisibility, lack of externality, and so on. This idealized abstract market is constituted in the mind, as is the global harmony to which markets and free trade should lead us. All actual markets – and especially the real-estate markets – are such a disappointment when you come at them in this way: the "imperfections" swamp the few elements which conform to the abstract model. Great effort and ingenuity are then required to adapt the model so it can be used: welfare and environmental economics, institutional economics, and so on (Dobb 1969; Pearce and Markandya 1991; Ive 1998).

The Origins of Property Markets

A much more constructive alternative is to approach the conceptualization and analysis of markets with more historical and material reality from the outset. This is especially true in the study of urban societies. Issues of location, competition for scarce locations, and payments made to occupy space are all central issues and all of them involve analysis of the power relations among those involved. The necessary focus on the analysis of relationships in the production and use of the built environment is evident in the monumental work of Chambert (Chambert 1997) and of others who have applied his ideas (Page 1996; de Magalhães 1998). In the background is a theoretical debate on theories of rent (Haila 1989; 1990).

One important starting point is to acknowledge that markets don't just arise "naturally" but are actively constituted by those involved, and often with the state and the law actively involved in defining what is to be traded, the units of exchange, the terms of contract, the enforcement of conditions, and so on. In the case of modern land and property markets, this history is often on record if we look for it: it took a great struggle by capital to create a market in land in England, against the tenacity of the old landed interests represented in the House of Lords (McMahon 1985). The fraught power relations between landlords and tenants, owners and occupiers, remain everywhere uneasy and subject to the state as referee. A case in point is the recent success of major British retailers (who are "tenants" in this context) in securing changes which reduce the bias in their leases which have always strongly favored their landlords – typically insurance companies and pension funds – by insisting that rents could only be revised upwards and that tenants would remain liable to pay rent even if they had passed on their liability to a new tenant who then defaulted. The privileged power position of the landed interest in the UK property markets (which probably explains why property investment here has been so strong) is now a little bit weakened.

The characteristics of markets are also often influenced by the producers, merchants, professionals, credit-providers, and others who take part: in our case by the valuers, mortgage lenders, lawyers, and so on. Examples of these influences operating internationally from the UK and USA to Brazil have been documented (de Magalhães 2000) and a lot of Western consultants are busy advising on how property markets should now be reconstituted in the former communist countries.

In the many countries which now have some sort of land use planning system, the provisions, standards, codes, and zoning rules of the plan are important in constituting markets and power relations in a number of ways. Planning defines permitted categories of activity, called "use classes" in the UK system, and equivalents elsewhere. These definitions tend to constitute submarkets – for agricultural land, for housing land, for offices, and so on – because the zoning injects some uniformity into what would otherwise be a market of totally unique and assorted plots of land. The standardization of zoning in the USA earlier this century was a key factor enabling a sustained boom in housing production to take place (McMahon 1986). Zoning systems designed to exclude poor residents (and thus Blacks from White areas) then became a common feature (Plotkin 1988). Zoning rules can enforce inequality in more subtle ways too. The labor government of the city of São Paulo recently noted that much higher densities of construction (and thus higher profits) were permitted on larger sites than on individual plots of land – which strongly favored large developers over individual families – and in their new plan they set a uniform density for all sites to redress the balance.

Planning also regulates infrastructure production and it links areas for permitted building production to the availability of infrastructure. That at least was the postwar norm in northwest Europe. In southern Europe, Latin America, and elsewhere the infrastructure sometimes followed rather than led, and we have had a recent taste of this sequence at Canary Wharf in London Docklands where key infrastructure is being fitted in after the commercial building it is designed to valorize. It was the developers of this rather inaccessible office complex who insisted that Mrs Thatcher's government go ahead with the very costly underground railroads and highway schemes which would guarantee their success. But whether the infrastructure comes first or later, it is typically financed or underwritten by the central or local state and generates major shifts and concentrations of realizable value, which are then commonly the subject of private appropriation. The biggest European instance is probably the French state investment (in roads, regional and high-speed trains, urban infrastructure, and cheap loans) which underpinned the Eurodisney theme park at

Marne-la-Valée (Balducci 1992). But every town has its examples: shopping centers beside the highway intersections, office parks beside the airport, stores and offices at railroad interchanges and so on (Bertolini and Spit 1998).

Nodes in the transport system thus focus and concentrate the possibilities of making money through real estate: the owners of land in such places can lay hands on a share of the national product and most recent European examples are ones where private owners are the main beneficiaries. But there are cases across Europe where some of the profits from collective investment in infrastructure has returned to the collective purse: in the original British new towns, in a few of the French developments such as La Défense and in the Netherlands.

We can, in other words, view the production of infrastructure and buildings as being – among other things – a means for investors to lay hands on some of society's total profitability. The buildings are analogous to the sponge or tissue with which we mop water from the floor. This, of course, affects architecture profoundly since the role of the architect is to produce the best sponges. For many architects, this role is incompatible with the creativity and the commitment to social and environmental needs in which they have been trained. Often they find themselves subordinated to project managers who are better at keeping costs down and to property consultants who are experts in maximizing the finished value of buildings. In these conditions architecture can be reduced to a cosmetic function (Ive 1995), the property development industry is seen as lacking in social or environmental awareness (by Prince Charles, for example) and is viewed by sophisticated people as essentially philistine.

An urban and regional planning regime sustained over a period of time can play a central role in reducing the overall supply of urban space. This limits competition between investors and owners and thus underwrites their profitability and/or land values. In Britain until the 1970s we saw this in the protection of town center shopping against the threat from out-of-town shopping centers, in the rationing of sites for out-of-town centers in much of the subsequent period, in the maintenance of scarcity in the central London office market up to 1985, when the Thatcher government deregulated it, and in many other spheres. While it was always in the interests of the individual investor to secure exceptions and departures from restrictive plans, it was in the collective interests of the owners of landed assets to retain this restrictive and predictable form of planning – thus the calls for a return to "plan-led" development control in the UK after 1989.

Social Polarization and Segregation

The neoliberal strategy of lowering labor costs through wage reduction, labor market "flexibility," and the opening up of developed markets to low-wage production from poorer countries has of course led to the well-documented growth of poverty in "developed" countries – countries previously characterized by relatively egalitarian distributions of income and wealth. The strongest form of this impoverishment in "Western" countries is clearly in the USA (Brenner 1998) but it is emerging in various forms throughout western Europe and is well summarized by the French urbanist Alain Lipietz who outlines the trend towards what he calls an "hour-glass" society: more people in the top and at the bottom of the income distribution, fewer in the middle (Lipietz 1992; 1996; Dunford 1997).

These changes in the living standards of labor (and of the reserve army of labor – people surplus to the requirements of the labor market) are, of course, implemented in actual places in direct and indirect ways. Falling money wages and high unemployment are the most obvious direct forms of impoverishment. Indirectly people can be made worse off by reductions in the social wage (education, health, and other public services) or through increases in living costs – especially housing expenses. There are local arguments about whether the changes in income distribution constitute relative or absolute "polarization," or should better be seen (at least in the London case: Hamnett 1994) as professionalization. For New York, attention has focused on how the high salaries in the finance sector lead to housing being no longer affordable by poor and middle groups (Fitch 1993). The ubiquitous experience, however, is of poor people (and in high-cost cities like London, middle-income people too) competing on worsening terms for housing space.

The social sifting and sorting of people is, of course, highly complex, affected by the full range of national practices on social housing, rent control, tenant security, divisibility of dwellings, and so on. But in all cases it is the markets for housing which convert the employment inequalities into concrete housing experiences (vol. 20 of the journal *Built Environment* presents a useful series of city-level studies and the Open University has just produced an invaluable survey: Pile, Brook et al. 1999). The most ambitious analysis of the cumulative process through which social classes get resorted, services shift, property values adjust, and classes transfer again is still the comprehensive study of Paris (Preteceille and Terrail 1985; Pinçon-Charlot and Preteceille 1986). Some of the work of Harloe on London and of Fainstein and Marcuse on US cities explores these themes (Fainstein, Harloe et al. 1992; Marcuse and van Kempen 1999). We could say that the housing market operates partly as a means by which people "buy" access to good public and private services, high environmental quality and other things they want. This can be seen as individualistic behavior by people pursuing their preferences in the light of what they can afford and what the market offers, as for example in the unique study of the English town of Reading (Cheshire and Sheppard 1995). The broader way in which class segregation would result was clearly apparent in the 1970s (Harvey and Chatterjee 1974; Stretton 1976; Hirsch 1977) and 1980s (Hooper 1985) and becomes even stronger today (Harvey 1996; Massey, Allen et al. 1999).

We have yet to start the analysis of how the privatization of transport and other infrastructure and of public services may affect these mechanisms in Britain. By gearing more forms of consumption (education, health, transport) to markets and thus to income, these changes can be expected to reinforce local inequalities in property prices, rents, and thus class segregation. The relationship, though, may not be a simple one. If a service is provided free then users enjoy it as an "externality" – a benefit not charged for – and may be willing to pay high rent to live where they can enjoy it. If the service is privatized and users have to pay charges then they probably would not be willing to pay so much rent (in addition to these charges) so rent differentials in such areas might become less strong. On the other hand, the rising public transport prices which come with privatization reduce accessibility and will thus tend to make these rent differentials stronger. It should be no surprise that contradictory tendencies are at work, making it difficult for empirical social science to sort out what is happening. Contradictions are an inherent feature of capitalist urban life (Berman 1982).

Containment of Urban Growth

In Southeast England we have an acute form of the familiar metropolitan problem of inadequate land supply, massively reinforced in our case by urban and regional planning. It can be characterized as a systematic structural barrier to fixed capital formation on most of the land in the region and it gives us

(1) a severely limited supply of development land which,
(2) combined with real growth of incomes (from earnings, profits, and rents) for perhaps half the population,
(3) combined with the income elasticity of demand for housing (meaning that as people's incomes grow their demand for housing grows even faster),
(4) creates a tendency towards relative retail and other price inflation in our region; living standards are thus depressed and/or salaries pushed up, reducing the competitiveness of employers in a wide belt around London, especially in the west. By the same logic it also increases the volatility of prices because fluctuations in demand cannot be met by quick adjustments of supply and must be soaked up mainly by price changes.
(5) Combined further with relative (and perhaps absolute) impoverishment of a large part of the population, the market price of housing will exclude a growing proportion of the population or force them into less space or worse conditions.
(6) There is a powerful distortion whereby actual investment (in new construction, repair and maintenance) is lower than it would be in conditions of easier land supply. For example, (a) For households there is the familiar experience that you pay so much to service your mortgage that you can't afford to maintain or extend your dwelling; (b) developers spend so much on sites that they are constrained to skimp on floorspace, garden space, and building quality (Cheshire, Sheppard et al. 1985; Evans 1988). Cullen (Cullen 1982) and the early work of Ball (Ball 1983) was very effective in explaining the configuration of social forces which generated this characteristic form of speculative housing. This very low standard of development may nowadays gain some legitimacy through its high density, but in most cases any "sustainability" benefits must be outweighed by the automobile dependency of these developments and their sheer low quality.
(7) Structurally, it means that our regional decentralization has been over long distances to towns (or nontown locations) where automobile dependence for trips within and between settlements is strong (Ota 1995).
(8) Within the towns, especially London, this mechanism produces pressure for densification of suburbs and infilling everywhere – often at the expense of the environmental qualities and other use-values enjoyed by established residents. This is politically very tense, and the contradictions emerge very strongly in the NIMBY politics of the region.
(9) So far as the house building industry is concerned, does this configuration of forces help to explain the declining role of the volume speculative house builders in generating additions to housing supply?

(10) The need for social housing becomes ever greater in these conditions because low and middle-income people cannot afford what the market offers. In the UK, social housing is hardly produced any more except by nonprofit, semi-autonomous, housing associations. For this housing association sector, the combination of
- high land prices,
- falling Housing Association Grant from government (HAG),
- rising proportions of open market borrowing

means that
- space and quality standards are under intense pressure;
- rents have to be high and rising;
- You can afford a housing association dwelling only if you are prosperous enough, or if you are poor enough to get housing benefit (HB). This is a problem for those excluded, for the occupiers, for management, and for the social composition of schemes.
- only HB underwrites the market risk for lenders – a weird paradox where bankers have to defend the welfare system.

But these are details: the essence of the point is that truly massive transfers of income and wealth take place, the inequality of living conditions is exacerbated, technologies we need for housing and transport are never developed or optimized and moves towards real environmental sustainability are ruled out of consideration.

In terms of class politics the outcome is far from clear: there is absolutely no general appreciation of the real consequences of the containment policy. The rather small number of beneficiaries (institutional lenders, established owner-occupiers in the protected areas, some developers, and land owners) have marshaled the support of all political parties from the Tory right through to the Greens in support of the sacred greenbelt and "countryside." Only a few economists (Evans and Cheshire referred to above) have noted the economic penalties and only a minority within the Green movement have noticed some of the real social and environmental penalties (Fairlie and This Land is Ours 1996). Fairlie has pointed out that in much of southern England the poor and middle-earners are prevented from getting housing but required to use automobiles.

Centralization Tendencies in Cities and Countries

It is very evident that the operation of real-estate markets is a key mechanism in the overconcentration of investment in commercial building in the prime areas of European cities, and in the central cities within European countries. Ever since Hotelling's powerful modeling of the behavior of ice-cream sellers on a beach, it has been clear that competitive locational behavior by retailers can produce overconcentration which is on no one's interests but their own. They protect themselves from competition by clustering together, although consumers would be better served by a spread distribution. When strong externalities begin to arise from co-location the effect is further reinforced (and extended to other functions) and the more so when we realize that investors in centralized concentrations can realize and appropriate value originating in earlier rounds of investment and in the state's investment in radial transport.

On top of all this "rational" behavior by investors is the irrational tendency which Richard Barras has examined for London offices where investors seem to go for the combination of low returns and high risk in their lemming-like enthusiasm (his analysis is unpublished but the evidence is clear in the annual surveys of the Investment Property Databank). Normally markets in investments show an inverse relationship between risk and return: high risk often comes with high return, and the safest investments are usually less profitable. But for some reason the banks and other institutions active in British property markets compete so hard with each other to obtain properties in central London that the rate of return is driven down to a low level – much lower than would be expected for such volatile and risky investments.

Just as property investment tends to be too concentrated in prime cities and locations, it also tends to be underrepresented in peripheral cities and locations – partly because investors are less informed about such places, partly perhaps because they expect high vacancy rates in such places. Certainly it appears that prospects of specially high returns are required to attract developers to provincial towns (Henneberry 1995).

Conclusions

I hope that this short sketch makes the point that real-estate markets are important elements in the operation of modern urban capitalism, more than just distributive mechanisms but part of the basic machinery which determines how economies work, what gets produced and how activity is generated, suppressed, displaced, and its value realized. The approach taken here has been essentially a Marxist one – a perspective which seems increasingly powerful in this postcommunist world (Harvey 1998) – and which is particularly useful in unraveling relationships which are at the same time social, economic, and geographical.

Among the outcomes of property-market operations are some of the phenomena of social polarization – "exclusion" and so on – which are such important urban experiences. Other outcomes include the disparities between core and periphery at various geographic scales, the surges of investment into and out of the built environment, and many of the influences acting on architecture.

What I am not trying to argue is that markets in general, or this market in particular, should be targeted as the culprit – as the sole object of attack – by those interested in social inclusion, equality, or democracy. The forces acting behind and through the markets are the important objects of study and it is the social relationships there that ultimately prevent social change. But property markets can be the cogwheels through which the system works and better regulation of those markets can have profound effects.

The task, then, is primarily a task of analysis and clarification in which the research community should be unraveling the mechanisms in order to show just what the forces are behind the property markets: who benefits and who is losing. One valuable result would be to cast light on some of the practical and legal issues in urban planning, design, and management – on issues like whether broad or narrow definitions of use classes are to be preferred, what sort of reforms in lease structures would have progressive or regressive effects, how the benefits of transport infrastructure investment can best be captured to finance other services, and so on, not to mention the issue of how to use the greenbelt. Unintended consequences of plans and policies abound – like the urban containment example sketched earlier in this chapter – so there is a lot to be done in the analysis of how planning interacts with markets.

The results are not obvious, and some of us as individuals will probably find ourselves in the winning camp on some issues and the losing camp on others. But the winning camp is, in general, capital. Gone are the days when the ownership of land and property lay with a distinct "landed class." Landed property is now just one the classes of capital assets owned by banks, companies, pension funds, rich and middle-income households. Ownership of capital is still important and to be a nonowner is still the most basic "social exclusion." Ownership of real estate is a distinctive form of capital ownership.

REFERENCES

Balducci, A. 1992: *Eurodisney*. Milano: Triennale di Milano.

Ball, M. 1983: *Housing Policy and Economic Power*. London: Methuen.

Berman, M. 1982: *All that is Solid Melts into Air: The Experience of Modernity*. London: Verso.

Bertolini, L. and Spit, T. 1998: *Cities on Rails: The Redevelopment of Railway Station Areas*. London: Spon.

Brenner, R. 1998: Uneven development and the long downturn: the advanced capitalist economies from boom to stagnation 1950–1988. *New Left Review*, 229, 1–262 (whole issue).

Chambert, H. 1997: *Urban Development and Metropolitan Housing Construction: A Spatial Analysis Approach*. Stockholm. Chamberts Förlag.

Cheshire, P. and Sheppard, S. 1995: On the price of land and the value of amenities. *Economica*, 62, 247–67.

Cheshire, P. C., Sheppard, S., and Hooper, A. 1985: The economic consequences of the British [land use] planning system: some empirical results. University of Reading, Discussion Papers in Urban Regional Economics, no. 29.

Cullen, A. 1982: Speculative housebuilding in Britain: some notes on the switch to timber-frame production methods. Proceedings of the Bartlett International Summer School on the Production of the Built Environment, 4, 4/12–4/18.

Dobb, M. 1969: *Welfare Economics and the Economics of Socialism*. Cambridge: Cambridge University Press.

Dunford, M. 1997: The hour-glass society: the sharing of work versus the disintegration of society. *City*, 8, 171–87 (contains a summary in English of Lipietz 1996).

Evans, A. 1988: *No Room! No Room! Costs of the British Planning System*. London: Institute of Economic Affairs.

Fainstein, S., Harloe, M., and Gordon, I. 1992: *Divided Cities: New York and London in the Contemporary World*. Oxford: Blackwell.

Fairlie, S. and This Land is Ours 1996: *Low Impact Development: Planning and People in a Sustainable Countryside*. Charlbury, UK: Jon Carpenter Publishing.

Fitch, R. 1993: *The Assassination of New York*. London: Verso.

Haila, A. 1989: Invocation of historical accident: a critical examination of recent discussions on the theory of land rent. Proceedings of the Bartlett International Summer School on the Production of the Built Environment, 10, 201–8.

Haila, A. 1990: The theory of land rent at the crossroads. *Environment and Planning D: Society and Space*, 8, 275–96.

Hamnett, C. 1994: Socio-economic change in London: professionalization, not polarization. *Built Environment*, 20 (3), 192–203.
Harvey, D. 1996: *Justice, Nature and the Geography of Difference*. Oxford: Blackwell.
Harvey, D. 1998: Globalisation and the body. In R. Wolff, A. Schneider, and C. Schmid (eds.), *Possible Urban Worlds: Urban Strategies at the End of the 20th Century*. Zurich: Birkhäuser Verlag for INURA, 26–38.
Harvey, D. and Chatterjee, D. 1974: Absolute Rent and the structuring of space by financial institutions. *Antipode*, 6 (1), 22–36.
Henneber, J. 1995: Developers, property cycles and local economic development: the case of Sheffield. *Local Economy*, 10 (2), 23–5.
Hirsch, F. 1977: *The Social Limits to Growth*. London: Routledge.
Hooper, A. 1985: The role of landed property in the production of the built environment. Proceedings of the Bartlett International Summer School on the Production of the Built Environment, 6, 4/17–4/21.
Ive, G. 1995: Commercial architecture in 1980s London: value engineering or conspicuous investment. In I. Borden and D. Dunster (eds.), *Architecture and the Sites of History: Interpretations of Buildings and Cities*. London: Butterworth, 372–86.
Ive, G. 1998: Systems of metropolitan housing production: an institutional approach to their study. Proceedings of the International Summer School on the Production of the Built Environment, 17, 155–75.
Lipietz, A. 1992: *Towards a New Economic Order: Post-Fordism, Ecology and Democracy*. Oxford: Polity Press.
Lipietz, A. 1996: La Société en Sablier: le partage du travail contre la déchirure sociale. Paris, eds la Découverte (see Dunford 1997 for an English summary).
Magalhães, C. de 1998: Economic instability, structural change and the property markets: the late 1980s office boom in São Paulo. *Environment and Planning A*, 30, 2005–24.
Magalhães, C. de 2000: International property consultants and the transformation of local markets. *Journal of Property Research*.
Marcuse, P. and van Kampen, R. (eds), 1999: *Globalizing Cities: Is There a New Spatial Order?* Oxford: Blackwell.
Massey, D., Allen, J., and Pile, S. (eds.), 1999: *City Worlds*. London: Routledge and the Open University.
McMahon, M. 1985: The law of the land: property rights and town planning in modern Britain. In M. Ball, V. Bentivegna, M. Edwards and M. Folin (eds.), *Land Rent, Housing and Urban Planning: A European Perspective*. London: Croom Helm, 87–106.
McMahon, M. 1986: Zoning, a contradictory form of regulation. Proceedings of the Bartlett International Summer School on the Production of the Built Environment, 7, 279–88.
Ota, M. 1995: Office decentralization: London and Tokyo. Ph.D. thesis, UCL, London.
Page, M. W. 1996: Locality, housing production and the local state. *Environment and Planning D: Society and Space* (April), 14, 181–202.
Pearce, D. and Markandya, A. 1991: *Blueprint for a Green economy*. London: Earthscan.
Pile, S., Brook, C., and Mooney, G. (eds.), 1999: *Unruly Cities?* London: Routledge and the Open University.
Pinçon-Charlot, M. and Preteceille, E. 1986: *Ségrégation urbaine: classes sociales et équipements collectifs en région parisienne*. Paris: Anthropos.
Plotkin, S. 1988: *Keep out: The Struggle for Land Use Control*. Berkeley: University of California Press.
Preteceille, E. and Terrail, J.-P. 1985: *Capitalism, Consumption and Needs*. Oxford: Blackwell.
Stretton, H. 1976: *Capitalism, Socialism and the Environment*. Cambridge: CUP.

Chapter 51

The Politics of Universal Provision of Public Housing

Chua Beng Huat

At the same time as western European countries are withdrawing from extensive provisions of social housing, some Asian countries are increasing state involvement in direct provision. While ex-socialist European countries are dismantling state ownership of land, as part of the transition to capitalist economy, in part to promote "freehold" private housing, some Asian countries are promoting leasehold, subsidized public housing, with land remaining in state ownership. Following the success of Singapore's national housing program, in which approximately 85 percent of the total households purchase a 99-year leasehold apartment directly from the state-run public housing agency, Hong Kong has announced that it will embark on a similar public housing home-ownership program to house the relatively poor. China has also begun to move away from a situation in which the population is dependent on rental apartments from different state sources to promote home-ownership of state-sponsored housing, the details of which remain unclear. The marked contrasts in housing strategies between these locations demand analysis. This chapter will focus on direct provision of housing units by the state rather than other forms of public assistance, such as rent, mortgage, or land subsidies. Hence the term "public housing" is used to refer exclusively to such housing.

State provision of housing has been conceptualized as a four-stage process: intervention, provision, quality, and withdrawal. According to Power, under conditions of rapid urban growth, the demand for minimal housing for each household generates intense pressures for state intervention.[1] Once this basic provision is achieved, provision shifts from quantity to quality. Finally, once the majority of the population is well housed, the state begins to attempt to withdraw from direct involvement, other than by social welfare assistance. According to this trajectory, current state interventions in selective Asian locations are the result of housing shortages due to rapid urbanization and the respective governments will progressively disengage themselves once shortages are solved. Yet evidence is to the contrary. Particularly in the case of Singapore, the government is constantly expanding its public housing supply in a progressively inclusive process, when housing quality for the entire population is already very high. Obviously, the four-stage historical process is not applicable to the Singapore case, warranting a different explanation.

The view that governments wait anxiously for the first opportunity to withdraw from housing provision may be said to be based entirely on fiscal considerations, without due attention to the politics of state assistance. This politics, however, has been undertaken within different frameworks, among which is the attempt to link public provisions to electoral behavior. Deriving from the British experience, it has been argued that state provision of housing and transportation as public service beside individuals providing for themselves as privately financed commodity consumption, has given rise to a political and electoral division along the two modes of consumption. These two modes constitute the basis of a vertical political cleavage that cuts across production-class positions, with state-dependents voting Left and the "self-financing" voting Right.[2] A plausible explanation is that national ideological structures "make available to individuals in different social locations particular perceptions of their interests vis-à-vis state policies and the interests of other social groups."[3] The ideological configurations tend to focus exclusively on pitching the interests of public-service-dependent consumers, in a zero-sum manner, against those who pay their own way; thus producing political and electoral divisions.

The political cleavage between consumption classes results, therefore, not from any intrinsic features of the state-provided goods or services, but from the two different modes of provision and consumption. This appears to be borne out by the fact that where there is near-universal state provision, such as health, education, and environmental services, in which private financing constitute tiny fractions of the respective total costs, the effects on electoral behavior are greatly minimized. Universal provision thus appears to "depoliticize," that is, remove politics from public provision.[4]

Conversely complete withdrawal of government provision would also remove the politics from consumption; as in the case of consumer goods. Precisely because complete withdrawal is another way to "depoliticize" consumption issues, the operationalization of politics of public provisions in terms of electoral behavior is not incompatible with the fiscal conception of state subsidy on public services. If all things were equal, fiscal considerations would compel any government to prefer no provision at all to universal provision. Again, Singapore's deviation from this general preference warrants an explanation.

In seeking to understand this deviation, we would also simultaneously augment our understanding of the spectrum and variations in the politics of state provision. To fashion an explanation for the Singapore case, we need to return to some of the conceptual issues raised by the above two existing frameworks of analysis.

The Fiscal and Depoliticization Theses

First, the fiscal "thesis" conceives of state provision of public goods and services as a one-way street; provision is a constant drain on the public purse and should therefore be terminated as soon and as quickly as possible. What is overlooked is the potential political advantages that could accrue to the government in power. This negligence arises in part from conceptualizing the issues in terms of an abstract "state," rather than in terms of the concrete "government in power";

potential political gains are important to the ruling politicians' desire to remain in power.

Next, we need to examine the idea of "depoliticization" in the context of (near-) universal state provision. That a significant activity of the state, such as universal provision of healthcare or education, can be conceived as "depoliticized" is itself curious. This is partly the consequence of operationalizing the "political" dimension of government provision in terms of electoral behavior. In so doing, it merely takes into account what Offe calls "the most superficial and most visible level of politics,"[5] that is, politics as practiced by various groups or classes of people united behind respective articulated interests, and entering into open negotiation or into class struggle, as projected by liberal democratic or Marxist analysis, respectively. In electoral politics, the electorate's voting behavior is taken as proxy, and read as reflections, of the result of the negotiations. Where overt negotiation or confrontation is not observable, nor deduced from electoral results, "depoliticization" is deemed to have occurred. This conception of "depoliticization" is ideological in at least two ways.

First, by equating electoral behavior with politics as such, "depoliticization" is used as a descriptive rather than an explanatory concept. So used, the concept glosses over rather than exposes and explains the political dimension of public provision. In contemporary nation-states, the body politic is far more deeply penetrated by administrative and government strategies than by the formality of periodic elections. Thus, from an electoral perspective, politics may have submerged from universal public provision but it has far from disappeared in the strategies of governance or governmentality. Those who stand to benefit from the reduction of public provision, including the ruling government, are merely kept in the wings of the political stage, waiting to make their reentry at the first opportunity, to "repoliticize" the issue. This is abundantly clear in the ruling government's own efforts to privatize any provision when so doing can be managed without losing the electoral majority. This is consistent with the above argument that, from a fiscal point of view, governments have a generalized preference to withdraw from provision.

Second, "depoliticization" as a descriptive concept reproduces precisely the way the ruling government would prefer to have its citizens believe and behave. It would encourage them to treat such provisions as purely technical and administrative matters, to confine their comments and criticisms to improving the bureaucratic effectiveness of the agencies entrusted with providing the goods and, preferably, not make political issues out of the provisions. This strategic division between technical administration and politics, with a preference for expanding the former and shrinking the latter, is part of the management procedures of the modern state.[6]

Contrary to the "depoliticization" thesis, it is argued here that, while the ruling government may indeed desire to administer the public provisions without political hindrance, it will not "depoliticize" provisions. This is because the electorate's satisfaction with and appreciation of the ruling government's successes in provisions are the very basis of building political capital, of maintaining the mass popular support that legitimizes the government in power. Thus, while extensive public provisions of goods and services are undoubtedly fiscal difficulties imposed on the ruling government, the successful management of these provisions, on the other hand, provides it with a political dividend and enables it to accumulate political capital, in terms of enhanced legitimacy to rule. Consequently, the ruling government will always attempt to make political capital out of such successes; conversely, it will distance itself from failures, blaming them on state functionaries. Indeed, it may be argued that, given the general preference for withdrawal from provision, the motivation by any government in power to extend provision universally is based precisely on the ability to enhance legitimacy to remain in power.

Thus, to balance the conceptualization of public provision of goods and service in fiscal terms as burdens on a government which is impatient to extract itself from more than necessary commitment, one must take into consideration the potential political returns generated by provision to the ruling government. One must recognize that every governmental/state intervention is a political act, even in instances where the political dimension is submerged. Such submersion should be conceptualized as an effect – "depoliticization" effect – achieved through precisely the strategies of state intervention, and the ways in which this effect is achieved and sustained should be analyzed. Singapore's national housing program is offered here as an illustrative example of the above argument that a government in power may be motivated to extend public provision because of the potential gains in political legitimacy to remain in power.

Singapore's National Housing Program

Established in 1960, the Housing and Development Board (HDB), Singapore's public housing authority was entrusted with the massive postindependence national housing program. It was given extensive powers in land acquisition, resettlement, town planning, architectural design, engineering works, and building material sourcing and production. In sum, it is responsible for all development work except actual building construction, which is undertaken by private contractors. With concentration of such powers and resources, the HDB has been able to provide housing at substantially lower cost than comparable accommodation in the private sector. Beginning modestly with provision of basic rental units for the poor who lived in slums at the urban fringe and in overcongested shop-houses in the central areas, a "home ownership" scheme was introduced in 1964. The rents and prices of the apartments are determined by the government in accordance with economic conditions while ensuring affordability. Large supplies of dwelling units have been sustained annually since. More than half a million high-rise apartments for sale and rent and a substantial volume of related facilities such as commercial spaces, light industrial parks, and recreational facilities have been completed, all within comprehensively planned new towns. Already 85 percent of the three million population lives in public housing, with an equal percentage as "home-owners." The government has proclaimed that its aim is for 100 percent home-ownership, giving substance to the phrase a "nation of home-owners." The impressive achievement has been made possible by the more than three decades of double-digit growth of the Singapore economy since the mid-1960s and also, of course, by a set of policy decisions.

From the supply side, several important policies should be noted. First, as land cost is one of the prohibitive features of extensive public housing, the government amended the colonial Land Acquisition Act in 1966 to enable it to acquire land with compensation rates determined by statute and far below market value, on account of the "national" development interest and in violation of common laws that govern property rights. As the economy expanded, compensation rates were adjusted upwards but it was not until the early 1990s that the market rate was used. By then, all the estimated land needed for national development was already in the hands of the Commissioner of Land, and any additional acquisition would have been minuscule. Throughout this process, affected landlords either accepted their losses with altruistic largesse or faced the losses with bitterness and alienation from the government. The popularity of the government's action among the overwhelming propertyless majority of the electorate enabled it to bear the rejection of the small minority of affected landlords.

Second, one of the "problems" in public housing is the propensity of residents to continue to live in the housing units even as their financial circumstances improve. This is because subsidized low rents mean increased disposable income to the residents, giving them comparative consumption advantages against nonpublic housing dwellers. This results in the government continually having to build new housing, without the ability to recover the capital cost of each cycle of construction. Such was the situation in ex-socialist nations.[7] Early introduction of the home-ownership program in Singapore managed to overcome this problem. Residents were not only encouraged to purchase a 99-year leasehold on their respective units but were entitled to sell the units after 5 years of residence and purchase a new and larger public housing flat, enabling older and smaller apartments to filter down to lower-income households in the resale market. Upgrading households were entitled to keep all the profits from the sale of their existing apartments as capital gains, without tax. The generous resale scheme in effect democratized property investment. As a result of the general economic growth and property price inflation, the economic gains had been very substantial for households who had entered the public housing sector early. In recent years, Singaporeans have grown so adept at making financial gains from public housing that the government was forced to change the resale rules to discourage excessive profits. The residential period before eligibility for new apartments has been extended from five to ten years. However, profit remains a possibility. The popularity of the home-ownership scheme, and its ability to generate political support, can be readily surmised even by those unfamiliar with the system.

The long-ruling government's commitment to universal provision is evident in the periodical raising of the monthly income ceiling for eligibility to purchase public housing, in step with the general economic growth, so as to include as many households as possible. In addition, the HDB would purchase older apartments from the resale market, refurbish them and sell them at greater subsidies, including cash grants, to families at the lower end of the income hierarchy. At the other end of the income strata, the government provided land subsidies to private developers to build better quality housing, in exchange for lower prices for apartments for young middle-class professionals who aspire to live in condominiums but cannot afford those in the private sector; cash grants are given to first-time home-owning families. The aim, as mentioned earlier, is what the government calls a "home-owning nation." Overall, then, the distinct small minority of Singaporeans who have not benefited directly from the universal public housing program are among the wealthiest in the city-state.

Significantly, this massive, inclusive public housing program has been managed without it becoming a constant strain on the national economy. Incomes from the sale of flats, along with rents derived from residential, commercial, and industrial premises, and revenues from ancillary services like parking lots, combine to ensure a significant return from the housing and attendent infrastructure investments. The return can then be ploughed back into the next cycle of new housing production. Inevitably, in the early phase of the program direct public subsidy was very substantial, However, as the program unfolded and when a critical mass of housing stock and attendent facilities had been built up, the margin of subsidy from the government shrank progressively; such that, by 1975, a brief ten years after the initiation of the home-ownership scheme, the subsidy was maintained at 2 percent of the national development budget till the mid-1980s.

Since then, doubts regarding actual subsidies to the ongoing public housing program have emerged publicly and are often raised by the few opposition members in parliamentary sessions. The government maintains that there is a "market" subsidy, that is, the selling price of a public housing apartment is lower than a comparable unit in the private sector. This response is not entirely satisfactory as it is an "accounting" response: subsidy is presumed in the relativity of prices, leaving the issue of actual construction cost subsidy, if any, unanswered. The significant larger lesson to be drawn, however, is that a national public housing program that aims at universal provision need not necessarily drain the public purse, but might even turn a profit or at least be fiscally healthy and viable.[8]

Political Legitimacy and Universal Provision

In a world where homelessness is common in both developing and developed nations, Singapore provides a unique and significant instance in which universal provision of public housing has been achieved without fiscal crisis or political divisiveness. It provides resources for rethinking of some extant explanations and arguments on universal provision; in this instance, an alternative to the idea of "depoliticization."

As argued earlier, questions of public goods provision must be posed not only as fiscal burden on, but also in terms of gains that accrue to, the ruling government. Since public provisions are to be delivered as nonprofit and redistributive practices, the gains are not or should not be economic in character but political. Accordingly, it is argued that successful delivery of public goods gives the ruling government popular support and political legitimacy. This seems to be prima facie unproblematic. The methodological issue is how to measure the extent of legitimacy that has accrued by any provision. The most obvious measure of electoral behavior is too clumsy because, assuming voting to be "rational," individuals would vote on the basis of an aggregate of issues; it would, therefore, be impossible to isolate public provision as the explanation for how one votes. It would seem that ideological evidence might be more useful, although admittedly less direct.

That there are national ideological structures that "made available to individuals in different social locations particular perceptions of their interests vis-à-vis state policies"[9] is a good starting point. Logically, with universal provision, such ideological structures would not be cast in terms of competing interests of the different groups but would appeal to an idea of the "collective," the "national" interest. Indeed the Singapore government appeared to require no more justification than the notion of the "national interest" for its housing program. In the early years of nation building, public housing provision was politically/ideologically embraced by the nascent government as testimony to its commitment to improving the material conditions of the newly enfranchised citizens of the city-state. After more than 30 years in power, this continues to be a fundamental of government; in the Prime Minister's words, "The best stake we can give to Singaporeans is a house or a flat, a home"; this populist and popular idea is seen as the sine qua non of political stability and economic growth and has seldom been publicly questioned.

That home-ownership has as one of its effects "the expansion of commitment to the prevalent social order by the development of personal stakes in its survival"[10] is not new. In Singapore, this is taken to its logical conclusion as the government belief that it will intensify national sentiments and strengthen national defense. The generalized tendency of home-ownership and the real capital gains that have been made by public housing residents up till now, among whom are the lower-income households who were also among the earliest to qualify for public housing, have intensified the population's ideological and material commitment to the system as a whole, and reinforced the popular support base of the ruling government.

The secure popular support base has enabled the government to underwrite other social policies through housing provision regulations. Among these are the following: to use housing policies to reinforce a traditional definition of family by excluding singles and unmarried mothers from eligibility; to disperse class-based communities by redistributing residents through the spatial mixing of different categories of flats; to disperse ethnic communities through a quota system of allocation to every block of apartments and, at its most politically problematic, to threaten to withhold upgrading and other ancillary services to electoral constituencies which voted against the ruling government, as in the 1997 general election. In these four illustrative instances, dispersing class-based and ethnic-based communities may be ideologically justified as the avoidance of the "ghetto" effect of public housing and, concurrently, the promotion of racial integration in the multiracial society. However, it is in the other two instances that we begin to get a glimpse into the extreme political effects of universal provision.

The exclusion of the single unmarried individuals is due to the pro-family social policies of the government. For example, the income ceiling for eligibility is raised very substantially and the waiting time significantly reduced, for younger families who choose to live with, or in close proximity to, any of their parents. Conversely, unmarried mothers are penalized for their "moral" crime of being out of wedlock. Finally, the threat of withholding upgrading as a means of coercing the citizens to continue to vote for the ruling party is too naked to require further explication. However, the ruling party considers it as "normal" politics. What is disclosed in these two instances is that universal provision has engendered an absolute dependency of the citizens on the ruling government for their basic housing needs, rendering them subjects of the latter's coercion. This is not "depoliticization" by any definition. It is, instead, the "paternalism" of the ruling government showing its authoritarian tendency, whenever the citizens "misbehave." It is the fulfillment of the Gramscian notion of hegemony, the concurrent incitement of both ideological leadership and the use of force by the wielders of state power.

Conclusion

It is argued here that while universal provision of public goods and services may apparently eliminate the political cleavage that emerges out of the consumption modes – the public service and the private commodity – of two classes of consumers, it does not by this apparent effect eliminate politics from such provision. Instead of being "depoliticized," universal provision is recast ideologically, by the government in power, as being in the "national" or "collective" interest. If this ideological reformulation is successful, it will not only gain legitimacy for the provision but also for its right to govern. Once provision is truly universal, citizens become absolutely dependent on the government as the monopolistic provider of the particular goods or service; thus, radically reducing their ability to resist, even negotiate, the terms of the provision itself. At this point, the government in power may be said to be in complete ideological hegemony in that specific sector of material life.

NOTES

1. Ann Power, *Hovels to High Rise: State Housing in Europe since 1850* (Routledge, London, 1993), pp. 3–4.
2. Patrick Dunleavy, "The urban basis of political alignment: social class, domestic property ownership and state intervention in the consumption process," *British Journal of Political Science*, 9, 409–43.
3. Patrick Dunleavy, *Urban Political Analysis: The Politics of Collective Consumption* (Macmillan, London, 1980), p. 74.
4. Dunleavy, "The urban basis", p. 412.
5. Claus Offe, *Contradictions of the Welfare State* (MIT Press, MA, Cambridge, 1984), p. 159.
6. Jürgen Habermas, Legitimation Crisis (Beacon Press, Boston, 1975).
7. Ivan Szelenyi, *Urban Inequalities under State Socialism* (Oxford University Press, New York, 1983).
8. For greater details regarding Singapore's public housing program see Chua Beng Huat, *Housing and Political Legitimacy: Stakeholding in Singapore* (Routledge, London, 1997); M. Castells, L. Goh and R. Y. -W. Kwok, *The Shek Kip Mei Syndrome: Economic Development and Public Housing in Hong Kong and Singapore* (Pion, London, 1990); Aline K. Wong and S. H. K. Yeh (eds.) 1985: *Housing a Nation: 25 Years of Public Housing in Singapore* (Housing and Development Board, Singapore).
9. Dunleavy, *Urban Political Analysis*, p. 74.
10. J. A. Agnew, "Home ownership and the capitalist order," in Michael Dear and A. J. Scott (eds.), *Urbanisation and Urban Planning in Capitalistic Society* (Methuen, London, 1982), p. 457.

Chapter 52

Reintegrating the Apartheid City? Urban Policy and Urban Restructuring in Durban

Alison Todes

Introduction

Current South African urban policy is founded on intentions to reintegrate cities, and to move toward more compact urban forms. Visions akin to the urbanist ideals of Jane Jacobs (1961) offering opportunities for higher-density living, proximity between home and work, land use mix, and social integration are prevalent. These city visions emerged as part of planners' critique of apartheid and their alternative of more developmental forms of planning (for example, Dewar and Uytenbogaardt 1991; Hindson et al. 1993). They appeared to accord with both resistance to urban apartheid and to the less divided urban forms which emerged as it broke down. Accepted within the inclusive forum processes which characterized the transitional period (Turok 1994; Watson 1998), and endorsed by neoliberal technocratic bodies such as the Urban Foundation (1990) and World Bank (1991), these ideas soon became a dominant discourse, and were embodied in legislation by the new government.

The compact integrated city ideal has however increasingly been questioned, as has been the case internationally. J. Robinson (1992, 1998) critiqued its technocratic discourse, suggesting that it could become another oppressive form of urban ordering – a physicalist metanarrative imposing a singular moral view of the good city. Further, the oppositional binaries contained within its narrative of the city limit perceptions of the diverse interactions across the city, and the way disconnections might, for example, have enabled economic activity in peripheral areas (J. Robinson 1998; see also Mabin 1998). Others have questioned its modernist assumptions that urban change can be controlled by policy (Simone 1998), and its prospects in a postmodern world where cities everywhere are increasingly characterized by division, fragmentation, and sprawl (Mabin 1995).

Rather than compaction or integration, empirical research on South African cities – focused mainly on Johannesburg, South Africa's largest city – suggests that new spatial divides are emerging along lines similar to patterns internationally (Mabin 1995; Murphy 1997; Beavon 1997; Tomlinson 1998). Compaction-integration appears to offer little to the urban poor on the periphery of the city (Tomlinson 1997).

The significance of compaction-integration is also being displaced politically at national level by a broader emphasis on developmental local government (Parnell and Pieterse 1998), and by a pragmatic politics focused on delivery and a reorientation to the market. A negotiated settlement may have played a role in the shift towards neoliberalism, but global markets provide a sharp discipline. Discourses of "competitive cities" are becoming increasingly common in the light of economic stagnation, growing unemployment, and South Africa's marginalization within current rounds of global economic restructuring. As Mabin (1998: 13) puts it, "there is wide agreement [among political parties] that urban policy should make cities safe for capitalism."

This chapter explores the prospects for compaction-integration against an analysis of current spatial restructuring in Durban, a city of three million people. I examine changing locational trends of residences, retail, and offices, considering the role of planning, and the extent to which new forms of planning are likely to achieve greater integration.

Durban is a city on South Africa's eastern seaboard. A branch plant manufacturing, port, commercial, and tourist city, it grew rapidly under import substitution policies from the boom years of the 1960s. Its position in the 1990s as South Africa opens to the global economy has been less secure: labour-intensive industries such as clothing have contracted substantially (Harrison 1998), while more capital-intensive industries have shed jobs through restructuring and repositioning (Valodia 1998). Durban's tourism position is also weakening as it is bypassed by international tourists, and as its traditional White middle-class market seeks seemingly safer and more varied experiences. These shifts, and the influence of a local growth coalition, underpinned an early emphasis on local economic development, largely focused on major projects, Durban's image and tourist roles (Freund 1998). Influenced by arguments that Durban could become one of South Africa's most internationally competitive cities (Centre for Development and Enterprise, CDE, 1996), economic regeneration and repositioning Durban as a "world class" city, is displacing the importance granted to spatial restructuring within planning agendas (Dominic 1998). Although strategies for economic regeneration include small firms, informal economic activities, and development within old township and informal areas, a greater "realism" is emerging, weakening support for forms of compaction-integration which contradict the market.

Housing and Urban Integration

In the late apartheid years, Durban's spatial form began to change, as rapid urbanization and weakening apartheid controls led to a massive growth of informal settlements on the periphery. Violence, overcrowding, and growing class differentiation also underpinned "decompression" into new middle-class housing areas and informal settlements within and on the edges of old African township areas (Morris and Hindson 1997). A few informal settlements emerged within central city areas as political instability undermined controls on settlement (Hindson et al. 1994). By 1994, informal settlements accounted for about a third of the Durban's population, but less than 4 percent were in central areas (Urban Strategy 1995).

Some of these settlements have densified, and a few land invasions have occurred since the 1994 elections, but a commitment by all levels of government to prevent land invasions has limited new growth. Urban growth has slowed (Urban Strategy 1995) as the economy stagnated (Cross 1996). Peripheral locales, such as unserviced tribal areas, defined beyond city limits in a recent (contested) demarcation, appear to provide important sites for households surviving through complex urban–rural linkages and marginal local employment (Cross et al. 1996).

Housing subsidies based on a capital grant to low-income households, and an initial application-based allocation system have largely reinforced apartheid patterns (Makhatini and Bedford 1998). Projects offering 73,300 housing opportunities had been approved by mid-1998, but most were in peripheral areas, reflecting the preexisting momentum of development, and the weight of informal settlement upgrading.

While the newly created Metropolitan Housing Service Unit is committed to restructuring the city along compact-integrated city lines, and has devised a number of innovative approaches to housing development, it is constrained by land cost and availability, competing claims to land, and resistance by adjacent communities. Vacant land is rarely "empty." Some 60 percent of housing development is likely to occur through informal settlement upgrading (Bedford 1998), following years of antiremovals struggles, and a recognition of the significance of people's investments in housing and social networks.

Centrally located informal settlements are a potential focus, and some projects have been developed, but they are often complicated by land ownership questions, and by the need to negotiate developments with adjacent – usually higher income – communities. Conflicts occur, for example, over service levels, impacts on property values, crime levels, race and culture. Although there is officially commitment to compaction policy by councillors, in practice the focus is on delivery, and constituency politics prevails, weakening the support for complex projects in central areas.

While Durban councils have largely avoided confrontations with high-income communities and landowners over the location of new low-cost housing – once an initial enthusiasm for more extensive redistribution was curbed by "economic realism" – some new developments defy an older race and class geography. Developments include those aimed at accommodating informal traders in the city center, Cato Manor, and infill on old buffer strips separating races. Justified by authorities in terms of antiapartheid discourses, such projects are usually contested along the lines suggested above. Claims by adjacent communities to housing developed in infill projects is a further source of contestation (Baskin 1998; Byerley 1998; Smit and Charlton 1998).

The case of Cato Manor, the largest and perhaps most important integrative project symbolically, exemplifies many of the tensions associated with policy directed attempts at urban integration and the challenges to planning imaginaries. Cato Manor is an area of 2,000 ha (900 developable), 7 km from the city center (P. Robinson 1994). It has "the most complex history of settlement... of any area in the city. It has been fiercely and often violently contested" (Edwards 1994: 415). The site of mass forced removals in the 1950s and 1960s, it remained largely vacant for decades, but land invasions began in the early 1990s. Emerging from a widely inclusive development forum, the Cato Manor Development Association (CMDA),

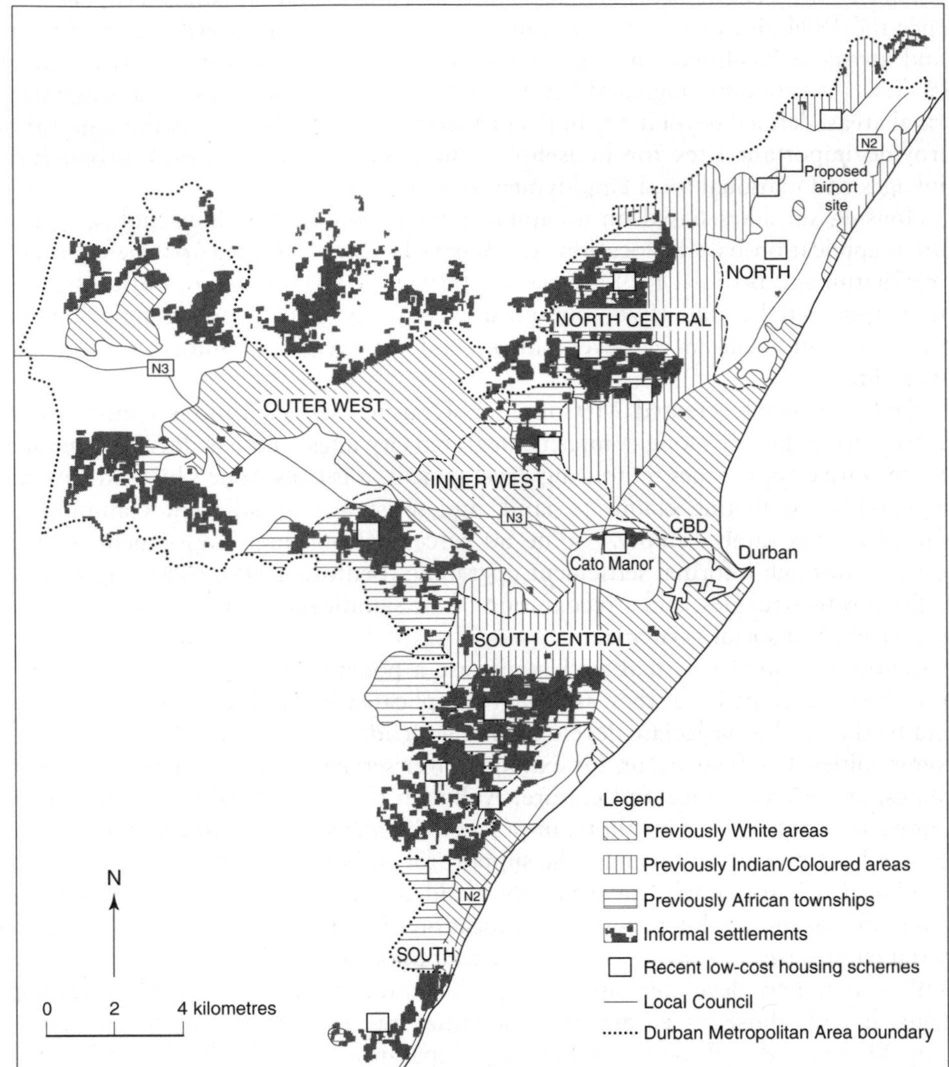

Figure 52.1 A reintegrating city? Racial zoning in Durban under apartheid, and recent developments

was created in 1993 to develop the area for around 170,000 mainly low-income people along compact-integrated city lines. By the end of 1998, some 2,000 sites had been developed, and another 8,000 were underway (CMDA 1998).

Despite its broad-based beginnings, its recognition as a Presidential Lead Project, its leadership by respected anti-apartheid planners, and international support, the project has been highly contested, slowing the achievement of objectives, and consuming considerable resources. Land invasions (Kahn and Maharaj 1998), unstable and weak leadership structures within informal communities, as well as crime and violence, have all impeded development (Foster 1998).

Figure 52.2 Centrally located informal settlements in Cato Manor, and, adjacent, higher-income areas (© Tony Smith Photography)

Further, conflict over site size – perhaps the most visible (and disliked) way in which compact city ideas are implemented – has cast planners within repressive roles. There are pressures to make proximate location available to more people through the formal system, but communities resist small sites on cultural grounds. Yet informal land markets and subletting result in far higher densities than those proposed, and high informal rents, posing questions as to whether the area can be maintained for low-income groups over the longer term (Foster 1998).

Development in Cato Manor has also been contested by competing claims to land by past victims of forced removals. Processes for land restitution – which involve lengthy validation of historical claims – only began once planning was well under-way. CMDA applied to have claims dealt with in other ways, but 400 of the potential 3,000 claimants demanded restitution and a lengthy court case ensued. Claimants appealed to historical identity and to ties to place. In the words of Agrippa Cebekhulu, "My roots are in Cato Manor. Any other place is not a home, but just a house" (cited in *The Mercury*, January 30, 1997). Planners were accused of insensitivity to history, echoing critiques of traditional planning. The outcome of the

Figure 52.3 The Cato Manor Development Project: one of the few opportunities for urban integration (© Tony Smith Photography)

court case was a mediation process, involving case-specific assessment by a panel, returning land where possible in terms of the development.

Other challenges to the form of development have come from the adjacent Greater Manor Gardens Residents Association (GMGRA), in terms of its "constitutional rights to protect and maintain property values, quality of life and safety and security" (GMGRA 1997). In the early years, an emphasis on extensive participatory processes, CMDA's weak institutional position and uncertain political support, as well as the presence of GMGRA on the CMDA Board, forced it to engage in extensive appeasement of local interests (Foster 1998). GMGRA's objections have more recently been marginalized by CMDA's incorporation into the municipality, greater representation of informal communities, and the growing focus on delivery in national development discourse.

A limited form of densification is underway, facilitated by revisions of Durban's town planning schemes (providing for control of physical development through zoning) in the early 1990s. Nevertheless, the old logic of limiting densities through fairly low maximum limits remains. Still, densities are far lower than allowed in central areas, and apart from small high-income developments, the pressure is rather to convert to higher-yielding business uses.

Walled housing complexes – developed in response to land costs and security concerns, as in other increasingly unequal societies (Soja 1997) – are becoming common. While higher-income complexes frequently extend the divided and sprawling city (perhaps densifying the edges), those at the lower end may represent a form of integration. There is considerable demand for well-located housing at the lower end of the private formal market, but banks, fearing nonpayment and abandonment, are unwilling to loan money to African people in sectional title developments – a problem also affecting multistory public housing developments (Supersad 1998). Mechanisms are being developed to respond to these issues at national level, however.

Where developments of planned housing complexes involve rezoning, and there is space for adjacent communities to object or appeal against favorable decisions, they are often resisted in terms of older planning discourses of amenity and property values. A fear of "others" is often an underlying theme. Although resistance does not necessarily stop developments, it slows them, reducing their viability. The shift to democratically elected local councillors is resulting in greater support for densification than before, but older Garden City visions and planning discourses are still influential within appeals bodies.

A Decentering City

A level of deracialization along class lines is occurring through the housing market (Saff 1994), but patterns of race separation largely remain. Older apartheid orders have broken down more substantially in the inner city. From the late 1980s, the racial composition of residential areas changed markedly (Maharaj and Mpungose 1994), albeit less extensively than in Johannesburg (Crankshaw and White 1995; Morris 1997), and informal economic activity grew rapidly. Council response in recent years has been facilitative, providing infrastructure to accommodate informal trade and housing, but there is also a greater emphasis on control as Council attempts to manage competing images of the city.

Perceptions of "crime and grime," of growing disorder, in part underpin a process of decentralization from the Central Business District (CBD), but some of this movement has been occurring for a much longer time, and resembles patterns internationally. Suburban shopping centers have grown rapidly since the 1970s, facilitated, inter alia, by growing automobile usage, extensive highways, and a relatively laissez-faire planning approach, concerned largely with local impacts and evidence of demand. By 1998, there were 18 centers of over 10,000 m outside the CBD (JHI, Property Services 1998) – largely in previously White suburbs, but recently also in old Indian areas, as incomes rose. Major regional centers have developed in the 1990s. Apart from some failed developments in the 1980s, such centers have avoided old African township and informal areas. Incomes and thresholds are seen as too low, and levels of crime and violence too threatening (Harrison et al. 1997). Instead, large wholesalers locate on the edges, servicing convenience needs provided by small township spaza shops (run from home) (Watkinson 1998), and shopping remains centered on the CBD. The CBD has reoriented to the large Black consumer market, dependent on public transport, for whom it remains the most central location – despite distances to residential areas. It is an exceptionally vibrant market, despite images of decline and degradation.

Offices have begun to move to suburban locations, but the shift is not as strong as in Johannesburg (see Rogerson 1997; Murphy 1997). Durban's business has historically been far more CBD focused, with as much as 85 percent of A and B grade space located there as late as 1990. Vacancy rates increased from 2 to 11 percent between 1990 and 1998 (SAPOA 1990, 1998), but 76 percent of such space remains concentrated there.

Decentralization began in the 1970s as largely small professional offices moved to the suburbs close to the CBD. It was resisted by planning authorities, attempting to protect both the CBD and residential "amenity," but some development was allowed around shopping centers and in deteriorating areas. This approach has been extended by current councillors, fearing loss of well-located, relatively affordable housing. In the 1990s, new waves of decentralization are occurring, as corporate head and regional offices move, and new office parks in suburban locations are developed far from townships and informal areas (apart from Cato Manor). Decentralized locations now account for 41 percent of A grade space, including developments presently underway (SAPOA 1998).

The growth of decentralized office parks follows trends internationally, but was also made possible by planning decisions under the past fragmented system of local government, and by provincial oversight based on market demand and local impact. Competing interests between areas have continued with consolidation of local government into six structures and a metropolitan authority, making it impossible for the Metropolitan Spatial Development Framework to take up issues such as the metropolitanwide distribution of commercial and office development.

Something like an "edge city" (Freund 1998) is developing in the North Local Council (NLC), but as Freestone and Murphy (1998) argue for the case of Sydney, its underlying dynamics and form are quite particular. Development is driven by Durban's major private landholder, Tongaat Hulett, which has huge tracts of land under sugar cane. It has been facilitated by past residential growth in the area, an underused highway, lower land costs, perceptions of CBD decline and insecurity, and growing demand for small owner-occupied office buildings expressing a strong company image. Such developments are intended to be coupled with a new regional shopping center, major entertainment complexes, golf estates, further high-income residences, and a new airport. The development of the NLC as a separated high-income world is presented in language of competitive cities, offering Durban a space to attract and appeal to Gauteng and foreign-based capital.

The recent Integrated Development Plan for the area also preserves this image. The area comprises a number of racially based small towns and settlements, all at some distance from one another. For nearly a decade now, Tongaat Hulett has proposed a plan based on dual corridors: a high-income corridor including its major developments along the coast, and another corridor comprising the old Indian towns and African townships, industrial development, and related economic activities. The spatial framework developed by the IDP does not depart very far from this idea, although Tongaat Hulett's own direct influence on the process appears to have been relatively confined, and a very extensive participatory process centered on stakeholders occurred. Participants for example agreed that no low-cost housing development should occur east of the highway where new developments are occurring (Williamson 1998), although two informal settlements may be upgraded. A rates shortage and lower representation of Africans in the area might have influenced decision making, but the extended spatial fragmentation of the area means that communities largely consider development priorities and needs within their own areas, and development where they are, rather than the potential for more abstract restructuring. Similar dynamics occur in other areas, perhaps in a less exaggerated way.

Nevertheless, a number of developments in the North have been slowed or thrown off-course by the politics around major projects, or by stagnant economic growth. The NLC's right to position itself as Durban's "jewel," monopolizing developments, is also being challenged by elements of the Metropolitan Council.

Durban remains far more centralized than Johannesburg. Durban's position as a branch plant economy, and smaller impact of buyout by international firms are probably important (see Goga, forthcoming). Informalization and disorder have been far more contained, and location remains a significant factor for firms in the CBD, particularly those linked to the port (Day 1998). Decentralization has also been limited by recessionary conditions and a shift away from property investments by major institutions as opportunities to invest in international markets opened up (Rode 1998). A plummeting rand and sharply rising interest rates, as the Asian crisis spilled over into South Africa, has exacerbated conditions. Investment in property development has been uneven, however: since the mid-1990s, investment in Durban declined relative to Gauteng and particularly Cape Town (Davies 1998), as the latter successfully positioned itself in the changing global and national environment.

Planning and Transformation

Current planning is attempting to integrate development spatially and sectorally through the mechanism of integrated development plans. A spatial development framework, embodying compaction-integration, and the use of development corridors and nodes to focus development, is being formulated. Concepts resemble those in other cities (see Watson 1998).

Although participatory processes have been extensive, it is not guaranteed that the ideas embodied in the plans are widely shared or commonly understood, as Watson (1998) shows for Cape Town. Concerns raised in the context of participatory processes are not always ones to which local government can respond (such as gangsterism, rape, child abuse), nor do demands necessarily take a strongly spatial form (Moonsammy 1998; Centre for Community and Labour Studies, CCLS 1998). Planning has been accorded the role of synthesizing local demands, and of reworking them into spatial form, giving planners the power to reinterpret them in ways which accord with current discourses (see also Watson 1998; Oosthuizen and van Huyssteen 1998). Such discourses can become dominating in this context, as Healey (1997) suggests, particularly given limited capacity within communities (CCLS 1998). Planning at the metropolitan scale is rather abstract, and political participation in the process has been weak. While formal commitment to the plan exists, in practice, a constituency politics – a politics of investment in "our areas" – remains.

Despite the grand ideals of the postapartheid reconstructionists, development regulation through the town planning schemes still embodies traditional discourses, which often jar with the new ideas. While the older discourses emphasize the role of planning in maintaining areas as they were – a sense of stasis – the new approaches emphasize fluidity and change, and would actively encourage change in many existing areas. The parameters and meanings of compaction-integration, and how they relate to older discourses, are not well developed at the level of regulation. While town planning schemes are to be reconsidered, older discourses of at least property values and amenity are still likely to be played out through the planning process at local level.

The repositioning of the city as "world class" is also likely to limit the achievement of the ideals of compaction-integration. In the face of the reality of continued disjunctures and inequalities, the language of compaction-integration is itself diffusing, and is at times being used in ways which perpetuate – or at least accept – apartheid divisions. In the NLC plan for example, the language of compaction-integration is used to mean concentration of development around existing centers, or along new corridors, but these remain divided, as the discussion above suggests. In other contexts, it is used to mean development outwards from townships and informal areas towards centers of economic activity, rather than in opposite directions; increasing densities within or on the edges of existing townships, perhaps along main routes, rather than well beyond city limits.

In some contexts as well, concepts of corridors and nodes become simulacra as suggested by Oosthuizen and Van Huyssteen (1998), promising but not delivering development. Corridors and nodes, together with the 1 km radius which surrounds them, cover some 40 percent of the city. These might help to focus bulk service development, influence the location of new low-cost housing and focus public transport, but there is also a promise that local economic activity, closer to homes, will be generated. Nodes and corridors in some areas incorporate office and retail developments, but they also run through townships and informal areas, as integrative elements. Understood in a weak way, there is some potential for these ideas to provide focal points for both informal and formal economic activities, which were in part undermined by poor spatial organization in the past (Harrison et al. 1997). Current planning focuses on the development of nodes which concentrate public investments (such as clinics, police stations, libraries) at interceptory locations, in order to provide thresholds for other economic activities. Some successes have been achieved, but there are immediate constraints as a consequence of a shortage of developable land (since much open land has been informally settled, or due to the complexity of ownership) and the chaotic administration and dysfunctional servicing which was inherited from the past (Moonsammy 1998).

Conclusion

This chapter has shown the limits of compact-integrated city ideas in the face of resistance to change and the emergence of new spatial disjunctures. The shift away from spatial restructuring toward competitive cities, the turn to pragmatism, and constituency politics all combine to weaken the prospects for the newer ideas. Nevertheless, there are important achievements and there has been a significant switch of resources to previously deprived areas such as townships and informal settlements. The more limited elements of compaction-integration are perhaps more plausible than grandiose urban reconstruction, which has rarely been implemented on the scale intended (Mabin and Smit 1997).

Nor is it clear that the vision of compaction-integration is much more than a planning ideal, a particular narrative of people's disadvantages in and experiences of the city. Yet despite its limitations, it is still useful in opening up a wider variety of spaces and opportunities. Further, it helps to avoid gross peripheralization of the urban poor, and to bring questions of accessibility to the fore. In addition, it focuses attention on the need to reconstruct township and informal areas, and does in part weaken old divides. Cities are of course dynamic, and processes of change opened up by current planning could be more significant than is immediately apparent.

ACKNOWLEDGMENTS

Thanks are extended to the many people interviewed, not all of whom have been cited here, and to Erwin Rode for the complimentary use of his database.

REFERENCES

Baskin, J. 1998: Metropolitan Housing Service Unit, Durban Metropolitan Council. Interview.

Beavon, K. 1997: A city and a metropolitan area in transformation. In C. Rakodi (ed.), *The Urban Challenge in Africa: Growth and Management of its Large Cities*. London: Bernan, 150–91.

Bedford, L. 1998: Metropolitan Housing Service Unit, Durban Metropolitan Council. Interview.

Byerley, M. 1998: Metropolitan Housing Service Unit, Durban Metropolitan Council. Interview.

Cato Manor Development Association 1998: Annual Report.

Centre for Community and Labour Studies 1998: Implementing integrated development planning in the Durban metropolitan area. Unpublished manuscript.

Centre for Development and Enterprise 1996: *Durban – South Africa's Global Competitor?* Johannesburg: Centre for Development and Enterprise.

Crankshaw, O. and White, C. 1995: Racial desegregation and inner city decay in Johannesburg. *International Journal of Urban and Regional Research*, 19, 622–38.

Cross, C. 1996: On migration and the country of the mind. Conceptualising urban/rural space in KwaZulu-Natal. Paper presented to the IAI/ISER Conference on Understanding Changing Settlement Patterns and Resettlement in Southern Africa. Grahamstown: Rhodes University.

Cross, C., Luckin, L., Mzimela, T., and Clark, C. 1996: On the edge: poverty, livelihoods and natural resources in rural KwaZulu-Natal. In M. Lipton, F. Ellis and M. Lipton (eds.), *Land, Labour and Livelihoods in Rural South Africa*. Durban: Indicator Press, 173–214.

Davies, K. 1998: Durban within the South African economy. A sinking ship? Unpublished paper for Moreland Developments.

Day, B. 1998: Is Durban central business district declining? B.Sc. (Construction Management) Dissertation, University of Natal, Durban.

Dewar, D. and Uytenbogaardt, R. 1991: *South African Cities: A Manifesto for Change*. Cape Town: University of Cape Town.

Dominic, T. 1998: Urban Strategy, Durban Metropolitan Council. Interview.

Edwards, I. 1994: Cato Manor: cruel past, pivotal future. *Review of African Political Economy*, 61, 415–27.

Foster, C. 1998: Cato Manor Development Association. Interview.

Freestone, R. and Murphy, P. 1998: Metropolitan restructuring and suburban employment centers: Cross-cultural perspectives on the Australian experience. *Journal of the American Planning Association*, 64, 286–97.

Freund, B. 1998: City hall and the direction of development: The changing role of the local state as a factor in economic planning and development in Durban. Paper presented to the City of Durban conference, Durban: University of Natal.

Goga, S. (forthcoming). Property development versus people's development. Ph.D. thesis, Rutgers University, New Brunswick.

Greater Manor Gardens Residents Association 1997: Comment on Draft Structure Plan for Cato Manor. Letter to the Cato Manor Development Association, July 29.

Harrison, K. 1998: Migrate, innovate or evaporate. The clothing industry in KwaZulu-Natal. Unpublished manuscript.

Harrison, P., Todes, A. and Watson, V. 1997: The economic development of South Africa's urban townships: realities and strategies. *Development Southern Africa*, 14, 43–60.

Healey, P. 1997: *Collaborative Planning: Shaping Places in Fragmented Societies*. London: Macmillan.

Hindson, D., Byerley, M., and Morris, M. 1994: From violence to reconstruction: the making, disintegration and remaking of an apartheid city. *Antipode*, 26, 323–50.

Hindson, D., Mabin, A., and Watson, V. 1993: Restructuring the built environment. Unpublished report to the National Housing Forum.

Jacobs, J. 1961: *The Death and Life of Great American Cities*. New York: Vintage Books.

JHI Property Services 1998: *The KwaZulu-Natal Property Market*. Durban: JHI.

Kahn, S. and Maharaj, B. 1998: Restructuring the apartheid city: Cato Manor – "a prime reconstruction opportunity"? *Urban Forum*, 9 (2), 1–24.

Mabin, A. 1995: On the problems and prospects of overcoming segregation and fragmentation in South African cities in the postmodern era. In S. Watson and K. Gibson (eds.), *Postmodern Cities and Spaces*. Oxford: Blackwell, 187–98.

Mabin, A. 1998: Commentary on "Vusani Amadolobha – Urban Regeneration and Integration Plan for City, Town and Township Centres." Paper presented to the Symposium Re-integrating the (post) Apartheid City, Johannesburg: University of the Witwatersrand.

Mabin, A. and Smit, D. 1997: Reconstructing South Africa's cities? The making of urban planning 1900–2000. *Planning Perspectives*, 12, 193–223.

Maharaj, B. and Mpungose, J. 1994: The erosion of residential segregation in South Africa: the "greying" of Albert Park in Durban. *Geoforum*, 25, 19–32.

Makhatini, M. and Bedford, L. 1998: The metropolitan context. Paper presented to the Housing in Metropolitan Durban Conference, Durban.

Moonsammy, S. 1998: Planning and Development, Durban North/South Central Council. Interview.

Morris, A. 1997: Physical decline in an inner-city neighborhood. A case study of Hillbrow, Johannesburg. *Urban Forum*, 8 (2), 153–75.

Morris, M. and Hindson, D. 1997: Class and household restructuring in metropolitan Durban. *Society in Transition*, 1, 101–21.

Murphy, S. 1997: The geography of commercial and industrial spaces on the central Witwatersrand: reinforcing the shape of the Apartheid city? Paper presented to the Conference on Environment and Development in Africa: An Agenda and Solutions for the 21st Century, Johannesburg.

Oosthuizen, R. and van Huyssteen, E. 1998: "The map precedes the territory." The cartography of "integrated development planning in South Africa." Paper presented to the AESOP Conference, Aveiro.

Parnell, S. 1997: South African cities: perspectives from the ivory tower of urban studies. *Urban Studies*, 34, 891–906.

Parnell, S. and Pieterse, E. 1998: Poverty alleviation and developmental local government. Paper presented to the City of Durban conference, Durban: University of Natal.

Robinson, J. 1992: Power, space and the city: historical reflections on apartheid and post-apartheid urban orders. In D. Smith (ed.), *The Apartheid City and Beyond*. London: Routledge, 292–302.

Robinson, J. 1998: "Planning the post-apartheid city": comments on the Metropolitan Development Framework – Cape Town. Paper presented to the Symposium Re-integrating the (post) Apartheid City, Johannesburg: University of the Witwatersrand.

Robinson, P. 1994: Cato Manor: a legacy of South Africa's past or a model for reconstruction. Paper presented to the Sixth International Planning History Conference, University of Hong Kong.

Rode, E. 1998: *Rode's Report on the South African Property Market*, vol. 11, no. 1, Cape Town: Rode and Associates.

Rogerson, J. 1997: The central Witwatersrand: Post-elections investment outlook for the built environment. *Urban Forum*, 8 (1), 93–108.

Saff, G. 1994: The changing face of the South African city: from urban apartheid to the deracialization of space. *International Journal of Urban and Regional Research*, 18, 377–91.

SAPOA 1990: *Office Vacancy Survey*. Johannesburg: South African Property Owners Association.

SAPOA 1998: *Office Vacancy Survey*. Johannesburg: South African Property Owners Association.

Simone, A. 1998: Discussion paper on "The Urban Development Framework." Paper presented to the Symposium Re-integrating the (post) Apartheid City, Johannesburg: University of the Witwatersrand.

Smit, D. and Charlton, S. 1998: The metropolitan housing context. Paper presented to the Housing in Metropolitan Durban Conference, Durban.

Soja, E. 1997: Six discourses on the postmetropolis. In S. Westwood, and J. Williams (eds.), *Imagining Cities: Scripts, Signs, Memory*. London: Routledge, 19–30.

Supersad, V. 1998: KwaZulu-Natal Provincial Housing Board. Interview.

Tomlinson, R. 1997: Urban sprawl problem hard nut to crack. *Business Day*. September 29.

Tomlinson, R. 1998: From exclusion to inclusion: rethinking Johannesburg's central city. Paper presented to the Associated Chartered Town Planners in South Africa conference New National and International Perspectives in Planning. Johannesburg: University of the Witwatersrand.

Turok, I. 1994: Urban planning in the transition from Apartheid, part 2. *Town Planning Review*, 65, 243–58.

Urban Foundation 1990: *Policy Overview: The Urban Challenge*. Urban Foundation: Johannesburg.

Urban Strategy Department 1995: *Settlement areas and population estimates, Durban Metropolitan Area*. Durban: City of Durban.

Valodia, I. 1998: Trade policy, industrial structure and growth in the industrial sector of Durban. Paper presented to the City of Durban conference, Durban: University of Natal.

Watkinson, E. 1998: Economic Development Unit, Durban Metropolitan Council. Interview.

Watson, V. 1998: Planning under political transition: lessons from Cape Town's metropolitan planning forum. *International Planning Studies*, 3, 335–50.

Williamson, A. (1998). Consultant. Interview.

World Bank 1991: South Africa. Urban Sector Reconnaissance. Unpublished World Bank Mission Report.

Index